# Space, Movement and t[
# Roman Cities in Italy and Beyond

How were space and movement in Roman cities affected by economic life? What can the study of Roman urban landscapes tell us about the nature of the Roman economy? These are the central questions addressed in this volume.

While there exist many studies of Roman urban space and of the Roman economy, rarely have the two topics been investigated together in a sustained fashion. In this volume, an international team of archaeologists and historians focuses explicitly on the economics of space and mobility in Roman Imperial cities, in both Italy and the provinces, east and west. Employing many kinds of material and written evidence and a wide range of methodologies, the contributors cast new light both on well-known and on less-explored sites. With their direct focus on the everyday economic uses of urban spaces and the movements through them, the contributors offer a fresh and innovative perspective on the workings of Roman urban economies and on the debates concerning space in the Roman world.

This volume will be of interest to archaeologists and historians, both those studying the Greco-Roman world and those focusing on urban economic space in other periods and places as well as to other scholars studying pre-modern urbanism and urban economies.

**Frank Vermeulen** is a professor of Roman archaeology and archaeological methodology at the Department of Archaeology of Ghent University, Belgium.

**Arjan Zuiderhoek** is an associate professor of ancient history at the Department of History of Ghent University, Belgium.

## Studies in Roman Space and Urbanism

*Series editor: Ray Laurence, Macquarie University, Australia*

Over the course of the last two decades, the study of urban space in the Roman world has progressed rapidly with new analytical techniques, many drawn from other disciplines such as architecture and urban studies, being applied in the archaeological and literary study of Roman cities. These dynamically interdisciplinary approaches are at the centre of this series. The series includes both micro-level analyses of interior spaces and macro-level studies of Roman cities (and potentially also wider spatial landscapes outside the city walls). The series encourages collaboration and debate between specialists from a wide range of study beyond the core disciplines of ancient history, archaeology and classics such as art history and architecture, geography and landscape studies, and urban studies. Ultimately the series provides a forum for scholars to explore new ideas about space in the Roman city.

**Water and Urbanism in Roman Britain**
Hybridity and Identity
*Jay Ingate*

**Urban Space and Urban History in the Roman World**
*Edited by Miko Flohr*

**Food Provisions for Ancient Rome**
A Supply Chain Approach
*Paul James*

**Urbanisation in Roman Spain and Portugal**
Civitates Hispaniae of the Early Empire
*Pieter Houten*

**Space, Movement and the Economy in Roman Cities in Italy and Beyond**
*Edited by Frank Vermeulen and Arjan Zuiderhoek*

For further information about this series please visit www.routledge.com/classicalstudies/series/SRSU

# Space, Movement and the Economy in Roman Cities in Italy and Beyond

**Edited by**
**Frank Vermeulen and Arjan Zuiderhoek**

Routledge
Taylor & Francis Group

LONDON AND NEW YORK

First published 2021
by Routledge
2 Park Square, Milton Park, Abingdon, Oxon OX14 4RN

and by Routledge
605 Third Avenue, New York, NY 10158

*Routledge is an imprint of the Taylor & Francis Group, an informa business*

*British Library Cataloguing-in-Publication Data*
A catalogue record for this book is available from the British Library

*Library of Congress Cataloging-in-Publication Data*
Names: Vermeulen, Frank, editor. | Zuiderhoek, Arjan, 1976– editor.
Title: Space, movement and the economy in Roman cities in Italy and beyond /
edited by Frank Vermeulen and Arjan Zuiderhoek.
Description: Abingdon, Oxon; New York, NY: Routledge, 2021. |
Series: Studies in Roman space and urbanism |
Includes bibliographical references and index.
Identifiers: LCCN 2020049902 (print) | LCCN 2020049903 (ebook) |
ISBN 9780367371562 (hardback) | ISBN 9780367757229 (paperback) |
ISBN 9780429352911 (ebook)
Subjects: LCSH: Cities and towns–Rome. |
Urbanization–Rome–History. | Rome–Economic conditions.
Classification: LCC DG82 .S627 2021 (print) |
LCC DG82 (ebook) | DDC 307.2/160937–dc23
LC record available at https://lccn.loc.gov/2020049902
LC ebook record available at https://lccn.loc.gov/2020049903

ISBN: 978-0-367-37156-2 (hbk)
ISBN: 978-0-367-75722-9 (pbk)
ISBN: 978-0-429-35291-1 (ebk)

Typeset in Times New Roman
by Newgen Publishing UK

# Contents

# Figures

# Tables

# Contributors

**Patrizia Basso** is a professor of classical archaeology at the Department of Culture e Civiltà of the University of Verona, Italy.

**Peter Campbell** is a lecturer in cultural heritage under Threat, Cranfield Forensic Institute, Cranfield University, UK.

**Cristina Corsi** is an associate professor of archaeology at the Department of Humanities of the University of Cassino, Italy.

**Katherine Crawford** is a postdoc at the School of Human Evolution and Social Change, Arizona State University, USA.

**Christopher P. Dickenson** is an assistant professor of Ancient History at the School of Culture and Society, Centre for Urban Network Evolutions (UrbNet) of Aarhus University, Denmark.

**Miko Flohr** is a university lecturer in ancient history at the Institute for History at Leiden University, the Netherlands.

**Adeline Hoffelinck** is a PhD student in classical roman archaeology at the Department of Archaeology of Ghent University, Belgium.

**Simon Keay** is a professor of Roman archaeology at the University of Southampton and Director of the Portus Project, University of Southampton, UK.

**Dorien Leder-Slotman** is a PhD student in ancient history at the Department of History of Ghent University and a researcher at the Sagalassos Archaeological Research Project at the University of Leuven, Belgium.

**Giuseppe Lepore** is an associate professor of classics at the Department of History and Cultures of Bologna University, Italy.

**Simon Malmberg** is a professor of classical archaeology at the Department of Archaeology, History, Cultural Studies and Religion of the University of Bergen, Norway.

**Maria del Carmen Moreno Escobar** is a lecturer in classical and applied landscape archaeology, Department of Archaeology, University of Durham, UK.

**Jeroen Poblome** is a professor of classical archaeology at the Department of Archaeology of the University of Leuven, Belgium.

**Thomas G. Schattner** is scientific director at the German Archaeological Institute–Madrid, Spain, and a professor of classical archaeology at the Justus-Liebig-Universität in Giessen, Germany.

**Michele Silani** is a junior assistant professor of classical archaeology at the Department of Humanities and Cultural Heritage of the University of Campania 'Luigi Vanvitelli', Italy.

**Devi Taelman** is a postdoctoral researcher at the Department of Archaeology of Ghent University, Belgium.

**Frank Vermeulen** is a professor of Roman archaeology and archaeological methodology at the Department of Archaeology of Ghent University, Belgium.

**Andrew Wallace-Hadrill** is an Emeritus Honorary professor of Roman studies in the Faculty of Classics, University of Cambridge, UK; Emeritus Fellow of Sidney Sussex College, Cambridge, UK; and a principal investigator of the ERC Advanced Project, 'Impact of the Ancient City'.

**Rinse Willet** is a collaborator of the Sagalassos Archaeological Research Project, Turkey, coordinating the survey programme in the central parts of the Ağlasun Valley.

**Arjan Zuiderhoek** is an associate professor of ancient history at the Department of History of Ghent University, Belgium.

# Acknowledgements

The editors wish to express their sincere thanks to all those individuals and institutions who contributed to the success of the international workshop that took place on September 12–15, 2018, in the municipalities of Porto Recanati and Treia (MC, Marche, Italy) and on which this volume is based. These are, in particular, the municipalities of Porto Recanati and Treia, the Ghent University Departments of Archaeology and History and the International Research Network 'Structural Determinants of Economic Performance in the Roman World' funded by the Research Foundation-Flanders. We also thank Amy Davis-Poynter, Ella Halstead and Elizabeth Risch at Routledge for all their help and support in shepherding this volume towards publication; Ray Laurence, the Series Editor of *Studies in Roman Space and Urbanism* for accepting the volume as part of his series and for his constructive feedback and Adeline Hoffelinck for her help with the list of abbreviations.

We dedicate this book to the late Guido Cittadini who for many years provided unwavering moral and logistical support to the archaeological research of Ghent University in Porto Recanati.

# Abbreviations

| | |
|---|---|
| *AE* | *L'Année Épigraphique* |
| *AGRW* | *Associations in the Greco-Roman World* |
| *AquilNost.* | *Aquileia Nostra* |
| *Arch. Class.* | *Archeologia Classica* |
| *ATTA* | *Atlante Tematico di Topografia Antica* |
| *AvP* | *Altertümer von Pergamon* |
| *BaBesch* | *Bulletin antieke Beschaving* |
| *BAR* | *British Archaeological Reports* |
| *BCAR* | *Bulletino della commissione Archeologica Communale di Roma* |
| *BEFAR* | *Bibliothèque des Écoles françaises d'Athènes et de Rome* |
| *CCSL* | *Corpus Christianorum, series Latina* |
| *CIG* | *Corpus Inscriptionum Graecarum* |
| *CIL* | *Corpus Inscriptionum Latinarum* |
| *CILA* | *Corpus de inscripciones latinas de Andalucía* |
| *Cod. Iust.* | *Codex Iustinianus* |
| *DdA* | *Dialoghi di Archeologia* |
| *Hep* | *Hispania Epigraphica* |
| *IGR* | *Inscriptiones Graecae ad res Romanas pertinentes* |
| *ILS* | *Inscriptiones Latinae Selectae* |
| *Inscr. Aq.* | *Inscriptiones Aquileiae* |
| *JRA* | *Journal of Roman Archaeology* |
| *JRS* | *Journal of Roman Studies* |
| *Lib. Colon.* | *Libri coloniarum* |
| *MAAR* | *Memoirs of the American Academy in Rome* |
| *MAMA* | *Monumenta Asiae Minoris Antiqua* |
| *MEFRA* | *Mélanges de l'École française de Rome (Antiquité)* |
| *Not. Scav./NSc* | *Notizie degli Scavi di Antichità* |
| *PBSR* | *Papers of the British School at Rome* |
| *PLRE* | *Prosopography of the Later Roman Empire* |

| *RE Suppl.* | *Paulys Realencyclopädie der classischen Altertumswissenschaft Supplement* |
| *Rend. Pont.* | *Rendiconti della pontificia accademia romana di archeologia* |
| *RIB* | *The Roman Inscriptions of Britain* |
| *SEG* | *Supplementum epigraphicum Graecum* |
| *Vulg. Luc.* | *Vulgata Evangelium Lucae* |

# PART I
# Introducing the themes

# 1 Introduction

## Space, movement and the economy in Roman cities

*Arjan Zuiderhoek and Frank Vermeulen*

'Location, location, location!' is the universal mantra of real-estate agents. Anyone who has ever tried to buy or sell real property will be all too familiar with its fundamental truth: *where* a building is located in relation to other aspects of its geographical environment, both natural and artificial, is a fundamental determinant of its value. At the same time, accessibility, that is the ease with which a house can be reached and its links to accessible networks of travel and transport, is vital. This is *a fortiori* true for firms that need good access to road networks, waterways, airports and the like to be able to operate. Given all this, it follows that closeness, that is reducing the friction of distance, pays. It is an empirically observable fact that in most complex societies, people and firms (production units) tend to concentrate and cluster geographically. Another empirically observable fact, noticed by economists, is that economic productivity tends to rise in tandem with increasing growth and concentration of population. This phenomenon is dubbed 'agglomeration economies', and it offers one possible explanation for the existence of cities. Economies of agglomeration have been variously attributed to transport cost reductions brought about by the concentration of population, to the productivity gains that result from pooling labour or to the increased speed in the circulation of ideas in cities, which fosters innovation and causes a rise in human capital, yet the debate continues.[1] What matters for our purposes, however, is that, potentially, this analysis has the power to integrate the four central themes of this volume, space (in the sense of place, location), movement (mobility, transport), economies and cities, into an overarching explanatory framework. In fact, a range of modern social scientific disciplines, such as spatial economics, location theory and urban economics, have been developed to study this particular nexus of space, mobility/transport and urbanism.

Yet, for students of pre-modern societies, such as historians and archaeologists of the Greco-Roman world, such an explanatory framework, with all of its barely hidden universalizing assumptions, raises more problems than it solves. The statements above, for instance, imply a well-functioning market economy. But can we simply assume the existence of a market for real property in antiquity? Did Greek and Roman producers operate within a system of interlinked supra-regional markets that required the sort of easily accessible and efficient transport networks emphasized above? Can we take it for granted that an economic explanation for city formation such as the agglomeration economies model just referred to is true for cities every-where, in all periods of history (if indeed it is correct for modern western cities)? Phrased in more general terms, to what extent were urban space and movement in Greco-Roman antiquity affected, shaped or determined by the needs and requirements of economic life, that is, by economic considerations? Can the study of these urban spaces and movements in turn tell us some-thing meaningful about what kind of economy and what sorts of economic behaviour were characteristic of the Greco-Roman world? These are the kinds of questions that motivated the editors and contributors to put together this collection of studies and to organize the conference from which it derives. As regards its chronological and geographical scope, even though this introduc-tion will range a bit wider at times, our contributors, an international mix of archaeologists and historians, all focus on different areas of the Roman Imperial world[2] broadly conceived, that is Italy and the provinces, including the East. We have chosen this focus not because Republican Italy or the pre-Roman Greek world are uninteresting but to keep our topic manageable and thematically coherent. That is, we are concerned with the study of economic aspects of space and movement/mobility in cities that were part of a single imperial political system that left its own specific material and monumental imprint on the urban landscapes within its domains, even if often primarily through the agency of cooperative local elites. This, at least, is a feature that all of the cities studied in this volume share. We focus on cities, furthermore, because, as allocation centres of agricultural surplus and as hubs of manufac-ture and exchange, they are the focal points of economic activity. Moreover, as almost entirely artificial landscapes, they are the places where space and movement can be most easily and visibly manipulated to serve specific soci-etal needs. The chapters in this volume thus present case studies of the links between space, movement and economic life in cities in various parts of the Roman world. They are followed by a concluding chapter in which each con-tribution to the volume is briefly discussed and where the main connecting threads are highlighted. In the following pages of this introduction, we pre-sent a brief overview of some of the various strands of debate associated with our theme, and we discuss some of the important issues that can and should inform research on economic space and movement in ancient cities.

## Ancient views

The Greek and Roman written sources do not present us with a uniform picture of the relationship between space and economic life in antiquity. In Plato's ideal polis as sketched in the *Laws* (952d–e), a strict spatial separation was to be maintained between traders visiting the city and the citizens them-selves; the magistrates in charge must receive traders 'at the agoras, harbours and public buildings *outside the city* (ἔξω τῆς πόλεως)' – a separate suburban landscape, it would seem, created especially for commerce. Aristotle famously wished to follow the example of the Thessalians in providing his ideal city with a 'free agora' forbidden to traders, artisans and farmers selling their produce, which was to be spatially separated from 'the agora for buying and selling', that is the city's commercial market (*Politics* 1331a–b). Other sources, mostly also focusing on the agora or forum, refer, however, to the intermingling of economic and other kinds of activities in civic space, rather than their spatial separation. Thus, Livy, relating how the Roman king Tarquinius Priscus supposedly refurbished the city, has him not only constructing porticos and workshops (*porticus tabernaeque factae*) along the forum area but also laying the foundations for the temple of Jupiter on the Capitol (1.35, 1.38) nearby. From a preserved fragment of a play by the fourth-century BCE playwright Euboulos, we learn that at Athens in the agora, everything was for sale: not only figs, grapes, turnips, roses, cottage cheese but also summons officers, witnesses, laws and indictments (fr. 74, in Athen. *Deipn.* 14.640b–c), a comedic reference to the spatial intermingling of diverse social spheres (politics, law, commerce) that was characteristic of the agora.[3] Yet even in such multilayered civic locations, where economic activity and economic spaces were enveloped within and combined with other forms of behaviour and spatial structures, there could still be signs of a considerable degree of economic and commercial specialization, which was generally expressed spatially. Thus, for instance, different parts or sections of the Athenian agora were devoted to distinct and well-defined types of commerce, and people would say: 'I went to the wine, the olive oil, the pots' or 'to the onions and garlic, to the clothes' (Pollux, 9.47–8). In the imperial city of Rome, the ancient world's only true megalopolis, the same principle held, but on a much grander spatial scale, in the form of numerous specialized markets, for selling cattle, vegetables, pork, fish, wine and so on.[4]

## Modern debates

As will be evident from this all too brief selection, a simple perusal of the ancient sources does not allow one to gain an easy understanding of the spatial economy of ancient cities. At first glance, modern literature does not offer much more comfort either. The topic indeed stands at the intersection of three complex and long-standing debates within ancient history and classical archaeology, which have only very recently begun to become more integrated: debates on space, on the character of the ancient city and, related to this, on the nature of the ancient economy.

While drawing inspiration from space-related scholarship on other historical periods and within the social sciences, the 'spatial turn' in the study of the Greco-Roman world received a lot of stimulation from archaeology, the spatial discipline *par excellence*. Close study of individual buildings and building types has led to an outpouring of research on domestic space, on public monuments, religious architecture.[5] In scholarship on the Roman world, the spectacular remains at Ostia, Pompeii, Herculaneum and Rome have prompted endless studies of the structures of civic space. Methodological developments, moreover, such as field survey, the analysis of aerial photography, geographical information systems (GIS) and, more recently, a variety of non-invasive techniques have all contributed a great deal to our understanding of the spatial structures of ancient landscapes and cities.[6] Historians and archaeologists have also increasingly focused on the *uses* ancient actors made of urban spaces, on their patterns of movement through buildings and urban landscapes, and on perceptions of civic space and its meaning in terms of providing contemporaries with a sense of identity.[7] This work has also brought into focus the reciprocal relationship that exists between people – that is society with its norms, values and institutions – and the urban landscape. People create urban landscapes that reflect their society's world view and patterns of behaviour, but this world view and these patterns of behaviour are in turn strongly supported, maintained and reinforced *through* the urban landscape. In the words of the urban design scholar Quentin Stevens, 'The built environment in general is a particularly durable part of *habitus* which inspires and gives structure to the actions of everyday life. Built forms tend to suggest what behaviour is "appropriate" or "desirable"'.[8]

Yet while analyses of urban space, both historical and archaeological, have explored many dimensions of urban life, be they social, political or religious, scholars for a long time did not pay much attention to the economic dimension of urban space. In particular, there was (and still is) not much interaction between scholarship on urban space and the long-standing debates on the nature of the ancient city and the ancient economy. Surveys of the material remains of ancient cities rarely deal with the strongly comparative debates on the economic structure and role of the Greco-Roman city. Conversely, while archaeological evidence plays an ever-increasing part in the analyses of the Greek and Roman economies, rarely have participants concerned themselves much with issues of urban space. Only comparatively recently has this changed, with the work of a new generation of scholars. We might, for instance, mention Miko Flohr's analysis of the material evidence of fullers' workshops (see also his chapter on *tabernae*, this volume, Chapter 3), his and Andrew Wilson's volume on the economy of Pompeii, Stephen Ellis's study of *tabernae*, the books by J.W. Hanson, Rinse Willet (see this volume, Chapter 5) and Luuk de Ligt and John Bintliff on urban systems, which take in economic aspects as well, and the work of field archaeologists explicitly interested in economic life such as, for instance, Jeroen Poblome and his team, working on Sagalassos in Pisidia, Asia Minor (see also Chapter 5, this volume) or Frank Vermeulen, one of the editors, working in the Potenza valley in Central Adriatic Italy (see also Chapter 1, this volume), and several other contributors to this volume.[9] With the present book, we explicitly wish to position ourselves as part of this trend and allow it to gain further momentum, placing spatial analysis at the centre of debates on the urban economy of the Roman world.

At first sight, however, it is rather strange that spatial aspects did not play a larger role in the debate over the nature of the ancient economy. For in his path-breaking *The Ancient Economy*, Moses Finley pointed explicitly to the absence in Greek and Roman cities of the types of buildings and structures (guildhalls, bourses, cloth halls ...) associated with the commercial capitalism and interconnected markets of the cities of later medieval and early modern Europe, an absence which for him signified the absence of a capitalist market economy in antiquity.[10] This clear spatial reference was, however, quickly snowed under in the subsequent debates, which mostly focused on the social position of artisans and traders, the extent of trading networks, the possible involvement of Greek and Roman elites in manufacture and commerce, and the nature of city–countryside relationships.[11] A more recent round of debate, specifically on the Roman economy, broadly divides those who would see a more or less integrated market economy during the late Republic and early Empire (with the imperial government ensuring that some necessary conditions were in place, such as a unified currency, a legal system and a road network but otherwise staying largely in the background) from those who envision a far less integrated economy, with markets playing a role but with greater emphasis on exploitation and non-market contexts of production and exchange, and with a greater role assigned to the government and rent-seeking political elites.[12] One major drawback of this debate is that it remains rather abstract, largely taking place at a very high level of generality, involving contrasting empire-wide models. It might be productive to focus more on the local urban contexts, as some recent studies have done (e.g. the above-mentioned books by Flohr and Ellis). Finley, for one, never denied the existence, in the Greco-Roman world, of local or regional markets or market exchange; he just did not think that in antiquity such markets were as interconnected, and that market exchange was as economically dominant, as in later Europe. So let us follow his example and focus on the local: what can a close study of markets – actual, *physical* urban markets – and other economically relevant urban spaces and structures in Roman cities actually tell us about the nature of the Roman economy?

## Urban space and economies

The geographer David Harvey once suggested that specific social orders tend to produce built environments that more or less match their economic needs, social hierarchies and social norms.[13] If we combine this idea with the insight of Quentin Stevens, quoted above, that the built environment inspires and constrains social behaviour in specific ways, then we do indeed have a good theoretical point of departure for using the analysis of Roman urban landscapes to inform us about the nature of the Roman economy. However, unlike the ancient sources on urban space and economic life discussed earlier, modern discussion about the Roman economy leaves us with a distinct duality: a Roman world where economic life was dominated by political and administrative structures (empire) versus one where the economy was dominated and integrated by market exchange. Are we condemned to approach Roman urban landscapes in a similarly Manichean fashion? As Harvey writes, '[T]he interactions between spatial form, symbolic meaning and spatial behaviour are probably very complex'.[14] Close study of the urban landscape in all its richness might actually offer us a way out of the deep dualism that characterizes the debate over the ancient economy in its various incarnations. For in the multifunctional palimpsest of the urban landscape, spheres of human activity constantly interact and overlap, as do the material contexts in which these activities take place. Hence, marketplaces, for instance, are never *just* economic markets, and sanctuaries (to give another example) are never *just* cult places: all kinds of other activities and interactions take place there as well. One implication of this is that 'economic space', that is spaces, places and buildings associated with economic activity are often (partly) encapsulated within spaces and structures relating to other spheres of social life and *vice versa* (see Zuiderhoek, Chapter 6, this volume). This statement, of course, begs a number of important questions: what, precisely, is urban economic space? How is it constituted, and how, exactly, can it inform us about the structures of Roman economic life? Can we identify a specifically (Greco-)Roman form or forms of economic space?

The chapters that follow in their own way represent attempts to answer these and other related questions. At the workshop from which this volume arose, we did not wish to pre-empt discussion by providing at the outset a clear-cut, comprehensive and uniform definition of 'Roman urban economic space' (if it is indeed even possible to come to such a formulation, especially given the wide chronological and geographical range of the chapters in this volume), and neither do we now wish to prejudice the reader by offering such a definition here. Instead, to conclude this introductory chapter, we shall briefly discuss a number of themes and issues that also cropped up during the workshop and that resonate with, and should, we think, inform research on the theme of economic space in Roman cities.

The first of these themes is movement and flow. Recent scholarship on urban space in the Roman world has, as we saw, paid particular attention to the way people move through buildings, streets, squares and other parts of the urban landscape, and this is an aspect that should also be central to the investigation of economic space, as is indeed made clear in a number of contributions in this volume. How did people, animals and goods move through urban (economic) spaces? What obstacles did they encounter? We should investigate the economic connectivity between various urban zones related to different aspects of production, distribution and consumption (e.g. movement of goods between ports, warehouses, *tabernae*, households), between city and countryside and between smaller and larger cities. Movement, or change, also has a chronological dimension, as urban landscapes and the economic spaces within them change and evolve through time. What can the evolution of urban economic space through time tell us about changes in economic life, at the micro- and macroscale?

Another issue that was much discussed during the workshop and that is central to several of the contributions in the volume is the importance of small towns to the study of the relationship between space and economic life in the Roman world. Urban behemoths such as the city of Rome, Carthage, Antioch or Alexandria, and even substantial provincial centres such as Ephesus or Lugdunum might easily deceive us, but in fact most Roman cities, in Italy as well as in the provinces, were (very) small indeed, numbering inhabitants in the thousands rather than tens of thousands. They often functioned as focal points and congregation hubs for substantial rural territories, and a good number of their more permanent residents may have been (part-time) agriculturalists as well. Some small cities also grew up around specific, highly localized forms of economic activity, such as the exploitation and working of metal at tiny Munigua in Baetica, discussed by Schattner in this volume (see Chapter 14). How did 'urban' economies in such small cities actually function? How did the relationship between 'urban' space and economic activity manifest itself there? These are important questions, since due to their numerical proliferation across the empire, small cities are far more likely to represent the 'typical' Roman urban experience than larger ones.

Related to this issue are two other concerns that frequently cropped up at the workshop. The first of these is the (in)applicability of what we might call the Vesuvian model of Roman urbanism, based on centuries of close study of the spectacular remains at Pompeii and Herculaneum, to the rest of the Roman world. Clearly models based on the structure and use of urban space at Pompeii can be very instructive for our understanding of Roman urbanism more broadly, as Wallace-Hadrill's chapter on the circulation of goods within the city demonstrates (Chapter 11). Yet the Vesuvian model can also be deeply deceptive, as becomes clear, for instance, in Flohr's chapter in this volume (Chapter 3): the rows of *tabernae* that, based on the Pompeian model, we tend to view as highly typical Roman economic spaces were by no means a universal feature in small-town Roman Italy. The second concern is that, given the prominence of modestly sized cities in the Roman world, Roman Imperial urbanization, especially but certainly not exclusively in the West, can largely be defined as the monumentalization of the small town. Virtually every Roman town, however slight, had its own monumental urban centre, often including most of the standard set of buildings typical of the Roman town (e.g. forum, basilica, temples, theatre …). In this way, large villages became 'cities' (*civitates*, *municipia* and *coloniae*) in the Roman definition, and in this sense Roman urbanism was very much a product of empire, even though it was mostly effected through the empire's local agents, the urban elites, who as office-holders and benefactors used both public and private money to embellish their communities to the required level of 'urbanness'. In doing so, they became at the same time the most important facilitators of the creation of economic space within their cities, which, as mentioned above, was often a (partially) embedded feature of the civic public architecture that formed the main focus of elite expenditure (see e.g. the Chapters 6 and 7 by Zuiderhoek and Dickenson, respectively).

One final issue that needs to be addressed is economic space at the supra-urban level, that is as manifested in connections between cities and between cities and regions. Empires tend to generate big cities, as rulers, elites and their large households cluster into urban centres, together with myriad artisans, traders, service providers and others drawn to the huge demand exercised by these wealthy elites. Thus, the first Greek cities with well over 100,000 inhabitants living within their walls are a phenomenon of the Hellenistic world with its imperial capitals, and similarly the Roman empire generated its own urban giants. Yet Empires often tend to generate only a few such cities. In fact, comparison with early modern Europe has shown that whereas the largest cities in the Roman Empire were much bigger than those in (politically fragmented) early modern Europe, the latter had far more cities of +10,000 inhabitants than the Roman world, where the majority of cities were (much) smaller than that. This is often interpreted as sign that the urban systems of the Roman world were less commercially integrated than those of later Europe.[15] While there might be some truth in this from an empire-wide perspective, the densely urbanized landscapes dotted with smaller cities discovered by archaeologists primarily in the central Mediterranean parts of the Roman world (see e.g. Vermeulen 2017, and Chapter 2, this volume) do, at the regional level at least, suggest another possibility as well. Namely that a dense and well-integrated network of smaller towns might be as commercially effective as a system consisting of one or two large regional centres and their satellite communities. Roman urbanization and, as we will see in the chapters that follow, Roman urban economic spaces, frequently differed from what we find in other societies, in medieval and early modern Europe but also elsewhere, yet it is precisely in the exploration of these differences between various pre-modern societies that a huge research potential lies for economic historians and archaeologists. This volume offers a range of detailed studies of Roman economic spaces, which, we hope, might facilitate such broader synthetic and comparative projects in the future.

## Notes

1  See Glaeser and Gottlieb, 2009: 984.
2  Some of the Italian examples in this volume also focus on the later Republican phases of the studied cities.
3  See Millett, 1998: 217.
4  Cattle: *forum boarium* (Livy 10.23.3), vegetables: *holitorium*, fish: *piscarium* (Varro, *de Lingua Latina* 5.146–47), pork: *suarium* (*CIL* 6.3728 and 9631), wine: *vinarium* (*CIL* 6.9181–82). See Broekaert and Zuiderhoek, 2012: 50.
5  For syntheses of recent work, see Gros and Torelli, 2007; Gates, 2011; Laurence, Esmonde Cleary and Sears, 2011; Zuiderhoek, 2017, esp. ch. 4. On domestic space, see Nevett, 2010. On Greco-Roman space in general, see Scott, 2012 for thoughtful discussion.

6 See, e.g. Bintliff and Snodgrass, 1988; Johnson and Millett, 2012; Vermeulen et al., 2012; Corsi et al., 2013.
7 See, e.g. Bon and Jones, 1997; Laurence and Newsome, 2011; Ostenberg, Malmberg and Bjørnebye, 2015.
8 Stevens, 2007: 49.
9 Flohr, 2013; Flohr and Wilson, 2016; Ellis, 2018; Hanson, 2016, see also Hanson et al., 2019; Willet, 2019; de Ligt and Bintliff, 2019; Poblome, 2016, 2020; Vermeulen, 2017.
10 Finley, 1999: 137, see Zuiderhoek, this volume Chapter 6.
11 For a survey of the post-Finley debates, including many pertinent contributions, see Scheidel and von Reden, 2002.
12 The debate is probably best exemplified by the contrasting analyses of Bang, 2008 and Temin, 2012.
13 Harvey, 1973: 32.
14 Harvey, 1973: 32.
15 See Zuiderhoek, 2017: 49–55 for references to the relevant literature and discussion.

## References

Bang, Peter Fibiger. *The Roman Bazaar: A Comparative Study of Trade and Markets in a Tributary Empire* (Cambridge Classical Studies). Cambridge: Cambridge University Press, 2008.

Bintliff, John and Anthony Snodgrass. "Mediterranean Survey and the City." *Antiquity* 62 (1988): 57–71.

Bon, Sara E. and Rick Jones, eds. *Sequence and Space in Pompeii.* Oxford: Oxbow, 1997.

Broekaert, Wim and Arjan Zuiderhoek. "Food Systems in Classical Antiquity." Pages 41–55 in *A Cultural History of Food in Antiquity*. Edited by Paul Erdkamp. London and Oxford: Bloomsbury, 2012.

Corsi, Cristina, Bozidar Slapšak and Frank Vermeulen, eds. *Good Practice in Archaeological Diagnostics. Non-invasive Survey of Complex Archaeological Sites* (Natural Science in Archaeology 69). Cham, Heidelberg, New York, Dordrecht, London: Springer International Publishing Switzerland, 2013.

de Ligt, Luuk and John Bintliff, eds. *Regional Urban Systems in the Roman World, 150 BCE–250 CE* (Mnemosyne Supplements 431). Leiden: Brill, 2019.

Ellis, Stephen J.R. *The Roman Retail Revolution: The Socio-economic World of the Tabernae.* Oxford: Oxford University Press, 2018.

Finley, Moses I. *The Ancient Economy* (Updated ed.) Berkeley: University of California Press, 1999.

Flohr, Miko. *The World of the Fullo: Work, Economy, and Society in Roman Italy* (Oxford Studies on the Roman Economy). Oxford: Oxford University Press, 2013.

Flohr, Miko and Andrew Wilson, eds. *The Economy of Pompeii* (Oxford Studies on the Roman Economy). Oxford: Oxford University Press, 2016.

Gates, Charles. *Ancient Cities: The Archaeology of Urban Life in the Ancient Near East and Egypt, Greece and Rome.* London: Routledge, 2011.

Glaeser, Edward L. and Joshua D. Gottlieb. "The Wealth of Cities: Agglomeration Economies and Spatial Equilibrium in the United States." *Journal of Economic Literature* 47.4 (2009): 983–1028.

Gros, Pierre and Mario Torelli. *Storia dell'urbanistica. Il mondo romano.* Rome: Laterza, 2007.

Hanson, John W. *An Urban Geography of the Roman World, 100 BC to AD 300* (Archaeopress Roman archaeology, 18). Oxford: Archaeopress, 2016.

Hanson, John W., Scott G. Ortman, Luís M.A. Bettencourt and Liam C. Mazur. "Urban Form, Infrastructure and Spatial Organisation in the Roman Empire." *Antiquity* 93 (2019): 702–718.

Harvey, David. *Social Justice and the City.* University of Georgia Press, 1973.

Johnson, Paul and Martin Millett, eds. *Archaeological Survey and the City.* University of Cambridge Museum of Classical Archaeology Monographs 2. Oxford: Oxbow, 2012.

Laurence, Ray and David J. Newsome, eds. *Rome, Ostia, Pompeii: Movement and Space.* Oxford: Oxford University Press, 2011.

Laurence, Ray, Simon Esmonde Cleary and Gareth Sears. *The City in the Roman West c.250 BC–AD 250.* Cambridge: Cambridge University Press, 2011.

Millett, Paul. "Encounters in the Agora." Pages 203–228 in *Kosmos. Essays in Order, Conflict and Community in Classical Athens.* Edited by Paul Cartledge, Paul Millett and Sita von Reden. Cambridge: Cambridge University Press, 1998.

Nevett, Lisa C. *Domestic Space in Classical Antiquity* (Key Themes in Ancient History). Cambridge: Cambridge University Press, 2010.

Ostenberg, Ida, Simon Malmberg and Jonas Bjørnebye, eds. *The Moving City: Processions, Passages and Promenades in Ancient Rome.* London and Oxford: Bloomsbury, 2015.

Poblome, Jeroen. "The Potters of Ancient Sagalassos Revisited." Pages 377–404 in *Urban Craftsmen and Traders in the Roman World* (Oxford Studies on the Roman Economy). Edited by Andrew Wilson and Miko Flohr. Oxford: Oxford University Press, 2016.

Poblome, Jeroen. "La Sagalassos romaine, avancées récentes de la recherche." Pages 427–440 in *Les mondes romains. Questions d'archéologie et d'histoire.* Edited by Ricardo Gonzalez-Villaescusa, Giusto Traina and Jean-Pierre Vallat. Paris: Editions Ellipses, 2020.

Scheidel, Walter and Sitta von Reden, eds. *The Ancient Economy.* New York: Routledge, 2002.

Scott, Michael. *Space and Society in the Greek and Roman Worlds* (Key Themes in Ancient History). Cambridge: Cambridge University Press, 2012.

Stevens, Quentin. *The Ludic City: Exploring the Potential of Public Spaces.* London and New York: Routledge, 2007.

Temin, Peter. *The Roman Market Economy* (The Princeton Economic History of the Western World). Princeton: Princeton University Press, 2012.

Vermeulen, Frank. *From the Mountains to the Sea: The Roman Colonisation and Urbanisation of Central Adriatic Italy* (BABESCH Supplement 30). Leuven, Paris and Bristol, CT: Peeters, 2017.

Vermeulen, Frank, Gert-Jan Burgers, Simon Keay and Cristina Corsi, eds. *Urban Landscape Survey in Italy and the Mediterranean.* Oxford: Oxbow, 2012.

Willet, Rinse. *The Geography of Urbanism in Roman Asia Minor.* Sheffield: Equinox, 2019.

Zuiderhoek, Arjan. *The Ancient City* (Key Themes in Ancient History). Cambridge: Cambridge University Press, 2017.

# 2 Economic space and movement between Roman towns, their suburbia and territories

## The regional perspective

*Frank Vermeulen*

## Introduction

The city and the sociopolitical and economic system associated with it are certainly some of the most fundamental hermeneutic categories through which we can understand the historical evolution of the communities living around the Mediterranean. The study of towns is central to any understanding of the Roman Empire, since they were the nodes through which the administration, economy and culture of the Empire were negotiated (Millett and Keay 2004). In particular, in Roman Italy, where one can locate a confusingly high number of town sites – probably around 500 depending on the definition (Sewell and Witcher 2015; Hanson 2016) – the study of towns remains quintessential for advancing the historical debate (e.g. Cornell and Lomas 1995; De Ligt 2011; Zuiderhoek 2016). During the past two decades, there is a distinct trend in the study of the Roman city, which shows a progression from description towards the analysis of patterns of behaviour. As is demonstrated in this book, considerations of economic space and movement in and around urban centres can be viewed as central to this scholarly evolution. Apart from the impressive work that has been carried out in this respect on prime cities as Ostia and Pompeii, there is a growing need for a geographical shift and for a focus on a range of other sites that have been neglected in this debate. The diffusion of a series of non-invasive field techniques and of researchers taking these approaches into consideration for serious urbanism studies promises now to create a fuller analysis of space and movement in ancient towns that allows to go beyond those two well-preserved and studied towns on the central Tyrrhenian coast. Simultaneously this shift in perception of geographical focus and of ways of data gathering creates opportunities for the in-depth study of economic space and movement between Roman towns, their suburbia and their territories, wherever we are in the Roman world. We can now find solutions to better explore how the spatial structures of Roman cities and the patterns of movement and mobility through and between urban spaces influenced Roman economic processes and developments and how urban spaces and their territories were shaped and moulded by the rhythms and demands of the regional or wider Roman economy.

Several current scholars of the subject (e.g. Kaiser 2000, 2011; Laurence 2007, 2008; Laurence and Newsome 2011; Poehler 2017; Hartnett 2017) have already pointed out that the spatial organization of a Roman town, and the ways one moved in them, can be interrogated in a number of ways, such as looking at the actual layout of the streets and how this affects the use of space, at the type of street cover and the wear and tear of pavements caused by wheeled traffic, at the underlying topography and visual markers (e.g. arches or prominent buildings) and at entry points or gates directing the flow of traffic into and out of the city. If the city was constructed on a major road, it is worth looking at the role of this long-distance route in the layout of the grid, which is often conditioned by this pre-existing feature (Laurence 2012: 88–89). As most Roman towns are situated on road arteries (or rivers) that are part of the wider regional or trans-regional road system, and as these same urban centres are generally the foci for local economic traffic within their respective territories, it is best to link the study of urban space and movement to these wider contexts. There is no doubt that such a resolute regional view on the spatial context of economic activities can stimulate the debate on the nature of the Roman economy, the role of urbanization in Roman economic development and the importance of space and mobility in the study of Roman society.

## A regionally based landscape approach

Archaeological research has in recent decades developed a set of tools that helps to demonstrate the urban impact on the countryside and vice versa. Traditionally this discipline with its focus on material culture has used the presence and dispersion of artefacts in towns and their neighbouring countryside, most often revealed through excavations, as the best way to complement the historical sources and the epigraphic evidence. But now modern archaeology has developed a more pronounced and integrated use of a whole set of non-destructive survey techniques on the towns and their territories to allow fast advancement of current knowledge on the town–country nexus in Roman times (e.g. Bintliff and Snodgrass 1988; Johnson and Millett 2012; Vermeulen *et al.* 2012; Corsi *et al.* 2013). Technologies, such as certain types of remote sensing and geophysical prospection (e.g. aerial photography, ground-penetrating radar), efficient tools for mapping and analysis like geographical information systems and specific geo-archaeologic- and landscape-based approaches to the past are starting to revolutionize our view on the use of space in the Roman World (Figure 2.1).

In almost all studied regions of the Empire, the Roman site network, be it urban or rural, is now being evaluated against local topography, road systems, ancient agricultural practice, pre-Roman settlement dynamics, the location and potential exploitation of raw materials and the impact of certain Roman concepts of organizing space (e.g. gridded land division systems). The current archaeological fieldwork approach, in particular in the well-studied central

*Figure 2.1* Non-invasive survey of the Roman city of *Mariana* in Corsica. Amazingly detailed image of structures buried at 75 cm depth: a street and lined buildings (e.g. houses, shops, etc.), obtained by ground-penetrating radar prospection in the south of the urban centre (GPR data by L. Verdonck).

and western Mediterranean, also shows that important regional differences can be distinguished. The latter are the results of a set of parameters, such as geographical location, geopolitical choices, specific historical events, economic suitability of the area, receptivity of indigenous societies and development of the regional road system. When looking at economic space and movement, it is essential for comprehending the nature of the cities and other central places we are looking at, that we pay attention to the influence of the economy of their respective territories and especially to the resource management responsible for the construction, success and evolution of the urban centre. The landscape surrounding each town is more than just a backdrop against which history is played out. It is a key driver in the formation of settlement patterns and socio-economic networks. Often it is a 'settlement chamber' where a whole dynamic of settlement behaviour and human movement over time can be observed (Bintliff 2013) and where the formation and subsequent life of a town is sometimes just a single and temporary event. In this context, it is of the essence to understand the 'site catchment' of a Roman town, in other words, to understand where a site (*in casu* the town) and its inhabitants acquired the raw materials, natural and agricultural resources and commodities to build a functioning urban society and make it successful over time. Such a fundamentally geo-archaeological and spatial approach, here applied to larger entities such as Roman towns, presents many opportunities for investigation. We know, for instance, that metallic minerals, stone, water, clay and wood were the most important natural materials used in antiquity. A simple perusal of Pliny's *Naturalis Historia* suffices to demonstrate this, as he left us a kind of inventory of the natural potential available for exploitation within the

Roman Empire. Many aspects and details of this imperialistic catalogue can now be archaeologically demonstrated: we can trace the trajectories between the place where the raw materials and resources were used, often as artefacts in an urban context, and their original position in nature, often the site of a quarry, a mine or another exploitation unit. In addition, systematic land evaluations, realized in the territories of ancient cities, together with a data-driven reconstruction of past realities and chronologies, allow interdisciplinary teams to provide a decent picture of the potential of Roman period's agricultural and pastoral exploitation of the countryside. Furthermore, we can try to understand the extent to which urban goods and services flowing to the countryside and vice versa may have changed in the course of Roman occupation. Changes in this transfer may not only be related to changes in intra-territorial connections and rural exploitation but also be connected with the economic and political success or failure of a certain city (Corsi and Vermeulen 2010).

Important in this respect is the development, since the last quarter of the twentieth century of systematic artefact surveys in and around Roman towns in Italy and beyond. Especially when this traditional approach of topographic survey is combined with more sophisticated techniques of remote sensing and intensive non-destructive surveys in the suburbia and the wider territories of the towns, in close connexion to city surveys, the role of space and movement in and around the city centre can be well-explained. Of course, to investigate the impact of towns on their territory implies a good knowledge of the rural settlement patterns, and there is no ideal way to delineate and understand fully the typology of the latter. The vexed question of farm/villa/*praedium* has, however, been posed in the past decades on a much more solid base, as the number of systematic regional surveys as well as rural site excavations has risen considerably. Also through a very detailed and better archaeologically documented morphological analysis of the landscape, zooming in on land divisions and normative systems like the *centuriatio*, we can understand the sometimes intensive reorganization of the land and the transport organization near the city. New ways of digitally deciphering such ancient grids, integrated with very specific field operations looking at field boundaries and local road systems, surely stimulate a better understanding of this process of systematic use of rural and suburban space. All elements at our disposal today indicate that this process must have altered the rural world in the vicinity of the new towns in a dramatic way. Often connected with this are also the observations denoting a radical change in the agricultural production system, in many areas demonstrating a shift towards large-scale wine and oil production. The impact on landscape transformation of such shifts is no less remarkable, as are the new and related ways of transporting goods and organizing services for movement.

The transformation of rural settlement patterns turns out to be the phenomenon that, together with the appearance of well-structured towns, marks best the slow so-called Romanization process of the later stages of the

Republic and the beginnings of the Imperial age in Italy. Intensive archaeological research spread over long periods, concerning both the pre-Roman
and the Roman occupations, can illustrate very well the strong and often
quite rapid impact of the city on the evolution of indigenous communities,
on the economic and social organization of the area and on the creation of a
new rural landscape. This impact is mainly linked with the construction of a
strong road network, with the rapid spread of villas and roadside villages and
with the implementation of those new land divisions. Many rural areas of the
ancient Italy and 'in-between town' areas of its countryside, roadside villages
(*vici*) and a series of deliberately created forum towns (*fora*) start, during the
later centuries of the Republic, to function as commercial interfaces between
the dispersed inhabitants of the countryside and the urban dwellers. Their
location is strictly linked with major thoroughfares, such as the *via Aemilia*
or the *via Flaminia*, and occurs often at crucial nodes in the road and river
network of the peninsula. Those service centres, generally based on a street-
village type of elongated plan, which often grew out of *praefecturae*, are also
ecologically well located. They generally occur in areas with sufficient fresh-
water provisioning and amidst good agricultural land, which provide a good
environment for a long-lasting function as a local centre. Some of these roadside villages will become real towns or *municipia* sometime before or after the
Social War, and from the Augustan era at the latest will become, together with
colonies and existing town centres, the urban backbone of Imperial Roman
Italy (Figure 2.2).

*Figure 2.2* Visualization of the Early Imperial phase of the town of *Septempeda* near
San Severino Marche shows how a small *municipium* in Apennine Italy
based on a Late Republican street village might have looked (by Klein and
Vermeulen).

Municipalization and 'deep' urbanization, as well as the full development of a more internationalized economy, have caused the relationships among the many towns in a specific region, and between the flourishing of towns and prosperity and density of rural settlements in their territory, to become complicated matters. Because of the *synoikismos* of small towns with their larger neighbours, eventually these interventions have affected the rest of the countryside as well. From the last phase of the Republic and most intensely from the Augustan period onwards, the thorough exploitation of the countryside by certain urban élites, and the fact that all cities were in varying degrees of 'consumer' cities in relation to their territories, must have placed intra-territorial connections at the forefront of economic success. The more intricate cityscapes on which we can focus from that time onwards reveal much about the transformation of the environment closest to the people who populated Italian territories. With expressions of power and social status as its driving force, many cityscapes let us read into the dynamics of the Roman world. Cities and other central places are excellent vehicles for studying acculturation processes, as they became instruments and symbols of Roman power. As space and society interact, a city's layout is a good basis for studying how political discourse was presented to its citizens. The study of its individual monuments, be it temples and buildings for spectacles, or even only food markets and certain domestic buildings, shows a redefinition of public and semi-private space and thus of society as a whole. In this sense, the topography, planning and materialization of some Roman towns can now be better read as a cognitive map within a mind frame conditioned by the local elite's perception of the religious and political ideals and structures of Rome and its leaders. We start to see from the Augustan era onwards a wider diversity between cities in the same region, which is partly a result of competition and comparison between towns. But the development of the urban form and the use of space in a city can also reflect the relation of that city with elite networks of patronage that could release economic resources for expenditure in that particular city. Other crucial parameters are the sustainability of the wider region and its population (Laurence *et al.* 2011: 6) and the specific geographical positions of individual towns versus the changing success of its infrastructure of movement and commerce, such as the road system, the river infrastructure and the sea ports.

## The urban system of central Adriatic Italy

To illustrate the contribution of the regional approach to this debate on the Roman spatial economy, we choose to focus on a particular area of Italy, the central Adriatic, which has in recent years become a good case study for the understanding of Roman regional networks and analysing space and movement. Recent results from large-scale non-invasive fieldwork operations on a series of towns and their countryside in this region (Vermeulen *et al.* 2017), combined with a region-wide analysis of all know cities here

(Vermeulen 2017), allow us to develop a model for studying topographic–economical patterns that can profitably be compared with other areas of the Roman world.

Urbanization, in particular not only as an instrument of colonial policy by Rome but also as a motor for the management and self-development of integrated socio-economic territories, reveals itself quite distinctly in the Adriatic. Especially in the area between the Apennines and the central Adriatic coast (Figure 2.3), or essentially the Early Imperial regions V and

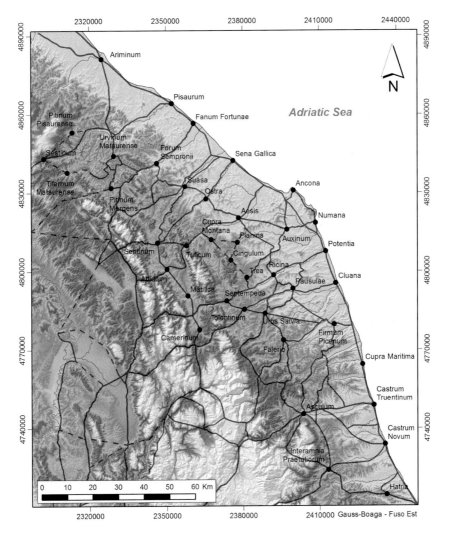

*Figure 2.3* The fully developed urban network and road system of central Adriatic Italy around the reign of Augustus (by Vermeulen and Taelman).

VI, where one of the highest concentrations of towns in the whole Roman Empire occurs, the role of urbanization in stimulating change and adaptation was enormous (Vermeulen 2017). The past two decades of fieldwork in central Adriatic Italy have seen an increasing sophistication of field methods and material studies as well as some theoretically informed desktop studies, which now succeed in mapping a wide range of forms of permanent human settlement and ritual activity in the landscape, from subsistence farms to complex urban settlements and from ritual cave sites to institutionalized sanctuaries. These studies show that the ten colonies founded by Rome in central Adriatic Italy during the third and second centuries BCE soon developed a strong link to their surrounding countryside. This new territory beyond the limits of the ritually delineated *pomerium* of Rome needed to be exploited for economic survival and soon allowed incorporation into the existing networks of trade and commerce over land and sea. The network of new cities is characterized by a series of strategically placed colonies and new urban creations located on and near the coast and its coastal road, and on or near a new inland road running parallel with the coast, the *Via Salaria Gallica*. Not surprisingly, the detailed planning of all of these new and strategically placed towns followed basic rules connected with the presence and orientation of crucial road connections, easy river crossings and newly constructed river mouth landings or sea ports. Fairly quickly, the new towns and their satellites of colonist villages and hamlets, as well as the great numbers of new rural colonists that joined the region via viritane allotments granted by the *lex Flaminia* (232 BCE), must also have integrated economically with local people still living in older centres and in rural settlements away from these new city centres dominated by the local and sub-regional élites and a very Roman lifestyle. In the course of the first century BCE, this gradual process of economic integration accelerated and intensified when the many newly created *municipia* (some 30 sites in total) developed into well-structured market centres, and new waves of veteran colonists joined many of them during the period of the Second Triumvirate and Augustus' reign. At the onset of the Principate, the role as economic foci for markets and trade fully defines these Roman towns now as places within the local economy, and as centres which became the engine for the better integration of the region in the international flows of goods. Within this system, there was a hierarchy determined above all by proximity to the main source of political, social and economic power: the city of Rome. But the metropolis was by no means the only force acting here, and a regional hierarchy of market centres should also be imagined, with some offering basic goods and services with a low demand threshold and others also providing higher order goods to a much wider area. Consequently consumers from all over the territory would visit their local town regularly and make occasional trips to a more important centre (Morley 1997).

Positions in the landscape, such as on the coast, near navigable stretches of rivers and on-road junctions, now became even more crucial than before. They would determine the flowering or decay of those small centres, with only a periodic market as the main base of existence, and they had a serious effect on the demographic balance of most towns and their territories. People could and did choose to go and live in town or in an expanding roadside settlement, where they would benefit from the growth in trade, transport and construction, and the many opportunities that those brought, but when opportunities were scarce, too many harvests in the towns' territory failed, and local economies dwindled, they would move away, often joining the poor masses in even larger cities and especially in Rome. The general economic situation of Italy and of this Adriatic region in particular, and also of every single town and its own territory, was, therefore, crucial to the potential of the urban centres to expand, provide comfort to their citizens and display wealth to locals and visitors alike.

The role of sea ports was fundamental in this regional system, as engines for coastal and also inland economies. Agricultural goods produced in their immediate hinterland, such as olive oil and wine, were from at least the late second century BCE onwards and produced on a wider than local scale, intended not primarily for local, on-site consumption but with an eye on surpluses that would have been shipped to Rome and to other, sometimes larger, neighbouring towns. All coastal towns were involved in an active Adriatic coasting trade conducted through a range of ports that was much more diverse than previously portrayed on the basis of historical sources. Some shipwrecks and many urban consumption contexts show that the coastal towns evidently functioned as transhipment ports through which local and regional trade goods passed, bound for other destinations and markets (e.g. Menchelli 2011). A special role was reserved here for the centrally placed harbours of *Ancona* and nearby *Numana*. Both are positioned on the impressive coastal Monte Conero promontory and had the best naturally protected locations in a very long stretch of coastline, which allowed them to harbour large marine ships. The other coastal ports, often positioned at the river mouths where the towns flourished, were mostly served from here by way of smaller boats for tramping or 'cabotage', probably distributing or receiving many overseas goods and commodities via these main harbours (Cardinali and Luni 2006).

But despite the pivotal role of the coastal centres, especially from the first century BCE onwards, the thorough exploitation of the inland countryside by, among others, new urban élites and the fact that the new central places were developing more and more into 'consumer' cities in relation to their territories must have placed intra-territorial and intra-regional connections at the forefront of economic success. Although the expansion of Roman roads since 220 BCE in this area first followed military developments, they soon became a new and privileged means of communication between different areas of the region, radically transforming the existing transportation system and generating new routes to serve the interests of the many towns and villages. The nodes of this network were formed by the new Roman and Latin colonies and both roads and cities played a major role in the emergence of a new political identity, contrasting with the character of indigenous intra-territorial connections. From Augustus onwards, the Roman roads became an Imperial project, inscribing a pattern of order on the landscape and a way of directing people between towns and road stations. Still these roads were also much structured by the landscape itself, with its hills, ridges and valleys; indeed, this landscape factor is, for this hilly region with the characteristic parallel-oriented deep valleys of *Picenum* and eastern *Umbria*, of major significance in fully comprehending the structures of mobility and accessibility. The major roads attested in the ancient sources, the *via Salaria* and the *via Flaminia*, were now not only interconnected along the coast and between the middle valleys of the many parallel rivers, but also a whole series of *diverticula* crossing other important valleys roads of lower rank and connecting the emerging cities were further developed, as well as many tracks and pathways that connected the countryside with these towns along mostly 'natural' lines and with ties to the dense spread of farms and hamlets. It is also clear, however, that the building of bridges or the creation of fording infrastructures on the many crossings of land and river roads played an essential role in communication and accessibility in this landscape. As the landscape of central Adriatic Italy is an environment that directs the movement into well-defined W-E-oriented corridors, the position of central settlements and bridges within the network can play an important role in the development of the settlement pattern and the economic success of individual towns and centres. The existing communities that are well-positioned in or near these nodes of access and passage can funnel more people, goods and substances and can, therefore, profit from their location. The organically developed system of communications of pre-Roman date has in this way developed into a well-organized, state and city-sponsored system of roads with regular inter-distances, with the implementation of monumental constructions such as bridges, with shifts in religious foci (temple sites now lying closer to the roads) and especially with better access to the towns and their many facilities (Vermeulen and Mlekuz 2012).

Increasingly during the Early Imperial period previously unparalleled scales of commerce were involved, with an important movement of food and associated goods from the region to Rome, or possibly at certain times (e.g. under Trajan from the port of *Ancona*) to the armies on the frontiers. This increase in commercial flow, occurring over an extended period of time, in the process stimulated and complemented smaller scale regional and local trading activity. Archaeologically and textually known exports from the region via these ports were among others: food products (wine, oil, grain, sweet bread, fruit, sausages, etc.), wool, wood and textiles (e.g. purple cloth from *Ancona*). Some of these must, in the Imperial period, have been handled by the *navicularii maris Hadriatici*, who are epigraphically attested in *Ostia* (Paci 2001: 77). At the same time, there are many archaeological indications of the wide variety and bulk import of goods, such as pottery, food products (wine, oil, fish sauce), building materials (e.g. decorative stone, brick and tile), luxury objects, and so on (Panella 2010). The majority of products handled through the towns of the region were essentially of local or regional origin; however, in particular, the mass of food products obtained from agricultural activity in the countryside, profitable exploitation of the sea and intensified activity in the high mountain areas, where the collective use of the *ager publicus* was indispensable for the practice of pastoral activities (e.g. Gabba and Pasquinucci 1979; Fortini 1991).

The recent synthesis of the topography and urban characteristics of the circa 40 small- to medium-sized towns in the region – with their urban centres ranging between 8 and 45 ha – revealed much about the use of economic space within the city walls where most of this commercial activity took place (Vermeulen 2017). The fundamental role of their fora, as well-structured and planned architectural spaces, where the Roman planners and local populations created a physical interface for controllable economic activity, is well evidenced by most of the towns where a more complete urban pattern has been revealed. At the moment, the origins of the forum as an architecturally defined, separate place can only be traced back to the second century BCE in the region, when there was a gradual evolution of central town areas concentrating their crucial economic processes, communal activities and political and religious display in and around a plaza. As can be seen in the second-century BCE colonies of *Potentia* (Vermeulen *et al.* 2017) and *Pollentia* (Perna *et al.* 2016), where some good archaeological data are now available, it can be assumed that most colonies established before the Social War received a planned forum that was well-integrated in the general layout of the regular town (Figure 2.4).

This first formal forum must initially has counted only few public buildings, such as one or more temples or *sacella*, while presumably also some houses were still clustered around the square. The economically essential *tabernae* and a *porticus*, added to these fora, from the start or only later, can be seen as additional binding elements: they defined the square and gave the forum its first typical inwards-oriented look conditioned by urbanistic principles and the rules of economic efficiency that the Romans held in high regard. At the same time, due to its focal position on a regular city grid that was well connected with the main roads leading to the colony, the central market place could easily be discovered and reached by traders and sellers coming from outside town. In the many towns in the region that more gradually grew out of road agglomerations during the first century BCE, the position of the forum is also evident: it was normally located along the dominant street and major thoroughfare of the settlement. Here influences from urban planning elsewhere initiated a transformation from a rather linear street village with some shops and other commercially important buildings spread without major focus to a more centralized type of town with a forum plaza mirroring the coastal colonies and urban life in other parts of the peninsula. Most importantly, this transformation served to create increasing conformity between the local urban organization and economic standards, and those of the City of Rome (Figure 2.5).

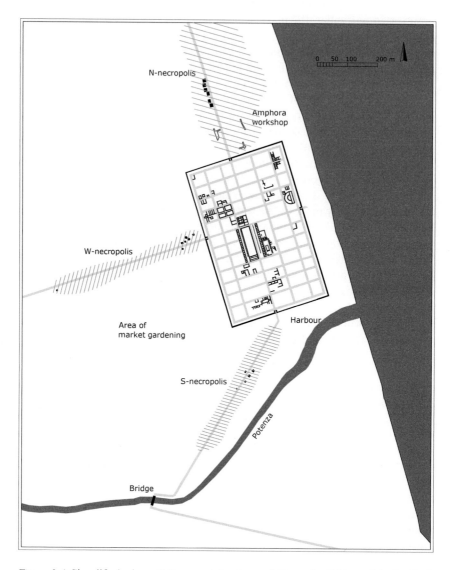

*Figure 2.4* Simplified plan of the coastal colony of Potentia (184 BCE) in its Early
Imperial phase, with the central location of the forum (D) and the clear
links of the street network and *suburbium* with the regional road system
(by Vermeulen).

While the planning of many fora in these mostly inland towns must have
happened soon after promotion to *municipium*, their full monumentalizing
often only took place during the reigns of Augustus and his successors in the
Julio-Claudian dynasty, with addition of other crucial buildings for economic

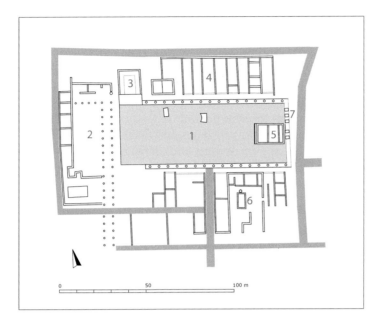

*Figure 2.5* Interpretation plan of the forum architecture discovered via geophysical survey and aerial photography in the Roman urban settlement of *Trea*. A row of tabernae was clearly identified on the northern side of the plaza (4) (by Vermeulen).

life, such as the sometimes attested *macella* and *basilicae* and probably also *horrea*. There is evidence that certain towns had a high concentration of *tabernae* on the forum (e.g. *Potentia*, *Suasa*), as a kind of spatial monopolization of all trade in one place, as can be seen in many Tyrrhenian contexts. In other instances, such as in *Ricina* where a series of shops seem linked to the access to the nearby river and bridge, or in *Trea* where a row of seemingly planned *tabernae* clusters near the gate to Ancona, evident topographical choices seem to prevail (Vermeulen *et al.* 2017, 90–98). Still retail landscapes are based on rational economic principles, and the distribution and location of shops are largely dependent on the motivation behind retail investment, such as regarding the question whether the return of a shop is higher than for houses or if shops are gifts to freedmen and, therefore, located near certain elite dwellings.

The gradual growth of the towns as significant central places for their territories continued into the second century CE, when still some of them are being provided with additional facilities for a prosperous municipal life such as theatres, amphitheatres, temples, aqueducts and public baths (Vermeulen 2017, 143, table 2). Created originally as somewhat artificial administrative centres (*praefecturae* or *coloniae*), many cities became flourishing centres of marketing and exchange, real magnets for strong ties between town and territory, where the named facilities became additional attraction poles for commercial transactions. Still it is striking and most interesting that not all the Roman towns provide the same functions. Although almost all of them shared the necessary attributes that define a town (such as walls, market, forum with justice hall and temple) and provided the basic socio-economic, commercial and administrative functions, there are huge differences between towns in this region. This is visible not only in terms of town size, size of their territory but also in other town attributes, such as the presence or absence of thermal public baths, temples, theatres and amphitheaters. Due to their size and monumentality of their public infrastructure, many inland towns seem to be servicing at least as much the surrounding countryside as the relatively small numbers of urban inhabitants living there, and town dwellers of nearby centres without a theatre or amphitheatre of their own could also easily reach these facilities (Figure 2.6).

In a relatively small town like *Ricina*, where a large bathhouse, a big amphi- theatre and a monumental theatre were discovered, it can be suggested that on market days and religious festivities a large part of the population from the surrounding countryside, and from smaller nearby towns like *Trea* and

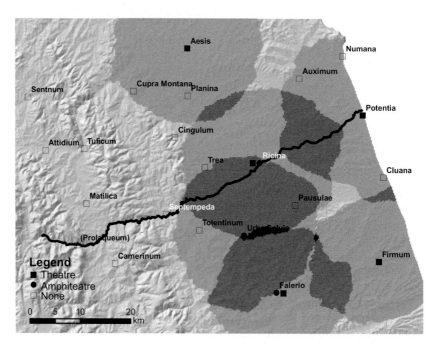

*Figure 2.6* A simulation of 4-h walk isochrones around the towns with archaeologic- ally attested theatres in northern *Picenum* illustrates the interconnectivity of the urban system in that area (by Mlekuz and Vermeulen).

*Pausulae* with probably fewer facilities, needed to be serviced. These buildings of entertainment thus might have served as powerful magnets to attract the countryside population into cities as well as townsfolk from other centres in northern *Picenum*. By attracting people into towns for major holidays and celebrations, they provided a setting for the containment of people. Containment is a technology of power, which together with *fora, macella* and other crucial economic facilities can be seen as a technology of control. They provide a physical envelope for a setting, separate the outside from the inside, and provide prescribed ways of movement and behaviour. They can crowd people, animals, things and substances together, mix them and hide them from view. Thus, spectacle buildings and other places for entertainment like large bath complexes do not only provide a physical setting for the indoctrination of people through display and performance of monumentality and spectacles but structures where people become obedient subjects by embodying the Imperial ideology through prescribed movement, postures and so on (Foucault 1975; Gros 1996). The desire of many a town to impress the traveller or visitor from other towns clearly had primacy over the needs of the local inhabitants and the creation of an environment for social and economic interaction in and around the forum. The dense urban network developed all over the central Adriatic area, with an average distance between towns of around 13 km, or *c.* 9 Roman miles, thus, allowed the population of this region to live in an economically well-organized and rather coherent settlement system, well-adapted to the local needs and traditional dynamics and, at the same time, integrate fully in the Roman lifestyle.

## Movement and connectivity in *suburbium* and countryside

The specific landscape and climate characteristics, together with evidence from ancient authors, indicate that the central Adriatic region had the potential to sustain a dense, partly urbanized population (Vermeulen 2017). Even if the region did not stay outside the major economic fluctuations that affected central Italy during the later phase of the Republic and the first two centuries of the Empire, with some towns and territories being greatly dependent on the Late Republican wine business boosted by huge investments by the Roman elite and with a remarkable decline visible from the mid-first century CE onwards as a result of international competition and shifting foci (e.g. Purcell 1985; Rosenstein 2008; Launaro 2011), it probably suffered less from these major fluctuations than other regions in the central and southern Italy. In the central Adriatic area, the more mixed economy was smaller in scale and less unpredictable and, thus, less affected by changes in modes of exploitation, helping to explain the quite visible growth and topographic continuity of rural and, therefore, also urban settlement throughout the general period of 90 BCE–200 CE. Based on the recent and current archaeological research on urban centres, rural settlement patterns, land use and infrastructure, we can now provide some more substantial data for these developments and on how they affected economic space and movements in the region.

The conditions for economic growth were rooted in the region's third- and second-century BCE colonial past, when investments in infrastructure were realized and it received colonists to exploit (new) land (*cf. supra*). The rural landscape of central Adriatic Italy remained, in general, well-inhabited and socio-economically stratified in Late Republican times. While inland towns and nucleated settlements (larger villages) were more and more surrounded by a dense network of roads and other infrastructures and the coastal towns of colonial foundations, often boasted some harbour facilities, the countryside thrived. There was a general continuity in this area in the presence of modest farmsteads densely spread over all types of landscapes (coastal locations, valley floors, slopes, hill crests, etc.) alongside the appearance of generally modest *villae* (Verdonck and Vermeulen 2004). Part of the lower and the mid-valley town's wealth would have derived from intensive farming in the centuriated or otherwise regularly organized valley floors and olive and wine cultivation mostly on the lower slopes of the bordering hills. Especially in the latter, we see the gradual development, mostly after the mid-first century BCE of somewhat larger *villae rusticae* better linked with maritime and international trade. Around many towns in coastal and lower valley areas, like *Potentia* (Vermeulen *et al.* 2017), *Urbs Salvia* (Perna and Capponi 2012) and *Firmum* (Menchelli 2012), topographic and archaeological studies have documented a dense rural infill of the surrounding territories. Many of these developments can be linked to the opening up of some valleys by the construction of or improvement in the diverticula of the *via Flaminia* and *via Salaria*, and the implementation of large-scale land divisions in the valley floors or on the river terraces by early rural colonists and later veteran colonists being settled here. The surveys suggest that the distribution of *villae*, which in central Adriatic Italy seems to gather momentum only during the first century BCE, was foremost a peri-urban phenomenon. But given the dense network of nucleated settlements developed in this region during the second half of the first century BCE, we can hardly expect a fall-off and the distribution of rural villas may eventually prove to be quite even over the landscape. Even then, the real *villae* formed only a fraction of rural settlement in the Late Republican and Early Imperial countryside of this region. Small farmsteads continued to exist side by side with *villae*, meaning probably that the rural free population must have constituted a considerable component in the demographic composition of the countryside.

While the archaeological and epigraphic records clearly demonstrate substantial elite investments in several town centres and the *ager* of all colonies from the mid-second century onwards (Delplace 1993; Paci 2008; Vermeulen 2017), in the form of urban embellishment, industrial activities and rural elite housing, economic well-being and connectivity on the level of individual households prove harder to attest, given the paucity of diagnostic materials. In some areas, it can be shown, however, that access to imported amphorae and fine table pottery, i.e. black gloss pottery, in even modest rural sites certainly was no exception, as was local production of these more widely traded food containers and table commodities. Site and off-site patterns from artefact surveys now reflect highly intensive land use, with the ceramic record of some sites clearly revealing specialization in wine production. This is especially remarkable in the coastal areas. Once the lower valley floors were drained and the nearby slopes better terraced and stabilized for intensive cultures by the first generations of colonists, more space in the lower valleys became available for agricultural expansion, an opportunity that was seized by the Romans, as the settlement evidence now shows. Doubtlessly the improved infrastructure of roads and drainage systems in the plains, and on the beach ridges and terraces along the coast, were highly conducive to investments for wine and oil production, and for implanting or improving the rural estates that are responsible for this partially market-oriented production. Findings of many amphora production sites and presses (Van Limbergen 2011) make it likely that the larger farmsteads and villa sites near the coast and surrounding some towns were engaged in the production of wine and oil for oversea markets, as do the ancient sources mentioning quality wines in the region (Van Limbergen *et al.* 2017). The major consumption regions of these wines are fairly well-documented: northern Italy, Dalmatia, Greece, Asia Minor, Alexandria and Rome were the main markets, but products have also been found in *Africa, Iberia, Gallia, Germania, Noricum* and *Pannonia*, demonstrating wide international distribution. The few larger villas near the central Adriatic coast (e.g. Dall'Aglio *et al.,* 1991; Campagnoli 1999; Verdonck and Vermeulen 2004) were clearly not only meant for *otium* but also most of all linked to exploiting the agricultural hinterland and the marine and other resources of the Adriatic coast.

We, therefore, need to turn to the archaeology of the landscapes immediately bordering the coastal towns to understand the impact of these economic patterns and fluctuations on the life of the urban centres as well as on the development of their suburban areas. The suburban infrastructure of a town is, partly like its urban infrastructure, a reflection of social processes related to economic and other types of activity. Its character is closely linked to the development and the necessities of the city, and, therefore, it has its own history of evolution and devolution (Antico Gallina 2000). Most newly founded Roman cities were clearly demarcated by walls and also by a peripheral communal area that was still considered part of the *pomerium* and thus public. Only with time could this strip be partially privatized for all kinds of functions connected with the life of the city and its inhabitants, and in general the hold of the town over its landscape environment tightened and expanded spatially. The *suburbium* essentially had a double function: it served for provisioning the town and was also a residential space (Lafon 2001), but many additional services and activities can be linked directly to the urban core. Most of the typical structures found in the *suburbia* of Roman towns in Italy have also here and there, depending on archaeological activity and chance finds, been brought to light outside the walls of a good number of central Adriatic towns. To associate these structures directly with town functions, we look mostly at zones with a maximum distance from the forum of some 6–8 km, which can be seen as the crucial area for the daily satisfaction of the alimentary needs of the city. Nevertheless, in many ways, it is better not to follow a simple and mathematically strict concentric model, as towns on the coast evidently have a very different suburban geography, as *suburbia* sizes should be measured according to the size and demographic reality of towns, and most of all, because a radial system linked to the roads leaving the town and regarding the cost and ease of travel makes much more sense.

Some of the features of Roman *suburbia* are clearly visible archaeologically, others need higher resolution research, such as via particular survey operations, ecological analyses and geomorphological observations. Recently, I identified the most important elements seen in the region's suburban landscape (Vermeulen 2017), and I remind the reader here of just a few archaeologically well-attested examples. A first group is related to connectivity: they are the many Roman roads leaving the gates of the towns in the region and a series of utilitarian or honorific structures connected with transport (bridges, milestones, arches). Some of these, such as the arch in *Ariminum*, mark the limits of the *pomerium*. In most towns, this linear system is opportunistically used for the residences of the dead, and most detected cemeteries, especially in the final decades of the Republic and during the first century CE, were lined with monumental structures (Stortoni 2008). The aqueducts and other utilitarian structures connected with water, such as monumental fountains, monumentalized sources and public cisterns, are also sometimes topographically close to the roads (Agostini 1987), as was seen with the Fonte Magna at *Auximum* (Gobbi 1999) and an aqueduct entering *Trea* from its western gate (Moscatelli 1988; Vermeulen *et al.* 2012). When a river or the sea is nearby, port installations and possibly storehouses might be encountered, as is the case in *Castrum Truentinum* near the mouth of the Tronto river (Staffa 2001). Along the extramural roads, certain service buildings can also be present, such as *tabernae*, *thermae*, sanctuaries or buildings for spectacles, such as the amphitheatre of *Urbs Salvia* and the recently discovered and in 2019 partially excavated *campus* complex of *Septempeda*. More polluting or dangerous, and, therefore, often banished to the suburbs, were sites of manufacturing or workshops for pottery, building materials, metal works, glass production, tanneries and so on, as located around a few towns, such as the pottery quarter found in *Septempeda* (Landolfi 2003) and a possible metal works in *Suasa* (Giorgi and Lepore 2010). Partly connected with this, and also with normal residential functions inside the towns, are the waste disposal areas or rubbish dumps, as suggested by a suburban survey in *Trea* (Vermeulen *et al.* 2012). This also applies to quarries and clay pits, perhaps surviving as ponds with a secondary function for watering cattle. Connected more with food production are the indications closer to the walls of market gardening areas, with their own paths and demarcations or enclosures, structures related to land division and hydrological land improvement (ditches and gullies for drainage or irrigation) and rural properties with or without farms or villas. Among the latter, a special place is taken by some suburban villa properties of high status and comfort to be seen as a direct extension of the rich housing in the town centre.

Much of these latter peripheral structures, connected with market gardening and the first agricultural exploitation outside city walls, were archaeologically revealed and partly mapped outside the coastal city of *Potentia* (Figures 2.4 and 2.6), where the phenomenon of suburban spacing and intercommunication could be well-studied (Vermeulen 2017; Corsi and Vermeulen, forthcoming).

Soon after its second century foundation (184 BCE), this colonial town was surrounded by a series of single farmsteads, particularly clustered on the hillslopes and near the edge of the valley plain. In the valley bottom of the Potenza river, where a *centuriatio* system divided the land, some farming occurred, even if here it seems densities were initially less. At the end of the Republic and during the first century CE, settlement and peripheral structures intensified in the suburban area. The first mile outside the city walls remained mostly free of rural habitation and seemed to have hosted a series of peripheral facilities and functions for the town. The three outgoing roads here were increasingly lined with funerary monuments and the corresponding cemeteries expanded now further away from these transport axes. The road south of the town, leading towards a bridge over the river that was possibly built here in Augustan times, also served an area where port installations near the river mouth are presumed, and some extramural settlement was located. South of the river, on the drier beach ridge, several amphora workshops have been detected along the coastal road (Monsieur 2009). Here the suburban tentacles of the town reached a greater distance, thanks to the functionality of the road and the port. Near the northern gate more industrial activity, including again a potters' workshop for amphora production, must have functioned for a time. Finally, the area immediately west of the town was shown by palynological analysis to combine, during the period considered here, some wet grassland for grazing livestock and mainly orchards for the town supply of fruits (e.g. plums, cherries, nuts) and vegetables (e.g. chicory, fennel, cabbage). Outside this first peripheral town zone, the wider agricultural land stretched over the centuriated valley bottom and the hills. An even denser network of Roman farms and some larger *villae rusticae* than in the previous period has been revealed here. Many farms and villas were typically located on the well-positioned hill ridges and slopes near the edge of the valley plain, where wine and olive cultivation on terraced slopes was favourable. On a few hillslope locations south of the valley, the associated amphora production has been demonstrated. A few larger terraced villas with sea views were particularly well located on half-slope locations where the terrain was less steep and where often a local source was captured, providing the inhabitants with water throughout the year. These villas, often surviving until Late Antiquity, kept a very good visual and material (road) link with the city and riverine and maritime port they depended on. Their spatial collocation and direct communication potential were very well equilibrated with their fundamental economic role for the city and its territory.

## Conclusion

In this chapter, we have argued for a definite regional approach to the debate on the Roman spatial economy and assembled some elements to show how our understanding of the movement of people and goods for economic purposes can be better understood. Our focus on archaeologically detectable material aspects of urban topography and regional landscape use considered the role of towns as prime market centres and also of their *suburbia* and rural territories as highly important study areas for revealing production and consumption patterns of the population concerned. Via a detailed case study in central Adriatic Italy, we could stress the very widespread Roman phenomenon of the prime importance of road and river networks as the arteries of economic movement, in close interplay with maritime connections and with the fundamental impact that a dense network of towns, villages and other transport nodes has on economic space. This exercise undoubtedly demonstrates that if we desire to answer on an Empire-wide scale such questions as 'how did spatial structures and movement dynamics in Roman cities influence economic processes?' and 'to what extent, and how precisely, did Roman economic activity shape and determine spaces, places and movements in and around cities?', we need to focus on regional diversity and look close enough at phenomena that help explain the functioning and dynamics of urban-based economic networks within their specific geographical and historical context.

## References

Agostini, Silvano. "Aquedotti romani sotteranei in area mesoadriatica: tema di una ricerca archeologica integrate", Pages 139–145 in *Atti II Convegno Nazionale di Speleologia Urbana*. Edited by CAI. Napoli, 1987.

Antico Gallina, Mariavittoria, ed. *Dal Suburbium al Faubourg: evoluzione di una realtà urbana.* Milano: ET Edizioni, 2000.

Bintliff, John. "Catchments, settlement chambers and demography", Pages 61–69 in *Counterpoint: Essays in Archaeology and Heritage Management in Honour of Professor Kristian Kristiansen.* Edited by Kristian Kristiansen, Serena Sabatini and Sophie Bergerbrant. British Archaeological Reports. International series 2508. Oxford: Archaeopress, 2013.

Bintliff, John and Snodgrass, Anthony. "Mediterranean survey and the city", *Antiquity* 62 (1988): 57–71.

Cardinali, Claudia and Luni, Mario. "La riscoperta nella regione medioadriatica delle trentacinque città romane", Pages 19–40 in *La forma della città e del territorio 3* (Atlante Tematico di Topografia Antica 15). Edited by Lorenzo Quilici and Stefanella Quilici Gigli. Roma: L'erma Di Bretschneider, 2006.

Campagnoli, Paolo. *La Bassa valle del Foglia e il territorio di Pisaurum in eta romana* (Studi e Scavi 7). Bologna: University Press Bologna, 1999.

Cornell, Tim J. and Lomas, Kathryn, eds. *Urban Society in Roman Italy*. London: Taylor & Francis, 1995.

Corsi, Cristina, Slapšak, Bozidar and Vermeulen, Frank, eds. *Good Practice in Archaeological Diagnostics. Non-invasive Survey of Complex Archaeological Sites* (Natural Science in Archaeology, 69), Cham–Heidelberg–New York–Dordrecht– London: Springer International, 2013.

Corsi, Cristina and Vermeulen, Frank. "Introduction", Pages 11–16 in *Changing Landscapes. The Impact of Roman Towns in the Western Mediterranean* (Proceedings of the International Colloquium, Castelo de Vide – Marvão 15th–17th May 2008). Edited by Cristina Corsi and Frank Vermeulen. Bologna: Ante Quem, 2010.

Corsi, Cristina and Vermeulen, Frank. "Suburbia and the town-territory relationship in the Roman West: theory, method and archaeological practice". *Orizzonti* XII (2021): 25–36, DOI: 10.19272/202107501002

Dall'Aglio, Pier Luigi, De Maria, Sandro and Mariotti, Amelia, eds. *Archeologia delle valli marchigiane Misa, Nevola e Cesano*. Perugia: Electa Mondadori, 1991.

De Ligt, Luuk. *Peasants, Citizens and Soldiers. Studies in the Demographic History of Roman Italy 225 BC–AD100*. Cambridge: Cambridge University Press, 2011.

Delplace, Christiane. *La romanisation du Picenum. L' exemple d'Urbs Salvia* (Collection de l École française de Rome 177). Rome: École française de Rome: 1993.

Fortini, Paulo. "Aspetti della vita economica del Piceno", Pages 95–116 in *Il Piceno in età romana dalla sottomissione a Roma alla fine del mondo antico, Atti del 3° Seminario di studi per personale direttivo e docente della scuola*. Cupra Marittima, 1991.

Foucault, Michel. *Surveiller et punir*. Paris: Gallimard, 1975.

Gabba, Emilio and Pasquinucci, Marinella. *Strutture agrarie e allevamento transumante nell'Italia romana*. Pisa: Giardini, 1979.

Giorgi, Enrico and Lepore, Giuseppe, eds. *Archeologia nella valle del Cesano tra Suasa e Santa Maria in Portuno (1996–2009), Atti delle giornate di studi in occasione dei venti anni di ricerche archeologiche dell'Università di Bologna nella Valle del Cesano (Castelleone di Suasa, Corinaldo 18 dicembre 2008 - San Lorenzo in Campo 19 dicembre 2008*. Bologna: Università degli studi Bologna, 2010.

Gobbi, Cecilia. "La "Fonte Magna" di Auximum". *ATTA* 8 (1999): 185–196.

Gros, Pierre. *L'architecture romaine. 1. Les monuments publics*. Paris: Picard, 1996.

Hanson, John William. *An Urban Geography of the Roman World, 100 BC to AD 300*. Oxford: Archaeopress, 2016.

Hartnett, Jeremy. *The Roman Street: Urban Life and Society in Pompeii, Herculaneum, and Rome*. Cambridge: Cambridge University Press, 2017.

Johnson, Paul and Millett, Martin, eds. *Archaeological Survey and the City* (University of Cambridge Museum of Classical Archaeology Monographs 2). Oxford: Oxbow, 2012.

Kaiser, Alan. *The Urban Dialogue: An Analysis of the Use of Space in the Roman City of Empúries, Spain*. Oxford: Archaeopress, 2000.

Kaiser, Alan. *Roman Urban Street Networks*. London: Routledge, 2011.

Lafon, Xavier. "Le suburbium". *Pallas* 55 (2001): 199–214.

Launaro, Alessandro. *Peasants and Slaves. The Rural Population of Roman Italy (200 BC to AD 100)*. Cambridge: Cambridge University Press, 2011.

Laurence, Ray. *Roman Pompeii: Space and Society*. London: Taylor & Francis, 2007.

Laurence, Ray. "City Traffic and Archaeology of Roman Streets from Pompeii to Rome", Pages 87–106 in *Stadtverkehr in der Antiken Welt. Internationales Kolloquium zur 175-Jahrfeier des Deutschen Archäologischen Instituts. Rom 21. bis 23. April 2004*. Edited by Dieter Mertens. Wiesbaden: Dr. Ludwig Reichert Verlag, 2008.

Laurence, Ray. *Roman Archaeology for Historians*. London & New York: Routledge, 2012.

Laurence, Ray and Newsome, David J. *Rome, Ostia, Pompeii: Movement and Space*. Oxford: Oxford University Press, 2011.

Landolfi, Maurizio. *Il Museo Civico Archeologico di San Severino Marche*. San Severino Marche, 2003.

Menchelli, Simonetta. "Anfore vinarie adriatiche: il Piceno et gli altri contesti produttivi regionali". *Ocnus* 19 (2011): 239–244.

Menchelli, Simonetta. *Paesaggi piceni e romani nelle Marche meridionali. L'ager Firmanus dall'età tardo-repubblicana alla conquista longobarda*. Pisa: University Press, 2012.

Millett, Martin and Keay, Simon. "General background", Pages 224–228 in Helen Patterson (ed.), *Bridging the Tiber. Approaches to Regional Archaeology in the Middle Tiber Valley*, Monographs of the British School at Rome. London: British School at Rome, 2004.

Monsieur, Patrick. "A Late Republican and an Early Imperial Amphora Workshop at Potenza Picena (Marche, Italy)". *BABESCH* 84 (2009): 93–95.

Morley, Neville. "Cities in context: urban systems in Roman Italy", Pages 40–58 in *Roman Urbanism: Beyond the Consumer City*. Edited by Helen M. Parkins. London & New York: Taylor & Francis, 1997.

Moscatelli, Umberto. *Trea*. (Forma Italiae 33). Firenze: Olschki, 1988. Staffa, Andrea. "Abruzzo: strutture portuali e assetto del litorale fra Antichità ed Altomedioevo", Pages 343–413 in *Strutture Portuali e rotte marittime nell'adriatico de età romana*. Edited by Claudio Zaccaria (Collection de L'Ecole Française de Rome 280, Antichità Altoadriatiche XLVI). Trieste/Roma: Editreg, 2001.

Paci, Gianfranco. "Medio-Adriatico occidentale e commerci transmarine (II sec. A.C.-II sec. D.C.)", Pages 73–88 in *Strutture Portuali e rotte marittime nell'adriatico de età romana* (Collection de L'Ecole Française de Rome 280, Antichità Altoadriatiche XLVI). Edited by Claudio Zaccaria. Trieste & Roma: École française de Rome, 2001.

Paci, Gianfranco. *Ricerche di storia e di epigrafia romana delle Marche* (Ichnia 11). Tivoli: Edizioni Tored, 2008.

Panella, Clementina. "Roma, il Suburbio e l'Italia in Età Medio- e Tardo-Repubblicana: Cultura materiale, territorie, economie". *Facta* 4 (2010): 11–124.

Perna, Roberto and Capponi, Chiara. "*Città e campagna nella valle del Chienti in età repubblicana ed imperiale. La carta archeologica della provincia di Macerata*", Pages 149–164 in *I Processi formativi ed evolutivi della città in area adriatica*. Edited by Giuliano de Marinis, Giovanna Maria Fabrini, Gianfranco Paci, Roberto Perna, Mara Silvestrini (BAR International Series 2419). Oxford: BAR Publishing, 2012.

Perna, Roberto, Cingolani, Sofia, Tubaldi, Valeria, Capradossi, Valentina and Xavier de Silva, Ludovica. "I contesti repubblicani della colonia di *Pollentia-Urbs Salvia*. L'area forense". *Rei CretariÆ RomanÆ FaVtorVm Acta* 44 (2016): 267–280.

Poehler, Eric, E. *The Traffic Systems of Pompeii*. Oxford: Oxford University Press, 2017.

Purcell, Nicolas. "Wine and wealth in ancient Italy". *JRS* 75 (1985): 1–19.

Rosenstein, Nathan. "Aristocrats and agriculture in the middle and late Republic". *Journal of Roman Studies* 98 (2008): 1–26.

Sewell, Jamie and Witcher, Rob, E. "Urbanism in Ancient Peninsular Italy: developing a methodology for a database analysis of higher order settlements (350 BCE to 300 CE)". *Internet Archaeology* 40 (2015).

Stortoni, Emanuela. *Monumenti funerari romani nelle province di Macerata, Fermo e Ascoli Piceno*. Macerata: Me Monacchi, 2008.

Van Limbergen, Dimitri. "Vinum picenum and oliva picena. Wine and oil presses in central Adriatic Italy between the Late Republic and the Early Empire. Evidence and problems". *BABESCH* 86 (2011): 71–94.

Van Limbergen, Dimitri, Monsieur Patrick and Vermeulen, Frank. "The role of overseas export and local consumption demand in the development of viticulture in Central Adriatic Italy (200 BC-AD 150). The case of the ager Potentinus and the wider Potenza valley", Pages 336–360 in *The economic integration of Roman Italy. Rural communities in a globalising world*. Edited by Tymon, C., A. De Haas and Gijs Tol. Leiden & Boston: Brill, 2011.

Verdonck, Lieven and Vermeulen, Frank. "A contribution to the study of Roman rural settlement in Marche". *Picus* XXIV (2004): 161–229.

Vermeulen, Frank. *From the Mountains to the Sea. The Roman Colonisation and Urbanisation of Central Adriatic Italy* (Babesch Supplement 30). Leuven–Paris–Bristol: Peeters Publishers, 2017.

Vermeulen, Frank, Burgers, Gert-Jan, Keay, Simon and Corsi, Cristina, eds. *Urban Landscape Survey in Italy and the Mediterranean*. Oxford: Oxbow, 2012.

Vermeulen, Frank and Mlekuž, Dimitri. "Surveying an Adriatic Valley: a wide area view on early urbanisation processes in Northern Picenum", Pages 207–222 in *Urban Landscape Survey in Italy and the Mediterranean*. Edited by Frank Vermeulen, Gert-Jan Burgers, Simon Keay and Cristina Corsi. Oxford: Oxbow, 2012.

Vermeulen, Frank, Slapšak, Bozidar and Mlekuž, Dimitri. "Surveying the Townscape of Roman *Trea* (Picenum)", Pages 261–282 in *Archaeological Survey and the City* (University of Cambridge Museum of Classical Archaeology Monographs). Edited by Paul S. Johnson and Martin Millett. Oxford: Oxbow, 2012.

Vermeulen, Frank, Van Limbergen, Dimitri, Monsieur, Patrick and Taelman, Devi. *The Potenza Valley Survey (Marche, Italy). Settlement Dynamics and Changing Material Culture in an Adriatic Valley between Iron Age and Late Antiquity* (Studia Archaeologica 1). Roma: Academia Belgica, 2017.

Zuiderhoek, Arjan. *The Ancient City* (Key Themes in Ancient History). Cambridge: Cambridge University Press, 2016.

# PART II
# Spaces

# 3 Beyond Pompeii and Ostia

## Commerce and urban space in Roman Italy

*Miko Flohr*

### Introduction

Scholarly discourse on Roman urban commercial topographies has been almost completely dominated by Pompeii and Ostia. From the lengthy discussion on the distribution of 'shops' over the urban topography of Pompeii by Ray Laurence (1994), via Janet DeLaine's seminal chapter on the commercial landscape of Roman Ostia (DeLaine 2005), through to recent approaches to the archaeology of Roman retail and commerce by Claire Holleran (2012) and Steven Ellis (2018) and, for Ostia, Schoevaert (2018), it is clear that the commercial landscapes of these two cities have received by far most of the attention. The role of other cities – including Rome itself – has remained much more limited, maybe with the partial exception of Herculaneum (Monteix 2010). This is, of course, for understandable reasons: Pompeii and Ostia (and to a lesser extent Herculaneum) are exceptionally well-preserved and well-documented Roman cities, where substantial parts of the urban landscape can be studied, both at one specific moment – the 70s CE for Pompeii (and Herculaneum) and the 130s CE for Ostia – and in their chronological development over time from the Middle Republic through to well into the Imperial period, and for Ostia even beyond.

Yet it is also clear that the strong focus on these two cities poses a significant methodological problem when one is interested in the commercial history of cities in Roman Italy at large: not only is two cities a small sample to work with anyway, but for all their qualities, Pompeii and Ostia barely represent the urban average in the peninsula. For Ostia, the metropolitan satellite, closely tied in its development to the city of Rome itself, the historical exceptionality is straightforward and undisputed, but it should not be forgotten that Pompeii, too, was a large city in a quite exceptional region. In De Ligt's survey of urbanism in Roman Italy in the Augustan period, both Ostia and Pompeii firmly belong to a group of 'large' cities with an urban area exceeding 40 ha in size (De Ligt 2012). While there are over 40 such cities in Roman Italy, particularly in *Latium*, *Campania*, and Cisalpine Gaul, they represent just over 10% of the total. Medium-sized towns of between 20 and 40 ha – a group to which, for instance, Herculaneum belonged, count

*Table 3.1* Towns of Roman Italy categorized according to size (based on De Ligt 2012)

|  | Large towns (>40 ha) | Medium-sized towns (20–40 ha) | Small towns (<20 ha) | Total |
| --- | --- | --- | --- | --- |
| Tyrrhenian Italy | 15 | 38 | 74 | 127 |
| Apennines | 4 | 25 | 80 | 109 |
| Southern Italy | 9 | 12 | 84 | 105 |
| Cisalpine Gaul | 15 | 31 | 32 | 78 |
| Total | 43 | 106 | 270 | 419 |

over 100, while a substantial majority of 270 towns in Roman Italy probably measured less than 20 ha (Table 3.1). While there was some urban growth in the Imperial period, these basic parameters of urbanism did not fundamentally change: most urban settlements in Roman Italy remained relatively small (De Ligt 2016). For Pompeii, it can be added that recent discourse on its urban economy has identified a range of regionally specific factors that make it that it should be seen, from early on, as a large and wealthy city in an exceptionally wealthy region (Flohr and Wilson 2017; Flohr 2013). Thus, it is essential for debates about the role of commerce in Roman urban space to address the question of the extent to which developments that can be observed in Pompeii and Ostia were actually mirrored elsewhere. Put differently: what was the effect of urban scale on the development of urban commercial space and on the presence of retail and manufacturing in the urban landscape? How can we build a bridge from the picture that can be reconstructed for Pompeii and Ostia to all those medium-sized and small towns that made up the bulk of cities in Roman Italy?

This chapter addresses these questions and explores a comparative framework for assessing the urban commercial landscapes of Roman Italy in all their varieties. It does so from the idea that it is essential for debates in Roman urban history to develop more and better tools to construct historical narratives by weighing archaeological evidence from multiple urban sites. Any successful approach, however, has to start from Pompeii and Ostia – simply moving away from these places does not connect them to the larger whole; the key is to find an approach to the evidence from Pompeii and Ostia that also works in the other known urban sites of Roman Italy. This chapter argues that one way to do this is to focus on the historical development of urban commercial landscapes and the changing patterns of investment, rather than to analyse the resulting commercial landscapes of the Imperial period, which outside Pompeii and Ostia can barely be meaningfully studied: the idea is that investment contexts rather than urban topographies make it possible to see which developments that can be encountered at Pompeii and Ostia were common throughout Roman Italy, and which were not, and, thus, ultimately, allow for a meaningful comparison of historical developments throughout the peninsula.

For this purpose, the following pages will first revisit the evidence from Pompeii and Ostia to assess what, actually, are the indicators for development in their archaeological records; then the evidence from a range of other cities from Roman Italy will be discussed to identify structural similarities and differences. This makes it possible to articulate a comparative framework for urban commercial landscapes in Roman Italy in the final section of this chapter, and to discuss the broader dynamics of commercial investment in the cities of the peninsula in the later Republican and Imperial period. This exercise will make clear that some of the developments at Pompeii and Ostia can be identified in some other cities as well, but that it is, at the same time, clear that they offer a focal point of limited value for addressing the history of urban commerce in Roman Italy in broader terms. Nevertheless, it will be argued that a model based on a critical confrontation of these two cities with evidence from other places offers considerable help in getting a grip on the commercial history of urban settlements in the Italian peninsula.

### Pompeii: *building* tabernae *in a large Roman city*

Pompeii offers the most detailed and varied archaeological environment for studying the historical development of investment in commercial facilities. The key to reconstructing the history of its commercial landscape lies in the city's architectural remains and in our relative dating of the materials and techniques used for their construction. The historical development of building practice is a methodological minefield in Pompeian studies with a substantial historiography (Mau 1900; Carrington 1933; Ling 1997; Adam 2007). While this is not the place for an exhaustive treatment, it may be argued that it is marked by two relatively undisputed watersheds that can be used to distinguish the main phases of Pompeii's urban history. The first of these is the emergence of mortar-based construction: initially, Pompeian walls were made from carefully stacked Stones within a larger framework of pillars – for both, a local travertine called 'sarno stone' would be used. Over the course of the second century BCE, this way of building gave way to a practice in which walls were increasingly held together by mortar. Precise dating is not available, but most scholars assume that the decisive turning point lies somewhere close to the middle of the second century BCE (Peterse 1999; Mogetta 2016). It is also clear that this change goes hand in hand with an increased variation in the building materials used: alongside Sarno stone, builders began to use grey lava and tufa in substantial quantities. The second watershed was the spread of brick-dominated construction techniques. This change does not so much concern the first appearance of brick (in columns, in the late second century BCE), but rather the increased use of brick-dependent building practices like *opus latericium* and *opus vittatum mixtum*; for Pompeii, this seems to be a development of the Augustan period (e.g. Fröhlich 1993). Starting from these watersheds, the history of Pompeii's commercial landscape can be discussed in three steps: an 'early' phase, traditionally referred to as the 'Samnite' period, up to around 150 BCE, a late Hellenistic and early Roman phase, between 150 BCE and ca. 25 BCE (but with an emphasis in the late second century), and an Early Imperial phase, between ca. 25 BCE and 79 CE.[1]

The commercial landscape of Samnite Pompeii is only fragmentarily known, and its interpretation remains complex, as there is no agreed way of (relatively) dating buildings within this period; especially in the city centre, almost everything has been overbuilt in later periods – it is relevant to note that most *tabernae* from the Samnite period have survived in the relative margins of Pompeii's urban landscape, where there was little development in later periods (Figure 3.1). Their remains make clear that the urban landscape *was* to some extent commercialized. As is known through a 1940s excavation by Maiuri, there was a row of *tabernae* along at least part of the east side the *forum*, and a number of houses constructed with building techniques typical for this period has *tabernae* around or next to their main entrance, though never more than one or two.[2] It seems that in this period, investment in *tabernae* is attested in a limited number of forms and appears to have taken place on a relatively small scale. It is also clear that even though there was some interest in building *tabernae* in Samnite Pompeii, the *taberna* was not the omnipresent phenomenon that it would become later on: many of the larger houses that we have from this period,

*Figure 3.1* Pompeii, house I 3, 25–26: Samnite period building with main entrance and *taberna* opening on a back street in the south of the city. Facade in Sarno stone.

*Figure 3.2* Pompeii, Samnite period house VI 14, 20 with a closed Sarno stone Facade.

such as the House of Orpheus (VI 14, 18–20, Figure 3.2) and the House of the Surgeon (VI 1, 10), were built without *tabernae*, even though they were in very central locations; other houses from this period only got their *tabernae* at a much later point in time, when the *cubicula* that originally had surrounded the main entrance corridor were converted into shops.[3] As it seems, Pompeii's commercial landscape before the mid-second century BCE was a bit less dense than it would become later on, and less clearly focused on the main roads.

The change between Samnite Pompeii and Late Hellenistic Pompeii was dramatic and can, when it comes to retail, rightly be thought of in terms of a 'retail revolution', as Steven Ellis has recently suggested (Ellis 2018, 127–147). As Ellis acknowledges, this retail revolution is part of a much broader historical development, which has left deep traces throughout Pompeii's urban landscape and which has been discussed in terms of a 'golden century' (Pesando 2006). In many ways, the urban landscape of Pompeii was decisively shaped in this period, and particularly, it seems, in the decades around 100 BCE. As far as Pompeii's commercial landscape is concerned, the evidence indicates a marked diversification in the contexts in which *tabernae* were being constructed and a sharp increase in the numbers of *tabernae* constructed within individual building projects. Three developments are worth outlining (Flohr 2011). First, there was an increase in the size of houses, and

*Figure 3.3* Pompeii, late Hellenistic facade with shops belonging to the Domus
Cornelia (VIII 4, 14–25).

an increased tendency to build *tabernae* on all sides of houses bordering on
the street. This led to higher numbers of *tabernae* associated with individual
houses – houses were being constructed with five, six, or ten *tabernae* rather
than with just one or two (Figure 3.3).[4] Second, *tabernae* started to appear
in public buildings, which often were designed with a facade with a row of
*tabernae*. This is true for the two large public bath complexes constructed
in this period – the Stabian Baths (ca. 100 BCE, Figure 3.4) and the Forum
Baths (ca. 70 BCE) – and for the first version of the *macellum*, which was also
constructed in this period (Pesando and Guidobaldi 2006). Finally, there
was an emergence of independent, purpose-built, rows of *tabernae* (Flohr,
2020a. Often, these were constructed on plots of land that appear to have
been earmarked for private house construction, thus suggesting substantial
investment by private individuals in commercial space (Figure 3.5). These
developments resulted in a very dense commercial landscape with a strong
focus on the urban thoroughfares. By the end of this period, most commercial possibilities alongside the main roads were actually being used, and it
is only in the more marginal locations in the city that houses were being
constructed with closed facades.

For the last century of Pompeii, up to and including the last decades
before the eruption, when the city seems to have been suffering from repeated

*Figure 3.4* Pompeii, late Hellenistic facade of the Stabian Baths.

*Figure 3.5* Pompeii. Row of Late Hellenistic *tabernae* alongside the Via dell'Abbondanza (VIII 5, 16–20).

*Figure 3.6* Pompeii. West facade of the Early Imperial Central Baths (IX 4).

seismic upheaval, the city's architectural remains suggest a gradual continuation of commercial intensification. Several larger construction projects that constructed *tabernae* on a scale not previously seen – particularly, this is true for the *porticus* with *tabernae* that, remarkably, was constructed just *outside* the main city gate on the north side of the city – the Porta di Ercolano (Pesando and Guidobaldi 2006, 266; Zanella 2020). Inside the city, there was an extension to the Stabian Baths, which included 12 *tabernae*, and the newly constructed Central Baths (Figure 3.6), which included 13 *tabernae*, albeit on a location where probably a similar or larger number of *tabernae* had stood before the houses in the city block were demolished to make space for the bath complex (De Haan and Wallat 2008).

At the same time, many houses were being built or rebuilt with *tabernae*, and there is ample evidence of originally domestic rooms being converted into *tabernae* in this period.[5] This extended, and intensified, but ultimately did not fundamentally alter Pompeii's commercial landscape. In terms of the nature of investment, existing models continued to be applied, but there was no real innovation. Indeed, the most fundamental change in Pompeii's commercial landscape in this period is the disappearance of *tabernae* from the east side of the *forum*, and the gradual isolation of the plaza from its urban context – even though this did not end the *forum*'s commercial role, it changed the dynamics of the commercial landscape in Pompeii's city centre (Poehler 2017, 49–51; Pesando and Guidobaldi 2006, 40–53).

### Ostia: *commercial investment in the shadow of Rome*

The archaeological remains at Ostia offer much less explicit a view on the long-term historical development of the city: they cluster in the first half of the second century CE. Virtually all earlier building activity is only fragmentarily known, and our knowledge depends on the amount of excavation activity underneath the floor levels of Trajanic and Hadrianic buildings (Figure 3.7).[6] Still the evidence for these earlier phases is just about explicit enough to allow for a discussion of the development of the city's commercial landscape in general terms. The working chronology at Ostia slightly differs from that at Pompeii: it makes sense to distinguish just one Republican phase, an Early Imperial phase up to the end of the first century CE, and the boom period of the first half of the second century CE.

While the walls of several third-century BCE *tabernae* have been preserved against the outer east wall of the *castrum* that formed the heart of the mid-Republican Roman colony (Calza and Becatti 1953, 98), a more complete picture only emerges from the later second century BCE onwards, when the city began to grow organically alongside the roads leading to and from the *castrum*. Remains of houses from this period have been excavated at several places, particularly along the western *decumanus* and in the *castrum* (Flohr 2018). Some of these houses seem to have included *tabernae*, but for most, their presence is actually hard to prove at the present state of our knowledge,

*Figure 3.7* Ostia, late Republican and Early Imperial structures underneath the second century CE floor level.

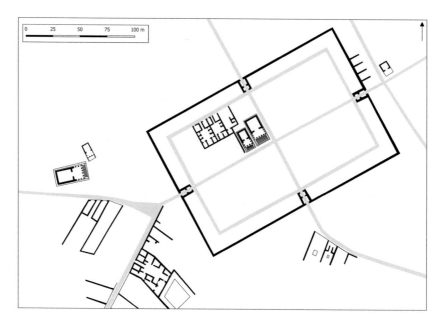

*Figure 3.8* Ostia, plan indicating the remains of the late Republican city.

as traces of entrances and thresholds are lacking.[7] They are mostly small-
to medium-sized *atrium* houses with room for the classic scenario of two
*tabernae* around the main entrance (Figure 3.8).

Investment on a larger scale could only be found east of the *castrum*, along
the eastern *decumanus*. Here the remains of a row of at least ten *tabernae*
were excavated underneath the later Horrea of Hortensius, some 200 m
from the *castrum* in an area that, at the time, clearly was suburban in character: just west of the *tabernae* are the remains of a late second-century BCE
tomb (Pavolini 2006, 234–235). Even further to the east, a large complex with
at least 15 *tabernae* was built north of the *decumanus* (Pavolini 2006, 35).
Probably, these large commercial complexes served the harbour rather than
the city: before the Trajanic and Hadrianic periods, basically no people were
living in this area, as building was restricted by official decree (Pavolini 2006,
49). Thus, at Ostia, there was a dichotomy between small-scale private investment in the city itself, and further to the east large-scale investment associated
with the supply system of Rome rather than with the still modest urban settlement around the harbour. Compared to Pompeii, the elite *domus* with large
numbers of *tabernae* was absent from late Republican Ostia, as is true for
public buildings with rows of *tabernae* – there were no large bath complexes
or a *macellum* in the city before the Imperial period.

From the Augustan era onwards, *tabernae* began to be built on a larger
scale within the urban area as well: rows of *tabernae* were built against the west
wall of the *castrum*, and along the western *decumanus*, and there is evidence

for commercial architecture along the inner pomerial road of the *castrum* (Calza and Becatti 1953). Even if the overall picture of urban development in the first century CE remains fragmentary, it seems that the city's commercial landscape in general became not only denser – more urban space was used for commercial purposes, and *tabernae* became a more central element in the urban landscape – but also vaster, extending over the entire area enclosed by the late Republican wall circuit and, already in the late first century CE, beyond, in the Flavian period, a large *domus* with six *tabernae* was built just outside the Porta Marina (III VII 3–4; Van der Meer 2005; Pavolini 2006, 174–176). Still the forms of investment stuck to the architectural models that were already known, and no *tabernae* were built in connection to the public urban architecture.

The Trajanic and Hadrianic building boom, which completely transformed Ostia's urban landscape, brought considerable diversification in investment, and a substantial level of innovation, also compared to late Republican Pompeii. The urban leap of scale brought about by the growth of the city in the early second century CE was first and foremost reflected in the vast size of some building plots, particularly in areas that had not been built up in earlier periods, or which were cleared for development by the government, such as the area between the *forum* and the Tiber. Moreover, particularly in the city centre, building projects were generally maximizing the commercial use of space, leading to the canonical Ostian *insulae* with *tabernae* and other forms of commercial space on the ground floor and apartments for living on upper floors (Figure 3.9).

*Figure 3.9* Ostia, Caseggiato di Diana (I III 3–4), a second-century CE *insula* building.

*Figure 3.10* Ostia, *Case a Giardino* (III IX): two *tabernae* opening off the inner plaza of the complex.

In addition to these broader trends, there were three specific developments in construction practice that led to a more fundamental change in the nature of Ostia's commercial landscape. The first of these is that several building projects (by far) surpassed the size of one building and basically involved the construction of entire urban quarters, with, so it seems, their own internal social dynamics, and an internal commercial landscape that seems to have functioned partially independently of the surrounding urban area. This is particularly clear in the case of the Case a Giardino development in the west part of the city, which included a substantial number of *tabernae* around its central inner courtyard (Figure 3.10; Stevens 2005; Pavolini 2006, 153–171). A second development concerns the role of *tabernae* in public architecture, which is further increased compared to late Republican and Early Imperial Pompeii: *tabernae* now occupy the area under the *cavea* of the theatre (Figure 3.11), and even open off the *palaestrae* of the two large bath complexes. The third 'innovation' that first emerged in  second-century CE Ostia is the *taberna* building with internal *tabernae*, away from the street. For instance, the so-called Caseggiato del Larario (Figure 3.12), close to the *forum*, was surrounded by nine *tabernae* on its outside, but, additionally, had ten *tabernae* around its small internal courtyard (Scocca 1994; Pavolini 2006, 113).

*Figure 3.11* Ostia, *tabernae* underneath the *cavea* of the theatre.

*Figure 3.12* Ostia. Central courtyard of the *Caseggiato del Larario* (I IX 3) with internal *tabernae*.

Other buildings, like III 1 7, had a central, internal corridor surrounded by *tabernae* (DeLaine 2005, 35). Some *tabernae* were also simply constructed along the open space inside the city blocks (e.g. *tabernae* IV 11 4; Stöger 2011, 153–155). Thus, compared to Pompeii, where only the *macellum* had internal *tabernae*, at Ostia, the retail and other forms of commerce were increasingly penetrating into the inner parts of the city blocks.

As we can see from this overview, the commercial landscape of Ostia developed according to different principles and at a different pace than that of *Pompeii*. Up to the late first century CE, Ostia essentially lagged behind: it did have *tabernae* along its streets, and in slowly increasing quantities; and it had seen a development towards larger forms of investment in the Early Imperial period, but it lacked the large *atrium* houses that drove the development of the commercial landscape of Late Hellenistic Pompeii; and, in this period, it also lacked *tabernae* associated with public buildings. With the exception of the zone along the eastern decumanus, which may have been dominated by Rome-based investors to serve the Roman market, commercial investment in late Republican and Early Imperial Ostia appears to operate on a smaller scale than Pompeii. This obviously changed in the second century CE, when types of investment emerged that at *Pompeii* had never existed. Perhaps, to some extent, these innovations reflect ways of thinking about commercial investment that had developed in, specifically, the Roman metropolis, though it has to be kept in mind that Ostia's building boom in many ways presented an occasion for unbounded urban development rarely paralleled in Rome itself, given the virtually flat area on which Ostia developed (Jansen 2002).

## Urban commercial landscapes in Roman Italy

The question raised at the start of this chapter was in which way, and to which extent, these developments in Pompeii and Ostia represent the broader direction of change in late Republican and Early Imperial Roman Italy. This issue cannot be assessed without looking at the actual archaeological remains of other cities, but it has to be stressed that this evidence, wherever it is available, is fragmentary, and structurally biased: with few exceptions, urban excavations in Italy have focused on a small subsection of the city including or in the direct environment of the *forum*, and it is generally very hard to understand what was happening elsewhere in cities, particularly along urban through roads further away from the city centre (Patterson 2006, 116–119). Still, it is occasionally possible to identify the existence and spread of certain investment scenarios.

Indeed, in some cities where modern excavations have targeted rather centrally located parts of the urban landscape, no or very few *tabernae* could be identified. Remarkably, this is true for two cities that were destroyed in the late Roman Republic, in the very period when commercial investment was booming at Pompeii. At *Fregellae*, destroyed by Lucius Opimius in 125

*Figure 3.13  Norba.* Street surrounded with *atrium* houses with closed facades.

BCE, the excavators have reconstructed a number of *atrium* houses along a road directly north of the *forum*, and while these show all characteristics of medium-sized Pompeian *atrium* houses, their architecture and their remains strongly suggest they did not have *tabernae*: most, instead, had two *cubicula* surrounding the main entrance (Battaglini and Diosono 2010). At *Norba*, a zone with *atrium* houses has been excavated along the major urban east-west axis, not far from the *forum*. Again, though the architecture of the houses closely follows the Italic conventions, entrance corridors are surrounded by *cubicula*, not by *tabernae*, which are entirely lacking in the excavated part of the site (Figure 3.13; Quilici Gigli 2003; Carfora et al. 2010).

The *forum* of *Norba*, unfortunately, remains unexcavated – it is possible, but by no means certain that it was surrounded by *tabernae* on its long sides; at *Fregellae*, the *forum* is known through geophysical survey, and this has strongly suggested that the plaza was not surrounded by *tabernae* (Sewell 2010, 58–60). Essentially, thus, there is no clear evidence for *any* investment in *tabernae* in these two cities in the late second century BCE. It has to be observed that neither *Norba* nor *Fregellae* was a small city – they were ranked as such by De Ligt, but that was after their treatments at the hands of the Roman army (De Ligt 2012, 308). Before Sulla, *Norba* measured 40 ha *intra muros*, and *Fregellae* appears to have been much larger than this and is explicitly referred to as a major regional centre by Strabo (5.3.10).

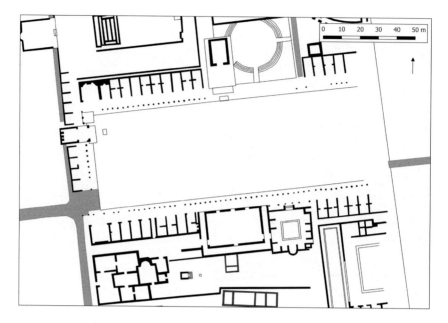

*Figure 3.14  Paestum.* Plan of the forum area.

At the same time, other cities, from early on, developed in a different direction. A place of particular significance is *Paestum*, which became a Roman colony in 273 BCE and was equipped with a large *forum* with over 60 *tabernae* a couple of decades thereafter (Figure 3.14; Torelli 1999; Greco et al. 1987; Greco and Theodorescu 1999). The large amount of *tabernae* around this *forum* may have limited investment elsewhere in the city: while there are *tabernae* along some of the excavated urban roads, many houses also have part of their *facades* closed: a common scenario for the larger houses was to have the main entrance surrounded by two cubicula, which then were followed by *tabernae* – at Pompeii, such houses would often have four *tabernae*; at *Paestum*, they have no more than two (Figure 3.15). Moreover, with one possible exception directly next to the *forum*, the *tabernae* along the city's roads were associated with house *facades*, not with commercial or public buildings.[8] Thus, while Republican *Paestum* developed a much more pronounced commercial landscape than *Norba* and *Fregellae*, it did not develop in the way Pompeii did; perhaps, Ostia – excluding the harbour area – is a closer parallel, but there are differences here too: contrary to Ostia, *Paestum* did have a massive *forum* with *tabernae*, and the largest *atrium* houses in the city were much larger than those at Ostia, suggesting a different type of local elite. Another relevant case is *Alba Fucens*. In this

*Figure 3.15 Paestum*. Large late Hellenistic *atrium* house with a partially opened facade with two *cubicula* and two *tabernae*.

city, founded as a Roman colony in 330 BCE, but developing its final urban form only in the late Republican period, excavations have targeted the central depression in the middle of the city (Mertens 1981). This area, which was surrounded by hills on three sides, contained the city's *forum* and a large set of public buildings. The two urban roads that surrounded the central zone had long rows of *tabernae* on their outer sides (Figure 3.16). These *tabernae*, which have been dated to the early first century BCE, were constructed on the land reserved for them when the city centre was planned – on both sides of the city centre, the *tabernae* occupy the area between the road framing the central public area and the first terrace wall (Mertens 1981, 39–40). It is likely that this was a publicly owned land and that the *tabernae* were public property. While the urban landscape of *Alba Fucens* remains mostly unknown, the enormous height differences between the *forum* zone and the rest of the city meant that movement through the city was limited (Flohr 2020b, 72). This would naturally have clustered a lot of commerce in the central valley where these *tabernae* were constructed, while, in the higher parts of the city, the incentive for investment in commercial space would have been much more restricted. This would suggest a picture similar to *Paestum*, where the *tabernae* in the central area were publicly owned, their centrality and sheer quantity restricting investment elsewhere in the city.

*Figure 3.16  Alba Fucens*, the so-called Via dei Pilastri, with a row of *tabernae* built on public land.

Yet, not all cities were developed and planned as Roman colonies. Particularly in the Early Imperial period, the processes of urbanization and municipalization created a category of cities that were both smaller and less consistently planned. Two examples of cities that emerged in this way are *Veleia* and *Saepinum*. They belong to the smallest category of cities catalogued by De Ligt and have an urban area of about half the 20 ha defining the upper end of this group. *Veleia*, perhaps, should not even be ranked as a true 'city' – it rather was a small settlement clustered around an Augustan era *forum* in the centre of an agriculturally rich river basin in the Northern Apennines. The small *forum* plaza was surrounded by *tabernae* (Figure 3.17), and there were *tabernae* in front of the three small houses that have been excavated immediately south of it – one house had two, the others had just one (Ward Perkins 1970; Albasi and Criniti 2006).

*Saepinum* was a bit larger, and a bit more strongly monumentalized, with a wall circuit, a theatre, and even a tiny *macellum*; otherwise, it was a rather similar settlement, in a rather similar place in the middle of an agriculturally productive valley (Benedittis et al. 1993; Barker 1995). As far as is archaeologically visible, the roads of the city were surrounded with sequences of *tabernae*, all belonging to very small private buildings – most of these were even strip buildings rather than true *atrium* houses (Figure 3.18). Even if the streets of *Saepinum* were densely commercialized, the socio-economic background of the *tabernae* differed radically from those at Pompeii and Ostia.

*Figure 3.17  Veleia. Tabernae* along the East edge of the *forum.*

*Figure 3.18  Saepinum.* View from the *forum* towards Porta Boiano with *tabernae* flanking the road.

## Comparing urban commercial landscapes: towards a historical framework

The question, of course, is to which extent this variation can be translated into a proper historical model. The evidence discussed in the last section confirms that Pompeii and Ostia represent a trajectory of development profoundly differed from the other cities discussed here, and it is also clear that the second-century CE building boom in Ostia represents a level of complexity that belongs to a different category than late Republican and Early Imperial Pompeii. As far as the other cities are concerned, it may make sense to distinguish cities like *Norba* and *Fregellae* without any identifiable commercial facilities from cities where reasonable numbers of *tabernae* can be found. On this basis, it makes sense to distinguish, for Roman Italy, a hierarchy of four types of cities: (1) cities where the *taberna* was a marginal phenomenon; (2) cities where the *taberna* was widespread but were mostly clustered around the *forum* or associated with private houses along the urban streets; (3) cities where *tabernae* were regularly constructed along the streets in larger numbers as part of public or commercial architecture; and (4) cities where *tabernae* were constructed in larger numbers in a large variety of contexts, including the internal parts of buildings.

### (1) Cities where the taberna was a marginal phenomenon

The *taberna* is a historical phenomenon, the emergence of which post-dated the emergence of both the *forum* and the *atrium* house by a considerable margin. The earliest urban *fora* known – such as the original *forum* of *Cosa* (Brown 1980) – were constructed without *tabernae*, and the reports by Livy (41.27) of Roman *censores* building *tabernae* around several urban *fora* of Roman Italy suggest that these *fora* already existed but without *tabernae*. The *taberna*, as a phenomenon, was an innovation, but as all innovations, its spread was uneven, slow, and not necessarily complete. Moreover, there always were alternatives: retail could be done on the street, or in temporary facilities on the street or on the *forum*, and many regular manufacturing processes can find a place in private houses (cf. Holleran 2011). Particularly in small face-to-face communities, the urgency to use architectural means to facilitate exchange may long have remained limited. Indeed, many Greek cities, up to the Late Hellenistic period, had very few shop-like facilities. Having *tabernae* was a strategic commercial choice, and, therefore, also a choice that in some places may never or only rarely have been made. The lack of identifiable *tabernae* in (late) Republican cities like *Fregellae* and, particularly, *Norba* suggests that, as late as the late second and early first century BCE, and perhaps later still, there were cities where most retail was taking place in temporary facilities on the *forum* rather than in privately owned *tabernae* lining the streets. Particularly in smaller urban centres, and particularly in contexts that remained relatively unaffected by social change and economic growth, urban landscapes that initially emerged without *tabernae* may have remained stable: there was a functioning local system of retail and manufacturing, and there were few people interested in making (additional) money by building commercial facilities.

### (2) Cities where the taberna *was widespread but investment remained modest in nature*

However, in most cities that are archaeologically known, and in almost all cities with evidence from the Imperial period, *tabernae* have been identified, and usually in numbers suggesting they were rather common. As a general rule, *tabernae* in these cities can be found around the *forum*, along urban thoroughfares, or in both locations. Generally, the land around *fora* was in public hands, and authorities used this to construct longer rows of *tabernae* – though these were by no means a universal phenomenon.[9] Elsewhere in the city, *tabernae* remained typically associated with private houses. The numbers of *tabernae* per building depended on the size of houses, and thus, on the social profile of the city. In many cases, however, the majority of *tabernae* belonged to houses of relatively modest size – small *atrium* houses or narrow strip buildings – suggesting that *tabernae* were built on an almost individual basis. A city like *Saepinum*, where all recognizable *tabernae* – except for the ones belonging to the city's small *macellum* – belonged to such houses, clearly falls within this group, but the same is true for the much larger city of *Paestum*, and for *Alba Fucens*. Outside the *forum* area, investment in *Paestum* was dominated by the owners of small- to medium-sized houses. Even if some larger *domus* with *tabernae* existed, they generally had *tabernae* only in the facade, and, as a rule, did not maximize the commercial use of facade space. At *Alba Fucens*, the only *tabernae* not associated with the rows of *tabernae* built on public land belonged to the only excavated elite house of the city and were part of the house's facade (Mertens 1981; Pesando 2010, 115–117). Typically, however, the part of the facade immediately surrounding the main entrance was closed and inwardly oriented, highlighting that maximizing commercial profit was not a key concern in building the house (Figure 3.19).

### (3) Cities where tabernae *were constructed in larger numbers*

Arguably, the cities of group (2) represented the majority in Roman Italy. They may be seen as the standard from which group (1) and groups (3) and (4) deviate – the first, because they lagged behind, the other two, because they surpassed the levels of investment seen in most cities. It is clear that at Pompeii, from the late Hellenistic period onwards, at least three developments can be identified that differ *fundamentally* from those in the cities belonging to group (2). In the first place, in private contexts, there is a consistent maximization of the commercial potential of the facades of houses – large and small – along through routes, and, additionally, houses situated on the corners of city

*Figure 3.19  Alba Fucens.* Elite house with *tabernae* and main entrance surrounded by a closed facade.

blocks had rows of *tabernae* constructed along their flanks. While in the cities of group (2), few houses had more than two *tabernae*, at Pompeii, over 20 houses had more than four. Second, the use of the facades of public buildings for constructing *tabernae* has no parallel in the cities of group (2): Pompeii had three bath complexes with at least ten *tabernae* in their facades, while almost all bath complexes known elsewhere in Italy – excepting Ostia and Rome – do not have *tabernae* at all (Cf. Nielsen 1990). Third, the emergence of purpose-built commercial architecture is not attested in most other cities of Roman Italy.

The more difficult question is which cities, other than Pompeii, were part of this group. This is hard to tell: there is no clear evidence of the three phenomena that separate Pompeii from group (2) in any other city outside the metropolitan region of Rome and its harbour cities. There is a case to be made for Herculaneum, which had one public–religious complex (the so-called Insula Orientalis) with a long row of *tabernae* in its facade (Figure 3.20; Monteix 2010, 255–288), and, possibly, a *taberna* building in the unexcavated part of the site (Wallace-Hadrill 2011, figure 3.1).

Herculaneum is much smaller than Pompeii, and its full urban development is Early Imperial rather than late Republican in date, but it is part of the same region and may have benefited from the same fortunate economic circumstances. As the presence of the Villa of the Papyri makes clear, capital

*Figure 3.20* Herculaneum. Insula Orientalis II, with a row of *tabernae*.

for investment was certainly available in the direct environment of the city
(Pesando and Guidobaldi 2006, 392–399). It may be supposed that at least
some of the other cities in the bay of Naples area saw similar developments
in commercial investment – one may think particularly of *Neapolis* and
*Cumae*.[10] Outside this region, it is very hard to see how common commercial
landscapes like that of Pompeii were. It may be argued that the circumstances
supporting developments like those at Pompeii were not very common elsewhere in Italy: investment capital was unequally divided over the peninsula,
and traditionally overwhelmingly concentrated in Southern Latium and
Campania. It is here, in the large cities of Latium and Campania – Capua,
Cales, Teanum, Aquinum – that one might suspect that developments similar
to those at Pompeii could be found – but very few of these cities are archaeologically known to an extent that makes it possible to check whether this is
actually the case.[11]

### (4) Cities with large-scale commercial investment

The fourth and final urban category bears some similarities to group (3) but
distinguishes itself through the increased scale of investment, and the pene-
tration of the *taberna* – and therefore of commerce – into the inner parts
of commercial and public buildings – as was attested at the second-century
CE Ostia. From the perspective of retail, particularly, the latter development

was a fundamental step ahead: no longer was the street the leading environ-ment – rather, commerce was increasingly taking place in built environments completely adapted to the needs of retailers and their customers. Indeed, this innovation to some extent resembles the emergence, in late eighteenth-century Paris, of the arcade, a covered pedestrian shopping alley that took shopping away from the street, and into the built environment – a major development in early modern commercial architecture (cf. Coquery 2014). At Ostia, the spread of these covered commercial buildings is remarkable: they can be found throughout the city and could include high numbers of *tabernae*. As far as the scale of investment is concerned, Ostia is clearly in a different league from Pompeii: while at Pompeii, the building with the largest number of *tabernae* was the *Porticus* outside Porta Ercolano with 14 shops, developments at Ostia reached a much higher level – there are 12 complexes with more than 15 *tabernae*, and, in total 34 buildings with ten or more *tabernae* – compared to just seven at Pompeii.

There can be no doubt that the picture emerging from Ostia is highly excep-tional. Arguably, there were strong similarities to developments in the Roman metropolis – both in terms of the scale of investment and in the development of inwardly oriented commercial architecture – the obvious example is the Markets of Trajan, even if this complex was partially used for other purposes (Holleran 2012, 167–169). This is unsurprising as both cities were part of the same economic environment and may have had overlapping urban elites (Bruun 2002; 2015, 350–351). Beyond Rome, however, there was no obvious parallel for Ostia in the Italian peninsula. It is perhaps possible that *Puteoli* came close, but even if *Puteoli* was a busy port city with some impressive public buildings, its known urban remains in Rione Terra and in the city's har-bour area do not necessarily suggest the same level of spatial and commercial pressure that can be seen at Ostia (De Caro and Gialanella 2002).

## Discussion

This chapter has tried to establish a framework for comparing the material remains of urban commercial landscapes in Roman Italy. Starting from Ostia and Pompeii, it has outlined the diverging developments in cities of which material remains are known. Even after the commercial boom of the late Hellenistic period, the *taberna* had not become omnipresent in every city in Italy – as has been argued in this chapter, the developments at Pompeii and Ostia clearly were a very locally specific materialization of broader historical trends; indeed the evidence discussed in this chapter suggests that, as global-ization theory suggests, the broader political and economic developments that shaped and transformed the Italian peninsula in the late Republican and Early Imperial period had very different local outcomes. This makes it hard to project the late Hellenistic investment boom visible at Pompeii onto the entirety of the Italian peninsula (*contra* Ellis 2018). It is from the differences between cities that the urban commercial history of Roman Italy has to be reconstructed. While the particular framework outlined in this chapter can undoubtedly be further refined, adapted, or replaced, the study of urban commercial history will need something closely resembling it in scope and structure to be able to capture urban commerce in Roman Italy in a credible historical narrative.

What, then, should this more abstract historical narrative look like? Starting from the points made about the different historical trajectories of the cities of Roman Italy in this chapter, it can be argued that, while Roman Imperial hegemony facilitated dramatic developments in the commercial landscapes of the Roman metropolis and its satellites, and in some larger cities in *Latium* and *Campania*, things were fundamentally different elsewhere in the peninsula and, particularly, in the Apennines – in the level of commercialization, but especially in the scale of investment. Phrased differently, it seems as if, as soon as the imperial, senatorial, and equestrian elites were physically beyond the horizon, *tabernae* remained clustered around *fora*, or associated with small houses. Thus, urban commercial development in Roman Italy could certainly be spectacular and reach unprecedented levels in terms of scale and complexity, but it was and did so in relatively few highly privileged places. It is an unfortunate coincidence that these are also the places that modern scholars first resort to when they study Roman urbanism and Roman urban commerce.

## Notes

1 There is a tendency in Pompeian scholarship to separate the phase between 62 and 79 CE from the preceding Early Imperial period because of the seismic upheaval in this period. For the present argument, however, this seems unnecessary. On this period, see Fröhlich and Jacobelli, 1993; Monteix 2017, 210–212.

2 For example, house I 3, 25 and I 4, 8–10. Cf. Peterse 1999. On the *forum*, see Maiuri 1942, 53–74.

3 Converted *cubicula*: particularly I 4, 1–3. See also Bulighin 2006 (House of Orpheus, VI 14, 20), Anderson and Robinson 2018 (House of the Surgeon, VI 1, 10), De Haan et al. 2005 (House of the Scientists, VI 14, 43).

4 For example, the house of the Faun in *insula* VI 12, and the *Insula Arriana Polliana* in *insula* VI 6.

5 For example, IX 3, 1–2, House of the Surgeon, VI 14, 10–12, I 4, 1–3.

6 Most of these excavations have focused on the area of the original castrum and the western *decumanus*. The most detailed discussion of the archaeology underpinning the reconstructions of the early phases in Ostia is still Calza and Becatti 1953, even if a lot of their conclusions have been contradicted by later excavations. For dating individual buildings, this chapter has relied on Pavolini 2006 and more recent bibliography.

7 For example, the reported remains of the *atrium* houses under the Casa Basilicale next to the forum reported by Calza and Becatti 1953 show the main outline of the house plan, but no imagery of the remains of their street front. The same is true for the Domus a Boucranes: it is possible, perhaps likely, that this house had *tabernae* but decisive evidence is lacking. Cf. Perrier et al. 2007.

8  I am referring to the north-east corner of the *insula* immediately south-west of the *forum*, which includes a structure with what may have been a large number of *tabernae*.

9  See e.g. the Imperial period *fora* of Volsinii and Rusellae. Cf. Gros 1983, Liverani 2011.

10  On Roman *Neapolis* see De Simone 1986. On *Cumae* see Caputo et al. 1996; Gasparri 2009.

11  Of these cities, *Aquinum* and *Cales* have never been overbuilt, but no large-scale geophysical survey has been done to map their remains, and only very small sections of these cities have been excavated. On *Aquinum* see Piro et al. 2011 and Ceraudo 2019; on *Cales* see Femiano 1990.

## References

Adam, J.-P. "Building Materials, Construction Techniques and Chronologies." Pages 98–113 in *The World of Pompeii*. Edited by J. Dobbins and P. Foss. London: Routledge, 2007.

Albasi, T., and N. Criniti. *Res publica veleiatium: Veleia, tra passato e futuro*. Parma: Monte università, 2006.

Anderson, M., and D. Robinson. *House of the Surgeon, Pompeii: Excavations in the Casa del Chirurgo (VI 1, 9–10.23)*. Oxford: Oxbow, 2018.

Barker, G. *A Mediterranean Valley: Landscape Archaeology and Annales History in the Biferno Valley*. London: Leicester University Press, 1995.

Battaglini, G., and F. Diosono. "Le domus di Fregellae: case aristocratiche di ambito coloniale." Pages 217–232 in *Etruskisch-italische und römisch-republikanische Häuser*. Edited by M. Bentz and Chr. Reusser. Wiesbaden: Reichert, 2010.

Benedittis, G.D., M. Gaggiotti, and M.M. Chiari. *Saepinum. Sepino*. Campobasso: Enne, 1993.

Bragantini, I. *Poseidonia-Paestum. V. Les maisons romaines de l'îlot nord*. Rome: École Française de Rome, 2008.

Brown, F.E. *Cosa: The Making of a Roman Town*. Ann Arbor: University of Michigan Press, 1980.

Bruun, C. "Ostia – una Roma in miniatura?" Pages 3–10 in *Ostia e Portus nelle loro relazioni con Roma*. Edited by Chr Bruun and A. Gallina Zevi. Rome: Institutum Romanum Finlandiae, 2002.

Bruun, C. "Civic Identity in Roman Ostia: Some Evidence from Dedications (Inaugurations)." Pages 347–369 in *Urban Dreams and Realities in Antiquity. Remains and Representations of the Ancient City*. Edited by A. Kemezis. Leiden: Brill, 2015.

Bulighin, G.P. "Il complesso d'Orfeo a Pompei (domus VI, 14, 18–20 e VI, 14, 12): quadro architettonico e cronologico." Pages 76–142 in *Contributi di Archeologia Vesuviana I*. Edited by N. Monteix and G.P. Bulighin. Rome. "L'Erma" di Bretschneider, 2006.

Calza, G., and G. Becatti. *Scavi di Ostia. I. Topografia Generale*. Rome: Libreria dello Stato, 1953.

Carfora, P., S. Ferrante, and S. Quilici Gigli. "Edilizia privata nell'urbanistica di Norba tra la fine del III e l'inizio del I secolo a. C." Pages 233–242 in *Etruskisch-italische und römisch-republikanische Häuser*. Edited by M. Bentz and Chr. Reusser. Wiesbaden: Reichert, 2010.

Caputo, P., R. Morichi, R. Paone, and P. Rispoli. *Cuma e il suo parco archeologico. Un territorio e le sue testimonianze.* Rome: Bardi Editore, 1996.

De Caro, S., and C. Gialanella. *Il Rione Terra.* Naples: Electa, 2002.

Carrington, R.C. "Notes on the Building Materials of Pompeii." *Journal of Roman Studies* 23 (1933): 125–138.

Ceraudo, G. *Le terme centrali o vecciane di Aquinum. Ambiente, archeologia e paesaggi.* Foggia: Claudio Grenzi, 2019.

Coquery, N. "Shopping Streets in Eighteenth-Century Paris: A Landscape Shaped by Historical, Economic and Social Forces." Pages 57–77 in *The Landscape of Consumption. Shopping Streets and Cultures in Western Europe, 1600–1900.* Edited by J.H. Furnée and C. Lesger. Basingstoke: Palgrave Macmillan, 2014.

DeLaine, J. "The Commercial Landscape of Ostia." Pages 29–47 in *Roman Working Lives and Urban Living.* Edited by A. MacMahon and J. Price. Oxford: Oxbow, 2005.

Ellis, S.J.R. *The Roman Retail Revolution. The Socio-Economic World of the Taberna.* Oxford: Oxford University Press, 2018.

Femiano, S.R. *Linee di storia, topografia e urbanistica della antica Cales.* Maddaloni: Centro Grafico Edit, 1990.

Flohr, M. "Tabernae, economische groei en stedelijke ontwikkeling in republikeins Pompeii." *Tijdschrift voor Mediterrane Archeologie* 46 (2011): 34–41.

Flohr, M. "The Textile Economy of Pompeii." *Journal of Roman Archaeology* 26 (2013): 53–78.

Flohr, M. "Tabernae and Commercial Investment along the Western Decumanus in Ostia." Pages 143–153 in *Ostia Antica. Nouvelles études et recherces sur les quartiers occidentaux de la cité Actes du colloque international ( Rome-Ostia Antica, 22–24 septembre 2014).* Edited by C. De Ruyt, Th Morard, and F. Van Haeperen. Rome: Institut historique belge de Rome, 2018.

Flohr, M. "Commerce and Architecture in Late Hellenistic Italy: The Emergence of the Taberna Row." Pages 7–17 in *Proceedings of the 19th Congress on Classical Archaeology. Cologne/Bonn 22–26 May 2018. Vol. 8.2. Shops, Workshops and Urban Economic History in the Roman World.* Edited by M. Flohr and N. Monteix. Heidelberg: Propylaeum, 2020a.

Flohr, M. "Hilltops, Heat and Precipitation: Roman Urban Life and the Natural Environment." Pages 66–85 in *Urban Life and the Built Environment.* Edited by M. Flohr. London: Routledge, 2020b.

Flohr, M., and A. Wilson. *The Economy of Pompeii.* Oxford: Oxford University Press, 2017.

Fröhlich, T. "La Porta di Ercolano a Pompei e la cronologia dell'opus vittatum mixtum." Pages 153–159 in *Archäologie und Seismologie, la regione vesuviana dal 62 al 79 d.C., problemi archeologici e sismologici.* Edited by T. Fröhlich and L. Jacobelli. Munich: Biering & Brinckmann, 1993.

Fröhlich, T., and L. Jacobelli. *Archäologie und Seismologie, la regione vesuviana dal 62 al 79 d.C., problemi archeologici e sismologici.* Munich: Biering & Brinckmann, 1993.

Gasparri, C. "Il Foro di Cuma dal I. sec. a.C. all'età bizantina." Pages 581–611 in *Cuma. Atti del Quarantottesimo Convegno di Studi sulla Magna Grecia.* Taranto: Istituto per la storia e l'archeologia della Magna Grecia, 2009.

Greco, E., and D. Theodorescu. *Poseidonia-Paestum. IV. Forum ouest-sud-est.* Rome: École Française de Rome, 1999.

Greco, E., D. Theodorescu, and A. Rouveret. *Poseidonia-Paestum. III. Forum nord.* Rome: École Française de Rome, 1987.

Gros, P. "Il foro di Bolsena: nota sull'urbanistica di Volsinii nel I secolo dopo Cristo." *Bollettino d'Arte* 17 (1983): 67–74.

De Haan, N., C. Peterse, S. Piras, and F. Schipper. "The Casa degli Scienziati (VI 14, 43): Elite Architecture in Fourth-Century B.C. Pompeii." Pages 240–256 in *Nuove ricerche archeologiche a Pompei ed Ercolano*. Edited by P.-G. Guzzo and M.-P. Guidobaldi. Naples: Electa, 2005.

De Haan, N., and K. Wallat. "Le Terme Centrali a Pompei: ricerche e scavi 2003–2006." Pages 15–24 in *Nuove Ricerche Archeologiche nell'Area Vesuviana (scavi 2003–2006)*. Edited by M.-P. Guidobaldi and P.-G. Guzzo. Rome: "L'Erma" di Bretschneider, 2008.

Holleran, C. "The Street Life of Ancient Rome." Pages 246–261 in *Rome, Ostia, Pompeii. Movement and Space*. Edited by R. Laurence and D. Newsome. Oxford: Oxford University Press, 2011.

Holleran, C. *Shopping in Ancient Rome: The Retail Trade in the Late Republic and the Principate*. Oxford: Oxford University Press, 2012.

Jansen, G.C.M. *Water in de Romeinse stad*. Leuven: Peeters, 2002.

Laurence, R. *Roman Pompeii – Space and Society*. London: Routledge, 1994.

De Ligt, L. *Peasants, Citizens and Soldiers: Studies in the Demographic History of Roman Italy 225 BC – AD 100*. Cambridge: Cambridge University Press, 2012.

De Ligt, L. "Urban systems and the political and economic structures of early-imperial Italy." *Rivista di Storia Economica* 32 (2016): 17–75.

Ling, R. *The Insula of the Menander at Pompeii. I. The Structures*. Oxford: Oxford University Press, 1997.

Liverani, P. "Il Foro di Rusellae in epoca romana." *Atlante tematico di topografia antica* 21 (2011): 15–31.

Maiuri, A. *L'ultima fase edilizia di Pompei*. Rome: Istituto di Studi Romani, 1942.

Mau, A. *Pompeji in Leben und Kunst*. Leipzig: Engelmann, 1900.

Van der Meer, L.B. "Domus Fulminata. The House of the Thunderbolt at Ostia (III, viii, 3–5)." *BABesch* 80 (2005): 91–112.

Mertens, J. *Alba Fucens*. Brussels: Centre belge de recherches archéologiques en Italie centrale et méridionale, 1981.

Mogetta, M. "The Early Development of Concrete in the Domestic Architecture of Pre-Roman Pompeii." *Journal of Roman Archaeology* 29 (2016): 43–72.

Monteix, N. *Les lieux de métier: boutiques et ateliers d'Herculanum*. Rome: École Française de Rome, 2010.

Monteix, N. "Urban Production and the Pompeian Economy." Pages 209–241 in *The Economy of Pompeii*. Edited by M. Flohr and A. Wilson. Oxford: Oxford University Press, 2017.

Nielsen, I. *Thermae et Balnea. The architecture and Cultural History of Roman Public Baths*. Aarhus: Aarhus University Press, 1990.

Patterson, J. *Landscapes & Cities. Rural Settlement and Civic Transformation in Early Imperial Italy*. Oxford: Oxford University Press, 2006.

Pavolini, C. *Ostia*. Rome: Laterza, 2006.

Perrier, B., S. Aubry, C. Broquet, C. Boucherens, T. Morard, and N. Terrapon. "La domus aux Bucranes à Ostie." Pages 13–109 in *Villas, maisons, sactuaires et tombeaux tardo-républicains. Actes du colloque international de Saint-Romain-en-Gal en l'honneur d'Anna Gallina Zevi*. Edited by B. Perrier. Rome: Quasar, 2007.

Pesando, F. "Il 'Secolo d'Oro' di Pompei. Aspetti dell'architettura pubblica e privata nel II secolo a.c." Pages 227–241 in *Sicilia ellenistica, consuetudo italica. Alle origini dell'architettura ellenistica d'Occidente*. Edited by M. Osanna and M. Torelli. Spoleto: Edizioni dell'Ateneo, 2006.

Pesando, F. "Alba Fucens fra case ed abitanti." *Quaderni di Archeologia d'Abruzzo* 2 (2010): 113–119.

Pesando, F., and M.-P. Guidobaldi. *Pompei Oplontis Ercolano Stabiae*. Rome: Laterza, 2006.

Peterse, C.L.J. *Steinfachwerk in Pompeji*. Amsterdam: Gieben, 1999.

Piro, S., G. Ceraudo, and D. Zamuner. "Integrated Geophysical and Archaeological Investigations of Aquinum in Frosinone, Italy." *Archeological Prospection* 18.2 (2011): 127–138.

Poehler, E. *The Traffic Systems of Pompeii*. Oxford: Oxford University Press, 2017.

Quilici Gigli, S. "Trasformazioni urbanistiche ed attività edilizia in epoca repubblicana: il caso di Norba." *Orizzonti* 4 (2003): 23–32.

Schoevaert, J. *Les boutiques d'Ostie. L'économie urbaine au quotidien. Ier s. av. J.-C. - Ve s. ap. J.-C.* Rome: École Française de Rome, 2018.

Scocca, L. "Nuovi elementi per l'interpretazione del Caseggiato del Lario a Ostia." *Archeologia Classica* 46 (1994): 421–440.

Sewell, J. *The formation of Roman urbanism, 338–200 B.C.: between contemporary foreign influence and Roman tradition*. Portsmouth RI: Journal of Roman Archaeology, 2010.

De Simone, A. "S. Lorenzo Maggiore in Napoli: il monumento e l'area." Pages 233–253 in *Neapolis, Atti del XXV Convegno di Studi sulla Magna Grecia*. Edited by G. Pugliese Caratelli and M. Gras. Taranto: Arte Tipografica Editrice, 1986.

Stevens, S. "Reconstructing the Garden Houses at Ostia. Exploring Water Supply and Building Height." *BABesch* 80 (2005): 113–123.

Stöger, H. *Rethinking Ostia: A Spatial Enquiry into the Urban Society of Rome's Imperial Port-town*. Leiden: Leiden University Press, 2011.

Torelli, M. *Paestum Romana*. Paestum: Istituto per la storia e l'archeologia della Magna Grecia, 1999.

Wallace-Hadrill, A. "The Monumental Centre of Herculaneum: in Search of the Identities of Public Buildings." *Journal of Roman Archaeology* 24 (2011): 121–160.

Ward Perkins, J.B. "From Republic to Empire: Reflections on the Early Provincial Architecture of the *Roman West*." *Journal of Roman Studies* 60 (1970): 1–19.

# 4 Market buildings in Asia Minor

## Old assumptions and new starting points

*Dorien Leder-Slotman*

## Introduction

During the Hellenistic Period, many cities in west and south-west Asia Minor constructed large, monumental structures that have come to be known as market buildings. Although defining this building type is complicated, in general, market buildings consisted of one to three storeys and were usually constructed against a slope, so that the top floor was accessible from the agora, while the ground floor could be entered from the road or plateau on the other side of the building (Figure 4.1). In this way, those market buildings that were multistoried made use of the height differences in the landscape. Both large halls and smaller rooms, sometimes combined, made up the inner arrangement of these substructures. As a building type, market buildings were seemingly unique to Asia Minor.

Market buildings are a relatively understudied phenomenon. Only three publications, from, respectively, 1970, 2005 and 2012, have considered the group as a whole (Lauter, 1970; Köse, 2005; Cavalier, 2012). Apart from these articles, they are mentioned, individually or as a group, in several other publications, but these discuss mostly their stylistic properties while their function receives little attention (e.g. Coulton, 1976; Machatschek and Schwarz, 1981). This is remarkable, because market buildings are a distinctive feature of many agoras in *Asia Minor* and they occupied a central place in the city.

Since the earliest discussions of the type, a relatively broad consensus about the function of market buildings developed, and this established opinion might be part of the reason that market buildings have been studied so little later on. This widely accepted interpretation of market buildings is that they were commercial buildings that contained shops and storage rooms, hence, the name 'market building'. Yet the way in which this perceived commercial function has been demonstrated in the past is questionable.

This chapter focuses on what I consider to be the two main problems concerning the study of market buildings: (1) the way they have been studied up until now, especially the handling of the epigraphic and material evidence and, from this, (2) the definition and categorization of market buildings. The first part of this chapter reviews past research on market buildings, based on the major publications on the subject and focusing on the evidence that has been used to demonstrate a commercial function. This overview will help to identify the main problems with the study of market buildings, after which a discussion of the problem of definition will follow. I will then present some initial ideas about the future of research on market buildings, with an eye to avoid the unfounded generalizations and definitional weaknesses that have characterized the discussion so far. I will do this by first discussing the theory about the meaning of buildings of architectural historian William Whyte. After this I will present several new avenues for studying the function of market buildings in the future.

With regard to the theme of this book, this chapter demonstrates that identifying economic space in Greco-Roman cities is not a straightforward task, even with buildings that seem obvious examples at first sight. Thus, my goal here is not to come up with entirely new results concerning the functioning of market buildings but to tentatively deconstruct what has been written about this group of buildings and to present some new directions for future studies. Part of this process is to critically evaluate the basis of common assumptions about the suitability of Greco-Roman buildings for economic purposes, in general, and, in other words, to rethink what is really 'economic' about buildings.

For practical reasons, I will keep using the term 'market building' throughout this chapter, as it is the most common name by which the building type is known. However, as we will see, more research is necessary to decide whether this is indeed a suitable designation.

## Commercial buildings? Reviewing the literature

Two of the first people to write about the market building type were Richard Bohn and Carl Schuchhardt, who, in their publication from 1889 about the city of *Aigai*, describe the remains of the local market building (Figure 4.1; Bohn and Schuchhardt, 1889: 15–27). Based on an early description of the site from 1886 by Michel A. Clerc who saw in the rooms 'des magasins, des dépôts' (Clerc, 1886: 287), they suggest that the rooms in the substructure were shops and that the whole building served 'dem Zweck des Marktverkehrs' (Bohn and Schuchhardt, 1889: 26). However, apart from the form and size of the rooms, no further evidence is given for this interpretation. From p. 26 onwards, Bohn and Schuchhardt consider mostly the architectural qualities of the building in *Aigai* and, in comparison, of a similar building in *Alinda*. Both buildings enlarged the terraces of the agoras at which they stood. No new arguments are given to support the notion that the buildings had a market function. Bohn and Schuchhardt do acknowledge, however, that this claim needs more substantiation (Bohn and Schuchhardt, 1889: 26).

### *Lauter*

These early assumptions have remained at the centre of the study of market buildings and have also led to the impression that the buildings, containing shops and/or storage rooms, were part of the commercial sphere in the city. Indeed, few other functions have been suggested. Hans Lauter conducted the first study of market buildings as a group. In his article, he concludes that the

Gez. v. R. Bohn.

*Figure 4.1* Reconstruction of the market building in Aigai, drawn by Richard Bohn (Bohn and Schuchhardt 1889: figure 24).

cellars of a Roman *basilica* in *Aspendos* belonged to an earlier, Hellenistic structure, on the basis of several architectural features. He considers this earlier structure to be a market building (Lauter, 1970: 77–81). To contextualize these Hellenistic remains in *Aspendos* and to support his statement that they were the remains of a market building, Lauter discusses some of the market buildings that were already known, with their properties (Lauter, 1970: 85–94), and formulates the following definition of market buildings: '*An der Hangseite kleinasiatischer hellenistischer Marktplätze befindet sich häufig ein Bau, der sich aus einem oder mehreren Untergeschossen und einer doppelschiffigen Halle auf dem Niveau des Platzes zusammensetzt*' (Lauter, 1970: 81). Although this is a rather neutral definition, it has become problematic in that it does not cover all of the structures that could now be regarded as market buildings. The building in *Selge* was triple aisled, for example (Machatschek and Schwarz, 1981: 58, see also below), while a possible early example from *Miletos* was single storied, thus lacking a substructure (Knackfuss and Rehm, 1924: 3–5, 43–7; Kleiner, 1968: 61; Köse, 2005: 140–1).

Lauter points to some of the architectural features and finds in and around the market buildings to suggest a commercial or administrative role for the building type as a whole. Concerning the rooms in market buildings, Lauter notes the variety in size of the rooms and the large round doors in *Alinda* as well as the darkness in the rooms of several market buildings. These are just individual details, however, leading to a rather superficial analysis and disputable suggestions about the use of the buildings. For example, with regard to the large, unlighted spaces in market buildings, Lauter concludes that these could only have been storage spaces. He compares them to free-standing warehouses in the Hellenistic period, suggesting that this older building type was possibly integrated in market buildings (Lauter, 1970: 95). Considering the building in *Aspendos*, he draws on the earlier article of Heinz Cüppers to show that its substructure had a storage function. Cüppers described a clever funnel system in the wall between two spaces in the substructure that could divide bags between the eastern and the western cellar. On the basis of this information, Cüppers went on to calculate the amount of grain that could fit in these spaces (Lauter, 1970: 77; Cüppers, 1961: 34). This system is indeed a strong indication that the building in *Aspendos* had a storage function at some point. This does not mean, however, that this applied to all market buildings, especially because only the example in *Aspendos* is known to have had such a system. The agora in *Aspendos* had two structures resembling market buildings on both the east and west side of the agora, but Lauter only considers one of these to be a market building, which makes it unclear, despite his definition, what are his criteria for the identification of market buildings (Lauter, 1970: 82). The presence of two market buildings on one agora is also attested in *Assos* (Coulton, 1976: 70, 219), but this is not common in other cities in Asia Minor. It can thus be asked what the implications of this configuration are for the purpose of both structures.

Another aspect of market buildings that Lauter concentrates on is their possible public nature. According to him, the building in *Aspendos* was a public building like the *basilica* that superseded it. He suggests that it was some kind of 'Börse' or exchange, a function which had also been suggested for Roman *basilicae* (Lauter, 1970: 85; Fuchs, 1961), especially because contrary to the building on the other side of the agora, this building had no separate rooms, at least not on the ground floor. To argue that 'Versorgungsanlagen' at the agora were not uncommon, Lauter refers to the cisterns located at the agora of *Termessos* (Lauter, 1970: 85). For Lauter, the dedication of the market building in *Aigai* to the *augusti*, *Apollo Chresterios* and the people is further proof that market buildings were public buildings (Lauter, 1970: 85; Köse, 2005: 156. For the inscription, see Clerc, 1886: 288–9; Bohn and Schuchhardt, 1889: 23–7). Moreover, comparing the double-aisled *stoa* of the market building in *Aspendos* to a *stoa* at the agora in *Priene* and a *stoa* at the port of *Miletos*, where, according to Lauter, financial transactions took place, he suggests the same function for the market building in *Aspendos* (Lauter, 1970: 95). He concludes, '*Es steht nichts im Wege, die Marktbauten in allen ihren Teilen für öffentliche Gebäude zu halten, die im Besitz der Stadt waren*' (Lauter, 1970: 95).

Furthermore, when considering the rooms in other market buildings, Lauter assumes that in some cases, these were storerooms. As indications for this use, he points to the differences in the size of the rooms in *Alinda* as well as the large doors, which, he argues, could be openings for carts. According to Lauter, however, the narrow rooms of a market building in *Herakleia* would be unsuitable for use as shops and the rooms in a market building at *Pergamon* too dark. Remains of shutters in the windows at *Aigai* would indicate a use as depot for costly products and the cisterns in the substructure of a market building at *Assos* could show that the building had a supply function (Lauter, 1970: 95). Finally, with regard to the substructure of the market building in *Alabanda*, Lauter claims that because of its crude-looking design it must have been a storage space (Lauter, 1970: 100). It is clear from these examples that the characteristics of market buildings highlighted by Lauter vary from city to city; and a systematic, consistent approach to market buildings as a group, considering their layout and architecture as well as the finds associated with them is lacking in Lauter's work.

In a later book, Lauter briefly discusses market buildings under the heading 'Bautypen und Gebäudegattungen', subheading 'Die Stoa und Verwandtes' (Lauter, 1986: 121–4). Here he considers market buildings next to the category of multistoried *stoas* and calls them an '"unechte" Gruppe' next to the '"echten" doppelgeschossigen Hallenbauten' (Lauter, 1986: 122–3). Lauter contrasts market buildings with double-storied *stoas* like the *stoa* of Attalos in Athens, by pointing out that market buildings did not consist of *stoas* on top of each other but that they had a substructure consisting of rooms and large halls.

### Machatschek and Schwarz

This attitude towards market buildings has been adopted on multiple occasions later on. An example is the elaborate description of the market building in *Selge*, *Pisidia*, by Alois Machatschek and Mario Schwarz, which is part of their publication about the remaining monuments in *Selge* (Machatschek and Schwarz, 1981). They introduce the building as having the character of 'eines nüchternen Zweckbaues' (Machatschek and Schwarz, 1981: 56). Their discussion of the market building is accompanied by multiple elaborate drawings and plans of its reconstruction and includes a detailed list of the pieces of the building found around the site (Machatschek and Schwarz, 1981: 56). In their reconstruction, the building was triple aisled, with a *stoa* on top and two levels of rooms below. They state that the *stoa* on top might have been a market hall, while the rooms in the substructure functioned as public storerooms or shops with storerooms in the rear (Machatschek and Schwarz,

1981: 57). Their arguments for these suggestions are the similarity of the market building at *Selge* to other market buildings and to Lauter's definition, as well as an inscription which mentions the restoration of the *chrēmatistēria*, a complex with shops, found nearby in the *Odeion* and probably dating to the first half of the third century CE (Köse, 2005: 153–5; Machatschek and Schwarz, 1981: 57; Lanckoronski 1890–1892: 234, nos. 248 and 250; Nollé and Schindler, 1991: 17). These claims, thus, partly depend on the belief that Lauter's article, the only more or less comprehensive study of market buildings as a building type at the time, had led to a steady definition of what exactly is a market building and which activities took place inside it. But, as we have seen above, this is not the case. Machatschek and Schwarz furthermore compare the market building at *Selge* to a building in *Herakleia* on the *Latmos*, especially because of the corridor that ran in front of the rooms. They likewise point to the market buildings in *Aigai* and *Assos* as parallels of the building in *Selge*, although they also mention the differences between these structures. On the basis of stylistic similarities, they tentatively place the market building in *Selge* in the tradition of terrace buildings in *Pergamon*, an idea that would be elaborated upon by Köse (see below). According to them, direct Pergamene influence in *Selge* cannot be proven, but the market building in *Selge* nevertheless indicates that a Pergamene building type was applied here (Machatschek and Schwarz, 1981: 57–8).

### *Köse*

A more recent publication to be discussed is the article by Veli Köse (Köse, 2005). Köse presents an overview of several remaining market buildings, together with a discussion of their possible predecessors, their continued use in Roman times and their possible function. Although this chapter gives more attention to the function of market buildings than earlier work on market buildings had done, here as well, the suggested functions are mostly commercial in nature and based on a rather superficial review of the evidence. Concerning a market building in *Pednelissos*, for example, Köse states 'The middle storey was probably a storage hall as usual' (Köse, 2005: 144), while no convincing evidence for this storage function has been presented yet up until that point in this chapter. He furthermore writes about the construction of market buildings in Asia Minor that '... they were mainly erected along the agora. This was probably because of their perceived function as market buildings. In other words, their function determined their location'. However, as no solid argument for a commercial function has been presented yet at this point in this chapter, nor in previous publications, as we saw, and as the location at the agora as such does not suffice to indicate a commercial function, one could ask what this connection to the agora really proves. Indeed, the fact that market buildings stood at the agora can be meaningful, but without any further evidence, it is not sufficient to prove a commercial function.

In his discussion of the functions of market buildings, Köse not only looks at architectural features, but also at epigraphical evidence. Epigraphical evidence is important for understanding market buildings, but the few remaining inscriptions have to be interpreted carefully. Köse discusses an inscription referring to the *stoa* on the eastern border of the south agora of *Miletos*, the so-called East Building. An inscription on a fragment of a Doric architrave found close to the northeast corner of the agora states that a son of *Seleukos* dedicated the building to the Didymaian *Apollo* (Knackfuss and Rehm, 1924: 43–7, no. 193a. See also Kleiner, 1968: 61–5). This son is probably *Antiochos* I, son of *Seleukos* I, who ruled from 280 to 261 BCE. Another inscription, found in *Didyma*, mentions how *Antiochos* I offered to build a *stoa* 'in the city', of which the revenue would be used to finance the construction of the new *Didymaion*. Because *Didyma* was an important religious centre for *Miletos*, it is probable that the inscription refers to the East Building in *Miletos* (Haussoulier, 1900: 245–6; Rehm, 1958: no. 479. See also Knackfuss and Rehm, 1924: 43–7; Kleiner, 1968: 61–5; Winter, 2006: 60). Köse, however, believes that this second inscription 'confirms that the predecessors of the building type discussed here were referred to as stoas in antiquity' (Köse, 2005: 155 and note 64). In this statement, Köse, on the one hand, assumes that the East Building was a predecessor to the market building type, which is questionable, and on the other hand, he generalizes from the information about a single building, indicating that all predecessors of the building type were referred to as *stoas*. Although these seem to be just small nuances in Köse's text, they are nevertheless important to point out, as they can ultimately lead to far-reaching conclusions about market buildings, based on unjustified extrapolations from the evidence instead of the evidence itself.

Köse furthermore concentrates on inscriptions that mention either the term *chrēmatistēria* or the term *ergastēria*. The term *ergastēria* is known from several Hellenistic and Roman inscriptions and it refers to complexes with (work)shops that were rented out, although Köse acknowledges that none of these inscriptions can be directly linked to one of the market buildings (Köse, 2005: 155; for the inscriptions see Fabricius and Schuchhardt, 1890: no. 40; *SEG* 34 (1984) no. 1250; Robert, 1984: 496–9; Gauthier, 1984: 81–111; *SEG* 39 (1989) 1285; Pleket, 1970: 73–4; Reynolds, 1996; *SEG* 46 (1996) 1393). Köse refers to three passages from, respectively, Diodorus, Plutarch and Strabo to make clear that the term *chrēmatistēria* indicated a place for trade and cash transactions (Köse, 2005: 155; Diod. Sic. 1.1.3, 14.7.2; Plut. *Caes.* 67.1; Strabo VII 1.20). Köse mentions three inscriptions with the word *chrēmatistēria* from *Miletos*, *Priene* and *Selge* (Köse, 2005: 153–5; Wilski, 1906: 77–9 no. 3; Hiller von Gaertringen, 1906: 82 no. 106; Machatschek and Schwarz, 1981: 57; Lanckoronski, 1890–1892: 234, nos. 248 and 250; Nollé and Schindler, 1991: no. 17). However, no direct relation between these inscriptions and the market buildings has been demonstrated yet, with the exception maybe of the inscription from *Selge* that might be connected with the market building there (see also p. 73). The inscription, probably dating to the first half of the third century CE, records how Publia Plancia Aurelia Magniana Motoxaris paid for the restoration of several buildings in the city, among which were the *chrēmatistēria*. Further references are parchments from *Dura-Europos*, again recording the word *chrēmatistēria* and indicating that it was a sort of record office. These, however, date to between 120 and 160 CE and *Dura-Europos* is located in a very different region (Köse, 2005: 155; Perkins, 1959: nos. 20–2 and 24).

Köse furthermore focuses on architectural, archaeological and spatial features to discuss possible functions for the buildings. Köse not only concentrates on a possible commercial function but also considers other options, like cultic or administrative activities. However, here as well, the argumentation is often hardly convincing and based on only one of the market buildings. For example, Köse suggests that because the rooms in the substructure of *Alinda* were connected to other rooms, they might be seen as public offices (Köse, 2005: 157). To support the idea of a commercial function, Köse notes that near the market building in *Assos*, two measurement blocks were found. There is furthermore evidence for hooks under the lintels of the doors in *Assos* to hang products from, as well as slots in the windows for wooden shutters. Here again, this evidence is derived from only one building. Köse additionally mentions the presence of windows and back rooms in market buildings as possible indications for the use of the rooms as shops (Köse, 2005: 157).

To demonstrate a possible cultic function for some of the rooms of the *stoas* surrounding the agora in *Magnesia* on the *Maeander*, he mentions two Athena statues and three *pudicitia* statues, as well as a table with marble feet shaped like lion's paws, found in one of those rooms. This room was also larger than most of the rooms in the same *stoa* and could be entered through two Doric columns. The other two possible 'cult rooms' Köse mentions are likewise relatively large and could be accessed through four Ionic columns. For these two rooms, Köse mentions no further evidence for a cult function (Köse, 2005: 156–7). However, the *stoas* in *Magnesia* on the *Maeander* are not explicitly designated as a market building by Köse and they are single storied, which means they do not seem to fit Köse's definition of market buildings. On the first page of his article, Köse describes market buildings as 'stoas with additional substructures and with rooms located below and behind the colonnades, which face onto civic agoras'. According to Köse's classification, the building in *Magnesia* on the *Maeander* would be a precursor, because on page 2 he writes: 'While cities on flat sites, such as *Miletos* and *Magnesia* on the *Maeander*, continued to build single-storey porticos with rooms behind, cities on sloping ground tackled the lack of space by building multi-storey structures with rooms on different levels'. Admittedly, Köse does not explicitly generalize from the evidence for cult practices to say anything about the building type as a whole. However, it remains debatable whether a possible, but uncertain idea about the cultic function of three rooms in a building that might not even be a market building can tell us much about possible cultic functions of market buildings.

### Cavalier

Finally, in an article from 2012, Laurence Cavalier discusses some of the market buildings already mentioned by Köse and three new examples, in *Smyrna*, *Xanthos* and *Tlos* (Cavalier, 2012). The descriptions of these buildings are followed by some thoughts about the link between these buildings and the public supply system.

The structures in *Xanthos* and *Tlos* that Cavalier discusses date to the Imperial period, but Cavalier states that the formula is derived from that of the market buildings, a formula in which, she argues, the terrace is extended by a monument with a substructure that both serves as a support and could be used for storage purposes (Cavalier, 2012: 251–4). In her introduction, she acknowledges the difficulty with the names 'Marktbau' and 'Marktgebäude', and their various interpretations, and states that she will not discuss all buildings belonging to these categories. Therefore, Cavalier opts to call the buildings she discusses in her article 'des portiques à sous-sol adossé' (Cavalier, 2012: 241).

In a small paragraph at the beginning of the article, Cavalier discusses the typology and function of market buildings. Based on work by Lauter, she states that the *stoa* on top might have fulfilled an official, possibly financial role (Cavalier, 2012: 243; Lauter, 1986: 93). Concerning the substructure, she states that the large halls were mostly used for storage, while the rooms, though often seen as shops, were also used for storage (Cavalier, 2012: 243). However, based on Lauter's article, she also suggests that in certain cases, the rooms were used for public institutions, for example, as archives. No additional evidence for these claims and ideas is presented. The cistern in the substructure of a market building in *Assos* is pointed out to suggest that the buildings were constructed as part of the public supply system (Cavalier, 2012: 243; Lauter, 1970: 88, 95).

After discussing the remains of market buildings in *Lyrbe*, *Selge*, *Pednelissos* and *Aspendos* as well as the three new examples, Cavalier elaborates some more on the possibility that the market buildings were part of the city's public supply system, particularly in the Imperial period. She points at the funnel system in the walls of the market building in *Aspendos* to sustain this idea. Moreover, she shortly discusses the phenomenon of *sitometroumenoi*, recipients of grain distributions, who are mentioned in inscriptions from *Xanthos*, *Oenoanda* and *Tlos* (Cavalier, 2012: 253–4; Balland, 1981: 173–224; Wörrle, 1988: 127–35; Ras, 1995: 30 no. 31; Hall and Milner, 1994: 34 no. 23; *IGR* III 492; Baker and Thériault, 2003: 433). This might indeed provide an interesting background to the construction of market buildings in Asia Minor during the Imperial period, the period in which the buildings in *Xanthos* and

*Tlos* were constructed. However, Cavalier does not connect these inscriptions directly to the market buildings in *Xanthos* and *Tlos* and only remarks that this institution required the availability of large quantities of grain, for which the substructures of the buildings in *Xanthos* and *Tlos* could provide space in the city centre (Cavalier, 2012: 254). So although she chooses to use the more neutral term 'portiques à sous-sol adossé' to describe market buildings, her suggestions about their use remain largely hypothetical.

## The problems

Do the critiques formulated above imply that the study of market buildings is doomed to fail? I would not have written this chapter if that would be the case. My goal here is not to just critique past scholarly work on market buildings, but to show that, in order to better understand their function, we need to re-evaluate the old assumptions about their use and find new ways to discover the meaning of these buildings. A first stage in this process is to deconstruct the foundations for the old assumptions, for which I have made some initial steps in the first part of this chapter.

It is clear from this overview that although there are certain indications that market buildings might have had a commercial or market function, the evidence that is presented up until now and especially the way it has been presented is flawed. In my opinion, there are seven general problems with the study of market buildings that arise from this literature review, which I will highlight in this section.

The first problem is that much of the evidence presented to suggest a commercial function, such as the presence of windows to provide light, could also support multiple other activities happening in the buildings. Lighted rooms are not only necessary for running a shop, but also for cooking, or for carrying out administrative activities, to name a few examples.

Second, many of the more specific details are only observed in one of the buildings. The evidence for hooks under the lintels of the doors in *Assos* to hang products from certainly forms an interesting feature, but this feature is not mentioned in these articles for any of the other market buildings. This is also the case with the large round doors in *Alinda* or the possible cult rooms in *Magnesia* on the *Maeander*. We are in fact dealing with very loose pieces of evidence plucked from buildings that, although maybe belonging to a certain building type, also exhibit many varieties and are located at considerable distances from each other. This might reflect differences in use, which makes it especially risky to apply an aspect characteristic of one market building to all market buildings.

The third problem is the tendency not only to ascribe to the building type functions on the basis of one or two elements observed in one of the buildings but also to come up with univocal, clear-cut functions: the spaces in the building were either shops, or public offices, or storerooms, etc. This way of reasoning ignores both the fact that many buildings were in use for a very long time and that they were part of a dynamic urban environment. The variety in internal arrangements and number of storeys show that cities adapted the building type to their own needs. It follows that, although the buildings might have conformed more or less to a specific type, the activities happening inside did not necessarily follow identical patterns. For example, the possible market building in *Sagalassos* was in use from the second century BCE until the sixth century CE. It underwent several changes in appearance and internal arrangement and might even have been turned into a *gymnasium* in Early Imperial times (Claeys, Alper and Arnaut, 2017: 1, 15, 16, 19 and figure X.4). Although the articles discussed do reflect on these kinds of variations, they do not recognize that it might be just the mix of different roles that defined these buildings. Commercial activities were part of everyday life in antiquity and businesses can be found integrated in all sorts of buildings. Good examples are the shops that were built in the East Gymnasium in *Ephesos* (Alzinger, 1970: 1614; Börker and Merkelbach, 1979: 162–3). One could say that the current analyses stay too one-dimensional for a multidimensional object.

A fourth problem with the current studies about market buildings is that most of them have either been excavated a long-time ago or have not been excavated at all. For information about their architectural and spatial features, as well as epigraphical and material finds in and around the buildings, we are mainly dependent on publications. This is not necessarily a problem, but these publications might not have recorded details that are crucial for understanding the function of the different spaces in the buildings, such as the presence or absence of thresholds, which can provide information about how these rooms were closed off, for example, by doors, shutters or something else. To gain more insight in the architecture and layout of market buildings, on-site research is of major importance.

The fifth issue is that research into market buildings needs a new impulse, as new buildings belonging to this group are still being discovered. Old ideas can be re-evaluated in the light of new evidence. A notable example is the possible market building on the east side of the agora in *Sagalassos*, which was discovered in 2015. In *Notion* as well, there is a building with a substructure such as those of market buildings on the south side of the agora (Martin, 1951: 429; Ratté, Rojas and Commito, 2017: 621). In both cases, further research is necessary to determine whether these examples belonged to the larger group of market buildings, but they can also be studied to gain more insight into the very idea of a 'market building type' itself.

The sixth aspect that is missing from previous studies of market buildings is the consideration of market buildings within the historical developments in Asia Minor. Why do we only find market buildings here? Their occurrence specifically during the Hellenistic period and continued use during the Roman period is another feature of interest. Market buildings were part of a changing urban environment as well as larger historical developments. What is their place in the monumentalization of agoras in Hellenistic cities, or the economic growth later perceptible throughout the Roman world? These are questions that have not been answered, or even posed, before.

Finally, having reviewed the literature on market buildings, perhaps the most urgent problem that we are presented with is the definition of market buildings. It might seem a strange choice to discuss the definition of a subject halfway into the chapter, instead of at the beginning. But the problem of definition forms the core of my argument and it is through the literature review that it emerges most clearly. What are we talking about when discussing market buildings? The four studies discussed above do not all focus on the same buildings, which is a clear sign of the confusion and incoherence surrounding the category, if indeed, we can call it a category. The selection of specific buildings by scholars in their articles not only exposes their ideas about what a market building constitutes, but it also shows that there is not one category with a fixed number of buildings. This has to do with the discoveries of new examples on the one hand but predominantly with the problem of definition.

*Figure 4.2* The remains of the western wall of the market building in *Selge*, seen from the west. The arched door gave access to the middle floor, while the almost completely buried rectangular door gave access to the ground floor (photo by author).

## Definition

As has become clear from the literature review above, no clear-cut definition of market buildings exists, which makes identifying a structure as a market building difficult. Yet, several buildings have been identified as such, albeit on the basis of changing and imprecise criteria. This means that some general, joint feeling of what a market building constitutes exists. So far, market buildings have been identified in more or less 15 different cities situated in the *Troad, Aeolis, Ionia, Caria, Lycia, Pisidia* and *Pamphylia*. Remarkably, market buildings seem to have been constructed not only in large well-known cities but also in small towns that possessed no other impressive structures at the time.

Naturally, on the one hand, a more specific definition than the one presented in the introduction might not be necessary, as market buildings constitute a fluid category which cities adapted as they saw fit, but on the other hand, identifying some characteristic aspects is necessary to decide whether this group of buildings can really be considered a type and, if so, to delimit the study object. In past research, ideas about the architectural properties of market buildings have differed rather widely. It has been theorized that market buildings developed from the terrace buildings observed in *Pergamon* (Köse, 2005: 141–3; Lauter, 1970: 96–7, 99–101). If this is accepted, then the multistorey aspect of market buildings can be seen as an integral characteristic. Such a categorization would include the buildings in *Priene, Assos, Lyrbe, Aspendos, Selge* (Figure 4.2), *Aigai, Pednelissos, Kapıkaya, Alinda, Herakleia on the Latmos,* and *Sillyon,* buildings which are discussed by the authors mentioned above. Another, related suggestion is that market buildings evolved from the *stoas* with rooms behind which are assumed to have been invented by Athenian architects (Köse, 2005: 140; Coulton, 1976: 86–9 and figure 24). With this idea in mind, one-storey structures could be included as well, such as the East *Stoa* in *Miletos* and the South *Stoa* in *Priene* (Köse, 2005: 140–1). Theories about the origin of market buildings are thus closely connected to theories about definition. However, Köse also mentions structures without a *stoa* as belonging to the market building category, such as the buildings in *Melli* and *Kapıkaya* (Köse, 2005: 148). Clearly, the 'category' of market buildings has been interpreted in different ways.

Theories about the development of building types are often based mainly on stylistic similarities, but this leaves many questions unanswered. It is true that the market buildings from, for example, *Alinda* and *Selge* resemble specific structures in *Pergamon*, but what does this actually mean? It is important to consider the concrete processes that constitute what is vaguely called 'influence', such as the exchange of ideas between people and the role of authorities in deciding on construction plans. The decision to construct a certain building and to follow a specific style is preceded by a complicated process full of contingencies. Concluding that a building style developed from another style based on stylistic comparison alone ignores the historical reality in which architectural ideas were developed and applied. Moreover, functional properties are as important for the evolution of a building type as are stylistic features. Cities probably do not construct new, expensive structures solely for aesthetic reasons, so it is important to investigate what was attractive about these kinds of buildings in functional terms.

It is furthermore questionable if the combination of *stoa* and rooms, whether in a one-storey building or in a building with a substructure should be seen as a 'unique' building type or as a combination of two already well-known structures. John J. Coulton has stated that the *stoas* were the main element in the building and that the substructure containing the rooms and halls was only built to make use of the space created when raising the *stoa* above ground level instead of filling up the space underneath with earth. The appearance of the substructure would thus be dependent on the design of the *stoa* on top. To Coulton, the market building is, therefore, still first and foremost a *stoa* and he sees the apparent storage facilities of the lower storeys as a sign of their being subordinate (Coulton, 1976: 93). To William B. Dinsmoor as well, the primary object of the substructure was 'the support of the terrace' (Dinsmoor, 1950: 293). However, this way of reasoning does not take into account that the building had to be planned as a whole from the beginning. The substructure did not just emerge as a natural consequence of the planning of the *stoa*, it was part of the original design. Architects had to think about the uses the substructure could have in designing the building. The varieties in the substructures show that their arrangement was adapted to local needs. To degrade the substructure, therefore, to a mere support of the *stoa*, is to ignore the intended use of the spaces underneath.

Is it then possible to come up with a set of characteristics that a structure has to have to fit the category of 'market buildings'? To answer this question, it is necessary to compile a database containing all structures that have been, in one or more publications, indicated as a market building, something that would exceed the scope of this article. Once all the available information from archaeological publications has been gathered, gaps will become visible. These gaps, wherever possible, should be filled by on-site observations. Even if these gaps cannot be filled due to a lack of information, it is important that they are observed and given a place in the record as well to allow for a balanced overview. This will make it possible to come up with a definition that is informed by a consistent data set instead of loose bits of information. Only once these basic prerequisites are covered will it be fruitful to discuss the possible functions as well as investigate the role of market buildings in the urban environment they were part of and the historical developments in Asia Minor.

In short, the study of market buildings needs to take a step back. Current studies have taken too many things for granted, among which are the origin of market buildings, their coherence as a type and, most importantly, their function. The next section of this chapter will take this step back, departing from a more theoretical perspective, after which some more concrete ideas for further study are presented.

## The meaning of buildings

How do we move forward from these insights in trying to understand market buildings? The difficulty with market buildings is that, except for the building itself, there is very little to go on. There are some epigraphical and literary references as we have seen above, but the information they give is indirect and fragmented. In my opinion, this situation is overlooked in much of the literature discussed above, in which too much value is attributed to the scarce literary and epigraphic evidence, leading to distorted conclusions. Instead, we need a fresh, more material-based perspective, using the building itself as the main chunk of evidence, with the scarce additional references as helpful extra data, which must be critically evaluated.

In this section, I will present a theoretical perspective on market buildings, based on the ideas of architectural historian William Whyte. Whyte tried to widen the scope of investigation in understanding the meaning of buildings. According to him, 'Architectural history thus deals not only with buildings, but also with those who built them, those who use(d) them, and those who sought or seek to understand them. It is also concerned with the process of designing and executing plans, with plans that are not carried out, and with the reception of the building, both at the time it was built and thereafter' (Whyte, 2006: 172).

The meaning of a building evolves throughout time and its purpose as seen by the creator, as well as the observer, can change. Whyte, making use of the literary theory of Mikhail Bakhtin, understood this evolution as 'a series of transpositions' (Whyte, 2006: 155, 173–4). A building can be understood within different genres, which, according to Whyte, 'embody differing ways of understanding reality' (Whyte, 2006: 173; Bakhtin, 1981). Genres can be, for example, the drawing of the plan, a visual portrayal of a building, the mentioning of the building in a conversation or the description of a building in an inscription. Each genre has its own conventions, rules and rhetoric, and every piece of evidence related to the building is shaped by the logic of the genre it belonged to (Whyte, 2006: 174–5). Whyte speaks of transposition each time the building is manifested in another genre, and this process shapes and changes the building itself. Consequently, to understand the meaning of buildings, the transpositions need to be studied (Whyte, 2006: 175).

Although the study of market buildings as discussed in this chapter is not strictly architectural history, these conditions also apply here. To understand how market buildings functioned in the urban environment they were part of, it is necessary to study the different genres these buildings were manifested in. Instead of taking one bit of evidence and trying to extract a specific function from that, all evidences related to market buildings need to be studied within its own genre. What were the rules, for example, for setting up an inscription recording who paid for the (restoration of a) market building? And how did these conventions determine how the building was described in the inscription? Genres also link to questions about the people involved with market buildings: who was responsible for construction works? Who paid for the building and who commissioned it? What was the public for these buildings, in other words, who were the people that were to eventually use the building? This entails not only the people that the building was initially meant for, but also those who used the building in the centuries after construction.

Of course, within ancient history this is no easy task, because we are left with a limited selection of evidence. Furthermore, as Whyte notes himself, this method will ask of the historian to gain a deeper understanding of each of the sources he/she studies, which is a complex and difficult undertaking (Whyte, 2006: 176). However, this perspective makes clear that evidence has a multifaceted character, which should be explored in a more thorough and fair way, ultimately disclosing the multifaceted character of buildings themselves. This is an important realization, especially in the context of research on market buildings, in which the evidence has often been handled too casually.

## New avenues for research

In this final part of the chapter, I will propose five concrete ways to broaden the scope of future research on market buildings. Research based on these ideas could build on the database imagined in an earlier paragraph.

A first avenue is to compare market buildings with antique buildings of which the purpose is known. This mostly concerns the architectural properties that made buildings suitable for a specific function. For the supposed function of grain storage, for example, this could be Roman *horrea*. Studying which properties made *horrea* suitable for grain storage can help identifying, or instead explicitly not identifying, those properties in market buildings. While this has been done in a superficial way already, as I have shown above (large, dark, halls in market buildings seem similar to the large empty spaces of warehouses), a more precise, methodologically explicit study is necessary to make sounder conclusions.

Second, market buildings should be studied in their urban context. Market buildings were not constructed individually but as part of a larger arrangement. As this environment changed during the years, so did the role of the market building in it. This approach entails studying which buildings usually stood in the vicinity of market buildings as well as their connection to the market building. It is furthermore possible to analyse the accessibility of market buildings. This is especially interesting with regard to the special layout of the building type, which had several entrances at different levels and sides but usually lacked a connection between the upper *stoa* and the substructure.

A third approach entails the spread of market buildings in Asia Minor. Market buildings appeared in cities in the west and south-west of Asia Minor and their construction was not limited to large and influential cities. One explanation for this situation might be the level of urbanization in *Asia*

*Minor*, but this is something that needs to be investigated better, because it is conceivable that other factors were at play as well, such as the presence and/ or influence of specific political powers.

A fourth theme that could be explored is related to the economic aspects of the construction of market buildings. It has often been assumed that market buildings themselves had an economic function, but the decision to construct these buildings had economic implications as well. Market buildings are monumental in nature and their construction required money, workforces and specialized craftsmen as well as technical knowledge and logistical organization. All of these aspects should be investigated better. For example, it could be analysed how much stone was needed to build market buildings, what it would take to transport this material and how much money would have been involved in this. Answering questions like these can provide insights about the impact of building large structures such as these on the cities they were built in. Analysing costs can demonstrate the importance of market buildings for cities as well. Especially for smaller cities, where the market building is one of the largest structures remaining, the construction must have been an enormous investment.

Lastly, although this has less to do with the material properties of buildings, a thorough, complete review of the epigraphic evidence is necessary to arrive at a better understanding of the context in which these buildings were constructed. Inscriptions have been used to interpret market buildings, especially by Köse, but here again, an inscription is described to make statements about the entire building type (Köse, 2005: 155). These epigraphic references are scarce and are often concerned with the restoration of a market building, such as in *Selge* or in *Aigai* (Lanckoronski, 1890–1892: 234 nos. 248 and 250; Machatschek and Schwarz, 1981: 55; Nollé and Schindler, 1991: 89–94 no. 17; Köse, 2005: 155; Bohn and Schuchhardt, 1889: 23–7, figs. 22 and 26; Köse, 2005: 156), but they can provide small pieces of information about, for example, the people involved with market buildings or the political context in which market buildings were built and restored. These inscriptions need to be put into perspective, however.

These approaches are only examples of ways in which market buildings can be studied. They nevertheless demonstrate the range of topics that have  not been addressed yet and, thereby, show the limits of previous work on market buildings. Naturally, these approaches will not provide a complete picture of the purpose of market buildings either. It is furthermore important to note that, as with all of history, the choice of which aspects to study is never neutral and will, therefore, unavoidably lead to a bias in what we will know about the buildings. A focus on the urban environment of buildings might lead to conclusions missing the point about the buildings' individual characteristics. What I have pointed out here, however, is that the current approaches lack depth and methodology and that new approaches such as those outlined above can both broaden and deepen our knowledge of market buildings.

## Conclusion

I hope I have made clear that, in the study of market buildings, it is necessary to break away from the rather haphazard way in which possible functions of market buildings have been proposed, among which is the habit of suggesting functions on the basis of individual details. Through a literary overview I have shown that a re-evaluation of these ideas is necessary, as the evidence under-lying them is either not there or used in an invalid way. New studies should start from the notion that these buildings were part of a versatile urban envir-onment which would be reflected in the buildings. In order to make this clear, I have discussed the theory of William Whyte on architectural history. I have furthermore proposed some new avenues for research about market buildings in the future. Approaching market buildings from these perspectives may shed new light on this central feature of many cities in ancient Asia Minor.

## References

Alzinger, Wilhelm. "Ephesos B." *RE Suppl.* XII (1970): 1588–704.

Baker, Patrick and Gaétan Thériault. "Prospection épigraphique: rapport sur la cam-pagne de 2002." *Anatolia Antiqua* 11 (2003): 431–5.

Bakhtin, Mikhail. "Forms of Time and of the Chronotope in the Novel." Pages 84–258 in *The Dialogic Imagination: Four Essays.* Edited by Michael Holquist. Austin: University of Texas Press, 1981.

Balland, André. *Fouilles de Xanthos VII: Inscriptions d'époque impériale du Létôon.* Paris: Klincksieck, 1981.

Bohn, Richard and Carl Schuchhardt. *Altertümer von Aegae.* Berlin: Georg Reimer, 1889.

Börker, Christoph and Reinhold Merkelbach. *Die Inschriften von Ephesos* II. Bonn: Habelt, 1979.

Cavalier, Laurence. "Portiques en bordure des agoras d'Asie Mineure à l'époque hellénistique et à l'époque impériale." Pages 241–56 in *Basiliques et agoras de Grèce et d'Asie Mineure.* Edited by Laurence Cavalier, Raymond Descat and Jacques des Courtils. Bordeaux: Ausonius, 2012.

Claeys, Johan, Ece Alper and Robin Arnaut. *Sagalassos 2017–Site UAE. Final Excavation Report.* Excavation report Sagalassos Archaeological Research Project. Leuven, 2017.

Clerc, Michel A. "Les ruines d'Aegae en Éolie." *Bulletin de Correspondance Hellénique* 10 (1886): 275–96.

Coulton, John J. *The Architectural Development of the Greek Stoa.* Oxford: Clarendon Press, 1976.

Cüppers, Heinz. "Getreidenmagazin am Forum in Aspendos." *Bonner Jahrbücher* 161 (1961): 25–35.

Dinsmoor, William B. *Architecture of Ancient Greece. An Account of its Historic Development.* London: Batsford, 1950.

Fabricius, Ernst and Carl Schuchhardt. *Inschriften von Pergamon. Altertümer von Pergamon 8.1.* Berlin: Verlag von W. Spemann, 1890.

Fuchs, Günter. "Die Funktion der frühen römischen Marktbasilika." *Bonner Jahrbücher* 161 (1961): 39–46.

Gauthier, Philippe. *Nouvelles inscriptions de Sardes II*. Geneva: Droz, 1984.

Hall, Allan S. and Nicholas P. Milner. "Education and Athletics. Documents Illustrating the Festivals of Oenoanda." Pages 7–47 in *Studies in the History and Topography of Lycia and Pisidia: in Memoriam A.S. Hall*. Edited by David French. Ankara: British Institute at Ankara, 1994.

Haussoullier, Bernard. "Les Séleucides et le temple d'Apollon didyméen." *Revue de philologie, de littérature et d'histoire anciennes* 24 (1900): 243–71.

Hiller von Gaertringen, Friedrich F. *Inschriften von Priene*. Berlin: Habelt, 1906.

Kleiner, Gerhard. *Die Ruinen von Milet*. Berlin: De Gruyter, 1968.

Knackfuss, Hubert and Albert Rehm. *Der Südmarkt und die benachbarten Bauanlagen. Milet I, 7*. Berlin: Schoetz–Parrhysius, 1924.

Köse, Veli. "The Origin and Development of Market Buildings in Hellenistic and Roman Asia Minor." Pages 139–66 in *Patterns in the Economy of Roman Asia Minor*. Edited by Stephen Mitchell and Constantina Katsari. Swansea: The Classical Press of Wales, 2005.

Lanckoronski, Karol. *Städte Pamphyliens und Pisidiens. 2. Pisidien*. Vienna: F. Tempsky, 1890–1892.

Lauter, Hans K. "Die hellenistische Agora von Aspendos." *Bonner Jahrbücher* 170 (1970): 77–101.

Lauter, Hans K. *Die Architektur des Hellenismus*. Darmstadt: Wissenschaftliche Buchgesellschaft, 1986.

Machatschek, Alois and Mario Schwarz. *Bauforschungen in Selge*. Vienna: Verlag der Österreichischen Akademie der Wissenschaften, 1981.

Martin, Roland. *Recherches sur l'agora grecque*. Paris: E. de Boccard, 1951.

Nollé, Johannes and Friedel Schindler. *Die Inschriften von Selge*. Bonn: Habelt, 1991.

Perkins, Ann Louise. *The Excavations at Dura-Europos. Final Report V, Part 1*. New Haven: Yale University Press, 1959.

Pleket, Henri W. "Nine Greek Inscriptions from the Cayster Valley: A Re-Publication." *Talanta* 2 (1970): 55–88.

Ras, M. "Oinoanda in Lykia, the Elite and Economy in the Roman Empire." *Lykia* 2 (1995): 22–38.

Ratté, Christopher, Felipe Rojas and Angela Commito. "Notion Archaeological Survey, 2014–2015." *Araştırma Sonuçları Toplantısı* 34 (2017): 617–38.

Rehm, Albert. *Die Inschriften. Didyma II*. Berlin: Verlag Gebr. Mann, 1958.

Reynolds, Joyce M. "Honouring Benefactors at Aphrodisias. A New Inscription." Pages 121–6 in *Aphrodisias Papers 3. JRA Supplement 20*. Edited by Charlotte Roueché and Roland R. R. Smith. Ann Arbor: Journal of Roman Archaeology, 1996.

Robert, Louis. "Documents d'Asie Mineure." *Bulletin de Correspondance Hellénique* 108 (1984): 457–532.

Whyte, William. "How Do Buildings Mean? Some Issues of Interpretation in the History of Architecture." *History and Theory* 45 (2006): 153–77.

Wilski, Paul. *Karte der milesischen Halbinsel*. Berlin: Reimer, 1906.

Winter, Frederick E. *Studies in Hellenistic architecture*. Toronto: University of Toronto Press, 2006.

Wörrle, Michael. *Stadt und Fest im kaiserzeitlichen Kleinasien*. Munich: C.H. Beck, 1988.

# 5 Do economic activities impinge on Roman urban matrices in Asia Minor?

## A new style/function debate

*Jeroen Poblome and Rinse Willet*

### Setting the scene

In his 2005 study, the American comparative economist Frederic L. Pryor set out to investigate, at a global scale, whether the number of economic systems was either limited or endless in time and space. With economic systems, he meant a clustering of institutions (the rules of the game) and organizations (the players of the game) that specify property relations and channel the distribution of goods and services in society. Based on the Standard Cross-Cultural Sample, compiled by George P. Murdock and Douglas R. White in 1969, Frederic Pryor developed a unified analytical approach and a taxonomy of economic systems for various types of (pre-)industrial societies, based on a combination of cluster and regression analytical methods. Not only could he identify a small number of coherent types of economic systems, he also argued that these systems were relatively independent of social, political and environmental influences, yet highly dependent on the level of economic development. His comparative perspective allowed to understand certain economic activities as integral parts of the economic system, whereas other activities could be viewed as unique aspects of the particular society.

As far as (past) agricultural societies are concerned, these featured four quite distinct economic systems. Societies were considered to be agricultural when 85% or more food was derived from own agricultural production. Avoiding the detail of the other three systems (the herding plus system, the egalitarian farming system and the individualistic market system), the case of the Roman Empire can best be regarded as an example of Pryor's 'semi-marketized farming economic system', featuring comparatively more trade, more wage labour, higher rents on land, less slavery, high land leasing rents, higher taxes and higher economic development compared to the other three types of agricultural societies. Importantly, other features related to physical environment, geographical location or social or political structure did not appear to determine the emergence of this economic system.

Even though the words 'Rome' or 'Roman Empire' are not to be found in the index of Frederic Pryor's (2005) book and he does not offer a single phrase on the constellation of this empire, we considered his study relevant to introduce the topic of our chapter. Indeed, when considering the many remaining manifestations of the Roman Empire, be these historical or archaeological, the question arises whether, as Pryor would suggest, its economic system was endemic to Roman society and an important topic of study in its own right being in a constant causal relationship in the functioning and development of the Empire?

In this chapter, we will approach this question from the specific theme of urbanism and, more specifically, develop thoughts on whether and how economic activities hold elements of causation for the development of Roman towns. The context of Asia Minor is our relevant and familiar study region.

In his 1988 book, Paul Bairoch investigated the *nexus* between cities and economic development from a long-term perspective. In his view, the existence of towns presupposed the availability of a substantial agricultural surplus and so implying a dialectical relationship with the countryside. Moreover, the surplus had to be sufficiently large to also be available for exchange, and not merely feed the townsfolk. This duality required the existence of certain social and technological 'structures' or, in this context, institutions. In the case of Rome, Paul Bairoch (1988) saw increased demographic pressure playing a role in the spread of more advanced agricultural methods throughout the Empire. He judged less equivocally on technological advances in Roman society. Although the variety, quality and availability of all sorts of products had clearly increased, the underlying technical processes had not necessarily done so. Nonetheless, Bairoch gave due importance to the so far unparalleled diffusion of technical knowledge and artisanal activities, which *en gros* meant economic development with towns providing the necessary leverage. On the whole, however, he concluded that the Roman urban phenomenon did not really instigate development as the accumulated resources, which could be considerable, were not invested in the mechanisms of economic growth but rather in policies of self-preservation such as maintaining the army and the imperial house or sustaining the *caput mundi*.

Clearly, Paul Bairoch was much inspired by the works of Moses I. Finley and Keith Hopkins in developing his rationale. Much more recently, Arjan Zuiderhoek has been revisiting some of these highly influential ideas in his 2017 study on the ancient city. He actually advocates to merge some of the main characteristics of the so-called consumer city model, featuring centrally in the Finley–Hopkins interpretation of the ancient world, with a complex, dynamic economic system. Even if, in our view, more effects should be considered in judging on the spending power of the average townsfolk, the fact that the economic relationship between city and countryside should be defined as non-reciprocal holds true. According to Zuiderhoek, basically any ancient economic activity should be seen as a consequence of the urban (elite) claiming of agricultural produce as a consequence of legal and political entitlements, and not in exchange for manufactured products and services provided to the countryside. We agree that this basic, structural feature of ancient society has no necessary consequences for whether these economies should be active or static, developing, developed or even generating economic growth. Now as in the past, the truth will very much be in the mix.

Notably, Arjan Zuiderhoek allocates a considerable role to activities related to manufacture, service provision and trade in ancient cities, so much so that in his view some towns can best be regarded as producer cities, even if these are the exceptions in antiquity. However, when such activities meant a lot to the well-being of the majority of the urban dwellers, no systematic incentive at investment in these sectors can be discerned. Civic authorities, according to Zuiderhoek, basically had concerns with two flip sides of the urban economy: gathering sufficient public revenue and ensuring adequate provisioning of the community. The institutions harnessing these functions were often the first to be housed in dedicated monumental structures, provided by the city and to some extent also private benefactors. Cities and their captains of society, in other words, did not develop truly economic policies, which keeps the conceptualization within the framework of the consumer city model. Importantly, however, notwithstanding the limited civic concerns for the urban economy, the latter quite often fared well in the sense that the sociopolitical organization 'provided a highly beneficial context for economic activity' (Zuiderhoek 2017: 146), which at times genuinely contributed to economic growth.

In these three overview and comparative studies, different concepts are being elaborated, scoring variable effects in interpreting the past relationship between urbanism and economic activities. We selected these studies as they step-wise zoom in on antiquity and the issue at hand. On the whole, these works do not connect the systematic elaboration of economic policies with the phenomenon of urbanism in the Roman Empire, even if they leave different margins in how active the economic behaviour and patterns could have been in the past. The question is whether and how archaeological evidence can contribute to this debate?

We propose to look into this matter by attempting a new style/function debate. Indeed, in the case of Roman urbanism, the physical result of the mentioned models is simply amazing: there is a strong level of conformity, considering the physical aspects of Roman towns throughout the Empire. The visual and functional townscapes are apparently similar, so much so that inhabitants of the eastern provinces would find their bearings in western provincial cities and the other way round. Embellished fora/agorai, theatres, temples dedicated to recognizable gods, in an iconographically readable context, sustained familiarity, even if the languages spoken in the streets would have been different. Similarities are also apparent at a more detailed level of how, for instance, terracotta water pipes were conceived or roofs tiled and iron nails made.

In the framework of restricted development of urban economic policies, what does this apparent conformity in townscapes and what do these similarities at different levels in functional and infrastructural terms mean? It all has to do with meaning, of course, and touches upon one of the most intricate problems in archaeological reasoning: the difference between things being the same or rather being similar. In other words, can we, in the case of Roman urbanism, observe analogous or homologous patterns? This problem was also at the basis of the renowned style/function debate, also known in archaeological literature as the (François) Bordes/(Lewis) Binford debate (Wargo 2009). The matter at hand concerned the interpretation of European Middle Palaeolithic Mousterian (160,000–40,000 BP) stone technology and was related to the question whether the attested different taphonomic groups of these artefacts revealed the identity of different cultural groups or rather toolkits with different functions? In case the stone artefacts are to be considered as the result of the same intellectual/cultural tradition, then these products share the same style and are basically homologous. In case the traits of this material culture truly converge, then they share the same function, and can we talk about analogies.

Even though this debate finds its origins in late nineteenth-century American archaeology, for a long time it lacked a theoretical foundation to explain why one particular process acted or produced either a stylistic or a functional trait. This theoretical framework was in fact created by Darwinian evolutionary archaeologists (Hurt and Rakita 2001) who saw function associated with evolutionary fitness and style to traits with no selective values/drift. Homologies, in this sense, are features similar in structure (not form) because of a common origin, giving rise to trait diffusion, e.g. pots with identical decoration of the same cultural heredity. Only functional traits, to be sure, could be analogies.

So in the case of urbanism in the Roman Empire, or at least in the case of Asia Minor, can we approach the apparent similarities as analogies or homologies, and, either which way, what does this say about whether economic activities impinged upon Roman urban matrices in Asia Minor?

## Urbanism in Asia Minor

Before diving into such matters, it is important to discuss the object under study. Although very few if any living being on this planet in the early twenty-first century would have no conceptualization of what a city is, a uniform definition of cities is not self-evident. In art, cities are represented in depictions, such as in Vermeer's *View of Delft*, or through abstractions, such as Mondriaan's *Broadway Boogie Woogie*. In music, the opening of Gershwin's *An American in Paris* or Kraftwerk's *Neon Lights* captures the different emotional states evoked by urban environments. As varied as these works of art conceptualize (parts of) urbanity, approaches in research to urbanism differ at least as much. The approach selected for this chapter allows for quantitative comparative studies.

Geographers typically use population levels to define towns and cities. This can be considered somewhat reductionist and foregoes the complexities that characterize cities. Shanghai clearly differs from Tokyo, London, New York, Paris, Brussels and Amsterdam in more ways than just size. However, it can also not be denied that the examples chosen here immediately conjure up images of large bustling agglomerations. Furthermore, for the questions at hand, demographic levels and economic aspects of urbanism are often linked, whereby higher population levels are associated with greater economic power and differentiation of activities (De Vries 1984; Scheidel 2001; Bowman and Wilson 2011). That this linkage is far from linear or simplistic has been successfully studied by Luis Bettencourt and Geoffrey West, who discovered the scalar properties that affect these aspects of urbanism (Bettencourt 2013; West 2017). Paul Krugman, too, pointed out that random growth of the cities was an important factor in shaping the differentiation of population levels between (modern) cities and that the initial conditions, in which the unevenness of the natural landscape must be included, introduced randomness to the development of groups of cities and thus are important for the trajectory of urban systems (Krugman 1996: 412, 416). Unfortunately, the study of ancient city sizes is not clear-cut as statistics on the number of inhabitants are lacking for antiquity. Proxies must, therefore, be employed, which are indicative of the variation in population levels. Surface area of settlements is commonly employed (Chamberlain 2006: 127–128).

Administrative status is often used as a defining factor for cities as well. Administrative status is the amount of political acting power a settlement, as a body of its inhabitants, had to determine and enforce rules, start building projects and levy taxes within a civic political framework in which the settlement exists. For antiquity, civic autonomy or the lack thereof is the most important differentiation between cities and other types of settlement. In practice, a city with civic autonomy held jurisdiction over a territory. It was responsible for levying taxes in its territory and from its urban inhabitants. The financial power which imbued civic autonomy was an attractive proposition for members of local elites. This is evidenced by an early fourth-century CE inscription found at Orkistos in which the inhabitants of the settlement make a plea for civic autonomy to Emperor Constantine (MAMA VII.305, the inscription is dated shortly after 30 June 331 CE). A more cynical read of some of the letters of governor Pliny the Younger to Emperor Trajan from Bithynia, describing various urban construction projects that turned into disastrous money pits, would suggest that civic taxation could (illegally) flow into the personal coffers of members of the urban elites as well (Plin. *Ep.* X.37–38; 39–40; 81–82; 90–91; see also Dio Chrys. *Or.* 40.33; 44.11; 45.6; 10ff). It is, therefore, perhaps of little surprise that many communities strived for or protected the legal privileges associated with civic autonomy.

Another important aspect of cities is their physicality, which is most clearly expressed through the presence of (public) buildings and monuments. As already mentioned, the monumentality of a city, and the conforming to or compatibility with an urban layout to an expected pattern of buildings, streets, squares, passages and gates, help the visitor to navigate the city. Monumentality certainly was a vital aspect of what made a city live up to aspiration in antiquity, as expressed by Pausanias (10.4.1). The ancient expectations on the differences in monumentality between self-governing cities and secondary agglomerations (i.e. villages, subject towns, hamlets etc.) are further mentioned by Tacitus. He describes how Agricola furnished the *civitas* capitals of Roman Britain with temples, a public square, houses, colonnades and bath buildings (Tac. *Agr.* 21). This founding and furnishing of new *civitates* by Agricola implies that autonomous cities should have certain specific types of buildings (Kolb 1993: 323 further notes that these are specifically noted buildings, whereas certain other types of 'urban' buildings are not mentioned, such as theatres, basilicae, libraries, circuses, amphitheatres, aqueducts, etc.). From this, Kolb (1993: 325) argued that for the new cities in Roman Britain, these buildings represented the basic array of amenities while conforming to what cities in the Roman West were expected to have. The inscription from Orkistos outlined the presence of basic public amenities as part of the plea for civic autonomy. Orkistos was located at a place where four official roads came together. It claimed to have a sizeable population, which easily filled its agora. It also had production facilities, as reference is made to numerous watermills. In other words, Orkistos had a function as a central place in an economic sense (Kolb 1993: 332–333). Furthermore, the inscription mentions the presence of a *mansio* or inn, a copious water supply, public and private bath buildings and a public square richly adorned with statues of previous *principes* (Kolb 1993: 328, 330 and Thonemann 2013: 32 argued that the stipulation of the presence of a large population is indicative of the deurbanization of the fourth-century CE Phrygia. The small scale of most cities in Asia Minor is discussed below). This monumentality was part of an expectation pattern for (proper) cities. Naturally, a major part of this was not only style but also certainly function. Towns and cities provided amenities to their inhabitants and visitors. Short-cycle markets were held at both cities and villages, for instance, but annual fairs and markets often coincided with religious festivals, courtdays and so on in cities. To some extent, but not completely, the amenities a city offered were reflected in its public buildings. Yet, we also must be careful to interpret the presence of these buildings in too utilitarian ways. An agora was as much a place of (political) display, while markets could as well be held on a simple field.

The cities discussed here all had civic autonomy, which is a (relatively) simple differentiation to establish in the context of Asia Minor. Under the Roman Empire, inscriptions attest to the presence of a council and the people. Also, large corpora have been compiled on minting cities. The data used for this analysis are the result of research on Roman urbanism in Asia Minor (Willet 2020). The sources consist of publications in archaeology and ancient history, combined with a careful analysis of ancient texts, epigraphy, numismatics and aerial photography. From this research, a total of at least 446 cities with civic autonomy have been collected for Roman Asia Minor (Figure 5.1). These were unevenly distributed over the landmass. The provinces of *Galatia et Cappadocia* (n=52) and *Bithynia et Pontus* (n=19) are sparsely dotted with cities. *Cilicia* (n=48) had a denser distribution pattern,

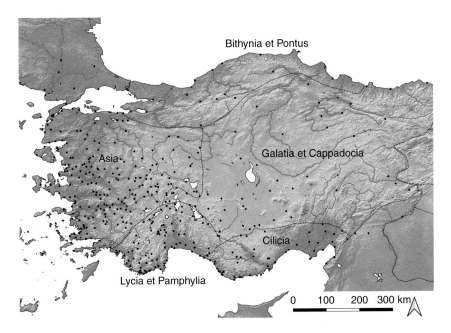

*Figure 5.1* Distribution of cities with civic autonomy. Of the 446 cities, 428 are located
and displayed on the map. Sagalassos (discussed in the following text)
is marked with the white dot.

while the provinces of *Asia* (n=198) and *Lycia et Pamphylia* (n=86) contained
most cities. Particularly the river valleys of western Anatolia, the Aegean and
Mediterranean coasts and the Pisidian lakes are correlated with the dense
distribution of cities. Asia Minor was highly urbanized, with a forthcoming
publication collecting only some 500 autonomous cities for Roman North
Africa (Morocco, Algeria, Tunisia, Libya), which was a vastly larger area
than Asia Minor (Hobson 2019). Spain, too, was home to a large number
of cities (430 in total), but their size was much smaller and the density of
cities (Lusitania: n=53–c. 118,500 km²; Citerior: n=213–c. 385,000 km²;
Baetica: n=164–c. 76,100 km²) was lower overall, although the Guadalquivir
river valley was indeed densely settled.[1]

Structural determinants partially explain this pattern for Asia Minor. The
coast was clearly an attractor, with 140–150 of the 428 located self-governing
cities situated within less than 15 km from the ancient coastline. Also, the
zones with most cities shared a Mediterranean climate. The distribution of
natural resources affected the urban pattern as well. Although there is plenty
of evidence from ancient sources and archaeological findings for the exploitation of a wide array of natural resources (timber, marble, etc.), the foundation of a city's economy must have been its agriculture. Agricultural potential
has been shown as a good predictor of urbanization for the Ottoman period,

for example (Faroqhi 1990: 147–148). Yet, we must be careful for the trap of geographic determinism in explaining the settlement patterns of Anatolia. The Hittite Empire, for example, had its powerbase in Anatolia anchored in palaces and settlements focused on the Central Plateau, in contrast to later periods. Shifts in climate in Anatolia influenced settlement patterns in the long-term (Haldon 2016). Sociopolitical, cultural and perhaps, most importantly, historical context are important elements in the establishment of the Roman Imperial pattern. Therefore, the dense pattern found in Roman western and southern Anatolia cannot be seen separate from the preceding Classical and Hellenistic periods.

The *Inventory of Archaic and Classical Poleis* by Mogens Hansen and Thomas Nielsen (2004) forms a solid and well-researched basis for reconstructing the Classical urban pattern. The *Inventory* lists 212 Greek-style self-governing cities for Asia Minor (Figure 5.2). It is clear that these are mostly focused on the coasts of western and southern Anatolia. This is to some degree the effects of the research topic (i.e. Greek *poleis*), as native settlements, often known mostly through archaeology, are not listed as exhaustively by the *Inventory*. However, the dense concentration of cities found on the coasts and relative paucity inland seems hard to ignore and was reflected in the subsequent Hellenistic and Roman Imperial phases.

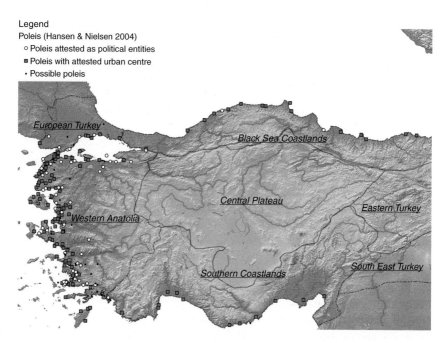

*Figure 5.2*  Greek-style autonomous cities (*poleis*) as recorded by Hansen and Nielsen's *An Inventory of Archaic and Classical Poleis*. These are the places listed as 'poleis attested as political entities' (n=60), 'poleis with attested urban centres' (n=127) and 'possible poleis' (n=39).

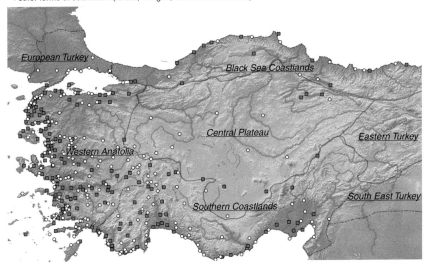

Legend
Tentative reconstruction Hellenistic urban pattern (Cohen 1995, Head 1911, Schuler 1998 etc.)
■ Greek style self-governing city
○ other forms of settlement (towns, villages, colonial foundations)

*Figure 5.3* Reconstruction of the autonomous cities in the Hellenistic period. The sources are ancient texts, inscriptions and coins, collected in individual publications on-sites and compendiums. See also Willet (2020).

Hellenistic urbanism has received relatively little attention in comparison with the Classical and Roman Imperial periods, with the works by Victor Tscherikower (1927) and Getzel Cohen (1995) still standing as important surveys. With the aid of these works and other volumes on Hellenistic towns, villages and settlements, and on coining, a tentative reconstruction can be made (Figure 5.3). This reconstruction is obviously biased by historically attested cities and settlements, which, at the same time, tend to be the larger and more monumentalized ones. In this way, Hellenistic Asia Minor numbered at least 169 Greek-style self-governing cities, together with 168 other towns, villages and colonial foundations. The pattern that emerges again displays a densely settled coastal area, although autonomous cities are clearly expanding inland. The Roman Imperial distribution of cities is, therefore, a reflection of the Hellenistic pattern. Finally, in a famous study on the economy of Roman Asia Minor from the 1930s, Thomas Broughton (1938) observed a change in the number of cities from the Late Republican period (n=265+; Broughton 1938: 497–702) to Flavian–Severan times (n=368; Broughton 1938: 737–739). Although he did not count nor map these places, the expansion clearly took place from a dense coastal to a further intensification of the inland distribution of cities. The path dependency of many Roman Imperial cities on the Classical and Hellenistic periods is striking and some of these cities would rank among the most monumental and sizable in the Empire (e.g. Ephesos, Pergamon, Miletos, Nikomedeia, Laodikeia on the Lykos, Alexandreia Troas and so on).

Yet, these famous names are but a few among the hundreds of autonomous cities. If the size of these places is considered, the striking fact is that the majority of cities were small. Table 5.1 contains all the measured cities of Roman Asia Minor. Due to the fact that many cities are archaeologically not well-researched, only for a limited number of the 446 cities a measurement could be made (n=169). The sizes range from less than 2 ha (Nephelis, Pogla) to 193 ha (Smyrna). On average, the cities measured c. 45 ha. The largest and most of the large cities are situated in *Asia* situated in relative close proximity (Figure 5.4). Large cities in the other provinces, particularly in *Galatia*

*Table 5.1* City sizes per size category

| Size category (in ha) | No. of measured cities with civic autonomy |
| --- | --- |
| Total | 169 |
| >160 ha | 4 (2.9%) |
| 81–160 ha | 24 (14.2%) |
| 41–80 ha | 38 (22.5%) |
| 21–40 ha | 42 (24.7%) |
| <20 ha | 61 (35.9%) |

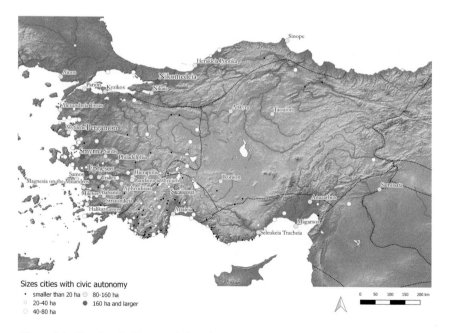

*Figure 5.4* City sizes in Roman Asia Minor.

*et Cappadocia*, are more isolated, such as Ancyra (113 ha), Taouion (150 ha) or Ikonion (120 ha). For *Lycia et Pamphylia*, the province with the densest distribution of cities with civic autonomy, the size of cities was comparatively small, on average 23 ha, with Attaleia being the largest (83 ha).

It is striking how many of these cities had monumental buildings. For the entirety of Asia Minor, the presence of public buildings belonging to different classes was tabulated (Table 5.2), based on extant archaeological remains, epigraphic references or ancient descriptions. Even though the majority of the places discussed here were not excavated or otherwise studied, in total a minimum of 262 out of 446 cities with civic autonomy have one or more public buildings attested (Figure 5.5) (Table 5.3). The full complexity of individual

*Table 5.2* Classes and building types

| Class | Building types |
|-------|----------------|
| Fortifications | City walls, Gates (freestanding) Defensive towers |
| Civic and commercial | *Agora*, Market Building, *Bouleuterion*, *Stoa*, Basilica |
| Water | Bath house, Gymnasium, *Nymphaion*/Fountain, Aqueduct, Cistern |
| Spectacle | Theatre, Amphitheatre, *Odeion*, Stadium |
| Religious | Temples |

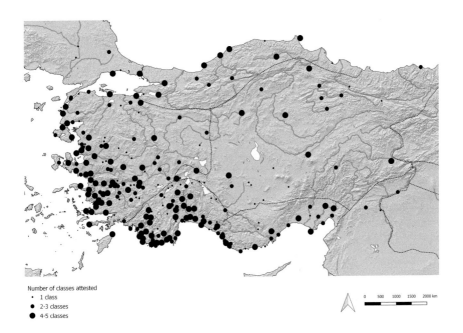

Number of classes attested
· 1 class
● 2-3 classes
● 4-5 classes

0  500  1000  1500  2000 km

*Figure 5.5* Cities with civic autonomy and attested public buildings.

buildings in functionality and style is obviously not captured with this method and the presence of more than one building within a single class (e.g. the presence of multiple spectacle buildings, such as a theatre, an odeion and a stadium) is not accounted for. Yet, these classes form a starting point for comparative analysis and must be regarded as a minimum indicator of urban monumentality. The majority of public buildings are attested in cities of south-western Asia Minor. In 26% of the cities, only 1 class of buildings is represented (20 – fortifications, 16 – religious buildings, 6 – civic and commercial buildings, 15 – water-related buildings, 11 – spectacle buildings). In 34%, 2–3 classes are attested. Importantly, for 41% of the cities, 4–5 classes are attested.

When considering the average size of these places, the larger cities tend to have more classes attested than the smaller ones (Table 5.4). Cities, particularly when they were (becoming) larger, had a propensity to monumentalize and diversify in public buildings. We consider this related to the economic power of a city. The fact that some cities possessed multiple buildings of each class and that there is variation in the level of finishing and decoration shows that cities were doing economically well in the Roman Empire. The city councils and the urban elites wanted to display this wealth in public monuments.

*Table 5.3* The number of cities with 1 to 5 classes attested per province

|  | Total | Asia | Lycia et Pamphylia | Cilicia | Galatia et Cappadocia | Bithynia et Pontus |
|---|---|---|---|---|---|---|
| 5 classes | 71 | 36 | 24 | 1 | 5 | 5 |
| 4 classes | 35 | 12 | 8 | 7 | 3 | 4 |
| 3 classes | 48 | 18 | 13 | 10 | 4 | 3 |
| 2 classes | 40 | 18 | 6 | 7 | 4 | 1 |
| 1 class | 68 | 26 | 16 | 6 | 12 | 3 |
| Total | 262 | 110 | 67 | 31 | 28 | 16 |

*Note*: Total includes cities in Asia Minor visible on the map but situated outside these four provinces, such as Thracia and Syria.

*Table 5.4* Average size for cities with 1–5 classes attested

| Average size combinations | Total | Asia | Lycia et Pamphylia | Cilicia | Galatia et Cappadocia | Bithynia et Pontus |
|---|---|---|---|---|---|---|
| Average city size 4–5 classes | 59.0 | 77.9 | 25.5 | 24.0 | 73.6 | 83.3 |
| Average city size 2–3 classes | 31.4 | 33.0 | 19.9 | 26.8 | 51.7 | n/a |
| Average city size 1 class | 28.3 | 53.0 | 26.6 | 15.0 | 10.8 | n/a |

*Note*: Sizes given in hectare. For *Cilicia* and *Bithynia et Pontus*, the number of measured cities with attested classes is too limited to result in reliable averages.

It was common for cities to have an array of buildings to fulfil a variety of functions, which is in line with ancient expectations on cities and monumentality. The highest variety of urban monumentality is found in proximity to the coast, where cities were situated in close proximity to each other and probably rivalled for prestige through public buildings (Tak 1990). Also along the river valleys in *Asia* and in inland Pisidia cities tended to have higher numbers of classes attested. Further inland, in *Galatia et Cappadocia*, the cities with higher monumentalization are spaced at greater distances. This could be indicative of these cities functioning as a central place providing amenities to visitors from a wider region (Bintliff 2002).

Apart from autonomous cities, many settlements existed in Roman Asia Minor which were not juridically independent. These consisted of many different types (villages, small towns, hamlets and so on). Ancient geographers distinguish various non-urban types of settlement in the region, and from epigraphy, many *komai* and *katoikiai* or villages/communities are known. With regard to monumentality, villages could have the same public buildings as a city, and they could erect with their own funds such buildings as temples, *agorai*, gymnasia and bathing complexes and defensive structures (Schuler 1998: 255–264; De Ligt 1990: 28f). The term secondary agglomeration is used to cover these places that do not have civic autonomy and were thereby subject to cities and obliged to pay taxes to these. We consider the number of these (mostly historically attested) secondary agglomerations as a minimum, as intensive archaeological surveying tends to reveal many more wherever conducted. However, the presence of epigraphy or the mentioning of a place in ancient sources hints at the fact that these places were in a tier higher in importance, function and, possibly, size.

For Asia Minor, a total of 743 secondary agglomerations are tabulated, of which 479 are located (Figure 5.6 and Table 5.5). Strikingly, the areas with few self-governing centres seem to be 'filled up' with secondary agglomerations, particularly on the Central Plateau and the Black Sea coast. Here the cities are situated along natural routes in the landscape and leave many areas empty. In these cases, the secondary agglomerations could have played a role as central places and foci of residence in a sparsely populated landscape, providing similar, if not the same, amenities as autonomous cities. In these sparsely settled areas, even estates have been the centres for short- or longer cycle markets, and many estates are indeed attested in Galatia.

Second, and more importantly, those areas where clusters of self-governing centres existed also have many secondary agglomerations, thereby making the clusters both larger and denser. This can in part be explained by their origins. The Hellenistic period saw intensive (re)founding of settlements in areas with good arable land. As a result, the areas with intense clusters of autonomous centres also saw an intensive pattern of secondary agglomerations. It is difficult to avoid the conclusion that the geographical distribution of natural resources was a major factor in shaping the settlement pattern. As the distribution of secondary agglomerations seems only partially aimed at 'filling in the gaps'

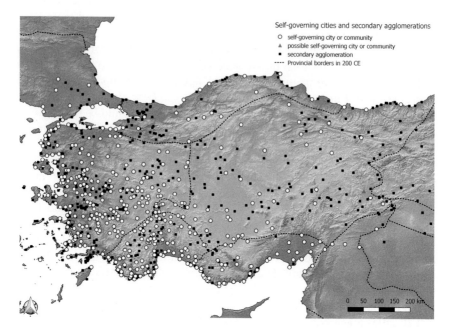

*Figure 5.6* Self-governing cities and secondary agglomerations in Roman Asia Minor.

*Table 5.5* Count of secondary agglomerations per province

| Province | No. of secondary agglomerations (% of total) | No. of located secondary agglomerations | No. of located self-governing cities and communities (% of total) | Ratio of self-governing cities and communities: secondary agglomerations |
|---|---|---|---|---|
| Asia | 299 (40.2%) | 188 | 198 (46.8%) | 1:1.51 |
| Lycia et Pamphylia | 82 (11.0%) | 59 | 86 (20.3%) | 1:0.95 |
| Cilicia | 38 (5.1%) | 23 | 48 (11.4%) | 1:0.79 |
| Galatia et Cappadocia | 216 (29.1%) | 112 | 52 (12.3%) | 1:4.15 |
| Bithynia et Pontus | 80 (10.7%) | 69 | 19 (4.5%) | 1:4.21 |
| Outside provinces | 28 (3.8%) | 28 | 25 (5.8%) | 1:1.12 |
| Total | 743 | 479 | | |

*Note*: These include roughly located settlements, which are not included for mapping or spatial analysis. Of the secondary agglomerations outside the provinces, 19 are situated in Thracia, 3 on Rhodos, 1 on Samos, 3 on Lesbos, 5 in Syria and 3 in the eastern part of Turkey, Armenia and Georgia. A further 110 secondary agglomerations are recorded.

on the maps, it seems that the availability of settlement chambers was a more important factor than the provision of goods and services from the primary and secondary agglomerations to the countryside. This demonstrates that urbanism in Asia Minor was a complex and highly regionalized phenomenon, which was shaped both by structural determinants and to a greater degree by the histories of settlement that the region underwent. Certainly, the high density of secondary agglomerations in areas with dense clusters of autonomous cities suggests a higher demographic pressure on the landscape in these areas and a greater agricultural exploitation.

In terms of size, for only 41 secondary agglomerations existing during the Roman Imperial period, a measurement could be obtained. This showcases that academic attention by archaeologists and historians for smaller towns and villages in Anatolia has been lacking. We advocate more research to be directed to these types of settlement. The average size for the 41 secondary agglomerations is c. 5.7 ha (range: 0.2–34 ha), from which we deduce that these settlements were much smaller than cities with civic autonomy. Quite possibly the unmeasured settlements would further lower this average. The monumentality of secondary agglomerations is also less pronounced than for autonomous cities. For only 149 secondary agglomerations, buildings belonging to classes 1–5 have been attested and only rarely multiple classes are attested. Fortification works are the most common type of public building attested for secondary agglomerations, and these tend to be dated mostly (if at all) to pre-Roman periods. All these findings support the idea that settlements in the territories of autonomous cities constitute the socio-economic foundation on which Roman urbanism in Asia Minor could emerge. Furthermore, autonomous cities showed great monumentality, which is linked to the size of the city. The largest cities tend to be focused on areas with the densest distribution of autonomous cities and secondary agglomerations (i.e. southwestern Anatolia). This seems to suggest that the investment in (elaborate, large and/or multiple) public buildings by civic authorities is closely related to the economic, demographic and territorial power base of these places. Furthermore, the monumentality and size of these places suggest that most wealth was flowing to these urban hubs. The greater density of secondary agglomerations also shows that the agricultural exploitation was more intense and made this flow of wealth possible, in tandem with rural economic development, or at the cost of it.

At this general level, the archaeology of the cities and secondary agglomerations of Asia Minor seems to align with the reasoning and conclusions put forward by the cited works by Paul Bairoch and Arjan Zuiderhoek, even if the relative independence of the economic system from environmental factors as put forward by Pryor must be questioned. Although geographic determinism is not what we advocate, to deny the relation between the proximity of the coasts and good agricultural lands on the distribution of cities and secondary agglomerations is unattainable. The story is a complex interplay of factors acting at different chrono-spatial levels. Let us, therefore, find out whether this also holds true at the more detailed level of a particular case study.

## Case study: ancient Sagalassos

When running a research programme in Classical Archaeology, such as at ancient Sagalassos, the phenomenon of urbanism forms part and parcel of the agenda. The advantage of simultaneously organizing fieldwork in the urban area of Sagalassos and in its extensive 1200 km$^2$ hinterland, mainly based on intensive archaeological surveying, is that a different light can be thrown on the role of towns. As a matter of fact, when considering constellations of organized community life in the long-term history of the region, urbanism was a limited phenomenon in time and impact. Even in the heydays of urban Sagalassos, the majority of people continued to live in the countryside.

With the incorporation into the Roman Empire of the kingdom of Galatia, including the region of Pisidia, in 25 BCE, Rome introduced some structural changes into what was basically a Hellenistic regional matrix. The laying out of the *via Sebaste* created improved conditions for connectivity, the foundation of a string of military *coloniae* implied immigration of new groups into the region introducing social models *à la romaine*, but most of all there was the sensation of the *pax Romana*.

### The urban framework

Nothing but a new Sagalassos was built (Waelkens 2018; Figure 5.7). During the reigns of the Julio-Claudian dynasty, the town acquired the typical range of monuments and buildings transforming Sagalassos into a quintessential Roman provincial city. The moving of the Potters' Quarter to the easternmost plateaus of the site represented a true measure of urban planning. This new quarter would soon transform into a very busy Eastern Suburbium, featuring at its heart the many workshops of Sagalassos red slip ware, the local tableware.

*Figure 5.7* View of the area of the Upper Agora of Sagalassos, campaign 2018.

In monumental terms, the zone of the Upper Agora was a prime development area. Not only was the square paved, but it also started to receive a collection of honorific monuments set up to pay respect to the gods, emperors, provincial governors, the local elite and the *demos*. The sides of the agora were furnished with porticos, shops, a fountain and possibly a Gymnasium. Along the west side some of the local institutions received their home, with a presumed Prytaneion and the Bouleuterion. All of these were crowned by the main sanctuary of the polis, the so-called Doric Temple, which was presumably dedicated to Zeus. The laying out of the Lower Agora possibly catered to more mundane, less representational needs, such as hosting markets. Also this square was crowned by a sanctuary dedicated to Apollo Klarios. On its other side, i.e. the east side, a bath house was built, and the construction of an Odeion was initiated to its north; its south side connected into an embellished Colonnaded Street. At the end of this phase of urban renewal, on the western outskirts of the city, a stadium was built hosting local Klareia games.

With the adoptive emperors and the Antonine dynasty, ambitious members of the local elite climbing the social ladder of the Roman Empire as well as the polis were to continue building their city, not in the least by providing a Macellum and a range of spectacular Nymphaea. As 'first city of Pisidia, friend and ally of the Romans', Sagalassos was granted the right to organize the official imperial cult. The associated festivals and games would have attracted throngs to the town, which responded by initiating building projects at a scale beyond the local community, such as the Imperial Bath–Gymnasium Complex, the Temple of Antoninus Pius and the Theatre. The completion of some of these projects took into Severan times.

This investment programme carried out by the local elite and the polis together was relatively impressive in comparison with the wider Pisidian region, which, as part of the *provincia Lycia et Pamphylia*, was a fairly dense urbanized region within the Empire. With an estimated 2600–3650 urban inhabitants, Sagalassos was no metropolis, however. On the contrary, Sagalassos ranges within the couple of thousand provincial cities with less than 5000 inhabitants found throughout the Roman Empire (Willet 2020).

Investments in Pisidian towns included the laying out of commercial infrastructure and to some degree developing a built framework for the urban economic activities (Willet and Poblome 2019b). Notable examples are the so-called Hellenistic Market Buildings, as identified at Pisidian Sagalassos (Figure 5.8), Melli, Kapıkaya, Pednelissos and Selge. Recently, however, the traditional definition of the function of these buildings has been deconstructed (Leder-Slotman, this volume). A functional symbiosis with the agora seems to be in play, but it is quite unclear how the supposed commercial and storage functions of these buildings would have worked in detail and to which benefits for the poleis. The presumed functions also do not seem to have been continued in Roman Imperial times in all cases, without an alternative providing the continuation of these presumed functions being available in the Roman urbanscapes. In the case of Sagalassos, a public latrina was installed around 100 CE in the remains of one part of the Middle Hellenistic

*Figure 5.8* Part of the east facade of the Middle Hellenistic Market Building(?), together with the original Upper Agora the oldest monuments at Sagalassos. The Hellenistic building was incorporated into a Gymnasium in Roman Imperial times and again into an unidentified structure in Late Antiquity.

Market Building and the complex as a whole seems to have been enlarged and redesigned as a Gymnasium.

In Roman Imperial times, the clearest example of investment in a commercial building is the Macellum at Sagalassos. This facility was erected during the final years of the reign of Emperor Commodus and financed partly by a local high priest of the imperial cult and partly by the city (Figure 5.9). To be sure, the Lower and Upper Agoras and their respective porticos as well as the colonnaded and potentially other streets of Sagalassos also featured (work)shops, but such infrastructure was not devised with only commercial purposes in mind.

Third party or civic investment in economic infrastructure is also attested in the other Pisidian towns, featuring market places, porticos housing shops, the occasional Macellum as well as institutional arrangements arranging exchange and trade. Taken together, these initiatives did not form part of openly mercantile policies, however, and urbanization mostly concerned catering to the gods, the defence of the own community and the organization of spectacles and festivals, apart from housing to be sure.

### The townsfolk

The largest part of the urban population of Sagalassos tried to create an income through professional activities. No doubt a lot of work was available

*Figure 5.9* The *tholos* and central courtyard of Sagalassos' Macellum, campaign 2019.

in constructing the many monuments and buildings of Sagalassos as well as in catering food to the population. Sagalassos, however, finds itself in a seemingly exceptional position in featuring an artisanal quarter as part of its Eastern Suburbium (Figure 5.10). This condition, however, could also be partly explained by the less systematic attention devoted to such quarters in the urban archaeology programmes of Asia Minor. In any case, the artisanate traditionally played an important role for this community.

The urban artisanate originated in Middle Hellenistic times, more or less in tandem with the process of urbanization. The installation of a limited amount of potter's workshops in the area of the later Odeion serves as a case in point. The laying out of this area went hand in hand with a developed *chaîne opératoire* and increased product differentiation, and these processes can be considered to reflect increasing complexity in society. For Roman Imperial times, the archaeological and interdisciplinary record of the Sagalassos Project has revealed many aspects indicative of increased production specialization in the agricultural as well as artisanal sector. Some degree of path dependency on earlier, Hellenistic patterns should be acknowledged, but much was also new, such as the mentioned installation of a sizeable Potters' Quarter to the east of the Theatre, producing local sigillata tableware (Poblome 2016). No doubt, this created opportunities for the craftsmen at Sagalassos and presumably also for those in the wider region, but to be sure contract/order/income instability possibly combined with winter conditions not conducive to year-round production meant that insecurity continued to be part of the artisans'

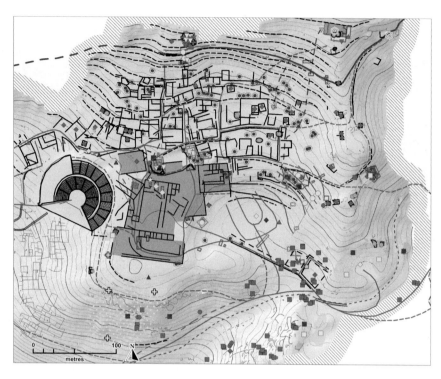

*Figure 5.10* The various activities attested in the Eastern Suburbium during Roman
          Imperial times. Walls and terrace walls, streets and (semi- )public
          buildings, aqueducts and waterways, attestations of funerary activities,
          artisanal activities, waste dumps and some modern features (Source:
          © Johan Claeys, KU Leuven).

lives. In this respect, a lot could have been at stake during the year markets
or other, religiously tied festivals, such as the emperor's cult at Sagalassos,
when the town was hoping to receive many visitors. These occasions probably aided in new pottery and new uses being introduced in Sagalassos
as well. Cooking wares, such as Pompeian Red Ware for instance, were
imported in early Roman Imperial times and improved locally (Bes *et al.*
2019). (Work)shops clearly needed to seize the moment when opportunities presented themselves. Other parts of the answer to managing insecur-
ities was limiting investment in production infrastructure and the working
of social buffering mechanisms by, for instance, placing the *familia* central
to the production organization and giving importance to the functioning
of professional associations. In the past years, a *schola* was excavated in
the Eastern *Suburbium*, catering to the congregation needs of local associations and other parties (Figure 5.11).

*Figure 5.11* View from the south-west on the *schola*.

### Meanwhile in the countryside

In antiquity, town and rural territory were one, and in most cases, the majority of people lived and worked in the countryside. For Sagalassos, recent demographic estimates envisage a total population ranging between 17,700 and 31,000 people for town and territory together. In Roman Imperial times, the maximum extent of the administrative territory of Sagalassos would be reached, including about 1200 km$^2$, and characterized by a wide variety of types of landscape. So far, about 10 Roman villages or secondary settlements were identified and in certain areas many more Roman hamlets and farmsteads. Three of these villages extended over 10 ha or more, about one quarter the size of Sagalassos (Vandam *et al.* 2019). Moreover, a range of Roman Imperial funerary monuments was registered with some of these sites, demonstrating the interests of the landed gentry in the countryside. As these site identifications are dependent on the planning of intensive archaeological surveying activities, the current numbers are best considered as a low estimate. In any case, it seems that at least a considerable part of the rural population was not directly dependent on urban Sagalassos for meeting their standard daily needs, with some of the villages, mainly in the southern parts of the territory, acting as the so-called secondary centres. The latter's role is exemplified by the Edict on *vehiculatio* issued by the governor of the

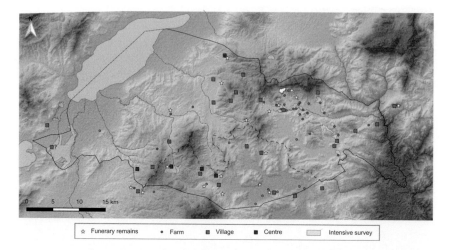

*Figure 5.12* General overview of Roman farmsteads, villages and funerary remains in the territory of Sagalassos (presumed area indicated in black line). The town and the Ağlasun Valley are in the upper right part of the map.

then *provincia Galatia*, Sextius Sotidius Strabo Libuscidianus, in 14/15 CE, according to which Roman authorities could make their own arrangements in the *chôra* of Sagalassos, without an inevitable mediating role for the town (Mitchell 1976). To be sure, local and regional markets and fairs, both urban and rural, taxation, the organization of courts and to some degree religion and the socio-political ambitions of the local elites represented a framework of potential integration between Sagalassos and its hinterland as well as between the local communities and the Roman Empire at large (Figure 5.12).

The countryside actually started at the doorstep of Sagalassos. At about 1 km southeast of Sagalassos, for instance, a Roman farmstead was identified and studied with a combination of intensive archaeological surveying and geophysical and geochemical soil pollution analyses. The farmyard contained a small battery of kilns, indicating how some of the crucial ingredients of town life were actually manufactured in the countryside, such as brick and tile and also cooking and storage vessels. Recent archaeological research in the quarters of the ilçe of modern Ağlasun along the course of the ancient southern access road to Sagalassos resulted in notable concentrations of Roman Imperial pottery, tessera, glass, coin, production waste, water pipe and tile and brick. Also, clusters of ancient stone architectural elements were registered as spolia in the traditional houses of Ağlasun or in their gardens, representing fragments of funerary monuments as well as containing inscriptions, ashlars and fragments of columns and capitals of non-funerary architecture (Willet and Poblome 2019a).

Except for the marginal landscapes in its eastern part, the Ağlasun Valley is dotted with traces of Roman hamlets, farmsteads and funerary monuments, typically 1 to 2 km apart. Clearly, this fertile valley, in close proximity to Sagalassos, was worked intensively. Examination of pollen and botanical remains, isotope analysis of faunal remains and pollution studies of the soil indeed show that most of the city's consumer goods came from this valley and its lower slopes. This area represented the primary catchment for the town, and Sagalassos the central marketplace for its produce. As with the artisanal sector, proxies indicate the Roman Imperial period as one of agricultural production specialization, resulting in a considerable ecological footprint, with the Ağlasun Valley as the most polluted part of the territory. During the Roman period, for instance, cattle became more important, which was probably a result of their use as beasts of burden. Roman farmers also raised more goats than sheep. This has been associated with changes in land use. Intensive agriculture and increased cattle breeding resulted in fewer grazing lands within the valleys for sheep (Poblome 2015). Consequently, farmers focused on goats, which could be herded on the mountain slopes. An arch-aeological survey of pastoralism on the Akdağ mountain east of Sagalassos indicated that, compared to previous centuries, more localities were occupied by shepherds in the Roman Imperial period, testifying to an intensive use of all available pockets in the landscape.

Recently, the agricultural carrying capacities of the study region of Sagalassos were approached and how these related to the societal and economic development in the region. Based on this data, food production seems not to have been a limiting factor, although some stress might have been present in case of adverse climatic conditions and the chosen field management strategies. The data modelling indicated that continuous cropping did not lead to dependable harvests. Instead, a scenario in which fields are cultivated every third year should have been preferable for the farmers of Sagalassos, resulting in far more constant yields and strongly decreased crop failure. Following this rotational cropping land use scenario, the production of food to sustain the inhabitants of Sagalassos and its territory in good years was probably not an issue. Under these conditions, there probably was some room for surplus production (Verstraeten *et al.* 2019).

To be sure, this setting was also a political landscape, in which Sagalassos acted as the uncontested city with not a single settlement in its territory approaching it in extent, facilities and appearance. A consequence of the embellishment of the urban centre with a range of Nymphaea and a considerable Bath–Gymnasium Complex, for instance, was an increased need for water, which the local natural sources could not sustain. Indeed, traces of aqueducts were discovered to the west and east of the city. Recent field-work resulted in the discovery of the source feeding the eastern aqueducts, the cistern capturing and distributing this resource, as well as many preserved sections of the channel. The source was located on the northeast flanks of the Akdağ, near the locality aptly called Başpınar. The entire length of the eastern aqueducts can now be measured at c. 24 km, completely encircling the higher flanks of the Akdağ, with a difference in height between source and the eastern edge of Sagalassos of around 100 m. Parts of the channel were worked into limestone outcrops or the flanks of the Akdağ and Ağlasun dağları, sometimes to a depth of several meters, with an average width of 0.4 m and watermarks at the average height of 0.5 m. Prior calculations arrived at estimates of water supply at an impressive 530 l per second or a total of nearly 45,000 m³ of water per day (Steegen *et al.* 2000). Apart from the eastern aqueduct being a testimony to the technical ingenuity of the time, its concept also symbolizes a landscape of power, whereby the town of Sagalassos managed to capture and guide one of the more important water sources in the entire region, mostly for its civic benefits. Furthermore, the runoff of these aqueducts contributed to the intensity of agriculture in the immediate vicinity of Sagalassos.

Agriculture remained very much at the core of the Pisidian social metabolism, however, providing the main framework of regional development. Therefore, the importance of the Ağlasun Valley and the secondary settlements to Sagalassos should not be underestimated. This countryside, to be clear, cannot be regarded as a uniform whole. Various forms of occupation have been attested, ranging from farmsteads to large villages. These settlements interacted, and constituted a network of occupation, wherein each location had its own character and function. The countryside as a singular concept did not exist. Behind this generic term a complex structure of human interaction and organization is hidden.

### Was this a sustainable model?

An important question is whether this seemingly symbiotic and productive landscape was also a sustainable one. An essential element in approaching sustainability is energy availability. In antiquity, this mostly comes down to approaching wood consumption, as wood was by far the most important fuel for all sorts of purposes. Recent research into the energy consumption of Sagalassos estimated the total wood consumption at 3650 to 12,775 tons per year within the city, requiring an area of 18,000 to 113,000 ha of forested land to sustainably provide wood to the inhabitants of Sagalassos and its territory. Based on palynological data, 20% of the territory would have been forested during the second century CE. Given the size and the nature of the territory of Sagalassos and its potential at growing forests, clearly, the energy consumption of the community of Sagalassos and its *chôra* was near the upper boundaries of sustainable use and was possibly stressing its territorial wood production potential during the second century CE (Janssen *et al.* 2017).

In general, in agricultural pre-industrial societies, the interplay of factors such as production specialization, urbanization and colonization of new territories could foster development, in the sense of growth, but such were discontinuous processes, mostly limited to aggregate growth and not resulting in metabolic change in the social–ecological system. On balance, a case could be made in favour of growth, at least in aggregate, for the community of Roman Imperial Sagalassos, as it was witnessing urban expansion, was controlling an extended territory and saw the artisanal and agricultural sectors developing processes of production specialization (Poblome 2015). The success of the latter, however, was dependent on external factors such as reaching the many markets of the Roman commonwealth as well as on a lasting *pax Romana*. Managing these external factors, however, was not necessarily easy for a provincial community of the scale of Sagalassos, especially since the crucial internal factor of energy availability represented a structural brake. So although the Pisidian landscapes are rich in mineral and natural resources, the flows of energy represented limits on the generation of wealth in the long-term. The wider region of ancient Sagalassos, in more ways than one, was partialized by the mountainous landscape symbolizing a locked potential for sustainable growth and wealth generation.

The open question is in how far this Pisidian pattern, displaying a delicate balance between potential and opportunities, and structural brakes within the own and the general Roman systems, should be valuable to approaching and understanding other regions in Asia Minor or the ancient world. It certainly is the case that Pisidia and Lycia too contained many natural settlement chambers due to the presence of mountains and hills. Indeed, in these regions many small- to medium-sized cities blossomed during the Roman centuries in terms of monumentality and size. It is also the case that the difference in city sizes was much greater in western Anatolia, where cities as Ephesos probably were parasitic in terms of food supply on neighbouring small cities like Metropolis and Hypaipa. Yet, the latter also flourished despite their 'subject' situation to Ephesos. Further inland and in the Black Sea Coastlands, cities were much more isolated, with very few becoming larger than Sagalassos. Moreover, Sagalassos and other Pisidian cities were in a relatively good position for connectivity with each other and other regions, yet at the same time protected enough by the natural landscapes to prevent one city becoming too dominant or parasitic. Even Pisidian Antioch would never grow much larger in terms of monumentality and size than Sagalassos, despite the fact that, as a *colonia*, it was institutionally favoured over Sagalassos.

## What does it all mean?

The focus of economic activities in the case of Sagalassos was agricultural. Even if the artisans employed in this town created genuine, specialized production and trade opportunities, the mainstay of the regional economy remained agricultural production. Apart from causing stresses in the regional social–ecological system, the importance of agriculture was not directly translated in the choices made in the local urbanization process. These economic activities did not directly impinge on the urban framework of Sagalassos. Of course, the city saw the construction of many important monuments. Arguably, most of the funding for these, private or official in origin, was based on agricultural surplus, but the monuments that were chosen to be built had little to do with boosting agricultural gain. The monumentalization of the towns of Roman Imperial Asia Minor was in large part the result of the intensification of agriculture and/or the exploitation of larger areas, but what was built did not act as a catalyst to further improve return on investment in agriculture. Possibly, the local artisans scored more effects in this regard, especially in the way the local potters occupied space in the Eastern Suburbium. Even then, though, a large part of the regional pottery production did not happen in Sagalassos itself, but on the farms and hamlets in the Ağlasun Valley, more or less in association with agricultural activities. In this respect, the townsfolk of Sagalassos as well as the dependent communities in its territory were developing specialized production activities to a relative degree of success but such did not result in their economic policies driving the local urbanization process.

From the discussion above, it is clear that as much can be said on similar processes in Asia Minor at large. As urbanization did not converge on economic functions, resulting from trajectories of evolutionary fitness, it is clear that townscapes in Asia Minor are best regarded as the outcomes of homologous processes, at least from an economic point of view. Similar structures enriched the townscape, but their origins are based on trait diffusion, rather than processes of selection or drift of characteristics or functions associated with economic behaviour and policies. The attested similarities noticeable in the towns in this region of the Roman Empire were based on the concepts of path dependency, ideology and social competition. These mostly result in stylistic similarities, and not functional analogies.

In general, even though Asia Minor can be counted as one of the most urbanized regions within the Roman Empire, urbanization as such was a weak phenomenon. Even though a point can be made for growth scenarios, even at per capita level, in particular cases, urbanization was not underscored by economic policies, and was limited by regional energy availability and carrying capacities, dependent on reaching external markets and remained socially tied. As a result, we hypothesize that many provincial cities in Asia Minor were hitting the limits of sustainability, explaining their relative size as well as the underestimated importance of secondary settlements. These conditions do not imply urban inhabitants or those of secondary settlements could not sustain certain qualities of life, even if for most income insecurity was perennial. All in all, these processes are best considered as homologous in nature as well as conceptualized under the umbrella of the consumer city as recently advocated by Arjan Zuiderhoek.

## Acknowledgements

This research was supported by the ERC funded project 'Empire of 2000 cities', the Research Fund of the University of Leuven, the Research Foundation Flanders and ANAMED Research Center for Anatolian Civilizations of Koç University.

# Note

1 The figures for Spain were graciously provided by Dr. P.H.A. Houten and are attested by ancient texts and/or epigraphic evidence.

# References

Bairoch, Paul. *Cities and Economic Development. From the Dawn of History to the Present*. Chicago: University of Chicago Press, 1988.

Bes, Philip, Willet, Rinse and Braekmans, Dennis. "All Sherds Great and Small." Pages 167–74 in *Meanwhile in the Mountains: Sagalassos*. Edited by Jeroen Poblome, Ebru Torun, Peter Talloen and Marc Waelkens. Istanbul: Yapı Kredi Yayınları, 2019.

Bettencourt, Luis M.A. "The Origins of Scaling in Cities." *Science* 340 (2013): 1438–41.

Bintliff, John L. "Going to the Market in Antiquity." Pages 209–50 in *Zu Wasser und Zu Land*. Edited by Eckart Olshausen and Holger Sonnabend. Stuttgarter Kolloquium. Stuttgart: Franz Steiner Verlag, 2002.

Bowman, Alan and Wilson, Andrew, eds. *Settlement, Urbanization, and Population*. Oxford Studies on the Roman Economy. Oxford: Oxford University Press, 2011.

Broughton, Thomas R.S. "Roman Asia Minor." Pages 499–919 in *An Economic Survey of Ancient Rome. Volume IV. Africa, Syria, Greece, Asia Minor*. Edited by Tenny Frank. New Jersey and New York: John Hopkins Press, 1938.

Chamberlain, Andrew T. *Demography in Archaeology*. Cambridge: Cambridge University Press, 2006.

Cohen, Getzel M. *The Hellenistic Settlements in Europe, the Islands, and Asia Minor*. Berkeley, Los Angeles: University of California Press, 1995.

de Ligt, Luuk. "Demand, Supply, Distribution. The Roman Peasantry between Town and Countryside: Rural Monetization and Peasant Demand." *Münstersche Beiträge zur antiken Handelsgeschichte* 9 (1990): 24–56.

De Vries, Jan. *European Urbanization, 1500–1800*. London: Methuen & Co., 1984.

Faroqhi, Suraiya. "Towns, Agriculture and the State in Sixteenth-Century Ottoman Anatolia." *Journal of the Economic and Social History of the Orient* 33 (1990): 125–56.

Haldon, John. *The Empire that would not die. The Paradox of the Eastern Roman Survival, 640–740*. Cambridge, MA: Harvard University Press, 2016.

Hansen, Mogens Herman and Nielsen, Thomas Heine, eds. *An Inventory of Archaic and Classical Poleis. An Investigation Conducted by the Copenhagen Polis Centre for the Danish National Research Foundation*. Oxford: Oxford University Press, 2004.

Hurt, Teresa D. and Rakita, Gordon F.M., eds. *Style and Function. Conceptual Issues in Evolutionary Archaeology*. Westport, Connecticut: Praeger, 2001.

Janssen, Ellen, Poblome, Jeroen, Claeys, Johan, Kint, Vincent, Degryse, Patrick, Marinova, Elena and Muys, Bart. "Fuel for Debating Ancient Economies. Calculating Wood Consumption at Urban Scale in Roman Imperial Times." *Journal of Archaeological Science: Reports* 11 (2017): 592–99.

Kolb, Frank. "Bemerkungen zur Urbanen Ausstattung von Städten im Westen und im Osten des Römischen Reiches anhand von Tacitus, Agricola 21 und der Konstantinischen Inschrift von Orkistos." *Klio - Beiträge zur Alten Geschichte* 75 (1993): 321–41.

Krugman, Paul. "Confronting the Mystery of Urban Hierarchy." *Journal of the Japanese and International Economies* 10 (1996): 399–418.

Mitchell, Stephen. "Requisitioned Transport in the Roman Empire: A New Inscription from Pisidia." *The Journal of Roman Studies* 66 (1976): 106–31.

Murdock, George P. and White, Douglas R. "Standard Cross-cultural Sample." *Ethnology* 8 (1969): 329–69.

Poblome, Jeroen. "The Potters of Ancient Sagalassos Revisited." Pages 377–404 in *Urban Craftsmen and Traders in the Roman World.* Edited by Andrew Wilson and Miko Flohr. Oxford Studies on the Roman Economy. Oxford: Oxford University Press, 2016.

Poblome, Jeroen. "The Economy of the Roman World as a Complex Adaptive System. Testing the case in second to fifth century CE Sagalassos." Pages 97–140 in *Structure and Performance in the Roman Economy. Models, Methods and Case Studies.* Edited Paul Erdkamp and Koen Verboven. Collection Latomus 350. Brussels: Editions Latomus, 2015.

Pryor, Frederic L. *Economic Systems of Foraging, Agricultural, and Industrial Societies.* Cambridge: Cambridge University Press, 2005.

Scheidel, Walter. "Roman Age Structure: Evidence and Models." *The Journal of Roman Studies* 91 (2001): 1–26.

Schuler, Christof. *Ländliche Siedlungen und Gemeinden im hellenistischen und römischen Kleinasien, Vestigia Beiträge zur alten Geschichte.* München: Verlag C.H. Beck, 1998.

Steegen, An, Cauwenberghs, Kris, Govers, Gerard, Waelkens, Marc, Owens, Edwin J. and Desmet, Philip. "The Water Supply to Sagalassos." Pages 635–49 in *Sagalassos V: Report on the Survey and Excavation Campaigns of 1996 and 1997.* Edited by Marc Waelkens and Lieven Loots. Leuven: Leuven University Press, 2000.

Tak, Herman. "Longing for Local Identity: Intervillage Relations in an Italian Mountain Area." *Anthropological Quarterly* 63 (1990): 90–100.

Thonemann, Peter, ed. *Roman Phrygia. Culture and Society, Greek Culture in the Roman World.* Cambridge: Cambridge University Press, 2013.

Tscherikower, Victor. *Die Hellenistische Städtegründungen von Alexander dem grossen bis auf die Römerzeit.* Philologus. Leipzig: Dieterich'sche Verlagsbuchhandlung, 1927.

Vandam, Ralf, Kaptijn, Eva, Willet, Rinse and Willett, Patrick T. "The Countryside. Where are the People?" Pages 271–9 in *Meanwhile in the Mountains: Sagalassos.* Edited by Jeroen Poblome, Ebru Torun, Peter Talloen and Marc Waelkens. Istanbul: Yapı Kredi Yayınları, 2019.

Verstraeten, Gert., Van Loo, Maarten, Broothaerts, Nils, Dusar, Bert and D'Haen, Koen. "The Sustainability of Agriculture in an Eroding Mediterranean Mountain Landscape." Pages 233–42 in *Meanwhile in the Mountains: Sagalassos.* Edited by Jeroen Poblome, Ebru Torun, Peter Talloen and Marc Waelkens. Istanbul: Yapı Kredi Yayınları, 2019.

Waelkens, Marc. "Archaeology of Sagalassos." Pages 1–32 in *Encyclopedia of Global Archaeology.* Edited by Claire Smith. New York: Springer, 2018.

Wargo, Melissa C. *The Bordes-Binford Debate: Transatlantic Interpretative Traditions in Paleolithic Archaeology.* University of Texas at Arlington: Unpublished Ph.D. thesis, 2009.

West, Geoffrey. *Scale. The Universal Laws of Growth, Innovation, Sustainability, and the Pace of Life in Organisms, Cities, Economies, and Companies.* New York: Penguin Books, 2017.

Willet, Rinse. *The Geography of Urbanism in Roman Asia Minor.* Sheffield: Equinox, 2020.

Willet, Rinse and Poblome, Jeroen. "Archaeological Surveying in the Western Part of the Ağlasun Valley and within Ağlasun, 2018". *ANMED. News of Archaeology from Anatolia's Mediterranean Areas* 17 (2019a): 255–61.

Willet, Rinse and Poblome, Jeroen. "Urbi et Orbi." Pages 67–78 in *Meanwhile in the Mountains: Sagalassos*. Edited by Jeroen Poblome, Ebru Torun, Peter Talloen and Marc Waelkens. Istanbul: Yapı Kredi Yayınları, 2019b.

Zuiderhoek, Arjan. *The Ancient City. Key Themes in Ancient History*. Cambridge: Cambridge University Press, 2017.

# 6 Elites and economic space in Roman Imperial *Asia Minor*

*Arjan Zuiderhoek*

## Introduction

What determined the shape of ancient urban landscapes in the Greco-Roman world, and of the economic spaces within them, and what caused urban landscapes (and the economic spaces within them) to change over time? In this chapter, I want to focus on one important factor arguably involved in these processes, namely, elite interventions in the urban landscape, more specific-ally, elite involvement in the creation of economic space. 'Economic spaces' I define as spaces within the city where economic activities (in the sense of the production and distribution of goods and services) took place and/or elements of the urban landscape which were strongly associated with such activities, whether these were spaces that were specifically designed for this purpose or not. After some brief remarks on the relationship between urban (economic) space and socio-economic structures, I focus on elite descriptions of, and elite interventions in, urban space. I conclude with some reflections on the (relative) cessation of such interventions in the third century CE. My case study for such elite interventions in urban landscapes during the first three centuries CE is *Asia Minor*.

Can the shape and character of a particular society's urban space (its civic landscape) inform us about the economic structure of that society and *vice versa*? I start with two quotations, one familiar and the other less so:

> It has been claimed, rather exuberantly, that such excavated districts as the potters' quarter at Corinth, evoke, in their physical appearance, 'the artisan quarters of medieval cities'. But it seems commonly to be overlooked that the excavators of Tarsus have found no Cloth Hall, that all ancient cities lacked the Guildhalls and Bourses which, next to the cathedrals, are to this day the architectural glories of the great medieval cities of Italy, France, Flanders, the Hansa towns, or England. Contrast the Athenian Agora with the Grande Place in Brussels.
>
> (Finley, 1999 [first ed. 1973]: 137)

> The production of space ... reflects the general economic structure and mode of production of the society which produces it. The space produced

by capitalism is different from the space produced by feudalism. Capitalist production is commodity production and the space inherited from feudalism emerges as a prime obstacle to the realization of profit ...

(Niemann, 2000: 71)

As we can see from these quotes, both Finley and Niemann suppose that space, urban space, is a clear product of social and economic forces. Especially Finley's remark is suggestive of the notion that a specific type of socio-economic formation – here, late medieval and early modern European commercial capitalism – would generate a specific and highly distinctive urban landscape. Niemann, who suggests a link between various socio-economic formations (or modes of production) in western history (feudalism, capitalism) and specific forms of social space, echoes this notion. Furthermore, following the geographer David Harvey, he also suggests that 'left-over' spaces generated by previous socio-economic formations could hem in and hinder the economic processes of subsequent formations – remnants of feudal space hindering capitalist profit making, for instance. The corollary of this, of course, is that social spaces that belong to a certain formation actually reinforce that socio-economic formation by influencing the behaviour of people in ways appropriate to that formation. Following Harvey and the spatial theorist Henri Lefebvre, and taking our cue from the quotes from Finley and Niemann, we might say that urban space not only is a product of social forces but also influences and 'creates' certain forms of social behaviour and limits others.[1] Finley, of course, famously argued that the *absence* in Greek and Roman cities of an urban landscape resembling anything like the urban landscape of medieval and early modern commercial capitalist cities implied that commercial capitalism as such was missing in Classical Antiquity.

## Civic elites and economic space

So what kind of socio-economic structure does the Greco-Roman urban landscape suggest? Or, what kinds of socio-economic behaviour might the ancient urban landscape have stimulated or suppressed? One way of coming to grips with this is to study closely Greek and Roman urban landscapes as they present themselves to us today, archaeologically, in their preserved, ruined state, and to figure out which kinds of buildings, structures and locations might most obviously have had something to do with processes of production, distribution and consumption, how these might have functioned and how they might have related to the rest of urban space. Another, complementary method is to try to use the written sources to gain a glimpse of how ancient actors perceived their cityscape. Many of these sources were written by and for the social and political elites of ancient cities. However, this potential weakness is, in a sense, also a strength, because social space, as we have learned from Lefebvre, Harvey and others, is not fixed, but it is subject to constant change over time, in interaction with the behaviour of those who create and use it. Space, in other words, is a process, and we happen to be reasonably well informed about the ways urban social space was envisaged, experienced and manipulated by the status group that constituted the most powerful generative force in the process of creating ancient social space by far: the urban elites. They controlled the largest quantities of land, capital and labour and were socially and politically pre-eminent. As private builders and as public benefactors and also as magistrates, priests and city council members in charge of sacred and public funds used for public construction, they collectively made the greatest mark on the urban landscape, fuelled by competition both internal, between local elite families, and external, between different cities in the same region. How did they view the urban landscape, what kinds of interventions in it did they make and can this tell us something about economic space in the ancient city? I start with a series of vignettes, some well-known, drawn from widely different periods of antiquity:

> But when we are about to enter the city (*polis*), around which runs a lofty wall, a fair harbour lies on either side of the city and the entrance is narrow, and curved ships are drawn up along the road, for they all have stations for their ships, each man one for himself. There, too, is their place of assembly (*agore*) about the fair temple of Poseidon, fitted with huge stones set deep in the earth. Here the men are busied with the tackle of their black ships, with cables and sails, and here they shape the thin oar-blades.
>
> (Homer, *Odyssey* 6.262–8; tr. A. T. Murray, Loeb)

> Imagine then, Athenians, that the country and its trees are appealing to you, that the harbours, dockyards and walls of the city are begging you for protection, yes, and the temples and sanctuaries too. Lycurgus, *Against Leocrates* 150, *c.* 330 BCE – from a court speech against an Athenian citizen accused of treason.
>
> (tr. J. O. Burtt, Loeb)

> They now started to climb the hill which loomed large over the city and looked down over the citadel opposite. Aeneas was amazed at the massive structures, where once there had been simply huts; he was amazed at the gates, the din of activity and the paved streets. The Tyrians were hurrying about busily, some tracing a line for the walls and manhandling stones up the slopes as they strained to build their citadel, others choosing the best site for a building and marking its outline by ploughing a furrow. They were establishing their laws and selecting their magistrates and respected senate. At one spot some were excavating the harbour, and at another a group of men were laying out an area for the deep foundations of a theatre. They were also extracting from quarries mighty pillars to stand

tall and handsome on the stage which was still to be built. Virgil, *Aeneid* 1.419–29 – the founding of Carthage.

(tr. Edmondson, 2006: 250)

From Chaeroneia it is twenty stades to *Panopeus*, a city of the Phocians, if one can give the name of city to those who possess no government offices, no gymnasium, no theatre, no market-place, no water descending to a fountain, but live in bare shelters just like mountain cabins, right on a ravine. Pausanias, *Description of Greece* 10.4.1, *c*. 170s CE.

(tr. W.H.S. Jones, Loeb)

For they [the inhabitants of *Orcistus*] assert that, in the course of a former age, their village had flourished with a city's splendour, so that it used to be adorned with magistrates' annual fasces, was famous for its *curiales* [members of the city council] and was filled with a populace of citizens …. There are there abundant streams of water, also their public and private baths, a forum adorned with statues of old-time leading men, and so crowded a populace of inhabitants that the seats that are in the said place can easily be filled… Letter of the emperor Constantine concerning the status of *Orcistus* in *Phrygia*, *c*. 320s CE, *CIL* 3.7000 = *MAMA* 7.305.

(tr. Johnson, Coleman-Norton and Bourne, 1961: 240, doc. 304, II, slightly adapted)

But our Emperor [Justinian], as if seeking to excuse his imperial predecessor's want of propriety, first of all observed that the city was suffering from shortage of water and was cruelly oppressed by thirst, and so he improvised a marvellous aqueduct and provided it with an unlooked-for supply of water, sufficient for the people there not only to drink but also to use for bathing and for all the other luxuries in which men indulge who have an unstinted supply of water. Besides this he made for them a public bath which had not existed before, and he rebuilt another which was damaged and lay abandoned, and already lay in ruin because of the scarcity of water which I have mentioned and because of neglect. Nay more, he built here churches and a palace and stoas and lodgings for the magistrates, and in other respects he gave it the appearance of a prosperous city. Procopius, *Aed.* 5.2.1–5, later 6th c. CE.

(tr. H.B. Dewing, Loeb)

This, to be sure, is a disparate selection of passages assembled from very different literary, documentary, historical, ideological and sociopolitical contexts, but taken together the texts do convey some sense, over more than a thousand years of ancient history, of the elements of the urban landscape emphasized or foregrounded by Greek and Roman elite writers when they wished to *describe* or *visualize* a city for their audiences. Thus, it can be argued that the passages offer us some cues to the conventional Greco-Roman elite view of civic space. It is interesting to note that among the buildings and structures selected for description we consistently find some that as modern observers, we would label 'economic' or 'quasi-economic' in their functionality, such as harbours, docks, market places, paved streets, water supply systems, mixed in with others that were primarily of a political, religious or defensive nature, or constituted civic amenities (government offices, temples, churches, walls, gates, theatres, gymnasia, public baths). It should be noted, though, that many of the public buildings, structures and urban spaces planned and constructed by urban elites and civic governments that were not ostensibly economic in nature nonetheless had some economic aspect to them, just as the structures that moderns would label 'economic' often had civic, political and/or religious functions and connotations as well. We might call this the 'architectural embeddedness' of economic spaces, which I suggest was highly characteristic of Greek and Roman cities. I will come back to this in a little more detail below, but one major implication for our analysis is that we would do best to cast our nets widely and take in the broad gamut of structures supported by ancient elites and civic governments, if we truly want to understand the spatial economy of ancient cities.

One possible approach is to turn to the rich epigraphic evidence for elite contributions to public buildings, which I shall now briefly discuss for Roman *Asia Minor*, during the first, second and early third centuries CE, the golden age of Greco-Roman urbanism in the east. Urban elites exercised control over the shaping of the civic landscape in two ways: first, as political actors, using (mostly) public funds, in their capacity as magistrates and council members (priests might use temple funds), and second, as public benefactors. These two forms might, of course, overlap, as magistrates were often expected to contribute to the cost of their office out of their own pockets, but here we are not so much interested in the sources of funding as in what kinds of structures elites supported, either as public actors or as private donors.

Publicly financed construction is less well-attested, epigraphically and otherwise, than euergetic contributions, since public funding was not subject to the strong competitive pressures that produced the widespread commemoration of munificent gift giving, but it is sometimes attested nonetheless.[2] The epigraphic evidence for elite euergetic contributions (i.e. building benefactions), by contrast, is particularly abundant. For Roman *Asia Minor* of a total of 305 contributions to public buildings compiled from inscriptions dating from the early first to the early third century CE, 24% were to religious structures, 21% to public baths and gymnasia, 14% to stoas, 10% to theatres, 5% to agoras, another 5% to governmental structures, about 2% to aqueducts and 1% or less each to *odeia*, *stadia*, libraries, *macella*, *nymphaea* and arches. Some 12% of contributions can be classified as 'miscellaneous': these include, for example, donations of statue groups, towers, gates, a public kitchen, a weighing house, storerooms, some street paving and a few booths. Some 6% cannot be specified, i.e. the type of public structure contributed to could not, or could no longer, be identified from the inscription. The category 'religious structures' consists of gifts towards temples, either donations of entire temples or contributions to or repairs/embellishments of existing temples (for example, adding columns, a *pronaos*, mosaics, statues). To this category also belong gifts of altars and (small) sanctuaries. The category 'governmental structures' comprises (contributions to) council houses (*bouleuteria*), basilicas and magistrates' offices (for example, for the *agoranomoi*).[3]

We can further flesh out the picture by taking a closer look at a few specific cases of euergetic building programmes in individual cities, turning to *Ephesos* first. The *Vedii* were a prominent Ephesian elite family, and generations of the *gens* devoted themselves to their city's public life, as magistrates, religious officials and benefactors. Particularly well known as benefactors are Publius Vedius Antoninus III (i.e. M. Claudius Publius Vedius Antoninus Phaedrus Sabinianus, also known in the German academic literature as the 'Bauherr') and his wife Flavia Papiane, their daughter Vedia Phaedrina and her husband the sophist Titus Flavius Damianus. Between them, they were responsible for the construction of an entire bath–*gymnasium* complex (the 'Vedius baths'), a thorough renovation of the Ephesian council house or *bouleuterion* (Vedius Antoninus III and Flavia Papiane, in the second half of the 140s CE), a splendid marble portico connecting the city with its famous temple of Artemis, and a lavishly decorated banqueting hall in the temple itself (Damianus and Vedia Phaedrina, in 160s and 170s CE), among other, less well-known building projects.[4]

In *Smyrna* around 124 CE, numerous elite individuals, men and women, including high-ranking local and provincial office holders and priests and priestesses (as well as, interestingly, a local Jewish association) contributed large sums for what seems like an impressive makeover of central elements of the civic landscape: the paving of a basilica, planting gardens in a palm grove, the paving of another basilica near the council chamber and the provision of it with bronze doors, the construction of a temple of Tyche in the palm grove, the gilding of the roof of the anointing room in the *gymnasium* of the *gerousia* (council/association of elders), columns with bases and capitals for a temple, further columns with bases and capitals for the palm grove and a sun room in the *gymnasium*, to all of which the emperor Hadrian, at the intervention of a local sophist, added further funding for a grain market, a *gymnasium* and a temple.[5]

At *Aphrodisias* during the later second century CE, a scion of an important local family, M. Ulpius Carminius Claudianus, similarly engaged in extensive public works: from an endowment fund that he established explicitly for the purpose of public construction, he financed the provisioning of seats for the theatre, renovated a street and, partly in cooperation with his wife Apphia, undertook a substantial renovation and embellishment of a *gymnasium* (the 'Gymnasium of Diogenes', providing an anointing room, walls, pillars, columns and lots of sculpture and statuary).[6]

Finally, at *Selge* in *Pisidia* in the early third century (220s or early 230s CE), the benefactress Publia Plancia Aurelia Magniana Motoxaris was responsible for an impressive overhaul of the city's upper agora ('Staatsmarkt'): she built an office for the *agoranomoi*, a sanctuary for Tyche and an *Odeion*, while she renovated what was presumably (possibly?) a market building (a structure with *chrematisteria*, i.e. 'spaces for business'), the 'slanting' or 'inclining' *stoa* and a *plintheion* ('rectangular building'?).[7]

As in the case of the city descriptions quoted earlier, from the material on elite investment in public buildings too, it is clear that elites did indeed occasionally invest in structures or undertakings that we would call economic or quasi-economic in terms of their functionality. We might mention, for instance, public weighing houses,[8] *macella*,[9] water supply systems, storage facilities, the office building for the *agoranomoi* and the 'business spaces' contributed by Motoxaris in Selge and the construction of the grain market at *Smyrna*, the funding for which was, admittedly, supplied by the emperor, but which came through the advocacy of a member of the local elite of *Smyrna*, the sophist Antonius Polemon.[10] For the most part, however, the 'economic space' produced by urban elites remained largely *implicit* within the broader civic structures that constituted the primary focus of their munificence or their activities as civic magistrates – this is what I have called the architectural embeddedness of economic space in Greco-Roman cities. Benefactors mostly contributed to temples, bath–*gymnasium* complexes, theatres, stoas, agoras and so forth, buildings that exemplified the communal ideals of the *polis* and constituted the amenities that were deemed necessary to the citizen good life, yet such structures in fact contained a great deal of economic space, even if this is mostly not mentioned in the honorific or building inscriptions that are our main sources of information. The fact that direct contributions to structures *we* would qualify as economic in function represent a distinct minority among euergetic gifts or civic public expenditures should, therefore, not mislead us: beneath the veil of civic ideology and euergetic public mindedness, urban elites in fact created a great deal of economic space. The bath–*gymnasium* complex that Vedius Antoninus III and Flavia Papiane donated to *Ephesos* (the 'Vedius gymnasium') is an obvious example: archaeological investigation has revealed that the entire south facade of the building and the southern part of its west facade were made up of workshops (*tabernae*).[11] Inscriptions found within the structure also demonstrate its close connections with various professional associations, and scholars have argued that the complex may purposefully have been constructed in an area of the city known for its commercial character, i.e. along the Sacred Way, *the* major traffic conduit of *Ephesos*, connecting the city with the *Artemisium*, in a neighbourhood where many workers' associations had their shops.[12] *Tabernae* were found at or near other bath–*gymnasium* complexes too and also featured in other structures frequently donated or contributed to by civic benefactors, such as stoas lining squares and streets.[13] Emblematic of the civic, communal ideals of the Greco-Roman city, the *stoa* was, of course, also a productive and commercial space *par excellence*, housing many shops and workshops. The agora too might be said to exemplify the structural embeddedness of politics, commerce and cultural/religious functions, as is well shown in Chris Dickenson's recent study of the agoras in Hellenistic and Roman Greece, whereas the many financial and commercial dealings of temples, frequent targets of building munificence, in Hellenistic and Roman *Asia Minor* have been extensively explored by Beate Dignas.[14]

Thus, we might note that the qualitative contrast once drawn by Finley between the commercialized medieval urban landscapes and the primarily 'civic' or 'political' ancient cityscapes is too stark. Ancient urban space was as vigorously economic as medieval and early modern European civic landscapes, but ancient productive and commercial spaces were often subsumed into spaces and structures primarily reflecting the collective ideology of the polis/ *civitas* community and the public achievements of the citizen-elite. This does emphatically *not* imply that Greek and Roman urban economies were any less sophisticated or productive than most later European ones, but that ancient economic activity and ancient markets took shape in, and functioned as part of, social, political and institutional configurations that were in many ways very different from the later European situation, and that the structure of ancient urban landscapes reflects this. There are more ways than one towards societal and economic complexity.[15]

## Third-century changes

If the structure of civic space, of urban economic space, is a product of the structures of civic society, then it follows that changes in civic space must be indicative of broader changes in civic society. Again, elite interventions in civic space function as our case study. Interestingly, in *Asia Minor* from the late second century CE onwards, euergetic expenditure on public buildings begins to decline.[16] It should be noted that this decline is not symptomatic of an overall tailing off of civic munificence: its onset coincides roughly with a general drop in the number of recorded benefactions during the reign of Marcus Aurelius, but this is followed by an impressive recovery of public gifts under the Severi. From roughly the 220s onwards, however, the numbers of recorded benefactions of all types in *Asia Minor* decline steadily.[17] To be precise: this is a decline in the number of surviving inscriptions recording benefactions by members of local urban elites. It seems, however, highly unlikely that public gifts continued unabated, but that they were simply no longer commemorated in public inscriptions. In essence, euergetism was a type of gift exchange, a form of political reciprocity between elite and non-elite citizens.[18] As public honours, honorific inscriptions were, therefore, an integral component of the institution of civic euergetism: in the exchange of public gifts for public honours between elite benefactor and the *dēmos*, the inscription constituted the crucial counter-gift that benefactors received in return for their donation, a publicly visible and enduring materialization of the prestige that they had earned. Thus, I would argue that a decline in the number of honorific and building inscriptions recording elite benefactions can serve as a good proxy for a decline of the institution of civic euergetism as such.[19] What we have here, then, is evidence for a profound change in urban elite behaviour. The implication is certainly not that *all* public building stopped; we have, for instance, continued evidence for defensive projects.[20] Yet a significant overall decrease in elite euergetic interventions probably means that in many cities, public construction was considerably diminished during much of the third century CE.

The picture is equally stark when we look at the data from individual cities. *Aphrodisias* continued to produce inscriptions until very Late Antiquity; yet whereas 1,500 of the extant inscriptions from the city date to the 300 years before the mid-third century CE, only 250 or so date to the period 250–550 CE. In contrast with the earlier material, among the later texts there are very few honorific inscriptions for benefactors from the local civic elite; most instead commemorate emperors or imperial officials.[21] Given that euergetism was the primary mechanism via which local elites intervened in the urban landscape, this change had important consequences for the development of civic space, including economic space, during the third century and later. *Perge* too is an instructive case. Numerous honorific and building inscriptions survive there for the first and second centuries CE, allowing detailed reconstructions of trends and developments in, among other things, public building and euergetic contributions to it. In the third century, however, the picture changes radically. The total number of surviving inscriptions drastically declines, public benefactions by private individuals practically cease and public building seems to come to a near standstill. Significantly, however, almost all honorific inscriptions that do survive from third-century Perge are for imperial officials.[22]

Now, what was the cause of these changes? At this point, large-scale explanatory frameworks might be invoked, such as demographic change (the Antonine Plague), or the standard third-century ailments such as market disintegration due to military unrest both internal and external, brigandage and inflation, but how important were such factors, and, crucially, how did they filter through into urban elite behaviour?[23] We may note, for instance, that if the drop in civic benefactions under Marcus Aurelius was a consequence of the Antonine Plague, the Plague's *direct* effects cannot have been very long-lasting, since we see an impressive recovery of munificence under the *Severi*. This recovery, however, mostly consisted of contributions towards festivals and games, arguably a cheaper form of euergetism (at least, when compared to gifts of whole buildings).[24] Then again, euergetism is admittedly only a rough proxy for elite wealth; the rich might spend their fortunes on something other than benefactions. One could also argue that, due to the second-century building boom, urban landscapes were by now more or less complete (how many *gymnasia* do you really need?), so that, within the overall economy of honours, the marginal return of prestige on donating yet another building was declining. Again, however, it should be noted that the cessation of building munificence was part of an eventual sharp *overall* decrease in civic euergetism, so this can hardly be a sufficient explanation.

I would suggest that the reasons for the change we see in the euergetic record during the third century should be sought in the changing social and political dynamics in the cities, which in turn were provoked by broader imperial-administrative, demographic and economic developments. As a result of these, elite behaviour changed. I can only discuss these changes and developments briefly and schematically here. Also, what follows is still very preliminary and needs to be investigated further. What I present are, therefore, only working hypotheses.

First, increasing government centralization, primarily in the fiscal sphere, for which we have evidence in *Asia Minor* in the form of increasing attestations of central government (semi-)military officials charged with fiscal tasks,[25] changed elite incentive patterns, in that it (partly?) robbed them of the social power associated with, and the wealth derived from, collective control over local tax resources, and, therefore, of their desire to keep central government interference in their cities to a bare minimum. Their primary strategy for preventing such interference, namely, employing civic munificence to keep local infrastructure and facilities in good condition and as a means to pacify the *dēmos* and to divert intra-elite competition to the non-violent euergetic sphere so as to avoid internal civic conflicts (which were sure to draw unwelcome imperial attention, see e.g. Plut. *Mor.* 814f–815a; Dio Chrys. *Or.* 46.14), was thus no longer as necessary as it had been before.

Second, the urban middling groups, well known from the first and second centuries and into the early decades of the third through the many inscriptions documenting the activities of professional associations (*collegia*), become considerably less visible in the cities of the east from the second half of the third century onwards (though *collegia* continued to be feature of late Roman cities).[26] These groups had been an important social force empowering the continuously functioning popular assemblies of the cities in the Roman east during the early and high empire, and had constituted a clear sociopolitical counterpoint for collective elite ambitions.[27] Declining market conditions caused by military unrest and broader economic changes,[28] as well as the diminishing importance of assembly politics in third-century eastern cities, may well have been behind the waning of such middling groups. With this, the need for elite individuals to forge links with them through munificence, and the advantages that might be derived by both parties from such links also disappeared.

Third, and most importantly, I would argue that with the Antonine Plague, the demographic expansion that had characterized the Mediterranean world since the late Republic basically ground to a halt.[29] Population growth had made urban elites, who were mostly large landowners, richer, as cultivable land became scarcer and rents rose. Arguably, it also made them broader, as more and more formerly middling landowning families eventually became wealthy enough to join the ranks of the urban elites during the first and second centuries CE. The intense intra-elite competition that we see in second-century and early third-century eastern Roman cities, which fuelled the boom in elite benefactions, was a likely result of this, as families within an ever broader, increasingly wealthier and increasingly internally stratified elite were struggling for power, prestige and a relatively fixed number of high-status positions.[30] This process came to an end with the end of the era of demo-graphic expansion; after the Antonine Plague, with fewer agricultural workers left, rents no longer rose, while military unrest and economic troubles in all likelihood adversely affected markets throughout much of the third century.[31] Particularly families belonging to the lower echelons of the urban elites would have been vulnerable. A relative drop in elite numbers would have eased com-petitive pressures, and thus the need for constant euergetic display, as did the other two factors mentioned above (increasing central government centraliza-tion and the dwindling of middling groups).

In his *The Romanization of Britain*, Martin Millett noted that acts of munificence by individual elite members were relatively scarce in Roman Britain (and in other northern provinces such as the Germanies). Lack of wealth was not the issue, since many of these people owned rich villas. Instead, he suggests that the solution was sociopolitical: the British *civitates* were controlled by small oligarchies of elite families, secure in their power, who had no incentive to compete with one another for power and prestige via euergetism.[32] The cake was big enough to satisfy all of the relatively small numbers of eaters. The intense intra-elite status competition, caused by upward social mobility, a broadening of elites and strong internal elite strati-fication that we see in the empire's Mediterranean provinces and in the east thus never took hold here. My suggestion is that, during the mid- and later third century, the cities of *Asia Minor* (temporarily?) reverted to a situation akin to the 'northern Roman pattern' sketched by Millett. The remaining civic elites in later third-century CE *Asia Minor* were probably no less wealthy than their second- and early third-century predecessors. However, the imperial-administrative, demographic and sociopolitical factors that had stimulated the intense euergetic competition among the latter during the early and high empire, and the spectacular interventions in the urban landscape that resulted from this, had now disappeared.

## Notes

1  Niemann (2000): 69–72; see Harvey (1985), Lefebvre (1974).
2  See Zuiderhoek (2013): 179–80 for references and discussion.
3  Zuiderhoek (2009a): 80, figure 5.3 and 160–4 for the data; Zuiderhoek (2014): 101–3.
4  Vedius bath–*gymnasium*: *I. Ephesos* 438; *bouleuterion* renovated: *I. Ephesos* 460. See Kalinowski (2002): 121–7. Damianus and his wife, cf. Philostr. *VS* 605–6.
5  *IGR* 4.1431 = *I. Smyrna* 697 = *AGRW* 194, with Philostr. *VS* 531.
6  *CIG* 2782, cf. Reynolds (1991), 20.

7 *I. Selge* 17.
8 For example, *I. Selge* 62; Waelkens, *Türsteine* 423 (Akmoneia); *CIG* 3705 (Apollonia ad Rhyndacus); *AvP* VIII.3, no. 30 (Pergamon).
9 *I. Perge* 193; *IGR* 3.351 = *I. Sagalassos* 25.
10 The wording of Philostr. *VS* 531, moreover, implies some agency on the part of Smyrna with regard to the uses to which the funds were to be put: Hadrian 'poured' (ἐπαντλῆσαι) money over Smyrna, 'and with this the grain market was built, a gymnasium ... and a temple ...' (ἀφ' ὧν τά τε τοῦ σίτου ἐμπόρια ἐξεποιήθη ... καὶ γυμνάσιον ... καὶ νεὼς ...).
11 Steskal and La Torre (2008): 301.
12 Kalinowski (2002): 125–7.
13 See Burns (2017): 280 on shops (*tabernae*) in colonnaded streets in the cities of the Roman east.
14 Dickenson (2017), Dignas (2004).
15 See Bang (2016).
16 Zuiderhoek (2009a): 170, appendix 3
17 Zuiderhoek (2009a): 18–19, figures 1.2 and 1.3.
18 On euergetism as gift exchange, see Zuiderhoek (2009a), Domingo Gygax (2016) and Domingo Gygax and Zuiderhoek (2021).
19 Zuiderhoek (2009a): 21–2.
20 Mitchell (1993): 235–6.
21 Roueché (1989): p. xx and *passim*; Liebeschuetz (1992): 4–6.
22 *I. Perge* II, pp. 1–2; Zuiderhoek (2009b): 40–1.
23 On the Antonine Plague, see Duncan-Jones (1996) and the contributions in Lo Cascio (2012); on third-century developments in *Asia Minor* see Mitchell (1993): 227–40, Zuiderhoek (2009b).
24 Mitchell (1990): 189–93; for recent discussion see Ng (2015).
25 Mitchell (1993): 228–34, Zuiderhoek (2009b).
26 On *collegia* in the Roman east see van Nijf (1997).
27 See Zuiderhoek (2008) for evidence and discussion.
28 See e.g. Poblome (2006) on the regionalization of ceramic production and distribution in third-century *Asia Minor*, probably indicative of market shrinkage due to disruption of trade and lower levels of (elite) investment and consumption.
29 On population growth, see e.g. Frier (2000): 811–6 (2001); Scheidel (2007).
30 Zuiderhoek (2009a): 53–70.
31 Zuiderhoek (2009b).
32 Millett (1990): 81–3. In her recent Leiden PhD thesis on communal dining financed by benefactors in the Roman west, Shansan Wen notes a similar contrast between the northwestern and the more central and Mediterranean provinces, see Wen (2018): 139–49.

# References

Bang, Peter Fibiger. "Beyond capitalism: conceptualising ancient trade through friction, world historical context and bazaars." Pages 75–89 in *Dynamics of production in the ancient Near East 1300–500 BC*. Edited by Juan Carlos Moreno García. Oxford: Oxbow, 2016.

Burns, Ross. *Origins of the colonnaded streets in the cities of the Roman east.* Oxford: Oxford University Press, 2017.

Dickenson, Christopher P. *On the agora: the evolution of a public space in Hellenistic and Roman Greece (c. 323 BC - 267 AD).* Leiden: Brill, 2017.

Dignas, Beate. *Economy of the sacred in Hellenistic and Roman Asia Minor.* Oxford: Oxford University Press, 2004.

Domingo Gygax, Marc. *Benefaction and rewards in the ancient Greek city: the origins of euergetism.* Cambridge: Cambridge University Press, 2016.

Domingo Gygax, Marc and Arjan Zuiderhoek, eds. *Benefactors and the polis: the public gift in the Greek cities from the Homeric world to Late Antiquity.* Cambridge: Cambridge University Press, 2021.

Duncan-Jones, Richard P. "The impact of the Antonine Plague." *Journal of Roman Archaeology* 9 (1996): 108–36.

Edmondson, Jonathan. "Cities and urban life in the western provinces of the Roman Empire, 30 BCE–250 CE." Pages 250–280 in *A Companion to the Roman Empire.* Edited by David S. Potter. Malden, MA, Oxford, Carlton: Blackwell, 2006.

Finley, Moses I. *The ancient economy.* Updated ed. Berkeley: University of California Press, 1999.

Frier, Bruce W. "Demography." Pages 787–816 in *The Cambridge ancient history vol. XI: the high empire, A.D. 70–192.* Second edition. Edited by Alan K. Bowman, Peter Garnsey and Dominic Rathbone. Cambridge: Cambridge University Press, 2000.

Frier, Bruce W. "More is worse: some observations on the population of the Roman Empire." Pages 139–159 in *Debating Roman demography.* Edited by Walter Scheidel. Leiden: Brill, 2001

Harvey, David. *The urbanization of capital: studies in the history and theory of capitalist urbanization.* Baltimore: Johns Hopkins University Press, 1985.

Johnson, Allan C., Paul Robinson Coleman-Norton and Frank C. Bourne. *Ancient Roman statutes.* Austin, TX: University of Austin Press, 1961.

Kalinowski, Angela. "The Vedii Antonini: aspects of patronage and benefaction in second-century Ephesos." *Phoenix* 56 (2002): 109–49.

Lefebvre, Henri. *La production de l'espace.* Paris: Anthropos, 1974.

Liebeschuetz, J. H. W. G. "The end of the ancient city." Pages 1–49 in *The city in Late Antiquity.* Edited by John Rich. London and New York: Routledge, 1992.

Lo Cascio, E. *L'impatto della "peste antonina."* Bari: Edipuglia, 2012.

Millett, Martin. *The Romanization of Britain: an essay in archaeological interpretation.* Cambridge: Cambridge University Press, 1990.

Mitchell, Stephen. "Festivals, games, and civic life in Roman Asia Minor." *Journal of Roman Studies* 80 (1990): 183–93.

Mitchell, Stephen. *Anatolia: land, men, and gods in Asia Minor. Volume I: the Celts and the impact of Roman rule.* Oxford: Clarendon Press, 1993.

Ng, Diana. "Commemoration and élite benefaction of buildings and spectacles in the Roman world." *Journal of Roman Studies* 105 (2015): 101–23.

Niemann, Michael. *A spatial approach to regionalisms in the global economy.* London and New York: Pallgrave Macmillan, 2000.

Poblome, Jeroen. "Mixed feelings on Greece and Asia Minor in the third century AD." Pages 189–212 in *Old pottery in a new century: innovating perspectives on Roman pottery studies. Atti del convegno internazionale di Studi Catania, 22–24 Aprile 2004.* Edited by Daniel Malfitana, Jeroen Poblome and John Lund. Catania: Bretschneider, 2006.

Reynolds, Joyce M. "Epigraphic evidence for the construction of the theatre: 1st c. B.C. to mid 3rd c. A.D." Pages 15–28 in *Aphrodisias Papers 2. The theatre, a sculptor's workshop, philosophers, and coin-types. Including the papers given at the Third International Aphrodisias Colloquium held at New York University at 7 and 8 April, 1989*. Edited by R.R.R. Smith and Kenan T. Erim. *JRA* Suppl. 2, Ann Arbor: Journal of Roman Archaeology, 1991.

Roueché, Charlotte. *Aphrodisias in late antiquity: the late Roman and Byzantine inscriptions including texts from the excavations at Aphrodisias conducted by Kenan T. Erim* (with contributions from Joyce M. Reynolds). *JRS* Monographs no. 5. London: Society for the Promotion of Roman Studies, 1989.

Scheidel, Walter. "Demography." Pages 38–86 in *The Cambridge economic history of the Greco-Roman world*. Edited by Walter Scheidel, Ian Morris and Richard Saller. Cambridge: Cambridge University Press, 2007.

Steskal, Martin and Martino La Torre. *Das Vediusgymnasium in Ephesos. Archäologie und Baubefund*. 2 Vols. (Forschungen in Ephesos XIV/1). Vienna: Österreichischen Akademie der Wissenschaften, 2008.

van Nijf, Onno M. *The civic world of professional associations in the Roman east*. Amsterdam: Gieben, 1997.

Wen, Shanshan. *Communal dining in the Roman west: private munificence towards cities and associations in the first three centuries AD*. Leiden: Unpublished PhD thesis, Leiden University, 2018.

Zuiderhoek, Arjan. "On the political sociology of the imperial Greek city." *Greek, Roman, and Byzantine Studies* 48 (2008): 417–45.

Zuiderhoek, Arjan. *The politics of munificence in the Roman Empire: citizens, elites and benefactors in Asia Minor*. Cambridge: Cambridge University Press, 2009a.

Zuiderhoek, Arjan. "Government centralization in late second and third century A.D. Asia Minor: a working hypothesis." *Classical World* 103.1 (2009b): 39–51.

Zuiderhoek, Arjan. "Cities, buildings and benefactors in the Roman east." Pages 173–92 in *Public space in the post-classical city*. Edited by Christopher P. Dickenson and Onno M. van Nijf. Caeculus 7. Leuven, Paris and Walpole, MA: Peeters, 2013.

Zuiderhoek, Arjan. "Controlling urban public space in Roman Asia Minor." Pages 99–108 in *Space, place and identity in Northern Anatolia*. Edited by Tønnes Bekker-Nielsen. Geographica Historica Band 29. Stuttgart: Steiner, 2014.

# 7 Making space for commerce in Roman Britain

## Re-evaluating the nature and impact of the forum/basilica complex

*Christopher P. Dickenson*

## Introduction

Towns occupy a paradoxical position in scholarship on Roman Britain. On the one hand, they are widely recognized as one of the most radical changes brought by Roman rule. The significance of the Iron Age *oppida* as a step on the road towards urbanization is still debated, but it was only under the Empire that real towns appeared: planned on a grid, relatively densely populated and offering a range of public amenities.[1] The impact of towns on the political, economic and cultural landscape of the province has been much discussed. On the other hand, while individual towns have been studied in detail comparative research – especially into the experience of urban life – has been thin on the ground.[2] Books on the province invariably include comparative chapters on towns, but John Wacher's *The Towns of Roman Britain*, published over four decades ago, though revised in 1995, remains the only major synthesis.[3] Evidence for crafts and trades within the towns has certainly not gone unnoticed but approaches to the towns have generally downplayed their economic function and have seen them as products of political and cultural concerns. The impact of economic activity on daily life and movement within the towns has yet to be seriously addressed.

Much commercial life within the towns of Roman Britain took place in shops: in the first century CE, typically small-scale rectangular strip buildings with their narrow side fronting streets, and from the second century onward rooms within grander houses more closely conforming to Mediterranean models.[4] It is often difficult to distinguish between shops, workshops and dwelling places and glimpses into the types of products made and sold are afforded only rarely through chance survivals of small finds. The row of shops in *Insula* XIV at St Albans, where it is possible to trace the history of crafts and trades over several successive phases of destruction and rebuilding is unique.[5] Not much can be said about how trades were distributed across the urban landscape in Britain but there are few grounds to suppose any clustering of different types of commercial activity. It would, therefore, not be particularly fruitful to explore the distribution of commerce in such private premises throughout the towns. Specialized public market buildings were also rare and problems of identification – too often glossed over – pertain to several of those that have been recognized. These buildings will be discussed in this chapter, but the main focus will be on the towns' most central and monumental public spaces, their forum–basilica complexes.

These complexes are widely accepted as serving as marketplaces yet their commercial function has generally been seen as secondary to their political and civic function. This chapter turns this interpretation on its head and argues that the market function of these complexes is crucially important for understanding why they were constructed and how they were used and experienced. I argue that not only commerce was accommodated in the central open space and shops behind the colonnades but also that their basilicas most likely served as market halls. Going further, the chapter explores the implications of this reassessment for understanding the role these buildings played in shaping urban society in Britain. The emphasis is on the second century CE, the high point of forum construction in Britain; the discussion draws most heavily on evidence from four of the best known towns of the province, Caerwent, Silchester, St Albans and Wroxeter. To set the stage, it is useful to first say something more about how the towns and forum–basilicas of Roman Britain have previously been approached and why this line of enquiry has not been pursued before.

## Emphasizing civicness

Issues that have featured prominently in discussions of Romano-British urbanism include town status, government and administration, the timing of urban development, Roman influence versus local agency, the relationship between towns and countryside and the towns' eventual decline.[6] The thread that ties these interests together is seeing the towns as manifestations of 'urbanism' and on that score assessments have tended to be rather negative. The fact that the towns remained under-monumentalized by comparison with those elsewhere in the Empire and that they largely disappeared when Rome withdrew from Britain in the fifth century has been held to prove that the towns were a purely political and cultural phenomenon, lacking the underlying socio-economic conditions that might have sustained them.[7] This vision is central to much thinking on ancient towns and cities, but it has arguably been taken to its most extreme for Britain.[8] This is surely one important reason why commercial life within the towns – and within their central public spaces, the forum-basilicas – has been downplayed.

There are other reasons. First, scholars interested in the economy of the province have tended to take a systemic approach seeing towns as nodes of production or consumption instead of zooming in to consider the impact of economy on their internal life.[9] Second, the evidence is extremely fragmentary: most of the towns lie beneath modern settlements and have been revealed only sporadically through rescue excavation. Economic activity is hard to read from architecture, small-find material is scant and traces of many trades simply would not survive anyway. There is, however, also a tradition of writing on the towns of Roman Britain that is strongly grounded in empirical fieldwork and which has arguably discouraged more theoretical discussions. Wacher's book, indispensable though it is, epitomizes the overall tone. Eschewing theory the book consists, for the most part, of a series of detailed site-by-site discussions of hard archaeological evidence. The 'spatial turn' has made few inroads into Roman Britain.[10] Michael Jones has gone so far as to suggest that the two-way relationship between architectural space and people that is the cornerstone of recent 'spatial scholarship' across the humanities and social sciences was less pronounced in Britain than elsewhere in the ancient world because there was so little monumental architecture.[11] It is worth recalling that Bourdieu's much cited discussion of the dialectic between space and society focused on the decidedly non-monumental houses of the Kabyle people.[12] If anything we should expect the transformative effect of public architecture to have been more profound in Britain than elsewhere because it was such a radical departure from earlier ways of life. Not for nothing did Tacitus, in the much cited passage of his Agricola in which he derides the Britons' enthusiastic adoption of the trappings of Roman urban life as a mark of their 'enslavement', include buildings: temples, bathhouses, houses and, significantly for present purposes, forums.[13]

The forum–basilicas of the towns of Roman Britain have certainly received much attention.[14] Most of them represent a variation in the typical forum design unique to the province: a fully enclosed courtyard, with rooms behind one or more of the colonnades, with a basilica lining one side opposite a single main monumental entrance (Figures 7.1 and 7.2). A long-lived and unresolved debate surrounds the possible influence of military *principia* on the design.[15] Religion is conspicuously absent.[16] Some contained small cult spaces, perhaps for the imperial cult, but no grand temples stood on any forum in Britain, with the exception of St Albans, which in any case is not of the fully enclosed type.[17] Forum–basilica complexes seem to have been a feature of all of the 25 or so fully fledged towns of the province. It has been possible to reconstruct the layouts of at least ten of these complexes. At several sites, a first-century timber phase of the forum has been discovered.[18] It was, however, in the second century that more permanent stone complexes were constructed at most towns.

These forum–basilica complexes are widely acknowledged to have accommodated public markets both in their central open spaces and in the small rooms around the edges. Reconstruction drawings of several of them exist replete with market stalls (Figure 7.3). However, the emphasis in modern discussions had been on their civic and political functions: on the courtyards serving as assembly spaces, on the basilicas as venues for legal hearings and on the rooms in the wings as accommodating the *curia*, magisterial offices or archives.

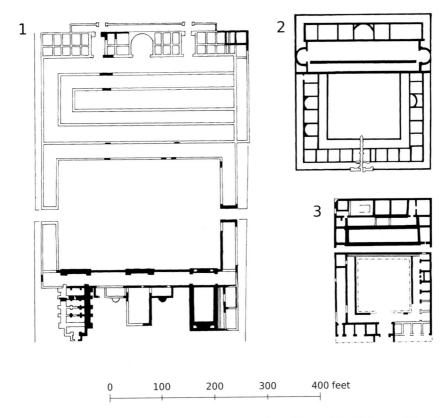

*Figure 7.1* Reconstruction map of the forums of St Albans (1), Silchester (2) and Caerwent (3) (from Wacher 1995: figures. 7, 8 and 9).

This emphasis of interpretation has a long history. In his 1876 translation of the passage of the Agricola just mentioned Alfred John Church rendered 'forums' as 'courts of justice'. Wacher stressed that commerce would have been a common sight on the forums – positioning himself against unnamed scholars who had argued the opposite – but he consistently emphasizes the political function as most important.[19] This vision has been reinforced even by scholars who have taken a more overtly theoretical approach to the towns of the province. Dominic Perring has argued that the wave of forum building in the second century was linked to an elite takeover of the towns at that time, seeing them as arenas for elite displays of Romanness.[20] This interpretation certainly moves away from the conservative tradition to consider the built environment and society as profoundly entwined, but it ultimately reinforces the old idea that the main civic centres of these towns were created through a top-down cultural imperative and downplays their use by ordinary townsfolk

:

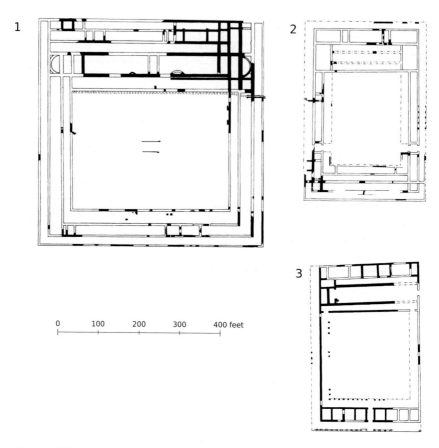

*Figure 7.2* Reconstruction map of the forums of London (1), Leicester (2) and
Wroxeter (3) (from Wacher 1995: figure 8).

for mundane business such as buying and selling. Louise Revell in a monograph and two important articles has recently offered some innovative and
sensitive readings of the relationship between local identity and the built
environment in Roman Britain, paying particular attention to the forums as
spaces where power was negotiated and where people in different towns found
different ways of being Roman.[21] She has, however, similarly emphasized the
civic and political function of these squares downplaying their commercial
significance and explicitly arguing that the basilicas were purely political
buildings.[22]

While the forum–basilica complexes of Roman Britain undoubtedly were
centres of government and administration, the primacy given to this civic
function in modern scholarship deserves reassessment.

*Figure 7.3* Reconstruction drawing of the forum and basilica at Leicester (Source: © Mike Codd/ Leicester Arts and Museums Service).

## The function of the forums of Roman Britain – politics versus commerce

In focusing on the political aspect of the forums, much effort has been made to identify *curiae*, record houses and magisterial offices.[23] Such identifications often rely primarily on inference from architecture though a convincing candidate for an archive or government office has been identified in a room at the rear of the basilica at Wroxeter, where writing equipment, wooden chests and part of a military diploma were discovered.[24] Two types of evidence more commonly found at forum sites, which might seem to hint at their civic importance and which, thus, deserve consideration here are dedicatory inscriptions to emperors placed above entrances and fragments of statues and statue bases from within the buildings.

Dedicatory inscriptions to reigning emperors from above forum entrances have been discovered at St Albans and Wroxeter – to Domitian and Hadrian, respectively – and possibly also at Silchester and Winchester.[25] Such inscriptions speak of power relations and might seem to hint at a largely political function for the squares. Market buildings dedicated to, or paid for by, emperors are, however, known at cities in other parts of the Empire such as Athens and Lepcis Magna.[26] Werner Eck has also recently argued that supposed dedications to emperors from basilicas in other parts of the Empire (previously thought to give the name in the dative) actually only mention the emperor's name (in the ablative) as a way to date the project.[27] The dedicatory inscriptions from Britain should then perhaps not give them too much weight in thinking about what the buildings were used for.

Other epigraphic and sculptural evidence from the forums of Britain is scant – as it notoriously is for the province as a whole – but Revell has recently convincingly demonstrated that it is sufficient to show that these spaces were no different to those elsewhere in the Empire in serving as venues for the display of statues and inscriptions.[28] At Silchester, in particular, fragments of statue bases and bronze sculpture from several different statues have been found.[29] That we do not have more such evidence from other sites probably says more about how much was later destroyed and reused than it does about genuine absence in Roman times.[30] Whether these statues represented local dignitaries or emperors is impossible to say but in either case they would have been decidedly political monuments that expressed relations of power. That is not, however, a reason to suppose that the political function of these squares was more important than the commercial one. On the contrary, such monuments would have made perfect sense in a setting that was home to a wide range of people and activities.

In the Greek East, statues certainly stood in spaces where commerce mingled with other activities and even in specialized market buildings.[31] Ephesos provides an instructive example. The city had two agoras, the more political so-called Staatsagora where the offices of government, the bouleuterion and prytaneion, were located and the Tetragonos Agora, which was clearly the city's commercial marketplace.[32] Strikingly, of the two, it is the Tetragonos Agora that has produced the most evidence for honorific statuary.[33] In emphasizing the honour of a local orator being buried on the Tetragonos Agora Philostratus refers to it as the 'epiphanestatos topos' (most visible place), a phrase often used to emphasize the prestige of locations of statues.[34] I have argued elsewhere that more account should be taken of the activities of daily life in thinking about the spatial context of public statues.[35] Statues and bases enjoy a prominence in the archaeological record that the ephemeral traces of daily life do not, which, combined with our modern familiarity with museums, makes it tempting for us to imagine that the places where Roman public statues were erected were purpose-built for their viewing.[36] However, in Roman towns, statues were more often part of the backdrop of daily life and quite deliberately so. Standing amid the hustle and bustle of daily life was where they were assured of the biggest audience and where they could most effectively communicate the importance of the people they represented. Imagining the forums of Roman Britain as bustling marketplaces would help to both explain why statues were set up there and to understand how such monuments were experienced in daily life. But are there more concrete grounds for deciding whether politics or commerce would have more prominent on these squares?

Hard evidence for either politics or trade is, unsurprisingly, hard to find. Wroxeter has, uniquely, produced some strikingly good evidence for commercial activity in the form of stacks of imported terra sigillata pottery and mortaria found *in situ* in front of one of the colonnades of the outer eastern side of the forum where they fell and were buried in the destruction layers of a mid-second century fire.[37] For our purposes, it is unfortunate that this evidence relates to the outside colonnade of the forum, but it at least attests to an association between the forum and commerce and absence of such evidence within squares is certainly not evidence of absence. Without disaster conditions such trade would not leave much trace. Shops within forums – assuming the rows of small rooms around the edges were shops – would have been kept clean and emptied when abandoned, and temporary stalls would have been cleared away at the end of a day's trading. The forums of Gloucester, Cirencester and Caerwent at least are known to have been paved, which meant that nothing that was dropped could be trampled into the ground for later discovery (Figure 7.4).[38]

I have suggested elsewhere that the ease with which paving can be swept clean made it particularly suitable for market squares.[39] This apparent touch of architectural splendour might then hint at the squares' use for accommodating markets rather than at some more lofty purpose. Political gatherings would have left even less trace though it is worth noting that no architectural provisions for meetings have been found – no postholes or cuttings on columns for voting enclosures or grandstands such as found on the forums

*Figure 7.4* The forum paving at Caerwent (photograph: C. Dickenson).

of several Republican cities in Italy,[40] and no remains of speakers' platforms such as those known at Rome and in some cities in the Greek East.[41] As already mentioned, apart from at St Albans, there were no temples on the forums from whose podia orators could have addressed a crowd as they did in Rome.[42]

At this point, it is important to address Dominic Perring's suggestion that the monumental forum–basilicas of the second century were built to express the Romanitas of a local elite who moved from the countryside to the towns in the second century, displacing the lower status inhabitants of the strip buildings and replacing their houses with grander courtyard buildings.[43] Perring links these developments to a purported contemporary decrease in evidence for commercial activity. The forum–basilicas, thus, evoked the grander civic centres of Roman towns to advertise the cultural identity of the local elite without actually accommodating the vibrant mix of activities found on such squares. Perring explicitly argues that the forums of the second century were somehow not truly public spaces.[44] The argument is elegant and thought-provoking and yet a simpler fit for the evidence is to take the forums at face value as spaces designed to be used by the whole community.

Rather than supposing that the courtyard houses represent a displacement of lower class town dwellers by an influx of rural elite, it is more straight-forward to see them as evidence of an improvement in urban prosperity and existing town folk improving their lot. Much of Perring's other evidence for economic decline actually dates to the third or even fourth centuries rather than the second century. The second century was a high point for the economic fortunes of the whole Roman Empire, which was reflected in a widespread building boom.[45] There is, therefore, no reason not to see the British forums as part of this wider phenomenon and constructed not as spaces purely for advertising identity but rather to fulfil the same purpose that they did elsewhere. Wacher has challenged the idea that courtyard houses of Britain did not contain workshops and shops.[46] But even if some commercial space was lost by the construction of these dwellings, the coincidence in the timing of the appearance of the forums could be read as suggesting not that trade disappeared but rather that it was relocated to these new monumental complexes. Elsewhere I have challenged the idea that enclosure of open spaces in ancient cities must signify a decline in publicness.[47] I return to that issue below, but it is worth noting at this point that Perring himself argues that the enclosed forums that emerged in Italy in late Republican and Early Imperial were the result of members of local elites asserting control over trade in cities whose economies were thriving; he does not see them as representational spaces devoid of commerce.[48] It is overly complicated to look for different motives behind the creation of Britain's forums and simpler to see them as the province catching up with trends that started much earlier in the heart of the Empire.

Ultimately common sense must play some role in deciding whether politics or commerce was a more important part of the function of these squares.

Knowledge of political life in the towns of the province is slight; for so many issues – size of councils, numbers and titles of magistrates, the competences of both – we are forced to assume that things worked in the same way as at towns elsewhere in the Roman West where documents such as town charters have been found.[49] For our purposes, what matters most is the role of citizens' assemblies since this would potentially explain the need for the central spaces that were the forums' defining features. There is no reason to assume that assemblies would have met often. Elections of magistrates (presumably two *duoviri* and two *aediles*) would have taken place annually; censuses would have been held every 5 years. Even allowing for fairly regular gatherings to hear news and discuss matters of popular concern, it is hard to imagine that this level of political activity would have required the investment in permanent premises that the forums represent. The business of buying and selling, on the other hand, would surely have taken place throughout the year.[50] These simple practical considerations make it hard to sustain the argument that these buildings would have been built primarily to serve as venues for politics.

## The basilica as a commercial building

Whereas past scholarship has only downplayed the commercial function of the main part of the forums of Roman Britain, for the basilicas that bordered these forums the commercial function has been completely rejected. Religion, in the form of the imperial cult, is accepted as accommodated within the small rooms, given particular prominence in the layout of several of these buildings but the emphasis in interpretation has been on their use as settings for political gatherings and legal hearings.[51] The tribunals found within these buildings and evidence for painting or marble ornamentation in some of them have lent weight to that interpretation.[52] Literary sources are our best evidence for the use of basilicas in the Empire and these do place emphasis on legal business. Given the preoccupations of the elite authors, this is hardly surprising.[53] There are, however, sources that refer to basilicas as multipurpose buildings that accommodated trade.[54] There is reason to think that those in Roman Britain housed markets as well as political business.

Splendid decoration is certainly no grounds for ruling out a commercial function. Grand buildings in other times and places – medieval churches and cathedrals spring readily to mind[55] – have been used for less than elevated purposes. The interior of the basilica at Aphrodisias in Caria was decorated with grand marble columns and sculpted friezes; and yet the display of Diocletian's Price and Currency Edicts on the facade on the side of its main entrance suggests a commercial connection, as Werner Eck has recently stressed.[56] The flexibility of basilicas in Britain is suggested by the fact that the supposed market building at Leicester (on which see below) included a basilica-like hall as did the bathhouses at Wroxeter and Caerwent[57]; at Wroxeter, there is even evidence to suggest that the bath basilica took over the administrative functions of the forum basilica in the fourth century.[58] Prior to that time, these halls must have housed functions connected to bathing and entertainment; they perhaps served as exercise halls. This at the very least proves that basilica architecture did not carry exclusively political connotations in Britain. Also potentially significant is the evidence that the basilicas on the forums at Silchester and Caerwent were used for bronze-working in the third century.[59] It is unlikely that metalworking had always taken place within these buildings but the introduction of this new activity might not represent the breakdown of civic life that it has been assumed to.[60] If these buildings had previously accommodated markets, metalworkers moving in would mark a less radical break with the past than if they had been purely courthouses. It is also worth considering the influence the British weather would have had on the types of public buildings the towns would have needed. Vitruvius recommended that '(b)asilicas should be constructed on a site adjoining the forum and in the warmest possible quarter, so that in winter *negotiatores* may gather in them without being troubled by the weather'.[61] Whether Vitruvius is referring to merchants, wholesalers or money lenders, he clearly envisages basilicas accommodating commerce and sees them as indoor extensions of the forum. In the frequently cold and wet climate of Britain, indoor market buildings would have been even more welcoming than in Italy, and not only in wintertime.

A connection with commerce can also be posited for the tribunals found within the buildings. Such platforms are attested, in Rome and elsewhere, being used in legal hearings; and there is no need to doubt that that is what they would have been used for in Britain too. But what type of legal business would have taken place in the towns of Roman Britain? Presumably disputes about land and inheritances and occasional criminal trials. Much such business probably fell under the competence of the higher magistrates – the *duoviri*. There would, however, also have been common petty disputes arising from interactions in the marketplace. These would have come within the sphere of the *aediles*, and *aediles* like higher magistrates are known to have sat atop tribunals in presiding over disputes.[62] In these relatively small, relatively poor communities such disputes would surely have been more common than the more exciting types of trials found in the literary sources and set in Rome. The forum basilicas of Roman Britain are relatively large spaces compared to the size of the towns. Most could have comfortably accommodated hundreds if not thousands of people. London's is the largest. Covering around 8,600 m², it could have held close to the entire urban population, an estimated 10,000–20,000 people.[63] Such large assemblies can hardly have been common. It is easier to envisage a large part of these halls being used for other business while small-scale hearings took place simultaneously in the immediate surroundings of the tribunals. At least three forum basilicas had two tribunals, one at either end, which favours the idea of simultaneous multiple usage of the buildings.[64] And since the most natural place for *aediles* to have presided over market disputes was actually in the marketplace – as attested elsewhere though admittedly for outdoor settings[65] – what other activity could have taken place in the main part of these basilicas except trade? Finally it is worth noting that at St Albans, whose forum is admittedly anomalous in so many ways, there was apparently no tribunal in the basilica but there was one on the opposite side of the square.[66] This suggests that this basilica at least may not have been used for legal hearings at all which gives extra reason to think that the functions of these buildings were broader than that which has traditionally been ascribed to them.

## *Macella* and other market buildings

Only four such buildings have been identified in Roman Britain – at Leicester, Cirencester, St Albans and Wroxeter – and the grounds for identifying all of them raise problems of interpretation that need to be addressed.[67] All these buildings have been generally referred to as *macella*, yet only the one at Wroxeter approaches the characteristic architectural form of that building type as a small rectangular courtyard surrounded by shops, 12 in this case (Figures 7.5 and 7.6).[68] The building at Wroxeter is incorporated within the bath complex immediately to the east of the forum.[69] At Wroxeter, a large open space has also been tentatively identified as a '*Forum Boarium*', a space where cattle were slaughtered for butchery and sale of their meat in the 'macellum'.[70] That label, however, borrowed from Rome, carries unhelpful connotations since there is no indication that the term was ever used outside the capital and since by the Imperial period, it is debated whether the *Forum Boarium* at Rome still functioned as a market.[71]

The supposed market buildings at Leicester and Cirencester resemble the design of Romano-British forums, though only a small part of either has been excavated; the first, as mentioned above, even included a basilica-like building. Pits containing sawn animal bones were found within the building at Cirencester which suggest that one thing the space was used for was butchery or sale of meat.[72] In both cases, however, the market interpretation has arisen purely because the main forum and basilica of the towns was believed to have been securely identified elsewhere. The interpretation of the function of buildings and parts of ancient cities too often relies on such apparently common-sense inferences. These identifications should cause us to question the appropriateness of ascribing single functions to buildings. Why not instead talk of Cirencester and Leicester having two forums? That these forum- and basilica-like structures have been considered as so eminently suitable for housing commercial markets should also lead us to ask why that function has been so downplayed for the towns' main forums and basilicas. The diversity and flexibility of use of ancient buildings and spaces are all too easily obscured by the labels we attach to them.

The building at St Albans is more unusual. It consists of a rectangular space approximately 40 × 20 m, running east to west, open at one of its short ends, lined with 'shops' on the long side and with a curious concrete foundation at the end opposite the entrance.

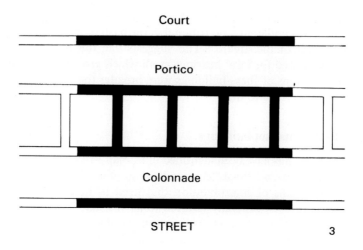

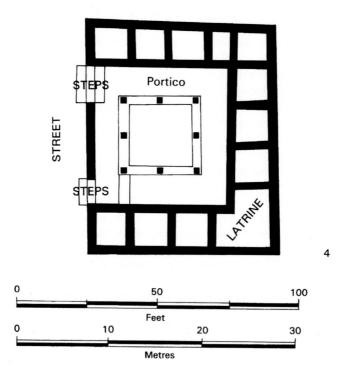

*Figure 7.5* Reconstruction map of the market buildings at Cirencester and Wroxeter.

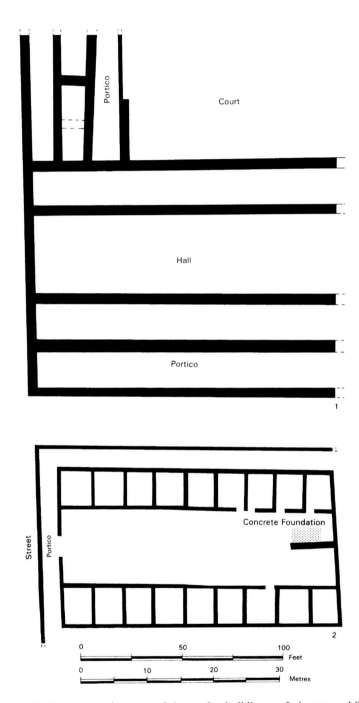

*Figure 7.6* Reconstruction map of the market buildings at Leicester and St. Albans.

It is tempting to imagine the foundation supporting a small shrine since, with the exception that it is not axially aligned with the entrance, the building calls to mind a religious complex like the – admittedly incomparably grander – Sebasteion at *Aphrodisias*.[73] Indeed Rosalind Niblett's monograph on the town includes a reconstruction drawing with a speculative relief of the god Mercury on the base.[74] She suggests he was a suitable god to have presided over trade and does not consider the possibility that the primary function of the building might have been religious.[75] Even if the complex was a sanctuary that would not, of course, rule out a commercial function for its supposed shops – the Sebasteion too had rows of rooms behind its colonnades that, at least, in Late Antiquity have been interpreted as shops. This complex at St. Albans again illustrates the difficulties in inferring function from form for ancient buildings.

Beyond the problems of identification that these four buildings illustrate, they are important to our concerns because if they are market buildings they represent the most significant step seen in Roman Britain towards the segregation of commercial space that I have argued was characteristic of the contemporary Greek East. Significantly here, as in the east, all of these buildings stood in close proximity to the forum. The buildings at St Albans (possibly) and Wroxeter (more certainly given the buildings' design) would possibly have housed markets for more exclusively elite products; Claire Holleran has recently argued that *macella* were generally buildings where a wealthy clientele purchased expensive meat and fish and that they were inaccessible to the less well-off.[76] If the structures at Cirencester and Leicester are market buildings, they must in contrast have accommodated trade on a fairly large scale, which would, of course, have repercussions for thinking about how much commerce would have been located on the main forum. On the whole, however, these four buildings do little to undermine the general impression that the main forum was the main focus of civic life, both civic and commercial, in most towns in Britain. Let us now consider the implications of my reassessment of the commercial function of the forums for how these buildings served to shape life within the towns.

## The implications of the argument – movement and space

The forum–basilicas of the second century CE seem, for the most part, to have been constructed in areas of open space that had fulfilled similar functions in the earlier years of the towns. At several sites, evidence for large timber predecessors of the later stone buildings has been found.[77] It is, therefore, important to ask what precisely was achieved by housing the forum's functions in monumental new fully enclosed complexes.

Perring, as mentioned, has seen the enclosure of squares elsewhere in the Early Empire as an elite strategy to exert greater control of economic life. Channelling entrance to single monumental gateways would have facilitated checking the quality of merchandise sold in the square and the collection of taxes. Perring downplayed the economic function of the second-century forums of Roman Britain, but there is no reason to doubt that this was also precisely what these buildings achieved. Controlling access to areas of urban space is always fundamentally about relations of power, since it reinforces inequalities between those who regulate access and those who seek to gain admission. I have elsewhere argued that enclosed market buildings in Roman Greece were one of several strategies by which members of the local elite sought to 'stage manage' (a phrase I borrow from Erving Goffman)[78] their interactions with the rest of the urban population. Elite disdain of the trading classes is seen persistently in Greek literary sources throughout Antiquity and in the fourth century BCE had led Aristotle and Xenophon to recommend cities having two agoras, one for politics and one for commerce to keep the riff-raff away from the business of government.[79] As public markets, the forum–basilicas of Roman Britain can hardly but have emphasized social distinctions between, on the one hand, the traders who came there to ply their wares and their lower-class customers and, on the other, the local elites who were presumably the driving force behind their construction. Channelling the passage of traders to the main entrances of these squares would have allowed their wares to be checked by magistrates or their assistants. Architecture and human interaction, thus, worked together to create a stark reminder of the differences in status between the two groups.

Inside the forums too, architecture and monuments worked to reinforce and mediate the relations of power. Members of the local elite were able to distinguish themselves from those lower down the social scale through privileged access to offices and meeting rooms that would have been off limits to traders. Louise Revell has astutely commented on the ways in which the tribunals within the basilicas served to accentuate differences in power, noting that these buildings were often equipped with minor entrances directly to the outside which would have allowed magistrates to reach the platforms without passing through the assembled throng, something that Goffman would have also classed as 'stage management'.[80] The position of the local elite was also emphasized by the presence of statues whether these represented members of that class or the emperors through which their local authority was legitimated. Accommodating different trades in different parts of a unified architectural complex could, furthermore, have worked to shape the relations of power among the trading class.[81] Permanent shops in the forums' wings would have quite likely sold more expensive or exotic merchandise with a long shelf life; perishable goods would have been more suited to being traded from open stalls in the centre. Evidence for doorways and thresholds of shops might confirm this suggestion if it showed that shops could be locked but unfortunately at most sites typically only the foundation courses of shop walls survive, so that we are largely in the dark regarding the question of movement in and out of them. Perring frames his discussion of the development of the forums in terms of 'exclusion' and 'inclusion'. I suggest that the term 'control' is preferable because it does not imply the presence or absence of certain types of people and allows a more nuanced consideration of how the buildings helped shape power relations.

Let us turn now to consideration of the place of the forum basilicas within the urban landscape to think about how they were approached and experienced from the outside. Lawrence, Cleary and Sears have noted a contrast with the situation in Gaul in the way that Britain's forums often deviated from the position and size that would have been dictated by the grid plan.[82] There is considerable diversity in their location which can be readily appreciated by considering the situation at five towns where the street system is fairly well-understood, namely, Gloucester, Colchester, Caerwent, St Albans and Silchester.

Only at the colony of Gloucester does the forum seem to have been situated in what might be termed a textbook situation, at the intersection of the '*cardo*' and '*decumanus*' *maximus*, though the location of the forum is not completely certain. Even at Gloucester, however, only one road – the north-east–south-east avenue – seems to have passed through the square, but the north-west–south-west avenue instead skirted along its northeast edge. At Britain's better known colony at Colchester, the forum seems to have been located in the western half of the city but its principle east-west and north-south avenues crossed at the square's south-west corner. At both cities, then any visitor entering the city would have naturally drifted towards the forum. Elsewhere, however, the situation was more complex. At Caerwent (Figure 7.7), the situation comes close to that at Gloucester with the forum located extremely centrally and the town's main east-west road passing along the forum's southern edge. The town's north and south gates, however, were offset by the width of an *insula*, so that there does not seem to have been a single main north-south road but people entering the city from those directions would have been led directly to, respectively, the forum's north-west and south-east corners.

At St Albans visitors from the south-west (from Silchester) and from the north-east would have been led directly to the forum's eastern edge. Visitors entering from the south (the direction of London) would have been led, via a left turn at a five-pointed intersection, to a road that took them, uniquely, directly into the middle of the forum in a situation that has been compared to the forums of Italy. Travellers entering the town from the north-west by contrast (the direction of Chester) before reaching the forum would have come first to a more confusing part of the city's civic centre where the theatre and a large temple were located before arriving at the rear of the forum's basilica. From there, they would only have been able to pass through the forum's main entrance after skirting the building, most quickly in a clockwise fashion. The arrangement was not particularly inviting to traffic from this direction even if the forum must have been easy enough to find. The approach from the direction of London was given special priority, particularly in view of the diagonal road that cut across the city's grid plan, creating the awkward space that came to be filled by the so-called 'Triangular Temple'.[83]

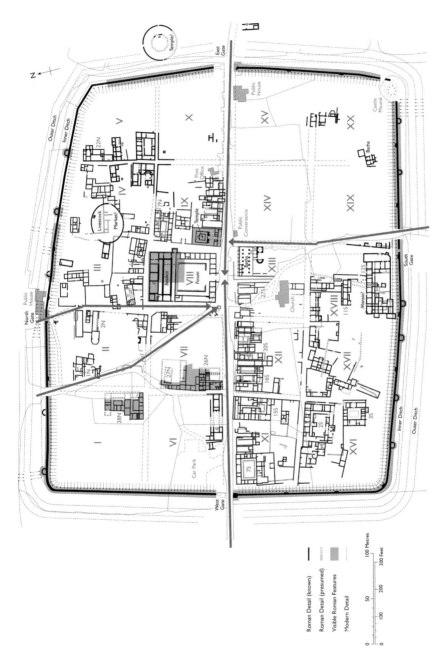

*Figure 7.7* Map of Caerwent showing main approaches to the forum.

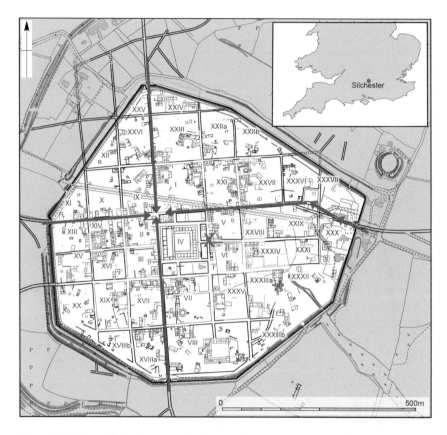

*Figure 7.8* Map of Silchester showing main approaches to the forum. After *Silchester, Changing Visions of a Roman Town: Integrating Geophysics and Archaeology: the Results of the Silchester Mapping Project 2005–10* (by J. Creighton with R. Fry. Britannia Monograph 28. Society for the Promotion of Roman Studies, London, 2016).

At Silchester, unusually, none of the town's main roads led directly to the forum's main entrance though all of them did skirt the multi-*insula* block on which the forum stood (Figure 7.8). The north-south road that connected the town to Dorchester and Leicester ran along the rear side of forum's basilica, in similar fashion to one of the roads at St Albans. The roads from London, Gloucester and Old Sarum on the other hand led directly past the forum and were separated from it by other buildings. The road from the forum's main eastern entrance led east to a T-junction at the entrance to a sanctuary containing two Romano-British temples. It is tempting to see this as a sacred way used in some local festival in which a procession passed from the forum to the sanctuary.[84] Although, as mentioned, there was little religious archi- tecture on the forums of Roman Britain, it is quite possible that in addition to the political and commercial functions discussed here their central open spaces also played a greater role in the religious life of the communities than has generally been suspected. At Silchester, the overriding impression is that the forum was positioned more for the benefit of the resident community than to draw in visiting strangers.

With the exception of at St Albans, all of the forums of Roman Britain whose outlines are known were fully enclosed spaces sometimes with minor entrances directly into the basilica or colonnades but all with one monumental entrance clearly designed to be used by most traffic. Their design made them, in short 'places to go to', rather than places 'to pass through' phrases that David Newsome has used to characterize the increasing enclosure of the *Forum Romanum* at the beginning of the Principate.[85] For the Greek East, similar enclosure of agoras in Hellenistic and Roman times has often been linked to a decline in the vitality of public space by the logic that restricted freedom of movement occurred in periods of reduced political freedom and that reduced traffic was detrimental to the spontaneity of these squares, a rather similar view to that proposed for the forums of Britain by Perring. I have challenged that view for the post-Classical agora[86] and do not believe it is a helpful way of thinking about Britain's forum–basilica complexes. Even if squares were primarily places to 'go to' what matters in assessing the vitality of public life is to ask what motivations people had to go there. My argument that the forums of Roman Britain were not primarily administrative and political centres but the central commercial spaces of their towns, means they would have been places that the entire community had more than incentive enough to frequent on a daily basis. Monumental entrances were a strategy to control entrance and thereby emphasize difference but this is not the same thing as discouraging people from going there.

As a corrective to the impression that the enclosed nature of the forum–basilica complexes would have isolated them from the life of the community, it is important to move away from ground plans to think about the built environment in three dimensions. The towns of Roman Britain were relatively under-monumentalized and many had considerable areas of open space within them. Several had multiple temples. Most had a bathhouse, some had a theatre, amphitheatre, circus or even a monumental arch but strikingly no town seems to have had more than one of any of these amenities. With the possible exceptions of Leicester and Circencester, as discussed above, no town is known to have had more than one forum. This means that their forum–basilica complexes would have been visible from far off, creating an imposing impression in contrast to the modest houses that made up most of the urban landscape.[87] Their looming bulk would have worked to draw in visitors from afar and would have perpetually reminded the town's inhabitants of the sights and sounds of public life that were played out within the buildings. The relationship of the forums to the rest of their urban environment might usefully be thought of as analogous to that of the towns to their surrounding countryside, as islands within which the expression and experience of 'being Roman' were intensified. Enclosing the forum completely by colonnades heightened its sense of place and set it apart, both physically and conceptually, from the rest of the town. Channelling and limiting access to the main entrance emphasized the transition from outside to inside and underlined this distinction.

## Conclusion

I have argued here that the past emphasis on the political function of the forum–basilica complexes of Roman Britain has unhelpfully downplayed their commercial function. Although the evidence will never allow certainty about how these buildings were used, I have made the case that these squares would have had more use as public markets than as political assembly places and that even their monumental basilicas served as indoor market halls. This argument is important because it casts a new light on – and I believe makes more sense of – both why these buildings were constructed and how they were experienced in daily life. Far from undermining the idea that these squares were also centres of administration and politics and – occasionally – venues for political gatherings of citizens, envisioning the forums as centres of trade restores an important part of the spatial context in which government and administration took place. Thinking about the presence of lowly traders and their customers who frequented the square and shops helps us to understand how the architecture of the forums and basilicas could be used by members of the local political class to 'stage manage' their actions on the public stage, to use Goffman's phrase. The proximity of politics to the hustle and bustle of daily life was clearly important, yet it was also necessary to develop strategies – locating administration in purpose-built offices, conducting legal hearings from raised tribunals, creating special entrances for people of importance – to demarcate differences in status and position. The erection of politically charged statues was also a strategy of communicating the realities of power and one that makes more sense in a setting where there would have been a truly public audience than in a venue reserved solely for elite representation. Enclosing commerce within a unified architectural complex controlled the movement of traders, which in addition to its practical advantages also served as a powerful reminder of difference. Looking at the position of the forums in reconstructed town plans, it is easy to suppose that they were isolated from their rest of the towns and yet, I have argued, their monumentality secured their visibility within the urban landscape and their mix of functions meant that people of a wide range of backgrounds had more than reason enough to visit them frequently. Enclosure cannot be read simplistically as symp-tomatic of a lack of public vitality, and there is no reason to doubt that the forums of Roman Britain were truly public spaces – perhaps more so than the forums and agoras of larger, more prosperous cities elsewhere since such places under the Empire exhibit clearer tendencies towards fragmentation and different functions being accommodated in specialized spaces. Emphasizing the importance of the commercial function of the forums of Britain and exploring the repercussions of this argument for how these complexes shaped the societies of their towns does nothing to diminish the political significance of these squares. On the contrary, the argument I have set out here broadens our approach to ancient politics beyond administration and government to think about how power relations were structured in daily life. And in that the forums of Roman Britain were profoundly political spaces.

## Acknowledgement

This work was generously supported by the Danish National Research Foundation under the grant DNRF 119 – Centre of Excellence for Urban Network Evolutions (UrbNet).

## Notes

1　For different views on the *oppida* and urbanism, with further references see Jones 1987, 47, Woolf 1993, Pitts 2010, Moore 2017.
2　Studies of individual towns, e.g. St Albans: Niblett 2001, Chester: Mason 2001, London: Wallace 2015 and now the expansive Hingley 2018. Silchester is arguably the best studied of all the towns of Roman Britain both through extensive early excavation (Boon 1957) and through Michael Fulford's intensive recent excavations of insula IX on which see, e.g. Fulford 2012.
3　Wacher 1995; though see also de la Bédoyère 1992. Book chapters include Mattingly 2006: chs 9–11, Creighton 2006: ch 4, Jones 2004, Revell 2016, Rogers 2016.
4　The fullest consideration of houses in Roman Britain is Perring 2002; on the strip houses pp. 55–60. Wacher stresses that the later houses like their predecessors often also accommodated trade Wacher 1995: 198.
5　Frere 1972: 5–112, Niblett 2001: 62–5.
6　For good overviews of the history of scholarship on the towns, see Jones 2004 and Rogers 2016.
7　Though cf. Dark 2000 and Rogers 2011.
8　For a useful overview of how pre-modern cities have been tended to be conceptualised as non-economic in nature, see Smith and Lobo 2019.
9　See for example Fulford 2004.
10　For a reflection on the impact of this paradigm shift, see Warf and Arias 2009.
11　Jones 2004: 168.
12　Bourdieu 1970.
13　Tacitus *Agricola* 21.
14　As a marker of Romannness, see Wacher 1995: 18, Frere 1987: 193.
15　Atkinson 1942, Goodchild 1946, Ward-Perkins 1970: 7–11, Frere 1971: 14–20.
16　The principle difference between these forums and those of neighbouring Gaul, see Goodchild 1946.
17　Temples at St Albans: Revell 2016: 772. For the fullest consideration of the forum at St Albans, see Frere 1983, 55–72. For the small cult places, see Wacher 1995, 63, Revell 2009, 94, Revell 2016, 772.
18　London, Castor-by-Norwich, Chichester, Wroxeter, Caerwent, Lincoln, Silchester, St Albans, Gloucester – see Wacher 1995: 43, 152, 223, 245, 259, 261, 276, 337.

19  On forum trade – Wacher 1995: 367; emphasizing the civic function – Wacher 1995, passim and especially 23 – referring to Frere 1987: 250.
20  Perring 1992.
21  Revell 2007, 2009, 2016.
22  For example, Revell 2016: 772: 'The forum had many purposes: economic, religious, social, but arguably the most important was the political'; for similar statements, see Revell 2007: 129 and 136.
23  On difficulties of identification, see Revell 2016: 769.
24  Atkinson 1942: 123–7, Wacher 1995: 43 and 366, Revell 2009: 40.
25  Wroxeter RIB 288; St Albans 3123, discussed fully by Frere 1983: 69–72. Revell (2009: 180) emphasises the political significance of the Wroxeter inscription. Wacher refers to a dedicatory inscription from Silchester that is too fragmentary to read – Wacher 1995: 276. For Winchester, Wacher mentions (1995: 296) two letters of the inscription with the largest letters known from Roman Britain. I (tentatively) suggest it might be the dedication of the forum.
26  The Roman Agora at Athens, paid for by Julius Caesar and Augustus – see Dickenson 2017a: 237–252 with references; the market building at *Lepcis Magna* was dedicated to Augustus but paid for by a member of the local elite – Mitchell 1987: 343.
27  Eck 2018: 9.
28  Revell 2016: 769–71 with references.
29  Revell 2007: 141–4 and Revell 2016: 771 and figure 37.2, drawing on Isserlin 1998.
30  Hope 2016, Croxford 2016.
31  Statues in a multipurpose space – e.g. the agora of Messene: Dickenson 2017b; statues in specialized market buildings in Asia Minor: Richard 2014: 259–60.
32  Scherrer 2000: 78–86 and 138–46.
33  Scherrer 2000: 144.
34  Philostr. *VS* 1.526.5–8; the grave was actually just outside the agora – see Cormack 2004: 42 with references. On the phrase: Ma 2013, 67–9.
35  Dickenson 2017c.
36  Dickenson 2017a: 438–42.
37  Atkinson 1942: 127, Wacher 1995: 63 and 367 Revell 2009: 40.
38  Gloucester: Wacher 1995: 155, Cirencester, *ibid* 321, Brewer 1997: 48.
39  Dickenson 2012: 259–6.
40  See Bossert 2018, with references.
41  On which see Dickenson 2017a: 157–70, 186–8, 194–9, 292–324.
42  See above.
43  Perring 1992.
44  Perring 1992: 296: 'There was, however, little need for public space, public buildings, and public interaction in these towns. Such cities were preserves of romanitas from which most aspects of the barbarian world could be excluded'.
45  See Wilson 2009: 74–8 and figures 2 and 3.
46  Wacher 1995: 125, 198, 285.
47  Dickenson 2018.
48  Perring 1992: 294. 'The direction of marketing into controlled public space, increasingly evident from the end of the Republic, can be seen as a reaction to mercantile success'.
49  On the political constitutions of towns in Roman Britain, drawing completely on evidence from elsewhere – Wacher 1995: 36–42.

50 On the frequency of Roman markets in general though there is no real evidence from Britain see de Ligt 1993 and, focusing on Rome, Holleran 2012: 181–9.

51 For example, Wacher 1995: 42, Frere 1987: 250. The incorporation of religion is stressed by Laurence, Esmonde Cleary and Sears 2011: 185–6 and Revell 2016: 772.

52 Revell 2016: 769. Revell 2009: 73 on the paintings and columns that articulated the tribunal in the basilica at Caerwent. On the use of imported marbles for decoration in several of the forums of Roman Britain see Isserlin 1998.

53 For example, Plin. *Ep.* 2.14 and 6.33; Quint. *Inst* 12.5.6.

54 On the function of basilicas Weinberg 1960: 106–9, though dated is useful. See also Cavalier and Descat 2012 and now Eck 2018.

55 Davies 1968.

56 For the building's architecture – Stinson 2008; for the price edict – Reynolds 1989; on the inscriptions' placement – Crawford 2002, Stinson 2008: 94–6. See also Eck 2018: 11–2.

57 Revell 2009: 175.

58 Wacher 1995: 375.

59 Jones 2004: 188. For Silchester see also Wacher 1995: 289; Brewer 1997: 52.

60 'Commandeered' for metalworking according to Jones – Jones 2004: 188.

61 Vitr. 5.1.4. Translation (modified) by F. Krohn 1912.

62 On Antiochus IV of Syria emulating this behavior see Polybius 26.1; see also Livy 41.20. See Dickenson 2017a: 163–4; for a platform of the *agoranomoi* (the Greek equivalent of the *aediles*) from the agora of Argos – Philippa-Touchais et al. 2000: 494. While these examples are both from the second century BCE see also the discussion of a representation of an *aedile* on a tribunal from Pompeii in Clarke 2003: 197.

63 For the most recent overview of the buildings with references, see Hingley 2018: 123–6. Using the convenient 1 person per 0.4 m$^2$ ratio that Hansen used to estimate the capacity of the Athenian Pnyx – Hansen 1996.

64 Silchester, Caerwent and Wroxeter. On Silchester: Revell 2016: 769; on Wroxeter: Wacher 1995: 366, on Caerwent: Wacher 1995: 381.

65 See above.

66 Wacher 1995: 225.

67 For all four buildings, Wacher 1995: 63–6 (refs); St Albans: Richardson 1944; Leicester: Wacher 1995: 63–66 and 352; Cirencester: Wacher 1962: 8 and Wacher 1995: 304 Wroxeter: Wacher 1995: 369, Ellis 2000, Grocock 2015. Revell also suggests that the supposed amphitheatre at Caerwent might really have been a market building – Revell 2009: 74, Revell 2016: 779. Wacher mentions a grand public building at Gloucester next to the forum and once taken to be the forum but which he does not seem to consider a potential market building – Wacher 1995: 158.

68 See for instance Wacher 1995 passim but esp. 66 and 91.

69 *Ibid n.* 66.

70 Grocock 2015: 169 with references.

71 See Holleran 2012: 93–4, who argues that it did keep its market function until the third century but with reference to those who have previously argued it did not.

72 Wacher 1995: 306.

73 For a full description of the Sebasteion's layout with a plan and reconstruction drawing see Smith 1987.

74 Niblett 2001: 115, figure 58.

75  Niblett 2001: 114.
76  Holleran 2012: 160–81.
77  Silchester, Exeter and Lincoln – Wacher 1995: 43.
78  Goffman 1956: *passim* and esp. p. 15.
79  Xen. *Cyr* 1.2.3; Arist. *Pol.* 1331a30–1331b4. Tracing elite disdain of traders into later periods – Dickenson 2012: 326–3.
80  Revell 2009: 151–61. For similar strategies in Roman Greece, see – Dickenson 2012: 313–559, Dickenson 2011.
81  For sharp ethnographic observations of such processes at work in a modern market, see Black 2013. I have commented on the issue for the Hellenistic and Roman period agora – Dickenson 2012: 324.
82  Laurence 2011: 184.
83  Niblett 2001: 78–85, 110.
84  As suggested by Cleary 2005: 8–10.
85  Newsome 2011.
86  Dickenson 2018.
87  That the monumentality of the forums should be seen in such relative terms has already been suggested by Revell 2007: 136.

## References

Atkinson, Donald. *Report on Excavations at Wroxeter: (The Roman City of Viroconium) in the County of Salop 1923–1927*. Oxford: Oxford University Press, 1942.

Black, Rachel. E. *Porta Palazzo: The Anthropology of an Italian Market.* Philadelphia, PA: University of Pennsylvania Press, 2013.

Boon, George. C. *Roman Silchester: The Archeology of a Romano-British Town.* London: Max Parrish, 1957.

Bossert, L. *Auf dem Forum – Die Temporäre Platznutzung in Antiken Städten Italiens.* Unpublished PhD Thesis, Humboldt-Universität zu Berlin, 2018.

Bourdieu, Pierre. "The Kabyle House or the World Reversed." *Social Science Information* 9(2) (1970): 151–70.

Brewer, Richard. J. *Caerwent Roman Town*. Cardiff: Cadw: Welsh Historic Monuments, 1997.

Cavalier, Laurence and Raymond Descat, eds. *Basiliques et agoras de Grèce et d'Asie Mineure*. Mémoires 27. Bordeaux: Ausonius, 2012.

Clarke, J.R. *Art in the Lives of Ordinary Romans: Visual Representation and Non-Elite Viewers in Italy, 100 B.C.–A.D. 315*. Berkeley, CA: University of California Press, 2003.

Cleary, Simon E. "Beating the Bounds: Ritual and the Articulation of Urban Space in Roman Britain." Pages 1–17 in *Roman Working Lives and Urban Living*. Edited by Ardle MacMahon and Jennifer Price. Oxford: Oxford University Press, 2005.

Cormack, Sarah. *The Space of Death in Roman Asia Minor*. Vienna: Phoibos, 2004.

Crawford, M. H. "Discovery, Autopsy and Progress: Diocletian's Jigsaw Puzzles." Pages 145–63 in *Classics in progress: essays on Ancient Greece and Rome*. Edited by T. P. Wiseman. London: The British Academy, 2002.

Creighton, John. *Britannia: The Creation of a Roman Province*. London and New York: Routledge, 2006.

Croxford, Ben. "Metal Sculpture from Roman Britain: Scraps but Not Always Scrap." Pages 25–46 in *The Afterlife of Greek and Roman Sculpture: Late Antique Responses and Practices.* Edited by Troels M. Kristensen and Lea M. Stirling. Ann Arbor, MI: University of Michigan Press, 2016.

Dark, Ken R. *Britain and the End of the Roman Empire.* Stroud, Gloucestershire: Tempus, 2000.

Davies, John G. *The Secular Use of Church Buildings.* London: SCM Press, 1968.

de la Bédoyère, Guy. *Roman Towns in Britain.* London: B.T. Batsford Ltd/English Heritage, 1992.

Dickenson, Christopher P. "The Agora as Political Centre in the Roman period." Pages 47–60 in *The Agora in the Mediterranean. From Homeric to Roman times. Proceedings of an International Conference Held at Kos 14–17 April 2011.* Edited by Angelikiki Giannikouri. Athens: Υπουργείο Πολιτισμού και Τουρισμού, Αρχαιολογικό Ινστιτούτο Αιγαιακών Σπουδών, 2011.

Dickenson, Christopher P. *On the Agora – Power and Public Space in Hellenistic and Roman Greece.* Groningen, Unpublished PhD thesis, 2012.

Dickenson, Christopher P. *On the Agora – The Evolution of a Public Space in Hellenistic and Roman Greece (c. 323 BC – 267 AD).* Leiden: Brill, 2017a.

Dickenson, Christopher P. "Public Statues as a Strategy of Remembering in Early Imperial Messene." Pages 125–42 in *Strategies of Remembering in Greece under Rome (100 BC – 100 AD), Publications of the Netherlands Institute in Athens VI.* Edited by Tamara M. Dijkstra, Inger N.I. Kuin, Muriel Moser and David Weidgenannt. Leiden: Sidestone Press, 2017b.

Dickenson Christopher P. "The Agora as Setting for Honorific Statues in the Roman Period Greek East." Pages 432–54 in *The Politics of Honour in the Greek Cities of the Roman Empire.* Edited by Onno M. van Nijf and Anna Heller. Leiden: Brill, 2017d.

Dickenson, Christopher P. "The Myth of the Ionian Agora – Combining Archaeological and Historical Sources to Investigate the Enclosure of Greek Public Space." *Hesperia* 88(3) (2018): 557–93.

Eck, Werner. "Basilcae und ihre epigraphischen Texte: Kommunikation nach außen und innen." *Zeitschrift für Papyrologie und Epigraphiek* 206 (2018): 3–19.

Ellis, Peter. *The Roman Baths and Macellum at Wroxeter: Excavations by Graham Webster 1955–85.* London: English Heritage, 2000.

Frere, Sheppard S. "The Forum and Baths at Caistor by Norwich." *Britannia* 2 (1971): 1–26.

Frere, Sheppard. *Verulamium Excavations. Volume I.* London: Society of Antiquaries of London (Distributed by Thames and Hudson), 1972.

Frere, Sheppard. *Verulamium Excavations. Volume II.* London: Society of Antiquaries of London (Distributed by Thames and Hudson), 1983.

Frere, Sheppard. *Britannia: A History of Roman Britain.* London and New York: Routledge & Kegal Paul, 1987.

Fulford, Michael G. "Economic Structures." Pages 309–26 in *A Companion to Roman Britain.* Edited by Malcolm Todd. Oxford: Wiley-Blackwell, 2004.

Fulford, Michael G., ed. *Silchester and the Study of Romano – British Urbanism. Journal of Roman Archaeology Supplementary Series 90.* Portsmouth, RI: Journal of Roman Archaeology, 2012.

Goffman, Erving. *The Presentation of Self in Everyday Life.* London: Penguin, 1956.

Goodchild, Richard G. "The Origins of the Romano-British Forum." *Aniquity* 20 (1946): 70–7.

Grocock, Christopher. "The Wroxeter Macellum: A Foodway in Every Sense." Pages 163–76 in *Food & Markets: Proceedings of the Oxford Symposium on Food and Cookery 2014*. Edited by Mark McWilliams (ed.). London: Prospect Books, 2015.

Hansen, Mogens H. "Reflections on the Number of Citizens Accommodated in the Assembly Place on the Pnyx." Pages 23–33 in *The Pnyx in the History of Athens – Proceedings of an International Colloquium Organized by the Finnish Institute at Athens, 7–9 October 1994*. Edited by Björn Forsén and Greg Stanton. Helsinki: Foundation of the Finnish Institute at Athens, 1996.

Hingley, Richard. *Londinium: A Biography: Roman London from its Origins to the Fifth Century*. London: Bloomsbury Publishing, 2018.

Holleran, Claire. *Shopping in Ancient Rome: The Retail Trade in the Late Republic and the Principate*. Oxford: Oxford University Press, 2012.

Hope, Valerie. "Inscriptions and Identity." Pages 285–302 in *The Oxford Handbook of Roman Britain*. Edited by Martin Millett, Louise Revell and Alison J. Moore. Oxford: Oxford University Press, 2016.

Isserlin, Raphael M.J. "A Spirit of Improvement? Marble and the Culture of Roman Britain." Pages 125–55 in *Cultural Identity in the Roman Empire*. Edited by Ray Laurence and Joanne Berry. London and New York: Routledge, 1998.

Jones, Michael J. "Cities and Urban Life." Pages 162–92 in *A Companion to Roman Britain*. Edited by Malcolm Todd. Oxford: Wiley-Blackwell, 2004.

Jones, R.F. "A False Start? The Roman Urbanization of Western Europe." *World Archaeology* 19 (1987): 47–57.

de Ligt, Luuk. *Fairs and Markets in the Roman Empire: Economic and Social Aspects of Periodic Trade in a Pre-Industrial Society*. Leiden: Brill, 1993.

Laurence, Ray A. Simon Esmonde Cleary and Gareth Sears. *The City in the Roman West, c.250 BC – c. AD 250*. Cambridge: Cambridge University Press, 2011.

Ma, John. *Statues and Cities: Honorific Portraits and Civic Identity in the Hellenistic World*. Oxford: Oxford University Press, 2013.

Mason, David J. *Roman Chester: City of the Eagles*. Stroud: Tempus Publishing Limited, 2001.

Mattingly, David J. *An Imperial Possession: Britain in the Roman Empire, 54 BC – AD 409*. London and New York: Allen Lane, 2006.

Mitchell, Stephen. "Imperial Building in the Eastern Roman Provinces." *Harvard Studies in Classical Philology* 91 (1987): 333–65.

Moore, Tom. "Beyond Iron Age 'towns': Examining Oppida as Examples of Low-Density urbanism." *Oxford Journal of Archaeology* 36(3) (2017): 287–305.

Newsome, David J. "Movement and Fora in Rome (the Late Republic to the First Century CE)." Pages 290–311 in *Rome, Ostia, Pompeii: Movement and Space*. Edited by Ray Laurence and David J. Newsome. Corby: Oxford University Press, 2011.

Niblett, Rosalind. *Verulamium: The Roman city of St. Albans*. Stroud: Tempus Arcadia Pub, 2001.

Perring, Dominic. "Spatial Organisation and Social Change in Roman Towns." Pages 273–94 in *City and Country in the Ancient World*. Edited by John Rich and Andrew Wallace-Hadrill. London: Routledge, 1992.

Perring, Dominic. *The Roman House in Britain*. London and New York: Routledge, 2002.

Philippa-Touchais, Anna, Gilles Touchais, Marcel Piérart, Patrick Marchetti, Maria Marchetti-Lakaki and Yvonne Rizakis. "Rapport sur les travaux de l'École française d'Athènes en 1999 – Argos." *Bulletin de Correspondance Hellénique* 124(2) (2000): 489–98.

Pitts, Martin. "Re-thinking the Southern British Oppida: Networks, Kingdoms and Material Culture." *European Journal of Archaeology* 13(1) (2010): 32–63.

Revell, Louise. "Architecture, Power and Politics: The Forum-Basilica in Roman Britain." Pages 127–51 in *Material Identities*. Edited by Joanna Sofaer. Malden: Blackwell, 2007.

Revell, Louise. *Roman Imperialism and Local Identities*. Cambridge and New York: Cambridge University Press, 2009.

Revell, Louise. "Urban Monumentality in Roman Britain." Pages 767–90 in *The Oxford Handbook of Roman Britain*. Edited by Martin Millett, Louise Revell and Alison J. Moore. Oxford: Oxford University Press, 2016.

Reynolds, J. M. *"Imperial regulations." Pages 252-318 in Aphrodisias in Late Antiquity.* Edited by C. Roueché. London: Society for the Promotion of Roman Studies, 1989.

Richard, Julian. "Macellum/μάκελλον: 'Roman' food markets in Asia Minor and the Levant." *Journal of Roman Archaeology* 27 (2014): 255–74.

Richardson, Katherine M. "Report on Excavations at Verulamium: Insula XVII, 1938." *Archaeologia* 90 (1944): 81–126.

Rogers, Adam. *Late Roman Towns in Britain: Rethinking Change and Decline.* New York: Cambridge University Press, 2011.

Rogers, Adam. "The Development of Towns." Pages 741–66 in *The Oxford Handbook of Roman Britain*. Edited by Martin Millett, Louise Revell and Alison J. Moore. Oxford: Oxford University Press, 2016.

Scherrer, Peter. *Ephesus: the New Guide.* Istanbul: Österreichisches Archäologisches Institut and Efes Müzesi Selçuk, 2000.

Smith, M.E. and J. Lobo. "Cities Through the Ages: One Thing or Many?" *Frontiers in Digital Humanities* 6 (2019). Doi: 10.3389/fdigh.2019.00012

Smith, Roland R.R. "The Imperial Reliefs from the Sebasteion at Aphrodisias." *Journal of Roman Studies* 77 (1987): 88–138.

Stinson, Philip. "The Civil Basilica of Aphrodisias: Urban Context, Design and Significance." Pages 107–26 in *Aphrodisias Papers 4: New Research on the City and its Monuments. JRA Supplementary Series 70.* Edited by Christopher Ratté and Roland R. R. Smith. Portsmouth, NH: *Journal of Roman Archaeology*, 2008.

Wacher, John S. "Excavations at Cirencester." *Antiquities Journal* 41 (1962): 1–12.

Wacher, John S. *The Towns of Roman Britain. Second Edition.* London: Batsford, 1995.

Wallace, Lacey. *The Origin of Roman London.* Cambridge: Cambridge University Press, 2015.

Ward-Perkins, John B. "From Republic to Empire: Reflections on the Early Imperial Provincial Architecture of the Roman West." *Journal of Roman Studies* 60 (1970): 1–19.

Warf, Barney and Santa Arias, eds. *The Spatial Turn: Interdisciplinary Perspectives.* London: Routledge, 2009.

Weinberg, Saul S. *The Southeast Building, the Twin Basilicas and the Mosaic House.* Corinth: Results of Excavations Conducted by the American School of Classical Studies at Athens 1.5. Princeton: American School of Classical Studies, 1960.

Wilson, Andrew. "Indicators for Roman Economic Growth: A Response to Walter Scheidel." *Journal of Roman Archaeology* 22 (2009): 71–82.

Woolf, G. "Rethinking the Oppida." *Oxford Journal of Archaeology* 12(2) (1993): 223–34.

# 8    The Roman colony of *Sena Gallica*

## Urban space and economic activities

*Giuseppe Lepore and Michele Silani*

### Before the colony: a commercial *emporium*?

Although it was an important stronghold on the Adriatic coast at the beginning of the third century BCE, *Sena Gallica* should certainly not be defined solely as a military fortress within the context of Rome's policy of expansionism in the Italian peninsula. Its strategic position definitely also depended on commercial interests stimulated by the desire for integration with the political and economical *élites* of central Italy.[1] A new coastal landing, which together with Ravenna and in probable partnership with Ancona, maintaining a position of allied state,[2] served as a link with the *Veneti* and their landing in *Altinum*. The known *askòs* fragment with the *Galicos colonos* stamp coming from *Spina*, which seems to indicate the presence of a workshop that began to operate for the colonists of the *ager Gallicus* immediately after 232 BCE, could represent the sign of the settlement's prior condition, that is, of commercial relations that were already active at the end of the fourth century BCE.[3]

The choice of *Sena Gallica*'s foundation site itself can be better understood if considered in relation to land travel routes, predating the creation of the backbone of the via Flaminia (220 BCE), which would *de facto* cut off the colony of *Sena Gallica* already at the end of the third century BCE and was justified in relation to the new bridgehead of the Latin colony of *Ariminum*, established in 268 BCE. Between these routes, the via Amerina could have had particular importance; constructed from Rome between 329 and 312 BCE, and originally ending at *Ameria*, it was later prolonged until *Perusia* during the first decades of the third century BCE, in connection to Marius Curius Dentatus' conquest of the *ager Gallicus* in 284 BCE.[4] From here, thanks to a *diverticulum* to *Iguvium*, through the Pass of Scheggia and the basin of *Sentinum*, it would have reached the maritime colony of *Sena Gallica* (Figure 8.1).[5]

This trans-Apennine route to the Adriatic coast was probably already active during a previous age, as a connection to pre-Roman *Sena*. This pre-Roman *Sena* is now better known, thanks to the recent archaeological investigations. It was a genuine settlement, located very close to the river Misa's last bend, characterized by sub-rectangular-shaped housing structures, with trellis elevations on hollow clay and gravel wooden beam foundations, paved with

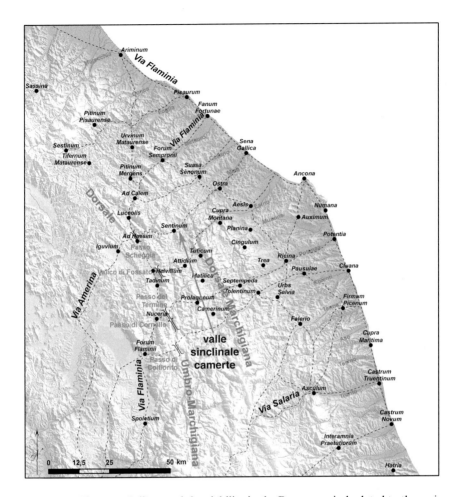

*Figure 8.1* The *ager Gallicus* and the viability in the Roman period related to the main morpho-structural units of the Umbrian-Marche Apennines (elaboration M. Silani).

pebbles; a technique typical of all swampy areas and well-attested in Padanian centres such as *Adria* and *Spina*.[6] Here the presence of a large number of fragments of Piceni pottery, along with diagnostic materials such as a few fragments of *skyphoi* with red figures, Attic pottery, high-Adriatic vases and leucitite grindstones from Lazio, allowed us to identify the settlement's three main life stages. The first, of proper Picene tradition, dates to the fifth century BCE (Piceno V), with the creation of the first core settlement, the second and third date to fourth century BCE (Piceno VI) and are characterized by more ethnic variety and a few structural changes.[7] Pre-Roman *Sena*, which already defines itself as a settlement between the fifth and fourth centuries BCE, perhaps soon acquired the characteristics of an *emporium*, where a new class in control of commercial and trade routes probably gained more and more influence within society, adapting to a new socio-economic reality probably created by the arrival of external communities such as the Senone Gauls or by the presence of Syracusans in the nearby city of *Ankon* (Ancona; Figure 8.2).[8]

## The colony: economy of living

Accordingly, the Roman colony was not founded *ex-nihilo* but in a place that had been settled at least since the fifth century BCE. The process of colonization not only brought vast political and institutional change but also introduced a technological revolution. The arrival of new peoples from the Tyrrhenian area and *Latium*, at first as *mercatores* and then as real colonists, is visible in the signs of new forms of dwellings, which are defined by different building techniques.[9] A tangible sign of such a revolution is the presence of *domus* characterized by the *fauces-atrium-tablinum* system, based on the Etrusco-Italic model, which were inserted into the urban network design, which was now extended to the whole floodplain (Figure 8.3).[10]

This technological revolution was only made possible, thanks to the specialized technical knowledge and expertise of colonists from *Latium*. Materials and building techniques for foundations were changed and adapted to the damp and marshy environment present in the floodplain of Senigallia so that they could support a higher structural weight. Clay brick walls were now built on a foundation of *c.* 50/60 cm of pebbles and stone blocks (sandstone), and thanks to the superimposition of 8–10 rows of ridged tiles lying on their flat side, the socket of which is filled with pieces of bricks sunk into a clay- and gravel-based mortar.[11]

A new sensitivity, which was artistic, emerges from the creation of pavements. A building technique was adopted, which consists in the realization of, first, a layer of small terracotta fragments (amphora and tiles) necessary in order to achieve isolation from the soil's humidity, then a layer of gravel or brick fragments finely chopped and lastly a layer of concrete conglomerate. Such stratification, which seems to respect Vitruvian prescriptions, is defined by a variable thickness of 20–30 cm and 5–10 cm, which is for the surfacing layer (*pavimentum*). The basic binder is lime, to which brick fragments of many colours were added (red–orange–yellow) or, in rare cases, dark-coloured shards or lithic fragments. The most common insertions are lithic (white limestone or black stone) of variable sizes. In the examples of the highest quality, the decoration is obtained through the insertion of white pieces into a nucleus of cement. The final result is a pavement with the typical pink–orange tone defined by the most widespread decorative motifs of the Republican age (Figure 8.4).[12]

The walls of the dwellings were now decorated with paintings in the so-called "first Pompeian style", not only displaying a new artistic sensitivity but also indicating the presence of specialists who could carry out the necessary plaster

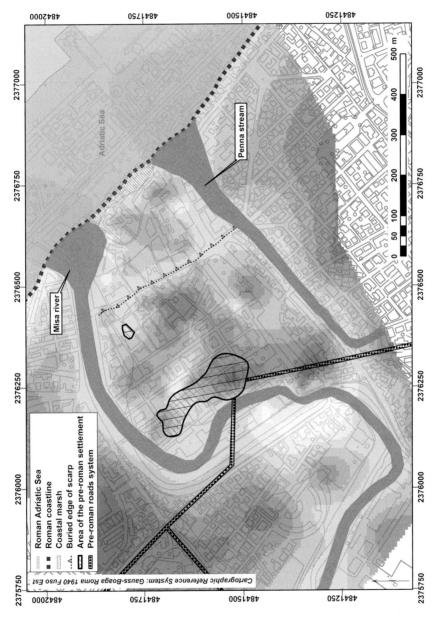

*Figure 8.2* The pre-Roman settlement: reconstructive hypothesis (elaboration M. Silani).

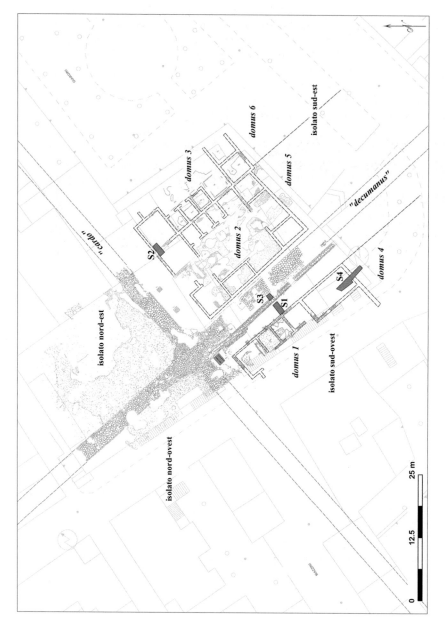

*Figure 8.3  Sena Gallica: domus* characterized by the Etrusco-Italic model, inserted into the urban system's design (area of Teatro "La Fenice") (elaboration M. Silani).

*Figure 8.4 Sena Gallica.* Pavement with the typical decorative motifs of the republican age (area of Teatro "La Fenice") (photo by M. Silani).

preparations (*tectores*) and create fresco painting (*pictores*).[13] Pavements and pictorial decorations both imply the use of lime, and, therefore, the techno-logical necessity of building kilns to bake limestone and maybe for quenching as well as the use of specific containers for transportation. These new forms of living also became a social indicator, highlighting the presence of a new ruling class, fully aligned with the dictates of the Hellenistic form of *luxuria*.[14]

## The colony: economy of building

All of the aforementioned elements suggest the organization and manage-ment of construction sites of a certain magnitude, the traces of which are not clearly visible but whose presence can be implied from the developments just described. The presence of specialists for every single activity is an indirect indication of the process of Romanization. The use of tiles in wall foundations and in the preparation of pavements adds to the presence of collapsed layers of bricks and tiles, which prove the use of such materials for coverings. Despite not having found wooden materials within the collapsed layers, it is obviously possible to hypothesize the creation of trusses for the support of roofs in important rooms such as Tuscan atriums with impluviums. The con-struction of such support systems for roofs necessarily implies the presence of *lignarii* or *intestinarii* for the processing of wood, as shown by the inscription of the *materiarius Lucius Pulpius Buccio* (C.I.L. XI 6212) in the first century BCE.[15] It is clear that wood processing is closely related to the exploitation of woodlands on the territory and the management of its transportation to the urban area. Parallel to this, the use of consistent amounts of brick material must necessarily imply the presence of kilns in the suburban areas of the city or in the territory.[16]

One illustration of the required degree of specialization during the initial phases of creation of the colony's structures are the remains of two wells, dated to the time of the colony's foundation, and built using superimposed big terracotta rings (diameter 70 cm, height 60 cm and width 4 cm; Figure 8.5).[17]

It is a kind of technology that we already see in the late-archaic phases of the temple of *Jupiter Capitolinus* in Rome, halfway through the sixth century BCE, and it was, thus, clearly derived from Latial models.[18] The overall dimensions of such rings suggest that they were locally produced, due to the severe difficulties that their transportation would have entailed. Accordingly, the importance of water management, storage and distribution ever since the very first life stages of the colony is clear. This aspect would face technological changes towards the middle of the first century BCE, when the building of filtering wells is documented, i.e. with the lining made of amphora necks for the filtering of waters in the soil within the cistern-well.[19]

The management of waters would, in all likelihood between the end of the first century BCE and the Augustan age, become an increasingly significant aspect of public life in the colony of *Sena Gallica*. A higher demand for water led to the creation of a city aqueduct, the traces of which are archaeologically

*Figure 8.5 Sena Gallica.* Well built using superimposed big terracotta rings (via Cavour, photo by M. Silani).

documented by the presence of a public fountain and the relative system of adduction with lead fistulas.[20] The fountain's tank, significantly placed at the crossing between two city axes, is built with tiny brick cubes intentionally cut into a square shape and carefully put into place. The brick cube technique comes from a more ancient tradition and is seen in Senigallia in second century BCE contexts and in the neighbouring colony of *Ariminum* in the third century BCE.[21]

Alongside the residential needs of the new colonists, there are clear archaeological traces of production activities carried out in rustic buildings in the peripheral parts of the urban area. They consist of a *torcular* base and *dolia defossa*, for the pressing and storage of their various products, most likely grapes or olives, another consequence of Romanization. Palaeo-carpological analysis reveals findings mostly attributable to farmed species, in particular cereals, legumes and vines.[22]

Rustic buildings are located next to the city walls, which constituted the most significant intervention at the time of the colony's foundation. The traces of the outer wall's spoliation have been identified in correspondence with the south-western area of the floodplain and also with the confluence of the river Misa and the smaller so-called Penna stream, which was probably still active in Roman times. Thanks to the geo-archaeological reconstruction of the palaeosoil in Roman times, it was possible to hypothesize the extension and perimeter of the outer walls, which adapt to the original morphology, taking advantage of the protection provided by the waterways Misa and Penna.[23] A significant intervention, unequivocally dated to the moment of the colony's foundation, was documented by the stratigraphic sequence from the dig in via Baroccio. Here a *sub divo* sanctuary clearly already frequented by the Romans since the end of the fourth century BCE was monumentalized and modified precisely in relation to the construction of the urban walls.[24] The finding of a few fragmented yellow sandstone blocks, i.e. calcarenite, in the spoliation pit, and the analysis of the reuse of squared blocks made of the same material visible in medieval buildings and mostly inside the Rovere Renaissance walls, make it possible to hypothesize with some certainty the elevation of the walls, which must have been defined by an embankment that was very clearly visible in the excavation section.[25]

In addition to the necessary effort involved in their construction, the technical expertise and skill needed to put those blocks in place must not be forgotten, as this task was probably carried out with the aid of machines for lifting and traction. At the same time, the use of such blocks is an indirect evidence of the nearby presence of stone quarries. In the case of *Sena Gallica*, the calcarenite quarry must have been located a few kilometres to the south-east of the city. In this regard, a plausible hypothesis is that it was located in the area nowadays known as San Gaudenzio, where *gessaie* have been documented since the nineteenth century, and indeed chalk quarries were a term used to describe yellow calcarenite during that time.[26] Regardless of the precise location of the extraction quarry, the presence of finely squared blocks to be put in place in the walls indirectly proves the technical skills related to both extraction and transportation of material. For the transportation of the blocks, use could have been made of the terminal part of the river Misa, with hauling systems and *naves caudicariae*, that is, medium-sized boats fit to be towed by both oxen and men. The use of sandstone as construction material, therefore, throws an interesting light on the initial occupational stages of the colony. The planning of the city grid and its relative zoning begins with the definition of the perimeter. Simultaneously, the external areas of the city, like the *necropoleis*, are defined. Thus, it is perhaps no coincidence that the only necropolis known for the colony of *Sena* from excavations at the beginning of the nineteenth century is characterized by "die-shaped" funerary monuments created from parallelepiped blocks of sandstone.[27]

Urban planning at the time of the colony's founding took place through the creation of the city's road axes throughout the third century BCE. The excavation of a crossroads and the reconstruction of the form of the original housing lot allowed the disposition of the colony's housing plots to be hypothesized (Figure 8.6).[28]

Medium- and small-sized flagstones were used in the construction of roads, on top of a foundation made of pressed clay and gravel. The presence of flagstones is a clear indicator of the town's capacity for the transport and import of these materials, probably from the inland Apennine area of Marche.[29] Ongoing research will determine their origin with more precision.

Recent investigations have also proved how in response to hydraulic issues, such as the waterlogging of depressed areas, the actual remediation systems were put in place in order to elevate the walking surface. Such remediation works imply a considerable technical knowledge especially if made on a large scale, as is shown by excavations in the archaeological area "La Fenice". It was possible to prove how, in this area within the urban zone, an initial road paving, probably put in place soon after the colony's foundation, was later restored and raised in height over a powerful remediation layer between the second and first centuries BCE. Such public intervention was also observed in private housing, where we see an elevation of the original pavements inside the *domus* facing the street.[30] This planning and zoning of the city grid, thus, respect some pre-existing structures and insert them into the road system, as in the case of the sanctuary of via Baroccio. Here the presence of a *sub divo* fully Roman sanctuary, characterized by the presence of epigraph-free sandstone altars and simple offerings directly laid on the ground (following the model of *Lucus Pisaurensis*[31]), is monumentalized with two *sacella* that respect the city grid's orientation. The altars and *sacella* represent the heart of the sanctuary, with the areas for depositions and offerings surrounding it since the first "open-sky" phase. The discovery of black gloss pottery in association with locally produced kitchenware, albeit deriving from Latial models, and the discovery of a cooking ring within the area of the sanctuary, together with archaeometric analysis of ceramics, demonstrate the presence of more production structures: kilns for pottery located on a strategic site

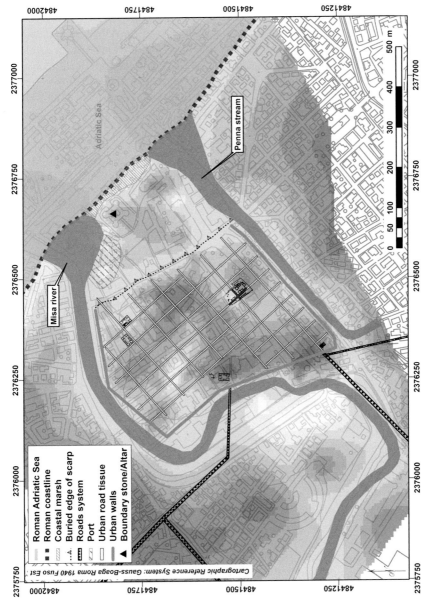

*Figure 8.6 Sena Gallica.* Hypothetical reconstruction of urban planning at the moment of the colony's deduction (elaboration M. Silani).

near the watercourse, clay pits and a higher ground location compared to the rest of the floodplain's topography. A fragment of a Rhodian amphora was recovered from the urban area, alongside locally produced materials. The fragment is defined by the presence of a circular stamp or cartouche, inside of which the radiant head of Helios and the epigraph Ευφράνορος are visible, demonstrating that *Sena Gallica* was already part of the commercial networks that developed through the Adriatic into the Mediterranean soon after the foundation of the colony. As a matter of fact such stamps were recovered not only in Rhodes but also in Athens, Lindos and Delos.[32] This commercial network remained active throughout the second century BCE as well, as proven by the activity of the Rhodian manufacturer *Hephaistion*, whose name can be seen on the Rhodian amphora stamp.[33] Commercial relations during the Imperial age appear less documented, but this might be due to an "archaeological bias": trade is in fact well-attested for the duration of the Middle Ages[34], and, therefore, we can credibly imagine some continuity of Senigallia in the use of port facilities and trade route networks.

## The *ager*: economy of the territory

From the very first stages of occupation, the socio-economic system connected to the foundation of the colony also applies to its *ager*. The colony's territory is delimited by the creation of a few benchmarks at the time of the foundation which, in the form of *vici* and *pagi*, demonstrate the presence of colonists. The *ager Senogalliensis* must have covered a great extent since the first phases, comprising the estuary areas of three rivers, Cesano, Misa and Esino, following the territory's morphology on the hills and incorporating the change in direction of river courses in the middle valley areas.

Aside from topographical analysis, the reconstruction of its extent is based on the equal orientation of newly installed agricultural divisions.[35] Between the third and second centuries BCE, we see the territory progressively taken into possession by way of installing traditional Roman agricultural divisions, according to the systems of *limitatio* and *centuriatio*, and by the construction of small farms and rustic villas. This new agricultural landscape is progressively structured and at the end of the first century BCE is even subject to still further divisions and distributions following triumviral law.[36] The presence of *agrimensores* with their theoretical–practical abilities for the creation of agricultural divisions must have been fundamental ever since the first occupational phase. The introduced management of space necessarily included unassigned areas, the so-called *subseciva,* mostly close to river courses, and also uncultivated areas for the communal exploitation of woodlands. This system of land management promoted economic production and the smooth agricultural administration of the territory.

Recent research carried out in the area of Madonna del Piano (Corinaldo), on the western margin of the colony's territory, allows the hypothesis of the existence of a *pagus* there, despite the absence of direct epigraphic evidence (Figure 8.7).[37]

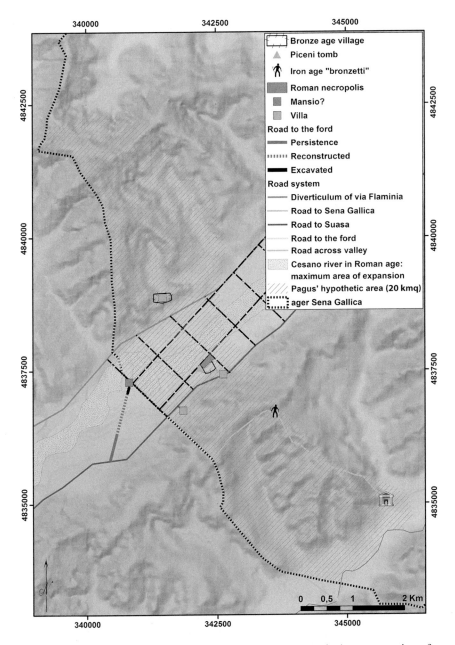

*Figure 8.7* Area of Madonna del Piano (Corinaldo): hypothetical reconstruction of a *pagus* in the *ager Senogalliensis* (elaboration M. Silani).

The presence of an important ford on the river Cesano within the same district and connected to the main valley traffic routes, of a large *villa rustica*, of an extensive cemetery area, of a series of kilns for the production of bricks, and of the epigraphic evidence for a shrine, all this corroborates such a hypothesis, even in the absence of a definite nucleus attributable to a *vicus*.

The discovery of containers for foodstuffs and Graeco-Italic amphorae, dated to the middle of the third century BCE, documents the production and commerce of either wine or olive oil. Among these, a fragment of a *dolium* from the area of S. Isidoro, neighbouring Madonna del Piano, has a 2-cm diameter stamp on the external margin of the rim. This rose-shaped stamp with eight stylized petals and eight more intercalary ones[38] seems iconographically linked to the ones found inside black gloss productions such as those from the *atelier des petites estampilles*, with comparisons in neighbouring *Aesis*, the seat of a black gloss pottery workshop dated to the first half of the third century BCE.[39] Our *dolium* specimen can, therefore, possibly at least be traced back to a third-century BCE dating.

The presence of the aforementioned containers, thus, documents *villae rusticae* for agricultural production in the area as early as the third century BCE. Recent archaeological research has allowed us to stratigraphically investigate the large villa located on the river ford. The complex is defined by the presence of secondary rooms that serve as storage or service areas and of a courtyard area with a large brick tank covered in good quality hydraulic mortar (Figure 8.8).

*Figure 8.8* Area of Madonna del Piano (Corinaldo): the large villa located on the river ford. The complex is defined by a courtyard area with a large brick tank (photo by M. Silani).

A constructed channel allowed water collection and management, and the localization of an outflow system, realized through the insertion of an amphora neck into the wall, avoided potential hydraulic issues. The whole complex can in this monumental phase be dated back to the second century BCE, while the phase of the greatest development starts from the first century BCE.

Traces of the technical abilities necessary for the storage and distribution of waters are also present in the territory. The management of water must have been an important sector as it is connected to flood terraces surrounding the river course, which were regularly subject to floods. The use of water is directly connected to the presence of kilns for the production of bricks, tiles and common pottery; and in the area of Madonna del Piano, seven such complexes of various sizes are documented along the main road system on the right side of the valley and in correspondence with the ford on the River Cesano.[40] The kilns with vertical air flow are proof of a large-scale production phase dated to the first and second centuries CE and appear as part of a genuine industrial quarter. The finding of a few stamps in relation to the *Aufidii gens*, an important senatorial *gens* originating from Pesaro, and the evidence of a freedman connected to them, may imply the presence of an *officinator* and a *figlina* property of the *Aufidii*, a point of reference in the management of the economic hub.[41] This suggests the existence of commercial networks making use of inland and river routes based on direct contact between the territory of the colony of *Sena Gallica* and that of *Pisaurum*.[42]

### Concluding remarks

The foundation of a colony is a complex operation: it is not just an urban, juridical, military or political phenomenon, but a combination of all the above. In addition to this, there is also the economic factor, which must have played a major role, as is visible in the case of *Sena Gallica*. As studies concerning the *apoikiai* from *Magna Graecia* and Sicily have shown for some time, one of the keys to the interpretation of the whole ancient colonial phenomenon, apart from chronological issues, is the connection that developed between the new city and its territory.[43] It is utterly clear that even in the Roman world they are two aspects of a single process: the creation of a *colonia* cannot be disconnected from the division and structuring of the pertaining *ager*. The integrated analysis of these two components allows us to reconstruct not only an urban picture but also a mostly economic one. The definition of a well-structured urban landscape represents the mark of a new *civitas*, a community of citizens, ready to meet the challenge of a new beginning inside a hostile territory (or one in the process of being "pacified") and, therefore, eager to improve their economic and social conditions.

The same military role which *Sena* must certainly have assumed for coastal defence will, therefore, have been devoted during an initial phase to consolidation and taking full possession of the territory, including in an economic sense.[44] Even if an Adriatic policy had not been well defined during the first years of the third century BCE, there was certainly no lack of existing commercial relations between the two Adriatic shores, relations involving Roman citizens, Latin allies and simple *foederati*.[45] Among the causes of the war that triggered the dissolution of the 302 BCE pact between Rome and Taranto and the taking of the city itself in 272 BCE is probably also Rome's desire to strengthen its territories, now seamlessly extending to the *Mare Superum*, and consequently to be able to reach them via the sea without the precluded passage of the Strait of Otranto.[46] The picture emerging from the analysis of data referable to the first years of the colony is that of a city conceived on a vast scale, in order to occupy all the available space within the chosen site or about 18 hectares if our hypothesis is correct. Right after the first preparations during the third century BCE, the settlement experienced a major urban and economic stimulus in the course of the second century BCE.[47] Unfortunately we do not know anything yet of the two main social and economic centres of the urban area of the colony, the forum with its monumental area and the port, heart of the life and survival of the city of Senigallia throughout its entire history; these nuclei shall be the objectives of our future research.[48]

## Notes

1  Our vision of the colonial phenomenon has been too uniform and standardized for far too long, reduced as it was to a bipartition (colonies according to Roman law/Latin law) that does not do credit to the complexity of the policy implemented by Rome during the most ancient phases of the Republic (see the legal texts in: *Expropriations et confiscations en Italie et dans les provinces: la colonisation sous la République et l'Empire*, published in MEFRA 127-2, 2015). Only recently, the archaeological study of single territories has finally shed some light on the great articulation and variability of the choices adopted, which is always linked to a common ideology of conquest (Torelli, 1988). The research activities on the colony of *Sena Gallica* also fall within this area of study, and more generically speaking, research on the *ager Gallicus* at the time of the conquest. The matter of the "double date" of the first Roman law colony on the Adriatic, mentioned more than once in previous studies (for a summary, see Lepore, 2014), can, therefore, be the indicator of a colonial phenomenon that proceeded in a smart way (and maybe also a cynical way), with moments of acceleration and phases of stasis, using every "available weapon" (for a summary of the first phases of the Roman colonization of the *ager Gallicus*, see Silani 2017: 3–72; Vermeulen 2017).
2  Malnati and Manzelli, 2015: 42–45.
3  Cornelio Cassai, 2015: 74.
4  Sisani, 2007: 117–121.
5  Silani, 2017: 70.
6  New data concerning the indigenous settlement preceding the Roman colony of *Sena* mainly come from the excavation in via Cavallotti. A recent revision of the stratigraphic context was submitted during the *Workshop Internazionale Piceniadi. L'archeologia del Piceno preromano*, Ancona 28–29 September 2018 (see Gaucci and Lepore, in press). Concerning the construction technique employed for the

building in via Cavallotti, a possible comparison also comes from the sixth century BCE agricultural structure uncovered at Moscosi of Cingoli.

7   Gaucci and Lepore, in press.

8   Silani, 2014: 403–407.

9   The presence of "fully Roman" materials already at the beginning of the third century BCE, not only at *Sena Gallica* but also elsewhere in the territory of the *ager Gallicus*, indicates the relocation of the first components from *Latium* and can be regarded as the starting point for the process of colonization and "Romanization" or "auto-Romanization". After a first frequentation possibly by *mercatores* or small groups of colonists starting from the beginning of the fourth century BCE, documented in the first expressions of religious sites (like at *Sena Gallica*), a free immigration in the form of *occupatio* followed, not regulated by the Roman state (cf. Bandelli, 2005; Silani, 2017: 253–257). A phase of Roman pre-colonization in the *ager Gallicus* already in the first half of the third century BCE is archaeologically documented by the site of Cattolica (Mazzeo Saracino, 2013: 357–389; Silani, 2017: 30–33).

10  Lepore *et al.*, 2014b: 1–32. The city of *Sena Gallica*'s best known living environment is the archaeological area of the Theatre "la Fenice", where the whole block with its relative *domus* was rebuilt. Even in the case of the *domus* of *Sena Gallica*, it is possible that *tabernae* for trading activities were located at the sides of the *fauces* at the house entrance. On this subject, see M. Flohr in this volume (Chapter 3).

11  Such a building technique is already documented for the territory in the third century BCE, in the *conciliabulum* of *Suasa* (Zaccaria, 2010a: 180; Zaccaria, 2010b).

12  Two types of decoration are attested in the colony of *Sena*: the rhombuses' grid and the dotted irregular pattern (for a detailed summary on the flooring of *Sena Gallica*, see Silani, 2018: 141–150). The closest comparison can be found in the *domus* 7 of *Fregellae* dated back to the first quarter of the second century BCE (Coarelli, 1995: 19–20).

13  Lepore *et al.*, 2014b: 1–32.

14  Marcattili, 2011: 415–424.

15  A *libertus* who was also a woodworker. The *gens Pupia* is mentioned in a second inscription (C.I.L. XI 6211) from Senigallia dated to the first century BCE (Gasperini, 2005: 129–138). Of major interest is the funerary epigraph pertaining to a tomb destined to house three *liberti* of the *gens Pupia* dated between the end of the second century BCE and the period of Sulla (Marengo, 1982: 131–135) and coming from the territory of the *ager Senagalliensis* (for the extension of the total area of the colony of *Sena Gallica*, see Lepore *et al.*, 2014a: 21–69, and Lepore and Silani, in press).

16  See *infra*.

17  The two wells were, respectively, found in the excavation sites of via Cavallotti and of via Cavour.

18  Wells of this kind were already widespread in pre-Roman times but of different sizes (see Curina *et al.*, 2010: 21–23; 55–58). For the temple of *Jupiter Capitolinus*, see Cifani, 2008: 87.

19  It is a construction functional to the collection of water of various provenance, since the system is able to channel, other than the water from the well itself, upwelling or external waters using the cavity located between the soil and the frame itself: the amphorae become a kind of "funnel" to channel such influxes into the reservoir. This type can be dated back to the mid-Republican Age, with

examples from the Marche and Emilia-Romagna regions; in particular, see the well discovered at Palazzo Massani in *Ariminum* (Ortalli, 2001). In general, regarding this subject cf. Vigoni, 2011: 19–52 and Antico Gallina, 1996: 85–86.

20  Salvini, 2003.
21  Attributable to the category of clay brick pavements, evidence of floorings made of small earthenware cubes at *Sena Gallica*, all from more or less recent excavations consist of a total of five specimens (Silani, 2018: 141–150). With regard to Rimini, see Ortalli and Ravara Montebelli, 2003. Such typology is largely widespread in all of Cisalpine Gaul.
22  Lepore *et al.*, 2012: 1–19.
23  Silani *et al.*, 2016.
24  Belfiori, 2016a: 181–191.
25  During the dig, a spoliation pit was located, 12.5 m long and 2.60 m wide, attributable with certainty to the removal of a big structure, like the colony's city walls (Silani 2017: 98–100). The progressive construction of the city walls was then paralleled by the realization of an embankment functional for both construction and defensive purposes, such as found, for example, in the city walls of the slightly posterior Latin colony of *Ariminum* (Ortalli, 2007). A similar embankment was recently found also in relation to the walls of *Potentia* (Vermeulen *et al.*, 2011: 192–193).
26  A systematic survey of yellow sandstone blocks reused in various buildings of the city of Senigallia is being carried out. It is quite possible that quarries of this kind of sandstone, easily recognizable due to its amber-like colour, consistence and lightness (a very important property, especially during the transportation phase), could be located in a suburban site, even along the path which, coming from S. Angelo, connected *Aesis* with *Sena*.
27  The colonists relocated to *Sena* were registered into the *Pollia* tribe, as shown by the late-Republican epigraph on the parallelepiped sandstone block pertaining to a die-shaped funerary monument, on which the personal details of the defunct are displayed: *M(arcus) Asullius/L(uci) f(ilius), Pol(lia tribu)* (Paci, 1982).
28  The elongated rectangular-like shape of 35 × 70 m, hypothesized for *Sena Gallica*'s block (Silani, 2017: 130–137), could be a clue to the antiquity of the urban plan of the colony itself. It well suits a foundation date towards the beginning of the third century BCE, since, as previously noted, already at the beginning of the second century BCE a process of rationalization and standardization of urban planning began, which after the Social War, and in particular during the Augustan age, would lead to a preference for the square module of 2 *actus* (Sommella, 2002: 799–803).
29  Concerning the importance of roads as economic factors and spaces, see C. Corsi in this volume (Chapter 13).
30  Ulterior interventions of reclamation within the urban area, regarding both public and private sectors, were found in the sites of via Gherardi and Piazza Garibaldi. For the latter see Belfiori, 2016b.
31  Belfiori, 2017.
32  Stefanini, 1994–1995.
33  Branchesi, 2011: 81–83. For an update of epigraphic documents concerning trade relations see Lepore *et al.*, 2015: 273–295.
34  Cirelli *et al.*, 2016.
35  Lepore and Silani, in press; Silani, 2017: 138–152.

36  *Lib. col.*, II, 258, 10–12 (Lach.).
37  Lepore *et al.*, 2013: 101–125.
38  Lepore *et al.*, 2013: 101–125.
39  Brecciaroli Taborelli, 1998; still in the Esino river valley, see the recent surveys carried out on the site of Angeli di Mergo, Ciuccarelli, 2008.
40  Lepore, 2010: 17–86.
41  Lepore, 2010: 17–86.
42  Lepore *et al.*, 2013: 101–125.
43  For a summary concerning the colonial worlds of *Magna Graecia* and Sicily, please refer to the volumes *Confini e frontiera nella grecità d'Occidente* 1999 and *Problemi della chora coloniale* 2001; see also Leone, 2011 and Osanna, 2015. In the structuring of the colonial landscapes of *Magna Graecia* and Sicily, sanctuaries scattered all over the area pertaining to each *apoikia* played a fundamental role: these locations, beyond the function of territorial cornerstones, must have constituted the meeting and trading points between indigenous communities and the newly arrived. In this regard, see Stek, 2009.
44  Jaia, 2013: 475–489.
45  Bandelli, 2003: 218.
46  It can be assumed, however, that the interests of Rome were not only commercial but also political, as suggested by the diplomatic relations between the Senate and an embassy from *Apollonia* in 230 BCE, which is probably when the first contacts with the Greek colony of *Lissa* were established, following their request for help against Illyrian pirates in 230 BCE and the subsequent Roman intervention. Within this wider picture of Rome's Adriatic policy, even the maritime colonies on the Adriatic coast must have played a major role, such as the alliances established with cities along the coast south of the delta of the river Po, like Ancona and certainly from 268 BCE the foundation of the Latin colony of *Ariminum* (Bertrand 2012: 87–102).
47  Silani 2017: 137–138. For an overall picture of the development of urban centres in the *ager Gallicus* and *Picenum*, see most recently Vermeulen 2017 and his contribution in this volume (Chapter 2).
48  At the current state of research and according to the few data in our possession, the most likely locale of the port is on the mouth of river Misa. On the subject of river ports, see the contributions by S. Malmberg and P. Basso in this volume (Chapters 15 and 9).

# References

AA.VV., "Confini e frontiera nella grecità d'Occidente", Atti del trentasettesimo Convegno di studi sulla Magna Grecia, Taranto 3–6 ottobre 1997, Taranto: Istituto per la Storia e l'Archeologia della Magna Grecia 1999.

AA.VV., "Problemi della chora coloniale dall'Occidente al Mar Nero", Atti del XXXX Convegno di Studi sulla Magna Grecia, Taranto, 29 settembre – 3 ottobre 2000, Taranto: Istituto per la Storia e l'Archeologia della Magna Grecia 2001.

Antico Gallina, Mariavittoria. "Valutazioni tecniche sulla cosiddetta funzione drenante dei depositi di anfore." Pages 67–112 in *Acque interne. Uso e gestione di una risorsa*. Edited by Mariavittoria Antico Gallina, Milano: ET Edizioni, 1996.

Bandelli, Gino. "Dallo spartiacque appenninico all'«altra sponda»: Roma e l'Adriatico tra il IV e il II sec. a.C." Pages 215–225 in *L'Archeologia dell'Adriatico dalla Preistoria al Medioevo, Atti del Convegno Internazionale, Ravenna, 7–9- giugno 2001*. Edited by Fiamma Lenzi, Firenze: All'Insegna del Giglio, 2003.

Bandelli, Gino. "La conquista dell'*ager Gallicus* e il problema della colonia di *Aesis*." *AquilNost* 76 (2005): 15–54.

Belfiori, Francesco. "Santuari centro italici e romanizzazione: valenze itinerarie e processi acculturativi." Pages 181–191 in *Santuari mediterranei tra oriente e occidente. Interazioni e contatti culturali*, Atti del Convegno 18–22 giugno 2014. Edited by Alfonsina Russo Tagliente and Francesca Guarnieri, Roma: Scienze e Lettere S.r.l., 2016a.

Belfiori, Francesco. "Archeologia urbana a Senigallia IV. I riti del costruire di *Sena Gallica*." *The Journal of Fasti on Line* 369 (2016b): 1–19.

Belfiori, Francesco. *«Lucum conlucare Romano more». Archeologia e religione del "lucus" Pisaurensis*. Bologna: Bononia University Press, 2017.

Bertrand, Audrey. "Conquête, appropriation, et gestion d'un territoire : le cas de colonies républicaines." Pages 87–102 in *Gérer les territoires, les patrimoines et les crises*, Actes du Colloque, Clermont-Ferrand, 20–22 octobre 2011. Edited by Mireille Cébeillac, Clara Berrendonner and Laurent Lamoine, Clermont-Ferrand: Presses universitaires Blaise-Pascal, 2012.

Branchesi, Fabiola. "Instrumentum domesticum inscriptum da *Sena Gallica*." *Picus* XXXI (2011): 69–90.

Brecciaroli Taborelli, Luisa. "Jesi (An). L'officina ceramica di *Aesis* (III sec. a.C.–I sec. d.C.)." *Nsc* 1996–1997 (1998): 5–25.

Cifani, Gabriele. *Architettura romana arcaica: edilizia e società tra monarchia e repubblica*. Roma: L'Erma di Bretschneider, 2008.

Cirelli, Enrico, Lepore, Giuseppe, Silani, Michele. "La tavola di duchi, vescovi e mercanti a Senigallia". Pages 132–137 in *In & Around. Ceramiche e comunità*, Secondo convegno tematico dell'AIECM3–Faenza, Museo internazionale delle Ceramiche 17–19 aprile 2015. Edited by Margherita Ferri, Cecilia Moine, Lara Sabbionesi, Firenze: All'Insegna del Giglio, 2016.

Ciuccarelli, Maria Raffaella. "La ceramica a vernice nera da Angeli di Mergo e qualche nota sulla romanizzazione dell'ager Gallicus". Pages 279–306 in *Sentinum 295 a.C., Sassoferrato 2006. 2300 anni dopo la battaglia. Una città romana tra storia e archeologia*, Atti del Convegno Internazionale, Sassoferrato, 21–23 settembre 2006. Edited by Maura Medri, *Studia Archaeologica* 163, Roma: L'Erma di Bretschneider, 2008.

Coarelli, Filippo. "Gli scavi di Fregellae e la cronologia dei pavimenti repubblicani", Pages 17–30 in *AISCOM II*, Atti del II Colloquio dell'Associazione italiana per lo Studio e la Conservazione del mosaico (Roma, 5–7 dicembre 1994). Edited by Irene Bragantini, Federico Guidobaldi, Bordighera: Istituto internazionale di studi liguri, 1995.

Cornelio Cassai, Caterina. "Askós con bollo "Galicos Colonos." Page 74 in *Brixia: Roma e le genti del Po. Un incontro di culture III-II secolo a.C.* Edited by Luigi Malnati, Valentina Manzelli, Firenze: Giunti GAMM, 2015.

Curina, Renata, Malnati, Luigi, Negrelli, Claudio, Pini Laura. "Alla ricerca di Bologna antica e medievale. Da Felsina a Bononia negli scavi di Via D'Azeglio." *Quaderni di Archeologia dell'Emilia-Romagna* 25 (2010): 21–23; 55–58.

Gasperini, Lidio. "Sul "materiarius" di "Sena Gallica" (C.I.L. XI 6212)." *Picus* XXV (2005): 129–138.

Gaucci, Andrea, Lepore, Giuseppe. "L'insediamento lagunare di Senigallia tra V e IV sec. a.c. nel quadro del popolamento fra i fiumi Misa e Cesano." in *Workshop Internazionale Piceniadi. L'archeologia del Piceno preromano*, Ancona 28–29 settembre 2018, in press.

Jaia, Alessandro Maria. "Le colonie di diritto romano. Considerazioni sul sistema difensivo costiero tra IV e III secolo a.C." Pages 475–490 in *Mura di legno, mura di terra, mura di pietra: fortificazioni del Mediterraneo antico*, Atti del convegno internazionale, Sapienza Università di Roma, 7–9 maggio 2012. Edited by Gilda Bartoloni, Laura Maria Michetti, *Scienze dell'Antichità*, n. 19.2/3, 2013.

Leone, Rosina. "Il sacro e la frontiera: ancora qualche considerazione sui luoghi di culto extraurbani in Magna Grecia." Pages 159–170 in *Finem dare. Il confine tra sacro, profano e immaginario: a margine della stele bilingue del Museo Leone di Vercelli* (Atti del convegno internazionale, Vercelli, cripta di S. Andrea, 22–24 maggio 2008). Edited by Gisella Wataghin Cantino, Collana "Studi umanistici" 22, Vercelli: Mercurio, 2011.

Lepore, Giuseppe. "Il territorio di Corinaldo in età romana e tardo antica. Il sito di S. Maria in Portuno." Pages 17–86 in *Corinaldo. Storia di una terra marchigiana. Età medievale*. Edited by Virginio Villani, Ostra Vetere: Il Lavoro Editoriale, 2010.

Lepore, Giuseppe. "La colonia di Sena Gallica: un progetto abbandonato?" Pages 219–242 in *Hoc quoque laborius premium. Scritti in onore di Gino Bandelli*. Edited by Monica Chiabà, *Polymnia*, Trieste: Edizioni Università di Trieste, 2014.

Lepore, Giuseppe, Ciuccarelli, Maria Raffaella, Assenti, Gilda, Belfiori, Franceschi, Boschi, Federica, Carra, Maria Letizia, Casci Ceccacci, Tommaso, De Donatis, Mauro, Maini, Emanuela, Savelli, Daniele, Ravaioli, Enrico, Silani, Michele, Visani, Fabio. "Progetto Archeologia Urbana a Senigallia I: le ricerche di Via Cavallotti." *The Journal of Fasti on Line* 248 (2012): 1–19.

Lepore, Giuseppe, Galazzi, Federica, Silani, Michele. "Nuovi dati sulla romanizzazione *dell'ager senogalliensis*: un *pagus* a Madonna del Piano di Corinaldo?" *Ocnus* 21 (2013): 101–126.

Lepore, Giuseppe, Galazzi, Federica, Silani, Michele. "Il territorio comunale di Ostra in età romana." Pages 21–69 in *Montalboddo la terra, Ostra la città. Dalle origini al Quattrocento*, vol. 1. Edited by Giancarla Raffaeli, Bruno Morbidelli, Fano (PU): Banca di Credito Cooperativo di Alba, Langhe e Roero, 2014a.

Lepore, Giuseppe, Mandolini, Emanuele, Silani, Michele, Belfiori, Francesco, Galazzi, Federica. "Archeologia urbana a Senigallia III: i nuovi dati dall'area archeologica "La Fenice." *The Journal of Fasti on Line* 308 (2014b): 1–32.

Lepore, Giuseppe, Antolini, Simona, Branchesi, Fabiola, Galazzi, Federica. "Novità epigrafiche da Senigallia." *Picus* 35 (2015): 273–295.

Lepore, Giuseppe, Silani, Michele. "Lo sviluppo di una conquista. Dalla fondazione della *colonia* di *Sena Gallica* all'organizzazione dell'*ager*." in *Roman Archaeology Conference*, Sapienza Università di Roma, 16–19 March 2016, in press.

Malnati, Luigi, Manzelli, Valentina. "La Cisalpina tra III e I secolo a.C. alla luce dell'archeologia. Il IIII secolo a.C." Pages 42–45 in *Brixia: Roma e le genti del Po. Un incontro di culture III-II secolo a.C.* Edited by Luigi Malnati, Valentina Manzelli, Firenze: Giunti GAMM, 2015: 42–45.

Marcattili, Francesco. "Primo stile e cultura della *luxuria*." Pages 415–424 in *Pittura ellenistica in Italia e in Sicilia. Linguaggi e Tradizioni*, Atti del Convegno di Studi (Messina 24–25 settembre 2009). Edited by Gioacchino Francesco La Torre and Mario Torelli, Roma: Giorgio Bretschneider, 2011.

Marengo, Silvia Maria. "Iscrizione latina inedita a Pianello di Ostra." *Picus* 4 (1982): 131–135.

Mazzeo Saracino, Luisa. "Indigeni e coloni nell'ager Gallicus e nel Piceno alla luce della cultura materiale." Pages 357–389 in *Epigrafia e Archeologia romana nel territorio marchigiano*. Edited by Gianfranco Paci. Tivoli: Edizioni Tored, 2013.

Ortalli, Jacopo. "Formazione e trasformazione dell'architettura domestica: una casistica cispadana." Pages 25–58 in *Abitare in Cisalpina. L'edilizia privata nelle città e nel territorio in età romana*. Edited by M. Verzàr-Bas, *Antichità Alto Adriatiche* XLIX, Trieste: Edizioni Editreg Srl, 2001.

Ortalli, Jacopo. "Tra storia e archeologia: quali coloni ad *Ariminum*?" *Arch. Class.* LVIII, n.s. 8 (2007): 353–369.

Ortalli, Jacopo, Ravara Montebelli, Cristina. *Rimini. Lo scavo archeologico di Palazzo Massani*, Rimini: Sistema dei Musei, 2003.

Osanna, Massimo. "L'entroterra lucano tra Bradano e Sinni nel III sec. a.C." Pages 621–657 in *La Magna Grecia da Pirro ad Annibale* (Atti del Cinquantaduesimo Convegno di Studi sulla Magna Grecia, Taranto 27–30 settembre 2012), Taranto: Istituto per la Storia e l'Archelogia della Magna Grecia, 2015.

Paci, Gianfranco. "Nuove iscrizioni romane da Senigallia Urbisaglia e Petritoli." *Picus* II (1982): 37–68.

Salvini, Monica. *Area archeologica e Museo La Fenice. Guida*, Senigallia: Ministero per i Beni e le Attività Culturali: Soprintendenza per i Beni Archeologici delle Marche, Comune di Senigallia, 2003.

Silani, Michele. "Sena Gallica: dall'abitato indigeno alla fondazione della colonia romana". Pages 403–407 in *Centro y periferia en el mundo clásico, XVIII* CIAC–Congreso Internacional Arqueología Clásica, 13–17 Mayo 2013. Edited by José María Álvarez Martínez, Trinidad Nogales Basarrate, Isabel Rodà de Llanza, Mérida (España): Museo Nacional de Arte Romano, 2014.

Silani, Michele. *Città e territorio: la formazione della città romana nell.* Ager Gallicus, Bologna: Bononia University Press, 2017.

Silani, Michele. "I pavimenti repubblicani della colonia romana di *Sena Gallica*: un quadro di sintesi." Pages 141–150 in Atti del XXIV Colloquio dell'Associazione Italiana per lo Studio e la Conservazione del Mosaico (AISCOM) (Este, 14–17 marzo 2018). Edited by Michele Bueno, Chiara Cecalupo, Marco Emilio Erba, Daniela Massara, Federica Rinaldi, Roma: Edizioni Quasar, 2018.

Silani, Michele, De Donatis, Mauro, Savelli, Daniele, Boschi, Federica, Lepore, Giuseppe, Susini, Sara. "Geo-archaeology of the Roman palaeosurface of *Sena Gallica* (Senigallia, Italy)." *Journal of Maps* (2016): 1–6.

Sisani, Simone. *Fenomenologia della conquista. La romanizzazione dell'Umbria tra il IV sec. a.C. e la guerra sociale,* Roma: Edizioni Quasar, 2007.

Sommella, Paolo. "Il fenomeno dell'urbanizzazione: dagli insediamenti protovillanoviani alla città nel mondo italico e romano." Pages 799–803 in *Il mondo dell'archeologia*, Roma: Enciclopedia Italiana - Treccani, 2002.

Stefanini, Stefania. "Rinvenimenti ceramici da *Sena Gallica*", in *Picus* XIV-XV (1994–1995): 23–52.

Stek, Tesse D. *Cult places and cultural change in Republican Italy. A contextual approach to religious aspects of rural society after Roman conquest.* Amsterdam: Amsterdam University Press, 2009.

Torelli, Marina. "Aspetti ideologici della colonizzazione romana più antica." *DdA* 6, 3ª s. (1988): 65–72.

Vigoni, Alberto. "Pozzi antichi nel Veneto: tipologia e diffusione." Pages 19–52 in *Archeologia e tecnica dei pozzi per acqua dalla pre-protostoria all'età moderna*, Atti del Convegno di Studi, Borgoricco (PD) 11 dicembre 2010, *Antichità Alto Adriatiche* LXX, Trieste: Edizioni Editreg Srl, 2011.

Vermeulen, Frank. *From the mountains to the sea. The Roman Colonisation and Urbanisation of Central Adriatic Italy.* Babesch, Leuven, Paris, Bristol: Peeters Publishers 2017.

Vermeulen, Frank, Destro, Marco, Monsieur, Patrick, Carboni Francesca, Dralans, Sophie, Van Limbergen, Dimitri. "Scavi presso la porta occidentale di *Potentia*: notizia preliminare." *Picus* XXXI (2011): 169–205.

Zaccaria, Mirco. "Tecnica edilizia in mattoni crudi." Pages 177–184 in *Archeologia nella Valle del Cesano. Da Suasa a Santa Maria in Portuno.* Atti del Convegno per i venti anni di ricerche dell'Università di Bologna (Castelleone di Suasa, Corinaldo, San Lorenzo in Campo, 18–19 dicembre 2008). Edited by Enrico Giorgi, Giuseppe Lepore, Bologna: Ante Quem, 2010a.

Zaccaria, Mirco. "Lo scavo delle strutture repubblicane." Pages 159–176 in *Archeologia nella Valle del Cesano. Da Suasa a Santa Maria in Portuno.* Atti del Convegno per i venti anni di ricerche dell'Università di Bologna (Castelleone di Suasa, Corinaldo, San Lorenzo in Campo, 18–19 dicembre 2008). Edited by Enrico Giorgi, Giuseppe Lepore, Bologna: Ante Quem, 2010b.

# 9 Aquileia's market spaces

*Patrizia Basso*

## Introduction

In June 2018, the University of Verona began archaeological investigation of the south-eastern sector of Aquileia (Udine), where the twentieth-century excavations had demonstrated the existence of commercial spaces dating to Late Antiquity. Our excavation was possible, thanks to ministerial concession[1] and financial support of Fondazione Aquileia. Even though we are talking about just the first season of work, we would like to present the main findings of the excavations – findings that, to date, have not been published or otherwise disseminated. First, however, we will present an overview of the commerce-related structures at Aquileia. We do this, even though these have been studied in depth in the past, because the city forms an interesting example for the study of urban commercial areas and their diachronic transformation.

One must note first of all that the city has a marked commercial character due to its geographical position: it is open not only to the Orient and the Mediterranean via the Adriatic but also to the Balkan and Continental Europe via such ancient routes as the Amber Road. Furthermore, as regards location, it should be noted that the city was not built on the coast where it would have been at risk of attack by the fierce Istrian pirates, but rather, in a more secure inland location, well linked to the sea by a river and a canal (see Figure 9.1). The river – about 50 m wide – is identified with the *Natiso cum Turro* (Natissa) mentioned by Pliny,[2] while the canal – given the name Anfora – runs from the western edge of the city and, after 6 km, reaches the modern-day Marano lagoon with access to maritime and endo-lagoonal routes[3].

The right bank of the main river was home to a large port, whose buildings were laid out in the middle of the first century CE and which extends over a frontage of several hundred metres (see Figure 9.2, n. 9). Over time, it grew to include ever-larger warehousing complexes and ramps leading into the urban centre, attesting to the strong long-term commercial vitality of Aquileia. At the end of the fourth century CE, the poet *Ausonius* celebrated them, along with the city walls, defining Aquileia to be *moenibus et portu celeberrima*.[4] Other, smaller, docks have been hypothesised in other parts of the city,

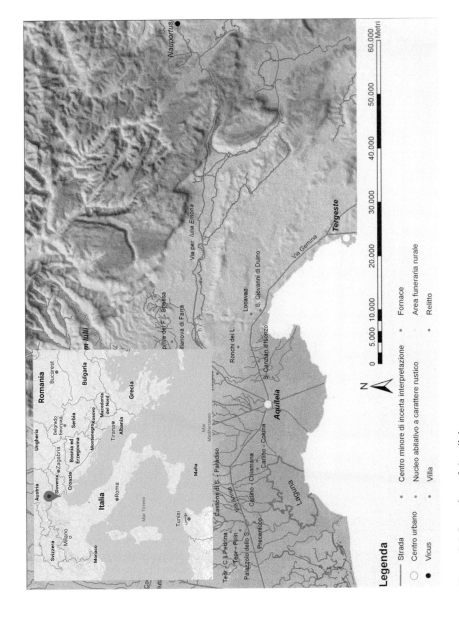

*Figure 9.1* Location of Aquileia.

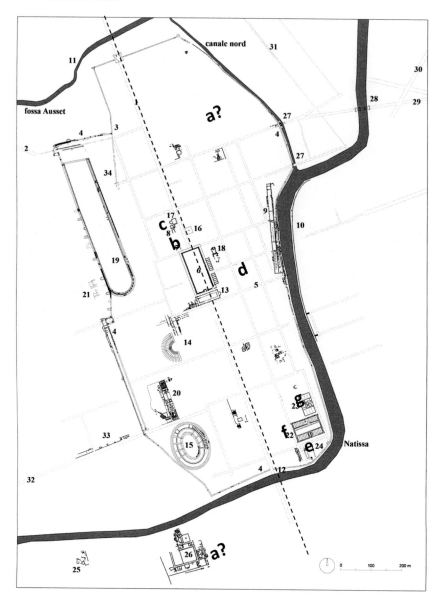

*Figure 9.2* Plan of the rivers, canals and principal structures of the Roman city: the via
Postumia is indicated with a dashed line; the letters (a–e) indicate the principal market structures referred to in this chapter; (f) indicates the location
of the *horrea* of Late Antiquity; (g) indicates the Palaeo-Christian basilica
(Patrizia Basso, on the basis of Ghiotto 2018).

which was surrounded on the north and west sides by a system of canals that provided a means to circumnavigate Aquileia.

Furthermore, literary sources also mention the city's role as an entrepôt, as can be seen in a famous passage from Strabo (5.1.8):

> The city served as a marketplace for the Illyrian peoples living along the Danube: they came to exchange slaves, animals and pelts for the products arriving by sea–wine that was put into wooden barrels on carts, and also oil.

This trade continued until the third century CE as Herodian tells us (8.2.3–4):

> Aquileia, near the sea, served as a marketplace for Italy. It gathered the products of the continent along land and river routes for sale to the seafarers and received from the sea those goods needed in the hinterland (those things that could not be produced due to the harsh climate) and sent them inland. Further, the region was very rich in vines and supplied large quantities of wine to peoples that did not cultivate vines.

Further confirmation comes from the numerous finds of foreign materials made during excavation of the urban areas. These provide evidence of exchange not only with the nearby territories of *Noricum*, *Histria* and *Pannonia* but also with north-eastern Europe, the Orient, Spain and North Africa. These data demonstrate the crucial role of the city as a crossroads of trade, with particular importance in the first century CE and then in the fourth century CE when it became the capital of the province of *Venetia et Histria*, reinforcing its political and military role.

## The marketplaces of Aquileia

The five known marketplaces of Aquileia across the city's history[5] can be seen in Figure 9.2, a–e. The oldest marketplace is attested in an inscription[6] from the middle of the second century BCE that records the construction, on the orders of the local Senate, of a 40-foot (12 m) wide connecting road between the cattle market that became known as the *forum pequarium* and the via *Postumia* (see Figure 9.3). The latter important route crossing northern Italy to connect Genoa to Aquileia had been built in 148 BCE and formed the north–south axis along which urban Aquileia was constructed (see Figure 9.2, dashed line). The inscription was found out of context and so cannot tell us where the market was located.

It is striking that other epigraphic sources that mention *fora pecuaria* in Italic territory (found at *Atina* and *Ferentinum* in region I; *Aeclanum* in region II and *Falerio Picenus* in region V – all centres in the heart of Apennine Italy where the pastoral economy was highly developed)[7] also refer to work

*Figure 9.3* (a, b) The inscriptions regarding the *forum pequarium* (from Lettich 2003).

on roads forming connections to the local cattle market or passing through it. This leads us to hypothesise that we are talking about important transit nodes located outside urban centres and probably directly linked to transhumance routes. We can thus hypothesis that Aquileia's cattle market was also extra-urban.

Archaeological research to date has not produced data that allow a more precise positioning. Luisa Bertacchi, one of the great interpreters of Aquileia archaeology, believed that the market occupied a vast complex south of Natissa[8] (see Figure 9.2,a?), in use from the late Republican to the Late Imperial periods, that was identified in the 1970s. It consisted of two large enclosures (800 × 350 m) that were hypothesised to be cattle enclosures, rooms with mosaics interpreted as offices and a long corridor. According to Bertacchi, the interpretation is confirmed by a Republican era votive inscription to Hercules found nearby,[9] given the strong connection between the god – protector of flocks and transhumance – and cattle markets. Such connections are seen in Rome at the *Forum Boarium* and hypothesised at *Tibur, Praeneste* and *Ferentinum*.[10] However, it must be remembered that the find spot of the inscription is somewhat uncertain and, moreover, that the building lacks findings securely datable to the Republican era. Further, when excavations were reopened in 1988, valuable high-status floorings were found, suggesting a residential use for the site.[11]

Another hypothesis puts the market to the north of the city where it would have had a more direct connection to the *Postumia* (as mentioned in the epigraphic source) and with transhumance routes (see Figure 9.2, a). The latter had been in use from the Iron Age – and perhaps earlier – bringing the salt that is indispensable for raising ovicaprids.[12] Further evidence would likely be provided by the presence of sanctuaries dedicated to Hercules such as the one at Sevegliano and finds like a vessel for boiling milk (mid-second to first century BCE) also found at Sevegliano.[13] A Republican era dedication to *T. Plausurnius* – who is also mentioned at Tivoli in connection with the reorganisation of the sanctuary of Hercules – found along the road from Monastero to Terzo,[14] has also made people think that there may have been a sanctuary to Hercules in the area between the *Postumia* and the Natissa, which could have been linked to the *forum pecuarium* of the inscription.

The commercial space dedicated to livestock seems to suggest an early specialisation of the spaces dedicated to buying and selling in the city (considering that the other *fora pecuaria* already cited are dated between the first century BCE and the second CE). It probably indicates the importance of this particular trade to Aquileia from the second century BCE on and may represent a continuation of activities among the indigenous precolonial communities.[15] It remains difficult to understand whether this was a space dedicated solely to ovicaprids (whose intensive rearing in the area is also confirmed by the flourishing wool processing activities) or also for cattle and pigs, given that the term *pecus* means all the animals that *pascuntur*. We cannot rule out this first market being an open space without buildings, similar to the livestock markets that could still be seen in the Italian countryside in the last century.

The second market was found to the north of the *forum*, behind the *comitium* and dates to the end of the second century BCE[16] (see Figures. 9.2, b and 9.4). It was identified as a *macellum* or space that (as numerous literary sources from Plautus to Saint Augustine testify) was to be used for the sale of foodstuffs.[17] This function would be supported by the large quantity of animal remains – mostly from cattle and pigs – recovered during the excavation.[18] We are talking about a square building (side length 35.4 m) divided

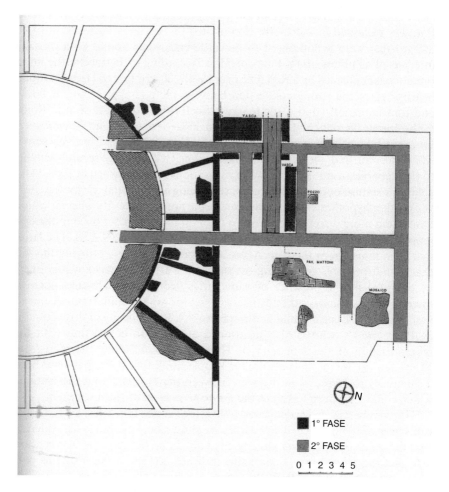

*Figure 9.4* Plan of the Republican *macellum* (from Maselli Scotti 1995).

by radial walls into a series of small spaces with brick floors surrounding a central circular open space with a diameter of 25 m. The central space has a floor of *opus spicatum* bordered by a stone kerb. There was a tank in *opus signinum* to one side, which some researchers believe was a sort of aquarium for live fish, given an inscription from Corinth that speaks of the existence of a *macellum cum piscario.*[19]

In many other cities in Italy and in the Empire, the presence of *macella* is hypothesised on the basis of epigraphic evidence and archaeological remains. It is of great interest that they are often located very close to the forum: this allowed the messy activities of commerce to be kept out of the main square, leaving it free for political life and administration, while keeping them close so that the magistrates could keep an eye on sales and, in particular, weights, prices and the freshness of the goods.[20] The *macellum* in the city, thus, indicates a clear desire to separate commercial activities according to a principal already evident in the traditions of Rome, with specialised markets for the sale of different products (the *forum Boarium*, the *Holitorium*, the *Piscarium*, etc.).

It should, however, be noted that the other *macella* found in Italian cities from the same epoch as that of Aquileia have in general a simpler rectangular plan with shops arranged around a central circular structure, as at Pompeii, Morgantina and *Alba Fucens* (first structure).[21] There are also examples very similar architecturally to the Aquileia building such as those found at *Aeclanum, Alba Fucens, Herdonia* and, more recently, *Castrum Truentinum*[22]: these, however, are constructions dating to the second century CE. The problem, thus, remains of understanding the reasons for the early presence of such a structure at Aquileia and the models from which it derived.

Between the first century BCE and the Julio-Claudian era, Aquileia strengthened its role as a port and commercial centre and experienced a period of particular economic vitality. In these years (and particularly around the middle of the first century CE), the *macellum* was demolished and covered with layers of gravel, sand and mortar.[23] A new building of rectangular plan was constructed on the site, with brick floors, channels and open spaces, one of which had a well (see Figure 9.2, c). Finds of bones in the use levels with traces of butchery allow us to hypothesise that this was still a market area, chronologically the third known in the city, expanding the Republican *macellum* to meet new urban needs.

The last mercantile spaces date to Late Antiquity, when Aquileia assumed an important political and economic role due to its strategic position as a frontier city. Directly connected to the Alpine defence system, the city was, so to speak, the gatekeeper at the "door" into Cisalpine Italy, menaced by the barbarian peoples. This role involved the presence of officials and soldiers working on the Danube border, a fact that must have provided incentives for trade in foodstuffs and other everyday products.

A first market has been hypothesised on the basis of recent investigations by the University of Trieste on the east side of the forum, between it and the port area (see Figure 9.2, d). The function of food market is suggested by its reduced dimensions, many ceramic finds and bones with butchery traces recovered during the excavation.[24] However, a certain caution in interpretation is required due to the partial nature of the excavation and the absence of channels and shops in the building. It seems to be characterised by several phases of use, beginning in the time of Constantine and lasting until the middle of the fifth century. In the last phase, it was expanded by the construction of an apse to the south of an open area and a new block, perhaps forming a vestibule for access from the north.

The second market area was the subject of our excavations and is located in the area known as "Fondo Pasqualis", from the name of the family that owned it for several centuries: the land was acquired by the state and given to the Aquileia Foundation when it was established in 2008 – it is open to public visits. It is in the extreme south-west of Aquileia (see Figure 9.2, e)

*Figure 9.5* Photo of the site from a drone, where the remains brought to light during
archaeological excavations carried out in the 1950s can be seen (Explora
s.r.l. drone survey, illustration Valeria Grazioli).

where, from the time of Constantine, buildings associated with both religious life (the basilica: see Figure 9.2, g) and civil life (the large *horrea* of the
time of Emperor Maximian modelled on those of Milan: see Figure 9.2, f)
concentrated. As expected, the area had already been partially investigated
by Giovanni Brusin in 1953–1954[25]: he identified important monumental
structures that were left open to public visitation.

   In particular, two areas paved in sandstone were uncovered, which were
interpreted as open spaces for the sale of goods, along with two parallel city
walls between them and the river Natissa (see Figure 9.5). A possible third
square may have been found by Brusin to the east of the other two. However,
some doubts remain as the poor state of preservation of its structures led to
it being back filled at the end of the excavations.

   Brusin left some drawings and sketches along with a series of black-and-
white photographs that are held in the archives of the National Archaeological
Museum of Aquileia: we retrieved and studied these before beginning our
fieldwork.[26] Despite the large amounts of data arising from those excavations,
many questions remain unanswered about this zone of major importance
for the story of the city in Late Antiquity. First, Brusin only excavated the
eastern part of the area: the western part was not investigated because, at
the time, vines were cultivated there (see Figure 9.5). Second, the presence
in the area between the two squares of the soil removed during excavation

has impeded our understanding of the relationship between them. Further, those excavations stopped at the Late Antiquity level and did not explore the Imperial and possible Republican phases of the site. Our investigations will now try to fill these gaps.

## New excavations at the "Fondo Pasqualis" site

Here we briefly present the first findings emerging from our work. It should be borne in mind that we are talking about preliminary data and that there is the possibility of reassessing them as the research proceeds. A heartfelt thank you goes to the Fondazione Aquileia that supported the research and to the entire team – and in particular to Diana Dobreva, who co-directed the excavation, taking charge of the materials lab, and to Maria Bosco, Valeria Grazioli, Fiammetta Soriano and Andrea Zemignani (the site supervisors) that worked hard in the field and in the laboratory.

Before excavation began we undertook a UAV survey of the walls remaining visible after the twentieth-century excavations (Esplora s.r.l.; see Figure 9.5). In July 2018, Frank Vermeulen and his Ghent University team undertook a geophysical survey of the entire area with magnetometer and georadar,[27] which revealed a double row of pillars to the west of the paved open areas (see Figure 9.7). This could be interpreted as another square with a portico.

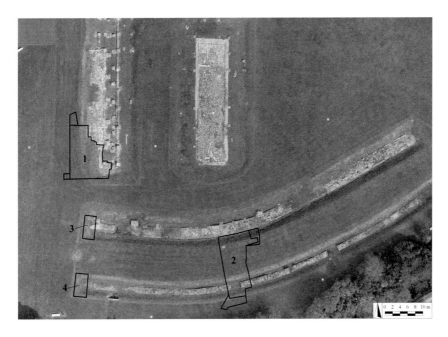

*Figure 9.6* The drone image of the excavation area showing the location of the trenches dug by the University of Verona (produced by Valeria Grazioli on the basis of drone images captured by Esplora s.r.l.).

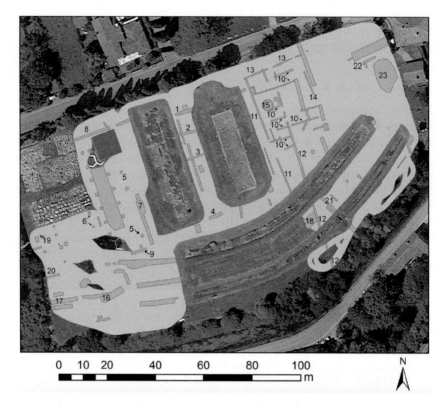

*Figure 9.7* The geo-radar anomalies revealed during the geophysical survey conducted by Ghent University (image by Frank Vermeulen and his team).

On the basis of these surveys and the historical questions that we wished to answer, we opened two trenches (see Figure 9.6, 1–2). Two other trenches (see Figure 9.6, 3–4) were opened to investigate the westward extension of the two southern walled structures. The work in this area has only just begun and will be completed in future field seasons: for this reason, we will not discuss it further here.

The first trench (100 m²) was placed at the south-west corner of the west square with the aim of investigating a stratigraphic basin that was untouched by modern excavation, so as to understand the various phases of construction, use and abandonment of the area. Further to this aim, we also undertook a general cleaning of the walled structures revealed by Brusin, with the purpose of understanding the construction techniques used and the stratigraphic relationships, so as to reconstruct the diachronic sequence (a task made more difficult by modern restoration work on the walls).

At least three phases of use were identified, from the Flavian age to the fifth century CE. The first phase was characterised by some walls and a pillar found beneath the layer that raised the floor in the next period. The limited extent of the further excavations and a rising level of groundwater have impeded our understanding of the structures and the associated levels. At the moment, then, we are looking only at limited traces. However, these most definitely constitute important evidence of use of the area as early as the Flavian period. The only way to better understand what is there is to enlarge the excavation area.

Above the level of the razing of the walls and pillars we found, as expected, layers of earth that served to raise the former floor level. The structures that we have revealed, considered together with two alignments of pillars already uncovered by Brusin and attributable to at least two different phases of construction (see Figure 9.8) suggest a first square, with a line of shops (each

*Figure 9.8* The two rows of pillars uncovered during Brusin's excavations to the east of the western square (photo: Patrizia Basso).

3.50 m × 2.80 m) along the sides, perhaps floored with brick (as suggested by a fragment found in one of the rooms excavated by Brusin). The dating of this first building remains uncertain and will be clarified as excavations continue.

At a later date (apparently the fourth century, as already proposed by Brusin), the square that is still visible today was constructed. It is about 25 m long and 4.40 m wide and is paved with stone slabs of various dimensions, most of which are rectangular, along with re-used architectural materials. The square was surrounded by a portico, 2.80 m in depth, and then a line of shops, with an access point to the north (see Figure 9.9). It should be remembered that, in the central square, Brusin unearthed two lines of stone bases close to the square, with quadrangular holes in their centres, which probably held wooden poles that supported a roof or canopy of some light material: it seems then that the two squares, characterised by different types of shops, sold different types of goods (see Figure 9.10).

The abandonment of the complex occurred after a fire: we found a layer of carbonised wood fragments across the surface of the trench, as had Brusin. These were the remains of the beams that supported the overhead coverings of the shops. The archaeological materials recovered in the levels linked to this period suggest a date between the mid- to late fifth century and the early sixth century CE. Of particular interest are some piles of cereal seeds (mostly barley and oats but the palaeobotanical analysis is still underway). These were probably originally contained in sacks, which would suggest that the space was specialised in the storage and sale of food products.

The second trench (80 m²) was opened between the two mighty southern walls: it revealed the previously unknown nature of their foundations and construction and prompted new thoughts about their significance in the overall picture of the history of the city. The inner wall (3.10 m thick; see Figure 9.11, a) was constructed using materials recovered from other urban monuments (bases of statues with inscriptions, parts of moulded cornices, columns, etc.). In this way, a robust fortification was created in a moment of defensive need: the wall is topographically linked to many other sections of wall uncovered in various parts of the city that are dated to a time before Julian's 361 CE siege, probably around the beginning of the fourth century CE.[28]

The external wall (see Figure 9.11, b) was much thinner (width 1.50 m) and was almost devoid of reused materials. It is characterised by a series of openings (2.60–3.20 m wide and, on average, 25 m apart) that seem likely to be aligned with landing places on the river and ramps leading up to the squares. It was, thus, not a wall that closed the city off but, rather, speaks to an openness and close relationship between the city and the river.

The external wall was built on a foundation of durmast oak poles and amphorae that were found in an excellent state of preservation (see Figure 9.12). These are dated to the first half of the fifth century CE. Hence, the construction of the wall and the ramps can be dated to the fifth century while the end of their use (with an accompanying build-up of fluvial sediment) seems to date to the first decades of the sixth century CE.

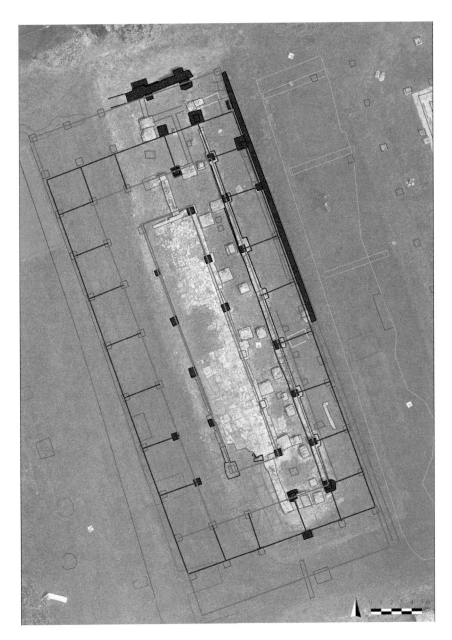

*Figure 9.9* Reconstruction of the western square with the portico and the shops in the final phase of use (drawing by Fiammetta Soriano).

*Figure 9.10* 3D reconstruction of the two market squares identified by Brusin in 1954 (drawing by Nudesign for the Fondazione Aquileia – used with permission).

*Figure 9.11* (a, b) View of the interior wall (on the left) and the exterior wall (on the right; photo: Patrizia Basso).

## Conclusion

While we wait to continue our work – enlarging the excavations, studying the materials, undertaking dendrochronological analyses of the wood and archaeobotanical and 14C analyses of the seeds and poles – we can at the

*Figure 9.12* General view of trench 2: the external wall with one of the openings, the ramp towards the squares and the consolidation of the riverbank with amphorae and wooden poles (photo: Valeria Grazioli).

moment synthesise the broad outlines of the story of the site, with important repercussions for the general use of economic space in the southern part of this ancient city.

Already in the first century BCE (and in particular in the Flavian age) if not before, the area was occupied by buildings, the functions of which are not yet understood. Around the fourth century, after various phases of use that we have so far only glimpsed, the system of three or four aligned squares was created. These constituted differentiated selling places with mobile coverings that could be accessed from the north along one of the city's *decumani* (unearthed in previous excavations) or from the south by river, through openings in the external wall and ramps identified between the two walls. To the north, the market must have had a functional connection to the large *horrea* uncovered south of the basilica and, along with them, formed a civil and economic space (a sort of new forum) for the urban centre now concentrated around the sacred centre. The inner wall (see Figure 9.13, M2), solid and closed, protected the city from the menace of outsiders but also from the clashes between legitimate emperors and usurpers for which Aquileia formed the backdrop several times in Late Antiquity. The outer wall was initially interpreted as part of a second curtain wall (see Figure 9.13, M3), 13–14 m outside the first that served to reinforce the eastern, southern and western sides of the city, even if this last section is rather dubious. But the

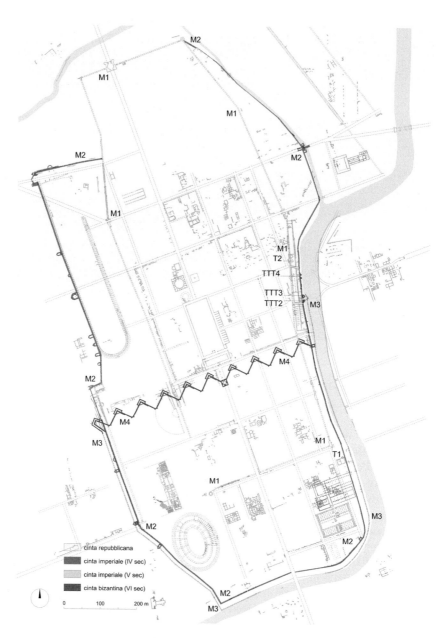

*Figure 9.13*  The hypothesised defensive walls of the city (from Bonetto 2009).

lesser thickness and the three openings already found by Brusin may suggest another hypothesis. Given its characteristics, the wall would seem to be readable as a dock and a containing wall/embankment for the Natissa, which Ammianus Marcellinus[29] says suffered a shift in its course after Julian's siege. Environmental analyses confirm a phase in which the current ran less strongly at the end of the fourth century.

It is possible that the inner wall lay directly on the banks of the river Natissa. The river was then diverted and its course moved further out and required the construction of an embankment that could also serve for the loading and unloading of goods from river transport.

It remains to be understood how goods were transported to the squares: were there gaps in the inner wall at a level higher than that to which it is preserved? Via the space between the two walls? We also need to understand the precise dating of the wall. On the basis of the amphorae, the foundations seem to date to the middle of the fifth century. Finally, the date at which the openings in the outer wall were filled in – an action noted by Brusin during his excavations – needs to be understood because it probably puts the entire operational system of the squares in crisis. At this point, the market, abandoned, would have experienced the fires and destruction seen in the excavations. This was followed by a long period of agricultural use lasting up until Brusin's excavations and attested to by a thick layer of organic accumulation and the holes for plants that were found above the collapse levels.

## Notes

1  Licence from Ministero per i beni e le attività culturali (protocol 0014409 – 28th may 2018).
2  Plin. *NH* 3.126.
3  Among the wide bibliography, see, most recently, Maggi et al. 2017.
4  Auson. *Ordo urbium nobilium*, 9.64–72.
5  For an extensive summary of Aquileia markets, see Tiussi 2004. See also Maselli Scotti and Rubinich 2009: 107–108; Ventura 2013.
6  CIL I² 2197 = CIL V 8313 = ILLRP 487 = SI 125 = Inscr. Aq. 53; Lettich 2003: 41, n. 34. This is a sandstone parallelepiped (166 × 52 × 25 cm) with the following inscription about hallway up: *De via Postumia in/ forum pequarium/ meisit lata p(edes) XXX[X?]/ de senatous sente(ntia)*.
7  On this topic, see Chioffi 1999: 106–109.
8  Bertacchi 1976: 12–16; Bertacchi 2000; Bertacchi 2003, tavv. 44–45, n. 102.
9  Bertacchi 1990: 645–647.
10  Bertacchi 2000: 77–84; Bonetto 2008: 692–693; Modugno 2000.
11  Maselli Scotti and Tiussi 1999; Bonetto 2008: 702–706.
12  Maselli Scotti 2014: 325.
13  On this topic, see Tiussi 2004: 258–263; Bonetto 2008: 695–696, together with the preceding bibliography.
14  Verzàr Bass 2006: 428–429.

15  Bonetto 2008: 697–698.
16  Maselli Scotti 1995; Tiussi 2004: 273–280; Maselli Scotti et al. 2007: 38–39.
17  On the *macella* and the sources concerning them, the summary in De Ruyt 1983: 226–227 remains useful. For additional references, see Chapter 10 (Hoffelinck) in this volume.
18  Maselli Scotti 1995: 160.
19  Tiussi 2004: 273–280.
20  De Ruyt 1983: 326–327.
21  De Ruyt 1983: 253–254; Tiussi 2004: 276–280.
22  De Ruyt 1983: 17–21, 30–35, 80–88, 286; Tiussi 2004: 277.
23  Maselli Scotti 1995: 159; Maselli Scotti and Rubinich 2009: 98.
24  Verzár Bass 1991; Verzár Bass 1994; Tiussi 2004: 300–302.
25  Brusin 1954 and 1955-56.
26  Special thanks go to the director of the Museum Marta Novello for kindly allowing us to study Brusin's documentation..
27  I take this opportunity to thank Frank Vermeulen and his *équipe*.
28  For an in-depth study of the walls of Aquileia and an expansive bibliography or prior work, see Bonetto 2004; Bonetto 2009; Bonetto 2013: 87–89. In particular, for the walls in Late Antiquity, see Buora 1988; Villa 2004; Buora and Magnani 2015; Buora 2016.
29  Amm. Marc. 21.12.17.

# References

Bertacchi, Luisa. "Il grande mercato pubblico a sud del Natissa". *Aquileia Chiama* 23 (1976): 12–16.

Bertacchi, Luisa. "La Venetia orientale". Pages 639–659 in *La Venetia nell'area padano-danubiana. Le vie di comunicazione*. Edited by Massimiliano Pavan Atti del Convegno Internazionale (Venezia 6–10 aprile 1988). Padova: CEDAM, 1990.

Bertacchi, Luisa. "Il grande mercato pubblico romano di Aquileia e S. Antonio Abate". *Aquileia Nostra* 71 (2000): 77–84.

Bertacchi, Luisa. *Nuova pianta archeologica di Aquileia*. Udine: Edizioni del Confine, 2003.

Bonetto, Jacopo. "Difendere Aquileia, città di frontiera". *Antichità Altoadriatiche* 59 (2004): 151–196.

Bonetto, Jacopo. "Allevamento, mercato e territorio in Aquileia romana". *Antichità Altoadriatiche* 55 (2008): 687–730.

Bonetto, Jacopo. "Le mura". Pages 83–92 in *Moenibus et portu celeberrima. Aquileia: storia di una città*. Edited by Francesca Ghedini, Michele Bueno and Marta Novello. Roma: Istituto Poligrafico dello Stato, 2009.

Bonetto, Jacopo. "Le difese di Aquileia nel IV secolo". Pages 72–74 in *Costantino e Teodoro. Aquileia nel IV secolo*. Catalogo della Mostra. Edited by Cristiano Tiussi, Luca Villa and Marta Novello. Milano: Mondadori Electa, 2013.

Brusin, Giovanni. "Gli scavi archeologici di Aquileia nell'anno 1954". *Aquileia Nostra* 28 (1954): 5–18.

Brusin, Giovanni. "Epigrafi aquileiesi in funzione di pietre miliari". *Atti dell'Istituto Veneto di Scienze, Lettere e Arti* 114 (1955–1956): 281–290.

Buora, Maurizio. "Le mura medievali di Aquileia". *Antichità Altoadriatiche* 32 (1988): 335–361.

Buora, Maurizio. "Nuovi dati sulle mura urbiche (repubblicane, dell'età di Massimino e tetrarchiche) di Aquileia dalla documentazione relativa agli scavi per le nuove fognature". *Quaderni Friulani di Archeologia* XXVI, 1 (2016): 9–19.

Buora, Maurizio, Magnani Stefano. "Il "Mur Forat". L'angolo delle mura nordoccidentali di Aquileia". *Memorie Storiche Forogiuliesi* XCIV-XCV (2014–2015): 11–40.

Chioffi, Laura. *Caro: il mercato della carne nell'Occidente romano. Riflessi epigrafici e iconografici*. Roma: L'Erma di Bretschneider, 1999.

De Ruyt, Claire. *Macellum, marché alimentaire des Romains*. Louvain-la-Neuve: Institut supérieur d'Archéologie et d'Histoire de l'Art, 1983.

Ghiotto, Andrea Raffaele. "Considerazioni sul teatro e sul "quartiere degli spettacoli". Pages 253–260 in *L'anfiteatro di Aquileia. Ricerche d'archivio e nuove indagini di scavo*. Edited by Patrizia Basso. Quingentole (Mantova): Sap Editoria, 2018.

Lettich, Giovanni. *Itinerari epigrafici aquileiesi*. Trieste: Editreg, 2003.

Maggi, Paola, Maselli Scotti, Franca, Pesavento Mattioli, Stefania, Zulini, Ella, ed. *Materiali per Aquileia. Lo scavo di Canale Anfora (2004–2005)*. Trieste: Editreg, 2017.

Maselli Scotti, Franca. "Nuove scoperte nella zona a nord-ovest del Foro di Aquileia". *Antichità Altoadriatiche* 42 (1995): 157–179.

Maselli Scotti, Franca. "Riflessioni sul paesaggio aquileiese all'arrivo dei Romani". Pages 319–330 in *Hoc quoque laboris praemium. Scritti in onore di Gino Bandelli*. Edited by Monica Chiabà. Trieste: Edizioni Università di Trieste, 2014.

Maselli Scotti, Franca, Tiussi, Cristiano. "Notiziario archeologico. Aquileia. Area occidentale dei cosiddetti mercati a sud del fiume Natissa, scavo 1988". *Aquileia Nostra* 70 (1999): 398–406.

Maselli Scotti, Franca , Rubinich, Marina. "I monumenti pubblici". Pages 93–110 in *Moenibus et portu celeberrima. Aquileia: storia di una città*. Edited by Francesca Ghedini, Michele Bueno, Marta Novello. Roma: Istituto Poligrafico dello Stato, 2009.

Maselli Scotti, Franca, Mandruzzato, Luciana, Tiussi, Cristiano. "Primo impianto coloniario di Aquileia: l'area fra foro e macellum". Pages 35–40 in *Forme e tempi della urbanizzazione nella Cisalpina (II secolo a.C. - I secolo d.C.)* Atti Giornate studio (Torino, 4–6 maggio 20006). Edited by Luisa Brecciaroli Taborelli. Sesto Fiorentino (Firenze): All'Insegna del Giglio, 2007.

Modugno, Isabella. "Alcune considerazioni sul culto di Ercole nel territorio di Aquileia fra protostoria ed età romana con particolare rifermento al fenomeno della transumanza". *Aquileia nostra* 71 (2000): 57–76.

Tiussi, Cristiano. "Il sistema di distribuzione ad Aquileia: mercati e magazzini". *Antichità Altoadriatiche* 59 (2004): 257–316.

Verzár Bass, Monika, ed. *Scavi ad Aquileia. I. L'area a est del Foro. Rapporto degli scavi (1988)*. Roma: Quasar, 1991.

Verzár Bass, Monika, ed. *Scavi ad Aquileia. I. L'area a est del Foro. Rapporto degli scavi (1989–91)*. Roma: Quasar, 1994.

Verzár Bass, Monika. "Riflessioni sui santuari extraurbani della colonia latina di Aquileia". Pages 423–438 in *Dúnasthai didáskein. Studi in onore di Filippo Cassola per il suo ottantesimo compleanno*. Edited by Michele Faraguna, Vanna Vedaldi Iasbez. Trieste: Editreg, 2006.

Ventura, Paola. "Mercati-horrea". Pages 94–99 in *Costantino e Teodoro. Aquileia nel IV secolo.* Catalogo della Mostra. Edited by Cristiano Tiussi, Luca Villa, Marta Novello. Milano: Mondadori Electa, 2013.

Villa, Luca. "Aquileia tra Goti, Bizantini e Longobardi: spunti per un'analisi delle trasformazioni urbane nella transizione fra tarda antichità e alto medioevo". *Antichità Altoadriatiche* 59 (2004): 561–632.

# PART III
# Movement

# 10 Finding your way towards the *macellum*

## The spatial organization of a Roman type of market building

*Adeline Hoffelinck*

## Introduction

The *macellum*, a permanent and enclosed building structure for the sale of fish and meat, according to the literary sources first appeared in Rome at some point towards the end of the third and the beginning of the second century BCE. There is some confusion in the ancient literature about the dating of the first *macellum*, since the words *forum piscatorium*, *forum* and *macellum* were often used to denote one and the same structure. However, Livy writes that in 209 BCE several buildings around the Roman forum, including the *macellum*, were reconstructed due to a fire the previous year. This indicates that a *macellum* was already in use in the third century BCE (Livy, XXVII, 11.16; Holleran, 2012: 162–163). Varro tells us more about the function of this type of building: 'After all these things which pertain to human substance had been brought into one place, and the place had been built upon, it was called a *macellum*' (Varro, *De Linguae Latina*, V. 147).[1] The buying and selling of foodstuffs was concentrated in one place, rather than spread over the different open *fora*. We can, thus, suggest that there was a need to bring market activities together into a single space and also within a permanent and enclosed building structure. The word, as well as the ground plan of the building, was derived from Greek traditions. The term originated in the Greek word μάκελλον, or *makellon*, which did not primarily have the meaning of a market building but of an *enclosure*, referring to the enclosed character of the building (De Ruyt, 1983: 226–227, 229; Holleran, 2012: 160).[2] It has been widely accepted that the lay out originated in Hellenistic cities, where from the late fourth century BCE the civic *agora*, with its main political and judicial functions, was cleared of all market functions and specific commercial *agorai* were being created. Such commercial squares were for instance present in *Miletus* and *Ephesus*, where they were built in the course of the third century BCE (De Ruyt, 1983: 280; Gros, 1996: 451).[3] *Macella* were more than a simple product of the Greek *agorai* alone, however. As Richard states very clearly, the *macellum* is rather the outcome of a 'long and flexible process of cross-fertilization between different types of courtyard-shaped commercial structures built in Greece and Italy in the Early Hellenistic period' (Richard,

2014: 256). The *macellum*, then, was often a quadrangular or rectangular building, but sometimes also circular or polygonal, with an enclosed court-yard and an internal colonnade surrounded by *tabernae*. In the middle of the courtyard, a round structure, or *tholos*, was sometimes placed. Even though *macella* had several standard architectural elements, their appearance varied greatly: no two *macella* in the Roman world were ever the same (Holleran, 2012: 161; Richard, 2014: 255; Evangelidis, 2019: 258–286). This remark-able variety forces us to grant more importance to other identifying criteria, such as the availability of a water supply, the presence of *mensa ponderaria* or weight installations, counters and tables for the selling of food, remnants of fish scales and animal bones, pottery, coins and of course inscriptions (Holleran, 2012: 161–162; Figure 10.1).

From the second half of the second century BCE, the *macellum* began to spread from Rome to other cities in Italy, and early examples were for instance found in *Pompeii* and *Alba Fucens* (De Ruyt, 1983: 30, 140).[4] From the reign of Augustus onwards, the market building also appeared in provincial towns. We could ask why it was necessary to create this type of market building when there existed already several market spaces in the Roman city, for example commercial *fora*, plazas and porticoes, where temporary stalls were set up. In one sense, the development of the *macellum* in the Roman cityscape can be seen as a reflection of certain requirements concerning the buying and selling of food products, such as better hygiene and quality, and greater con-trol, elements that are reflected in the archaeological remains and inscriptions. In addition, the building was certainly important for tax collection, and it also was a means for the elite to gain prestige in a city (De Ruyt, 1983, 358; Lomas, 2003: 41; Holleran, 2012: 176–177).[5] In the 1983 synthesis study by De Ruyt, seventy-eight such building structures were identified across the Roman world.[6] Over the past decades, archaeological research in Roman cities has brought to light many more examples. Today, a total of 145 *macella* are known in Italy and its provinces.[7] Even though De Ruyt's work definitely stimulated interest in the study of the *macellum* within the broader field of research on Roman cities and their architecture, something that is reflected in the large number of in-depth studies published on the matter, there is still a lack of an updated synthesis study which incorporates the increasing data of the past few years.[8] Integrating the old and new research material would enable the *macellum*, as a landmark in many Roman towns, to be re-examined thoroughly. Some of the functions attributed to the building should be re-evaluated in such an analysis, such as the relationship between the building and sacrifices and the sale of sacrificed meat.[9] In addition, more attention should be paid to pre-viously understudied elements, such as the presence of hydraulic infrastruc-ture in the building or the organization of transport towards the building.[10] Strangely, even though there is a reasonable amount of knowledge on the management of buying and selling inside the *macellum*, no real study has been done concerning the movement and transportation towards the *macellum*. We can assume that, as one of the main market buildings in a Roman town, the

*Figure 10.1  Macella* across the Roman world, showing the great variety (Sources: Richard, 2014: figure 1, 257 [after De Ruyt, 1983], by permission).

building must have generated an important flow of movement, not only of people but especially of food products, transported there by several means, such as carts and donkeys. There has also been only little examination of the location and spatial organization of the *macellum* in the Roman city. An important question is: 'Did the location of the *macellum* affect traffic and transportation within the city, and if so, how?' I will attempt to answer this question (or at least attract scholarly attention to it) by looking at a series of Roman town plans. Before doing so, I will first take a closer look at the history of the study of movement in Roman cities.

## Movement in the Roman city

In the late 1980s, a paradigm shift was taking place in the study of Roman urbanism. While the focus before then had generally been on the analysis of the orthogonal grid plan and individual monuments and buildings, leaving aside their mutual spatial relationship, attention was now drawn to the study of the broader urban environment of cities. In 1986, MacDonald introduced the concept of the city as an *armature*, thus rejecting the idea that a Roman city was just a random collection of streets and buildings. On the contrary, a city was centred 'around a clearly delineated, path-like core of thoroughfares and plazas, that provided uninterrupted passage through the town and gave access to its principal public buildings.' There was a spatial logic, in which movement was an essential parameter (MacDonald, 1986: 3, 5). Zanker developed the idea of a *townscape*, implying that urban space was a reflection of society and that buildings needed to be studied in the wider context of public space (Zanker, 1998: 3). Granting more importance to the analysis of the spatial context of buildings could thus lead to more information about society itself, as 'the political, economic, social and religious functions of the city are reflected in its public buildings and their location within the urban environment' (Owens, 1991: 3). This trend is referred to as the Spatial Turn of the twentieth century.[11]

Studies on the organization of movement, transport and traffic within specific Roman cities have become increasingly popular specifically during the last two decades. From the beginning, the main focus has been on *Pompeii*, with important studies by Tsujimura on the presence of wheel ruts, and Poehler investigating the traffic system in one specific region (Tsujimura, 1991; Poehler, 2006). Van Tilburg has provided us with a general study of traffic in Roman cities, with special attention to the street network of *Pompeii*, although other cities, for instance Xanten, were also discussed (Van Tilburg, 2007, 2015). In 2000, Kaiser shifted the focus by putting the street networks of *Ampurias* and *Emporiae* in the spotlight. In 2011, he added the cities of *Pompeii*, *Ostia* and Silchester to his analysis and also presented a more general discussion of Roman street networks and the regulation of traffic in Roman towns. In these studies, Kaiser made use of the Space Syntax methodologies, which calculate the relationship of streets within a street network and evaluate which ones carried the most movement (Kaiser, 2000, 2011a). Also in 2011,

Laurence and Newsome published a volume with important contributions on several traffic systems, not only in *Pompeii* but also in Rome and *Ostia*. More recently, Poehler published '*The Traffic Systems of Pompeii*,' which is the most complete work on this theme for *Pompeii*. In addition, Poehler examines several other cities in the Roman world, mostly to compare them with the traffic system of *Pompeii* (Poehler, 2018). In total, he was able to recognize evidence for traffic in twenty-four other sites. Nonetheless, he concluded that, apart from *Pompeii*, no complete traffic systems can be observed, since the evidence from the studied sites is very fragmentary (Poehler, 2018: 221). This leads us to the first problem regarding the study of traffic and transport within Roman cities: a lack of complete archaeological evidence outside *Pompeii*. We know that in *Pompeii*, vehicular traffic was hindered by the multiple narrow streets and especially the placement of impediments on these streets (Kaiser, 2011b: 179). Hence, the question arises, and Poehler also discusses this, of whether the street network of *Pompeii* was exceptional in the Roman world or whether such strict traffic regulations were copied in other cities. Yet, Poehler's comparison with the city of Thamugadi clearly shows that traffic there was taken more into account during its construction (Poehler, 2018: 216, 227–232). We can, thus, conclude that the measurements for traffic organization in *Pompeii* were not applied in every Roman town. In order to learn something about other, less well-preserved, towns, we could take a look at the written sources; but here the second problem arises, namely, the relative lack of ancient texts on traffic regulations and the often exclusive focus on the city of Rome in the written material that we do have.

Our knowledge is mainly based on laws and charters that were issued by emperors or consuls aimed at banning vehicular traffic in the city, or passages by elite authors expressing their antipathy towards carts and traffic (Kaiser, 2011a: 56; Poehler, 2018: 4). One of the most interesting, but at the same time enigmatic, laws, is the *Lex Iulia Municipalis* issued by Caesar in 45 BCE (Newsome, 2011: 14).[12] This law banned *plostra*, heavy wagons, in the city of Rome until the tenth hour of the day, unless they were used for a religious purpose or a public construction. Lighter carts were probably still allowed (Kaiser, 2011a: 56; Hartnett, 2017: 37). Through a passage in the *Historia Augusta*, we learn that Hadrian also banned the entry of carts with a heavy load into the city (*Historia Augusta*, Hadrian 22.6). Newsome notes that vehicular traffic within the city was probably not restricted and that ancient texts refer more to transport between cities (Newsome, 2011: 20). Numerous authors write about the negative consequences of carts in the city: the noise and dust they create, their potential dangers and the shouting of the drivers (Kaiser, 2011a: 24; Hartnett, 2017: 36).[13] Other ancient references demonstrate that the street must be kept clean and more importantly passable for vehicles. This is described in the *Digest*:

> They (the city overseers, *curatores urbium*) must see to it that nothing is left outside workshops, except for a fuller leaving out clothing to dry, or

a carpenter putting out wheels; and these are not by doing so to prevent a vehicle from passing.

(*Digest* [Papinian], 43.10.1.4)[14]

It is fair to conclude that we need to maintain a critical attitude when studying ancient texts. Especially in a crowded and chaotic city like Rome, traffic must have prompted disdain in elite authors; their attitude, however, does not teach us anything about the actual organization of traffic and transport within cities. Moreover, even though legal texts were aimed at limiting or banning traffic in the city, goods must have still been transported on a daily basis. It is, therefore, important to emphasize that not all transport were provided by vehicles and that more frequently pack animals, like donkeys or mules, were used to transport goods (see Wallace-Hadrill in this volume). These were certainly much cheaper than wheeled traffic, could carry loads between 80 and 150 kg and could pass the streets relatively easily. On top of this, much transport was probably provided by human portage (Adkins and Adkins, 1994: 184; Raepsaet, 2008: 601; Adams, 2012: 230). Since goods often had to be distributed to a large number of locations in the city, it was more convenient to let several people and pack animals deliver them, rather than one cart (Laurence, 2012: 254). It is clear that there must have been a great contrast between daily products delivered by pack animals and human carriers, and *plostra* transporting larger loads (Laurence, 2008: 87–88).[15]

## Movement towards the *macellum*

Hartnett identifies the transportation of goods and supplies as one of the most important uses of streets (Hartnett, 2017: 44). Indeed, we can be sure that products must have entered the city from outside daily, coming from *villae* or farms through the roads or arriving as commercial transaction via river or sea. However, goods were also produced within the city walls itself, from where they were brought to their final destination. For the delivery of goods in *Pompeii*, Poehler defines monumental buildings as significant landmarks requiring a large amount of supplies. According to Poehler, the *macellum* was certainly one of these buildings (Poehler, 2011: 196), and even though Pompeii's street network has been heavily studied already, transportation towards the *macellum* has not yet been at the centre of attention, neither for *Pompeii* nor for any other Roman town. A number of key questions regarding this topic, therefore, remain unanswered: for example, how accessible were *macella* within the street network? Where were products transported from and how was this transport regulated within the city? In this part of the chapter, I will try to determine, by looking at some specific street networks, whether the specific location of the *macellum* had an effect on traffic and transportation.

De Ruyt stated that the *macellum* occupied a central and privileged position in Roman towns, usually directly on or close to the forum, or at the crossing of the two most important city streets, the so-called *Cardo Maximus* and *Decumanus Maximus*. In this way, the market facilitated access for customers and the delivery of goods (De Ruyt, 1983: 326, 328–329). Richard confirms this location and refers to these streets as *major traffic axes*. A position near the city gates or, in harbour cities, near the port, also facilitated the delivery of fresh products (Richard, 2014: 266). An essential factor for the location of the *macellum* in the city was thus definitely its degree of accessibility. The market had to be easily accessible from inside as well as outside the city: not only for its own residents but also for visitors and principally for the supply of products. For people visiting the city, we can assume that the market must have been relatively easy to find, as they probably knew, from their own town or visiting other towns, that it was usually located close to the forum or on one of the main streets. Let us now take a look at some specific case studies, spread over Italy and the rest of the Roman world, to assess the (in)accessibility of the *macellum* in the cityscape. First, several harbour cities will be discussed, after which attention will be devoted to inland cities.

*Minturnae* was founded in 296/295 BCE as a maritime colony on the *via Appia*. With the presence of the *Liris* river and its access to the coast, the city soon turned into an important trading centre (Campbell, 2012: 301). The *macellum*, built in the second century CE, was located on the forum but its main entrance was towards the *via Appia*. The market had high accessibility: a cart driver could enter the city through the main road and easily stop in front of the entrance to drop off their goods (Laurence, 2012: 144–145; Figure 10.2).

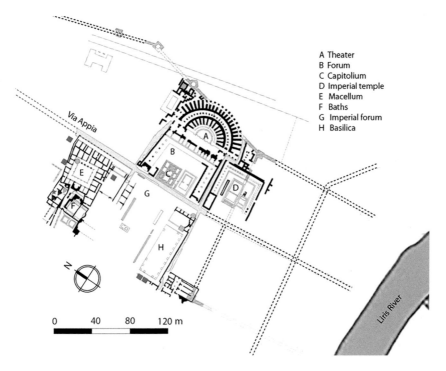

*Figure 10.2* The *macellum* (E) of *Minturnae* with main entrance towards the *via Appia* (Sources: Yegül, Favro 2019: figure 7.2, 413. Image courtesy of F. Yegül and D. Favro).

In the north Italian harbour town of *Aquileia*, located on the *Natiso* River, a *macellum* was built at the end of the second century BCE on the main north-south street, the *Cardo Maximus*. It was divided from the forum by a street and the *comitium*. The market, probably rebuilt under Tiberius, was perfectly positioned within the cityscape. It was located between the eastern and western harbour, which was recently discovered by geophysical survey, and also on the main road, making the building directly accessible from almost all gates (Tiussi, 2004: 282; Figure 10.3).[16]

In the second century BCE coastal town of *Potentia*, in *Picenum*, the *macellum*, probably dating to the Late Republican or Augustan period, was embedded on the eastern side of the forum. In the west, it must have opened directly to the *porticus* onto the *Cardo Maximus* and to the north

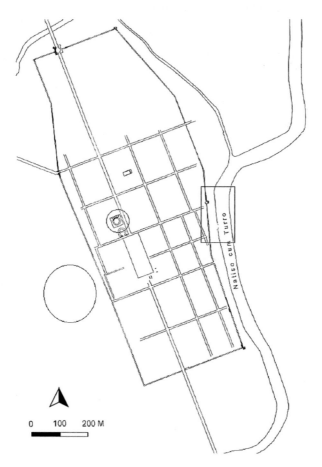

*Figure 10.3* The *macellum* of *Aquileia* (middle circle) located in between the two harbour complexes (outer black structures) (Sources: Maselli Scotti et al., 2009: figure 1, 236).

it probably had an entrance on the *Decumanus Maximus*. In this way, the market building was well connected with the four gates of the city and, thus, with the harbour and River *Potenza,* at that time located to the south of the city (Percossi Serenelli, 2001: 84–85; Vermeulen, 2012: 77, 82). The *macellum* of another coastal town in *Picenum, Castrum Truentinum*, was situated about 50 m south of the *Tronto* river and very close to the ancient port structures (Staffa, 2009: 47–49). The market in Neapolis, on the site of the San Lorenzo Maggiore church, occupied the south-eastern sector of the forum. Apart from an entrance to the forum, there was also an entrance towards the eastern *via dei Tribunali*. The building was thus quite easy to reach from the gates and harbour (De Simone, 1986: 245–246).

The *macellum* of the Roman-Iberian town of *Baelo Claudia*, located on the edge of the forum, stood in direct relationship to the *Decumanus Maximus*, to which it had its main entrance. In this manner, the building could be reached directly from the eastern gate to *Carteia* and the western gate to *Gades*. The market also seems to have been connected with a street coming from the harbour, passing the salt factories and winding up on the *Decumanus* (Figure 10.4).

In *Ampurias*, the Augustan market building was located in the centre of the town but separated from the forum by a *cryptoporticus*. The fact that the building was not located immediately on the forum facilitated its accessibility, since traffic was impeded on the forum by steps and gates. The building was located along a secondary street. When Kaiser evaluated the streets of *Ampurias*, he noted that these were about 4 m wide, enabling cart traffic to pass in two directions (Kaiser, 2011a: 194, 197). During the Flavian age, two *macella* were constructed at *Valentia*, one in the northern part of the city and one next to the forum. The first was located outside the administrative centre, close to the river and the small river port in the north, which facilitated the transport of goods arriving at the harbour (Torecilla Aznar, 2007: 251).

In several north African harbour cities, the *macellum* has been quite exceptionally preserved. The oldest example is found in *Leptis Magna*, where it was dedicated by a magistrate in 9 or 8 BCE. It was due to the commercial relationship with Rome that several local families accumulated a lot of wealth, such as the family of Annobal Tapapius Rufus who financed the *macellum* and, several years later, the theatre. Perhaps this is also the reason why the two buildings are located in close proximity to each other. The market bordered the *Cardo Maximus*, eventually leading from the western gate to the port in the east, which facilitated the provision of goods. The building was also easily accessible for the public, as there were several secondary entrances on the flanking minor streets (De Ruyt, 1983: 259–260; Young, 1993: 117). In the towns of *Hippo Regius* and *Gigthis*, the *macellum* was probably deliberately placed between the forum and the harbour. In the former, the building is located about 150 m north-east of the forum, in between two secondary streets and the *Decumanus*, but, probably not with an entrance towards it. It has been suggested, due to its location, that the market specialized in selling

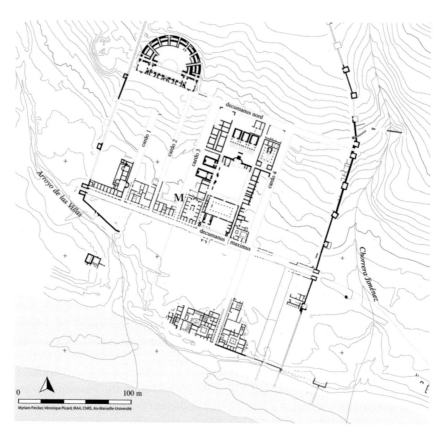

*Figure 10.4* The location of the *macellum* (M) in *Baelo Claudia* (Source: Bernal-Casasola et al., 2017: figure 11, 329, which is based on the updated cartography of the site by M. Fincker, V. Picard and S.L. Tecnocart).

fish (Young, 1993: 113, 123). In *Gigthis*, the second century CE market can be found 150 m south-west of the forum, where it bordered on a street, one of the main traffic axes, going towards the coast. We can assume that fish must have been one of the main products on sale, since there was a direct connection with the harbour (Young, 1993: 112; Grebien, 2016: 51). In Meninx, a *macellum* was discovered in the coastal zone by geophysical survey. It was surrounded by other coastal structures, such as *horrea*, and a main street aligned the building. This street probably headed all the way up to the port in the south (Lambers et al., 2017: 155–157; Ritter et al., 2018: 367). In the northern Greek city of *Thasos*, a market, built on a similar older Hellenistic structure, was embedded on the south-eastern border of the *agora*. Even though it was connected to the *agora* with a monumental passage, a secondary entrance towards a square was probably associated with a street going directly to the port (Marc, 2012: 225, 228). It is clear that in harbour and river port cities, the *macellum* was most often located closer to the harbour than to the forum or right in between both structures. This must have created a favourable transport situation: the products did not have to be brought near the forum, which would have been a busy place but were instead immediately transported on one of the main roads to the market. As mentioned, *macella* in harbour cities must have been oriented more towards the sale of fish, and, thus, a close connection with the harbour was necessary and its relationship with the forum was probably less important.

After focusing on these harbour cities, I would like to shift attention to the situation in inland towns and towns located some distance from the ancient coastline. Especially at *Pompeii*, where the street network is well preserved, some observations can be made on transport to the *macellum*. Here the building was located on the northern corner of the forum, with an entrance towards it, one on the *via degli Augustali* and an additional one on the *vicolo del Balcone Pensile*. As already discussed, multiple studies of *Pompeii*'s street net-work have demonstrated how cart traffic was obstructed by the large number of small streets, closed off streets, impediments on the streets and how some zones, including the forum, were even completely closed off to traffic (Kaiser, 2011b: 177–178).[17] Kaiser's map of the traffic system of *Pompeii* demonstrates how difficult transport towards the market must have been (Figure 10.5).

Not only was traffic possible in only one direction on the streets surrounding the *macellum*, but these streets were at a certain point even completely closed

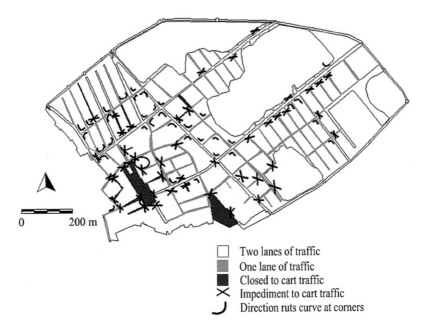

*Figure 10.5* Map of traffic patterns at *Pompeii* by Kaiser and after Tsujimura (1991) and Poehler (2006). Location of *macellum* encircled (Source: Kaiser, 2011: figure 3.6, 94).

off to cart traffic due to impediments. On the *via degli Augustali*, how-ever, right before the entrance of the forum, traces of wheel ruts of 1.40 m interdistance were found, confirming that this street might have been accessed by a cart driven by a single horse (Kaiser, 2011b: 182–184). Bearing in mind all the obstacles of the Pompeian street network, cart drivers must have known the city quite well. The case study of *Pompeii* shows us how difficult it must have been to transport products in such a complicated and dense street network. The central location of the market might have made it easily accessible for citizens, but it certainly did not improve its accessibility for cart traffic. Nonetheless, with these types of street networks, we should certainly bear in mind that products could have been delivered by pack animals and human porters. At *Alba Fucens*, the *macellum* was separated from the forum by the *basilica* and a small street. This street provided access to the two main traffic axes of the city: the *via dei Pilastri* and the *via del Miliario*, both well connected with the city gates. In Imperial times, however, and especially in the third century CE, the back of the market came to be incorporated in the *basilica*, which led to the closure of the small street. An entrance was now installed on the eastern side of the building, connecting it directly to the *via dei Pilastri*, while the entrance on the *via del Miliario* was closed off. Goods could now only be delivered through one street. There was probably also an entrance on the southern side of the building towards the sanctuary (Mertens, 1969: 66; De Ruyt, 1983: 32; Figure 10.6).

The market at *Herdonia* seems to have been very much closed off from the street network, as the building was located in the southern angle of the forum, with only one entrance directly towards the forum. We can assume that goods were transported here over the busy and crowded forum plaza. Luckily, the forum was accessible through two streets immediately connected to the nor-thern and north-eastern gate (Mertens and De Ruyt, 1995: 197). The same situation can be noted in *Paestum*: the forum had to be crossed in order to deliver products to the market (De Ruyt, 1983: 327). North of the forum of *Trea*, a small *municipium* in the middle Potenza Valley (*Picenum*), a pos-sible *macellum* was detected using non-invasive survey techniques. A street, connected to the northern gate, bordered the market and separated it from the *tabernae* on the forum. The market probably had its main entrance on this street which ultimately directed traffic to the important Adriatic harbour of Ancona (Vermeulen et al., 2017: 91; Figure 10.7).

The city of *Thamugadi* was furnished with two markets, one situated inside the town walls and one outside. The central market was placed east of the forum, with its principal facade on the *Decumanus Maximus*, in close prox-imity to the eastern gate. The market of *Sertius* was positioned right outside the western gate, also with a main entrance towards the *Decumanus Maximus* and an entrance towards the street going to the *Capitolium*. Poehler compared the street network of *Pompeii* to that of *Thamugadi*, even though the latter was founded centuries later. He concludes that in *Thamugadi*, movement was much more facilitated than in *Pompeii*, through the presence of wide streets

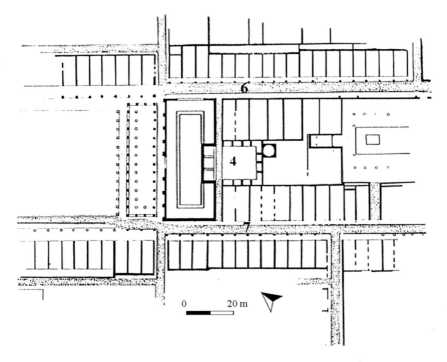

*Figure 10.6* The Republican *macellum* of *Alba Fucens* (4) connected to the *via dei Pilastri* (6) and the *via del Miliario* (7) through a small street. In Imperial times, the entrance through the *via del Miliario* was closed off (Source: Di Cesare and Liberatore, 2017: figure 4, 5 [after Mertens 1981]).

and colonnades, sidewalk space for pedestrians, a lack of stepping stones and only two-way streets (Poehler, 2018: 227–230). In *Thuburbo Maius*, a *macellum* complex, comprising three connected buildings, is found on the southern angle of the forum. The markets were bordered by the so-called *Rue du Labyrinthe* and the *Rue de l'Aurige*; however, this network of streets gives the impression of being rather complicated and irregular (De Ruyt, 1983: 207–212). The market building of *Cuicul* was more easily accessible, as it was located on the forum with its entrance on the *Cardo Maximus*. Moreover, there was a close connection with the northern gate.

  *Lugdunum Convenarum* or modern Saint-Betrand-de-Comminges, located in the foothills of the Pyrenees and probably founded in 72 or 71 BCE, has a very irregular street pattern but is dominated by no less than five important routes. Its *macellum*, built at the foot of the hill, was strategically positioned at the crossing of the *Cardo Maximus* and a principal *Decumanus*. The *macellum* was well connected with the street network on all sides (Fabres and Paillet, 2009: 49; Laurence, 2011: 96, 98). In Wroxeter, the *macellum* was part of a large complex, in which a bathing and exercise space were integrated. It was

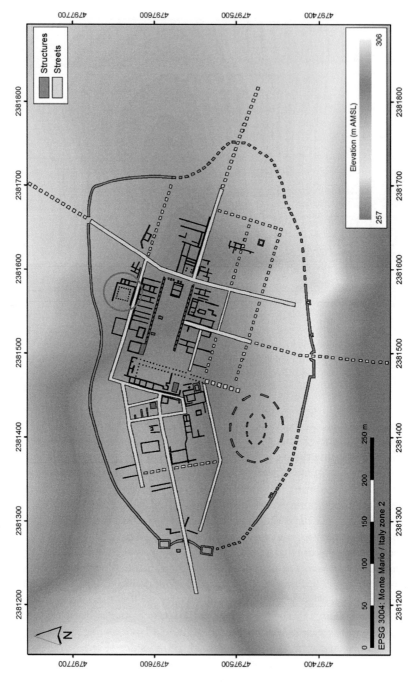

*Figure 10.7* The *macellum* of *Trea* (Source: Vermeulen et al., 2017: figure 57, 88).

separated from the forum by the *Cardo Maximus*, and it was connected to the town gates through this street (Grocock, 2015: 151). The *tholos* in *Aezani*, belonging to a larger market complex, was situated on the right side of the *Rhyndakos* river, which separated the building from the centre of the city. This location guaranteed a closer relationship with the river and facilitated the delivery of products (De Ruyt, 1983: 23). Finally, the bizarre location of the *macellum* of *Sagalassos* should be mentioned. The building is situated on the south-eastern angle of the *agora* and is placed on an inferior level. The market was only accessible through the stairs leading from the *agora*, which created a difficult situation for the delivery of products. Three theories have been proposed about this location. First of all, since the market was one of the last large buildings to be constructed in the monumental centre, there might not have been much room left after its construction. Second, the vicinity of residential zones might have been more important than accessibility for cart traffic. Third, the location of the building can be interpreted in terms of competitive display: the financer may have chosen this location to compete with one of their family members who had donated the *nymphaeum* on the north side of the *agora* (Richard and Waelkens, 2012: 83, 87–88).

The *macella* in inland towns appear to have had a strong connection with the main roads, through which they were immediately related to the gates; however, as we have seen, in some cases, the *macellum* was located in less accessible zones in the city. In *Herdonia* and *Paestum*, one needed to cross the forum to deliver products, while in *Pompeii* and *Thuburbo Maius*, the characteristics of the street pattern definitely complicated the supply of goods. In *Alba Fucens*, the *macellum* became more inaccessible in the Imperial period and in *Sagalassos* cart traffic to the market was impossible. Admittedly, *macella* had a privileged position, in the most monumental part of the city and along roads, but this did not always benefit the organization of transport. We can conclude that the accessibility of these market buildings was strongly affected by their location within the street network.

There is one more element affecting the *macellum*'s accessibility that needs to be discussed. Characteristic of *macella* was the presence of monumental entrances, often adorned with large and wide arches and stairs. Often, the entrance to the building was placed on a slightly higher level than the floor level of the street. Even though markets were often located on main streets and were thus accessible for carts, the actual building was not. It was, thus, impossible for wheeled traffic to enter the building, making it exclusively accessible for pedestrians (Richard, 2014: 267). In some cities, these entrances must have had only minimal effect on the delivery of goods. At *Baelo Claudia*, for example, the entrance on the *Decumanus Maximus* was marked by three steps, and carts could easily stop and the goods be carried inside the market. At *Saepinum* and *Paestum*, the access to the *macellum* was also provided by three steps. In north African cities, these entrances were the most monumental, and we can understand why the delivery of products must have been more complicated here. In *Thuburbo Maius*, *Thamugadi*, *Cuicul* and *Thugga*, a flight of steps provided entrance to the building. In the latter two cities, these stairs numbered 17 and 19 steps, respectively (Young, 1993: 102).

The organization of traffic towards the *macellum* was, of course, also highly dependent on where goods were specifically delivered from. We can imagine that products from inside the city were probably better delivered on foot or using pack animals. Meat from butchered animals could be brought in from the local butchery, but if the animals were to be butchered inside the *macellum*, as is shown by the evidence in some contexts, then they must have been brought in by carts.[18] Many products essentially came from outside the city, however, for instance from the harbour or the villa estates. Especially concerning the latter, some information is provided in Varro's *De Re Rustica*. In a dialogue between Merula and Axius, we learn that wild boars from the villa estate of Seius were sold to the *macellarius* and must have been for sale inside the *macellum* (Varro, *De Re Rustica*, 3.2.11; Holleran, 2012: 173).[19] Varro also mentions the presence of fish ponds on villa estates, thus suggesting that fish were kept in enclosures filled with either fresh or salt water, after which they were brought to the market (Varro, *De Re Rustica*, 3.4).[20] These fish ponds are, for instance, well-attested along the Thyrrenian coast, from where they were certainly brought to the *macella* of Rome. But fish could also have been transported directly from the harbour to the market. Columella informs us that fish coming from these ponds were much cheaper than fish from the sea: 'For unless the fish is fattened with food provided by its owner, when it is brought to the fish market its leanness shows that it has not been caught in the open sea but comes from a place of confinement and because of this a large sum is detracted from the price' (Marzano and Brizzi, 2009: 226, 228; Columella, *De Re Rustica*, 8.17.15). These fish were transported in tanks, so that they were still alive when they got to the market (Holleran, 2012: 178).[21] Many products probably derived from the *villae* and Holleran even see the emergence of the *macella*, especially in Rome, as a phenomenon linked to changes in the agricultural landscape and the production on villa estates for the cities (Holleran, 2012: 174).

## Conclusions

In the last two decades, several studies have drawn attention to the organization of movement, transport and traffic in Roman cities. The *macellum*, as an example of one of the buildings in the city requiring a large supply of goods, has been completely ignored in these studies, and, therefore, this chapter aimed to shed light on the spatial organization of the *macellum* and its effect on traffic and the transportation of goods by discussing several city plans in Roman Italy and the Roman provinces. Based on this, we can conclude that the embedding of *macella*, their relationship with the streets, other public buildings and city gates, surely must have had an impact on the regulation of transport. From the examples of *Pompeii*, *Herdonia*, *Paestum* and *Thuburbo Maius*, it is clear that the *macellum*'s privileged position on the forum did not always have a positive effect on the delivery of goods but rather complicated the transport process. Mostly, however, the market buildings were oriented with their main entrance towards an important street, providing easy access for carts or pack animals. Nonetheless, these carts or animals could not enter the market itself as the entrance was often arranged around stairs, and the goods were thus carried into the market on foot. It is noteworthy that in harbour or river port cities, the *macellum* was frequently built somewhere between the forum and the harbour, to facilitate the delivery of goods from ships. Comparing several Roman street networks enables us to reveal different patterns of transport in different cities. Such a study should in the future be supplemented by an analysis of the street networks using Space Syntax, a methodology that makes it possible to detect those streets that facilitated most of the movement in a city. Examining how the *macellum* and other public and private buildings were related to these streets could potentially provide us with important insights into Roman urban planning.

## Notes

1  '*Haec omnia posteaquam contracta in unum locum quae ad victum pertinebant et aedificatus locus, appellatum Macellum,…*': Translation in Kent, 1938, 138–139.
2  In its turn, the word is derived from the Semitic word *mikla* (enclosed space).
3  Aristotle in his *Politics* (VII, 11.2: 1331a-2) explains this:
   '*It is convenient that below this site should be laid out an agora of the kind customary in Thessaly which they call a free agora, that is, one which has to be kept clear of all merchandise and into which no artisan or farmer or any other such person may intrude unless summoned by the magistrates.*' (Translation: http://www.perseus.tufts.edu).
4  An exception is the *macellum* of Morgantina in ancient Sicilia.
5  Under Augustus and Tiberius, a tax was issued on food sold in the *macellum*. Even though Suetonius tells us (*Cal.* 40) that this was in force in the entire city, Pliny the Elder (*HN* 19.56) refers to (probably) this tax as *macellum vectigali*, thus confirming that it was a tax associated with the market. The tax caused a lot of dissatisfaction and was, therefore, cancelled, possibly under Nero (Holleran, 2012, 177). The presence of a strong elite financing this building and the wish to enhance not only their own status but also that of their city, by outbuilding neighbouring cities, must certainly have been one of the reasons for its construction.
6  This study remains the only synthesis publication on the *macellum*.
7  Forty-three in Italy and 102 in the provinces. This number has been achieved through an in-depth study of the existing literature and excavation reports on *macella*. Because of the large variation in evidence, nine categories were created, on the basis of which *macella* have been identified and studied: excavation, inscriptions, inscriptions and excavation, geophysical survey, geophysical/aerial survey and excavation, ancient literature and inscriptions, ancient literature, inscriptions, ancient literature and excavation and uncertain.
8  Several studies focused on the building in single cities: Didierjean et al., 1986; Uscatescu and Martin-Bueno, 1997; Láng et al., 2014; Fabre and Paillet, 2009; Marc, 2012; Morena López et al., 2012; Richard and Waelkens, 2012; Olivito,

2014; Ciliberto, 2015; Grocock, 2015, while others analysed its distribution in specific provinces: Young, 1993; Torrecilla Aznar, 2007; Hamdoune, 2009; Richard, 2014; Cristili, 2015.

9  Van Andringa, 2007: 49 described the *macellum* as main distributor of sacrificed meat. As there is still no definitive conclusion on this matter, the evidence should be summarized and discussed.

10  The lack of attention to water supply has already been pointed out by Richard, 2017.

11  For more information on this Spatial Turn, I refer to Newsome, 2011: 1–54 and Östenberg et al., 2015: 1–9.

12  A partial copy of this law has been found in Heraclea (*Tabula Heracleensis*) in southern Italy.

13  These refer to the writings of, for instance, Juvenal, Horace and Martial.

14  Translation in Hakim, 2014: 5.

15  Through Vitruvius we know that these two-wheeled carts were mostly used for the transportation of agricultural produce: Vitruvius, *De Architectura*, 10.1.5.

16  For the geophysical survey, see Groh, 2012.

17  Impediments included blocking stones, extending kerbs and sidewalks, or buildings or fountains extending onto the street.

18  Inside the *macellum* and porticoes of Wroxeter, pits have been found containing animal bones, which show signs of butchery, and iron hooks. Bones of butchered animals are also abundant in Segesta. Recently, it has been claimed that the *tholos* of Morgantina was used to butcher animals. See Ellis, 2000: 330: Grocock, 2015: 169; Olivito, 2014: 31–35; Sharp, 2015.

19  Translation at http://penelope.uchicago.edu/Thayer/E/Roman/Texts/Varro/de_Re_Rustica/3*.html

20  Translation at http://penelope.uchicago.edu/Thayer/E/Roman/Texts/Varro/de_Re_Rustica/3*.html

21  De Ruyt, 1983: 313 and Richard, 2017: 344 claim that fish were even kept alive in the *macellum*, yet there is no hard evidence for this assumption.

## References

Adams, C. "Transport." Pages 2018–2240 in *The Cambridge Companion to the Ancient Economy*. Edited by Walter Scheidel. Cambridge: Cambridge University Press, 2012.

Adkins, Lesley and Roy A. Adkins. *Handbook to Life in Ancient Rome*. New York: Infobase Publishing, 1994.

Bernal-Casasola, Darío, José A. Expósito, José J. Díaz, Nicolas Carayon, Kristian Strutt, Ferréol Salomon and Simon Keay. "Baelo Claudia, Puerto pesquero, commercial y de viajeros. Nuevas perspectivas." Pages 309–344 in *Los Puertos Atlánticos Béticos y Lusitanos y su relación commercial con el Mediterráneo*. Edited by Juan M. Campos Carrasco and Javier Bermejo Meléndez. Roma: L'Erma di Bretschneider, 2017.

Campbell, Brian J. *Rivers and the Power of Ancient Rome*. Chapel Hill: University of North Carolina Press, 2012.

Ciliberto, Fulvia. "Nugae sepinati I. Il macellum di Sepino." *LANX* 21 (2015): 41–53.

Cristili, Armando. "Macellum and Imperium. The relationship between the Roman State and the market-building construction." *Analysis Archaeologica* 1 (2015): 69–86.

Di Cesare, Riccardo and Daniela Liberatore. "Le tabernae di Alba Fucens." *The Journal of Fasti Online* 379 (2017): 1–26.

Didierjean, François, Claude Ney and Jean-Louis Paillet. *Belo III: Le Macellum.* Paris: De Boccard, 1986.

De Ruyt, Claire. *Macellum: marché alimentaire des Romains.* Louvain-La-Neuve: Publications d'Histoire de l'Art et d'Archéologie de l'Université Catholique de Louvain, 1983.

De Simone, A.S. "Lorenzo Maggiore in Napoli: il monumento e l'area." Pages 233–253 in *Neapolis: Atti del venticinquesimo convegno di studi sulla Magna Grecia, Taranto 3–7 Ottobre 1985.* Taranto: Istituto per la Storia e l'Archeologia della Magna Grecia, 1986.

Ellis, Peter. *The Roman Baths and Macellum at Wroxeter. Excavations by Graham Webster 1955–85.* London: English Heritage, 2000.

Evangelidis, Vasilis. "Macella and Makelloi in Roman Greece: The Archaeological and Textual Evidence." *Hesperia* 88 (2019): 283–318.

Fabres, Georges and Jean-Louis Paillet. *Saint-Bertrand-de-Comminges. Vol. 4, Le Macellum.* Pessac: Éditions de la Fédération Aquitania, 2009.

Grebien, Matthias. "Das Macellum von Gigthis, eine Imitation der Trajansmärkte in Rom." Pages 51–55 in *"Ich bin dann mal weg" Festschrift für einen Reisenden Thuri Lorenz zum 85. Geburtstag.* Edited by Gabriele Koiner and Ute Lohner-Urban. Vienna: Phoibos Verlag, 2016.

Grocock, Christopher. "The Wroxeter Macellum: A Foodway in Every Sense." Pages 151–170 in *Food & Markets: Proceedings of the Oxford Symposium on Food and Cookery 2014.* Edited by Mark McWilliams. London: Prospect Books, 2015.

Groh, Stefan. *Research on the Urban and Suburban Topography of Aquileia.* Internet publication http://ceur-ws.org/Vol-948/paper4.pdf, 1–11, 2012.

Gros, Pierre. *L'architecture romaine du début du IIIe siècle av. J.C. à la fin du Haut-Empire. Les monuments publics.* Paris: Picard, 1996.

Hakim, Besim S. *Mediterranean Urbanism: Historic Urban/Building Rules and Processes.* Berlin: Spring, 2014.

Hamdoune, Christine. "Les *macella* dans les cites de l'Afrique romaine." *Antiquités Africaines* 45 (2009): 27–35.

Hartnett, Jeremy. *The Roman Street: Urban Life and Society in Pompeii, Herculaneum, and Rome.* Cambridge: Cambridge University Press, 2017.

Holleran, Claire. *Shopping in Ancient Rome: the Retail Trade in the late Republic and the Principate.* Oxford: Oxford University Press, 2012.

Kaiser, Alan. *The Urban Dialogue: An analysis of the use of space in the Roman city of Empúries, Spain.* Oxford: Archaeopress, 2000.

Kaiser, Alan. *Roman Urban Street Networks.* New York: Routledge, 2011a.

Kaiser, Alan. "Cart Traffic Flow in Pompeii and Rome." Pages 174–193 in *Rome, Ostia, Pompeii: Movement and Space.* Edited by Ray Laurence and David J. Newsome. Oxford: Oxford University Press, 2011b.

Lambers, Lena, Jörg W.E. Fassbinder, Stefan Ritter and Sami Ben Tahar. "Meninx–Geophysical Prospection of a Roman Town in Jerbia, Tunisia." Pages 135–137 in *12th International Conference of Archaeological Prospection.* Edited by Benjamin Jennings, Christopher Gaffney, Thomas Sparrow and Sue Gaffney. Oxford: Archaeopress Archaeology, 2017.

Láng, Orsolya, Alexandra Nagy and Péter Vámos. *The Aquincum Macellum. Researches in the Area of the Macellum in the Aquincum Civil Town (1882–1965).* Budapest: Phoibos Verlag, 2014.

Laurence, Ray. *The Roads of Roman Italy: Mobility and Cultural Change.* London: Routledge, 1999.

Laurence, Ray. "City Traffic and Archaeology of Roman Streets from Pompeii to Rome." Pages 87–106 in *Stadtverkehr in der Antiken Welt. Internationales Kolloquium zur 175-Jahrfeier des Deutschen Archäologischen Instituts. Rom 21. bis 23. April 2004.* Edited by Dieter Mertens. Wiesbaden: Dr. Ludwig Reichert Verlag, 2008.

Laurence, Ray and David J. Newsome. *Rome, Ostia, Pompeii: Movement and Space.* Oxford: Oxford University Press, 2011.

Laurence, Ray. "Traffic and Land Transportation in and near Rome." Pages 246–261 in *The Cambridge Companion to Ancient Rome.* Edited by Paul Erdkamp. Cambridge: Cambridge University Press, 2012.

Lomas, Kathryn. "Public Building, Urban Renewal and Euergetism in Early Imperial Italy." Pages 28–45 in *Bread and Circuses: Euergetism and Municipal Patronage in Roman Italy.* Edited by Kathryn Lomas and Tim Cornell. London: Routledge, 2003.

MacDonald, William L. *The Architecture of the Roman Empire. Volume II: An Urban Appraisal.* New Haven: Yale University Press, 1986.

Marc, Jean-Yves. "Un macellum d'époque hellénistque à Thasos." Pages 225–239 in *Basiliques et agoras de Grèce et d'Asie Mineure.* Edited by Laurence Cavalier, Raymond Descat and Jacques Des Courtils. Bordeaux: Ausonius Éditions, 2012.

Marzano, Annalisa and Giulio Brizzi. "Costly Display or Economic Investment? A Quantitative Approach to the Study of Marine Aquaculture." *Journal of Roman Archaeology* 22 (2009): 215–230.

Maselli Scotti, Franca, Luciana Mandruzzato and Cristiano Tiussi. "La prima fase dell'impianto coloniario di Aquileia. La situazione attuale degli studi e delle ricerche." Pages 235–277 in *Aspetti e problemi della romanizzazione: Venetia, Histria e Arco Alpino Orientale.* Edited by Giuseppe Cuscito. Trieste: Editreg Sas, 2009.

Mertens, Joseph. *Alba Fucens I: Rapports et études.* Brussels: Institut Historique Belge de Rome, 1969.

Mertens, Joseph. *Alba Fucens.* Brussels: Centre belge de recherches archéologiques en Italie centrale et méridionale, 1981.

Mertens, Joseph and Claire De Ruyt. "La piazza forense in epoca imperiale." Pages 185–203 in *Herdonia. Scoperta di una città.* Edited by Claire De Ruyt, Joseph Mertens and Giuliano Volpe. Brussels: Institut Historique Belge de Rome, 1995.

Morena López, José A., Antonio Moreno Rosa and Rafael M. Martínez Sánchez. *El macellum de la Colonia Ituci Virtus Iulia (Torreparedones. Baena-Córdoba).* Baena: Excmo. Ayuntamiento de Baena, 2012.

Newsome, David J. "Introduction. Making Movement Meaningful." Pages 1–54 in *Rome, Ostia, Pompeii: Movement and Space.* Edited by Ray Laurence and David J. Newsome. Oxford: Oxford University Press, 2011.

Olivito, Riccardo. "Dynamics of 'Romanization' at Segesta: the Case of the Macellum." Pages 1507–1511 in *Centre and Periphery in the Ancient World. Proceedings of the XVIIIth International Congress of Classical Archaeology, Vol.II.* Edited by José M. Alvarez, Trinidad Nogales and Isabel Rodà. Mérida: Museo Nacional de Arte Romano, 2014.

Östenberg, Ida, Simon Malmberg and Jonas Bjørnebye. "Introduction" Pages 1–10 in *The Moving City: Processions, Passages and Promenades in Ancient Rome*. Edited by Östenberg I, Simon Malmberg and Jonas Bjørnebye. London: Bloomsbury, 2015.

Owens, Edwin J. *The City in the Greek and Roman World*. London: Routledge, 1991.

Percossi Serenelli, Edvige. "Appunti per una *forma Urbis*." Pages 72–87 in *Potentia: quando poi scese il silenzio…: rito e società in una colonia romana del Piceno fra Repubblica e tardo Impero*. Edited by Edvige Percossi Serenelli. Milano: Motta, 2001.

Poehler, Eric E. "The Circulation of Traffic in Pompeii's Regio VI." *Journal of Roman Archaeology* 19 (2006): 53–74.

Poehler, Eric E. "Where to Park? Carts, Stables, and the Economics of Transport in Pompeii." Pages 194–214 in *Rome, Ostia, Pompeii: Movement and Space*. Edited by Ray Laurence and David J. Newsome. Oxford: Oxford University Press, 2011.

Poehler, Eric E. *The Traffic Systems of Pompeii*. Oxford: Oxford University Press, 2018.

Raepsaet, Georges. "Land Transport, Part 2: Riding, Harnesses, and Vehicles." Pages 580–605 in *The Oxford Handbook of Engineering and Technology in the Classical World*. Edited by John P. Oleson. Oxford University Press: Oxford, 2008.

Richard, Julian and Marc Waelkens. "Le Macellum de Sagalassos (Turquie): un marché "romain" dans les montagnes du Taurus? Compte-rendu préliminaire des fouilles archéologiques menées depuis 2005." Pages 81–102 in *Tout vendre, tout acheter: structures et éuipements des marches antiques: actes du colloque d'Athènes, 16–19 juin 2009*. Edited by Véronique Chankowski and Pavlos Karvonis. Athens: École Française d'Athènes, 2012.

Richard, Julian. "*Macellum*/μάκελλον: 'Roman' Food Markets in Asia Minor and the Levant." *Journal of Roman Archaeology* 27 (2014): 255–274.

Richard, Julian. "Water for the Market. Hydraulic Infrastructure at the Roman Macellum of Sagalassos, SW Turkey." *BABesch Supplement* 32 (2017): 343–350.

Ritter, S., Sami Ben Tahar, Jörg W.E. Fassbiner and Lena Lambers. "Landscape Archaeology and Urbanism at Meninx: Results of Geophysical Prospection on Jerba (2015)." *Journal of Roman Archaeology* 31 (2018): 357–372.

Sharp, Henry K. "Nuove ricerche sul macellum di Morgantina. Funzioni pratiche e metaforiche." Pages 172–178 in *Morgantina Duemilaequindici: la ricerca archeologica a sessant'anni dall'avvio degli scavi*. Edited by Laura Maniscalco. Aidone, Sicily: Museo Regionale, 2015.

Staffa, Andrea R. *Guida all'Antiquarium di Castrum Truentinum*, Martinsicuro, Castellalto, 2009.

Tiussi, Cristiano. "Il sistema di distribuzione di Aquileia: mercati e magazzini." Pages 257–316 in *Aquileia dalle origini alla costituzione del ducato longobardo. Topografia, urbanistica, edilizia pubblica*. Edited by Giuseppe Cuscito and Monika Verzár-Bass. Udine: Editreg, 2004.

Torrecilla Aznar, Ana. *Los Macella en la Hispania Romano. Estudio arquitectonico, Funcional y Simbolico*. Unpublished PhD dissertation Universidad Autónoma de Madrid, 2007.

Tsujimura, Sumiyo. "Ruts in Pompeii: the Traffic System in the Roman City." *Opuscula Pompeiana* I (1991): 58–90.

Uscatescu, Alexandra and Manuel Martín-Bueno. "The Macellum of Gerasa (Jerash, Jordan): From a Market Place to an Industrial Area." *Bulletin of the American Schools of Oriental Research* 307 (1997): 67–88.

Van Andringa, William. "Du sanctuaire au macellum: Sacrifices, commerce et consummation de la viande à Pompéi." *Food & History* 5 (2007): 47–72.

Van Tilburg, Cornelis. *Traffic and Congestion in the Roman Empire*. London: Routledge, 2007.

Van Tilburg, Cornelis. *Streets and Streams. Health Conditions and City Planning in the Graeco-Roman World*. Leiden: Primavera Pers, 2015.

Vermeulen, Frank. "Potentia: A Lost New Town." Pages 78–95 in *Urbes Extinctae: Archaeologies of Abandoned Classical Towns*. Edited by Neil Christie and Andrea Augenti. Farnham: Ashgate, 2012.

Vermeulen, Frank, Devi Taelman, Francesca Carboni and Wieke De Neef. "Intra-site Surveys on Protohistoric and Roman Central Places in the Potenza Valley." Pages 67–111 in *The Potenza Valley Survey (Marche, Italy): Settlement Dynamics and Changing Material Culture in an Adriatic Valley between Iron Age and Late Antiquity*. Edited by Frank Vermeulen, Dimitri Van Limbergen, Patrick Monsieur and Devi Taelman. Rome: Academia Belgica, 2017.

Yegül, Fikret and Diane Favro. *Roman Architecture and Urbanism. From the Origins to Late Antiquity*. Cambridge: Cambridge University Press, 2019.

Young, Alexis M. *The Roman North African Macella: their Chronology, Typology, Urban Placement and Patronage*. Unpublished PhD dissertation McMaster University, 1993.

Zanker, Paul. *Pompeii: Public and Private Life*. Harvard: Harvard University Press, 1998.

Varro, *On the Latin Language*, Volume I: Books 5–7. Translated by Roland G. Kent. Cambridge, MA: Harvard University Press, 1938.

# 11 How open was the Roman city?

## Movement and impediments to movement in the street system

*Andrew Wallace-Hadrill*

## Introduction

The ancient city, in the standard view, was different in kind from the medieval city, whether of Western Europe or the Islamic world.[1] Yet there is something paradoxical about the way the contrasts are constructed. On the one hand, the ancient city is supposedly characterised by an open street network: preferably a rationally organised grid pattern, but in any case, a system of capillary connections whereby the main roads ran from the gates to the centre, opening up the city to communication locally and externally, with a place of exchange, agora or forum, at its heart.[2] By contrast, the medieval city is supposedly characterised by winding alleys and dead ends. As Averil Cameron (1985) puts it:

> All over the empire, archaeology shows that a transformation was occurring during the sixth century. The open spaces of the classical city — the baths, fora and public buildings which Procopius records … were giving way to the crowded and winding streets of the medieval souks; the houses were soon rather to be found huddling round the fortified citadel enclosing the bishop's palace and the main church.

The contrast between the straight streets of antiquity and the winding alleys of the Middle Ages stretches from Francis Haverfield to Hugh Kennedy's 'Polis to Medina'.[3] Arjan Zuiderhoek in his admirable survey of the Ancient City in his last chapter, 'The end of the ancient city?', cites Kennedy:

> the wide colonnaded streets typical of the ancient Greco-Roman city 'were invaded and divided up by intrusive structures, both houses and shops, and became more like narrow winding lanes', especially in the East as stoas developed into souks.[4]

Inescapably it sounds like a story of decline: the ancient and especially Roman city has been offered up since the early nineteenth century as a model of rational urbanism, one from which modern town planning is invited, as by Haverfield, to learn lessons.

But there is a second standard contrast, that developed by Moses Finley on the basis of Max Weber.[5] Here the ancient city is characterised by the dominance of a landowning elite, which uses the city as the place to display its power and wealth and takes no interest in trade, unless incidentally to support its luxury lifestyle. This city is contrasted with that of medieval Europe (just when and where are never fully clear) in which the separation of town and country permits the emergence of a distinctive urban economy and an urban elite of merchants and traders. I do not want to stoke up the embers of the 'consumer city' debate (though the fires lie ever close to the surface) but simply to point out that it is paradoxical in terms of mobility and trade that we should regard the ancient city as ideally planned for mobility and exchange, and yet suppose that the ruling elites had little interest in trade and see the tangled streets and inaccessible ghettos of the medieval city as the ground that fostered trade. We need not subscribe to either aspect of the traditional contrast, that is, either the medieval winding street model or the ancient consumer city model. But it provides a good spur to reflect more seriously on the relationship between Roman street networks and trade.

## Movement and impediments to movement

Let us ask ourselves, then, how far the street layout of a Roman city promoted or inhibited commercial activity. Here we have the advantage of a series of monographs in the recent years of Roman street systems, with some focus on Pompeii, starting with Ray Laurence on Pompeii, followed by Alan Kaiser on *Roman Urban Street Networks*, and, more recently, Eric Poehler's *The Traffic System of Pompeii* and Jeremy Hartnett's *The Roman Street*, together with two important conference proceedings on streets and traffic edited by Dieter Mertens and Catherine Saliou.[6] Cumulatively, these studies suggest that Roman municipal authorities devoted considerable attention to ensuring smooth traffic flow in their cities and, if Poehler is right, evolved fairly sophisticated traffic management systems. Among elements that can be taken to have promoted traffic flow are the width of main thoroughfares, their metalling with basalt pavers and attention to keeping roads and pavements clear, whether of rubbish and filth, or actual encroachments, like the activities of the barbers and salesmen that Martial so vividly evokes.[7] Evidence that responsibility for keeping the roads clear devolved on the aediles or other municipal magistrate stretches from the *lex Julia municipalis* of the *Heraclea* tablets to the Digest (Figures 11.1–11.3).[8]

But equally interesting are interventions which actually inhibit the flow of traffic. I have long been struck by the ingenuity and thoroughness with which wheeled traffic was excluded from the forum areas of both Pompeii and Herculaneum. Anyone traversing the main east/west axis of Pompeii through the Forum, from the Porta Marina to the Via dell'Abbondanza, must be

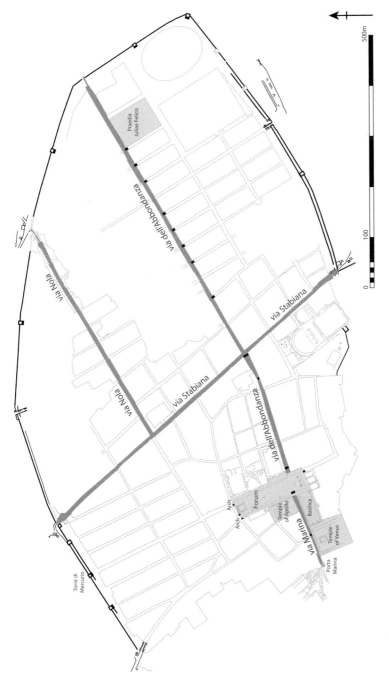

*Figure 11.1* Pompeii: plan of the main streets with indications of traffic impediments and the main sites mentioned in this chapter (after a plan provided by Archaeological Park of Pompeii), drawing by Sophie Hay.

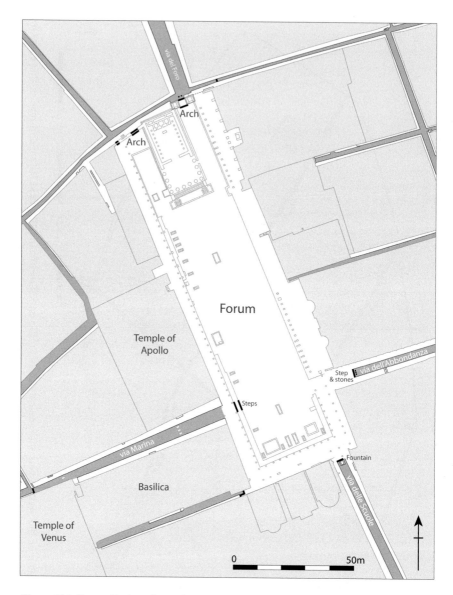

*Figure 11.2* Pompeii: location of forum impediments (after a plan provided by Archaeological Park of Pompeii), drawing by Sophie Hay.

struck by the way it is deliberately rendered impassable to wheeled traffic. The steep road up from the Porta Marina, which puts so many tourists to the test, was evidently impossible for carts to negotiate; and as if to make the matter absolutely clear, the precinct wall of the temple of Venus actually extends over

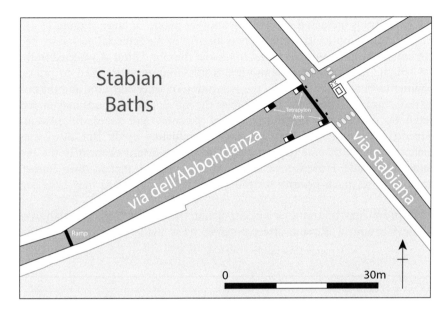

*Figure 11.3* Pompeii: impediments near the Stabiana crossroads (after a plan provided by Archaeological Park of Pompeii), drawing by Sophie Hay.

the road, narrowing it to less than a cart's width, while the pavement on the opposite side is elevated in such a way as to rule out ramping up one wheel over the pavement. The road broadens outside the temple of Apollo and the Basilica, but not for the benefit of carts, which would have had to negotiate steps down to the forum. The exits from the Forum to the north are blocked by two monumental arches with steps, while that to the south is cut off by a colonnade and a strategically located fountain in the centre of the road. On the east side, the entrance to Via dell'Abbondanza is blocked by three upright stones and a step; these apparently replaced a monumental gateway that was no less hard to negotiate.[9] Further down the Via dell'Abbondanza, at the crucial intersection with the Via Stabiana, the road broadens out into a piazza and is rendered impassable by a combination of a steep step and an honorific monument.

The Herculaneum Forum, of which we have only a fragment,[10] is cut off from the three '*cardines*' that lead down to the sea: Cardo III is blocked by a large podium, Cardo IV by a deep drop in level of the road, a water tower and a fountain, while the junction of Cardo V with the Decumanus Maximus is constricted by a fountain and a block of stone, though this is wide enough not to block traffic entirely. Elsewhere too in Herculaneum and Pompeii, fountains are placed on the road, narrowing if not entirely blocking the highway: the intersection of the lower Decumanus and Cardo V outside the Palaestra is narrowed by the fountain, though in compensation, the road width outside the Palaestra is increased, so creating another piazza or largo (Figure 11.4).

It is clear in both cities that there is an urge in the Imperial period to 'pedestrianise' the city centre or rather to restrict the circulation of wheeled traffic. Of course, modern pedestrianisation is not a strategy designed to prevent commerce but to promote it by the separation of wheeled traffic and the pedestrian shopper. The traffic that enables the movement of goods may impede retail by obstructing the movement of persons, and successful planning depends on the delicate management of conflicting needs. But all of these mean that impediments to traffic may be an important element in the promotion of trade. However, we may question whether ancient town councils gave quite so much priority to trade, and their motivations may have been different.

Impediments to traffic is an important theme that runs through Alan Kaiser's study of Roman street systems, as is made clear by his preface,

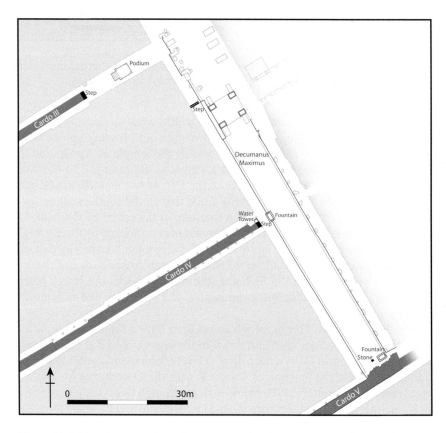

*Figure 11.4* Herculaneum: impediments on the decumanus maximus (after plan provided by Massimo Brizzi/HCP), drawing by Sophie Hay.

in which he recounts his experience at Empuries of discovering that 'impediments to traffic, such as narrow roads and stone slabs and fountains blocking routes, were much more common than I ever would have expected based on the modern literature about Roman cities' (xvi). His insight is a valuable one, for the literature has indeed been more concerned with traffic flow than obstructions, and the impression is often generated that the ideal Roman grid city was perfectly permeable to wheeled traffic.

Kaiser may have pushed his case too far in seeing virtually every street south of the Via dell'Abbondanza in Pompeii as blocked to traffic,[11] and Poehler in much greater detail reads as ramps and water-management systems many features that Kaiser sees as blockages.[12] As a consequence, Poehler has wheeled traffic running over most of Pompeii in one-way systems that change over time.[13] Undoubtedly Poehler's painstaking observations of differential wear to kerb stones, building on Tsujimura's pioneering study of rut patterns,[14] have transformed our understanding of traffic movements. But worn kerb stones are fine-tuning. The most fundamental point to grasp is the underlying contrast of broad and narrow streets, and it is clear that unless obstructed by steps and other obstacles, broader streets were generally more accessible to wheeled traffic, and narrow side streets less so.

Here Kaiser's analysis of the language of Latin (and occasionally Greek) texts is illuminating. It has long been known that the standard contrast of *decumani* and *cardines* has no roots in ancient usage, being a misappropriation of the language of the agrimensores in dividing plots of land. Despite the protests of authorities as respected as Ward-Perkins and Castognoli, this language is still applied not only to ancient sites like Herculaneum (and I have already, perforce, used this language) but also to modern Naples, where the *decumani* give a false patina of antiquity to roads that do indeed follow the original Greek colonial layout, but with a label for which there is no ancient evidence. These bogus labels would not matter if they did not overlap with and distract from a different and more important contrast, between the main, broad streets and narrow neighbourhood streets. The main routes could be called *viae*, like the trunk roads leading into the city, but the dominant term is the Greek term *plateae*, which persists in Latin usage from Vitruvius until at least the seventh century in Isidore's Visigothic Spain,[15] and in Italian cities until the crucial point, which Henrik Dey identifies as in early twelfth century Italy, when the term piazza emerges.[16] In contrast to the *plateae* are the narrow lanes whose width is reflected in the Greek term *stenopoi*, and its Latin calque *angiportus/a*, but whose function of serving a neighbourhood is emphasised by the much commoner *vici* (the term constantly met in Rome itself).

Cities like Herculaneum and Naples have allowed the inference to be smuggled in that *decumani* were always broad *plateae* and *cardines* narrow *vici*, but this cannot be right, since a principal function of *plateae* was to link the gates of the city and the world beyond to its centre (even if they did not always reach the forum itself because of pedestrianisation). This is already clear in Diodorus Siculus' account of the foundation of *Thurii* in 440 BCE, where four *plateae* divide its length (i.e. running north/south) as well as three dividing its breadth (i.e. east/west).[17] This must have been the case in Naples too, where the Via Duomo provides the essential north/south link, and in passing the Duomo passes the intersection with the central east/west thoroughfare, Via dei Tribunali, and in antiquity the agora/forum, and similarly to the west Via Costantinopoli/Via Mezzocannone, which albeit broken preserves the lines of a principal axis between the acropolis and the port.

The important distinction between road types is not their direction but whether they serve through traffic or simply local, neighbourhood needs. It is this that determines their width. Neighbours, *vicini*, do not want through traffic. I suggest that rather than thinking in terms of city authorities trying to make sense of their frustratingly narrow side streets by introducing one-way systems, we should think of quiet side roads that want peace and a minimum of traffic. One-way systems are not always to the advantage of neighbourhoods, because they facilitate the flow of traffic. It is sometimes better for the neighbours to have two oncoming vehicles stuck, logjammed because they are too wide for these little roads.

The contrast between the broad and narrow roads can be very stark and is not always reflected in published plans of ancient cities. Most small-scale plans of Pompeii draw no distinction between the main thoroughfares, Via dell'Abbondanza, Via Stabiana, Via di Nola, etc., and the narrower side streets. One advantage of Poehler's analysis of one- and two-way streets is to make quite clear the *plateae*. The distinction is fundamental, because it is on the *plateae* that the shops and bars and indeed, as Laurence showed, the electoral programmata cluster. These are the roads with the highest footfall, and commerce always wants footfall. Insofar as there are commercial premises on the *vici*, they are not retail outlets looking for customers but workshops looking for lower rents. The shops of Herculaneum cluster on the falsely named *decumani*, both major thoroughfares, and *Cardo* V, which is a significant north/south route leading from the Suburbans baths and the shore to the edge of the centre of town.

Wheeled traffic is relatively discouraged by narrow roads (whether or not they had the advantage of a one-way system) and what the pattern of the Roman city, with its *plateae/vici* rhythm, achieves is to channel wheeled traffic, which I think we should assume is principally external, entering through the gates to the main areas of the city, while allowing neighbourhoods some peace and quiet. But if this is right, what happens when the forum itself is cut off by obstacles? One of the interesting features of the street system of Pompeii is that it preserves older patterns that have been abandoned. The forum lies at the intersection of a major north/south with a major east/west axis. But the original gate at the Torre di Mercurio has been closed, while any access to the harbour to the south has been cut off by the constructing grand houses on multiple levels going down to the sea. The roads preserve their ancient dignity as *plateae* in their width but are no longer through routes. Instead, the Via Stabiana takes over the function of the major north/south axis, and the two principal east/west routes intersect with it in such a way as to divide it into precise thirds. This makes it possible to cut off the 'Altstadt' from the system of through traffic and pedestrianise the forum and its approaches. But then, we ask, how do you get goods delivery vehicles to the commercial outlets in the centre of town? Are we seeing the impact of a landowning elite that cares so little about commerce that it actually impedes it by cutting off the roads?

It is at this point, I think, that we have to wean ourselves of the modern assumption that wheeled traffic is essential for access. Long ago, Richard Bulliet in his *The Camel and the Wheel* showed the deep impact made on Islamic cities by the choice of the camel as the principal means of transport over the waggon.[18] The camel, though it can carry at best half the weight of a waggon, is cheaper to maintain, does not suffer mechanical breakdown and can handle more adverse terrains. The streets between souks could indeed be narrow and winding because the camel could cope with them, in a way which would have defeated the waggon. But for the Roman world, the ox- or mule-drawn waggon was not the only alternative. Mules individually could carry significant weights. Mules can carry up to 200 kg (the state limit in India), though the US Army recommended a maximum of 150 kg: the Diocletianic price edict implies a mule would normally carry half the load of a camel.[19] I have always been struck by the carrying capacity of the mule, which we excavated in the house and bar of Amarantus. The house contained hundreds of empty amphorae, but in the atrium, next to the mule's stable, were 60 Cretan amphorae, neatly arranged in rows.[20] It seems a fair inference that they represent a single shipment, in contrast to the many other amphorae, and that they made their way from the port to this bar on mule back. Needless to say, the mule could negotiate obstacles designed to block off wheeled vehicles, including the steep incline from the Porta Marina.

Remains of carts, and even stabling suitable to house them, are exceptional in Pompeii, the classic case being the house of the Menander.[21] Much commoner are remains of equids, whether horse, mules or donkeys. I suggest that they played a significant role in the distribution of goods within the city. The ruts tell us that waggons still rolled, but alongside them must have been hundreds of equids, doing, as Apuleius' *Golden Ass* remains us, most of the heavy lifting. But there were also human porters, *saccarii*. We encounter them, like the *muliones*, in several electoral programmata.[22] We also meet them in depictions, like the pair of terracotta plaques, found by no coincidence at the entrance of the Forum, one showing a mule, the other two men carrying an amphora on a pole over their shoulders.[23] A full amphora, at 40–80 kg, might be a struggle for a single man, but quite possible for a pair of porters, while a mule could manage two heavy amphorae, perhaps more (Figure 11.5).

*Figure 11.5* Terracotta plaque of *saccarii* from outside the Forum of Pompeii (photograph Sophie Hay).

## Conclusion

Where do these observations take us? I want to offer three provisional conclusions. First, that in our anxiety to construct the classical orthogonal city and the Islamic or western medieval city with its tangle of winding alleys as opposites, we are overlooking the common factors. Both typologies are based on a distinction between principal, broad, thoroughfares that lead to central spaces, whether the forum or the mosque or the cathedral, and the minor roads that branch off them and lead to private domestic spaces. The narrow *angiportus* or *vici* of the Roman city were in their own way far less accessible to traffic and especially through traffic. If we repopulate them in our minds with balconies overhanging the pavements, sometimes less than the legally prescribed 10 feet from their neighbours on the opposite side,[24] populate the pavements and even the roads with domestic activity spilling out of the house, fill the roads not just with waggons but pack animals and porters pushing and shouting, we have something far less like the well-ordered city of the *plateae*, far more of a fire hazard (as numerous fires at Rome confirmed), far more of a challenge to the aediles to police.

Second, we should stop thinking of the cart as the only method of moving goods and put it alongside the mule and the slave porter. These are still a far cry from Bulliet's camel, which could do the job of both cart and mule. But it does help us to see that absence of cart ruts is not equivalent to the absence of movement of goods and trade. Eric Poehler has made a brave attempt to think about the Roman street network systematically and read the traces not just of ruts but of warn curb stones as signs of passing carts. But there is a simple reason for scepticism about his one-way systems: they cannot work without signage, and of signage there is no sign. Alan Kaiser was doubtful about the idea that a Roman town council involved itself in the level of micro-management presupposed by a one-way system. But above all, it was not even necessary. Anyone trying to negotiate drive down the roads of the crowded communities around the Bay of Naples knows that you have to negotiate. At Ercolano, they have switched off the traffic lights at crossroads, and each time there is a four-way negotiation. Everyone knows you have to negotiate: if someone has already embarked on the one available lane, you wait and let them past. Most of the roads of Pompeii had the advantage of being straight, and a cart driver could simply wait at one end until the road had cleared of the oncoming traffic. This in my view better explains the contradictory signs of traffic moving in *both* directions than a one-way system subject to constant revision. This may make the Roman city a tad more chaotic and less centrally organised, but, *pazienza!*, it works OK.

Third, I ask again what conclusions we can draw about the attitudes of the ruling elite of the Roman city to commerce. We have seen how wheeled traffic was largely excluded from the heart of Pompeii. I drew attention some years ago to the relative absence of ruts from the upper stretch of the Via dell'Abbondanza approaching the Forum and suggested it was the outcome of a conscious decision to exclude certain activities, seen as morally undesirable, from the central spaces of the city.[25] Whether that is plausible, and bars and brothels were pushed away into side roads, I do not want to read it as an exclusion of commerce. We are lucky enough to have the friezes from the Praedia Juliae Felicis to convince us that the Forum was packed with traders as well as official notices and honorific statues (Figures 11.6 and 11.7).

To me the exclusion seems to be of heavy goods vehicles, for the good reason that they can be lethally dangerous to pedestrians, as Juvenal evoked.[26] Caesar's exclusion of *plostra* from Rome in daylight hours doubtless sets the

*Figure 11.6* Frieze from the Praedia Juliae Felicis Julia Felix (photograph: Sophie Hay. MANN inv. No 9057).

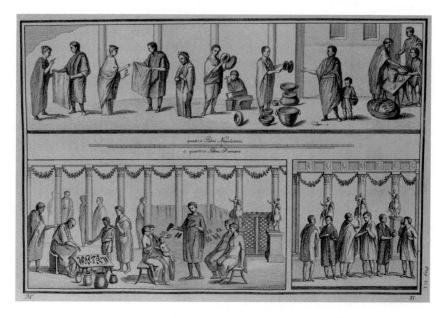

*Figure 11.7* Drawing of frieze from the Praedia Juliae Felicis Julia Felix (Morghen,
Filippo 1762. Le pitture antiche d'Ercolano e contorni incise con qualche
spiegazione. Tomo terzo p. 227 TAVOLA XLIII)

model.[27] As in Rome, there is a premium on *dignitas* in the central, public
spaces of the city.[28] That may lead to the exclusion of some types of activity,
but not of commerce as such.

I continue to find the image of a landowning elite that despises commerce
deeply implausible.[29] The same rich people who owned country estates owned
urban property and drew revenue from businesses, whether by direct or indirect
involvement through *institores* or from rent. They had no motive to discourage
trade, and the sheer density of commercial premises in Pompeii, let alone Ostia
or Rome itself, is incompatible with an attitude of official discouragement.
Kaiser reckons on 904 commercial premises in Pompeii and observes that they
are found predominantly on the primary streets of the town, those that connect
to city gates and forum (100–101). That is a prodigious number of commercial
premises for a city of 12,000 (+/–) inhabitants, let alone for one which was hostile to commerce. (Note that Miko Flohr comes up with different numbers: 468
tabernae out of 1,130 independent units, with 533 hypothesised to allow for
the unexcavated area – a much safer calculation, and still a very high number,
see Flohr 2016.) But elite residences also cluster on primary streets. Far from
shunning commerce, they were in the midst of it. Of course, there are also
residences which shunned the centre, like the great houses looking out over the
seawall of Herculaneum. Yet in the same *insulae*, there are numerous commercial and rental premises: who owned them if not the rich people with sea views?

## Acknowledgement

The research for this chapter was undertaken with the support of the ERC Advanced project, The Impact of the Ancient City. This project received funding from the European Research Council (ERC) under the European Union's Horizon 2020 research and innovation programme (grant agreement no. 693418). I am grateful for comments to the conference participants and also to Eric Poehler who generously left space for disagreement. I owe the illustrations, as well as the benefit of deep knowledge of Pompeii, to Dr Sophie Hay.

## Notes

1  For a fine overview of the debate, Zuiderhoek 2017: 1–19.
2  The classic account of Haverfield 1913 is challenged and revised by Kaiser 2011, Laurence, Esmonde-Cleary and Sears 2011.
3  Kennedy 1985, see also Avni 2011 for an update.
4  Zuiderhoek 2017: 184.
5  Finley 1981; see for the debate, Zuiderhoek 2017: 10–2; for my earlier thoughts, Wallace-Hadrill 1991.
6  Laurence 1994/2007, Kaiser 2011, Poehler 2017, Hartnett 2017, Mertens 2008, Saliou 2008.
7  Martial 7.61: Abstulerat totam temerarius institor urbem/inque suo nullum limine limen erat./Iussisti tenuis, Germanice, crescere vicos,/ et modo quae fuerat semita, facta via est./Nulla catenatis pila est praecincta lagoenis/ nec praetor medio cogitur ire luto./Stringitur in densa nec caeca novacula turba/ occupat aut totas nigra popina vias./ Tonsor, copo, cocus, lanius sua limina servant./ nunc Roma est, nuper magna taberna fuit.
8  *Tabula Heracleensis* 20–3 (*Roman Statutes* xxx): Quae viae in urbe Roma propiusve u.R. p. M, ubei continente habitabitur, sunt erunt, quoius ante aedificium earum quae via erit, is eam viam arbitratu eius aed(ilis) quoi ea pars urbis h.l. obvenerit tueatur; isque aed. curato uti quorum ante aedificium erit, quamque viam h.l. quemque tueri oportebit, ei omnes eam viam arbitratu eius tueantur, neve eo loco aqua consistat quominus commode populus ea via utatur. Digest 43.11 de via publica et itinere publico reficiendo; see Saliou 1994.
9  Existence of such a gateway was documented by (still unpublished) excavations in the 1990s by S.C. Nappo.
10  See Wallace-Hadrill 2011.
11  Kaiser 2011: 94, map 3.6.
12  Poehler 2017: esp. 18, n.65.
13  Poehler 2017: 172–3, figures 6.5–8.
14  Tsujimora 1991; Poehler 2017, 9.
15  Vitruvius *Arch.* 1.6: Moenibus circumdatis secuntur intra murum arearum divisiones platearumque et angiportuum ad caeli regionem directiones. Dirigentur haec autem recte, si exclusi erunt ex angiportis venti prudenter. Qui si frigidi sunt, laedunt; si calidi, vitiant; si umidi, nocent; Isidore *Etymologiae* 15.2.22–3: vicus, ut praedictum est, ipsae habitationes urbis sunt; unde et vicini dicti … Plateae

perpetuae ac latiores civitatum viae sunt, iuxta proprietatem linguae Graecae a latitudine nuncupatae; πλατύς enim Graeci latum dicunt.

16  Dey 2016.

17  Diodorus Siculus 12.10.7: τὴν δὲ πόλιν διελόμενοι κατὰ μὲν μῆκος εἰς τέτταρας πλατείας, ὧν καλοῦσι τὴν μὲν μίαν Ἡράκλειαν, τὴν δὲ Ἀφροδισίαν, τὴν δὲ Ὀλυμπιάδα, τὴν δὲ Διονυσιάδα, κατὰ δὲ τὸ πλάτος διεῖλον εἰς τρεῖς πλατείας, ὧν ἡ μὲν ὠνομάσθη Ἡρῴα, ἡ δὲ Θουρία, ἡ δὲ Θουρῖνα. τούτων δὲ τῶν στενωπῶν πεπληρωμένων ταῖς οἰκίαις ἡ πόλις ἐφαίνετο καλῶς κατεσκευάσθαι.

18  Bulliet 1975.

19  Diocletianic Price Edict ch. XVII on costs of transport: 1,200 lb waggon load, 20 denarii per mile; 600 lb camel load, 8 denarii per mile; ass load, 4 denarii per mile.

20  Berry 1997: 110, 114.

21  Ling 1997: 105–32; Poehler 2017: 104–9.

22  Mouritsen 1988: 174–5 registers three citations each for *muliones* and *saccarii*.

23  Poehler 2017: 198.

24  *Codex Justinianus* 8.10.11: Maeniana quae Graece exostas appellant sive olim constructa sive in posterum in provinciis construenda, nisi spatium inter se per decem pedes liberi aeris habuerint, modis omnibus detruncentur. In his vero locis in quibus aedificia privatorum horreis publicis videntur obiecta obstructione maenianorum, quindecim pedes intervalla serventur.

25  Wallace-Hadrill 1995, cf. Laurence 1994/2007: 70–5; challenged by McGinn 2004: 240–55.

26  Juvenal *Sat.* 3.254–6: longa coruscat/serraco veniente abies, atque altera pinum/ plaustra vehunt; nutant alte populoque minantur; cf. Horace *Serm.* 1.6.43f.: at hic, si plaustra ducente/concurrantque foro tria funera.

27  Tab.Heracl. 56–61, cf. Robinson 1992: 73–4.

28  Varro *de vita populi Romani* 2.72 (Nonius 523M): hoc interuallo primum forensis dignitas creuit atque ex tabernis lanienis argentariae factae.

29  Wallace-Hadrill 1994: 141.

# References

Avni, G. (2011), '"From Polis to Madina" revisited – urban change in Byzantine and early Islamic Palestine', *Journal of the Royal Asiatic Society* 21.3, 301–29.

Berry, J. (1997). 'The conditions of domestic life in Pompeii in AD79: a case-study of houses 11 and 12, insula 9, region I', *Papers of the British School at Rome* 65, 103–25.

Bulliet, R.W. (1975). *The Camel and the Wheel* (Cambridge, MA: Harvard University Press).

Cameron, A. (1985). *Procopius and the Sixth Century* (London: University of California Press).

Dey, H. (2016). 'From "street" to "piazza": urban politics, public ceremony, and the redefinition of *platea* in communal Italy and beyond', *Speculum* 91/4, 919–43.

Finley, M.I. (1981). 'The ancient city: from Fustel de Coulanges to Max Weber and beyond', in B.D. Shaw and R.P Saller (eds), *Economy and Society in Ancient Greece* (London), 3–61.

Flohr, M. (2016). 'Quantifying Pompeii', in A. Wilson and M. Flohr (eds), *The Economy of Pompeii* (Oxford: Oxford University Press).

Hartnett, J. (2017). *The Roman Street. Urban Life and Society in Pompeii, Herculaneum and Rome* (Cambridge: Cambridge University Press).

Haverfield, F. (1913). *Ancient Town Planning* (Oxford: The Clarendon Press).

Kaiser, A. (2011). *Roman Urban Street Networks* (London: Routledge).

Kennedy, H. (1985). 'From polis to Madina: urban change in late antique and early Islamic Syria', *Past & Present* 106, 3–27.

Laurence, R. (1994/2007). *Roman Pompeii: Space and Society* (London: Routledge).

Laurence, R., S.E. Cleary and G. Sears. (2011). *The City in the Roman West, c.250 BC–c. AD 250*. (Cambridge: Cambridge University Press), 6.

Ling, R., P.R. Arthur. (1997). *The insula of the Menander at Pompeii. Vol. 1, The structures.* (New York: Clarendon Press).

McGinn, T.A.J. (2004). *The Economy of Prostitution in the Roman World. A Study of Social History & the Brothel* (Ann Arbor: University of Michigan Press).

Mertens, D., ed. (2008). *Stadtverkehr in der antiken Welt: internationales Kolloquium zur 175-Jahrfeier des Deutschen Archäologischen Instituts Rom, 21. bis 23. April 2004* (Deutsches Archäologisches Institut, Rome).

Mouritsen, H. (1988). *Elections, Magistrates and Municipal Elite: Studies in Pompeian Epigraphy* (An.Inst.Dan., Rome: L'Erma di Bretschneider).

Poehler, E.E. (2017). *The Traffic Systems of Pompeii* (Oxford: Oxford University Press).

Robinson, O.F. (1992). *Ancient Rome: City Planning and Administration* (London: Taylor & Francis).

Saliou, C. (1994). *Les lois des bâtiments: voisinage et habitat urbain dans l'Empire romain: recherches sur les rapports entre le droit et la construction privée du siècle d'Auguste au siècle de Justinien* (Beyrouth: Institut français d'archèologie du Proche-Orient).

Saliou, C., ed. (2008). *La rue dans l'antiquitè: définition, aménagement et devenir de l'orient méditerranéen à la Gaule: actes du colloque de Poitiers, 7–9 septembre 2006* (Rennes: Université de Poitiers).

Tsujimora, S. (1991). 'Ruts in Pompeii: the traffic system in the Roman city', *Opuscula Pompeiana* 1, 58–86.

Wallace-Hadrill, A. (1991), 'Elites and trade in the Roman town', in J. Rich and A. Wallace-Hadrill (eds), *City and Country in the Ancient World* (London: Routledge), 241–69.

Wallace-Hadrill, A. (1994). *Houses and Society in Pompeii and Herculaneum* (Princeton: Princeton University Press).

Wallace-Hadrill, A. (1995). 'Public honour and private shame: the urban texture of Pompeii', in T. Cornell and K. Lomas (eds), *Urban Society in Roman Italy* (London), 39–62.

Wallace-Hadrill, A. (2011). 'The monumental centre of Herculaneum: in search of the identities of public buildings', *Journal of Roman Archaeology* 24, 121–60.

Zuiderhoek, A. (2017). *The Ancient City* (Cambridge: Cambridge University Press).

# 12 Transport and trade

## An energy expenditure approach for the distribution of marble in Central Adriatic Italy in Roman times

*Devi Taelman*

### Introduction

Complex societies are characterised by an increased importance of the movement of material culture since the production of goods tends to be distributed geographically among all members/locations of society. A good example of such a complex society is the Roman one. The Roman Empire spanned large parts of the present-day Europe, North Africa and the Middle East and could only function, thanks to a well-developed communication and transport network. Roman society is particularly known for its well-developed trade systems where goods – such as food, wine, olive oil, pottery and stone – were moved in enormous quantities and over long distances. How this Roman trade system exactly functioned still remains the subject of scholarly debate; see, for example, the discussions concerning the nature and general performance of the Roman economy. This debate is, in essence, framed between formalist/modernist and primitivist/substantivist views or fitted within market-driven vs. predation-driven models (Bang, 2008; Scheidel, 2014; Temin, 2013). Through the study of the provenance, spatial distribution and consumption of material culture, archaeology and archaeological modelling have the potential to deliver new insights into this long-standing discussion and to increase our understanding of how Roman trade and its economy functioned.

In this chapter, I wish to look at effect of transport (constraints) on the differential consumption, distribution and trade of marble. By comparing the results of geospatial transport cost modelling to the archaeologically observable distribution of marbles in Roman Central Adriatic Italy, I want to examine the degree to which transport, in particular energy requirements of transport, acted as a variable in structuring the Roman landscape and the Roman marble trade. As recently noted by Russell (2018: 131), studies of the Roman marble economy tend to focus on either the quarrying and carving or provenance determination and consumption of marble objects. How production and consumption are connected through 'trade', i.e. the movement in physical and social space of these goods, generally, receives less scholarly attention. Particularly for the aspect of the movement in physical space this is surprising, given that the distribution of voluminous and heavy goods – such as marble and other types of building material – is to a large extent related to the costs of their transport.

## Transport of marbles and other stones

Transport constituted a major expense in construction projects in pre-industrial times, in some cases even exceeding the costs of the actual raw material and its quarrying and carving. This is, for example, demonstrated by DeLaine (1997: 219–220) in her study of the economics related to the building of the Baths of Caracalla in Rome. The importance of transport in the building industry is also noted by Roman writers like Vitruvius[1] and Cato the Elder[2] who warn specifically for the costs and difficulties of transporting stones over long distances. The latter author mentions that the 6-day transport of a millstone costs around 20 % of its purchase price (72 HS for transport vs. 400 HS for the millstone). In a second case, he notes the transport costs for a similar millstone at slightly over 70 % of the purchase price (280 HS for transport vs. 384 HS for the millstone). These passages illustrate how geographical situation and transport constraints greatly conditioned the degree into which people could engage in trade and economy, certainly in relation to trade of heavy bulk goods.

It is common knowledge that transporting bulk goods over water is more cost-effective than transporting over land, especially for medium to long distances. As noted by Russell (2013a: 356), ships can carry larger individual blocks as well as higher total loads than any land vehicle. Moreover, ships do not depend on the quality of roads and require less manpower or animal power. However, sea and river transport also have drawbacks, such as the threat of piracy and wreckage, and seasonality due to sea currents, river flood regimes and flow rates (Russell, 2013b: 95–140; 2018: 136–139). The exact degree to which sea and river transport was advantageous over land transport is, however, less straightforward to determine and depends on multiple factors, such as the type and weight of goods transported, the terrain over which transport took place, sea currents, upstream vs. downstream river transport, transport technology and chronological period. Cost ratios for maritime, riverine and land transport derived from Roman legal texts, medieval and post-medieval building accounts as well as studies on pre-industrial transport modelling report divergent figures (Table 12.1). Despite the divergence, these figures illustrate the great difference in transportation costs between maritime, riverine and land transport as well as the importance of maritime transport for the transport of bulk goods. The importance of seaborne transport is further also illustrated by the large number of shipwrecks known from the Mediterranean carrying stone cargoes (Russell, 2011) and by the location of many of the most intensively exploited marble quarries on or near the seaside, such as the white marble quarries of Thasos, *Proconnesos* and Carrara (Russell, 2008: 108). Moreover, sudden changes in maritime accessibility could have far-reaching implications for quarries. The silting up of the harbour at *Luna* in the third/fourth century CE, for example, is considered a crucial contributing factor to the diminished importance of Carrara marble in Late Antiquity (Russell, 2008: 108–109; Walker, 1988: 191).

While it is clear that we should not underestimate the role of maritime transport in the Roman marble trade, we should also be careful not to over-estimate its importance. Easy access to sea transport appears not to have been an absolute necessity for marble producing areas as some major marble quarries were not located near accessible seaports. The most notable examples in this case are the *Dokimeion* quarries in inner Turkey or the quarries in the Egyptian Eastern Desert. Moreover, archaeological evidence shows that almost all Roman towns, even towns located in inland areas that were not accessible by sea, participated in the trade of marble, implying that a multimodal transport system, combining, sea, river and land transport, was in many cases, if not most cases, inevitable.

Closely related to the aspect of multimodal transport is the problem of transhipment (Russell, 2008: 114–115). For cargoes of heavy and indivis-ible marble objects, transhipment can be costly and technologically challen-ging. Difficulties relate primarily to the lifting and manoeuvring of stone blocks and the associated need for specialist infrastructure. This is particu-larly true for architectural elements such as large architraves or monolithic columns. Textbook examples are the colossal column shafts of the portico of the Pantheon in Rome that each weigh up to 70 tonnes. All sixteen shafts were carved in stone from Egypt, five in granite from the Aswan quarries along the Nile and 11 in granodiorite from the *Mons Claudianus* quarries in the Eastern Desert (Wilson Jones, 2009: 208). As for the transportation, this means that the massive column shafts had to be transhipped at least twice or, for the *Mons Claudianus* ones, even three times, i.e. once from the quarries to the Nile, once in Alexandria where they were transferred from river barges onto sea-going vessels and a final time in Rome where they were loaded onto carts or rollers again for the final transport stretch until the construction site. Figures for the construction projects in provincial towns are equally impres-sive, given the non-imperial nature of most of these projects. For example, the Roman theatre in Urbino, a small- to mid-sized town in Roman Italy, was decorated with monolithic columns carved in *cipollino verde* marble. With a diameter of 50 cm, an estimated height of 5 m (Taelman *et al.*, 2019) and a volumetric mass density of 2,740 kg/m$^3$ for *cipollino verde* marble, the weight of the columns can be calculated at around 2,690 kg per column.

## The case of Central Adriatic Italy

### *Urbanism and marble consumption*

Roman presence in Central Adriatic Italy is the result of a series of events that started in late fourth/early third century BCE, including the famous decisive

*Table 12.1* Cost ratios of sea to river and overland transport in pre-industrial times

| Source | Sea:river | Sea:land | River:land | Reference |
|---|---|---|---|---|
| Fourth century BCE – Greece | / | 1:14 | / | Yeo, 1946: 232–233 |
| Roman world | 1:3.4 (6.8) | 1:43.4 | 1:12.8 (6.4) | de Soto, 2019: 283 |
| Diocletian's Price Edict | 1:6 | 1:55 | 1:9.2 | Hopkins, 1983: 303 |
| Diocletian's Price Edict | 1:6 | 1:60 | 1:10 | Hopkins, 1978: 46–47 |
| Diocletian's Price Edict | 1:3.9 (7.7) | 1:42 | 1:10.8 (5.5) | DeLaine, 1997: 211; Erim and Reynolds, 1970; Russell, 2018: 136, 2013b: 95–96 |
| Diocletian's Price Edict | 1:4.9 | 1:42 | 1:8.6 | DeLaine, 1997: 211; Duncan-Jones, 1974: 368 |
| ORBIS (based on re-evaluation of DPE) | 1:5 (10) | 1:52 | 1:10.4 (5.2) | Scheidel, 2014: 9–10 |
| c. 1,160 CE – Song (China) | / | / | 1:7 | Scheidel, 2014: 10 |
| 1,202 CE – China | | | | Scheidel, 2014: 10 |
| Thirteenth century CE – Norwich (England) | 1:2 | 1:34 | 1:17 | Russell, 2018: 136, 2013b: 95–96; Salzman, 1967: 119 |
| Fourteenth/Fifteenth century CE – France | / | / | 1:7 | Dubois, 1986: 290; Scheidel, 2014: 10 |
| Sixteenth century CE – Cambridge (England) | / | / | 1:8.1 | Alexander, 1995; Russell, 2013b: 95–96 |
| Sixteenth century CE – Carrara (Italy) | / | 1:35 | / | Klapisch-Zuber, 1696; Russell, 2013b: 95–96 |
| Sixteenth century CE – Sens (France) | / | / | 1: 12.5 | Cailleaux, 1997; Russell, 2013b: 95–96 |
| Eighteenth century CE – England | 1:4.7 | 1:22.6 | 1: 4.8 | Duncan-Jones, 1974: 368; Russell, 2018: 136, 2013b: 95–96; Scheidel, 2014: 10 |
| Eighteenth century CE – England | / | / | 1: 5 | Masschaele, 1993: 277; Scheidel, 2014: 10 |
| Unspecified | 1:5.9 | 1:62.5 | 1:10.6 | de Soto, 2019: 283; Künow, 1980: 23 |
| Unspecified | 1:5.8 | 1:39 | 1:6.7 | de Soto, 2019: 283; Deman, 1987 |

Source: updated from Russell (2008: 114–116; 2013b: 96; 2018: 136–137).

battle of the Third Samnite War in *Sentinum* in 296–295 BCE, and culminated in a growing urbanisation in the form of colony foundations in third and second centuries BCE and the establishment of a series of municipal centres in the second and first centuries BCE (Vermeulen, 2017: 61–107). During the Late Republican and Imperial periods, many towns in the region were monumentalised with temples, *basilicae*, theatres and amphitheatres (Vermeulen, 2017: 110). These events resulted in the region of Central Adriatic Italy becoming one of the most densely urbanised regions of the Roman world, with figures comparable to those for *Latium, Campania* on the Italic Peninsula and *Baetica* on the Iberian Peninsula, the most densely urbanised regions of the whole Roman Empire (Bekker-Nielsen, 1989; de Ligt, 2012b: 187–188; Vermeulen, 2017: 111–113) (Figure 12.1A). A particular characteristic of the urbanisation of Central Adriatic Italy is that, despite the very dense urban landscape, the urban centres are on average much smaller than those in, for example, *Latium* and *Campania* (de Ligt, 2012a; 2012b: 188; Van Limbergen and Vermeulen, 2017; Vermeulen, 2017: 111–113) (Figure 12.1B). Moreover, in these small towns, we are confronted with a phenomenon of an over-sizing of public spaces. For example, the case of Roman *Trea* presents a modest town of c. 11 ha, where the forum complex, including *basilica*, takes up more than 10 % of the total intramural space. Due to the size and monumentality of these sites, we can argue that these towns acted as a kind of service centres aimed at impressing the urban inhabitants as well as travellers or visitors from the surrounding countryside or neighbouring towns (Vermeulen, 2017: 158–159). Overall, this dense urbanisation in the region in the Late Republican and Imperial periods resulted in an increased market not only for goods such as wine, olive oil, etc. but also for decorative stones. Since no stone resources of sufficient quality for use as decorative material characterise the regional geology, all high-quality decorative stones and crystalline marbles had to be imported.

Marble studies have illustrated the widespread use of architectural marble essentially between the late first century CE and early third century CE, when many new monumental buildings were erected and the existing buildings were redecorated using ornamental stones. Notable examples of the large-scale use of architectural marble are the *oecus* of the house of the *Coiedii* in *Suasa* (Castelleone di Suasa; early second century CE, with adjustment in the third century CE; Capedri *et al.*, 2001; Dall'Aglio *et al.*, 2007: 192–193, 200), the second century CE marble renovation of the theatre of *Urvinum Mataurense* (Urbino; Taelman *et al.*, 2019) and the marble panoramas of towns like *Sentinum* (Sassoferato), *Trea* (Treia), *Potentia* (Porto Recanati), *Ricina* (Villa Potenza), *Forum Sempronii* (Fossombrone) and *Urbs Salvia* (Urbisaglia; Antonelli *et al.*, 2014; Antonelli and Lazzarini, 2013; Taelman, 2017). With marbles imported from Italy, Greece (mainland and Aegean islands), *Asia Minor*, Egypt and North Africa, the region shows a strong integration in the wider Mediterranean marble trade.

Aside from this general image for the wider Central Adriatic Italy, we can observe some clear site- or context-specific trajectories of marble consumption. For example, the marble assemblages of the *augusteum* in *Forum Sempronii*, the house of the Coiedii in *Suasa* and the theatre of *Urvinum Mataurense*, three more or less contemporary assemblages of the second century CE show clearly differential consumption patterns for marble, with marble types of different provenances occurring in dissimilar proportions (Figure 12.2).

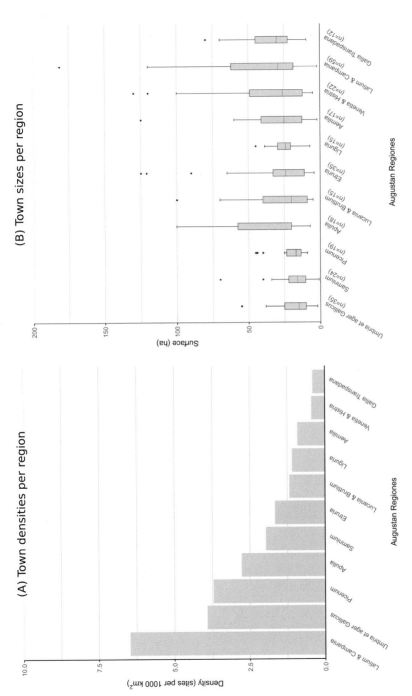

*Figure 12.1* Urbanisation figures for Central Adriatic Italy (corresponding to 'Umbria et ager Gallicus' and 'Picenum') in comparison with other regions in Roman Italy. (A) Bar graph showing the number of urban centres per 1,000 km² (based on Bekker-Nielsen, 1989; de Ligt, 2012b: 187–188; Vermeulen, 2017: 111–113). (B) Box plot of town sizes (in hectare; boxes are ordered from small to large, according to the median surface per region; based on de Ligt, 2012a; 2012b: 188; Van Limbergen and Vermeulen, 2017; Vermeulen, 2017: 111–113).

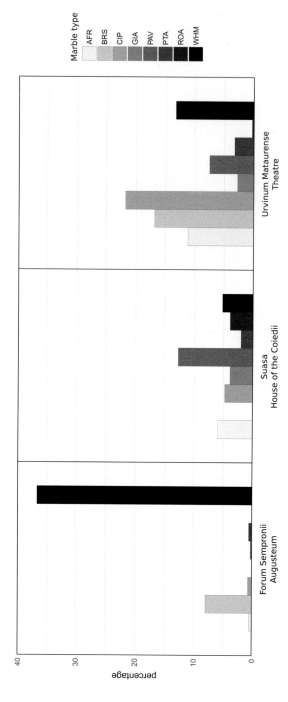

*Figure 12.2* Bar graphs showing dissimilar marble assemblage compositions for the eight most common marbles for the augusteum in Forum Sempronii, the house of the Coiedii in Suasa and the theatre of Urvinum Mataurense. AFR = africano, BRS = breccia di Sciro, CIP = cipollino verde, GIA = giallo antico, PAV = pavonazzetto, PTA = portasanta, ROA = rosso antico and WHM = white marble.

Prime questions regarding this differential distribution and consumption of marble deal with 'Why can we observe differences in the distribution of marble?' and 'Can these differences be related to differences in transport costs?' The underlying question here is whether the distribution of marbles in Central Adriatic Italy was guided by essentially a market-driven exchange or whether other factors such as state intervention, ideology or fashion influenced the movement of these high-quality, luxury goods.

### Distributing and moving marble

For Roman Central Adriatic Italy, we can imagine that marbles were imported overseas and arrived in the region through the town of *Ancona*, a major port of the Roman Adriatic or through one of the smaller harbour towns spread along the coast. From here, marble objects were distributed in the regional hinterland. This hinterland has a very diversified topography, consisting of three main N-S trending geomorphic regions, which without doubt had great impact on transport possibilities. The inland mountainous area of the Apennine Mountains, in the west, is made up of two anticline ridges with elevations between 1,000 and 1,500 m AMSL (Coltorti *et al.*, 1996: 34). Through deep and narrow transversal gorges, a network of relatively short, parallel rivers with small drainage basins crosscuts the Apennines to enter the central hilly landscape. This mid-valley sector is characterised by moderate to high hills oriented parallel to each other and to the river network, and by gradually widening alluvial plains that slope gently towards the Adriatic Sea. Rivers are labelled as small-sized, with mean annual discharges lower than 20 m³/s, as measured for the Metauro, Misa, Potenza and Tronto rivers, four main rivers in Central Adriatic Italy (Appiotti *et al.*, 2014: 2018–2019).[3] At present, the rivers show high slope gradients with a single channel in a narrow valley in their upper valleys. In the middle valley, the slope gradients drop and the rivers take a meandering channel with a valley width between 10 and 100 m. In the lower valley, the rivers change from a meandering to a braided regime, with valley floors reaching up to 4 km in width. Geomorphological and geoarchaeological studies have illustrated that the rivers had downcutting fluvial regimes characterised by meandering channels with tight loops in Roman times (Figure 12.3; Coltorti, 1991; 1997: 317; Goethals *et al.*, 2005; 2009; Luni *et al.*, 2009).

Landscape morphology, fluvial regimes, low mean annual discharges and the absence of archaeological evidence of inland port infrastructure point towards limited possibilities for large-scale river transport in Roman times, certainly in the dry season and in the more torrential middle and upper courses. For the lower courses, we cannot exclude limited navigability directed to the presence of port facilities near the river mouths. The limited navigability of the Central Adriatic rivers is also illustrated by a twelfth-century CE reference for the town of Jesi referring to the non-navigability of the Esino river, one of the main rivers in the region (Luconi, 2011: 54). Even though

*Figure 12.3* Hydrology of the river Potenza, one of the main rivers in Central Adriatic
Italy: (A) remains of a meandering palaeo-channel with tight loops;
(B) present-day shallow river mouth illustrating the low mean annual
discharge.

no direct evidence exists for river transport and land transport most likely was the norm in Central Adriatic Italy, it is without doubt that the main river valleys in the region acted as important corridors of movement linking the coastal area with the Apennine mountains (Vermeulen, 2017: 9–10), and we cannot fully exclude yet that some rivers were, at least partially, navigable, perhaps until the mid-valley sections as suggested by Coltorti (1991: 75).

To determine the relationship between transport costs and the differential distribution and consumption of marble in Central Adriatic Italy, and the underlying nature of Roman marble trade, reliable quantification of transportation costs are needed. Costs of pre-modern transportation can be expressed in several forms, the principal of which are distance, time, speed, energy expenditure and financial cost. The relevance of these cost measures depends primarily on the nature or reason of transport. For example, speed and time are particularly relevant for the movement of troops, the trade in perishable goods and the transfer of information, while the calculation of energy expenditure is preferred for non-perishable bulk goods, such as marbles, as it is a direct measure of the effort that humans and/or animals have to make for the movement to take place, irrespective of the speed at which the transport takes place. Ultimately, energy runs out and needs to be replenished with food and rest and, as such, it poses a limit to the amount of time that can be spent on movement and, thus, on the distance that can be covered. To simulate these energetic costs of transporting goods overland in a landscape, a geospatial cost model was developed in a geographical information system (GIS) environment based directly on Newtonian mechanics and biomechanics. The development of the geospatial transport cost model consisted of four main steps[4]:

1. Energy source: calculation of the potential draught force of the energy source. Throughout history, oxen and ox-drawn carts have been the preferred source of force/energy for transporting heavy and indivisible loads overland, given their relative strength and trainability. Still today, oxen are the major source of energy for heavy transport in developing countries such as India or on the African continent (Wilson, 2003: 21). While oxen are relatively strong in comparison with, for example, horses and donkeys, the amount of draught force they can generate is not unlimited and depends on biological and mechanical factors, the most important of which is animal weight.[5] Put simply, larger animals can generate higher draught forces than smaller animals. Vall (1998) illustrated that, in normal weather conditions, well-conditioned oxen can exert a continuous or sustained draught force (throughout the day) of an average 10–15 % of their body weight, with a maximum of 25–30 % of their body weight for shorter periods. Increasing the number of animals in a span naturally increases the total draught capacity. In theory, this means that any load can be moved if the team is large enough. However, increasing the number of animals in a span does not increase draught capacity by

a constant amount. The more animals added in a team, the less each contributes individually due to a loss of efficiency as a result of coordination problems (Chawatama *et al.*, 2003: 427).

2. Force requirements: calculation of the draught force needed to move a certain load over a certain terrain. Irrespective of the transport medium, moving objects require energy. For an object to be moved, work needs to be produced, i.e. an external force needs to be exerted on an object to move it over a certain distance. The amount of force that has to be applied to move the cart needs to be higher than the gravitational and frictional force that the cart experiences. In other words, to put a cart in movement, an external (draught or tractive) force must be exerted on the cart that exceeds the cart resistance that depends essentially on topography, rolling resistance and obviously the mass of the load to be transported, where the latter is a sum of cart mass and load mass. Pulling upslope requires more force than moving downhill or on flat terrain. For these reasons, strategies adopted for ascending can be very different from those for descending. Rolling resistance depends primarily on the type of wheels, the material of which they are made and the surface upon which is moved. Pulling over paved roads requires less force than pulling over muddy tracks.

3. Movement and energy: by comparing the potential force of the ox team (step 1) and the required force for moving (step 2), accessible and inaccessible parts of the landscape are determined for a particular team pulling a particular load over a particular terrain. For accessible parts of the landscape, as a cart is moved, an animal (team) produces a tractive force; and as it moves, it performs work and expends energy. The amount of work an animal needs to deliver and the amount energy expended is a direct relation between the draught force it has to exert for the cart to move and the distance of movement. Oxen, however, not only expend energy for carting loads. They also need energy to move their own body mass. Calculation of the energetic cost and speed of walking for oxen is based on physiological experiments by Dijkman and Lawrence (1997), Lawrence (1991) and Vall (1998).

4. Least cost paths and total energy expenditure: in a GIS environment, the optimal or least-effort path between any two locations in the landscape was computed by minimising energy requirements (as expressed in megajoule, MJ) for carting. For the resulting paths, the total energy costs, distance costs and time costs were calculated. The use of optimal or least-effort paths assumes that carting always uses the least costly route in the landscape. The movement of trade goods between two locations, however, is not defined ad hoc but by the topology of pre-existing roads. Trade goods were moved from one location to another over pre-defined paths, using an existing road network. The workflow was, therefore, adapted to simulate movement along an existing road network.

Using this workflow, energy expenditure, travel distance and travel time for transporting marbles using ox-drawn carts can be computed for multiple scenarios. In this version, the model links the main Roman urban centres in Central Adriatic Italy (53 sites), by means of c. 3,170 km of roads. Information on the Roman road network and the location of roads was gathered from archaeological evidence (bridges, preserved road sections, etc.) as well as archaeological–historical hypotheses of road trajectories (such as for the *via Flaminia*, *via Salaria*, etc.). Unknown sections of the road network were computed using the least-cost principle. As illustration, the results of the least-cost route between the harbour town of *Ancona* and the inland town of *Camerinum* based on the transport cost simulation for three scenarios: scenario 1 with a cart load of 0 kg (empty cart), scenario 2 with 1,000 kg and scenario 3 with 1,500 kg are presented in Table 12.2. Team size was two oxen for scenarios 1 and 2, and four oxen for scenario 3. Other input parameters for the model were ox mass, cart mass and road surface. For this case study, the mass of the typical 'Roman' ox is estimated at 500 kg. This figure is slightly higher than the 350–400 kg that Raepsaet (1985: 1427) suggests for cattle in general in the Roman period and takes into account a selection of larger (stronger) animals for transport. Modern breeds of *Bos taurus*, the European subspecies of domesticated cattle, range in mass between 455 and 1,365 kg (Conroy, 2017). However, the results of zooarchaeological studies show that Roman oxen were smaller than their modern equivalents. Moreover, regional differences and variability in size between different breeds were very common, as illustrated by zooarchaeological studies (for example, Davis, 2008; Kron, 2002; Trentacoste *et al.*, 2018) and by Columella (*De Agri Cultura* VI.I.1–3). Archaeological and iconographic data show that heavy loads were generally moved in four-wheeled carts, such as the wagon of Langres which was estimated as weighing around 500 kg when empty and was capable of carrying a maximum load of 1,500 kg (Molin, 1984: 106; Raepsaet, 1985: 1440). Larger wagons existed for exceptional loads. Road surface was set as paved with a rolling resistance coefficient of 0.07 for pre-modern carts on paved roads (Baker, 1914).

*Table 12.2* Simulated transport costs between the harbour town of Ancona and the inland town of Camerinum

| Scenario | Energy cost (MJ) | Distance cost (km) | Time cost (h) | Time cost (days)* |
|---|---|---|---|---|
| 1 | 235.1379 | 83.21 | 25.51 | 4.25 |
| 2 | 316.6602 | 83.09 | 34.63 | 5.77 |
| 3 | 551.8031 | 83.13 | 30.24 | 5.04 |

*Assuming a 6-h workday.

### Transport costs and marble distribution

For Central Adriatic Italy, we can imagine that marble arrived in the study area overseas through one of the regions' coastal harbour towns. The price of marble material at this point would equal the sum of the price for the raw material, the costs of manufacturing and the costs of transport from quarry to harbour. From these harbours, the objects were distributed in the study area. The price of the marble objects would finally be determined by the transport costs from harbour to the final site of consumption. The effect on the price of the marble objects of this second step of their distribution involves that the differences in price between cheaper and more expensive marbles becomes smaller when the transport costs become higher. In other words, less prestigious marbles will be transported over shorter distances as the labour/energy inputs required to move these items quickly become too high. This also means that it becomes relatively cheaper to import expensive marbles if transport is more costly (Figure 12.4). Markets or towns with higher transport costs should, therefore, at least theoretically, have a relatively higher amount of rare, expensive material. If the hypothesis that transport costs affected the degree to which a town (or a market) could participate in marble trade holds true, this should be reflected in the marble assemblages.

This approach presents us, however, with two problems: (1) we have no direct knowledge on the price of individual marble types, apart from the 301 CE Price Edict of Diocletian, which is very problematic for use in relation to marbles as we have no idea what these prices refer to – what type of object (veneer, columns, m³, m²) – and if they indicate prices for Rome, other towns or prices upon leaving the quarry[6]; (2) due to the complex depositional and

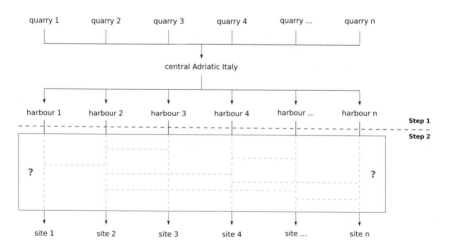

*Figure 12.4* Schematic representation of the distribution of marble in Central Adriatic Italy in the Roman period.

post-depositional processes that influence the formation of the archaeological marble record, a direct comparison of archaeological assemblages is impossible and makes very little sense. To overcome these two issues, the marble assemblages were not compared directly but through three specific statistical measures: the size of the assemblages, the richness of the assemblages (i.e. the number of different marble varieties present) and evenness (Shannon–Wiener diversity index) of the assemblages. This last statistic looks essentially at the relative proportion of each material category in the assemblage and accounts for the higher probability of rare types in larger assemblages, simply because of their larger size and, therefore, allows different-sized assemblages to be compared directly (Baxter, 2001; Kintigh, 1984; McCartney and Glass, 1990).

If the transport costs played an important role in the distribution and consumption of marble, in the sense that higher transport costs promote an increased use of rare, prestigious and expensive marbles, we should see a correlation between transport cost (expressed as energy values) and evenness of the marble assemblages, preferably with a higher richness. Sites with lower transport cost values should display evenness values that are lower than for sites with higher transport cost values. As sites take in a more peripheral location in the transport network, it would become relatively cheaper for them to import expensive marbles, and thus they should present more even marble assemblages.

The marble assemblages, in particular the richness and evenness values, of twenty-two contexts (dated between the late first century CE and early third century CE) from eight sites[7] in Central Adriatic Italy as obtained through an in-depth quantitative study of marble veneer were compared with the results of the ox-cart energyscape model (Tables 12.3 and 12.4, Figure 12.5). All sites show a wide range of marble types that were used for their embellishment,

*Table 12.3* Simulated transport cost to reach the eight case-study sites from the nearest harbour town

| Site | Harbour | Energy cost (MJ) | Distance (km) | Travel time (h) | Travel time (day)* |
|---|---|---|---|---|---|
| Forum Sempronii | Fanum Fortunae | 68.8402 | 22.36 | 8.87 | 1.48 |
| Ostra | Sena Gallica | 57.2895 | 19.45 | 7.60 | 1.27 |
| Potentia | Potentia | 0.0000 | 0.00 | 0.00 | 0.00 |
| Ricina | Potentia | 71.1946 | 24.13 | 9.43 | 1.57 |
| Sentinum | Sena Gallica | 159.5053 | 48.62 | 19.63 | 3.27 |
| Suasa | Sena Gallica | 82.7699 | 26.17 | 10.46 | 1.74 |
| Trea | Potentia | 127.4385 | 41.23 | 16.32 | 2.72 |
| Urvinum Mataurense | Pisaurum | 147.6814 | 39.84 | 16.39 | 2.73 |

*Assuming a 6-h workday.
*Note*: Costs were calculated using a standard ox-cart transport (2 oxen, ox mass = 500 kg, cart mass = 500 kg, cart load = 1,000 kg, paved roads).

*Table 12.4* Diversity measures of the studied marble assemblages

| Site | Context | Fragment count | Richness | Evenness (weight based) |
|---|---|---|---|---|
| Forum Sempronii | Augusteum | 738 | 15 | 0.462966 |
| Forum Sempronii | Bathhouse | 77 | 5 | 0.625689 |
| Forum Sempronii | Marble taberna | 1,092 | 13 | 0.704297 |
| Forum Sempronii | Structure B26 | 5 | 3 | 0.728831 |
| Ostra | Sector 1 | 85 | 12 | 0.590968 |
| Ostra | Sector 2 | 17 | 9 | 0.704938 |
| Ostra | Sector 4 | 33 | 8 | 0.601428 |
| Ostra | Structure 4 | 193 | 16 | 0.678306 |
| Ostra | Structure 40 | 49 | 9 | 0.650464 |
| Ostra | Unnamed structure | 50 | 11 | 0.524635 |
| Potentia | Site survey | 68 | 11 | 0.721636 |
| Potentia | Western gate | 10 | 3 | 0.196704 |
| Ricina | Forum survey | 94 | 11 | 0.728598 |
| Sentinum | Santa Lucia excavation | 267 | 16 | 0.710053 |
| Suasa | Forum | 8 | 4 | 0.577337 |
| Suasa | House of the Coiedii | 1,421 | 20 | 0.799952 |
| Suasa | House sector 1 | 28 | 10 | 0.729171 |
| Suasa | Unnamed structure | 31 | 9 | 0.619979 |
| Trea | Basilica survey | 130 | 4 | 0.707503 |
| Trea | Forum survey | 194 | 14 | 0.705035 |
| Trea | Site survey | 206 | 17 | 0.817891 |
| Urvinum Mataurense | Theatre | 1,916 | 25 | 0.738656 |

including different varieties of the most expensive types of decorative stone used and traded in the Roman period, extracted notably in Greece, *Asia Minor*, Egypt, Italy and North Africa. A comparison of the results of the transport model and the marble distribution in the study area seems not to show a clear positive correlation illustrating that energetic considerations were not the main factors in the distribution of marble decoration, and, thus, that distribution and consumption of marbles, specifically in Central Adriatic Italy, were not guided by pure market-driven exchange, but that other factors such as state intervention, fashion or ideology intervened in the movement of these high-quality, luxury goods (Figure 12.6).

## Conclusions

Heavy and indivisible goods such as building stone and marbles are difficult and costly to transport. Nevertheless, marbles and other decorative stones were traded in enormous quantities and over long distances, especially in the Mediterranean where they are found in nearly every urban centre. Although significant effort was involved in quarrying, cutting and fitting marble slabs, blocks and columns in the constructions of elite architecture, the transport of marbles from quarry to building site generally consumed great amounts

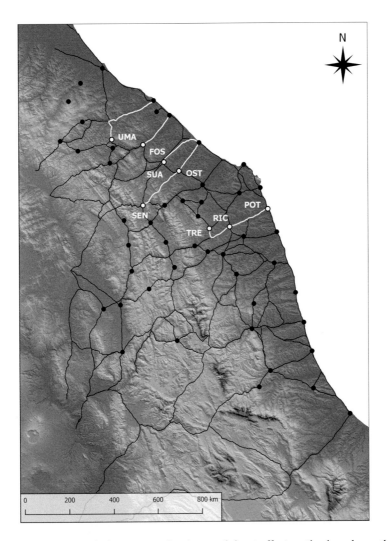

*Figure 12.5* Map of the case-study sites and least-effort paths based on the ox-
cart energyscape model. FOS = Forum Sempronii, OST = Ostra,
POT = Potentia, RIC = Ricina, SEN = Sentinum, SUA = Suasa,
TRE = Trea and UMA = Urvinum Mataurense.

of energy. The use of marble implied a massive investment in labour to bring
stones from distant sources. The economic and political dimensions of this
undertaking must have been considerable, as indicated by the sheer amount
of labour consumed. Considering the cost-effectiveness of water transport
over land transport, the majority of the transport of these luxury goods will
surely have taken place over water (sea or river). Overland transport could not

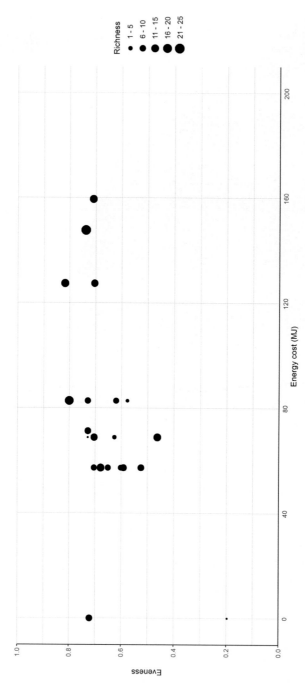

*Figure 12.6* Comparison of the evenness, richness values of the twenty-two marble assemblages studied to the energy transport costs as obtained through the ox-cart energyscape model.

always be avoided, however, and a multimodal transport system, combining, sea, river and land transport, was in many cases, if not most cases, inevitable.

Pre-industrial transportation by water largely depended on wind and current, while overland transport required energy provided by humans and/or animals. This reliance of overland transport on energy provided by humans and/or animals imposed serious constraints on the movement of goods, increasing the cost of these goods and directly influencing the degree to which people could participate in their trade. The question addressed in this chapter was to what extent this hypothesis is also valid for marble, a material that has a very distinct social and ideological function.

To test this hypothesis, an ox-cart energyscape model was developed in a GIS environment that simulates the energy costs of transporting marbles in Central Adriatic Italy and that allows for a deeper understanding of the importance of the energy requirements as a variable for structuring the trade of marble in the region in Roman times. The results of transport model and an in-depth study of the marble distribution in Central Adriatic Italy showed no clear or direct connection between marble consumption and transport costs, suggesting that distribution and consumption of marbles, specifically in Central Adriatic Italy, were not guided by pure market-driven exchange, but rather that other factors such as state intervention, fashion or ideology intervened in the movement of these high-quality goods.

As final note, we need to point out that the ox-cart energyscape model entails several assumptions and simplifications (for example, ox mass and cart mass) and that the results are derived from simplified biomechanical and physiological principles. The model and its results should, therefore, be approached merely as an analytical tool for understanding the costs of movement and transport, which can be used to gain better understanding of the nature of Roman trade, and not as an exact representation of the reality of transport costs.

## Acknowledgements

The research is conducted in the framework of a Post-doctoral Fellowship of the author, supported by the Research Foundation – Flanders (FWO) (12N8219N) based at Ghent University (Belgium) that studies the mechanisms and structure involved in the Roman marble trade in the Mediterranean.

The author thanks the participants of the international workshop 'Space, movement and the economy in Roman cities in Italy and beyond' that was held in Porto Recanati and Treia (Marche, Italy), September 12–14, 2018, for the fruitful discussions and their constructive feedback on the first draft of this chapter.

I am particularly grateful to Dimitri Mlekuž for his assistance in developing the preliminary algorithms of the ox-cart energyscape model that was used as the basis for the algorithms which are presented in this chapter.

## Notes

1  De Architectura I.2.8 – *Distributio autem est copiarum locique commoda dispensatio parcaque in operibus sumptus cum ratione temperatio. haec ita observabitur, si primum architectus ea non quaeret quae non poterunt inveniri aut parari nisi magno. namque non omnibus locis harenae fossiciae nec caementorum nec abietis nec sappinorum nec marmoris copia est, sed aliud alio loco nascitur, quorum comportationes difficiles sunt et sumptuosae.*

2  De Agri Cultura 22.3 – *Trapetus emptus est in Suessano HS CCCC et olei P. L. Conpsturae HS LX; vecturam boum, operas VI, homines VI cum bubulcis HS LXXII; cupam ornatam HS LXXII, pro oleo HS XXV; S.S. HS DCXXVIIII. Pompeis emptus ornatus HS CCCXXCIIII; vecturam HS CCXXC; domi melius concinnatur et accommodatur, eo sumpti opus est HS LX: S.S. HS DCCXXIIII.*

3  In comparison, the Tiber, Ebro, Po, Rhône and Rhine rivers have the present-day mean annual discharges of 225, 320, 1,470, 1,700 and between 2,300 and 2,600 m$^3$/s, respectively (Iadanza and Napolitano, 2006: 1214; Ibañez *et al.*, 1997: 89; Kwadijk *et al.*, 2016: 139; Montanari, 2012: 3739).

4  Details on the (bio)mechanical and physiological principles and algorithms of the cost model will be published elsewhere.

5  Other biological factors include animal breed, health, fitness, experience, training, stress and temperament. Mechanical factors include essentially the harnessing system which determines the efficiency of energy transfer from animal to cart. For ox-drawn carts, the harnessing system was a yoke which has evolved only little since Antiquity (Brownrigg and Crouwel, 2017).

6  For a detailed discussion on the difficulties on the use of the Price Edict of Diocletion for marble pricing, see Russell, 2013b: 33–36.

7  The studied sites are *Forum Sempronii, Ostra, Potentia, Ricina, Sentinum, Suasa, Trea* and *Urvinum Mataurense.*

## References

Alexander, J.S. "Building Stone from the East Midlands Quarries: Sources, Transportation and Usage." *Medieval Archaeology* 39(1) (1995): 107–135.

Antonelli, F., Columbu, S., Lezzerini, M. and Miriello, D. "Petrographic Characterization and Provenance Determination of the White Marbles Used in the Roman Sculptures of Forum Sempronii (Fossombrone, Marche, Italy)." *Applied Physics A. Materials Science and Processing* 115(3) (2014): 1033–1040.

Antonelli, F. and Lazzarini, L. "White and Coloured Marbles of the Roman Town of Urbs Salvia (Urbisaglia, Macerata, Marche, Italy)." *Oxford Journal of Archaeology* 32(3) (2013): 293–317.

Appiotti, F., Krzělj, M., Russo, A., Ferretti, M. and Bastianini, M.M.F. "A Multidisciplinary Study on the Effects of Climate Change in the Northern Adriatic Sea and the Marche Region (Central Italy)." *Regional Environmental Change* 14 (2014): 2007–2024.

Baker, I.O. *Treatise on Roads and Pavements*, New York: Wiley, 1914.

Bang, P.F. *The Roman Bazaar. A Comparative Study of Trade and Markets in a Tributary Empire*. Cambridge: Cambridge University Press, 2008.

Baxter, M.J. "Methodological Issues in the Study of Assemblage Diversity." *American Antiquity* 66(4) (2001): 715–725.

Bekker-Nielsen, T. *The Geography of Power. Studies in the Urbanization of Roman North-West Europe.* Oxford: Archaeopress, 1989.

Brownrigg, G. and Crouwel, J. "Developments in Harnessing and Draught in the Roman World: Equid Harnessing and Draught." *Oxford Journal of Archaeology* 36(2) (2017): 197–220.

Cailleaux, D. "Un chargement de pierres de Saint-Leu pour le chantier de la cathédrale de Sens à la fin du Moyen Âge." Pages 191–198 in *Pierres et carrières. Géologie, archéologie, histoire. Textes réunis en hommage à Claude Lorenz.* Edited by J. Lorenz, P. Benoit and D. Obert. Paris: Association des géologues du Bassin parisien, 1997.

Capedri, S., Venturelli, G., De Maria, S., Uguzzoni, M.P.M. and Pancotti, G. "Characterisation and Provenance of Stones Used in the Mosaics of the Domus Dei Coiedii at Roman Suasa (Ancona, Italy)." *Journal of Cultural Heritage* 2(1) (2001): 7–22.

Chawatama, S., Ndlovu, L.R., Richardson, F.D., Mhlanga, F. and Dzama, K. "A Simulation Model of Draught Animal Power in Smallholder Farming Systems. Part I: Context and Structural Overview." *Agricultural Systems* 76(2) (2003): 415–440.

Coltorti, M. "Modificazioni morfologiche oloceniche nelle piane alluvionali marchigiane: Alcuni esempi nei fiumi Misa, Cesano e Musone." *Geografica Fisica e Dinamica Quaternaria* 14(1) (1991): 73–86.

Coltorti, M. "Human Impact in the Holocene Fluvial and Coastal Evolution of the Marche Region, Central Italy." *Catena* 30 (1997): 311–335.

Coltorti, M., Farabollini, P., Gentili, B. and Pambianchi, G. "Geomorphological Evidence for Anti-Apennine Faults in the Umbro-Marchean Apennines and in the Peri-Adriatic Basin, Italy." *Geomorphology* 15(1) (1996): 33–45.

Conroy, D. *Oxen. A Teamster's Guide to Raising, Training, Guiding & Showing,* Storey Publishing, 2017.

Dall'Aglio, P.L., De Maria, S. and Podini, M. "Territory, City and Private Life at Suasa in the Roman Age." *Journal of Roman Archaeology* 20 (2007): 177–201.

Davis, S.J.M. "Zooarchaeological Evidence for Moslem and Christian Improvements of Sheep and Cattle in Portugal." *Journal of Archaeological Science* 35(4) (2008): 991–1010.

de Ligt, L. *Peasants, Citizens and Soldiers. Studies in the Demographic History of Roman Italy, 225 BC–AD 100,* Cambridge: Cambridge University Press, 2012a.

de Ligt, L. "Urban Archaeology, Urban Networks and Population Dynamics in Roman Italy." Pages 183–196 in *Urban Landscape Survey in Italy and the Mediterranean.* Edited by F. Vermeulen, G.-J. Burgers, S. Keay and C. Corsi. Oxford: Oxbow Books, 2012b.

de Soto, P. "Network Analysis to Model and Analyse Roman Transport and Mobility." Pages 271–289 in *Satellite Image Analysis: Clustering and Classification.* Edited by Borra, S., Thanki, R., M., and Dey, N. Singapore: Springer Singapore, 2019.

DeLaine, J. *The Baths of Caracalla. A Study of the Design, Construction, and Economics of Large-Scale Building Projects in Imperial Rome,* Portsmouth: JRA, 1997.

Deman, A. "Réflexions sur la navigation fluviale dans l'antiquité romaine." Pages 79–106 in *Histoire economique de l'antiquité. Bilans et contributions de savants belges présentés dans une réunion interuniversitaire à Anvers.* Edited by T. Hackens and P. Marchetti. Louvain-la-Neuve: UCL Institut supérieur d'archéologie et d'histoire de l'art Séminaire de numismatique Marcel Hoc, 1987.

Dijkman, J.T. and Lawrence, P.R. "The Energy Expenditure of Cattle and Buffaloes Walking and Working in Different Soil Conditions." *Journal of Agricultural Science* 128(1) (1997): 95–103.

Dubois, H. "Techniques et coûts des transports terrestres en France aux XIVe et XVe siècles." Pages 279–291 in *Trasporti e sviluppo economico, secoli XIII-XVIII*. Edited by A.V. Marx. Firenze: Le Monnier, 1986.

Duncan-Jones, R. *The Economy of the Roman Empire: Quantitative Studies*, Cambridge: Cambridge University Press, 1974.

Erim, K.T. and Reynolds, J. "The Copy of Diocletian's Edict on Maximum Prices from Aphrodisias in Caria." *Journal of Roman Studies* 60(1) (1970): 120–141.

Goethals, T., De Dapper, M. and Vermeulen, F. "Geomorphology and Geoarchaeology of Three Sites in the Potenza Valley Survey (The Marches, Italy): Potentia, Montarice and Helvia Recina." *Revista de Geomorfologie* 7 (2005): 33–49.

Goethals, T., De Dapper, M. and Vermeulen, F. "Geo-Archaeological Implications of River and Coastal Dynamics at the Potenza River Mouth (The Marches, Italy)." Pages 415–448 in *Ol' Man River. Geo-Archaeological Aspects of Rivers and River Plains*. Edited by M. De Dapper, F. Vermeulen, S. Deprez and D. Taelman. Ghent: Academia Press, 2009.

Hopkins, K. "Economic Growth and Towns in Classical Antiquity." Pages 35–77 in *Towns in Societies: Essays in Economic History and Historical Sociology*. Edited by P. Abrams and E.A. Wrigley. Cambridge: Cambridge University Press, 1978.

Hopkins, K. "Models, Ships and Staples." Pages 84–109 in *Trade and Famine in Classical Antiquity*. Edited by P.D.A. Garnsey and C.R. Whittaker. Cambridge: Cambridge University Press, 1983.

Iadanza, C. and Napolitano, F. "Sediment Transport Time Series in the Tiber River." *Physics and Chemistry of the Earth, Parts A/B/C* 31(18) (2006): 1212–1227.

Ibañez, C., Pont, D. and Prat, N. "Characterization of the Ebre and Rhone Estuaries: A Basis for Defining and Classifying Salt-Wedge Estuaries." *Limnology and Oceanography* 42(1) (1997): 89–101.

Kintigh, K.W. "Measuring Archaeological Diversity by Comparison with Simulated Assemblages." *American Antiquity* 49(1) (1984): 44–54.

Klapisch-Zuber, C. *Les maîtres du marbre: Carrare, 1300–1600*, Paris: SEVPEN, 1696.

Kron, G. "Archaeozoological Evidence for the Productivity of Roman Livestock Farming." *Münstersche Beiträge Zur Antiken Handelsgeschichte* 21(2) (2002): 53–73.

Künow, J. *Negotiator et ventura: Händler und transport im freiem Germanien*, Marburg: Philipps-Universität Marburg, 1980.

Kwadijk, J., Arnell, N.W., Mudersbach, C., de Weerd, M., Kroon, A. and Quante, M. "Recent Change—River Flow." Pages 137–146 in *North Sea Region Climate Change Assessment. Regional Climate Studies*. Edited by M. Quante and F. Colijn. Cham: Springer, 2016.

Lawrence, P.R. "Nutrient Requirements of Working Ruminants." Pages 61–79 in *An Introduction to Working Animals*. Edited by L. Falvey. Melbourne: MPW, 1991.

Luconi, G. *Storia di Jesi*, Jesi: Edizioni Jesi e la Sua Valle, 2011.

Luni, M., Mei, O., Nesci, O., Savelli, D. and Troiani, F. "Geomorphology and Archaeology: An Integrated Heritage along the Roman Via Flaminia in the Mid Metauro River Valley (Central Italy)." *Memorie Descrittive Della Carta Geologica d'Italia* 87 (2009): 99–108.

Masschaele, J. "Transport Costs in Medieval England." *The Economic History Review* 46(2) (1993): 266.

McCartney, P.H. and Glass, M.F. "Simulation-Models and the Interpretation of Archaeological Diversity." *American Antiquity* 55(3) (1990): 521–536.

Molin, M.M. "Quelques considérations sur le chariot des vendanges de Langres (Haute-Marne)." *Gallia* 42(1) (1984): 97–114.

Montanari, A. "Hydrology of the Po River: Looking for Changing Patterns in River Discharge." *Hydrology and Earth System Sciences* 16 (2012): 3739–3747.

Raepsaet, G. "Attelages ruraux de nos Régions dans l'Antiquité." *Revue de l'Agriculture* 6(38) (1985): 1423–1443.

Russell, B. "The Dynamics of Stone Transport between the Roman Mediterranean and Its Hinterland." *Facta: A Journal of Roman Material Culture Studies* 2 (2008): 107–126.

Russell, B. "Lapis Transmarinus: Stone-Carrying Ships and the Maritime Distribution of Stone in the Roman Empire." Pages 139–155 in *Maritime Archaeology and Ancient Trade in the Mediterranean*. Edited by D. Robinson and A.I. Wilson. Oxford: School of Archaeology, University of Oxford, 2011.

Russell, B. "Roman and Late Antique Shipwrecks with Stone Cargoes: A New Inventory." *Journal of Roman Archaeology* 26 (2013a): 121–145.

Russell, B. *The Economics of the Roman Stone Trade*. Oxford: Oxford University Press, 2013b.

Russell, B. "'Difficult and Costly': Stone Transport, Its Constraints and Its Impact." Pages 131–150 in *Roman Ornamental Stones in North-Western Europe. Natural Resources, Manufacturing, Supply, Life & After-Life*. Edited by C. Coquelet, G. Creemers, R. Dreesen and E. Goemare. Namur: Agence wallonne du Patrimoine, 2018.

Salzman, L.F. *Building in England down to 1540. A Documentary History*, Oxford: The Clarendon Press, 1967.

Scheidel, W. "The Shape of the Roman World: Modelling Imperial Connectivity." *Journal of Roman Archaeology* 27 (2014): 7–32.

Taelman, D. "The Changing Material Culture of a Valley. Marbles and Other Stones Used as Luxury Material." Pages 194–198 in *The Potenza Valley Survey (Marche, Italy). Settlement Dynamics and Changing Material Culture in an Adriatic Valley between Iron Age and Late Antiquity*. Edited by F. Vermeulen, D. Van Limbergen, P. Monsieur and D. Taelman. Rome: Dià Cultura, 2017.

Taelman, D., Delpino, C. and Antonelli, F. "Marble Decoration of the Roman Theatre of Urvinum Mataurense (Urbino, Marche Region, Italy): An Archaeological and Archaeometric Multi-Method Provenance Study." *Journal of Cultural Heritage* 39 (2019): 238–250.

Temin, P. *The Roman Market Economy*, Princeton - Oxford: Princeton University Press, 2013.

Trentacoste, A., Nieto-Espinet, A. and Valenzuela-Lamas, S. "Pre-Roman Improvements to Agricultural Production: Evidence from Livestock Husbandry in Late Prehistoric Italy." *PLoS One* 13(12) (2018): 1–33.

Vall, E. "Capacités de travail du zébu, de l'âne et du cheval au Nord-Cameroun. Concept d'adéquation du couple animal-outil." *Annales de zootechnie, INRA/EDP Sciences* 47(1) (1998): 41–58.

Van Limbergen, D. and Vermeulen, F. "Appendix: Topographic Gazetteer of Roman Towns in Picenum and Eastern Umbria et Ager Gallicus." Pages 165–202 in *From the Mountains to the Sea. The Roman Colonisation and Urbanisation of Central Adriatic Italy*. Edited by Vermeulen, F. Leuven: Peeters, 2017.

Vermeulen, F. *From the Mountains to the Sea. The Roman Colonisation and Urbanisation of Central Adriatic Italy*, Leuven: Peeters, 2017.

Walker, S. "From West to East: Evidence for a Shift in the Balance of the Trade in White Marbles." Pages 187–195 in *Classical Marble: Geochemistry, Technology, Trade*. Edited by N. Herz and M. Waelkens. Dordrecht: Kluwer Academic Publishers, 1988.

Wilson Jones, M. *Principles of Roman Architecture*, New Haven-London: Yale University Press, 2009.

Wilson, R.T. "The Environmental Ecology of Oxen Used for Draught Power." *Agriculture, Ecosystems & Environment* 97(1–3) (2003): 21–37.

Yeo, C.A. "Land and Sea Transportation in Imperial Italy." *Transactions and Proceedings of the American Philological Association* 77 (1946): 221–244.

# 13 "This mule will ruin me"

## The economy of mobility in Roman towns

*Cristina Corsi*

### Introduction: defining the matter

The question of "how did spatial structures and movement dynamics in Roman cities impact on economic processes, and to what extent, and how precisely, did Roman economic activity shape and determine spaces, places and movements in cities", asked by the organisers of the Porto Recanati meeting "Space, movement and the economy in Roman cities in Italy and beyond" (September 2018), suggested to me that I should look into the question of how the need for transport and mobility arising from the economic processes impacted on Roman cities, and the extent to which these activities, connected to transport and mobility, shaped the material fabric and the social structure of the urban space.

The starting point will be the definition of the material objects of this study, roads and streets, often considered only as artefacts or as means to connect destinations and settlements, as "spaces in between" or dividing lines to mark portions of landscape (e.g. blocks of urban settlements or plots of land divisions). Instead, roads and streets are not only activity spaces where movement and trade take place, but they are also public places for a variety of contacts and social life, locations for meaningful movement, like processions, and venues for many activities, including self-representation.[1] In particular, urban streets can be described as economic spaces, which provided citizens with the channels through which goods and people flowed, moving from urban centres to the countryside, from production sites to markets, from shops and workshops to domestic spaces.[2]

An analysis of the Latin vocabulary clearly shows that in the Roman perception there were two distinct categories of streets, a distinction based not that much upon the physical nature of streets but rather upon the types of activities that could take place along them. *Viae* and *plateai* clearly contrasted with *angiporti* and *semitae*, as only the first category could accommodate crowds and, therefore, work also as stages for gaining popularity (Kaiser 2011: 117–118; Wallace-Hadrill, this volume: Chapter 11). This new awareness of the economic and social role of urban street networks has brought them into the spotlight, raising a debate[3] that in the last 20 years has been paralleled by phenomenological, sociological (Witcher 1998: 60) and numerical approaches.[4] These contributions have also revitalised scholarly inquiry about the role that Roman roads played in the process of cultural change, moving far beyond simple analysis of the relationship between communication networks and political and economic history. Indeed, if towns remain the nodes of the web that wraps the sprawling *oikumene*, even a superficial look at the *Tabula Peutingeriana* can resolve the contradiction between the theory that considers towns as the main agency of the cultural change and the paradigm that sees movement and connectivity as the key factor in Roman history (Laurence 1999: 2; Harris 2007: 535). The tenet of mobilities, a contemporary paradigm focused on how movement (of people, things and ideas) affects contemporary and past societies and how those movements generate social implications, is just as much increasingly governing the acknowledgement of the historic and contemporary importance of movement for individuals and society, and of movement as an agent in several socio-economic and cultural processes (Corsi forthcoming).

Shifting to the economic implications of movement and exchange that took place along roads, here we will briefly refer to the revisited model of the consumer city that – already 25 years ago – led to highlighting the relevance of trade and exchange inside the city.[5] However, while some aspects of production and consumption and their implications for the general framing of urban economic life have been increasingly featuring in essays, some other components of this lively exchange system have been underestimated. Indeed, all those activities of production and consumption require transport and distribution; therefore, they generate a parallel economy, which could be labelled "transport and logistics", or – as I called it, mostly referring to movement of people – "economy of mobility". In this specific application, my field of study is more limited than the one encompassed in the definition of "transport economy", which embraces all trade and exchange-related activities.[6] Indeed, the first accounts for certain operations that are not necessarily connected with trade, while the second includes activities that do not necessarily imply mobility of people or might be just limited to a sort of commuting. Furthermore, the economy of mobility also includes activities that were carried out independently or only partially in relation to trade, like festivals, athletic or artistic contests, religious gatherings, possibly combined with periodical markets, and political events or judicial assizes, which generated business, mostly in the "hospitality business" (MacMullen 1970: 338). The definition adopted here also differs from what is labelled "movement economy", theoretically defined by Hillier (1996), interpreted by Hanna Stöger as the effect of movement along the urban street network generating hierarchies in locations and patterning the spatial distribution of "movement seeking" activities.[7]

Several sectors could be examined as individual compartments contributing to the overall budget of the "economy of mobility", such as horse breeding and feeding of other types of beasts of burden (Mitchell 2014), production of animal feed, vehicle manufacturing and upkeep, vehicle leasing and renting, driving or "valeting" vehicles and chauffeuring (Poehler 2017: 189–215), in addition to the strong revenues coming from the diversified sector of the "hospitality business".[8] Even in the event of requisition from the provincial populations, it is evident that these items were relevant budgetary headings in the general imperial economy. On this occasion, however, I will limit my analysis to the so-called "hospitality business", known in French as *accueil mercantil*.

## The social landscape of the economy of mobility

Most of these commercial enterprises were connected to what has been labelled as a deviant behaviour, defined as "behaviour that is condemned by a substantial proportion of the population, but is not considered to be beyond the limits of toleration by many people" (Laurence 1994: 70). In literary sources, the preferred location where deviants – legally brought together under the category of *infames*: slaves, drunks, thieves, gamblers, prostitutes, people working in the "entertainment industry" like gladiators and any other sort of lower status workmen employed in the transport sector and haulage business – are pictured carrying out their loathsome trade was in the brothels and *popinae*.[9] Obviously, this is a cliché that depicts the category of the *infames* as very marginal to citizenship and urban life, and it is strictly related to what can be defined as the "moral geography of a city" (Wallace-Hadrill 1995: 39). Even if some perplexities remain about the archaeological identification of pubs and bars, several surveys carried out in Pompeii show that these sorts of commercial operations were not necessarily concentrated around public buildings, notwithstanding the fact that they acted as foci of public activities (Wallace-Hadrill 1995: 43–45). This patterning argues for restrictions enforced by official regulations that would have pushed most of these businesses to back and side streets (Wallace-Hadrill 1995: 45–46, 54). On the other hand, it is likely that in reality "the provision of services by the *infames* may have been a necessary feature of the structure of Roman society" (Laurence 1994: 70), even if it is possible that the commercial operation related to deviant behaviour, such as prostitution, public drinking and gambling, was confined to urban sectors where it was tolerated (Laurence 1994: 70–71, specifically for Pompeii). Indeed, prostitution was an activity quite regularly performed at taverns and inns, not only in urban environments. However, the legal formulation of prostitution may have been superficial and "generalising", at least as far as can be deduced from the definition expressed by Ulpian in the Digest, where it seems to include, in addition to the staff of brothels, all women working in – if not just attending – a *caupona*.[10]

The "elitist" attitude towards the commercial enterprises related to the hospitality business (including prostitution) could be confirmed by the low number of bars and inns structurally dependent on any nearby elite houses, especially in the last phase of Pompeii between the earthquake and the eruption. However, this occurrence could also be connected to the fact that these activities did not require high investment and were poorly staffed and therefore stirred the hopes of their owners for a fast economic recovery after the traumatic event of the earthquake of AD 62. (Robinson 2005: 101). If transferred to the urban layout scale, in relationship to the above-sketched division of urban streets into two categories, this discriminatory attitude made the *angiporti* and *semitae* places where people who were keen to hide perpetrated acts that they did not want to be witnessed.

And here we come to the epigraphic document that was chosen to introduce this chapter. In this exceptional inscription from Isernia, reporting the dialogue between a customer and an innkeeper, the customer, who is clearly provided with a riding animal, also pictured on the stele, is charged for wine, bread, gruel, fodder for the mule and a girl[11] (Figure 13.1). The peculiarity of this stele is striking, since it fixes on stone a sort of satirical cartoon, more easily imaginable scratched as a graffito, where the customer complains only about the cost of the fodder, clearly considering it an accessory travel expense. Anyhow, the connection between inns, bars or diners and prostitution is openly

*Figure 13.1* Paris, Musée du Louvre. Inscription with dialogue between a traveller and an innkeeper, with the bas-relief depicting the traveller with the mule negotiating with a woman (a *copa*?), from Contrada Trinità (?), Isernia (Italy). After Corsi 2000.

stated here (Laurence 1994: 78). This document, although relatively popular in literature, has attracted only a few commentators. Among them, MacMullen (1970: 339) erroneously said it came from Pompeii and interpreted it as a scene of a farmer returning from the market where his merchandise would have been sold, since the mule appears unloaded. In reality, it is not even sure that it can be referred to as an inn, since there is no mention of payment for the night's stay, while most attention is addressed to sex-related issues, starting from the name of the *copo*, Calidius Eroticus and (his partner?) Fannia Voluptas (indeed, the person that collects the money from the customer might be a woman). In any case, even if the context of discovery is not clear,[12] this billing scene offers us an insight into the turnover of these small commercial enterprises. For a social analysis of the figure of the innkeeper, I refer to the most recent work of Marie-Adeline Le Guennec.[13] It will be enough here to recall the fact that in ancient literary sources there is an insistent recurrence of the *topos* of the dishonest mischievous host. This bad reputation did not spare the innkeepers of the road stations spread along the roads of the Empire, but since a stopover in the course of a journey was a necessity and – at least in some of these stations – the State ensured a certain level of service, the city taverns, and specifically the *popinae*, are the places where, as in contemporary bars and pubs, men lingered drunkenly, gambling, partaking in lewd conversation and singing, fighting and consuming junk food, attracting the judgemental comments of moralists (Laurence 1994: 78). The "social proximity" of deviant activities with the hospitality business often resulted in a spatial contiguity, as happened with the large *caupona* at Pompeii, with its main entrance just opposite to the town's largest brothel. The latter, however, was not far from the *macellum* and the *forum*, thereby confirming how these commercial activities associated with hospitality, trade and mobility were strictly interconnected (Frayn 1993: 38–42; Laurence 1994: 80).

## A competition among driving forces

When analysing the spatial distribution of a wide range of business activities associated with transport economy in town, it is necessary to start from the conceptual point of view and to question the political dimension of the management of the urban space. Modern essays are laced with the use of the terms "public" and "private" to label certain compartments of the urban space, but the original duplicity of these terms should be noted. "Public" versus "private" could be intended as a clash of the interests of the community versus those of individuals, but the concept of "public" is also linked to the idea of opening, as the essence of "privacy" is associated with the notion of enclosure. At the same time, the closure of the urban centre is competing with the economic need to open the town to exchange (Leveau 2017: 225). These two forces will challenge each other on the urban ground as well as in the social dynamics inside the civic body, but, unlike in contemporary urban planning, where a separation between traffic routes and residential compounds is sought, in the ancient city the interaction between traffic flow and private life took place in the street.[14]

The exceptional case studies of Pompeii and Ostia offer a privileged perspective to examine the interaction between traffic flow and daily activities. Assuming that the width of the street and its provision of sidewalks heavily influenced the intensity of (possibly two-way) vehicular and pedestrian traffic, leaving aside the changes that might have occurred with works in progress or with the construction of buildings with different volumetric characteristics, the "level of interaction" of each street has been measured by counting the doors and gates opening onto the frontage of the *insulae* bordering the street itself. The density of these openings is, therefore, considered an indicator of the high or low intensity of traffic and, accordingly, of social interaction. Predictably, the patterning of the counting of the front doors shows that the streets with the highest density of openings (i.e. >1/10 m) coincided with the main thoroughfares, connecting the city centre with the gates (Laurence 2008: 89–91). These streets with their high density of doorways also became the locations of most *cauponae* and *popinae* (showing, therefore, that the activities that took place there were not inappropriate). Other elements concur in highlighting the relevance and the popularity of these "hot spots" (most of all the intersections) of the urban space, such as shrines, water fountains, baths, benches and prestigious houses (Laurence 2008: 91–92). Undoubtedly, the intersections between popular streets worked as "nodes" and, therefore, attracted facilities and certain categories of retail shops. Other factors played a role in the hierarchy of urban thoroughfares, e.g. whether they were accessible to wheeled traffic – and this was more or less flowing – and the connectivity with the main points of attraction in town (Laurence 2008: 92). However, a spatial analysis of the distribution of bars and restaurants in those places that Kleberg labels as the "smartest locations" shows how rare they were in the hottest spots of Pompeii. This can again be explained by the underlying "moral dimension" of the urban texture (Wallace-Hadrill 1995: 46–51).

## Urban traffic and the economy of mobility: defining a transport property

To appreciate the spatial behaviour of the operations related to the economy of mobility, it is necessary to investigate their relationship with the urban street network and with public spaces.[15] The density of activities and the flow of traffic along the main thoroughfares and crossroads were clearly influenced by material and immaterial factors. Features like the city walls and their limited number of accesses through the gates, the presence of topographical impediments such as rivers, seaside and steep slopes and the obligatory passages like bridges undoubtedly affected the use of space in the Roman city and its consequent practice of social interaction (Laurence 2008: 98, 104). Furthermore, the traditional interpretation of the fragments of legislation regarding the traffic regulation in the urban environment (e.g. Gros 2008) has led several authors to argue that restrictions to the urban traffic pushed the location of the infrastructure for travellers to the margins of urban spaces.[16] Nevertheless, this regulation probably did not affect small-scale distribution and was not evenly adopted in Roman Italy. In any case, even in Rome, where vehicular traffic was generally excluded from the city during daylight hours, the circulation of pack animals and human porters was allowed.[17] Unfortunately, since these means of transport did not result in material features such as ruts and worn street pavements, their presence is not easily detectable in archaeological contexts (Wallace-Hadrill, this volume: Chapter 11). Even when the presence of draught or pack animals is witnessed by the presence of elements such as mangers, it cannot be related automatically to the use of animals in the transport sector. Therefore, to identify complexes that were involved in the "transport economy", whether vehicular or non-wheeled traffic, we have to rely upon the presence of architectural features such as ramps.[18] The latter allowed carts to leave the space of the streets and reach a parking area inside a building; these inner spaces to which ramps might have led[19] are generally identified by stables (Poehler 2011: 195; Poehler 2017: 214–215). Indeed, the presence of a ramp "signals the specific need for a large volume of material to be brought into and/or out of the property or for a high number of vehicles to be staged within the property" (Poehler 2011: 196), while the presence of a stable, given the high cost of building land, implies that it was more convenient for the holder of the real estate to own (and to be able to park and stable) his means of transport than hire them, or that the complex was operating as an inn with stabling services (Poehler 2011: 196). These properties, labelled "transport properties", are commonly identified with inns when they are served by a paved ramp (Poehler 2011: 196), while the presence of ruts ramps is usually connected to the rear entrances of houses or suburban estates where production took place. In Pompeii, for instance, estates characterised as "transport properties" are evenly spread either around the city gates (i.e. the large estates near the *Porta di Sarno*) or across the intramural space (Poehler 2011: 201). This pattern is mainly due to the fact that the category of "transport properties" includes private residences, where it was considered convenient to invest in large loading and unloading bays (Poehler 2011: 203). Although not fulfilling the prescription of Vitruvius (6.5.2, suggesting that stables had to be positioned at the rear of the building), stables and other spaces clearly devoted to stabling the animals have been identified in Pompeii. Stables, hay storage, storerooms and warehouses have been recognised, for example, on the front side of the Houses of Menander, of Faunus, of Labyrinth, of Pansa, of the Centenary, in most cases provided with an independent driveway (Callebat 2007: 79). In the House of Menander (Figure 13.2), for example, a room with a characteristic low door that could host up to four horses opened onto a small court, where a cart was found buried under the ashes (Figure 13.3). These findings show that this inner court was accessible to wheeled vehicles, as confirmed by the characteristics of the separate gate of the stable yard (I 10, 14). Four more rooms were accessible from the court (one is a *latrina* and

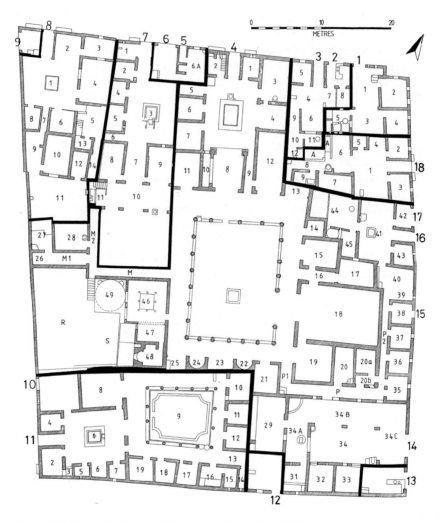

*Figure 13.2* Pompeii, House of Menander (after Ling 1990).

one is a shop), where there were other facilities such as a manger and a cistern (Callebat 2007: 79). The spatial organisation sealed by the ashes of the 79 CE eruption was the result of a piecemeal development, but the residential core was always kept separated from the two service areas of the kitchen (west) and the stable yard and staff quarters (south-east). This functional zoning confirms that the complex can be identified by "an agricultural operation outside the city" (Ling 1997: 47). As anticipated, most of these transport properties had to be considered private estates, which eventually underwent some commercial developments (*infra*).

*Figure 13.3* Pompeii, House of Menander. Reproduction of a cart in the stables (Creative Common, License CC BY-NC-SA 2.0).

## Architectural features

As with the wide terminology used for road stations, as well as in urban taverns and inns, there seems to be no direct relationship between the different terms featuring in several types of sources and the archaeological evidence.[20] For instance, Marie-Adeline Le Guennec has shown how the expected distinction between *caupona* and *stabulum* based on the accessibility or not to vehicles and mounts is not always confirmed by ancient sources (Le Guennec 2014: mainly 221–222) but can be detected on the basis of certain indexes.[21] Somehow, our typified idea of an inn, which seems to be more commonly termed a *caupona*, is inspired by the literary sources. The idyllic description of the place where the hostess Surisca of the piece *Copa*, included in the *Appendix Vergiliana*, graciously flirts with customers (Corsi 2000: 15, 35, 71), echoes the material evidence from Pompeii. Here, some of the largest inns (e.g. *insula* VII, 11.11/14), in some cases resulting from the adaptation of a former typical *atrium* house, offered the amenity of an inner garden, and sometimes also a larger garden at the rear of the building might have been in use as an orchard. Rooms for guests (up to 50) were usually found on the ground and upper floors (Laurence 1994: 79–80). However, it should be taken into account that a recent review of the Pompeian complexes recognised as inns for travellers provided with a mount or a vehicle has narrowed down the trustworthy identifications to only two (I, 1, 6–9 and VII, 12, 34–35, Fig 13.4: Le Guennec 2016: 87), not by chance located in the vicinity of the town gates.

Furthermore, as argued above, the places of business connected with the economy of mobility and the hospitality industry are not necessarily

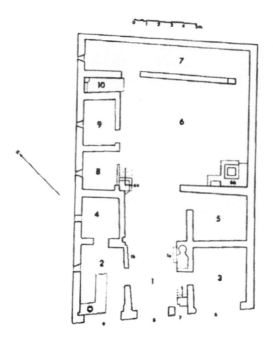

*Figure 13.4* Pompeii, I, 1, 6.7.8.9. Commercial operation devoted to the sale of food and beverages (after Le Guennec 2019).

architecturally definable as transport properties. The urban inns, if their function was only as lodgings for customers, often had a simple plan, without an entrance hall and court. Conventionally, on the ground floor, one could find the basic facilities, such as latrines, the kitchen, a dining room or a restaurant, sometimes a reception hall and sometimes a few bedrooms, while most of the bedrooms were located on the second floor (Kleberg 1957: 34–35; Casson 1974: 207). Conversely, most *stabula*, a term that clearly refers to accommodation for customers provided with a mount or a vehicle,[22] in addition to the characteristics listed above (an entrance hall or antechamber, flanked on either side by relatively small rooms that could have been equipped as a kitchen, dining room and reception room, with the addition of a latrine), had to be provided with a driveway, leading to a courtyard at the rear of the building, where wagons could be unharnessed and animals could be stabled. In the most common case of a two-storey building, the upper floor was reserved for bedrooms, some of which might also have been sited on the ground floor (Casson 1974, 207). In Pompeii, one of the most popular identifications of an inn for travellers with vehicles and/or mounts is the *stabulum* of Hermes (I, 1, 6–9), with its driveway accessing the inner courtyard (Figure 13.4). Here rooms 2 and 3 worked as *tabernae*, but no counters are preserved; room 7 is interpretable as a stable. On the second storey, there were some dormitories and two independent units.[23]

## Location in and around towns: spatial and economic analysis

The spatial analysis of the location in town of the commercial operations related to the economy of transport and mobility leads to interesting remarks about the economic strategies (e.g. the ratio between investments, property market and revenues) as well as about the social urban landscape (e.g. the relationship between areas where public activities are carried out versus alleys for secluded activities; residential districts versus more "touristic" sectors). As anticipated, in Pompeii, a survey of the preferred locations for *popinae* and *cauponae* shows that while the former, fulfilling the needs of a diversified clientele, composed mainly of citizens, seems to be evenly spread throughout the urban area, the inns, mainly targeting the public of travellers, were concentrated around the city gates, especially *Porta di Stabia* and *Porta di Ercolano*. Clearly, this hints that the thoroughfares that connected these two gates were those with the highest concentration of traffic and activities connected to mobility. Predictably, the area east of the forum (*regio* VII) also shows a certain concentration of *cauponae*, again suggesting a link with transport and logistical deeds (and, of course, with the largest city brothel: Laurence 1994: 81).

In the Vesuvian area, another suburban complex, identified by an infrastructure for travellers, has been excavated on the northern bank of the river Sarno, 600 m SW of the walls of Pompeii (De Simone and Nappo 2000; Nappo 2001: 845–846). It is divided into two parts, a thermal sector (west) and a *porticus triplex* (east), connected by a corridor (n. 7). At least three identical richly decorated *triclinia* (A, B, C; another three might have been located on the eastern side) were displayed on the northern side of the *porticus*, where there was also a kitchen (F). This sector probably had a second floor, where more rooms could have been found. The *porticus*, opening onto a *viridarium* and scenically positioned on the River Sarno, along the Via Stabiana (Nappo 2001, 852), might have accommodated a higher ranked public of travellers (Nappo 2001: 891–892, Figure 13.5). Following this interpretation, it has been addressed as the *Hospitium dei Sulpicii*. In the same area, another building, which included at least eight *tabernae* (or rooms with an independent entrance), the so-called *Edificio B di Murecine* (Nappo 2012), also considered an inn, confirms the economic vocation of the district.

This pattern seems to be replicated in other towns, where taverns and bars have been identified in "downtown" locations (e.g. in Petra, where they were positioned along the main streets, or in Sardis, where most taverns clustered around the bath–gymnasium complex, or in *Sagalassos* and *Cyrene*, where they lined the side of the main square, or Corinth, where bars and restaurants crowded around the theatre) or alongside the principal thoroughfares leading to the gates (Putzeys and Lavan 2007: 97–100). This latter positioning complied

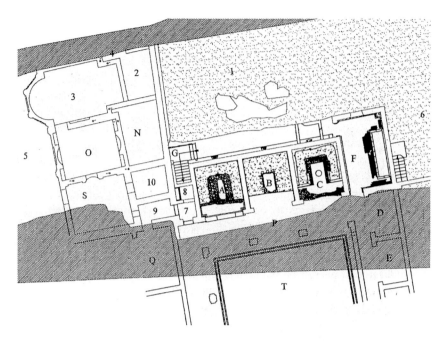

*Figure 13.5* Pompeii, loc. Murecine. Plan of the building labelled as "*Hospitium dei Sulpicii*" (after Nappo 2001).

better with those restrictions on intramural traffic referred to above and is clearly motivated by several practical reasons, not least the cost of building land. The location of inns at the gates or in the immediate *suburbium* of towns finds confirmation in a few epigraphic and literary sources, such as tales of miraculous events or criminal acts or other sorts of anecdotes (Constable 2003: 20: on the location of *pandokeia*), and in fragmentary archaeological evidence.

Apart from the exceptional case studies of Pompeii and Ostia, indeed, there is not much archaeological evidence to be discussed about inns in Roman towns. Moreover, as for road stations, the identification of excavated complexes with inns remains, in most cases, just hypothetical.

A first example comes from *Comum*, in northern Italy. Located in the modern Via Benzi at the crossroads with Viale Varese, the building has been investigated in the framework of a large archaeological intervention, spread over an area of around 6000 m², with archaeological evidence covering the phases from the first to the fifth centuries (Figure 13.6, Cecchini 2004; Blockley and Niccoli 2004). Here the analysis of several buildings sheds light on the organisation and evolution of the south-western *suburbium* of the town, starting from the first century CE (Blockey and Niccoli 2004: 19). This sector is crossed by main roads connecting the town to important destinations

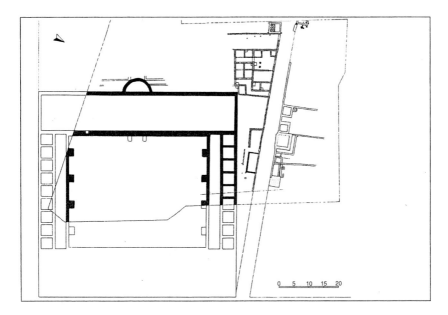

*Figure 13.6* Como, via Benzi. Plan of the building identified with an inn. Phase IIIA (in pale grey): Construction of Buildings A (*mansio*), D, E; Phase IV (in dark grey): construction of Building B (after Blockey and Niccoli 2004).

(the *glareata* road, the so-called *Via Regina*) as well as by a secondary road linking the southern quadrant of the *suburbium* to the port. It was just after the first reclamation of the area and the opening of the road with its lines of monumental tombs, and in connection with a first raising of the walking level, that – starting from the end of the first century CE and before the mid-second century CE – the construction of Building A, identified by the *mansio*, was carried out (phase IIIA). Building A, also known as "the inn", replaced another construction (Building C), probably a workshop or already a tavern, which lined the southern edge of the road. It was almost square (measuring 15 by at least 14 m) covering a total surface of c. 210 m² (Cecchini 2004: 195) and likely had two storeys. Outside its eastern wall, there was an open space that gave way from the road to the rear of the inn, where there was possibly a yard to park the vehicles and stable the animals (Blockey and Niccoli 2004: 60). During its main phase (IIIA), the plan was organised around a central large room (*ambiente* C), interpreted as a kitchen, at the sides of which there were two more small rooms (*amb*. T and U) that could have been used as storerooms. On the eastern side, there was another large room, probably a dining room. All other rooms (*amb*. A, G, K, L, M, N, P, Q, R and S), which were rather small, likely functioned as bedrooms, accessible by means of the two corridors (corridor D/E/F). After an additional raising of the deck of the road in the course of the second half of the second century (phase IIIB), some

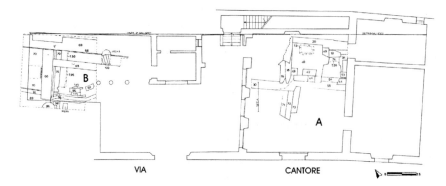

*Figure 13.7* Verona, Porta dei Borsari-via Cantore 18. Plan of the building identified
with a hostel (after Gottardi *et al.* 2016).

transformations were made to Building A (in connection with the construction of the nearby gigantic Building B (phase IV, Cecchini 2004: 197–210),
which was finally destroyed by fire between 236 and 255 CE (phase V, Blockey
and Niccoli 2004: 23–24, 98–99).

In Verona, archaeological research in the south-western *suburbium*, just
outside the city gate known as *Iovia* (nowadays *Porta Borsari*), and in close
connection with the *Via Postumia*, which entered the walls turning into the
main urban thoroughfare, has brought to light part of an archaeological complex that has been interpreted as a *mansio* (Gottardi *et al.* 2016). Known by
the name of its modern address (Via A. Cantore 18), the building is part of
an urban block fragmentarily investigated (Figure 13.7). Other finds in the
surrounding area of the *Via Postumia* included a segment of the town walls
traditionally attributed to the Gothic king Theodoric (end of the fifth–beginning of the sixth centuries CE), which run parallel to the late-republican walls,
with just a few metres in between, some ruins of a small temple, portions
of buildings interpreted as storerooms (sites: Via Cantore 15–Via Oberdan
18 and Via Cantore 6), a structure of unknown function (site: Via Oberdan
13), in addition to segments of paved roads, sewers and mosaics. Of the two
sectors into which the excavation area was divided, Area A presented some
underground rooms that were interpreted as a hypocaust, the use of which
ceased during the third century CE. Conversely, Area B (originally divided into
three underground rooms decorated with frescoes dating to the second century CE) was affected by an early medieval occupation, with Lombard burials
cut into the abandonment layers. The Roman complex has been interpreted
as an inn on the basis of the inscription mentioning staff usually related to
the transport economy (*supra*), of the link with Mercury, protector divinity
of trade and merchants, pictured in the frescoes, and ultimately of the close
connection with the *Via Postumia*.

In Gaul, a fashionable wave of research has brought many archaeological
complexes, both urban and rural, in most cases rather fragmentarily known,

to be identified with infrastructures for travellers.[24] At Clermont-Ferrand (ancient *Augustonementum*), in the proximity of the old bus station, a large building (269 m[2]), bordering an important road axis contouring the hill of Clermont, has attracted the attention of researchers because of its peculiar division into small rooms, accessible by way of a corridor opening onto the street (Ollivier *et al.* 2016). The rooms were heated and decorated by wall paintings. The identification as an inn seems to be confirmed by a fragmentary inscription of a wooden plate (dated by means of dendrochronology to the second century CE), with the word *viator* (Leveau 2017: 230 with references).

A better documented case study remains the complex from the Cité Judiciare at Bordeaux, excavated in the framework of some preventive archaeology activities, carried out between 1994 and 1995 at the car park of the new tribunal of the city near the river Gironde (Sireix 2014: 75). Here at a crossroads at the southern edge of the Roman *Burdigala* (Sanchez 2008: 31), there was originally a vast space where artisanal and manufacturing activities, almost exclusively iron working, took place. At the end of the first century CE, a building, identified as an inn, was built along the so-called *cardo* (Figure 13.8). The building, which had a rectangular shape, was organised, at ground level, into four rooms, one of which was a drive-through hall (*porte charrettière* C), giving access to an inner courtyard. The main building was flanked by annexes of some kind, on one side by kitchens and on the other by a smelting workshop (Sireix 2014: 75). The kitchens, served by a water channel, were equipped with two ovens. Although comparative research does not find a perfect match, it is possible that the oven complex functioned as a smokehouse for meat (Sireix 2014: 81–82). The building had an upper floor, protruding from the facade, sustained by the pillars in brick of a portico, covering the sidewalk (Sanchez 2008: 31; Sireix 2014: 79). On the southern

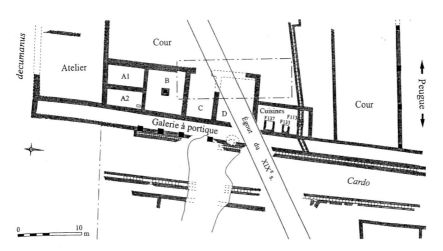

*Figure 13.8* Bordeaux, Cité Judiciaire. Plan of the building identified with an inn (after Sireix 2014).

side, there was an open courtyard (ca. 100 m²), delimited by walls on all sides. The beaten earth floor retains traces of combustion and waste that link this space to an atelier, which, however, did not practise specialised metallurgical activity like that of the first phase but rather seems to have provided services for the daily needs of the inhabitants of the block (Sireix 2014: 83). On the western side, there was another open courtyard, also paved in beaten earth; the side opening onto the river Peugue was bordered by a clerestory colonnade. The compound was served by some wooden water conduits, bearing the inscription *R(es) P(ublica) B(iturgum) V(iviscorum)* on the tubing (Sireix 2008: 60; Leveau 2016: 282–283; Leveau 2017: 230 with additional references). The complex did not undergo substantial changes between the second half of the second and the first half of the third century CE, but at the end of the third it was almost completely dismantled. The area was temporarily occupied by carvers and the manufacturing of wooden, bone and ivory objects. In general, the whole area around the *cardo* seems to have been used mainly "to quarry" materials for reuse in the construction of the late Roman town (Sireix 2008: 62–69). Since the findings have been studied without the distinction of provenience, it is not possible to underline any specific characteristic of the assemblage, but Stephanie Raux has stressed the link with activities connected to transport. On a more detailed level, it is worth noting the large number of writing instruments (Raux 2008: 148, 151).

Other fragmentary evidence informs us about the spatial organisation of the activities related to transport economy in and around towns.[25] Some inscriptions mentioning guilds of *iumentarii* (like the one found in Verona) come from the *porta Vercellina et Iovia* at Milan (*CIL* V 5872 = *ILS* 7295) and the *porta Gallica* at Fossombrone (*CIL* XI 6136 = *ILS* 7294; see Basso 2010). This delocalisation of the places of business for the economy of mobility might also be linked to some substantial changes in the spatial relationships between the intramural and extramural street network. Indeed, with the intensification of traffic along the Roman roads, at least some of the through traffic was diverted from crossing the town to the bypasses and beltways around urban centres.[26]

## Conclusions: *ad limina civitatis*

Although a thorough critical revision of the buildings that have been archaeologically connected with establishments related to the hospitality business is much needed, the spatial and social analyses described above might lead to the conclusion that there was a neat separation between the spaces devoted to most of the activities carried out in the framework of the economy of mobility and the "smartest areas" of towns. It might be argued, therefore, that the place for visitors to the city was at the margins of towns, a sort of liminal space, a "buffer zone" to keep out the strangers. However, several practical aspects have to be taken into account. The real-estate market and the prices of building land, vehicular traffic constraints and regulations, and the availability of stocking areas and services like porters in a sort of inter-change area are all factors that might have affected the spatial location of these operations. Nevertheless, the spatial distribution of all types of business related to the economy of mobility as it is documented in Pompeii clearly shows that "the whole of the urban landscape was charged with ideology" (Wallace-Hadrill 1995: 39). The struggle between the two driving forces of the citizenship unfolded mainly on the urban ground. The aristocratic snobbish disgust towards humble trade and menial commercial activities contended with the buzzing of the city economy, concealing in the backstage such a lively productive sector (Wallace-Hadrill 1995: 56), shaping the material and social urban landscape as well as the perception of the streetscape in Roman towns. We can underline the extent to which commercial activities related to the economy of mobility in general, and specifically the hospitality industry, impacted on the planning of urban space, its use and practice.

The "dichotomies between wide and narrow, observed and unobserved, open and secret, *via* and *platea* versus *angiportum* and *semita*" (Kaiser 2011: 118) find a perfect match in the spatial distribution of places of business characterised by a "mobility-seeking" behaviour only when not too openly linked to a "deviant behaviour". In other words, the wish to be clearly visible or conversely not to be seen impacted on the material fabric of the city as well as its social landscape.

Ultimately, this survey focused on some more practical aspects of mobility, highlighting the role of urban commercial enterprises connected to mobility in the general economy of Roman towns. We can observe that enough clues shed light on the impact that transport and mobility activities had on the urban space and the social fabric of small- and mid-sized towns. Of course, Pompeii and Ostia are exceptional case studies, but, while Ostia embodies an above-average context in relation to the transport economy, the snapshot taken in a mid-scale "provincial" town like Pompeii can bring us very close to grasping the essence of this global phenomenon of the economy of mobility.

From the archaeological point of view, we cannot but stress how ambiguous and misleading material evidence can be. This ambiguity is a direct conse-quence of the immaterial indistinctness of certain economic activities, where "private" and "public" businesses overlapped and supported each other. The complexes that underwent structural and functional transformations show that in the transport economy sector, urban investment strategies were fluid and responsive to market fluctuations. Moreover, in general, investments in commercial operations related to transport (such as inns and taverns) but also in simple infrastructures related to transport and logistics (such as ramps, loading bays and stables) prove how strong the impact of this economic sector on the urban tissue was. After all, the economy of mobility stands as one of the driving forces in the development of cityscapes, from the spatial as well as from the social point of view (Poehler 2011: 214), materialising a cultural construct that can be read through the filigree of the urban fabric.

## Notes

1  Witcher 1998: 60. E.g. Hartnett 2017: 1 investigates "how Romans came into contact, interacted, and sought to present themselves in the most used, yet least studied, of urban spaces: the street".

2  Hartnett 2017: 60. Referring to the work of Claire Holleran (2012: 194–231), Hartnett stressed that "the space between buildings also was a critical economic zone in its own right, as those hawking their wares were eager to profit from the street's crowds".

3  MacDonald 1986: 32–51, with emphasis on the architectural and functional connection between streets, squares and buildings; Favro 1994, on the structuring of urban routes following the definition of processional paths; Laurence 1994; Wallace-Hadrill 1995; Saliou 1999; Ellis 2004, specifically for Pompeii; Kaiser 2011: 115.

4  An excellent introduction to the latter is provided by Paliou 2014.

5  See the recent general review of literature by Zuiderhoek 2017: 11–12, 131–148.

6  See the definition of MacMullen 1970: 333.

7  Stöger 2011: 228–229: "movement economy is intended to group all those economic activities that have a movement-seeking behaviour, responding to peak pedestrian flows".

8  For example, a full essay has been devoted by Thomas McGinn (2004) to the "economy of prostitution".

9  Ancient sources ironically insist on this *topos*: e.g. Juv. 8, 172–176.

10  *Dig.*, 23.2.43 *praef* and 9. But see Le Guennec 2016: 87

> la prostitution n'entrait pas dans la définition de l'offre de services des *caupones* romains, puisqu'aux yeux du droit classique son exercice faisait basculer ces derniers dans les catégories professionnelles distinctes des *lenones/lenae* (*proxénètes*) ou des *qui/quae corpore quaestum faciunt* (prostitué(e)s).
> *Dig.* 3.2.4.2; *Dig.* 23.2.43.8–9; *Cod.Iust.* 4.56.3

11  *CIL* IX; 2689; MacMullen 1970, Viti 1989. The dialogue has been translated in English as follows: "–Mine host, let's settle the bill – You have a flagon of wine, and bread, one as; gruel, 2 asses–Agreed–For the girl, 8 asses–Agreed, again–And fodder for the mule, 2 asses–That mule will ruin me!" but the translation of the last sentence remains uncertain.

12  The stele is said to have been found at the Macchia d'Isernia, along the road connecting *Aesernia* with *Venafrum*, nowadays in Molise (Italy): Buonocore 2003.

13  Le Guennec 2019. The research is focused on the commercial activity related to the *accueil mercantil.*

14  Laurence 2008, 87. The reference work is predictably that one by Henri Lefebvre (1970) who first pointed at the "social" role of streets as public spaces and who stressed the need of balancing the requirements of a fluid flow of traffic, both vehicular and pedestrian, and the use of these spaces as places for social interaction.

15  This approach was applied by Stöger to the analysis of the spatial distribution of the *scholae* in Ostia: Stöger 2011, 213.

16  For example, Kleberg 1957, 48–60; Colleoni 2016b, 7; Leveau 2014, 36–40, and 40–44 for a more general discussion. This theory will be discussed below, against several case studies.

17 Mules, that can be loaded up to 100–135 kg, have also the advantage that they can easily overcome obstacles such as steep roadways, steps, thresholds and kerbstones (Laurence 2008: 87).

18 Ramps can be divided in two categories: the side ramps ("sections of the street where the kerbstones have been removed and replaced by an area of paving stones, usually inclined, in order to provide a place for wheeled vehicles to park out of the space of the street") and ramps that lead to a stable area: Poehler 2011: 196.

19 Indeed, the side ramps (see note 18) were only functional to facilitate the pull-off of goods needed to perform that specific commercial activity, especially in front of bakeries: Poehler 2017: 214.

20 Ellis 2004. Several attempts to typify the Latin terminology into a consistent classification of operations devoted to the hospitality business have been done but the resulting discrepancies argue for their uselessness: see Packer 1978: 5; Calabrò 2012: 73 and the criticism of Wallace-Hadrill 1995: 45–46 about the lack of grounding of these rankings in the usage of the sources.

21 Le Guennec 2016: 86–87. See also Corsi 2021. A good example of this inconsistency comes again from Pompeii: e.g. the bar (?) at Pompeii I 10, 2, where archaeological data seem to point at the presence of a "snack bar" that, given the absence of spaces for lodging and the tight link with the atrium house I 10, 3, and since it was probably operated by some "intermediary" of the householder, should be labelled as *thermopolium* (see figure 2). However, epigraphic evidence could lead to the definition of *caupona*: Ling 1997: 41–42. An archaeological survey of the spaces, equipment and architectural features of the operations devoted to food trade, restaurant and catering services and retail in *Herculaneum* is provided by Monteix 2010: 89–132.

22 The term *stabulum* – even in official documents like commemorative inscriptions (e.g. *CIL* VI 1774 = *ILS* 5906) – appears to be a synonym of *mansio* but is more explicit in referring to the presence of riding, pack or track animals (see most recently: Le Guennec 2014 and Crogiez 2016: 24; the latter thinks that "*stabulum* serait ainsi l'équivalent de *mutatio*"). In the Gospel, the place of the nativity is also labelled as *stabulum*, but – oddly – it is a proper stable of a *deversorium*, where Mary and Joseph are exceptionally lodged during their journey (*Vulg.* Luc. 2.7; Hier, *Hom. de natiuitate Domini*, 10–15 (*CCSL*, LXXVIII, 524)).

23 Packer 1978: 6–9. Also the two-storey building VII, 12, 34–35 is considered a typical *stabulum* partly on the basis of the presence of a neighbouring *cella meretricia* (Packer 1978: 9–12).

24 For example, Narbonne (along the *via Domitia*, graffiti and frescos that can be linked to an inn at the southern limit of the town: Leveau 2017: 230 with references), Aix-en-Provence, along the *voie d'Italie* (Leveau 2016a); Nîmes and La Croix de Fenouillet in proximity of the river Gard (Buffat 2009: 348–350, Leveau 2014: 27); Barzan in Charente-Maritime (Bouet 2011: 251, 979).

25 For example, an inscription from *Cales* (that, among other things, shows that streets had no name) mentions "the incline from the gate to the *cisiarios* [a station for a certain type of vehicle] at the *Porta Stellatina* (*CIL* X, 4660: *clivom ab ianu ad gisiarios porta*[e] *Stellatinae*"; Hartnett 2017: 34. Anna Stöger, commenting on the mosaics from the *Terme dei Cisiarii* (Baths of the Coachmen, II.2.3) at Ostia, located close to the *Porta Romana*, remarked how the representation of the walls of the town, albeit stylised, underlines the difference between narrow

gates (probably only for pedestrians) and larger gates for wheeled traffic: Stöger 2011: 223), confirming that associations of porters could have been stationed at the town's entrance.

26  See Gros 2008. E.g. Nimes, Aix, Vienne, Arles, etc., where even the crossing of the River Rhone is outside the urban centre.

# References

Basso, Patrizia. "Le stazioni di sosta lungo le strade della Cisalpina romana: problemi e prospettive di ricerca". Pages 155–168 in *Città e territorio: la Liguria e il mondo antico. Atti del IV Incontro Internazionale di storia antica (Genova, 19–20 febbraio 2009)*. Edited by Bertinelli, Maria Gabriella and Donati, Angela. Roma: G. Bretschneider, 2010.

Basso, Patrizia and Zanini, Enrico. eds. *Statio amoena: sostare e vivere lungo le strade romane*. Oxford: Archaeopress, 2016.

Blockley, Paul and Niccoli, Chiara. Lo scavo di via Benzi: stratigrafia per fasi. Pages 19–172 in *Extra moenia 1 - ricerche archeologiche nell'area suburbana occidentale di Como romana* (= Rivista Archeologica dell'Antica Provincia e Diocesi di Como 186). Edited by Anonymus, Como: New Press, 2004.

Bouet, Alain, ed. *Barzan III. Un secteur d'habitat dans le quartier du Moulin du Fâ à Barzan (Charente-Maritime)* (coll. Mémoires, 26; coll. Suppl. à Aquitania, 27). Bordeaux: Ausonius, Fédération Aquitania, 2011.

Buffat, Loïc. "De la prospection à la fouille: autour de quelques expériences réalisées en Languedoc". Pages 347–360 in *Les formes de l'habitat rural gallo-romain. Terminologies et typologies à l'épreuve des réalités archéologiques. Colloque AGER VIII. Toulouse 2007*. Edited by Philippe Leveau, Claude Raynaud, Robert Sablayrolles, Frédéric Trément. Bordeaux: Fédération Aquitania, 2009.

Buonocore, Marco. *Molise: repertorio delle iscrizioni latine. V,2. Aesernia: il territorio e la città*. Campobasso: Palladino, 2003.

Callebat, Louis. "Structure et organisation des espaces animaux de la villa". Pages 77–84 in *La médecine vétérinaire antique: sources écrites, archéologiques, iconographiques: actes du colloque international de Brest, 9–11 septembre 2004*. Edited by Cam, Marie-Thérèse. Collection "Histoire". Rennes: Presses Universitaires de Rennes, 2007.

Calabrò, Antonio. "Pompeian *Cauponae* in their Spatial Context: Interaction between Bars and Houses". Pages 73–91 in *Privata luxuria: towards an archaeology of intimacy*. Edited by Anguissola, Anna. Munich: H. Ultz, 2012.

Casson, Lionel. *Travel in the ancient world*. London: Allen and Unwin, 1974.

*CCSL* LXXVIII = Morin, German D., ed. *S. Hieronymi presbyteri opera*, II, Turnhout: Brepols, 1958.

Cecchini, Nicoletta. "La *mansio* (edificio A)". Pages 195–210 in *Extra moenia 1– ricerche archeologiche nell'area suburbana occidentale di Como romana* (= Rivista Archeologica dell'Antica Provincia e Diocesi di Como 186). Edited by Anonymus, Como: New Press, 2004.

Colleoni, Fabien ed. *Stations routières en Gaule Romaine: architecture, équipements et fonctions* (= Gallia 73.1 2016). Paris: Editions du Centre National de la Recherche Scientifique, 2016a.

Colleoni, Fabien. "Stations routières en Gaule Romaine: architecture, équipments et fonctions". Pages 3–9 in Colleoni 2016a.

Constable, Olivia Remie. *Housing the stranger in the Mediterranean world. Lodging, trade and travel in Late Antiquity and the Middle Ages*. Cambridge: Cambridge University Press, 2003.

Corsi, Cristina. *Le Strutture di Servizio del Cursus Publicus in Italia: Ricerche Topografiche ed Evidenze Archeologiche* (BAR International Series, 875). Oxford: John and Erica Hedges/Archaeopress, 2000.

Corsi, Cristina. "Stop and go. Men, animals and vehicles at Roman road stations in Gaul". Pages 181–194 in *Les modes de transport dans l'Antiquité et au Moyen-Âge. Mobiliers d'équipement et d'entretien des véhicules terrestres, fluviaux et maritimes. Actes du rencontres internationales Instrumentum (Arles 14–16 juin 2017)*. Edited by Raux, Stephanie. Drémil-Lafage: Editions Mergoil, 2021.

Corsi, Cristina. "Conceptualising Roman road stations. New perspectives for an innovative approach to mobility in the past". in *Aquitania, supplément*. Forthcoming.

Crogiez, Sylvie. "Les *mansiones* et *mutationes* dans les textes juridiques de l'Antiquité et du Haut Moyen Âge", Pages 16-26 in Basso and Zanini 2016.

De Simone, Antonio and Nappo, Salvatore, eds. Mitis Sarni opes. *Nuova indagine archeologica in località Murecine*. Napoli: Denaro libri, 2000.

Ellis, Steven J.R. "The distribution of bars at Pompeii: archaeological, spatial and viewshed analyses". *JRA* 17,1 (2004): 371–384.

Favro, Diane G. "The street triumphant. The urban impact of Roman triumphal parades". Pages 151–164 in *Streets. Critical perspective on public space*. Edited by Çelik, Zeynep, Favro, Diane G. and Ingersoll, Richard. London: University of California Press, 1994.

France, Jérôme and Nelis-Clément, Jocelyne, eds. *La statio: archéologie d'un lieu de pouvoir dans l'empire romain* (Scripta antiqua; 66). Bordeaux: Ausonius, 2014.

Frayn, Joan M. *Markets and fairs in Roman Italy: their social and economic importance from the second century BC to the third century AD*. Oxford: Clarendon Press, 1993.

Gottardi, Tecla, Zanetti, Cecilia and Zentilini, Elisa. "Lo scavo di via Cantore 18 a Verona: ipotesi di una stazione di sosta alle porte della città/The *statio* of the via Cantore 18 site in Verona: a hypothetical *mansio* at the edge of the Roman city". Pages 147–158 in Basso and Zanini 2016.

Gros, Pierre. "Entrer dans la ville ou la contourner? Remarques sur les problèmes posés par les tronçons urbains des voies de communication sous le Haut-Empire". Pages 145–163 in Mertens 2008.

Harris, William V. "The late republic". Pages 511–539 in *The Cambridge economic history of the Greco-Roman world*. Edited by Scheidel, Walter, Saller Richard P. and Morris Ian M. Cambridge: Cambridge University Press, 2007.

Hartnett, Jeremy. *The Roman street. Urban life and society in Pompei, Hercolaneum and Rome*. Cambridge: Cambridge University Press, 2017.

Hillier Bill, "Cities as Movement economies". *Urban Design International* 1/1 (1996): 41–60.

Holleran, Claire. *Shopping in ancient Rome: the retail trade in the late Republic and the Principate*. Oxford: Oxford University Press, 2012.

Kaiser, Alan. "What's a via? An integrated Archaeological and Textual approach". Pages 115–130 in *Pompeii: art, industry, and infrastructure: [108th annual meeting of the Archaeological Institute of America, held in San Diego, Calif.,2007]*. Edited by Poehler, Eric, Flohr, Miko and Cole, Kevin. Oxford–Oakville, CT: Oxbow Books, 2011.

Kleberg, Tönnes. *Hôtels, restaurants et cabarets dans l'antiquité romaine: études historiques et philologiques*. Uppsala: Almqvist and Wiksells, 1957.

Laurence, Ray. *Roman Pompeii: space and society*. London: Routledge, 1994.

Laurence, Ray. *The roads of Roman Italy: mobility and cultural change*. London–New York: Routledge, 1999.

Laurence, Ray. "City traffic and the archaeology of Roman streets from Pompeii to Rome. The nature of traffic in the ancient city". Pages 87–106 in *Mertens* 2008.

Laurence, Ray and Newsome, David J. eds. *Rome, Ostia, Pompeii: movement and space*. Cambridge-New York: Cambridge University Press, 2011.

Le Guennec, Marie-Adeline. "Le *stabulum* romain, écurie ou établissement hôtelier? La langue juridique et l'usage à Rome". Pages 215–227 in *Aux sources de la Méditerranée antique: les sciences de l'Antiquité entre renouvellements documentaires et questionnements méthodologiques. Actes du colloque tenu à la Maison Méditerranéenne des Sciences de l'Homme à Aix-en-Provence les 8 et 9 avril 2011*. Edited by Le Guennec, Marie-Adeline, Rossi, Lucia and Carrive, Mathilde. Marseille: Presses universitaires de Provence, 2014.

Le Guennec, Marie-Adeline. "Identifier une auberge romaine: quelques réflexions méthodologiques". Pages 81–90 in Basso and Zanini 2016.

Le Guennec, Marie-Adeline. *Aubergistes et clients. L'accueil mercantile dans l'Occident romain (IIIe s. av. J.-C. - IVe s. ap. J.C.)*. (BEFAR 381). Rome: École française de Rome, 2019.

Lefebvre, Henri. *La révolution urbaine*. Paris: Gallimard, 1970.

Leveau, Philippe. "Stations routières et *stationes viarum*. Une contribution à l'archéologie de la station en Gaule Narbonnaise et dans les provinces Alpines vosines". Pages 17–55 in France and Nelis-Clément 2014.

Leveau, Philippe. "Périphérie urbaine et lieux d'accueil des voyageurs et des marchands". Pages 281–294 in *Franges urbaines, confins territoriaux: la Gaule dans l'empire*. (Mémoires, 41) Edited by Besson, Claire, Blin, Olivier and Triboulot, Betrand: Bordeaux, 2016.

Leveau, "Philippe. Hospitalité publique, hospitalité privée dans la ville". Pages 225–249 in *Spazi pubblici e dimensione politica nella città romana: funzioni, strutture, utilizzazione: Clermont-Ferrand 30 marzo 2015, Bologna 27 ottobre 2015*. (CHEC) Edited by Franceschelli, Carlotta, Dall'Aglio, Pier Luigi and Lamoine, Laurent. Bologna: Bononia University Press, 2017.

Ling, Roger. *The insula of the Menander at Pompeii, I: the structures*. Oxford: Clarendon Press, 1997.

MacDonald, William L. *The architecture of the Roman Empire: 2. An urban appraisal* (Yale Publications in the History of Art 35). New Haven–London: Yale University Press, 1986.

MacMullen, Ramsay, "Market-days in the Roman empire. Phoenix". *Journal of Classical Association of Canada. Revue de la Société canadienne des études classiques* 24 (1970): 333–341.

McGinn, Thomas A.J. *The economy of prostitution in the Roman world: a study of social history and the brothel*. Ann Arbor: University of Michigan Press, 2004.

Mertens, Dieter, ed. *Stadtverkehr in der antiken Welt: internationales Kolloquium zur 175–Jahrfeier des Deutschen Archäologischen Instituts Rom, 21. bis 23. April 2004*. Wiesbaden: Reichert, 2008.

Mitchell, Stephen. "Horse-breeding for the *Cursus Publicus* in the later Roman Empire". Pages 247–261 in *Infrastruktur und Herrschaftsorganisation im Imperium*

*Romanum: Herrschaftsstrukturen und Herrschaftspraxis III. Akten der Tagung in Zürich 19.-20.10.2012, Berlin.* Edited by Kolb, Anne. Berlin: De Gruyter, 2014.

Monteix, Nicolas. *Les lieux de métier: boutiques et ateliers d'Herculanum.* Rome: École française de Rome, 2010.

Nappo, Salvatore. "La decorazione parietale dell'*hospitium* dei Sulpici in località Murecine a Pompei". *MEFRA* 113.2 (2001): 839–895.

Nappo, Salvatore. "L'edificio B di Murecine a Pompei: un esempio di architettura ricettiva alla foce del Sarno". *Rivista di Studi Pompeiani* 23 (2012): 89–101.

Ollivier, Julien, Blondel, François, Foucras, Sylvain, Hallavant, Charlotte, Le Guennec, Marie-Adeline, Longepierre, Samuel and Pédoussaut, Laëtitia. "Le site de la Scène nationale (Augustonemetum/Clermont-Ferrand, Puy-de-Dôme): une auberge et son enseigne peinte". Pages 189–216 in Colleoni 2016.

Packer, James E. "Inns at Pompeii. A short survey". *Cronache Pompeiane* 4 (1978): 5–51.

Paliou, Eleftheria. "Introduction". Pages 1–17 in *Spatial analysis and social spaces. Interdisciplinary approaches to the interpretation of prehistoric and historic built environments* (Topoi–Berlin Studies of the Ancient World 18). Edited by Paliou, Eleftheria, Lieberwirth, Undine and Polla, Silvia. Boston: De Gruyter, 2014.

Poehler, Eric. "Where to park? Carts, stables and the economics of transport in Pompeii". Pages 194–214 in *Laurence and Newsome, 2011.*

Poehler, Eric. *The traffic systems of Pompeii.* Oxford: Oxford Academic Press, 2017.

Putzeys, Toon and Lavan, Luke. "Commercial space in Late Antiquity". Pages 81–109 in *Objects in context, objects in use: material spatiality in Late Antiquity.* Edited by Lavan, Luke, Swift, Ellen, Putzeys, Toon and Gutteridge, Adam. Leiden–Boston: Brill, 2007.

Raux, Stephanie. "Le mobilier métallique". Pages 145–153 in Sireix 2008.

Robinson, Damian. "Re-thinking the Social Organisation of Trade and Industry in First Century A.D. Pompeii". Pages 88–105 in *Roman Working Lives and Urban Living.* Edited by MacMahon, Ardle, and Price, Jennifer. Oxford: Oxbow Books, 2005.

Saliou, Catherine. "Les trottoirs de Pompéi: une première approche". *BABESCH* 74 (1999): 161–218.

Sanchez, Corinne, ed. *La voie de Rome, Entre Méditerranée et Atlantique.* Bordeaux: Ausonius, 2008.

Sireix, Christophe, ed. *La cité judiciaire: un quartier suburbain de Bordeaux antique.* Pessac: Fédération Aquitania, 2008.

Sireix, Christophe. "L'auberge de la Cité judiciaire à Bordeaux". Pages 75–84 in *France and Nelis-Clément* 2014.

Stöger, Hanna. "The Spatial Organization of the Movement Economy". Pages 215–242 in Laurence and Newsome 2011.

Viti, Angelo. "*Ad Calidium.* L'insegna del piacere nel rilievo di Lucio Calidio Erotico". *Almanacco del Molise* 2 (1989): 115–135.

Wallace-Hadrill, Andrew. "Public honour and private shame: the urban texture of Pompeii". Pages 39–62 in *Urban society in Roman Italy.* Edited by Cornell, T.J. and Lomas, Kathryn. London: UCL Press, 1995.

Witcher, Robert E. "Roman roads: phenomenological perspectives on roads in the landscape". Pages 60–70 in *TRAC 97 (Proceedings of the seventh annual Theoretical Roman Archaeology Conference, April 1997, Nottingham).* Edited by Forcey, Colin, Hawthorne, John and Witcher, Robert E. Oxford: Oxbow Books, 1998.

Zuiderhoek, Arjan. *The ancient city.* Cambridge: Cambridge University Press, 2017.

# 14 Munigua's place in the operational chain

## Some considerations regarding the movement of people and goods and the division of labour in the lower Guadalquivir Valley during the Roman period

*Thomas G. Schattner*

## Introduction

The Hispano-Roman *Municipium Flavium Muniguense*, the modern-day Munigua (Villanueva del Río y Minas, Province of Seville), is certainly a good case study for the topic of this book. In the first and second centuries CE, Munigua was known as the largest producer of copper and iron in the Sierra Morena, developing exceptional economic power that enabled the development of the city with imposing religious and public buildings.[1] The most important among these is, without a doubt, the Terrace Sanctuary on the hill above the city, but the Temple of the Podium halfway up the hill, the two-storey portico with the temple of Mercury, the *forum* with its temple and the adjacent basilica, and not least, the baths also bear witness to the fact that the urban elite had the appropriate means to develop the city during this period. The large number and variety of these buildings, especially the religious buildings, which can be seen in Helio Ruipérez's hypothetical 3D illustration of the reconstruction (Figure 14.1), might at first glance suggest a monumentality, the size and reach which the city did not actually possess. With an area of just 3.8 ha contained within its walls, it is one of the smallest cities of Roman Spain.[2] As a consequence, the number of residential houses is also very limited, as the actual available city area only has space for around 15–18 houses or city villas.[3] The number of inhabitants must, therefore, have been correspondingly low. The *curia*, for example, which has the smallest floor area known in *Hispania*, has a maximum of 44 seats[4]; therefore, the number of decurions and, thus, the number of households are probably close to this number.[5]

A small city size and a limited number of inhabitants are nevertheless likely to have characterised many of the 175 cities that were recorded in Augustan times in the province of *Baetica*, which is home to almost half of the 400 Roman cities in *Hispania*.[6] In Roman municipalities, the external

*Figure 14.1* Hypothetical 3D reconstruction of the city (Visualisation H. Ruipérez; DAI Madrid, Munigua-Archive H. Ruipérez).

appearance of the fora, temples and baths is similar to one another, as are their economic foundations which, as elsewhere in much of *Hispania*, were generally based on agriculture and mineral resources, namely, mines and quarries. In Munigua, however, this balance was weighed differently: mining operations were by far the most important, followed by agriculture and quarrying. This can be concluded, first, based on the measurable extent of the mines; second, based on the examination of the soil quality which, being granite sand, is unsuitable for agriculture[7]; and, third, because of the small scale of the quarries.[8] The city's location in the Sierra Morena, far from the traffic artery of the Guadalquivir Valley, where hardly any other Roman cities can be found, provides further evidence (Figure 14.2). The existence of copper mines in this area was certainly the trigger for the con- struction of a settlement at this site, which had probably existed atop the hill since the late fourth century BCE under the native name of Munigua[9] and was only demolished when the terrace sanctuary was built in the time of Vespasian.[10]

Munigua is located in the Lower Guadalquivir Valley agglomeration area and had economic power due to its mines, all of which are located in the surrounding area. These are copper and iron mines, with copper exploitation being dominant since prehistoric times. Towards the middle or second half of the first century CE, however, there was a marked change towards iron.[11]

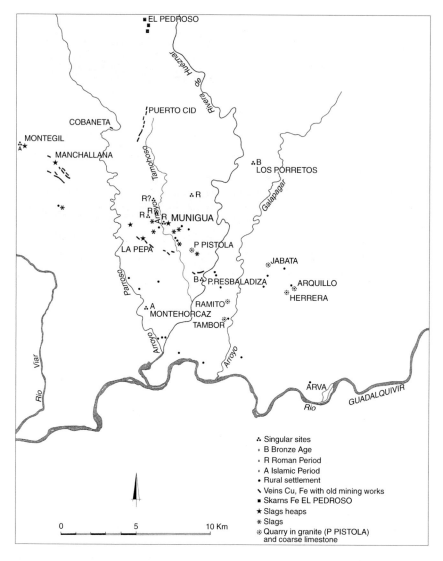

*Figure 14.2* Munigua and its territory in the lower Guadalquivir Valley (DAI Madrid, Munigua-Archive G. Ovejero).

This chapter is an attempt to determine Munigua's place in the production chain of the goods that the city itself produced or that came into and out of the city. To begin with, the assumptions and methods employed in the analysis are set out, followed by a description of the city's goods based on archaeologically documented evidence. The Roman Imperial period, especially during Flavian times, when the city experienced its heyday, is a decisive time frame, since most of the above-mentioned buildings were built during this period. The baths were built earlier, during Claudian times, but they also experienced a phase of construction in the Flavian period.[12] Only the Podium temple, which appears to date from the second century CE, was built afterwards.[13] The final part of this chapter attempts to provide a theoretical framework with the objective of including Munigua in the common models for work chains.

## Premises and methods

Economy and business result in movement and trade. In other words, economy is development.[14] It is one of the empirical findings of economic geography that technical progress, together with a developing population and a good infrastructure, form the basis for the diversification of labour, as was undoubtedly present in the population agglomeration of the lower Guadalquivir Valley. According to Adam Smith, increasing specialisation and division of labour are growth factors.[15] This means an increasing spatial separation of production and consumption, especially in this period of the Roman Empire. These factors intermesh and result in a change in the distribution pattern, which will become a larger and more diverse system with many players involved in trading, intermediate trading and possibly further processing.[16]

The objective of this contribution is a first attempt to determine Munigua's place and to classify the city against this background. Methodologically, several approaches are possible. In addition to the well-known concept of the *chaîne opératoire*, which was developed in the pioneering work of André Leroi-Gourhan in the first half of the twentieth century and has been used for the representation and reconstruction of manufacturing chains in the field of classical studies,[17] there are also the modern concepts of the "value chain", the "corporate environment" and other theoretical approaches such as the "*filière*-concept" or "network theory". It quickly becomes apparent, however, that none of these approaches are in themselves able to adequately describe the specific situation at hand, that is, of the locally produced and incoming and outgoing goods of an ancient city such as Munigua. Since it is mostly used in prehistoric contexts, the very open concept of the *chaîne opératoire*[18] in practice lacks the spatial dimension, which, however, is indispensable in relation to an agglomeration area such as that in the Guadalquivir. The "value chain" or the "*filière*-concept" models are too much geared towards modern needs, requiring specific figures such as economic indicators, national accounts, population, productivity (gross national product), profitability and many other factors to get the most out of them, factors that are fundamentally absent for antiquity. The purposes for which these models were designed are also not always compatible with ancient circumstances. For example, Michael Porter's value chain instrument was created primarily to give companies competitive advantages. As Porter points out, an analysis of value chains only makes sense at the level of individual companies in a branch of trade.[19] The conditions in Munigua provide no basis for any of this because the information related to them is simply unknown (as in other ancient cities). If the subject is nevertheless pursued here, this can only be done for certain goods and only in a rudimentary fashion, because the data gap between modern and ancient economics seems to be too large due to the described lack of knowledge. In addition, this chapter is written in full consciousness of the old debate on the applicability of modern criteria and economic terminology to the ancient world.[20] However, despite the lack, in the ancient world, of empirical data for most of the assumptions implicit in the modern theoretical approaches discussed in the section, it is argued here that we can still employ the statistical or quantitative methods associated with these approaches to analyse the archaeological data from Munigua.

## Economic goods in Munigua

Goods are the means for satisfying human needs.[21] Separated into tangible goods (Table 14.1) and services (Table 14.2), the economic goods in Munigua are listed in separate columns, according to whether they have been found in the town itself or in its territory, and whether as an individual finding and thus archaeologically attested (Column 1) or through indirect indications of their existence (Column 2). In Table 14.1, Column 3 is followed by an indication of the context in which the find or estate is located; this can be public, private or a sanctuary. The corresponding bibliographic citation appears in Column 4.

Immovable property, that is, buildings and facilities in Munigua include both sanctuaries and temples, public buildings such as the *forum*, the *curia*, and the double-storey hall as well as private dwellings/townhouses and the workshop buildings.[22] To these, we must add the farmsteads and the mines in the surrounding area, where a number of which were engaged in underground mining operations. The country roads that connect them also form part of this group as these are often accompanied by structural features, such as roadsides and fords or bridges. Finally, the furnaces and ovens/kilns are included, of which those for metal, bread, glass (Figure 14.3) and apparently also for pottery are attested in the city. While they are situated in public spaces or shops, the oil mills are located in the private areas of the houses. In the case of movable goods, the subgroup of manufactured goods is characterised by the existence of raw metal or metal ingots. Unfortunately, no ingot has ever been found in the course of the excavations and research in Munigua, which goes back as far as the sixteenth century, or at least no such find has ever been recorded.[23] The mines with their processing stations and furnaces do nonetheless bear witness to smelting, as do workshop buildings in the city. The final product of smelting is raw metal in the form of ingots. These, however, are only indirectly attested. In contrast, charcoal, which means firewood, has come to light in the excavations almost everywhere. This material is to

*Table 14.1* Tangible goods in Munigua (DAI Madrid E. Puch Ramírez and author)

| *1*<br>*Goods* | *2*<br>*Indirectly indicated* | *3*<br>*Context* | *4*<br>*Bibliography* |
|---|---|---|---|
| **Material goods**<br>**immobile, real estate** | | | |
| All buildings | | Public and private | Schattner 2003, 25–115 |
| Sanctuaries, temples | | Public and private | Hauschild 1992; Schattner 2003, 27–52 |
| Curia, forum, two-storied porticus, tabularium | | Public | Gimeno Pascual 2003 |
| Public thermae | | Public | Martini, in Mulva VIII |
| Town villas | | Private | Meyer, in: Mulva IV |
| *Officinae* | | Private | Schattner 2003, 115 |
| Farms in urban hinterland | | Private | Mulva VII |
| Mines in urban hinterland | | Private | Mulva VII |
| Country tracks | | Public and private | Mulva VII |
| Metal furnace | | Public | Mulva VII |
| Pottery kilns | | ? | Fabião 2006 |
| Bread furnace | | Public | Schattner, in: Mulva VIII |
| Oil mills | | Private | Hanel 1989 |
| Glass furnace | | Private | Newly found not published |
| **Material goods**<br>**Mobile**<br>**Material goods** | | | |
| **Producer goods, durable Consumer goods** | | | |
| Raw metal, ingots | Metalurgical process *officinae* | Private | Mulva VII |
| Firewood, charcoal | | Public and private | Mulva VII |
| **Material goods**<br>**Non-durable consumer goods** | | | |
| Metal vessels and tools | | Public | Mulva VI |
| Ceramic vessels | | Public and private | Vegas 1969; Vegas 1975; Vegas 1984; Basas, in: Mulva IV |
| Glass vessels | | Public and private | Mulva II, 38–47; Schattner 2003, 163–177 |
| Loom weights | | Private | Teichner, in: Mulva IV 2001, 322 Nr. O1–O7 Abb. 40 |
| Altars, statue pedestals, sculptures | | Public and private | Beltrán Fortes 1988, 84. 109; Hertel, in: Mulva III; Schattner, in: Mulva VIII |

(*continued*)

*Table 14.1* Cont.

| 1 Goods | 2 Indirectly indicated | 3 Context | 4 Bibliography |
|---|---|---|---|
| **Material goods** | | | |
| **Producer goods Durable Consumer goods** | | | |
| Building materials, stone, wood, stucco | | Public and private | Mulva VII |
| Colour balls Egyptian blue, haematite | | Public and private | Schattner, in: Mulva VIII, 1 |
| Meat | Animal bones | Public and private | Boessneck and von den Driesch 1980 |
| Bread, flour | Bakery furnace | Public and private | Schattner, in: Mulva VIII |
| Oil | Oil mill | Private | Hanel 1989 |
| Fish sauces | Amphorae | Private | Fabião 2006 |
| Wine | Amphorae | Private | Fabião 2006 |

be expected in all cities, as it was essential for the functioning of civic life in many respects.

Consumer goods include metal, ceramic and glass containers and loom weights, as well as sculptures and altars (grave and votive altars). As consumables, building materials such as stone, wood and stucco/plaster are preserved in the buildings, while colour balls of Egyptian blue and a vessel with blood-red hematite indicate the existence of dyers. Food can only be attested indirectly: meat from the animal bones, bread and flour from the bread ovens, oil from the oil mills and fish sauces and wine from the corresponding amphorae.

Table 14.2 contains a list of personal or factual services. In Column 1, the service is named, and in Column 2, the archaeological find from which the service was deduced is indicated. Column 3 contains an indication of the public (O) or private (P) character of the final object resulting from the context. Column 4 lists the relevant profession to which the benefit can be attributed, and Column 5 refers to the bibliography.

The discovery of medical equipment testifies to the existence of personal services. Certainly at this point, activities from other areas such as sanctuaries and temples, *thermae* or public administration could be cited. However, for the sake of simplicity, these are listed under pertinent services, since the factual reference may account for most of the work involved. The list continues with housekeeping work in the city villas, the drivers of mule or donkey caravans (transporters) and farmers and farm workers on the farms in the city's territory. It ends with the usual operations that can be expected in any city. Work in many workshops, such as metal foundries, metal furnaces, glassworks or weaving mills, was also been strongly geared to making repairs (Figure 14.3). In this respect, the tinker's profession indicated in Table 14.2 seems appropriate.

*Table 14.2* Services in Munigua

| *1*<br>Provision of services | *2*<br>Archaeological find | *3*<br>Context | *4*<br>Profession | *5*<br>Bibliography |
|---|---|---|---|---|
| **Provision of services individual related** | | | | |
| Medical care | Medical tools | Private | Medical doctor | Krug, Mulva VI, 33–35 |
| Tax farming | Inscription on bronze tablet | Public | Publicani, financier | Nesselhauf 1960; Schattner 2013, 348 |
| **Provision of services issue related** | | | | |
| Building business | Buildings | Public and private | Builder, mason, plasterer, carpenter, etc. | Schattner 2003, 25–115 |
| Cult service | Sanctuaries, temples | Public and private | Cult personnel | Hauschild 1992; Schattner 2003, 27–52 |
| Thermae service | Thermae | Public | Personnel | Martini, in Mulva VIII, 1 |
| Public administration | Curia, forum, two-storied porticus, tabularium | Public | City clerks | Gimeno Pascual 2003 |
| Housekeeping | Town villas | Private | Housekeeping personnel, cooks | Meyer, Teichner in: Mulva IV |
| Transport | Country tracks | Public and private | Transporters | Mulva VII |
|  | Farms in urban hinterland | Private | Farmers, peasants | Mulva VII |
| Mining and metallurgical process |  | Private | Miners, Mine workers | Mulva VII |
| Smelting, forge | *officinae* | Private | Metal workers, forgers | Mulva VII |
| Metal foundry | Metal furnace | Private | Metalurgist, tinkerer | Mulva VII |
| Pottery | Pottery kiln | Private | Potter | Fabião 2006 |
| Bakery | Baker furnace | Public | Baker | Schattner, in: Mulva VIII |
| Glaziery | Glass furnace | Private | Glazier | Newly found, not published |
| Opus spicatum floor | Oil press | Private | Oil miller | Hanel 1989 |
| Weaving | Loom weights | Private | Weaver | Teichner, in: Mulva IV |
| Sculpting | Altars, statue pedestals, sculptures | Public and private | Sculptor, chiseler | Beltrán Fortes 1988, 84. 109; Hertel, in: Mulva III; Beltrán Fortes 2006; Schattner, in: Mulva VIII,1 |
| Dye works, wall painting | Colour balls Egyptian blue, haematite | Public and private | Dyer, limer | Boessneck and von den Driesch 1980 |
| Meat market | Animal bones | Public and private | Butcher, shepherd, hunter | Fabião 2006 |
| Food trade (oil, fish sauces, wine) | Amphorae | Private | Trader |  |
| Forest care and charcoal burning | Charcoal | Public and private | Lumbermen, charcoal burner | Pérez Macías and Schattner 2018 |

*Figure 14.3* Distribution map of furnaces and ovens in Munigua: metal, bakery and glass (DAI Madrid, Munigua-Archive D. Schäffler).

In Figure 14.4, movable goods and services are arranged in the context of the traffic going in and out of Munigua. Intangible transport, such as the transfer of knowledge, is not included.

In terms of outgoing and incoming people, there are some reliable statements. These relate to father and son L. Quintius Rufinus and L. Quintius Rufus who donated pedestals with identical inscriptions for statues of Hercules both in Munigua and near the Strait of Gibraltar.[24] Also recorded is Quintia Flaccina, priestess (*flaminica*) of the imperial cult in the provincial capital of *Corduba*.[25] Whether Servilius Pollio of Carmona,[26] who leased the tax payments in Munigua, was ever really in town is unknown. Visits of specialists to the city can probably be assumed: the doctor, who, perhaps routinely, would have come from time to time, and the cabinet makers, builders and sculptors who would have carried out specific assignments. There must have been constant comings and goings among the drivers of the mule or donkey caravans, peasants, farm labourers and slaves.

Among the exported goods, only metal ingots as unit goods as well as firewood and charcoal as bulk goods can be mentioned. This material was taken from the wooded area around Munigua, which in antiquity, as nowadays, had a stock of trees, consisting mainly of holm and cork oaks. Charcoal burning, which was a profitable industry in this area until the 1960s, was associated with environmental maintenance. This was important for the pig industry because of the acorns that fall from these trees, and they are still a quality marker in the diet of the black pigs of the Sierra Morena (*jamón ibérico*). Most imported bulk goods consisted of food and produce. While the amphorae with the fish sauces originated predominantly from the Bay of Cádiz and thus had to be brought from a greater distance, flour and olives may have come from the Guadalquivir Valley. The fact that flour had to be imported is clear from the circumstance that mills, especially the well-known round-turning hand mills, are nearly absent in Munigua. The Guadalquivir Valley is the second largest supplier of amphorae, and their contents were probably wine and oil.

Gilt bronze statues[27] and bronze candelabra with silver inlays were imported as special items. It is precisely these kinds of findings that can be considered a measure of the taste prevailing in the city and of the financial power of some families.[28] Taking this in consideration, even more luxury goods may be expected such as, perhaps, fine towels, clothes and so forth. Metal and special ceramic vessels should also be mentioned at this point[29] as well as scales, writing utensils, furniture, fibulae and so on.[30] The agglomeration area of the lower Guadalquivir Valley could be presumed as the source of supply for these goods, whereas for particular marbles[31] or for the colour balls (small balls of Egyptian blue) and the gems/amulets, a more distant source must be assumed.

Meat certainly originates from Munigua's surroundings as do common stone building materials, clay brick and lumber. If the suspected pottery kilns are confirmed, then the production of utility ceramics or loom weights can be considered local. The newly discovered, unpublished glass furnace testifies

<table>
<tr><td colspan="9">traffic in Munigua</td><td>local manufacture</td></tr>
<tr><td rowspan="7">immaterial traffic (Knowledge transfer etc.)</td><td colspan="2">people</td><td colspan="6">goods, freight</td><td rowspan="7">loom weights<br>altars<br>building material (stone, wood, stucco)<br>glass<br>meat<br>ceramic vessels<br>(amphorae)<br>wine</td></tr>
<tr><td rowspan="2">outgoing</td><td rowspan="2">incoming</td><td colspan="2">outgoing</td><td colspan="4">incoming</td></tr>
<tr><td>bulk</td><td>pieces</td><td colspan="2">bulk material</td><td colspan="2">piece goods</td></tr>
<tr><td colspan="2" rowspan="2">transporters<br>farmers<br>peasants</td><td rowspan="4">firewood<br>charcoal</td><td rowspan="4">metal<br>ingots</td><td>from nearby</td><td>from far away</td><td>from nearby</td><td>from far away</td></tr>
<tr><td colspan="2">cloth</td><td colspan="2" rowspan="2">metal vessels<br>ceramic vessels<br>sculptures<br>furnishings<br>fibulae<br>scales<br>writing utensils<br>candelabra<br>equipment/machines<br>inscription tablets</td></tr>
<tr><td rowspan="2">L. Quintius Rufinus<br>L. Quintius Rufus<br>Quintia Flaccina</td><td rowspan="2">medical doctor<br>specialists<br>builders<br>cabinet makers<br>sculptors<br>Servilius Pollio?</td><td rowspan="2">flour<br>olives<br>olive-oil<br>wine<br>firewood<br>charcoal</td><td rowspan="2">fish-sauces</td></tr>
<tr><td>tools</td><td>marble<br>colour balls<br>(aegyptian blue,<br>haematite)<br>gems<br>votives/amulettes</td></tr>
</table>

*Figure 14.4* Traffic in Munigua (based on Die Ladezone im Blickpunkt, Anforderungen an die Güterversorgung in Köln und Leverkusen [Köln 2018] 10, Abb. 4, see www.ihk-koeln.de/upload/IHK_Studie_Ladezone_Onlinefassung_66820.pdf [accessed on 28 July 2018]; DAI Madrid E. Puch Ramírez and author).

to glass production, which has long been suspected.[32] The altars with tendril decoration have led José Beltrán to consider the possibility of the presence of a workshop in the city itself or in the region, due to the frequency of the motif in Munigua (four pieces) with simultaneous rarity in Baetica,[33] but they could also have been produced by a traveling workshop.

In summary, we can say that Munigua produced metal bars and firewood/charcoal as commodities. Foods were imported as both commodities (flour) and consumer goods, with olives, wine and fish sauces being imported as commodities in bulk. Luxury items such as bronze statues, bronze candelabra, statues or furniture were likely also imported.

## Models for work chains and theoretical framework

### Value chain

Metal extraction and processing has a long tradition in *Baetica* and has been an essential source of value for the regional economy since the dawn of metal working, especially in the mountainous regions of the Sierra Morena. Thus, it was always a topic of high practical and political relevance. As in Munigua, where metal ingots and firewood/charcoal appear to be the only goods that were exported (Figure 14.4), the industry must have already offered added value through its metalworking factories alone, insofar as the ingots circulated within wider regional networks of distribution and negotiation in which several actors participated and were normally paid for with money, not bartered.

Over the past 20 years, a variety of practical studies and theoretical approaches have dealt with developments in agricultural and other production systems,[34] and value chain approaches in particular have made an important contribution to explaining the organisation, coordination and structure of these complex systems.[35] In principle, a value chain can be understood as the connection between the raw material, the manufacturing process and the sale of a product.[36] In antiquity, this can be observed primarily in the vertical direction, in the sense that the temporally successive processing steps can be understood.[37] These steps are listed for the metal extraction in La Pepa (copper) and El Pedroso/Navalázaro (iron) in Figure 14.5, separated by copper and iron. The main difference is that the copper was made entirely into bullion at the mine in La Pepa itself and thus came into the city as a finished ingot, while the iron ore was brought as raw material from El Pedroso/Navalázaro to the town of Munigua for further processing. Proof of this is provided by the corresponding slag heaps, which in the case of copper lie in the vicinity of the mines and in the case of iron are located in the city itself.[38] This statement must be refined, however, since the observation allows us to conclude that there is a difference in the organisation of the extraction and processing of copper and iron, which gives reason to briefly consider the particular and quite exceptional situation in Munigua. Thus, the organisation of production seems to have been essentially determined by the distance to

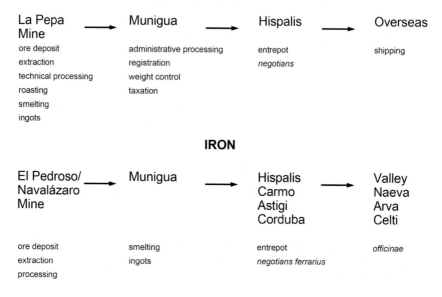

**METALS IN MUNIGUA**
**Operational chain**

**COPPER**

| La Pepa Mine | → | Munigua | → | Hispalis | → | Overseas |
|---|---|---|---|---|---|---|
| ore deposit | | administrative processing | | entrepot | | shipping |
| extraction | | registration | | *negotians* | | |
| technical processing | | weight control | | | | |
| roasting | | taxation | | | | |
| smelting | | | | | | |
| ingots | | | | | | |

**IRON**

| El Pedroso/ Navalázaro Mine | → | Munigua | → | Hispalis Carmo Astigi Corduba | → | Valley Naeva Arva Celti |
|---|---|---|---|---|---|---|
| ore deposit | | smelting | | entrepot | | *officinae* |
| extraction | | ingots | | *negotians ferrarius* | | |
| processing | | | | | | |

*Figure 14.5* Metals in Munigua. Operational chain based on the extraction of metals from La Pepa (copper) and El Pedroso/Navalázaro (iron) (DAI Madrid, Munigua-Archive E. Puch Ramírez and author).

the city of Munigua. If the mines were located somewhere in the city's near surroundings, such as the copper mine of La Pepa (2 km away), the largest of the copper mines, the processing was carried out at the mine itself. However, if the mines were located at a distance of about 8 to 10 km, such as Puerto Cid and Manchallana (both copper) or up to 20 km, such as Navalázaro and El Pedroso (largest iron mines), the entire processing may have taken place in the *municipium* of Munigua. Unfortunately, we have no information concerning the legal and owner relationships between the mines and the smelting and processing industry in the city. These, however, seem to have had nothing to do with the exploration system. Thus, the existence of not one, but of four large slag heaps in the Munigua town area, shows that it was a diversified system; for if this had been centralised, then the assumption would be the presence of a single slag heap. The distribution of the slags in different areas of the city, therefore, speaks in favour of the participation of several groups in iron and, to a lesser extent, copper production. It can be assumed that each of the groups worked in one area of the city and dumped their slag there. Apparently, several groups of producers could gain their living in this way, given that mines appear to have been rich enough to sustain these various groups. It is also noteworthy that, given the size of the Navalázaro and El Pedroso iron mines, there was no permanent settlement at or near these sites, as might be expected with mines of this size. This observation clearly demonstrates the real role of the *municipium* of Munigua. Apparently, the legal structure was such that the city of Munigua had priority over the mining area and did not allow, or may have even obstructed, the separate development of these mining districts. The absence of a settlement at these mines implies, first, that Munigua's production groups did not intend to develop or control those mining areas themselves, and second, that the production could not be directed or taxed in these places. These mining areas, thus, present themselves as free zones in which each of the groups took care exclusively of providing the raw material that was necessary for their own production. The Roman mining area of Navalázaro and El Pedroso, therefore, formed a kind of free zone, which was organised by neither shafts nor concessions; because these would have required at least some minor infrastructures in the mining area. There are no traces of, or hints for, such control or mining organisation from, neither the public sector (municipal or fiscal) nor the private sector (mining settlements). It seems that the families in Munigua who lived off the iron production were solely dedicated to the management of iron smelting and of the blacksmiths in the city of Munigua and not to the extraction of ore in the mines. Evidently it was an approach that had nothing to do with the usual mining practice, which had strict rules for prospecting, mining and management, as demonstrated by the famous *Vipasca* tablets.

We, therefore, have to assume that in the mining districts of Munigua, anyone would have been able to visit the mine, extract ore and sell it. This was easily possible because the ores in this area bloom on the surface, so that mining could be operated at the surface and in an open cast system. No installations in the vicinity of the veins suspected to have hosted miners. It is also unclear whether they lived at the mine, or whether they commuted to the mine for the working day and then brought the ore for smelting to Munigua. The distance from Munigua to Navalázaro (18 km) makes it possible to go back and forth to the mine in one working day and transport ore. The system perhaps seems strange but has strong parallels in the nineteenth/twentieth centuries.[39]

How the metal proceeded from Munigua, where and through what routes the Muniguian bars were delivered and who the contact partners were remains completely unknown. It can be assumed that the bars were brought from Munigua to the river valley with the usual donkey or mule caravans travelling to the Guadalquivir.[40] The nearest Roman moorings are documented in *Naeva*/Cantillana, downstream to the west, and in *Celti*/Peñaflor, upriver to the east,[41] but such moorings must have existed in each of the Roman cities along the river,[42] and are also supposed for *Canama*/Alcolea del Río or Villanueva del Río (with unknown ancient name), which are technically the nearest to Munigua. The riverboats would go as far as *Hispalis*/Seville, where the recent excavations in the port area have identified warehouses.[43] Perhaps one of them belonged to the epigraphically documented Titus Rufonius Brocchinus in *Hispalis*, the only *negotians ferrarius* known from Hispanic inscriptions.[44] Such traders could have further marketed the Muniguensian metal in other major cities in the Guadalquivir Valley such as *Carmo, Astigi* and *Corduba*. The sale of Muniguan iron to the valley for the production of agricultural implements has been accepted following many years of research into the economic base of the city of Munigua.[45]

The copper will also have taken this route to *Hispalis*/Sevilla. From here, however, it would have been loaded on seaworthy vessels and shipped across the Mediterranean to be used mainly in Roman coinage.[46] It seems probable, according to the research so far, that copper from Munigua was part of the major copper shipments recently found in shipwrecks in the form of copper ingots. The ships sailed routes in the western Mediterranean and transported copper from the Hispanic mines of the southwest and the Sierra Morena up to the Gulf of Lion.[47] There is currently an attempt to determine Munigua's role in this business through appropriate analysis.[48] In the case of Munigua, reference can only be made to the production chain in Figure 14.5 without any further details regarding Porter's emphasis on connecting a company with the upstream and downstream value-added activities of suppliers and customers.

The macroeconomic importance of both antique and modern metal-working lies in the fact that this production activity is closely intertwined with other economic sectors. It is often found at the beginning of the value-added chain and, as a wholesale supplier, represents an important cross-section and key industry. Due to the dependence on deposits, raw materials are delivered over great distances in certain areas. Spatial proximity contributes enormously to confidence building in this context and promotes the emergence of cooperation relationships.

### Corporate environment

The statement that every company forms an open system from which it communicates with its environment applies equally to antiquity. Dicken and Lloyd have described this environment as "a series of levels similar to the skins of an onion", and they distinguished three levels.[49] The inner plane is the task environment; our Figure 14.6 shows an attempt at a graphical representation. This consists of an effective level of communication on all sides, negotiating with the suppliers and with the customers, the government regulator (governor) and the other possible customers. The outer levels of impact, which include the potential actors with whom the company might come into contact, are presented here as the outermost level of the macro environment, which includes the social and global environment.[50] This is because the level of the task environment is particularly well able to illustrate the exchange of raw materials, goods and information, since the spatial component is shown in a corresponding separation of tasks, such as contact partners.

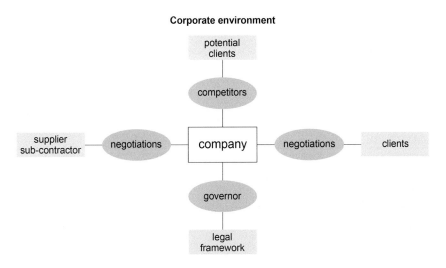

*Figure 14.6* Corporate environment (DAI Madrid, Munigua-Archive E. Puch Ramírez and author on the basis of Dicken and Lloyd 1999, 221).

In the small city of Munigua the Great Families, such as the *Aelii, Licinii, Quintii, Valerii* and *Aemilii Pudentes,* are known by name (Figure 14.7), and also relatives by marriages can be traced. The organisation of mining operations in Munigua is unknown. Whether the detailed organisational structure of the mines of *Vipasca*, as reflected in the local mining laws,[51] can be transferred to the situation in Munigua, remains to be seen. Of course, there will have been a (state?) procurator who acted as a higher authority and thus as a regulator (the governor in Figure 14.6). There must have been firewood and charcoal suppliers as well as the toolmakers or the produce suppliers. Customers must include the above-mentioned *negotiantes* in *Hispalis*, and other potential customers, who may also have had their offices in other cities. The metal industry, with the high proportion of metalworkers in the Sierra Morena and in the Lower Guadalquivir, should determine the structure, and the concentration would have been conducive to the training of special knowledge. Perhaps the strange metal furnace found in Munigua and possibly used for the extraction of silver from silver-bearing copper ores belongs to this context. The furnace documents an extraction process known as the *Seigerhütten process*. This was previously considered a technical innovation of the late Middle Ages, but according to the Muniguan testimony, it was apparently already known on the Iberian Peninsula.[52]

Certainly, the spatial configuration of value creation activities, which Porter calls the "geographical spread", has fuelled this development.[53] As part of his observations on the work chain, he notes the geographical distribution of these activities in different regions. He also notes that upstream value chains of a company are mostly independent of the sales market. In

**VALERII**

LVCIVS VALERIVS FIRMVS
Miembro del senado municipal

LVCIVS VALERIVS CELERINE
Patron

LVCIVS VALERIVS AELIVS SEVERVS
Sacerdote, liberto de Lvcivs Valerivs y Aelia Thallusa

**AELII**

LVCIVS AELIVS FRONTVS
Magistrado municipal

QVINTVS AELIVS VERNACLVS

AELIA THALLVSA

AELIA PROCVLA L. F.
Patrona

**LICINII**

LVCIVS LICINIVS ANNIANVS

LICINIVS VICTOR

GAIVS LICINIVS VICTOR ANNIANVS

**QVINTII**

LVCIVS QVINTIVS RVFINVS
Miembro del senado municipal

LVCIVS QVINTIVS RVFVS
Miembro del senado municipal

QVINTIA FLACCINA
Sacerdotisa

QVINTIO QVINTIANO

**AEMILII PUDENTES**

FVLVIA

LVCIVS AEMILIVS PVDENS
Miembro del senado municipal

LVCIVS AEMILIVS PVDENS

**FABII**

FABIA URSINA
Patrona

MAMERCVS

MARIVS

SALTIVS

TERTIVS

PSYCHE
Libertos de Fabia Ursina

**ANTONII**

LVCIVS ANTONIVS NERVA
Patron

ANTONIA OCELLIA
Liberta de Lvcivs Antonivs

ANNIVS CALLISTVS

NVMERIA FESTA

RVFINA

FLAVIVS BAETICVS
Liberto

LVCIVS FVLVIVS GE (NIALIS)
Sacerdote liberto

*Figure 14.7* Munigua's Great Families and their relationships (DAI Madrid, Munigua-Archive E. Puch Ramírez on the basis of San Martín Montilla and Schattner 2006, 40).

contrast, downstream value chains are often geographically close to the customer.[54] These are obviously economic cultural constants. In this respect, it is legitimate to ask these questions here, even if Munigua's ancient findings cannot provide any answers. The focus is on the scientifically based provenance analyses, which may perhaps provide approximate values in the future.

### *The filière concept*

The *filière* concept was conceived in the 1970s by French and Swiss scientists. It is an extension of Porter's value chain and, therefore, has some analogies to it. Its product-related view allows a structured view of production and distribution processes. Since it is primarily a descriptive analytical tool that allows for the derivation of further analyses and the preparation of hypotheses, it appears, for the time being, to be suitable for ancient findings.[55] Characteristic of the *filière* concept is the division of the value chain into segments. Figure 14.8 is an attempt to show the metal extraction in Munigua

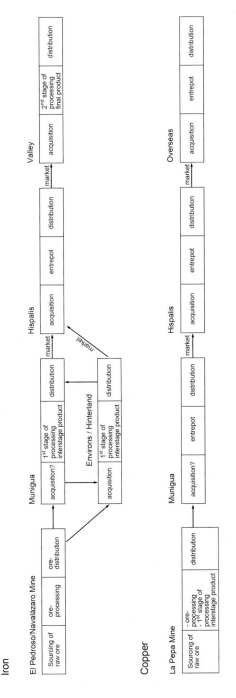

*Figure 14.8* The *filière*-concept with regard to the situation in Munigua (DAI Madrid, Munigua-Archive E. Puch Ramírez and author on the basis of Lenz 1997, 22; Kulke 2006, 63).

graphically. Each segment contains the "input – transformation – output" triad and represents a coherent production section.[56] The first segment, thus, depicts the situation at the mine.

In the case of the La Pepa (copper), the basic material is recovered at the mine and processed on the spot until the metal bar is produced. This will then be transferred to Munigua (next segment), where it will be refined, temporarily stored, administrated, marked and transported. In view of the situation described above, the target can only be an overseas port, namely, *Hispalis* (next segment). This action is probably linked to a positioning in the market. In other words, the billets may either have been sold from delivery to delivery point or have found their way to one, through the same dealer in *Hispalis* for a long period of time due to the long-term supply contracts. From there they were then loaded onto ships and shipped overseas (last segment). The transition from Munigua to *Hispalis* can be extended by any number of other segments, which in turn indicate the production of intermediate stages. The *filière* concept, thus, also includes the environment of the chain segments and the respective interfaces, in addition to the company-internal processes.[57] Through its ability to analyse, these interfaces both internally and externally, the relation of the *filière* concept to the transaction costs theory becomes clear.[58] Although the correspondent findings are not available in Munigua, the *filière* concept can be used to uncover all relevant relationships and actors.[59]

In the case of iron, the metal takes a similar path. The difference, however, is in the function of the city of Munigua. Because it was home to the workshops where the raw product was processed, Munigua was the production site. Hence, not only management, trans-shipment and onward transport took place or started from within its walls, but also the production and, thus, almost the entire chain of operations. In this form of production organisation, a modern trait can be recognised, which distinguishes the Roman chains of work from the older ones.[60] Such longer *filières* with the most diverse diverging and converging connections are characteristic of industrial productions, while short *filières* are found mainly in the agricultural sector.[61] By organising production in close proximity, regular face-to-face contacts are possible and costs can be kept low. Building trust in the reliability of trading partners reduces the uncertainty and the likelihood of opportunistic behaviour.

### Network theory

A look at the *Vitae* of Cicero or Caesar shows the extent of network organisations in Rome. Therefore, there is no need to provide a specific argument to justify assuming the existence of networks in Munigua. The metal trade in Munigua will have worked via such links. As actors we know the Great Families (Figure 14.7), on the one hand, and a dealer in Sevilla, on the other hand. Of course, this picture only reflects part of the reality and, therefore, it cannot be limited to Munigua. The Great Families, in particular the *Aelii*, may have been present in several cities in *Baetica*, especially in Seville, further refining the complexity of the system. The network theory briefly described below and the associated extensions can thus be transferred informally to the Muniguensian conditions and thus enable us systematically to re-imagine the ancient conditions.

Networks represent a combination of market and hierarchy organisation and describe the framework for the organisation of inter-company forms of cooperation. The guiding idea of network theory is that economic action cannot be considered in isolation but always takes place in the context of the social economy in which the economic actors are embedded.[62] A network is made up of nodes and edges. Nodes are the actors of a network. Actors can be individuals, groups, organisations and nations. Edges describe the relationships, activities or interactions between actors.[63] Four main characteristics of networks are as follows[64]: (1) reciprocity, (2) loose interrelations, (3) interdependence and (4) power asymmetries. The mutual exchange relationship between the actors is designated as reciprocity. At the same time, network relations are fundamentally long-term.[65] Since there are often no legally binding foundations for cooperation in networks, the ethical category of trust is of high importance.[66] Mutual relations are often governed by informal arrangements.[67] In contrast to hierarchical organisation, in a network companies are connected together by a web of loose links. They act legally and economically independently and the degree of vertical and horizontal integration remains low. This avoids the generation, over time, of fixed, and perhaps blocked, situations for the actors which would severely restrict the flexibility of the network and diminish its openness.[68] Loose interrelations enable redundancies as well as collective innovation and learning processes.[69] In contrast to pure market relationships and hierarchies, mutual dependencies arise in network relationships. These adaptation processes are called interdependence. Interdependencies increase the stability of the network and are mentioned in context with the generation of synergy effects. There is, thus, a direct correlation between the duration of network relationships and the degree of interdependence.[70] Power asymmetries are a constitutive feature of economic networks. They can reduce the complexity of coordination processes and are, therefore, necessary for handling interdependencies. The actors try to optimise their own position of power in the course of cooperation.[71] Networks are presumably subject to a life cycle, so that questions about the preservation and the end of networks are often ignored.[72] Network theory is strongly influenced by the socio-economic research approach. Since economic action always takes place in a specific context, Granovetter has extended the network approach to the concept of embeddedness.[73] Relational embeddedness refers to the quality of the relationship between two actors, and structural embeddedness characterises the quality of relationships between multiple actors. Due to the important role played by reputation with third parties, such embeddedness reduces the risk of opportunism. The concept of embeddedness from a spatial perspective becomes apparent at different levels of scale by examining the social context of companies.[74] In economic geography, embeddedness is often viewed from a spatial perspective only as a local or regional phenomenon.[75] Unfortunately, due to the lack of evidence described above, it is not possible to base these statements directly on the specific circumstances and situations in Munigua.

## Conclusion

In this chapter, we presented a summary of incoming and outgoing goods in Munigua (Figure 14.9) and thus of Munigua's place in the production chain. The picture is characterised, on the one hand, by the intake of a whole range of goods, among which foodstuffs such as fish sauces, wine and flour are most important, and expensive construction materials (marble), sculptures (altars, sculptures) and luxury goods (bronze *candelabrum*). Its incoming goods will not have differed significantly from those imported into other cities in the region. Its exports of metals, however, gave Munigua a special status. It must have been the reason for the wealth of the city and its inhabitants, which is reflected in the buildings and luxury goods. This wealth was on a quite modest scale, however. For example, marble was used extensively as a wall cladding of the Terrace Sanctuary but only on three sides.

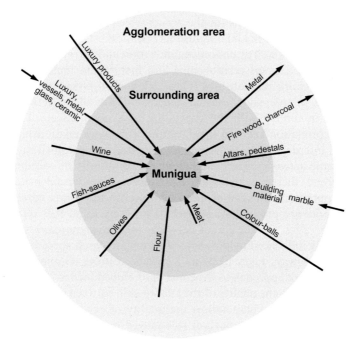

*Figure 14.9* Overview: imported and exported goods in Munigua (DAI Madrid, Munigua-Archive E. Puch Ramírez and author).

Marble was also used for some capitals or statues, but bronze statues were more common. The *forum* had a wooden entablature and pilaster capitals made of terracotta. The *forum* is too small to accommodate a market, which was anyhow not documented at Munigua. Instead, market activity is assumed to have taken place in the shops of the Thermengasse. There probably was a tinker, a baker and a paint dealer. The alley is very broad, so that one could surmise that this place was intended from the outset as a market. Deals would have also been made in the baths building, which lies next to it. The state authority, Rome, is archaeologically visible in all the contexts in the Imperial Gallery of Emperors' statues, which are situated in front of the double-storey hall, in which the bronze plaques of the city law were probably displayed.[76]

## Notes

1 For a current overview of the 60 years of research by the archaeologists of the Madrid Department of the German Archaeological Institute, see most recently Schattner 2019, with many illustrations. My thanks to Ch. Bashore/Granada for the revision of the English text.

2 Meyer 2001, 102.

3 The calculation is based on Meyer 2001, 102; Schattner 2013, 360. It is based on the floor plan size of houses 1 and 6, respectively. It is known that in Munigua not all of the area *intra muros* could have been used as building land. Since the necropolis (eastern necropolis) occupies a substantial part of it, it considerably reduces the available space. The boundary line between this necropolis and the residential city is a summer-dry stream with a parallel path that crosses the city from south-east to north (Figure 14.1). The situation described raises the question of the course of the city boundary, because it cannot be identical to the course of the wall; for more regarding the problem, cf. Schattner 2003, 60.

4 Schattner 2013, 354–364, Abb. 3.

5 Schattner 2013, 360–362.

6 Castillo Garcia 1975, 614–624.

7 This has been common knowledge among the local population since remote times. It is currently being quantified in the context of a master's thesis of the University of Hildesheim by Paul Matras under the direction of Professor A. Kirchner.

8 Pérez Macías, Ovejero Zappino and Schattner, Mulva VII (in press).

9 For the date of foundation, cf. Schattner 2006, 46–48; for the philological roots of the name Munigua, cf. Untermann 1961.

10 Griepentrog 1991.

11 Schattner et al. 2004, 365 as is shown by the stratigraphic profile alongside the corresponding ceramic findings. Schattner 2003, 78 figure 46; Schattner, Ovejero and Pérez Macías 2004, 357 s. figure 3.

12 cf. Martini, in: Mulva VIII, 1 2021, 228.

13 Hauschild 1992, 140; Schattner 2003, 39–42.

14 "Der fundamentale Vorgang in einer kapitalistischen Wirtschaft ist... Entwicklung" (Schumpeter 2006).

15 Adam Smith introduced and described the term "The division of labour" in the first chapter of The Wealth of Nations (1776).

16  Fundamental to these questions, for example Bathelt and Glückler 2003; Kulke 2008.

17  Leroi-Gourhan 1943–1945.

18  For the history of this concept, see Djindjian 2013; Coupaye 2015.

19  Porter 2000, 63.

20  The debate has existed since the early twentieth century in the controversy between the economist Karl Bücher who regarded the ancient economy as fundamentally different from the modern one, and Eduard Meyer who, with regard to antiquity, was already operating with the modern concepts of capital or factory and thus constructed a modernist picture (see Schneider 1990). Even later, in the discussions between the Russian historian Mikhail Ivanovich Rostovtseff and Moses I. Finley as the representative of the neo-primitivists, the assessment played a role again and again (see Drexhage et al. 2002, 19–21). With regard to the problem, cf. also the reviews of recent reference works such as Scheidel et al. 2013 or Scheidel and von Reden 2002; for a review, cf. M. Silver: http://eh.net/book_reviews/the-ancient-economy/ (accessed on 25 August 2018).

21  Definition as well as the corresponding subdivisions of the term according to the Bundeszentrale für politische Bildung: www.bpb.de/nachschlagen/lexika/lexikon-der-wirtschaft/19579/gueter (access on 28 August 2018).

22  The bibliographic citations for the individual archaeological findings and found objects discussed below are given in the table itself, so that a separate reference in this text commentary is unnecessary. The quotations mention the main works or the first publication, or the one that contains all of the older bibliography.

23  For the history of investigation in Munigua, cf. Schattner 2005.

24  HEp 12, 2002, 97; AE 2002, 730 (thanks to A. U. Stylow/Madrid for this indication).

25  AE 1966, 183.

26  Nesselhauf 1960, 153.

27  Krug 2006, 166 Nr. K1 Abb. 1 a.

28  Krug, Mulva VI 2018, 37. 257 Nr. B08a, 04 Taf. 26. 71a.

29  For example, a bronze bucket, Krug, Mulva VI, 2018, 195 Nr. B01a, 01 Taf. 4. 57. 62b.

30  Krug, Mulva VI, 2018, 256–266.

31  Grünhagen 1978; Schattner and Ovejero Zappino 2009; Pérez Macías et al., Mulva VII (in press).

32  Raddatz, Mulva I, 34.

33  Beltrán Fortes 1988, 84, 109; Schattner 2003, 195; Beltrán Fortes 2006, 99.

34  In summary, Kulke 2007.

35  Gereffi et al. 1994; Gereffi et al. 2005.

36  Porter 2000; Kulke 2008.

37  By contrast, statements about vertical integration in terms of shortening the chain by reducing the number of actors cannot be made. At this point, there are a whole series of developments and problems, which are unsolved not only for the present case study of Munigua but also for the ancient world as a whole. Thus, as a rule, no statements are possible regarding a horizontal concentration, i.e. a reduction in the number of participants/workshops in a single processing stage. Also questions regarding the respective power relations as well as the associated coordination and control mechanisms (for example, standards and contractual obligations) find no answer and, therefore, remain hidden.

38 Schattner et al. 2004, 369.
39 For all the exposed questions, cf. Pérez Macías et al., Mulva VII (in press).
40 Such caravans could be observed until the 1960s in the Sierra Morena, cf. for example, Schattner 2003, lám. 6a. The mining law from *Vipasca*/Aljustrel (Portugal) shows clearly that in a mining district fees were charged for almost everything and that no action was left without taxation (Flach 1979; Domergue 1983). This continued until the announcement by the crier (*praeco*). The fees were staggered. The announcement of a material value was rewarded with 1 *denarius* but that for the sale of pack animals with 3 *denarii* (Flach 1979, 433).
41 Abad Casal 1975, 71.
42 Abad Casal 1975, 73.
43 Ordóñez Agulla and González Acuña 2011.
44 CILA González 1991, Nr. 69; Gimeno Pascual and Stylow 1999, 85–87 Nr. 1.
45 Schattner et al. 2004, 369; Pérez Macías 2006, 104.
46 Pérez Macías 2006, 104.
47 "Le cuivre hispanique paraît donc régner en maître dans l'Occident romain", Jézégou et al. 2011, 67. Current distribution map of the wrecks that transported the metal bars from the Hispanic SW at Rico 2011, 43 figure 1.
48 The analyses are carried out by the Deutsches Bergbaumuseum (German Mining Museum) in Bochum under the direction of A. Hauptmann and S. Klein.
49 Dicken and Lloyd 1999, 220.
50 McDermott and Taylor 1982, 18.
51 Domergue 1983.
52 Kraus et al., in: Mulva VII.
53 Porter 1989, 25.
54 Porter 1989, 24 ff.
55 Lenz 1997, 20 ff.
56 Lenz 1997, 21.
57 Kulke 2006, 63; Tucher 1999, 8; Lenz 1997, 20 ff.
58 Hess 1998, 86.
59 Nuhn 1993, 141.
60 Compare the very similar situation of silver mining in the Orientalising period, in which the low processed raw material was not distributed at the mine itself but in the settlements of the surrounding area and processed there, s. Pérez Macías and Schattner 2018, 324–329.
61 Lenz 1997, 23.
62 Pfützer 1995, 52.
63 Kutschker and Schmid 2002, 518.
64 Hess 1998, 66 s.; Rehner 2003, 79 s.; Haas and Neumair 2005, 563 s.
65 Blau 1964, 6.
66 Kadritzke 1999, 75.
67 Hess 1998, 66.
68 Grabher 1993, 9.
69 Pfützer 1995, 55.
70 Hess 1998, 67; Rehner 2003, 79; Håkanson and Johanson 1993, 40.
71 Håkanson and Johanson 1993, 42.
72 Schamp 2000, 68.
73 Granovetter 1985.
74 Bathelt and Glückler 2003, 160 s.

75 Oinas 1997, 29.
76 Munigua, like the other peregrine cities of *Hispania*, probably possessed such tablets, which were on public display, Stylow 1999, 231.

# References

Abad Casal, Lorenzo, *El Guadalquivir, vía fluvial romana* (Sevilla: Diputación Provincial, 1975).
Bathelt, Harald – Glückler, Johannes, *Wirtschaftsgeographie. Ökonomische Beziehungen in räumlicher Perspektive* (Stuttgart: Eugen Ulmer, 2003).
Beltrán Fortes, José, *Las arae de la Baetica, resumen de tesis doctoral* (Málaga: University of Málaga, 1988).
Beltrán Fortes, José, "Pedestales, altares y placas", 98–99., in: San Martín Montilla – Concepción Schattner, Thomas G. (eds.), *Munigua. La colina sagrada*, Exposiciones Museo Arqueológico, Sevilla del 19–05-2006 al 20–07-2006 (Sevilla: Junta de Andalucía, Consejería de Cultura, 2006).
Blau, Peter M., *Exchange and Power in Social Life* (New York: J. Wiley, 1964).
Boessneck, Joachim – von den Driesch, Angela, "Knochenfunde aus dem römischen Munigua (Mulva), Sierra Morena", 160–185, in: *Studien über frühe Tierknochenfunde von der Iberischen Halbinsel* 7 (München: Institut für Palaeoanatomie, Domestikationsforschung und Geschichte der Tiermedizin der Universität München, 1980).
Castillo Garcia, Carmen, "Städte und Personen der Baetica", 601–654, in: *Aufstieg und Niedergang der römischen Welt* II 3 (Berlin, New York: W. de Gruyter, 1975).
CILA, González Fernández, Julián, *Corpus de inscripciones latinas de Andalucía* II 1 (Sevilla: Consejería de Cultura y Medio Ambiente de la Junta de Andalucía, 1991).
Coupaye, Ludovic, "Chaîne opératoire, transects et theories. Quelques reflexions et suggestions sur le parcours d' une methode classique", 69–84, in: P. Soulier (ed.), *André Leroi-Gourhan »l'homme tout simplement«* (Paris: Éditions de Boccard, 2015).
Dicken, Peter – Lloyd, Peter, *Standort und Raum. Theoretische Perspektiven in der Wirtschaftsgeographie* (Stuttgart: Eugen Ulmer, 1999).
Djindjian, François, "Us et abus du concept de »chaîne opératoire« en archéologie", 93–107, in: S. Krausz – A. Coli – K. Gruel (eds.), *L'âge du Fer en Europe, mélanges offerts à Olivier Büchsenschütz*, Ausonius Éditions, Mémoires 20 (Bordeaux: Ausonius, 2013).
Domergue, Claude, *La mine antique d'Aljustrel (Portugal) et les tables de bronze de Vipasca*, Publications du Centre Pierre Paris 9, Collection de la Maison des pays ibériques 12 (Talence: Université de Bordeaux III, Centre Pierre Paris, 1983).
Drexhage, Hans-Joachim Konen – Heinrich Ruffing, Kai, *Die Wirtschaft des römischen Reiches (1. bis 3. Jahrhundert). Eine Einführung* (Berlin: Akademie Verlag, 2002).
Fabião, Carlos, "Las ánforas romanas", 106 s., in: C. San Martín Montilla – Th. G. Schattner (eds.), *Munigua. La colina sagrada*, Exposiciones Museo Arqueológico, Sevilla del 19–05-2006 al 20–07-2006 (Sevilla: Junta de Andalucía, Consejería de Cultura, 2006).
Flach, Dieter, "Die Bergwerksordnungen von Vipasca", *Chiron* 9 (1979): 399–448.
Gereffi, Gary – Korzeniewicz, R. P. – Korzeniewicz, Miguel, "Introduction. Global Commodity Chains", 1–14, in: Gereffi, Gary – Korzeniewicz, Miguel (eds.), *Commodity Chains and Global Capitalism* (Westport: Praeger, 1994).

Gereffi, Gary – Humphrey, John – Sturgeon, Timothy, "The governance of global value chains", *Review of International Political Economy* 12, 1 (2005) 78–104

Gimeno Pascual, Helena, "La sociedad de Munigua a través de sus inscripciones", 177–192, in: Armani, Sabine – Hurlet-Martineau, Bénédicte (eds.), *Epigrafía y sociedad en Hispania durante el Alto Imperio. Estructuras y relaciones sociales*, Actas de la mesa redonda organizada por la Casa de Velázquez, el Centro CIL II de la Universidad de Alcalá de Henares, 10/11 April 2000 (Alcalá de Henares: *Universidad de Alcalá*, 2003).

Gimeno Pascual, Helena – Stylow, Armin U., *Analecta epigraphica hispanica. Manuscritos, calcos, dibujos, duplicaciones*, Sylloge Epigraphica Barcinonensis 3 (Barcelona: Universitat de Barcelona, Departament de Filologia Llatina, 1999), 85–112.

Grabher, Gernot, "*Rediscovering the Social in the Economics of Interfirm Relations*", 1–31, in: Grabher, Gernot (ed.), *The Embedded Firm. On the Socioeconomics of Industrial Networks* (London, New York: Routledge, 1993).

Granovetter, Mark, "*Economic Action and Social Structure. The Problem of Embeddedness*", *American Journal of Sociology* 91 (1985): 481–510.

Griepentrog, Markus, "*Munigua 1989. Die Grabung in der Heiligtumsterrasse*", *Madrider Mitteilungen* 32 (1991): 141–152.

Griepentrog Markus, *Mulva V. Die vormunizipale Besiedlung von Munigua*, Madrider Beiträge 29 (Wiesbaden: L. Reichert, 2008).

Grünhagen, Wilhelm, "Farbiger Marmor aus Munigua", *Madrider Mitteilungen* 19 (1978): 290–306.

Haas, Hans-Dieter – Neumair, Simon M., *Internationale Wirtschaft. Rahmenbedingungen, Akteure, räumliche Prozesse* (München, Wien: R. Oldenbourg, 2005).

Håkanson, Håkan – Johanson, Johan, "The Network as a Governance Structure. Interfirm Cooperation beyond Markets and Hierarchies", 35–51, in: Grabher, Gernot (ed.), *The Embedded Firm. On the Socioeconomics of Industrial Networks* (London, New York: Routledge, 1993).

Hanel, Norbert, "Römische Öl- und Weinproduktion auf der Iberischen Halbinsel am Beispiel von Munigua und Milreu", *Madrider Mitteilungen* 30 (1989): 205–238.

Hauschild, Theodor, "Munigua. Ausgrabungen an der Stützmauer des Forums –1985", *Madrider Mitteilungen* 27 (1986): 325–343.

Hauschild, Theodor, "Los templos romanos de Munigua (Sevilla)", *Cuadernos de arquitectura romana* 1 (1992): 133–143.

Hertel, Dieter, "Die Skulpturen", in: Blech, Michael – Hauschild, Theodor – Hertel, Dieter, 123-124 (eds.), *Das Grabgebäude in der Nekropole Ost. Die Skulpturen. Die Terrakotten, Mulva III*, Madrider Beiträge 21 (Mainz: Ph. von Zabern, 1993).

Hess, Martin, *Glokalisierung, industrieller Wandel und Standortstruktur*, Wirtschaft und Raum 2 (München: Verlag V. Florentz, 1998)

Jézégou, Marie-Pierre – Wenzel-Klein, Sabine – Rico, Christian, "Les lingots de cuivre de l'épave romaine 'Plage de la Corniche 6' á Séte et le commerce du cuivre hispanique en Méditerranée occidentale", *Revue archéologique de Narbonnaise* 44 (2011): 57–70.

Kadritzke, Ulf, "Herrschaft in Unternehmensnetzwerken. Vom Schwinden einer Kategorie in Theorie und Praxis", 63–98, in: Sydow, Jörg – Wirth, Carsten (eds.), *Arbeit, Personal und Mitbestimmung in Unternehmensnetzwerken* (München, Mering: Rainer Hampp Verlag, 1999).

Kraus, Stefan – Bartelheim, Martin – Pernicka, Ernst, "Ein Seigerofen in Munigua?", in: *Mulva VII* (in press).

Krug, Antje, "Munigua: Der Anfang vom Ende: die Aussage der Bronzeskulpturen und anderer Funde", *Madrider Mitteilungen* 47 (2006): 152–168.

Krug, Antje, *Die Kleinfunde, Mulva VI*, Madrider Beiträge 36 (Wiesbaden: Reichert, 2018).

Kulke, Elmar, *Wirtschaftsgeographie* (Paderborn: Schöningh, 2006).

Kulke, Elmar, "The Commodity Chain Approach in Economic Geography", *Die Erde, Journal of the Geographical Society of Berlin* 138,2 (2007): 117–126.

Kulke, Elmar, *Wirtschaftsgeographie. Grundriss Allgemeine Geographie* (Paderborn: Schöningh, 2008).

Kutschker, Michael – Schmid, Stefan, *Internationales Management* (München: R. Oldenbourg, 2002).

Lenz, Barbara, "Das Filière-Konzept als Analyseinstrument der organisatorischen und räumlichen Anordnung von Produktions- und Distributionsprozessen", *Geographische Zeitschrift* 1 (1997) 20–33.

Leroi-Gourhan, André, *Le Geste et la Parole 1. Technique et Langage 2. La Mémoire et les Rythmes* (Paris: Albin Michel, 1943–1945).

Martini, Wolfram, "Die Thermen", in: Martini, Wolfram – Schattner, Thomas G. *Die Thermen, Das Forum*, Mulva VIII (Wiesbaden: Reichert Verlag, 2021), 1–245.

McDermott, Philip – Taylor, Michael, *Industrial Organization and Location* (Cambridge: University Press, 1982).

Meyer, Katharina, E., "Die Häuser 1 und 6", 1–150, in: Meyer, Katharina, E. – Basas, Carlos – Teichner, Felix, *Die Häuser 1 und 6, La cerámica de la casa n. 6, Das Haus 2, Mulva IV*, Madrider Beiträge 27 (Mainz: Ph. von Zabern, 2001).

Mulva I, cf. Raddatz 1973.

Mulva II, cf. Vegas 1988.

Mulva III, cf. Hertel 1993.

Mulva IV, cf. Meyer, Basas, Teichner 2001.

Mulva V, cf. Griepentrog 2008.

Mulva VI, cf. Krug 2018.

Mulva VII, cf. Pérez Macías – Ovejero Zappino – Schattner (in press).

Mulva VIII, cf. Martini, Schattner (Wiesbaden: Reichert Verlag, 2021).

Nesselhauf, Herbert, "Zwei Bronzeurkunden aus Munigua", *Madrider Mitteilungen* 1 (1960): 142–154.

Nuhn, Helmut, "Konzepte zur Beschreibung und Analyse des Produktionssystems unter besonderer Berücksichtigung der Nahrungsmittelindustrie", *Zeitschrift für Wirtschaftsgeographie* 3/4 (1993): 137–142.

Oinas, Päivi, "On the socio-spatial embeddedness of business firms", *Erdkunde* 51 (1997) 23–32.

Ordóñez Agulla, Salvador – González Acuña, Daniel, "Horrea y almacenes en Hispalis. Evidencias arqueológicas y evolución de la actividad portuaria", 159–184, in: Arce, Javier – Goffaux, Bertrand (eds.), *Horrea d'Hispanie et de la Méditerranée romaine*, Collection de la Casa de Velázquez 125 (Madrid: Casa de Velázquez, 2011).

Pérez Macías, Juan Aurelio, "La producción metálica", 104 s., in: San Martín Montilla, Concepción – Schattner, Thomas G. (eds.), *Munígua. La colina sagrada*, Exposiciones Museo Arqueológico, Sevilla del 19–05-2006 al 20–07-2006 (Sevilla: Junta de Andalucía, Consejería de Cultura, 2006).

Pérez Macías, Juan Aurelio – Schattner, Thomas G., "Wege zur Küste. Werkkette, Metallgewinnung und Infrastruktur in den südwesthispanischen Minendistriken von Tharsis und Riotinto in orientalisierender Zeit", 315–335, in: Marzoli, Dirce – García Teyssandier, Elisabeth (eds.), *Die phönizische Nekropole von Ayamonte. Die Ausgrabung im Jahre 2013 und ihre Vor- und Begleituntersuchungen*, Madrider Beiträge 37 (Wiesbaden: Harrassowitz, 2018).

Pérez Macías, Juan Aurelio – Ovejero Zappino, Gobain – Schattner, Thomas G., *Die Wirtschaftsgrundlagen der Stadt*, Mulva VII, Madrider Beiträge (in press).

Pfützer, Stephanie, *Strategische Allianzen in der Elektronikindustrie. Organisation und Standortstruktur*, Wirtschaftsgeographie 9 (Münster: Lit, 1995).

Porter, Michael E., "Der Wettbewerb auf globalen Märkten. Ein Rahmenkonzept", 17–68, in: M. Porter (ed.), *Globaler Wettbewerb. Strategien der neuen Internationalisierung* (Wiesbaden: Gabler, 1989).

Porter, Michael E., Wettbewerbsvorteile (Competitive Advantage). Spitzenleistungen erreichen und sich behaupten (Frankfurt: Campus-Verlag, 2000).

Raddatz, Klaus, *Die Grabungen in der Nekropole in den Jahren 1957 und 1958*, Madrider Beiträge 2 (Mainz: von Zabern, 1973).

Rehner, Johannes, *Netzwerke und Kultur. Unternehmerisches Handeln deutscher Manager in Mexiko*, Wirtschaft und Raum 11 (München: Herbert Utz Verlag, 2003).

Rico, Christian, "Réflexions sur le commerce d'exportation des métaux à l'époque romaine", 41–64, in: Arce, Javier – Goffaux, Bertrand (eds.), Horrea d'Hispanie et de la Méditerranée romaine, Collection de la Casa de Velázquez 125 (Madrid: Casa de Velázquez, 2011).

Schamp, Eike W., *Vernetzte Produktion. Industriegeographie aus institutioneller Perspektive* (Darmstadt: Wissenschaftliche Buchgesellschaft, 2000).

Schattner, Thomas G., *Munigua. Cuarenta años de investigaciones*, Colección Arqueología (Sevilla), serie Monografías 16 (Sevilla: Junta de Andalucía. Consejería de Cultura, 2003).

Schattner, Thomas G., "Die Wiederentdeckung von Munigua. Abriss der Forschungsgeschichte", *Madrider Mitteilungen* 46 (2005) 267–288.

Schattner, Thomas G., "Cerámica ática y escultura romana calcárea en Munigua: formas de recepción", 43–53, in: Vaquerizo, Desiderio – Murillo, Juan F. (eds.), Vaquerizo, Desiderio (coord.), *El concepto de lo provincial en el mundo antiguo*. Homenaje a la profesora Pilar León Alonso (Córdoba: Imprenta San Pablo, 2006).

Schattner, Thomas G. – Ovejero Zappino, Gobain, "Mármol en Munigua", 285–312, in: Nogales, Trinidad – Beltrán, José (eds.), *Marmora Hispana. Explotación y uso de los materiales pétreos en la Hispania romana Roma*, Coloquio Internacional Marmora Baeticae et Lusitaniae, Sevilla y Mérida 2006, Hispania antigua, Serie arqueològica 2 (Roma: L'Erma, 2009).

Schattner, Thomas G., "Wo in Munigua tagte der Senat?" *Madrider Mitteilungen* 54 (2013): 348–370.

Schattner, Thomas G., *Munigua. Un recorrido por la arqueología del Municipium Flavium Muniguense,* con visualizaciones de H. Ruipérez (Sevilla: Ed. Universidad de Sevilla, 2019).

Schattner, Thomas G. – Ovejero Zappino, Gobain – Pérez Macías, Juan Aurelio, "Zur Metallgewinnung von Munigua", *Madrider Mitteilungen* 45 (2004): 351–370.

Scheidel, Walter – von Reden, Sitta (eds.), *The Ancient Economy* (Edinburgh: Edinburgh University Press, 2002).

Scheidel, Walter – Morris, Ian – Saller, Richard P. (eds.), *The Cambridge Economic History of the Greco-Roman World* (Cambridge: Cambridge University Press, 2013).

Schneider, Helmuth, "Die Blücher–Meyer Kontroverse", 417–445, in: W. M. Calder III A. Demandt (eds.), *Eduard Meyer, Leben und Leistung eines Universalhistorikers,* Mnemosyne Suppl. 112 (Leiden: E. J. Brill, 1990*)*

Schumpeter, Joseph A., *Theorie der wirtschaftlichen Entwicklung* (Berlin: Duncker und Humblot, 2006).

Stylow, Armin U., "Entre edictum y lex a prósito de una nueva ley municipal flavia del término de Ecija", 229–237, in: González, Julián (ed.), *Ciudades Privilegiadas en el Occidente Romano*, Congreso Internacional, Serie Historia y geografía 42 (Sevilla: Secretariado de Publicaciones, Universidad de Sevilla, Diputación de Sevilla, 1999).

Tucher, Mathias von, *Die Rolle der Auslandsmontage in den internationalen Wertschöpfungsnetzwerken der Automobilindustrie*, Wirtschaft und Raum 5 (München: Verlag V. Florentz, 1999).

Untermann, Jürgen, "Zum Namen von Munigua", *Madrider Mitteilungen* 2 (1961): 107–117.

Vegas, Mercedes, "Munigua. Römische Keramik des 1. Jhs. n. Chr", *Madrider Mitteilungen* 10 (1969): 199–250.

Vegas, Mercedes, "Tafelware aus Munigua", *Madrider Mitteilungen* 16 (1975): 281–302.

Vegas, Mercedes, "Munigua, Haus 6. Datierende Funde aus den Räumen und aus dem Brunnen", *Madrider Mitteilungen* 25 (1984): 181–196.

Vegas, Mercedes, *Mulva II. Die Südnekropole von Munigua: Grabungskampagnen 1977 bis 1988, Madrider Beiträge 15* (Mainz: P. von Zabern, 1988).

# 15  Understanding Rome as a port city

*Simon Malmberg*

## Introduction

For several centuries, Rome was the largest city of the ancient Mediterranean world. From the Late Republic until Late Antiquity, the population was probably in the range of between 800,000 and 1,200,000 inhabitants, with a peak population in the second century CE (for a recent overview, see Lo Cascio, 2018). A massive infrastructure comprising aqueducts and a road network was necessary to be able to sustain such a huge population. The Tiber and its harbours were the most important part of this supply organisation. Cicero summed it up most eloquently:

> [Rome] finds, in the same [Tiber] river, a communication by which it received from the sea all the productions necessary to the conveniences and elegancies of life, and possesses an inland territory beside, which furnishes it with an exuberant supply of provisions.
>
> (Cic. *Rep.* 2.10)

The Tiber connected Rome with both the sea and the inland regions, while many of the roads and highways intersected with the river or ran parallel to it. The Tiber, thus, intertwined local and regional movements with a Mediterranean-wide network. River and city interfaced at the banks, which developed into the port of Rome.

It is important to understand the dimensions of Rome's harbour facilities, and to study not only single buildings, but also the port as a whole, and its relation to other parts of the urban infrastructure. This will allow us to better gauge the port's role in the organisation of the city, which ultimately shaped the urban structure of Rome, by setting the limits for its demographic and spatial expansion.

Often Ostia or Portus are presented as the ports of Rome, which tends to overshadow the city of Rome as a major port in its own right. Within the urban area of Rome, along 18 km of the Tiber, there is a concentration of large-scale archaeological remains related to the port. Through an examination of these remains, this contribution will try to demonstrate that the city of Rome might have been one of the major port cities of the ancient Mediterranean world. The study aims to demonstrate the size of the port not only by providing an overview of most of the known port facilities, mainly based on archaeological finds, but also by using the evidence provided by ancient literary and legal texts, inscriptions, and the marble plans of Rome. It will focus on the time which saw a great expansion of the port, beginning in the early second century BCE, until it reached its maximum extent, in the middle of the second century CE. This contribution is part of an ongoing project on Rome as a port city. The project has so far mapped physical remains of the port. This compiled information has formed the basis for the present study, which attempts to provide a better understanding of the port as a whole.

Several important studies of Rome's port have already been undertaken. Quilici (1986) has provided an overview of the northern urban port area, while Castagnoli (1980), Maischberger (1997), and, especially, Mocchegiani Carpano (1975–76; 1981; 1982, etc.) have published fundamental works about the port downriver from Ponte S. Angelo. De Caprariis' (1999) work on the Late Antique development of the port is also of importance. A short but useful overview of the port as a whole has been produced by Pavolini (2000). Maischberger (2000) and Maiuro (2008) have provided entries on the Tiber as part of the *Lexicon Topographicum Urbis Romae* series. Although both of these are of high quality, they are constrained by the restricted length afforded each entry, and the artificial limits of the series, which splits up Rome between areas on either side of the Aurelian walls. Put together, however, the two studies give a good overview of the current state of the art. The only in-depth study of the whole of Rome's port area is still the magisterial work by Le Gall (1953; 2005). Originally written in 1953, it is now dated in some respects, although the author worked on a somewhat updated version until 1990, which was eventually published in 2005.

A very welcome additions to these works are the first overviews of the port of Rome written in English. This marks an important step forward in recognizing the importance of the Tiber and its urban harbours in studies of the city of Rome. In his book on floods in Rome, Aldrete (2007) also touches upon the port, while Tuck (2013) and Rice (2018) provide introductory and useful texts to the harbour system. Keay (2012) gives an excellent overarching survey not only of Rome's harbours but also of their context in the whole system of port cities of the region. I have also addressed the port of Rome in a recent contribution (Malmberg, 2015).

Recent studies of the port capacity of Rome have estimated the total length of quays in Rome, in one case, to c. 1,500–3,000 m, and in another, to c. 2,000 m. This would make Rome's port similar in size to that of Ostia, and only between a fifth and a seventh of the quay length estimated for Portus (Keay, 2012: 34, 43–4; Keay, 2015: 50; Rice, 2018: 206). This study will show that these estimates of the size of the port of Rome should most probably be radically increased.

Before we are able to measure and compare the size of Rome's port, we need to address the possible limits of the port. Did the port indeed have any limits, or was it rather like the city itself in the Imperial period, sprawling into the surrounding countryside, constantly adding new structures to its *continentia tecta*, similar to a modern megalopolis (Dion. Hal. *Ant. Rom.* 4.13.4; see also Malmberg and Bjur, 2011; Malmberg, 2014; Stevens, 2017)? One could use the limits of the city walls to define the port area, like some studies have done recently. But the Servian-Republican and the Aurelian walls would be anachronistic for the time period under study, when large parts of the port operated beyond both of them, and the Aurelian walls were of course built after the period studied by this contribution. I will instead use the 18 km of urban river which was demarcated by the Tiber boundary stones between Ponte Milvio and Magliana as a means to define the area under investigation. The area demarcated by the stones also coincides with a concentration of remains of the ancient harbours (Figure 15.1).

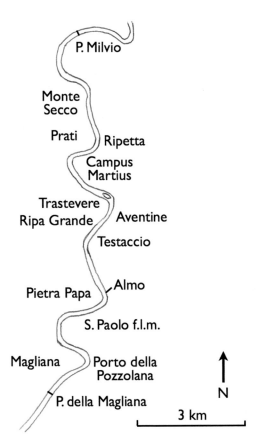

*Figure 15.1* Overview of the part of the Tiber under study (by author).

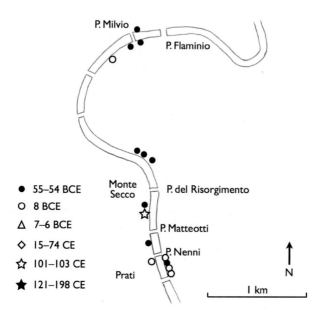

*Figure 15.2* Tiber boundary stones between Ponte Milvio and Ponte Nenni (by author).

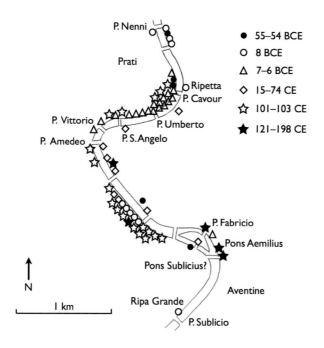

*Figure 15.3* Tiber boundary stones between Ponte Nenni and Ponte Sublicio (by author).

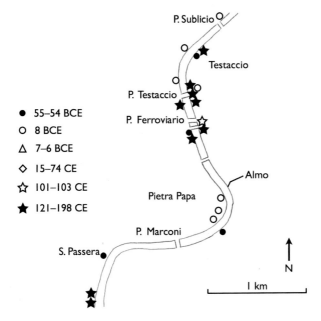

*Figure 15.4* Tiber boundary stones between Ponte Sublicio and Santa Passera (by author).

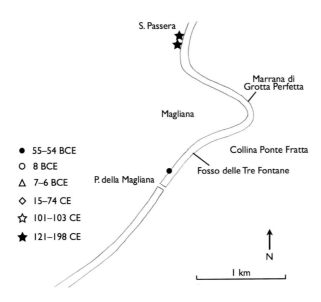

*Figure 15.5* Tiber boundary stones between Santa Passera and Ponte della Magliana (by author).

## Curating the Tiber

Due to its massive size, the city of Rome demanded a large urban administration. The river, being such an important part of the infrastructure, also had its own administrative organisations that probably handled river and port maintenance, shipping traffic, loading and unloading, storage, and distribution. Few details of these administrations are known, with glimpses provided by a few literary texts and laws but mainly by inscriptions. Much of the epigraphic information directly related to the port is derived from the Tiber boundary stones erected by the officials that headed the river administration. The stones do preserve not only these texts but also important spatial information when they were found in situ along the river, demarcating the area for public use along it and keeping the riverbanks clear for port activities. In total, 119 of these stones have been recovered between 1495 and 2013, erected in the period from 55 BCE to 198 CE (Figure 15.2–5).

The censors of 55–54 BCE set up a series of boundary stones along the Tiber, of which 21 have been found, between the Ponte Milvio in the north and the Ponte della Magliana in the south, for a total of 18 km along the river. A new series of stones were set up by the consuls of 8 BCE, 23 of which have been found between Ponte Milvio and Pietra Papa. The following year, Augustus himself added at least 22 more stones, primarily found on the right riverbank in Prati di Castello between Ponte Cavour and Ponte Vittorio.

In 15 CE, Tiberius created a collegium of five senators, known as the curators of the banks and bed of the Tiber (*curatores riparum et alvei Tiberis*; Dio Cass. 57.14.7–8; Tac. *Ann.* 1.76, 79; see also Suet. *Aug.* 30, 37; Lonardi, 2013: 8–9; Malmberg, 2015: 192). Members seem to have been appointed for 1 year and led by a consular. The high number of senators on the board, compared to other *collegia* created at this time, might indicate the importance and complexity of their task. In the same year as their creation, the curators added their inscriptions to 14 of the existing Tiber stones, mostly those of 8 BCE, probably to confirm their continued validity. In the following century, the curators also erected new boundary stones along the Tiber, 17 of which have been found. The delimitation programs seem to have been limited in scope, and they mostly renewed stones in areas that had been previously marked. The exception was four stones that have been found along the right bank of the Fiume Morto at Ostia, which were erected in 23–41 CE (*CIL* XIV 4704a–c, 192).

Sometime between 44 and 72 CE, the collegium was replaced by a single curator who from the time of Trajan was appointed for 3 years instead of 1 year. During Claudius, the curator had a subordinate staff consisting of a prefect and a procurator, but this was replaced by *adiutores* from the reign of Trajan (*CIL* X 797, XIV 172, 5345; *CIG* III 3991; *AE* 1923: 67, 1952: 156; Lonardi, 2013: 18). In 101–103, a major renewal program of boundary stones in Rome was undertaken, with 23 new stones, put up by the curator Julius Ferox, unearthed along the Tiber, between Ponte Matteotti and Ponte

Ferroviario. After this time, there were only limited renewals of the Trajanic project in 121–124 (8 stones), in 161 (5 stones), and in 198 (1 stone).

The boundary stones were normally at least the height of a human and had an inscription on one side that showed the names and title of the officials, and ended with the verb "have delimited" (*termin(averunt)*) (Figure 15.6). If the stone was a renewal of an older one, it ended with the statement "have restored" (*restituerunt*). A stone found in situ in 2013 had the text highlighted in red paint (Gregori, 2015: 443–5). What was then delimited by the stones? From the middle of the first century CE onwards, the stones often included a reference to the riverbank (*ripam cippis pos[itis]/ terminaverunt,* or *terminavit ripam*). A marker, set up in Ostia, provided the extra information that it delimited "without prejudice the [rights of the] state or private individuals", *sine praeiudic(io)/ publico aut / privatotorum* (!) (*CIL* VI 4704c; Lonardi, 2013: 35). As is stated by Gaius in the *Digest* 1.8.5 "The right to use riverbanks is public by *ius gentium* just as is the use of the river itself ... But ownership of the banks is in those to whose estates they connect", to which Paul, *Digest* 43.12.3 added "Public rivers are those which are always flowing, and their

*Figure 15.6* Tiber boundary stone *CIL* VI 40857 from 55–54 BCE at Ponte Milvio in 1959 (Quilici, 1986: figure 5).

banks are public ... Along the banks not all places are public, because the banks begin where the slope first starts to bear down to the water from level ground" (trans. Watson, 2009). It is often inferred that the boundary stones marked the limits of public ground, but as becomes clear from the inscription and the passages of the *Digest* cited above, rather than ownership, they defined the public right to *use* the riverbanks (Lonardi, 2013: 32).

Boundary stones found in situ show that the text was turned towards the river and, thus, primarily addressed people moving on or along the river. The only exception was the stone set up in 55–54 BCE next to Ponte Milvio, between the river and the Via Flaminia, which ran just next to the river at this point. This stone had almost identical inscriptions on two opposite sides, so it could be read from both river and road (*CIL* VI 40857). Two of the stones erected by the censors were found in situ exactly 100 Roman feet apart, which might imply that the stones in the first phase were placed at regular intervals in a line along the river (*CIL* VI 37026, 37027, see also 31541c–d; Lonardi, 2013: 36).

In the Augustan and later stones, the distance to the next stone on the right was given in Roman feet, varying between 6 and 386 feet, which showed that the stones were no longer placed at regular intervals. The distance information on the Augustan stones could be applied to the front, either side, or the back of the stone, indicating that the boundary formed a jagged rather than a straight line, which might be due to the accumulation of buildings along the banks. The pressure from buildings and activities along the river can also be demonstrated by several of the stones having small holes on their sides, into which metal clamps were attached with molten lead. Similar traces of metal clamps were also inserted at regular intervals in the travertine pavement between the markers, probably for a wooden or metal screen, attached to the boundary stones that formed a continuous barrier along the river (Marchetti, 1890; Lonardi, 2013: 38–40). The pressure on the river at this time is well illustrated by Suetonius who writes that Augustus "widened and cleared out the channel of the Tiber, which had for some time been filled with rubbish and narrowed by jutting buildings" (Suet. *Aug.* 30).

That the boundary was indeed respected is shown by stone markers erected in 8 BCE at Pietra Papa. Here, a bathhouse and a cemetery were built right next to the line of stones, but no construction went past a straight line drawn between the markers (*CIL* VI 40860, 40861; Jacopi, 1940: 98–9; Jacopi, 1943: 24–8; Le Gall, 1953: 172–3; Lonardi, 2013: 37). The stones were also in some cases respected long after they were erected, which were demonstrated by the one still in situ in the basement of Palazzo Farnese, where both later buildings and pavements avoided to disturb the stone erected in 55–54 BCE (*CIL* VI 40858). In a couple of cases, later stones were erected right next to earlier ones, similar to how Roman milestones by different emperors can sometimes be found together (e.g. *CIL* VI 31549a). When a Tiber stone was renewed, pains were often taken to point this out, sometimes even referring to a specific earlier curator (e.g. *CIL* VI 31553).

The jurisdiction of the Tiber curators extended from Rome to Ostia, as demonstrated by the boundary stones erected by the curators in Ostia. This might remind us of the four boundary stones raised by the urban praetor Gaius Caninius at the end of the second century BCE along the Via Ostiensis between the *castrum* and a point just outside the later Porta Romana at Ostia, which delimited land for public use between the road and the river, most probably related to the Tiber traffic as well (*CIL* XIV 4702a–d; discussion summarized by Stevens, 2017: 218–20). The jurisdiction of the Tiber curators at Ostia are further underlined by two inscription by a *corpus* of ferrymen at Ostia, documenting permissions from the curator to construct buildings close to the river (*CIL* XIV 254, 5320, see also XIV 5384).

Inscriptions show that the curators were not only demarcating the area of public use but also responsible for building and restoring the banks and harbours at Rome. In 15 CE, the curators had overseen and approved the building of an embankment or mole at Rome. In 286–293 and 324 CE, they were responsible for restoring quays and a bridge (*CIL* VI 31543, 31556; *AE* 1975: 135; Aldrete, 2007: 201; Lonardi, 2013: 56).

## Three Tiber demarcation efforts

There were three main demarcation programs along the Tiber, in 55–54 BCE, 8–6 BCE, and 101–103 CE. In addition, there were continually ongoing efforts of demarcation on a more limited scale up to 198 CE. The possible reasons for the chronological concentration of the programs to these three short periods deserves to be briefly addressed.

The first large undertaking in 55–54 BCE should be viewed in the context of Pompey being given complete command of the grain supply in 57–52 BCE, with the task to resolve the supply crisis of Rome. The efforts of the censors can, thus, be interpreted as one of the many efforts in these years to improve the infrastructure and organisation of the city's supply. By liberating the banks of the river from encroaching buildings, the censors made additional space available for docking, loading, and unloading (Rickman, 1980: 55–8).

The next large intervention, in 8–6 BCE, coincided with Augustus' second term as censor, and his large administrative reforms of the city, which saw the creation of the 14 urban regions and a reorganisation of the urban *vici*, together with the new cult of the Lares Augusti (Lott, 2004: 8; Maiuro, 2008: 150). After decades of civil war and neglect of the urban infrastructure, the work on the Tiber banks that had been done in the time of Pompey was probably in dire need of renewal.

The third large demarcation effort happened in 101–103 CE, probably in connection with the large harbour works at Portus that were initiated at this time (Lonardi, 2013: 43). The new Trajanic harbour at Portus probably increased the river traffic significantly. The subsequent need for additional harbour space in Rome might have made it necessary to overhaul the embankment boundaries to clear the way for an enlargement of the port facilities. As we have seen, the term of the curator was from this time onwards prolonged from 1 to 3 years. This was probably necessitated by the new complexity of administering the river infrastructure, which, by this time also came to include the sewers, also helped by the creation of a new staff of assistants to the curator. A similar development can be observed for the time of Claudius, when the posts of procurator and prefect of the Tiber were created to assist the curator, possibly because of the demands posed by the first phase of harbour works at Portus.

It is noteworthy that none of these great efforts can be directly linked to inundations in Rome. Only the creation of the collegium of curators in 15 CE was a direct result of severe flooding, with the task "to look after the river, so that it should neither overflow in winter nor fail in summer", according to Dio Cassius (57.14.8). Of course, fulfilling the curators' tasks of strengthening the banks and keeping the river channel clear simultaneously facilitated the supply organisation and lowered the risk for flooding.

In view of the jurisdiction of the curators spanning the whole length of the Tiber between Ponte Milvio and Ostia, why do they only seem to have bothered with erecting boundary stones along two stretches: between Ponte Milvio and Ponte della Magliana in Rome, and at Ostia? Did not the rest of the river need demarcation efforts? In my view, the demarcation in Rome seems directly related to the pressure of buildings and activities along the riverbanks. As will be demonstrated at length below, there is ample evidence for port facilities in Rome between Ponte Milvio and Ponte della Magliana, but much less both upriver from Ponte Milvio and between Magliana and Ostia (Maiuro, 2008: 153; Fedeli, 2013). The boundary stones, first put up in 55–54 BCE, and continually renewed for 250 years, thus seem to define the harbour area of the city of Rome.

## A review of port facilities in Rome

As stated previously, the aim of this chapter is to demonstrate the size of the port of Rome. To properly understand the size and workings of the port, we would need to study storage and market space, distribution centres, road networks, sources of production and demand, administrative resources, and a variety of harbour workers, just to mention a few categories that would give the whole picture of harbour size and character. In addition, there are differences between how seaports and river harbours work, and how this might affect the use of quays (e.g. with broadside mooring being more common at river harbours). This study should be seen as only a starting point in the mapping of port facilities at Rome. The focus in this contribution will be on the river quays and directly associated buildings. The length of the archaeologically known quays will also work as a simple tool of comparison with recent studies of Rome and some other Mediterranean ports. The following section is an attempt to provide as complete an overview as possible of the

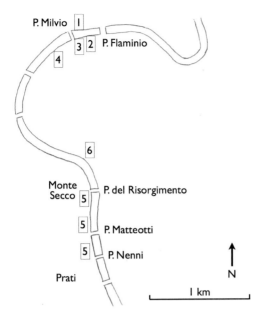

*Figure 15.7* Ancient harbours between Ponte Milvio and Ponte Nenni. Numbers denote entries in Table 1 (by author).

quays and associated buildings found along the Tiber between Ponte Milvio and Magliana.

### Ponte Milvio

Ponte Milvio most probably marked the northern limit of the port area of Rome, with no indications of port facilities for several kilometres upstream (Figure 15.7). The bridge marked the point where the *viae* Clodia, Cassia and Flaminia all converged before continuing into Rome. The bridge might have been first built in wood simultaneously with the construction of the Via Flaminia in 220 BCE, later rebuilt in stone in 109 BCE, some parts of which still are included in the present bridge. Augustus commemorated his restoration of the Via Flaminia by erecting an arch at the bridge crowned by a statue of himself ([Aur. Vict.] *De vir. ill.* 72.8; Amm. Marc. 27.3; Dio Cass. 53.22; Virgili, 1985; Galliazzo, 1994: 32–6).

Ponte Milvio was also the first bridge travellers moving downriver along the Tiber encountered when arriving at Rome. As the first obstacle across the river, it probably became a natural stopping point, a location where authorities could exert control over river traffic and perhaps also levy customs dues. This in turn attracted commercial and entertainment activities, of which we receive a rare glimpse from Tacitus, when he writes that Nero often went there because "the Mulvian Bridge at that period was famous for its nocturnal attractions ..." (Tac. *Ann.* 13.47).

There is, thus, no surprise to find extensive remains of port facilities along both riverbanks, both up- and downriver from the bridge. At the right river-bank, for the whole length between Ponte Milvio and Ponte Flaminio, has been observed a quay constructed in blocks of tufo lined with travertine, c. 400 m long (Figure 15.7 no. 1). Along the quay was a roadway paved with blocks of basalt, probably the Via Flaminia. Close to the bridge, between the quay and the road, was in 1819 found one of the Tiber boundary stones set up in 55–54 BCE, still preserved in situ, and, uniquely, with inscriptions towards both the river and the road (Figure 15.6). On the other side of the roadway were in 1907 and 1947 found remains of storage and commercial buildings built in *opus latericium* with tessellated floors, but the excavations were unfor-tunately never published, and the buildings were destroyed to make way for the new Tiber walls, the muraglioni. Parts of the quay could still be clearly seen in 1959 but have subsequently become mostly covered in silt and vege-tation (*CIL* VI 40857; *Not. scav.* 1907: 86; Mocchegiani Carpano, 1982: 159; Virgili, 1983; Quilici, 1986: 200) (Figure 15.8).

During excavation in 2017–18 along the right bank, just downriver from the bridge at Via Capoprati, remains of storage and commercial buildings in *opus latericium* were found along the river. They could be dated to the first

*Figure 15.8* Harbour remains on the right bank upstream from Ponte Milvio in 1959 (Quilici, 1986: figure 3).

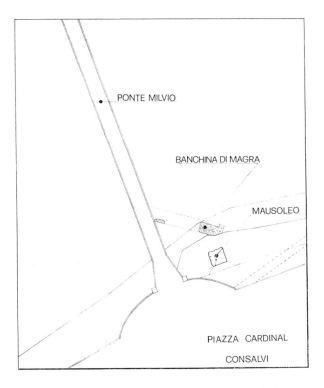

*Figure 15.9* Mole excavated in 1982 at Ponte Milvio (Virgili, 1983: figure 1).

century CE and were later replaced by a decorated villa in the third century (*La Repubblica* 27.11.2017; 13.7.2018).

At the opposite, left bank, of the Tiber, quays and associated storage buildings along the whole stretch between Ponte Milvio and Ponte Flaminio, for a distance of c. 400 m, were discovered during construction works in 1947 (Figure 15.7 no. 2). Just upriver from Ponte Milvio were remains of a mole excavated in 1982. The mole was set at an oblique angle towards the river (Figure 15.7 no. 3; 15.9). Its first part, 11 m long, joined the left bank with the second pylon of the bridge. The mole could also be observed downstream from this pylon and, thus, continued at least several metres beyond the bridge, further into the river channel. The first and second pylons from the left bank, with their connecting arch, fully preserve the original building phase of the stone bridge, datable to 109 BCE. The mole cannot have been built before the bridge, since it used the bridge pylon as an anchor point. The mole consisted of blocks of tufo dell'Aniene lined along the outside edges with travertine blocks. These are similar materials as the quays on the opposite bank, as well as the bridge itself, which had a nucleus of blocks of tufo di Grotta Oscura with outer layers in tufo dell'Aniene, with the outside of the pylons and arch lined with blocks of travertine. Unfortunately, it has not been possible to investigate the foundations of either the mole or the bridge, to establish whether the construction had a base of hydraulic concrete. A Tiber boundary stone of 55–54 BCE was found at the left bank just upriver from Ponte Milvio in 1724, while another of the same date was found 30 m downstream from the bridge in 1894 (*CIL* VI 31540b–c; *Not. scav.* 1894: 142–3, 170; Virgili, 1983; Quilici, 1986: 200).

About 300 m downstream from the Ponte Milvio, 15 m inland from the present left bank, massive remains of a concrete quay faced with *opus reticulatum*, excavated for a length of 73 m, were found in 1893. At the southern end, the quay made a sudden shift at right angles to the east, where it was excavated for a further 12 m. This probably formed a sheltered bay, which was equipped with a stairway flanked by stone pilasters. There was also a series of storage buildings facing the quay. This complex has been dated to the Augustan period. A river boundary stone of 8 BCE was found nearby in 1676 (Figure 15.7 no. 4; *CIL* VI 31541a; *Not. Scav.* 1893: 196; Quilici, 1986: 203; Maiuro, 2008: 153).

### Monte Secco

One of the largest harbour quarters of ancient Rome might also be one of the least known. The area that was known as Monte Secco consisted of a 16-m-high and 850-m-long ridge between the northern end of Lungotevere Oberdan and Ponte Matteotti. When the ridge was removed in the 1880s for the development of the new urban quarter of Prati, it was discovered that it was completely artificial. Monte Secco was made of discarded sherds from mainly amphorae and *dolia*, but the finds were never published, Figure 15.7 no. 5; 15.10–11; (*Not. scav.* 1884: 392–3; Quilici, 1986: 201–2).

A few years later, in 1892–94, during the building of the muraglioni in this part of Prati, was discovered a massive quay structure, 850 m long, built in tufo dell'Aniene and lined with travertine, that stretched from about 100 m upriver from Ponte del Risorgimento down to Ponte Nenni. The majority of this port was, thus, built between the Tiber and the Monte Secco ridge. The building technique was similar to that of the quays found along both banks at Ponte Milvio. Between the quays and the ridge were discovered several warehouses that, based on brickstamps, could be dated to the second century CE. Several amphorae were found near the right bank during river dredging in the 1890s. One of the Tiber boundary stones from 55–54 BCE was found in situ at the ancient quay just south of Ponte Matteotti in 1892. Another was discovered nearby the following year, used as a threshold, when the Osteria Montesecco was torn down. In 1779, a boundary stone of 8 BCE was found near the present Ponte Nenni, while another, set up in of 101 CE was found just south of Ponte Matteotti in 1930 (*CIL* VI 31540e–f, 31541e, 40862; *Not. scav.* 1892: 266; *Not. scav.* 1893: 517; *Not. scav.* 1894: 95; Quilici, 1986: 201–2; De Caprariis, 1999: 231–3).

Major remains of quays in *opus reticulatum* were also found in 1897 along the opposite left bank, from Via Raffaele Stern and southwards for 135 m.

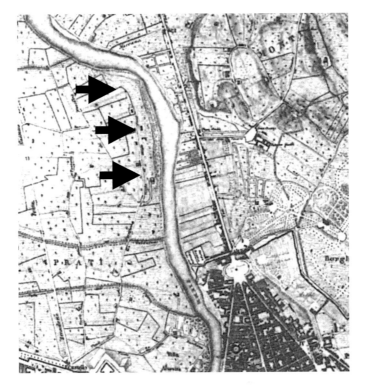

*Figure 15.10* Monte Secco in 1839, before its demolition in 1884–85 (Frutaz, 1962: tav. 503).

There were also traces of buildings behind the quay that might have been used for storage. Along the quay were found three river boundary stones of 55–54 BCE (Figure 15.7 no. 6; *CIL* VI 37026–37028; *Not. scav.* 1897: 9–10; Quilici, 1986: 202–3).

### *Ripetta*

At the location of the medieval and early modern port of Ripetta, there was also an ancient forerunner located next to the mausoleum of Augustus. It is mentioned in connection with events in 20 CE. Remains of the port structure were unearthed during the construction of the new Ripetta harbour in 1703. A 50-m stretch of the ancient quay was found, which was built in blocks of stone and paved in travertine. A Tiber marker from 8 BCE, renewed in 15 CE, was found at the Ripetta in 1750 (Figure 15.12 no. 7; Tac. *Ann.* 3.9.2; *CIL* VI 31541f; Maischberger, 1997: 106; De Caprariis, 1999: 220–1).

In 1906, 150 m downriver from the Ripetta, near Piazza Nicosia, a quay was found built in blocks of travertine. More blocks were unearthed in 1938, and part of what was probably the travertine paving of the quay was

*Figure 15.11* Map made in the 1670s showing the Tiber at Monte Secco, with via Flaminia at the bottom (Meijer, 1683).

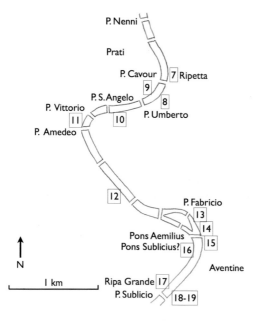

*Figure 15.12* Ancient harbours between Ponte Nenni and Ponte Sublicio. Numbers denote entries in Table 1 (by author).

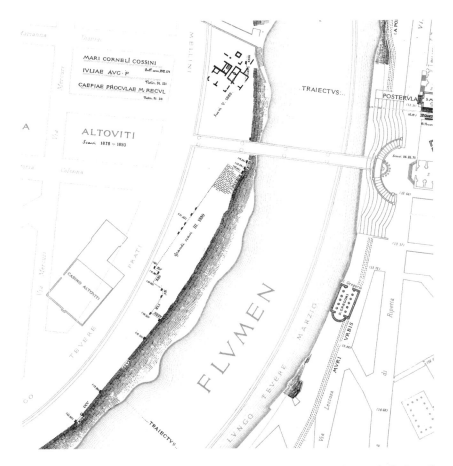

*Figure 15.13* Archaeological finds in 1889–92 along the Tiber in Prati di Castello (Lanciani, 1901: pl. 8).

discovered in 1956. A Tiber boundary stone set up in 16–23 CE was found nearby. In the medieval period, this was the location of a postern river gate in the Aurelian walls called Posterula della Pila, a name that suggests the existence of a mole. It has been suggested that this might have been the location of a port known as the Ciconias, used for unloading and registering wine connected to the Temple of the Sun, attested by an inscription from c. 300 CE. Close to this port was another artificial mound of pottery sherds, the Monte Citorio (Figure 15.12 no. 8; *CIL* VI 31544c, 1785; *Not. scav.* 1906: 356; *BCAR* 1906: 316; *BCAR* 1938: 271–3, 299–300; Le Gall, 1953: 202, 288–90, 314–6; Lega, 1993; Maischberger, 1997: 105; De Caprariis, 1999: 220–1, 225–6; Malmberg, 2015: 198–9).

In the 1890s, on the opposite right bank, at the Ponte Cavour, was discovered a large square paved with travertine. A similar, or perhaps the

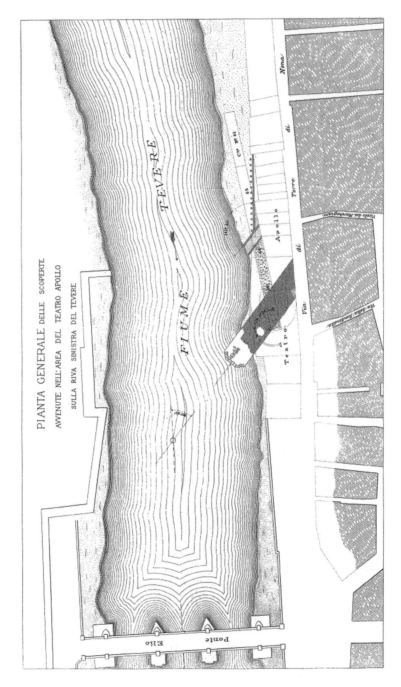

*Figure 15.14* Harbour excavated at Tor di Nona in 1890–91 (Marchetti, 1891: tav. 3).

same, square was also observed during unusually low water in 1956, when also several adjacent buildings were recorded. It has been suggested to be used for handling goods. Near this square two boundary stones from 55–54 BCE and three from 101 CE were found in 1890–92. A further series of 11 boundary stones erected in 7 BCE were found in 1890–91 in situ along the right bank in this area, starting just upriver from Ponte Cavour down to Ponte Umberto. During the construction of Ponte Umberto in 1890, the remains of a quay built in blocks of tufo were found (Figure 15.12 no. 9, 15.13; *CIL* VI 31540g–h, 31549a–c, 31542a–l; *Not. scav.* 1889: 188–9; *Not. scav.* 1890: 187, 322–3, 389–91; Marchetti, 1890; *Not. scav.* 1891: 91, 130–1, 164–5; *Not. scav.* 1892: 233–4, 316; Le Gall, 1953: 203–4; Mocchegiani Carpano, 1981: 143; Quilici, 1986: 202; Maischberger, 1997: 105; Maischberger, 2000: 72; Maiuro, 2008: 154; Muzzioli, 2015).

### Tor di Nona

A large mole was excavated in 1890–91 at Tor di Nona, 160 m upstream from Ponte S. Angelo. The mole, 50 m long, had protruded into the river at an oblique angle. It was made up of stone blocks, with the lower courses in tufo dell'Aniene, the upper ones in tufo di Grotta Oscura, and a pavement in travertine. The foundation consisted of a watertight cofferdam of interlocking oak beams with lead sheathing, into which was poured a concrete foundation. The use of concrete in the foundations of the mole is decisive for the dating. The oldest examples of underwater use of concrete are from the harbour at Cosa and can probably be dated to around 80 BCE or later, possibly from the Augustan period. The mole at Tor di Nona should, thus, probably not be dated earlier than the 80s BCE, and could conceivably have been built in the Augustan period (Figure 15.12 no. 10, 15.14 *Not. scav.* 1890: 153; *Not. scav.* 1892: 110–1; Marchetti, 1891; Cressedi 1949–51; Le Gall, 1953: 201–2; La Rocca, 1984: 63; Flambard, 1987: 203–4; Maischberger, 1997: 100–4; Gazda, 2008; Malmberg, 2015: 195).

### Villa Farnesina

In 1970–72, along the right bank from just upriver Ponte Vittorio down to Ponte Amedeo, for a distance of circa 300 m, several remains of an inclined concrete quay or embankment wall faced with *opus reticulatum*, with a foundation in wooden piling still preserved were unearthed or observed. Downriver from Ponte Amedeo, further ancient quays in concrete had been noted before their destruction in 1961–62. Here two river boundary stones set up in 101 CE were found (Figure 15.12 no. 11; *CIL* VI 37029, 40863; *Not. scav.* 1956: 56; Mocchegiani Carpano, 1981: 144).

During excavations undertaken in the grounds of the Villa Farnesina in 1878–81, a vast warehouse was discovered at the right riverbank, which was built in *opus mixtum* and dated by brickstamps to the early second century CE. The warehouse consisted of several parts, with elongated storage rooms grouped around porticoed courtyards paved with black and white mosaics. Several *dolia* and marble weights were discovered. An inscription, dated to 102 CE, identified the complex as the *Cella Vinaria Nova et Arruntiana Caesaris*. It was evidently a major state-operated centre for the handling of wine. No quay was found, but it is very plausible that one existed along the 150 m of riverfront of the complex. Five Tiber boundary stones set up in 8 BCE (four of which had been renewed in 15 CE), one in 73 CE, four in 101 CE, and one erected in 198 CE were found nearby (Figure 15.12 no. 12; *CIL* VI 31541g–l, 31547, 31549f–i, 31555, 8826; Le Gall, 1953: 120, 259; Palmer, 1980: 232; Rodríguez-Almeida, 1993; Mari, 2007).

### Portus Tiberinus

Downstream from the Tiber Island was the oldest of Rome's ports, identified from a passage by Varro as the Portus Tiberinus. In the Archaic period, the Tiber went at least 100 m further to the east, thus forming a sheltered natural harbour which was gradually moved westwards by successive embankment efforts from the sixth century BCE down to the second century CE. This was also the site of the first bridge across the river, the *Pons Sublicius*, as well as the first Tiber bridge in stone, the *Pons Aemilius*, which was completed in 142 BCE. The new stone bridge needed a sturdy embankment, which is probably the wall in tufo dell'Aniene that was excavated in the 1930s between the temple of Portunus and the river. Another part of the embankment, also built in tufo blocks, might have been found in 1886, beginning at Ponte Fabricio and going downriver for 30 m, which might be contemporary with the bridge, erected in 62 BCE. Here was also found an in situ Tiber boundary stone erected by Augustus in 7–6 BCE and restored in 15 CE, and another stone set up in 161 CE as a renewal of a Trajanic one (Figure 15.12 no. 13; Varro, *Ling.* 6.19; Livy 40.51.4; *CIL* VI 31542s, 40867; *Not. scav.* 1886: 273–4; Borsari, 1889: 169; Le Gall, 1953: 202; Colini, 1980; Castagnoli, 1980: 35; Ammerman, 2018: 407–8).

The old port facilities were damaged by flooding in the 90s and again in 105 CE, which led them to be completely replaced by a new harbour quarter built by Trajan, obliterating almost any trace of the previous port. Equally important for the construction of the new facilities was probably also the simultaneous development of the new Trajanic harbour at Portus. The new quarter, excavated in 1935–39, consisted of eight or nine large *horrea* buildings in *opus latericium* with floors in *opus spicatum* divided by streets in a strict orthogonal pattern. Brickstamps dated the buildings to the first decade of the second century CE. Two river boundary stones set up in 121–124 CE, which were renewals of previous Trajanic ones, were found close to the river. An inscription dated to 161 CE found during the excavations mentions a *Cella Lucceiana*, which might have been a warehouse for wine. No traces of quays were found, but this might have been due to the erosion of the riverbank since Antiquity (Figure 15.12

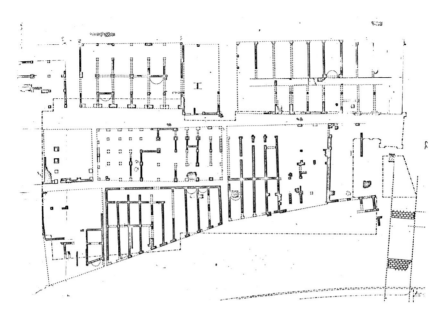

*Figure 15.15* Horrea excavated at Portus Tiberinus in 1935–39 (Colini, 1980: figure 10).

no. 14, 15.15; *CIL* VI 31552ad; *AE* 1971: 29; Colini, 1980; Pisani Sartorio, Colini and Buzzetti, 1986; Chioffi, 1993b; Buzzetti, 1999).

South of the Portus Tiberinus, outside the Porta Trigemina in the Severan/Republican walls, the aediles in 193 BCE built a portico and a wharf (*emporium*). Two years later, the *curule* aediles constructed a portico for timber merchants, or in the timber merchants' quarter, outside the same gate. In 179 BCE, the censor M. Aemilius Lepidus built the pylons of the *Pons Aemilius*, together with a port (*portum*), and also a portico outside the Porta Trigemina. Four years later, the censors enclosed the wharf (*emporium*) outside the same gate with paling, paved it with stone, and built a stairway from the Tiber to the wharf. They also repaired the portico built by Aemilius (Livy 35.10.11–12; 35.41.10; 40.51.4–6; 41.27.8–9).

The building projects of 193–174 BCE may represent the first major expansion of the Portus Tiberinus southwards and can probably be connected with a major population growth and increase in imports from overseas at Rome following the second Punic war. The specific location of these buildings has been fiercely debated, with many scholars placing them in Testaccio, which would be about 1 km outside the gate. In my view, this seems excessive, and a location much closer to the gate might be warranted, in the area between the Tiber and the foot of the Aventine, as suggested by e.g. Lanciani, Harmansah and Tucci. Just downstream from the Cloaca Maxima, a 25-m stretch of submerged quay built in blocks of tufo di Grotta Oscura was observed in

1887 and again in the 1970s. In 1879, a big step in travertine was found just downstream from the Cloaca Maxima with an inscription that the *curule aedile* Barronius Barba had restored it, which was dated to the middle of the first century BCE. It has been suggested this was a later repair of the stairway between the river and the emporium mentioned by Livy (Figure 15.12 no. 15; *CIL* VI 31602; *BCAR* 1880: 21; Borsari, 1889: 169; Mocchegiani Carpano, 1981: 145; Harmansah, 2002; Tucci, 2011–12: 198).

### *Via Anicia marble plan*

Reaching this part of the Tiber, it is worth looking more closely at the unique overlapping of two different marble plans of Rome, which might give us further insight into the arrangements along the Tiber in the area just north of the Portus Tiberinus. The *Forma Urbis* marble plan showed most of the city of Rome. It was created in the first decade of the third century CE and was displayed at the Forum Pacis. Several fragments of the plan show buildings adjacent to the Tiber. Among them are fragments 32ghi, discovered in 1562, and 31ll, unearthed in 2000, displaying a section along the river just above Ponte Fabricio. They depict a portico behind which is a long building with a row of narrow, elongated rooms facing the river. Between the portico and the river is an unidentified rectangular building on a platform (Figure 15.16; Filippi and Liverani, 2014–15: 78).

The fragments found in the Via Anicia in Trastevere in 1983 overlap with the area described above but in addition depict the riverbank itself. The plan was probably made in the first or in the beginning of the second century CE. It is drawn to the same scale as the *Forma Urbis* (1:240) but has a much higher degree of detail, with walls drawn with two lines, and the ownership of private buildings provided with names in the genitive. The plan also shows both the lower and the upper limits of the Tiber, i.e. the area defined as the riverbank by Roman law. In this area, there is the rectangular building also shown in the *Forma Urbis*. Normally the riverbank would be kept clear of buildings, but as shown by the permission given by the Tiber curators at Ostia, exceptions could be made. Along the upper limit there is a portico along the river, behind which there are two buildings. The left, northern one, has a broad stairway leading to a large inner room. South of this entrance is a row of *tabernae* facing the portico, presumably for storage or commercial use, and with presumably the owner's name in the genitive. The southern building consists of a row of similar small rooms facing the portico, with the inscription *Corneliae/ et soc(iorum)* ([owned by] Cornelia and associates) and a staircase indicating the existence of an upper storey. The two buildings are separated by a narrow alley. A series of numbers are provided along the portico: 99, 6, 54, and 51. These might denote the length in Roman feet of each section of the portico, with the short section of 6 feet corresponding to the narrow alleyway (Figure 15.17; Rodríguez-Almeida, 2002: 43–9; Muzzioli, 2007; Maiuro, 2008: 151; Muzzioli, 2009; Meneghini, 2016: 180–2).

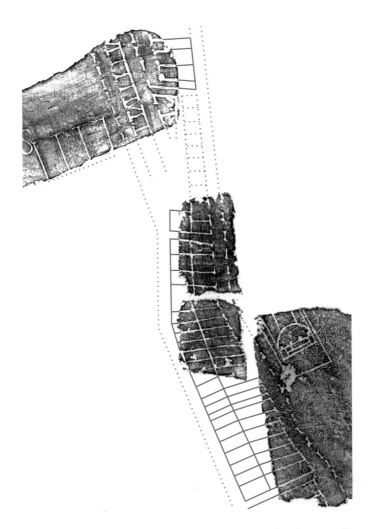

*Figure 15.16* Buildings along the Tiber in Campus Martius shown on fragments 32ghi and 31ll of the Forma Urbis (Filippi and Liverani, 2014–2015: figure 5).

However, the measurements displayed along the portico facing the Tiber on the Via Anicia fragments might not be as straightforward as has been previously suggested. Why are not any other buildings on the fragments depicted with measurements? Why is the building owned by Cornelia and associates provided with two different measurements, in spite of the whole building seemingly having the same owner? The measurements are only provided at the upper limit of the riverbank, which is also where the Tiber boundary stones would be displayed. As we have seen, the boundary stones from the time of Augustus onwards prominently displayed the distance in feet to the next stone. These

*Figure 15.17* The marble plan found at via Anicia in Trastevere in 1983 (Wikimedia Commons, Carole Raddato, cropped).

distances could vary greatly, from just 6 feet to as much as 386 feet. It has been suggested that the Via Anicia plan might have had a legal function as a cadastral map, delineating the borders of ownership. If that is the case, it would be intriguing to speculate that including information about the position of the Tiber boundary stones on this map would make sense, since the stones marked the legal boundary of the public use of the riverbank. Many of the stones had identical inscriptions, except for the measurements. To include that information on the map would, thus, make it easier to separate individual stones, and replacing stones that might be lost due to flooding or illegal damage. Of course, with only a small part of the plan preserved, this remains a very tentative suggestion for an alternative interpretation of the measurements provided on the fragments that to my knowledge has not been previously proposed.

### Along the Aventine

Downriver from the *Pons Aemilius*, fragments 27a-f of the *Forma Urbis* show both banks of the Tiber. On the left bank is depicted a columned portico along the river, which might have had a roadway or quay in front of it,

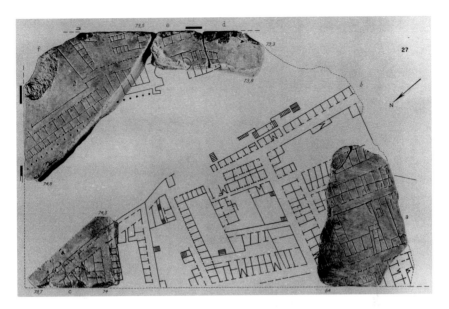

*Figure 15.18* Both banks of the Tiber downstream from Pons Aemilius shown on fragments 27a–f of the Forma Urbis (Carettoni et al., 1960: tav. 26).

similar to the arrangement in the Via Anicia plan. Further to the south is shown what might be interpreted as an L-formed mole together with a small harbour basin with *exedrae*. Along the right bank is also shown a portico with *tabernae* along the river, with what looks like quays in front. A complex stairway is also depicted, with two levels down to the river from the quays (Figure 15.18; Carettoni et al., 1960: 85–6; Rodríguez-Almeida, 1980: 108; Castagnoli, 1980: 35; Aldrete, 2007: 195; Muzzioli, 2018: 32–3).

Near the stairway shown on the *Forma Urbis*, at the church of S. Maria in Capella, downriver from *Pons Aemilius* and on the right bank, were several archaeological remains connected to a river harbour recorded. After the unusually strong flood of 1870, just upriver from the church, the remains of an ancient concrete quay faced with bricks with three mooring stones in travertine in the shape of lions' heads were discovered. One of them was destroyed during the construction of the muraglioni, while the other two were retrieved during an excavation here in 1979 and are now displayed at the river wall. In 1871, during excavation behind this quay, remains of a *horrea* building were found. In the 1880s, an open space paved with travertine slabs, together with two inscriptions was also unearthed. The first was erected by Avianius Symmachus as *praefectus annonae* and dedicated in 340–350. The stone includes a depiction of a Tiber transport ship, a *navis caudicaria*. Avianius' own house is known to have been located in the vicinity. Closeby was another inscription dedicated by a collegium of fishermen and divers of the Tiber. Another stone, a river

*Figure 15.19* Harbour discovered at Santa Maria in Capella in 1870, with Ponte Rotto in the background (Le Gall, 1953: pl. 10).

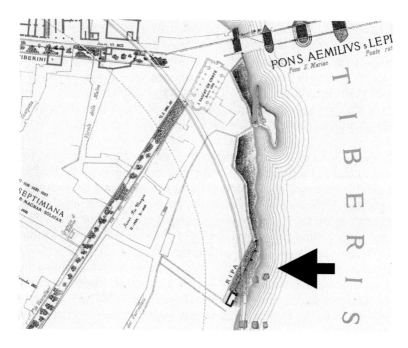

*Figure 15.20* Quay with mooring stones at Santa Maria in Capella in Trastevere (Lanciani, 1901: pl. 28).

boundary stone erected in 55–54 BCE, was found in the vicinity. In connection with the building of the muraglioni in this area in the 1880s, Lanciani reports the finding of an inclined concrete quay clad with bricks, with a rectangular mooring stone in travertine of the same type previously found at Testaccio (see below), found in situ still forming part of the quay. He also reported that further north, near Via dei Vascellari, the remains of a quay or embankment wall in travertine were found (Figure 15.12 no. 16, 15.19–20; *CIL* VI 31540i, 36954, 29702; *PLRE* I: 863–5; *Not. scav.* 1880: 128; *Not. scav.* 1885: 187–8; *Not. scav.* 1886: 362–3; *BCAR* 1887: 16–17; *BCAR* 1888: 387–9; Borsari, 1889: 169; Lanciani, 1901: pl. 28; Le Gall, 1953: 202–3; Castagnoli, 1980: 36; Tucci, 2004: 197–8).

A further 300 m downstream, at the medieval and early modern harbour at Ripa Grande, the remains of ancient harbour structures were also uncovered. In 1901, here 15 m of quay built in tufo blocks were found. Three of the blocks could still be observed in situ in 1947. In 1913, near the quay, a series of rooms built in *opus latericium*, with floors in white *tesserae* was unearthed. Adjacent to the rooms were found rows of *dolia* and a dedicatory inscription to Mercury in marble. In the riverbed nearby, a Tiber boundary stone from 8 BCE was discovered. At the Via del Porto di Ripa Grande, that goes along the river, an altar dedicated in 111 CE to Silvanus by the *vilicus* of the *Cella Civiciana* was discovered. This was presumably a *cellae vinaria*, a storage facility for the handling of wine, probably located nearby (Figure 15.12 no. 17; *CIL* VI 31541n; *AE* 1937: 61; *Not. scav.* 1901: 399–400; *BCAR* 1901: 284–5; *Not. scav.* 1913: 117; *BCAR* 1934: 177–8; Le Gall, 1953: 203; Chioffi, 1993a).

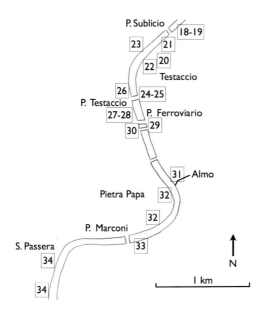

*Figure 15.21* Ancient harbours between Ponte Sublicio and Santa Passera. Numbers denote entries in Table 1 (by author).

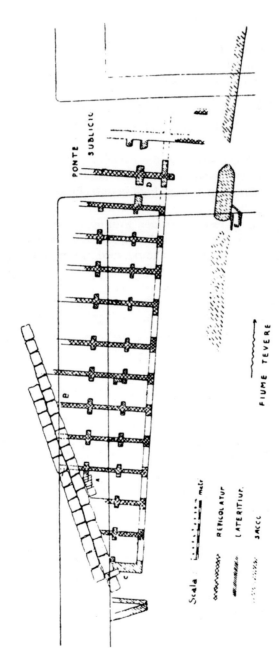

*Figure 15.22* Harbours excavated upstream from Ponte Sublicio in 1919–20 (Cressedi, 1956a: figure 1).

*Figure 15.23* Republican period harbour with animal-shaped mooring stones excavated upstream from Ponte Sublicio in 1919–20 (Gatti, 1936: figure 5).

*Figure 15.24* Imperial period harbour excavated upstream from Ponte Sublicio in 1919–20 (Mocchegiani Carpano, 1981: tav. 29).

### Testaccio

Across the river from Ripa Grande, on the left bank just upriver from the modern Ponte Sublicio, substantial remains of a quay built in large blocks of tufo di Grotta Oscura were discovered in 1919–20, which were preserved for a length of about 60 m. It was equipped with two converging stairways in peperino, which connected the riverbank with the upper level of the quay.

It also had large travertine mooring stones cut in the shape of animal heads. A date in the second or first century BCE has been suggested for this quay. It has been observed that this quay is built at a different angle than the modern Tiber embankment, which might indicate the presence of a sheltered basin in front of the so-called *Porticus Aemilia* building in the Republican period. This first harbour was replaced by a new quay in concrete faced with *opus mixtum* and with parts of the wooden foundation piling still preserved. The later quay was excavated for 75 m and was built at the same angle as the present Tiber embankment. Behind the quay were constructed a series of storage rooms in *opus reticulatum*, with floors in *opus spicatum*, travertine door frames, and elaborate locks. The construction technique and brickstamps dated the later quay and storage building firmly to the first decades of the second century CE (Figure 15.21 no. 18–19, 15.22–24; Gatti, 1934: 141; Gatti, 1936: 77–82; Le Gall, 1953: 102–3, 199; Cressedi, 1956a: 19–21; Castagnoli, 1980: 36; Mocchegiani Carpano, 1981: 146; Meneghini, 1985; Aguilera Martín, 2002: 58–60; Claridge, 2010: 404; Tucci, 2011–12: 200).

A building in Testaccio, since the early 20th century usually identified as the *Porticus Aemilia*, merits a mention here, because it has been suggested that it was used as a *navalia*, i.e. ship sheds for the Roman navy. It was constructed in the *opus incertum* technique, which would probably date it to the second century BCE. The building originally measured 487 m in length and 60 m in width and was divided into 50 bays probably covered by barrel vaults. Today, the remains are removed from the river by c. 80 m, but it has been suggested that there might have been a sheltered river basin in front of the building during the Republican period, which is indicated by the angle of the Republican quay mentioned above and the lack of any remains from the Republican period in front of the building. However, the identification as naval ship sheds is not without its problems, as has been demonstrated by excavations in 2011–13. The gradient from the river might have been too steep to use the building for this purpose. On the other hand, these conclusions are not secure since no findings were made of the use of the building in the Republican period: neither its original floor, nor any stratigraphic layer, or artefacts. What the excavators could establish, however, was the use of the building for storage and redistribution in the Imperial period, which also involved major rebuilding in the first and second centuries CE. The building continued to have a commercial function until the fifth century (Figure 15.21 no. 20; Gatti, 1934: 140, 145; Cozza and Tucci, 2006; Coarelli, 2007; Claridge, 2010: 403–4; Tucci, 2012; Rankov, 2013: 40; Malmberg, 2015: 192–3; Burgers *et al.*, 2018).

Just downriver from the Ponte Sublicio, between the so-called *Porticus Aemilia* and the Tiber, a 125-m-long complex on three levels has been revealed by excavations in 1952 and 1979–84. The quay was formed by an inclined wall that is not preserved, behind which were found enclosed substructures in *opus mixtum* filled with earth, dated to the first part of the second century CE. A series of vaulted rooms faced the quay, which was paved in travertine and was equipped with travertine mooring stones. In a first phase, dated to the first century CE, these vaulted rooms had large openings towards the

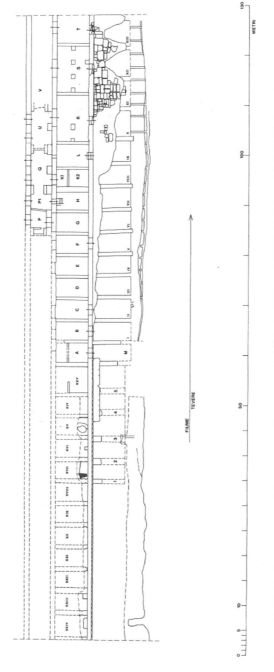

*Figure 15.25* Harbour excavated downstream from Ponte Sublicio in 1952 and 1979–84 (Meneghini, 1985: figure 3).

*Figure 15.26* Harbour excavated downstream from Ponte Sublicio in 1952 and 1979–84 (Meneghini, 1985: figure 1).

landward side. In the second-century rebuilding, they had smaller doorways on this side that led to an at least 250-m-long cryptoportico with another series of rooms on its other side. On top of the vaulted rooms was a third level, added in the second century, consisting of a series of rooms with a tile roof. These rooms, interpreted as offices, opened towards the landward side and were paved with black-and-white mosaics. They faced an open space paved with black *tesserae* built on top of the cryptoportico (Figure 15.21 no. 21, 15.25–27; Le Gall, 1953: 200; Cressedi 1956a; Cressedi, 1956b; Mocchegiani Carpano, 1981: 148; Mocchegiani Carpano, Meneghini and Incitti, 1986; Aguilera Martín, 2002: 60–2; Bianchi, 2007).

Further downstream, another harbour structure about 130 m long was excavated in 1868–70. On the riverbank an inclined wall was constructed, which was built in *opus mixtum* and could be dated to the Trajanic period based on the brickstamps. Five ramps linked the riverbank and the upper quay. Large mooring stones in travertine were built into the outer walls of the ramps and the main quay wall. At this quay was also found a Tiber boundary stone of 55–54 BCE and one of 121–124 CE. The structures were covered in silt after the 1870 flooding, and the last remains were destroyed in 1955. Excavations in 1955 found quays further south in the same building technique and along the same line as those excavated in 1868–70 but partially destroyed by the Aurelian wall (Figure 15.21 no. 22, 15.28–29; *CIL* VI 31540k, 40864; Gatti, 1936: 194–201; Le Gall, 1953: 196; *Not. scav.* 1956: 15–16; Cressedi 1956a: 36–52; Castagnoli, 1980: 36; Maischberger, 1996; Aguilera Martín, 2002: 62–6; Bianchi, 2007).

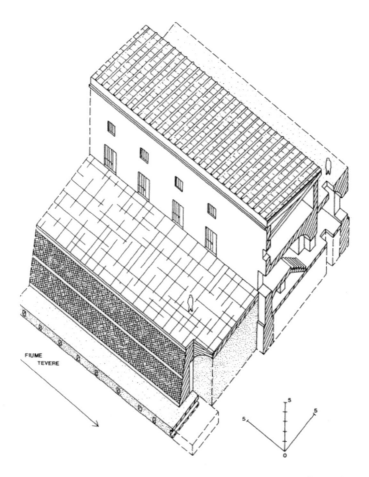

*Figure 15.27* Reconstruction of the harbour downstream from Ponte Sublicio (Meneghini, 1986: figure 283).

In 1868–70 during the excavations, 1,238 large blocks and columns of marble were found, which were piled in rows around the loading ramps, together with at least 26,000 sawn marble plaques. Of the blocks, only 31 (2.5%) had consular dates, upon which the chronological use of the quay is based. According to earlier interpretations, marble handling stopped here after Trajan and moved downriver to the area of S. Paolo fuori le mura. However, in my view, this is too small a sample to provide any conclusive evidence (Gatti, 1936: 63; Maischberger, 1997: 77, 80; Fant, 2001: 188, 192–3).

### Trastevere opposite Testaccio

Again, we have several pieces of the *Forma Urbis* that cast some light on the topographical situation along the Tiber in this area. The fragments 24cd

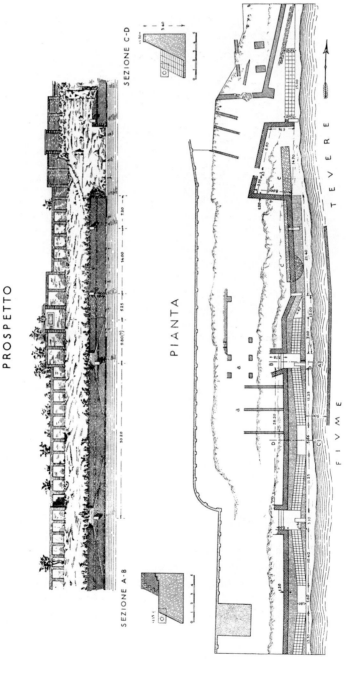

*Figure 15.28*  Harbour excavated in Testaccio in 1868–70 (Gatti, 1936: tav. 1).

*Figure 15.29*  Harbour excavated in Testaccio in 1868–70 (Gatti, 1934: tav. 5).

show buildings between the so-called *Porticus Aemilia* and the river on the left bank. Fragments 28abc show the opposite right bank, with a continuous line along the river that might indicate a quay or embankment wall. They also show several large *horrea*, one with its own set of stairs down to the Tiber (Figure 15.30; Carettoni et al., 1960: 87–8; Rodríguez-Almeida, 1980: 102–5, 108; Muzzioli, 2018: 34–5).

Some archaeological findings fill out the picture in this area. About 250 m south of the modern Porta Portese, the remains of a *horrea* with *dolia* that could be dated to the end of the fourth century CE were unearthed in 1997. About 50 m further south, in 1893, a large open space was found that stretched along the river for 60 m and was paved with travertine slabs. A roadway, presumably the Via Campana, ran parallel to the river behind the paved open space. At the southern end of this open space, during works on a drainage channel in 1888, a 25-m-long inclined concrete quay faced with *opus reticulatum* came to light. A large rectangular, pierced mooring stone in travertine protruded from the quay. Steps in travertine formed a stairway between the river and the quay. Behind the quay was excavated a portico, at least 30 m long, with walls in *opus latericium*, columns in peperino clad with stucco, and a paving of black-and-white tesserae. A brickstamp dated to 134 CE suggests that the portico was built in the middle of the second century CE. On the other side of the portico, a 18-m stretch was discovered of what might be the Via Campana. The roadway, paved with basalt blocks, was 9 m wide with sidewalks on both sides of the road in tufo and travertine. Further south, bisected by the Aurelian wall between the Porta Portuensis and the river, the remains of a warehouse built in brick and a Tiber boundary stone set up in 8 BCE were discovered

*Figure 15.30* Fragments 24cd and 28ab of the Forma Urbis, showing both banks of the Tiber in Testaccio and southern Trastevere (Carettoni et al., 1960: tav. 24 and 27).

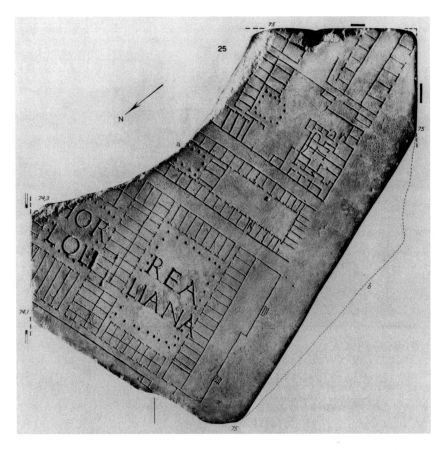

*Figure 15.31* Fragment 25a of the Forma Urbis, showing left bank of the Tiber with the Horrea Lolliana in southern Testaccio (Carettoni et al., 1960: tav. 25).

(Figure 15.21 no. 23 Borsari, 1889: 170; *BCAR* 1892: 286–7; *Not. scav.* 1892: 116–17; *Not. scav.* 1893: 420; Le Gall, 1953: 203; Imperatori, 2003: 61, 89–91).

### The Mattatoio area

Fragments 25ab of the *Forma Urbis* show the area just north of the former Mattatoio in Testaccio. They depict the *Horrea Lolliana*, a large *horrea* that faces directly onto the Tiber via a broad quay with two stairways down to the river. Downriver are two series of rows of *tabernae* facing the river separated by what has been interpreted as a bath building (Figure 15.31; Carettoni et al., 1960: 83–4; Rodríguez-Almeida, 1980: 106; Coarelli, 1996; Aldrete, 2007: 195; Muzzioli, 2018: 36).

In 1938–43, during work on the bridge known today as the Ponte Testaccio, well-preserved remains of port structures came to light on the left, Testaccio, side of the river. The remains mostly belong to two main phases. The first phase showed the remains of a quay preserved to a length of 54 m. Unfortunately, the building technique or materials used in this wall were not recorded. At this quay a Tiber boundary stone erected in 8 BCE was found. In the second phase, a new quay was built about 10 m further to the west, perhaps due to the movement of the riverbank in the intervening years. This later quay was preserved for a length of 42 m and was built in *opus mixtum*, very similar to the quay excavated upstream in 1868–70. The top of the quay was paved with stone slabs. Near this quay was found a Tiber boundary stone set up in 121–124 CE, and two stones set up in 161 CE, all restorations of earlier Trajanic ones. Behind this quay were two brick buildings. The southern building was 15 m in length with a row of *tabernae* facing away from the river. The northern building was excavated to a length of 20 metres but seems to have continued further north. It consisted of two separate rows of *tabernae*, one facing the river and the other away from it, with a corridor in between. This building overlaps with the southernmost part of the fragment 25a of the *Forma Urbis*, which also shows a building with the same layout (Figure 15.21 no. 24–25, 15.31; *CIL* VI 31552b, 40859, 40867, 40868; Caprino, 1948; Marcelli, 2014).

In 1935, excavations unearthed an inclined concrete quay along the right, Trastevere, side of the river, a few metres upriver from Ponte Testaccio. The inclined wall was supported by a series of barrel-vaulted rooms that had been filled with earth, similar in technique to the quay found downriver from Ponte Sublicio. In the 1970s, traces of a partially submerged ancient quay could be observed at low water upriver from Ponte Testaccio, which might have been the remains of the same quay. In the 1930s, behind the quay a broad road was found, presumably the Via Campana, lined with commercial buildings and a horrea in *opus quadratum*. Near this location a Tiber boundary stone set up in 8 BCE and renewed in 15 CE was found in 1700 (Figure 15.21 no. 26; *CIL* VI 31541o; Mocchegiani Carpano, 1975–76: 243; Mocchegiani Carpano, 1981: 151; Imperatori, 2003: 87, 97; Marcelli, 2014).

In 1909, in Via Niccolò Bettoni, on the right bank 150 m north of Ponte Testaccio, a cryptoportico in *opus reticulatum* with a floor in *opus spicatum* was found, which was dated by the excavator to the first century CE. The cryptoportico measured 4.2 m in width and 3.3 m in height. Another part of this cryptoportico was excavated in 2011, just a few metres away, and was dated by the excavators to the first century BCE or the first century CE. Downriver from the Ponte Testaccio, between the Via degli Stradivari and the Via Panfilo Castaldi, the remains of a cryptoportico were discovered in 1909, which was 26 m long parallel to the Tiber and 36 m long at right angles going away from the river. It was built using the same technique and with the same dimensions in width and height as the one discovered some 200 m to the north. Many amphorae and *dolia* were found stacked inside it. The two cryptoporticoes, found 200 m apart, were so similar that it must be conceived that they either formed part of a single, enormous structure, or were separate structures erected as part of the same building program (*Not. scav.* 1909: 444–7; *BCAR* 1909: 302–3; Marcelli, 2014).

About 60 m of ancient quay was demolished in 1941 on the right bank during the construction of Ponte Testaccio. A quay in blocks of tufo di Grotta Oscura was excavated in 1981 just downriver from the bridge. Test trenches in 2011–12 along the right bank at Lungotevere degli Artigiani, about 200 m downriver from the Ponte Testaccio, unearthed a concrete quay preserved for a length of at least 60 m at which point the test area was blocked by the Ponte Ferroviario to the south. In 1935, in the vicinity of this quay, a Tiber boundary stone of 161 CE was also discovered, and a statue base dedicated to Liber Pater at the *Cella Saeniana* (presumably a wine warehouse) by M. Lucceius Certus in the first half of the second century CE. This could have been the same Lucceius who might have built the Cella Lucceiana, mentioned at Portus Tiberinus in 161 CE (Figure 15.21 no. 27–28; *CIL* VI 40867; *AE* 1971: 29–30; Mocchegiani Carpano, 1981: 151; Chioffi, 1993b; Chioffi, 1993c; Imperatori, 2003: 128; Granino Cecere, 2008; Marcelli, 2014).

In 1981, during an enlargement of the Ponte Ferroviario, on the left bank a concrete quay faced with brick was observed. At this site, a Tiber boundary stone set up in 101 CE was found in 1886, and a stone erected in 161 CE was unearthed at this location in 1834. On the opposite, right bank, 20 m of an embankment or quay wall was found in 1981. It was unique among the recorded Tiber quays, built in *opus incertum* with stones in tufo dell'Aniene, and was dated by the excavators to the second century BCE. About 50 m south of this quay, in 1894, a Tiber marker was found which had been set up in 55–54 BCE and renewed in 15 CE, together with another erected in 121–124 CE, which was found in 1837 (Figure 15.21 no. 29–30; *CIL* VI 31540l, 31551, 31552c, 31554b; Mocchegiani Carpano, 1981: 152; Imperatori, 2003: 84, 123; Maiuro, 2008: 154, 128).

### Pietra Papa

At the ancient confluence of the Almo with the Tiber, just west of the Centrale Montemartini, the remains of a quay built in blocks of tufo together with 26 large marble blocks and columns and a river boundary stone of 55–54 BCE were found in 1897 and 1936. The quay was found about 50 m east of the current channel of the Tiber, which demonstrates the degree of movement that the river has experienced in this area since Antiquity. Just south of Centrale Montemartini, storage buildings in *opus mixtum* with floors in *opus spicatum* were excavated. An ancient bridge across the Almo was also recorded close to the harbour, west of the main Almo bridge used by the Via Ostiensis (Figure 15.21 no. 31; *CIL* VI 37025; *Not. scav.* 1897: 252; *BCAR* 1938: 299–300; Le Gall, 1953: 201; Quilici, 1996: 56; Marcelli, Matteucci and Sebastiani, 2009: 112–3).

At the Tiber bend at Pietra Papa, across the river from S. Paolo fuori le mura, major findings of port structures have been made. During drainage work in 1892, the finding of a long quay in *opus mixtum* with a stairway with

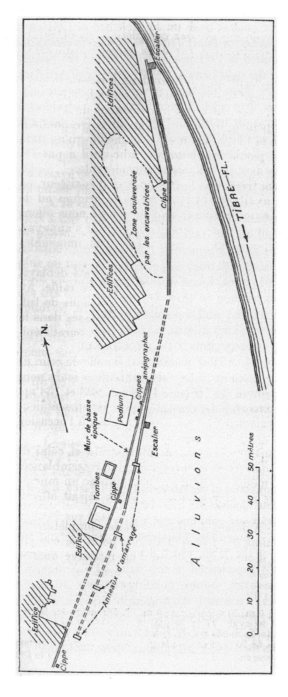

*Figure 15.32* Harbour excavated at Pietra Papa in 1938–40 (Le Gall, 1953: figure 8).

steps in travertine connecting the river to the top of the quay was recorded. Behind the quay were observed several ancient burial monuments. Major excavations were undertaken in 1938–40, which found an inclined concrete quay faced in *opus mixtum*, several large, perforated mooring stones in travertine, and two stairways in travertine 126 m apart that connected the river with the top of the quay. About 2 m from the edge of the quay, three river boundary stones of 8 BCE were found in situ, together with several other cippi without inscriptions. Marks from ropes on two of the inscribed stones showed that they had also been used as mooring stones. Near the southern end of the quay was found a boundary stone of the *Horti Cocceiani et Titiani*. A date in the reign of *Claudius* for the construction of the quay has been suggested. However, brickstamps from 123 and 134 CE seem to provide a construction date in the early second century CE (Figure 15.21 no. 32, 15.32–34; *CIL* VI 29772, 31541p, 40860, 40861; *BCAR* 1939: 185; Jacopi, 1940; Jacopi, 1943; Le Gall, 1953: 172, 196–7; 258–9, 271; Mocchegiani Carpano, 1975–76: 243–4; Castagnoli, 1980: 37–8; Palmer, 1981: 383; Taylor, 2000: 197–8; Imperatori, 2003: 164–5).

The total length of the excavated quay at Pietra Papa is debated. The excavator recorded a length of 206 m, but with the caveat that the ends of the quay had not been found neither upstream nor downstream. In 1947, Le Gall could follow the partly buried remains of the quay for 250 m, still with no signs of it terminating in either direction. Mocchegiani Carpano observed partially

*Figure 15.33* Aerial photograph of the excavations at Pietra Papa in 1940 (Palmer, 1981: figure 14).

submerged remains of the quay further north and noted a total length of at least 400 m for the quay. It might also be observed that the northern part of the quay was partially submerged, while the southern part was removed by up to 50 m from the present channel of the Tiber. This demonstrates, similar to the area at Centrale Montemartini, the scale of movement of the river since Roman times (Figure 15.34; Jacopi, 1943; Le Gall, 1953: 196; Mocchegiani Carpano, 1981: 152).

Behind the quay, a large villa has been excavated, which was built in the first century BCE and restored in the early second century CE. There were also two bathhouses and a large cistern, workshops, a marble fountain, and many remains of burials, some of them monumental. Surprisingly, there is no evidence of any large-scale buildings for commerce or storage. In contrast to the big ramps found at harbours in Testaccio, only two stairways, placed well apart, were found. Put together, this seems to indicate that the harbour at Pietra Papa was not used for the unloading or storage of merchandise (*BCAR* 1939: 216; Le Gall, 1953: 259; Palmer, 1981: 383–93). The large size of the quay at Pietra Papa points to an important role in the river traffic, but it is not possible to determine the function of the harbour without further excavation.

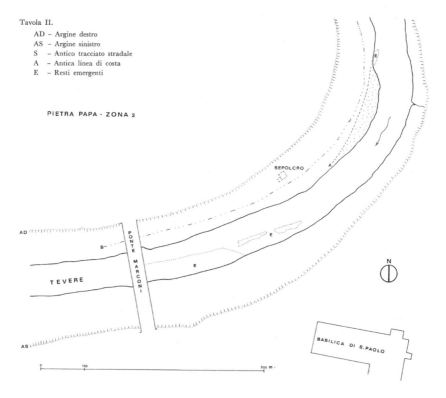

*Figure 15.34* Harbour remains at Pietra Papa and upstream from Ponte Marconi (Mocchegiani Carpano, 1975–76: tav. 2).

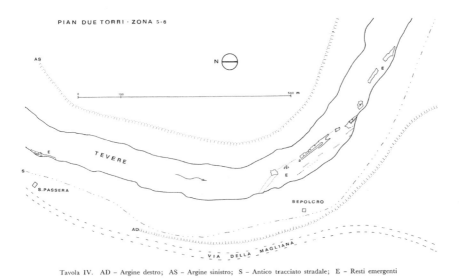

Tavola IV.  AD – Argine destro;  AS – Argine sinistro;  S – Antico tracciato stradale;  E – Resti emergenti

*Figure 15.35* Harbour remains at Santa Passera (Mocchegiani Carpano, 1975–76: tav. 4).

Some quays might have had other functions than unloading and storage, such as administrating different port functions, levying customs, and controlling the traffic (Palmer, 1981; see also Malmberg and Bjur, 2011).

In the 1970s, remains of a concrete quay were observed on the left bank just upriver from the later Ponte Marconi, in the middle of the present river due to the erosion and movement of the Tiber channel since Antiquity (Figure 15.21 no. 33, 15.34 Mocchegiani Carpano, 1975–76: 243; Castagnoli, 1980: 37; Mocchegiani Carpano, 1981: 152).

### Santa Passera

Downriver from the little church of S. Passera, in the next bend of the river, major remains of a port structure along the former right bank were found in the 1970s. Concrete quays faced with *opus reticulatum* or stone blocks were observed along the present right bank and then in the middle of the current river channel due to the erosion of the ancient right bank, for a total length of about 1,000 m. In the northern part, close to the Via Campana, one Tiber boundary stone set up in 55–54 BCE was found in c. 1820. Another two Tiber markers erected next to each other in 124 CE were discovered in the southern part of the harbour in 1915. The southernmost part, partially submerged in the river, was excavated for a length of about 100 m, which unveiled two parallel structures. Closest to the present right bank were a double row of wooden beams that formed rectangular sections, in which were found traces of concrete. Parallel to this structure, now in the middle of the river, was a concrete quay, 5.6 m thick, with a foundation of wooden piling. The concrete quay had an outer facing of stone slabs in tufo di Monteverde, and the top of the quay was paved with tufo and travertine. At regular intervals, holes for the insertion of mooring stones in travertine were found, one of which was still present at

*Figure 15.36* Mooring stone at harbour south of Santa Passera (Mocchegiani Carpano, 1975–76: figure 7).

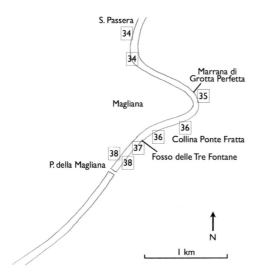

*Figure 15.37* Ancient harbours between Santa Passera and Ponte della Magliana. Numbers denote entries in Table 1 (by author).

the quay. Carbon testing of the wood piling gave a date for this quay in the period 30–70 CE. The wooden sections closer to the right bank was dated by the excavators as being slightly earlier, probably Augustan or late Republican in date. Parallel to the quays in the northern part of the port complex, which were still on land, traces of ancient road paving were found, which might have been the Via Campana. The excavations were, however, limited to the riverbank itself and did not go beyond the ancient roadway. Thus, they did not record any remains of storage or commercial buildings, which makes it impossible to know whether the port was used for these activities, although the excavators deemed it likely (Figure 15.35–36, 15.37 no. 34; *CIL* VI 31540m, 40865, 40866; *Not. Scav.* 1916: 318–20; Mocchegiani Carpano, 1975–76: 244, 250, 253, 257–61; Mocchegiani Carpano, 1981: 152: Maiuro, 2008: 154).

### *Porto della Pozzolana*

In 1897, at the southern end of the Prati di S. Paolo, near the mouth of the Marrana di Grotta Perfetta, and about 20 m removed from the present Tiber bank, an inclined concrete quay, 22 m long, faced with *opus mixtum* was found. The same construction technique was used as at the quays in Testaccio and Pietra Papa, and a dating in the early second century CE is probable. Parts of the same quay was found again during construction work in the 1980s (Figure 15.37 no. 35; *Not. scav.* 1897: 195–6; *BCAR* 1897: 275–6; Maiuro, 2008: 155).

Further south, the Tiber makes a bend around the Collina Ponte Fratta, at the location known until the middle of the nineteenth century as the Porto della Pozzolana, because of the pozzolana that was mined from the hillside and loaded onto river craft at this point. In 1891, between the river and the foot of the hill, a large concrete quay faced with brick for a length of at least 200 m was found. Facing the quay were warehouses and commercial buildings with doors framed in travertine and floors in black-and-white mosaics. Behind these buildings was excavated a long stretch of the Via Ostiensis, with road boundary stones still in situ. Other buildings were unearthed on the other side of the road in 1823 and 1882–83, among them a bath complex, habitations, and tombs, most of which were dated by the excavators to the first and second century CE, but also showed traces of a mid-Republican settlement. An altar dedicated to Silvanus could be dated to 147 CE. The quay could be followed, although much eroded by the river, until it reached the Fosso delle Tre Fontane, which the Via Ostiensis crossed on an ancient bridge. The port has been tentatively identified with the *Vicus Alexandri* mentioned by Ammianus Marcellinus as the location where the obelisk shipped to Rome in 357 was unloaded to be taken on the Via Ostiensis into the city (Figure 15.37 no. 36; Amm.Marc. 17.4.14; *Not. scav.* 1882: 67, 114, 413–4; *Not. scav.* 1883: 130–1; Lanciani, 1891; Mocchegiani Carpano, 1975–76: 246; Barbini, 2001).

Just downriver from the confluence of the Fosso delle Tre Fontane with the Tiber, 21 large blocks of marble were discovered during dredging work in the river in 1951. In the 1970s, columns in tufo were observed in the riverbed (Figure 15.37 no. 37; Mocchegiani Carpano, 1975–76: 246).

About 300 m upriver from the Ponte della Magliana, several large blocks in tufo di Grotta Oscura were observed in the 1970s along the right bank. The blocks seemed to form a structure that might have been a pylon for a bridge, either a road bridge or possibly an aqueduct bridge. A similar pylon could also be observed on the left bank. More blocks were found in the riverbed between the pylons during dredging work in the Tiber in 1957, together with a river boundary stone from 55–54 BCE. Remains of an ancient paved roadway were found along the right bank. Being the first obstacle across the river that met travellers moving upriver from Ostia or Portus, this point and Vicus Alexandri above it might have developed into a natural stopping point. It could also have functioned as a point of control for the river authorities, similar to Ponte Milvio at the northern entrance to Rome (Figure 15.37 no. 38; *CIL* VI 40856; Mocchegiani Carpano, 1975–76: 246–8; Mocchegiani Carpano, 1981: 153; Taylor, 2000: 212–25; Maiuro, 2008: 155–6).

## Problems in interpreting port development

The archaeological remains that have been found along the river listed above are proving challenging to interpret and understand. Securely dating the quays and their associated facilities is a big obstacle in providing an overview of port development and mapping quays in simultaneous use. Some quays can be dated with a high degree of certainty, due to brickstamps, inscriptions, or types of concrete facing. Stone quays are the hardest to date. Traditionally, type of stone has been used for approximate dating, with e.g. the use of tufo di Grotta Oscura, often seen as a sign of an early construction. The mole at Tor di Nona is a good demonstration of this debate, with suggestions ranging from the fourth century BCE onwards, due to the prominent use of Grotta Oscura in the structure. In fact, the use of hydraulic concrete in the foundation precludes a date before the 80s BCE, with an Augustan date the most probable. The use of stone in a quay could be used as an indication of an early construction date. However, I would argue that, after hydraulic concrete came into common use by the Augustan period, the choice to use *opus quadratum* could equally be a functional, rather than a chronological phenomenon, related to the types of craft that used the quays and the goods they handled.

The problems with dating quays and associated structures are most often due to the low quality of excavation and documentation along the river during the construction of the muraglioni in the late nineteenth and the first half of the twentieth centuries, often without the involvement of trained archaeologists. This lack of information makes it very difficult to piece together a coherent picture of the chronological development of the ancient port, and to what degree it was planned and coordinated by the Republican and imperial authorities. Indeed, the port at Rome has been described as built in a sporadic fashion and without a systematic plan (Aldrete, 2007: 193; Tuck, 2013: 243).

However, Bianchi has convincingly shown, through a study of construction technique and brickstamps, that a chronological–spatial approach is possible. She demonstrated that the quays excavated in Testaccio in 1868–70, 1979–84, and 1919–20 had been built starting with the southernmost quay in the first decade of the second century CE, then the middle complex in the 110s, with the northernmost quay built in 124–125 CE. This series of quays could, thus, be seen as a united project, contemporary with the construction of the new Trajanic harbour at Portus (Bianchi, 2007: 122–3). The quays at Ponte Testaccio, Pietra Papa, the northern part of the complex at Santa Passera, and the quays at Porto della Pozzolana also seem so similar in technique to the three quays in Testaccio that they, in my view, might be conceived as the product of the same construction programme.

## Two types of harbours at Rome

I argue that there were two types of harbours at Rome. One type was adapted to the river craft arriving from the inland regions to the city's northern harbours, while another type in the southern part of Rome catered to larger ships going upstream from Portus and Ostia or arriving directly from the Mediterranean.

The third-century CE inscription *codicari nav[iculari] infra pontem S[ublicium]* ("heavy river craft below the *Pons Sublicius*") should in my view be interpreted as confirmation that these heavy vessels, moving upriver from Ostia and Portus, were normally only used as far upriver as the first bridge over the Tiber, probably due to the difficulties in passing beneath Rome's bridges. Upriver from Rome, probably smaller and lighter river craft were used, which also provided the ability to navigate the upper reaches of the Tiber in the dry summer months. This division of the port at Rome to accept two types of river craft might be an important factor in the differences between the northern and southern harbours (*CIL* VI 1639, XIV 185, see also XIV 131; Le Gall, 1953: 257; Malmberg, 2015: 196).

Below the *Pons Sublicius*, Rome was dominated by large-scale harbours in concrete, with inclined walls. Mooring stones in travertine were provided to secure the heavy ships in the current, while stairs and ramps were constructed to handle the large and heavy loads. The northern harbours, on the other hand, were dominated by quays built in stone. They did not need large mooring stones or ramps, because the ships were light and the loads small. It is in the north that we find moles projecting into the river, at Tor di Nona and Ponte Milvio, or sheltered bays, such as downriver from Ponte Milvio and at the pre-Trajanic Portus Tiberinus, probably to provide protection against the river current for light, fragile craft.

There was a continued use of stone quays into the Imperial period at the northern harbours shown by the construction of adjacent warehouses that can be securely dated by concrete building technique, brickstamps and dedicatory inscriptions, and the continued demarcation of the quays by boundary stones into the second century CE. Stone might have continued to be the preferred building material, perhaps because of generous access to quarries north of Rome, where blocks could be shipped down the river with relative ease. The use of concrete might have been reserved for the southern harbours to facilitate a swifter construction pace in the large-scale projects that dominated in the southern part of Rome's river harbour during the Imperial period.

## Size of the port of Rome

We still lack an in-depth and up-to-date study of the port of Rome as a whole, although studies of high quality exist in different parts. Two recent studies present interesting estimates of the overall size of the port based on quay length, thus for the first time making it possible to compare the size of the harbours at Rome to other ancient ports. In a fundamental study, Keay has argued for the size of the principal areas of the river port in the Imperial period comprising the Portus Tiberinus and Testaccio areas, with quays running for a distance of 1.5 km, and a possible similar distance for quays on the Trastevere side. In an introduction to the river harbour at Rome by Rice, it is argued that the port had expanded by the second century CE to extend for approximately 2 km (Keay, 2012: 34, 39; Keay, 2015: 50; Rice, 2018: 206).

In these estimates, harbours at e.g. Ponte Milvio, Monte Secco, Prati di Castello, Pietra Papa, Santa Passera, or Porto della Pozzolana are not included, which seem to implicitly limit the "principal port area" described to within the area enclosed by the future Aurelian wall. The port area of Rome was never limited by this wall in Antiquity, neither before nor after its construction. Indeed, the absolute majority of harbour structures found at Rome in the Imperial period lie outside the line of the Aurelian wall. Neither did the construction of the Aurelian wall seem to generally have had much impact on the use of extramural port facilities, with most of them probably being in use until the early fifth century. The demise of most of the harbour, both intra- and extramural, could rather be seen as related to the diminished population of Rome in the course of the fifth century (Malmberg, 2015: 196–201).

Rather than inventing an artificial limit for the harbour area, we should let the physical remains of the port define its extent. Based on the review above of known quays and associated harbour features along the Tiber, it can be concluded with a fairly high degree of certainty that the port area of Rome comprised the length of the Tiber from Ponte Milvio in the north to just upriver from Ponte della Magliana in the south, a distance of 18 km. This is the area demarcated already by the first river boundary stones erected in 55–54 BCE and subsequently kept up by the curators during the following 250 years.

The importance to include the outlying areas of the port has also been underlined by several Italian scholars, most recently Maiuro who writes that "Il dato storico e topografico che maggiormente sorprende è la serie di scali portuali attrezzati e di grandissime dimensioni lungo il tratto che va dalla basilica di S. Paolo alla Magliana" (Maiuro, 2008: 154). My view of the size of the port area of Rome is also clearly reflected by Maischberger who concludes that "Der gesamte Tiberverlauf von der heutigen Magliana ... bis zum *Pons Milvius* war ein durchgehender Flußhafen" (Maischberger, 1997: 107; see also e.g. Castagnoli, 1980: 37; Pavolini, 2000: 169, 174).

The total length of archaeologically known quayside length that I have been able to map within the 18 km between Ponte Milvio and Magliana comprises c. 5,265 m (see Table 15.1). To this number, excavated quays with an unknown length have to be added. It also does not take into account known port facilities where we lack physically confirmed quays, such as at Portus Tiberinus. It can be argued that some of the structures identified as quays might rather have been river embankments, but if such a structure is accompanied by stairways, ramps, mooring rings, paved squares, or warehouses, it would most probably have to qualify as a quay.

All the known quays were, of course, not in use simultaneously. At the probable peak of the port of Rome, in the middle of the second century CE, if we subtract quays that were at this time out of use, converted, or replaced by later structures, the total length of known quays might still be around 4,644 m. To this number we can add several instances of probably contemporary but unmeasured quays, and quays potentially destroyed or not yet discovered. The actual length of quays in second-century Rome was, thus, most probably much larger.

There is, thus, no doubt that Rome had a very large port in the Imperial period. By mapping the quay lengths of Rome's port as a whole, it becomes meaningful to compare Rome to other ancient ports and contextualize its size. This is, however, a blunt measure of port capacity and needs to be complemented by a variety of other factors. Keay estimated that the quay length at Ostia was c. 2,400 m, while that of Portus was 13,890 m (Keay, 2012: 43–4). In a similar endeavour, Hurst compared the quays at Carthage (c. 2000–2,500 metres) with those at Portus (Hurst, 2010: 65–6). Blackman has made similar comparisons between the quay lengths at the Herodian harbours at Caesarea (1,100 m), Leptis Magna and Terracina (both 1,200 m), Hellenistic Delos (1,700 m), and Hellenistic Alexandria (3,000 m; Blackman, 2008: 650; see also Malmberg, 2016 for a study of Ravenna's port). The criteria applied in mapping quays at these different ports may vary considerably.

## Conclusions

The most important contribution this study makes to understanding Rome as a port city is by providing a detailed overview of the known port facilities along the whole area between Ponte Milvio and Magliana. To view the area between these two points as the port area of Rome is not a new opinion, but I hope that this study is able to argue convincingly for these limitations. The contribution provides an overview of the known length of river quays at Rome. This in turn allows a comparison with other ancient port cities where similar studies have been made. It can be concluded that the size of the port of Rome is larger than have been suggested in recent studies and probably was one of the major ports of the Roman Empire.

This study is a first attempt at providing a fuller understanding of the port of Rome. Future contributions will also need to address how the port worked, how it was integrated with the overall infrastructure of the city and its hinterland and its context within the imperial network. The Tiber harbours were an integral and fundamental part of the urban structure and development of the city of Rome, which we cannot hope to understand fully until we include the port in studies of the Urbs.

*Table 15.1* Tiber quays at Rome

| Map no. | Location, bank | Length | Quay technique | Related finds | Date |
|---|---|---|---|---|---|
| 1 | Ponte Milvio, right | c. 400 | Tufo and travertine blocks | Storage and commercial buildings, boundary stone, Via Flaminia | ? |
| 2 | Ponte Milvio, left | c. 400 | Tufo and travertine blocks | Storage and commercial buildings | ? |
| 3 | Ponte Milvio, left | c. 15 | Mole, tufo dell'Aniene and travertine blocks | Boundary stones | 109 BCE or later |
| 4 | Ponte Milvio, left | 85 | Opus reticulatum | Sheltered bay, storage buildings, boundary stone | Augustan |
| 5 | Ponte del Risorgimento to Ponte Nenni, right | c. 850 | Tufo and travertine blocks | Storage buildings, large mound of broken pottery, boundary stones | Second c. CE? |
| 6 | Via R. Stern, left | 135 | Opus reticulatum | Storage buildings, boundary stones, Via Flaminia | ? |
| 7 | Ripetta, left | c. 50 | Travertine and other blocks | A port according to Tacitus, boundary stone | Existed by 20 CE |

*Table 15.1* Cont.

| Map no. | Location, bank | Length | Quay technique | Related finds | Date |
|---|---|---|---|---|---|
| 8 | Piazza Nicosia, left | ? | Travertine blocks | A port according to texts, mound of pottery | ? |
| 9 | Ponte Cavour to Ponte Umberto, right | ? | Tufo and other blocks | Large paved square, buildings, many boundary stones | ? |
| 10 | Tor di Nona, left | 50 | Mole, tufo di Grotta Oscura and dell' Aniene, travertine, concrete foundation | Mound of pottery | Augustan? |
| 11 | Ponte Vittorio to Ponte Amedeo, right | c. 300 | Opus reticulatum | Boundary stones | Imperial period |
| 12 | Villa Farnesina, right | c. 150 | Probable quays, not confirmed | Wine warehouse, inscription, several boundary stones | 102 CE |
| 13 | Ponte Fabricio, left | 30 | Tufo blocks | Boundary stones | 62 BCE? |
| 14 | Portus Tiberinus, left | ? | No quays found | Port according to literary sources, horrea, wine warehouse, inscriptions, boundary stones | Rebuilt c. 110 CE |
| 15 | Emporium, left | 25 | Tufo di Grotta Oscura and travertine blocks | Port according to Livy | 193 BCE onwards |
| | Infra pontem Sublicium | | | | |
| 16 | S. Maria in Capella, right | ? | Opus latericium, travertine mooring stones | Horrea, paved square, inscriptions, boundary stones | Imperial period |

(*continued*)

*Table 15.1* Cont.

| Map no. | Location, bank | Length | Quay technique | Related finds | Date |
|---|---|---|---|---|---|
| 17 | Ripa Grande, right | 15 | Tufo blocks | Storage or commercial building, dolia, inscriptions, boundary stone | ? |
| 18 | Ponte Sublicio, left | 60 | Tufo di Grotta Oscura blocks, stairs in peperino, travertine mooring stones | Via Ostiensis | Second–first c. BCE? |
| 19 | Ponte Sublicio, left | 75 | Opus mixtum | Storage building, Via Ostiensis | 120s CE |
| 20 | Porticus Aemilia/ Navalia, left | 487 | Opus incertum | Naval shipsheds according to literary sources, later storage and commercial | Second c. BCE |
| 21 | Lungotevere Testaccio, left | 125 | Opus mixtum, paving and mooring stones in travertine | Storage and admin. buildings, crypto-portico, open square | First c. CE, rebuilt 110s CE |
| 22 | Marmorata, left | 130 | Opus mixtum, ramps, travertine mooring stones | Boundary stone, huge amount of marble blocks and plaques, storage | First decade second c. CE |
| 23 | South of Porta Portese, right | 25 | Opus reticulatum, stairway and mooring stone in travertine | Horrea, paved square, portico, Via Campana, boundary stone | Mid-second c. CE |
| 24 | Ponte Testaccio, left | 54 | ? | Boundary stone | |
| 25 | Ponte Testaccio, left | 42 | Opus mixtum, stone paving | Storage or commercial buildings, boundary stones | Imperial period |

*Table 15.1* Cont.

| Map no. | Location, bank | Length | Quay technique | Related finds | Date |
|---|---|---|---|---|---|
| 26 | Ponte Testaccio, right | ? | Opus mixtum | Commercial buildings, cryptoportico, Via Campana, boundary stone | Imperial period |
| 27 | Ponte Testaccio to Ponte Ferroviario, right | 60 | Tufo di Grotta Oscura blocks | | ? |
| 28 | Ponte Testaccio to Ponte Ferroviario, right | 60 | Concrete | Wine warehouse, inscription, boundary stone | Imperial period |
| 29 | Ponte Ferroviario, left | ? | Opus latericium | Boundary stones | Imperial period |
| 30 | Ponte Ferroviario, right | 20 | Opus incertum in tufo dell'Aniene | Boundary stones | Second c. BCE? |
| 31 | Centrale Montemartini, left | ? | Tufo blocks | Storage buildings, boundary stone, marble blocks, Via Ostiensis | ? |
| 32 | Pietra Papa, right | c. 400 | Opus mixtum, stairways and mooring stones in travertine | Boundary stones | Hadrianic |
| 33 | Ponte Marconi, left | ? | Concrete | | ? |
| 34 | Santa Passera, right | c. 1,000 | Opus reticulatum and concrete faced with slabs of tufo di Monteverde, travertine mooring stones | Via Campana, boundary stones | north second c. CE, south 30–70 CE |
| 35 | Marrana di Grotta Perfetta, left | 22 | Opus mixtum | | Second c. CE |
| 36 | Collina Ponte Fratta, left | c. 200 | Opus latericium | Port according to Ammianus, storage/ commercial buildings, Via Ostiensis | Imperial period |

(*continued*)

*Table 15.1* Cont.

| Map no. | Location, bank | Length | Quay technique | Related finds | Date |
|---|---|---|---|---|---|
| 37 | Fosso delle Tre Fontane, left | ? | No quays found | Marble blocks | ? |
| 38 | Ponte della Magliana | ? | No quays found | Road or aqueduct bridge?, boundary stone, roadway right bank | ? |
| | Total known quay length: | c. 5,265 ms | The quay length in probable use by mid-second century CE: | c. 4,644 m | |

## Acknowledgements

I wish to express my gratitude to Frank Vermeulen and Arjan Zuiderhoek, for inviting me to contribute to the conference "Space, movement and the economy in Roman cities in Italy and beyond", and the subsequent volume this spawned. I also want to thank all the other participants for their presentations and lively discussions during those days in September 2018. Astrid Capoferro, Manuela Michelloni, and Mona Johansen deserve my deepest thanks for all their help. I also want to extend my gratitude for the support I have received from Paolo Liverani, Giorgio Filippi, Renato Sebastiani, and Alessia Contino. The financial support of the Meltzer Foundation made possible my research visits to Rome, for which I am grateful.

## References

Aguilera Martín, Antonio. *El Monte Testaccio y la llanura subaventina*. Rome: Escuela Española, 2002.

Aldrete, Gregory. *Floods of the Tiber in ancient Rome*. Baltimore: Johns Hopkins University Press, 2007.

Ammerman, Albert. "The east bank of the Tiber below the island: two recent advances in the study of early Rome." *Antiquity* 92 (2018): 398–409.

Barbini, Palmira Maria. "Alexandri vicus." Pages 42–3 in *Lexicon topographicum urbis Romae. Suburbium*. Edited by Adriano La Regina, vol. 1. Rome: Edizioni Quasar, 2001.

Bianchi, Elisabetta. "I bolli laterizi del porto fluviale romano di lungotevere Testaccio." *BCAR* 108 (2007): 89–124.

Blackman, David. "Harbors." Pages 638–70 in *The Oxford handbook of engineering and technology in the classical world*. Edited by John Peter Oleson. Oxford: Oxford University Press, 2008.

Borsari, Luigi. "Di un'epigrafe spettante alla arginatura delle ripe del Tevere." *BCAR* 17 (1889): 165–72.

Burgers, Gert-Jan et al. "The afterlife of the Porticus Aemilia." *Fasti Online* (2018) (www.fastionline.org/docs/FOLDER-it-2018-400.pdf)

Buzzetti, Carlo. "Portus Tiberinus." Pages 155–6 in *Lexicon topographicum urbis Romae*. Edited by Eva Margareta Steinby, Vol. 4. Rome: Edizioni Quasar, 1999.

Caprino, C. "Roma. Cippi terminali del Tevere rinvenuti presso il ponte d'Africa (Testaccio)." *Notizie degli Scavi*. (1948): 139–40.

Carettoni, Gianfilippo et al. *La pianta marmorea di Roma antica*. Rome: Comune di Roma, 1960.

Castagnoli, Ferdinando. "Installazioni portuali a Roma." *MAAR* 36 (1980): 35–42.

Chioffi, Laura. "Cella Civiciana." Page 256 in *Lexicon topographicum urbis Romae*. Edited by Eva Margareta Steinby, vol. 1. Rome: Edizioni Quasar, 1993a.

Chioffi, Laura. "Cella Lucceiana." Page 257 in *Lexicon topographicum urbis Romae*. Edited by Eva Margareta Steinby, vol. 1. Rome: Edizioni Quasar, 1993b.

Chioffi, Laura. "Cella Saeniana." Page 257 in *Lexicon topographicum urbis Romae*. Edited by Eva Margareta Steinby, vol. 1. Rome: Edizioni Quasar, 1993c.

Claridge, Amanda. *Rome: an Oxford archaeological guide*. Oxford: Oxford University Press, 2010.

Coarelli, Filippo. "Horrea Lolliana." Page 43–4 in *Lexicon topographicum urbis Romae*. Edited by Eva Margareta Steinby, vol. 3. Rome: Edizioni Quasar, 1996.

Coarelli, Filippo. "Horrea Cornelia?" Pages 41–6 in *Res bene gestae*. Edited by Anna Leone, Domenico Palombi and Susan Walker. Rome: Edizioni Quasar, 2007.

Colini, Antonio Maria. "*Il porto fluviale del Foro Boario.*" *MAAR* 36 (1980): 43–53.

Cozza, Lucos and Tucci, Pier Luigi. "Navalia." *Archeologia Classica* 57 (2006): 175–202.

Cressedi, Giulio. "I porti fluviali in Roma antica." *Rend. Pont.* 25–26 (1949–51): 53–65.

Cressedi, Giulio. "Roma. Sterri al Lungotevere Testaccio." *Not. scav.* (1956a): 19–52.

Cressedi, Giulio. "Magazzini fluviali a Marmorata." Pages 113–21 in *Amor di Roma*. Rome: Te Roma Sequor, 1956b.

De Caprariis, Francesca. "I porti della città nel IV e V secolo d.C." Pages 216–34 in *The transformations of Urbs Roma in late antiquity*. Edited by William Harris. Portsmouth, RI: Journal of Roman Archaeology, 1999.

Fant, Clayton. "Rome's marble yards." *JRA* 14 (2001): 167–91.

Fedeli, Marta. "Le presenze archeologiche lungo le rive: approdi e navigazione a valle di Roma." in *CIRILI*. Edited by Giulia Vertecchi and Catherine Virlouvet. Rome: École française de Rome, 2013. (https://romatevere.hypotheses.org/436#_ftn5)

Filippi, Giorgio and Liverani, Paolo. "Un nuovo frammento della Forma Urbis con il Circus Flaminius." *Rend. Pont.* 87 (2014–15): 69–87.

Flambard, Jean-Marc. "Deux toponymes du Champ de Mars: ad Ciconias, ad Nixas." Pages 191–210 in *L'Urbs: espace urbain et histoire*. Rome: École Française de Rome, 1987.

Frutaz, Amato Pietro. *Le piante di Roma*. Rome: Istituto di Studi Romani, 1962.

Galliazzo, Vittorio. *I ponti romani*. Treviso: Canova, 1994.

Gatti, Guglielmo. "Saepta Julia e Porticus Aemilia nella Forma severiana." *BCAR* 62 (1934): 123–49.

Gatti, Guglielmo. "L'arginatura del Tevere a Marmorata." *BCAR* 64 (1936): 55–82.

Gazda, Elaine. "Cosa's hydraulic concrete." Pages 265–90 in *The maritime world of ancient Rome*. Edited by Robert Hohlfelder. Ann Arbor: University of Michigan Press, 2008.

Granino Cecere, Maria Grazia. "Saeniana cella." Page 33 in *Lexicon topographicum urbis Romae. Suburbium*. Edited by Vincenzo Fiocchi Nicolai, vol. 5. Rome: Edizioni Quasar, 2008.

Gregori, Gian Luca. "Documenti epigrafici dal contesto di largo Perosi in Campo Marzio: due nuovi termini del Tevere e altri reperti." Pages 443–51 in *Campo Marzio. Nuove ricerche*. Edited by Fedora Filippi. Rome: Edizioni Quasar, 2015.

Harmansah, Ömur. "Emporium." Page 118 in *Mapping Augustan Rome. Edited by Elisha Dumser*. Portsmouth, RI: Journal of Roman Archaeology, 2002.

Hurst, Henry. "Understanding Carthage as a Roman port." *Bollettino di archeologia online* 1 (2010): 49–68.

Imperatori, Paolo. *Contributi per la carta archeologica del comprensorio Portuense-Magliana*. Rome: Università di Roma "La Sapienza", 2003.

Jacopi, Giulio. "Scavi e scoperte presso il porto fluviale di S. Paolo." *BCAR* 68 (1940): 97–107.

Jacopi, Giulio. "Scavi in prossimità del porto fluviale di San Paolo località Pietra Papa." *Monumenti antichi* 39 (1943): 1–178.

Keay, Simon. "The port system of imperial Rome." Pages 33–67 in *Rome, Portus and the Mediterranean*. Edited by Simon Keay. London: British School at Rome, 2012.

Keay, Simon. "I porti di Roma." Pages 41–61 in *Nutrire l'impero. Storie di alimentazione da Roma e Pompei*. Edited by Claudio Parisi Presicce and Orietta Rossini. Rome: L'Erma di Bretschneider, 2015.

La Rocca, Eugenio. *La riva a mezzaluna. Culti, agoni, monumenti funerari presso il Tevere nel Campo Marzio occidentale*. Rome: L'Erma di Bretschneider, 1984.

Lanciani, Rodolfo. "Miscellanea topografica. Il Vicus Alexandri." *BCAR* 19 (1891): 217–22.

Lanciani, Rodolfo. *Forma Urbis Romae*. Milan: Hoepli Editori, 1901.

Le Gall, Joël. *Le Tibre: fleuve de Rome dans l'antiquité*. Paris: Presses Universitaires de France, 1953.

Le Gall, Joël. *Il Tevere: fiume di Roma nell'antichità*. Rome: Edizioni Quasar, 2005.

Lega, Claudia. "Ciconiae." Pages 267–69 in *Lexicon topographicum urbis Romae*. Edited by Steinby, Eva Margareta, vol. 1. Rome: Edizioni Quasar, 1993.

Lo Cascio, Elio. "The Population." Pages 139–53 in *A companion to the city of Rome. Edited by Claire Holleran and Amanda Claridge*. Hoboken: Wiley-Blackwell, 2018.

Lonardi, Anna. *La cura riparum et alvei Tiberis. Storiografia, prospografia e fonti epigrafiche*. Oxford: Archaeopress, 2013.

Lott, Bert. *The neighborhoods of Augustan Rome*. Cambridge: Cambridge University Press, 2004.

Maischberger, Martin. "Marmorata." Page 223 in *Lexicon topographicum urbis Romae*, vol. 3. Rome: Edizioni Quasar, 1996.

Maischberger, Martin. *Marmor in Rom. Anlieferung, Lager- und Werkplätze in der Kaiserzeit*. Wiesbaden: Reichert, 1997.

Maischberger, Martin. "Tiberis." Pages 69–73 in *Lexicon topographicum urbis Romae*, vol. 5. Rome: Edizioni Quasar, 2000.

Maiuro, Marco. "Tiberis." Pages 148–56 in *Lexicon topographicum urbis Romae. Suburbium*. Edited by Vincenzo Fiocchi Nicolai, vol. 5. Rome: Edizioni Quasar, 2008.

Malmberg, Simon. "Triumphal arches and gates of piety at Constantinople, Ravenna and Rome." Pages 150–89 in *Using images in late antiquity*. Edited by Stine Birk, Troels Myrup Kristensen and Birte Poulsen. Oxford: Oxbow, 2014.

Malmberg, Simon. "Ships are seen gliding swiftly along the sacred Tiber. The river as an artery of urban movement and development." Pages 187–201 in *The moving city. Processions, passages and promenades in ancient Rome*. Edited by Ida Östenberg, Simon Malmberg and Jonas Bjørnebye. London: Bloomsbury, 2015.

Malmberg, Simon. "Ravenna: naval base, commercial hub, capital city." Pages 323–46 in *Ancient ports: the geography of connections*. Edited by Kerstin Höghammar, Brita Alroth and Adam Lindhagen. Uppsala: Uppsala University Press, 2016.

Malmberg, Simon and Bjur, Hans. "*Movement and urban development at two city gates in Rome: the Porta Esquilina and Porta Tiburtina*." Pages 361–85 in *Rome, Ostia and Pompeii: movement and space*. Edited by Ray Laurence and David Newsome. Oxford: Oxford University Press, 2011.

Marcelli, Marina. "Lungotevere tra Ponte Testaccio e Ponte dell'Industria. Dati archeologici sulle rive del Tevere (2011)." *BCAR* 115 (2014): 366–73.

Marcelli, Marina, Matteucci, Renato and Sebastiani, Renato. "Il sistema informativa territoriale per la gestione del patromonio storico-archeologico del quartiere Ostiense-Marconi." Pages 105–17 in *Suburbium II. Il suburbio di Roma dalla fine dell'età monarchica alla nascita del sistema delle ville ( V-II secolo a.C. )*. Edited by Rita Volpe. Rome: École française de Rome, 2009.

Marchetti, Domenico. "Prati di Castello." *Not. Scav.* (1890): 82–88.

Marchetti, Domenico. "Di un antico molo per lo sbarco dei marmi riconoscuito sulla riva sinistra del Tevere." *BCAR* 19 (1891): 45–60.

Mari, Zaccaria. "Nova et Arruntiana cellae vinariae." Pages 118–19 in *Lexicon topographicum urbis Romae*. Suburbium vol. 4. Rome: Edizioni Quasar, 2007.

Meijer, Cornelis. *L'arte di restituire à Roma la tralasciata navigatione del suo Tevere*. Rome: Stamperia Varese, 1683.

Meneghini, Roberto. "Scavo di lungotevere Testaccio." Pages 433–*41* in *Roma. Archeologia nel centro*, vol. 2. Rome: De Luca, 1985.

Meneghini, Roberto. "Lungotevere Testaccio." *BCAR* 91 (1986): 563–86.

Meneghini, Roberto. "La Forma Urbis e le altre cartografie marmoree di Roma antica alla luce delle ultime ricerche e scoperte." *BCAR* 117 (2016): 179–91.

Mocchegiani Carpano, Claudio. "Rapporto preliminare sulle indagini nel tratto urbano del Tevere." *Rend. Pont.* 48 (1975–76): 239–62.

Mocchegiani Carpano, Claudio. "Indagini archeologiche nel Tevere." *Archeologia laziale* 4:5 (1981): 142–55.

Mocchegiani Carpano, Claudio. "Tevere. Premesse per una archeologia fluviale." *Bollettino d'Arte* (1982): 150–66.

Mocchegiani Carpano, Claudio, Meneghini, Roberto and Incitti, Mauro. "Lungotevere Testaccio." *BCAR* 91 (1986): 560–95.

Muzzioli, Maria Pia. "Sui portici raffigurati nella lastra di via Anicia." Pages 219–37 in *Res bene gestae*. Edited by Anna Leone, Domenico Palombi and Susan Walker. Rome: Edizioni Quasar, 2007.

Muzzioli, Maria Pia. "Le piene del Tevere e la sistemazione delle ripae a Roma: il contributo delle pianta di via Anicia." Pages 389–407 in *Societé et climats dans l'empire romain*. Edited by Ella Hermon. Naples: Editoriale scientifica, 2009.

Muzzioli, Maria Pia. "La riva destra del Tevere tra i ponti Cavour e Margherita." Pages 163–74 in *Humanitas. Studi per Patrizia Serafin*. Edited by Alessandra Serra. Rome: Universitalia, 2015.

Muzzioli, Maria Pia. "Le ripae di Roma in età imperiale: qualche evidenza dalla pianta marmorea severiana." *Riparia* 4 (2018): 28–45.

Palmer, Robert. "Customs on market goods imported into the city of Rome." *MAAR* 36 (1980): 217–33.

Palmer, Robert. "The topography and social history of Rome's Trastevere (southern sector)." *Proceedings of the American Philosophical Society* 125 (1981): 368–97.

Pavolini, Carlo. "Il fiume e i porti." Pages 163–81 in *Roma antica*. Edited by Andrea Giardina. Rome: Laterza, 2000.

Pisani Sartorio, Giuseppina, Colini, Antonio Maria and Buzzetti, Carlo. "Portus Tiberinus." *Archeologia Laziale* 7.2 (1986): 157–97.

Quilici, Lorenzo. "Il Tevere e l'Aniene come vie d'acqua a monte di Roma in età imperiale." *Archeologia Laziale* 7:2 (1986): 198–217.

Quilici, Lorenzo. "I ponti della via Ostiense." *Atlante tematico di topografia antica* 5 (1996): 51–79.

Rankov, Boris. "Roman shipsheds." Pages 30–54 in *Shipsheds of the ancient Mediterranean*. Edited by David Blackman and Boris Rankov. Cambridge: Cambridge University Press, 2013.

Rice, Candace. "Rivers, roads, and ports." Pages 199–217 in *A companion to the city of Rome*. Edited by Claire Holleran and Amanda Claridge. Hoboken: Wiley-Blackwell, 2018.

Rickman, Geoffrey. *The corn supply of ancient Rome*. Oxford: Clarendon Press, 1980.

Rodríguez-Almeida, Emilio. *Forma urbis marmorea. Aggiornamento generale* 1980. Rome: Edizioni Quasar, 1980.

Rodríguez-Almeida, Emilio. "Cellae vinariae Nova et Arruntiana." Page 259 in *Lexicon topographicum urbis Romae*, vol. 1. Rome: Edizioni Quasar, 1993.

Rodríguez-Almeida, Emilio. *Formae urbis antiquae. Le mappe marmoree di Roma tra la repubblica e Settimio Severo*. Rome: École française de Rome, 2002.

Stevens, Saskia. *City boundaries and urban development in Roman Italy*. Leuven: Peeters, 2017.

Taylor, Rabun. *Public needs and private pleasures. Water distribution, the Tiber river and the urban development of ancient Rome*. Rome: L'Erma di Bretschneider, 2000.

Tucci, Pier Luigi. "Eight fragments of the mable plan of Rome shedding new light on the Transtiberim." *PBSR* 72 (2004): 185–202.

Tucci, Pier Luigi. "The Pons Sublicius: a reinvestigation." *MAAR* 56–57 (2011–12): 177–212.

Tucci, Pier Luigi. "La controversa storia della 'Porticus Aemilia'." *Archeologia classica* 63 (2012): 575–91.

Tuck, Steven. "The Tiber and river transport." Pages 229–45 in *The Cambridge companion to ancient Rome*. Edited by Paul Erdkamp. Cambridge: Cambridge University Press, 2013.

Virgili, Paola. "Opere in arginatura a Ponte Milvio." *Archeologia laziale* 5 (1983): 124–26.

Virgili, Paola. "Ponte Milvio. Studi e restauri." *Quaderni del centro di studi per l'archeologia etrusco-italica* 11 (1985): 145–48.

Watson, Alan, ed. *The digest of Justinian*. Philadelphia: University of Pennsylvania Press, 2009.

# 16 Space, accessibility and movement through the *Portus Romae*

*Simon Keay, Peter Campbell, Katherine Crawford and Maria del Carmen Moreno Escobar*

## Introduction (Simon Keay)

Ports are often studied as monumental settings for commercial interactions between shippers and merchants. Such approaches prioritize basic commercial activities over the physical constraints offered by ports, and they overlook issues related to accessibility to them by sea, land and river as well as movement within and between harbours and the built-up areas of ports. In doing this, there is a danger that one adopts too simplistic an understanding of ports, of their role in the articulation of Roman Mediterranean commerce and, arguably, also of its scale. The objective of this chapter, therefore, is to explore the issue of movement through ports from the perspective of the evidence from the *Portus Augusti* during the high empire, as a corrective form. As the maritime port of Imperial Rome, it holds lessons for other ports across the Mediterranean basin.

Since coastal progradation since antiquity has ensured that Portus now lies entirely inland, previous scholarship has focused upon its topography, principal buildings and their development by means of geophysics and excavations. Geoarchaeological studies of the sedimentary sequences of its basins and canals have added important information about the main water spaces. Notwithstanding the importance of these studies, the authors of this article recognize the need to experiment with more formal approaches to the analysis of the terrestrial and maritime spaces relating to the port. The aim of the chapter, therefore, is to attempt this by drawing upon several key data sets created over the past 14 years. The first is the first overall map of the port derived from an interpretation of an extensive magnetometry survey undertaken between 1998 and 2004 (Keay *et al.* 2005). The second is a computer graphic model of the same area, which incorporates the results of excavations at the centre of the port undertaken between 2007 and 2015 by the Portus Project (Earl *et al.* 2020). The third is a geographical information system (GIS) which comprises key elements of the first two data sets, as well as Portus Project results of a geophysical survey of the Isola Sacra, and information relating to published sites along the Tiber between Portus and Ponte Galeria.[1]

This chapter begins by considering the current state of knowledge relating to the topography of Portus and its related water spaces. It then reflects upon the likely impact of diurnal wind patterns and currents on the approaches to, and within, the harbours and canals. This is followed by access and network analyses of the built spaces of the port together with cumulative viewshed analyses of the broader riverine environment of the port as a way of exploring its relationship to both Ostia and Rome. The chapter concludes with a brief assessment of the implications that these kinds of approach hold for our understanding of the accessibility and permeability of Portus to commercial traffic, its ability to process ships, boats and their cargoes on a large scale and, ultimately, its success as a hub for the import of food supplies to Rome and for the export and redistribution of a range of other goods to the Mediterranean at large.

## The topography of Early Imperial Portus (Simon Keay)

Portus has the advantage of being one of the more intensively studied Roman ports in the Roman Mediterranean as well as being the main maritime hub for the empire as a whole (Figure 16.1). Unlike Ostia, it was not an 'urbanized' port with a large residential population. It was instead an artificial complex

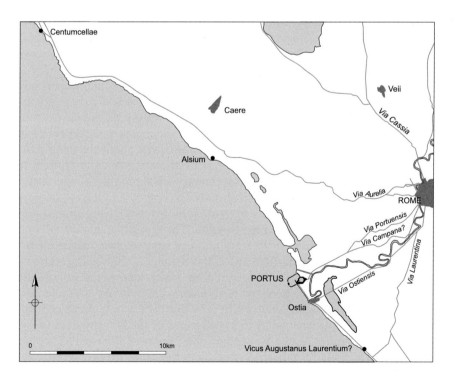

*Figure 16.1* Map showing the location of Portus (Portus Project).

built by the emperor, whose role and topography were structured around its primary functions of anchorage, transhipment, storage and the movement of boats between Ostia and Rome. By the later second century CE, therefore, it was dominated by its three great water spaces. The earliest, the Claudian basin, encompassed c. 200 ha. with a maximum depth of 9 m and was enclosed by two massive *opus caementicium* moles that projected out into the sea. Ships entered it on either side of the artificial island that lay between them and supported the monumental lighthouse or *pharos* (Morelli *et al.* 2011; Figure 16.2). This basin is generally understood to have acted primarily

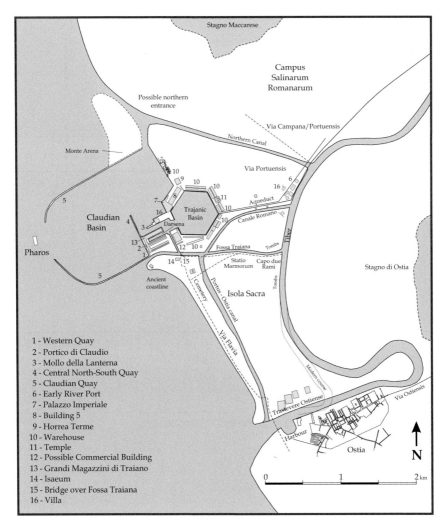

*Figure 16.2* Overall map of Portus and the Isola Sacra and sites mentioned in the text (P. Wheeler).

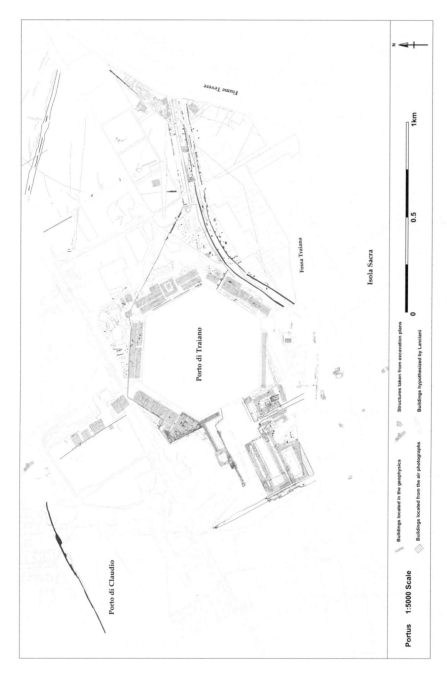

*Figure 16.3* Interpretation of the geophysical results from the 1998–2004 magnetometer survey of Portus (Keay *et al.* 2005: Pull-Out 2).

*Figure 16.4* Reconstruction of the Trajanic basin Portus in the later second century CE, with part of the Claudian basin in the foreground (Portus project/ Artas Media).

*Figure 16.5* Aerial view of the centre of the archaeological site of Portus (S. Keay/ Portus Project), with the Trajanic basin in the foreground and the Claudian basin in the mid and background; the northern mole runs across the top right of the picture (S. Keay/Portus Project).

as a space for the anchorage of sea-going ships, within which their cargoes would have been transhipped on to lighters. A smaller 1.07 ha. rectangular basin (Darsena) with a depth of c. 7 m and of similar date was located a short distance to the south-west side of the Claudian basin and was presumably used by lighters (*naves caudicariae*) ultimately bound for Rome. A third basin which encompassed 32 ha. and was 7 m deep was situated immediately to the east of the Claudian basin (Keay *et al.* 2005). Construction of this and its associated buildings had begun during the reign of the emperor Trajan in c. 112 CE and had probably finished shortly after his death in 117 CE.

All three harbour basins were connected to each other as well as to the Tiber and the sea by a network of six canals. These were

(1) the Fossa Traiana (the modern Canale di Fiumicino) that ran between the Tiber at Capo Due Rami along the south side of the Claudian basin and into the sea;
(2) the Northern Canal that ran from the Tiber into the sea to the north of the port;
(3) the Canale Romano that ran from the Tiber past the hexagonal basin and flowed into the Fossa Traiana (Salomon *et al.* 2014);
(4) the Canale Traverso that ran northwards from the Fossa *Traiana* past the Darsena and into the centre of the port;
(5) the Canale di Imbocco del Porto di Traiano that ran from the Claudian basin past a 300-m north-south mole and along an east mole (Molo della Lanterna) at the centre of the port and into the hexagonal basin (Keay *et al.* 2005). Lastly, Portus as a whole was connected with Ostia by a large canal
(6) that ran south across the Isola Sacra from the Fossa Traiana (Germoni *et al.* 2011; Salomon *et al.* 2016b).

The high degree of connectivity across the port that was afforded by these canals was complemented by a network of roads that ran along the river to Rome by means of the Via Campana/Portuense and across the Isola Sacra by the Via Flavia.

The most important administrative buildings in the port lay on a narrow isthmus of land that at once defined the northern side (II) of the hexagonal basin and the south side of the Claudian basin and which was thus central to the whole port. The first was the Palazzo Imperiale, a three-storey imperial palace or villa complex covering 3.5 ha. that overlooked the hexagonal and Claudian basins (Keay *et al.* 2011; Keay 2020). It was on a truly palatial scale, with a magnificent colonnade gracing its western facade, a series of luxuriously appointed and architecturally innovative peristyles and a bath block on its first floor together with mosaic floors, marble sculptures and monumental inscriptions. It seems likely that the complex was used by the emperor on those occasions when he passed through the port. The discovery of a small amphitheatre dating to 200–220 CE on the eastern side of the complex, similar to those known from later second century CE imperial palaces and *villae* near Rome, is perhaps an argument that it may have been visited by one of the Severan emperors. It was also an administrative complex probably used in the early third century CE by the *procurator portus utriusque*, an official under the direct authority of the *praefectus annonae*. The staff working for this official probably registered incoming and outgoing ships, allocated mooring bays, coordinated the unloading and registration of cargoes, allocated warehouse space and collected customs dues (*portoria*) from the incoming ships. The discovery at the Palazzo Imperiale of a lead stamp of the kind used to track marble blocks from imperial quarries destined for Rome is indicative of this. Immediately adjacent to the south-west side of the Palazzo Imperiale was the Grandi Magazzini di Settimio Severo, a late second century CE complex that is usually interpreted as a large warehouse (Rickman 1971: 128–30). However, its unusual architectural form and central position within the port suggest that its role was closely associated with those of the Palazzo Imperiale (Keay 2020). To the north-east of the Palazzo Imperiale was a building identified as the Imperial *navalia*. This was a massive (240 m × 58 m) late Trajanic complex that was probably originally designed to harbour official galleys (Keay *et al.* 2012) but which was converted entirely or in part to provide storage space in the later second century CE.

A recent survey suggests that by the later second century CE, there may have been c. 145,072 m$^2$ of warehouse space at the port (Keay *et al.* 2005: table 9.1). Warehouses around the sides of the hexagonal basin were oblong in plan, unlike those at Ostia and Rome, an unusual arrangement that suggests that the auctions and other buying and selling activities that often took place in the courtyard of warehouses at Ostia did not occur here. It was possibly during the Severan period that an internal wall pierced periodically with narrow doorways was built around the hexagonal basin, presumably to keep track of the transfer of unloaded cargoes from ships on the quaysides to the oblong warehouses behind them. The best known warehouses are the so-called Grandi Magazzini di Traiano located between the Fossa Traiana, Canale Traverso and Canale di Imbocco del Porto di Traiano (Bukowiecki *et al.* 2012, 2013; Bukowiecki 2016). This gigantic complex covered c. 10 ha., of which nearly 7 ha. was dedicated to storage. It comprised three parallel blocks of building on two stories connected by a fourth block of rooms along the maritime facade that was fronted by a long colonnade (Portico di Claudio). Initially constructed under Claudius, its original layout around the so-called Strada Colonnata was retained until the late second and early third centuries CE when, like other warehouses at Portus and Ostia, it was reorganized to significantly increase its capacity at the expense of its monumental and aesthetic appearance; intercolumnar spaces were systematically blocked to enable storage in circulatory spaces. Furthermore, wide quays were added along all of those sides of the complex in contact with water.

Grain was one of the main cargoes imported to Portus and stored in these warehouses, and by the later second century CE, the shipments transported from Alexandria and Carthage were a key annual event in the calendar of the port. The many Egyptians commemorated on inscriptions from both Portus and Ostia (Keay 2010) were probably involved in this. Similarly, the names of African families from Ostia are probably to be explained by their involvement in importing grain from *Africa Byzacena*. Analysis of ceramics from excavations at Portus confirms the importance of North African imports, with olive oil, fish sauce and other products not only from *Africa Byzacena* but also from the ports of *Oea* and *Leptis Magna* in *Tripolitania*. Olive oil from *Hispania Baetica* was another major import in the Severan period, the volume of which can be gauged by the surviving dated amphora sherds at Monte Testaccio in Rome. Imports of fish sauce from *Baetica*, wine from *Gallia Narbonensis*, *Hispania Tarraconensis* and different parts of the eastern Mediterranean, while also present in volume, were perhaps less important (Keay 2012b).

There is as yet little evidence as to the whereabouts of the port these commodities may have been stored. As at Ostia and Rome, one cannot assume that any one warehouse would always store the same commodity, and one should also expect that whatever was stored one year could have been very likely changed in the next, particularly if a warehouse was rented out to different merchants. While grain is usually assumed to be the principal commodity stored in them, it is only those lying on side III of the hexagonal basin and the Grandi Magazzini di Traiano which provide good evidence for this, with the widespread evidence of raised floors (Bukowiecki *et al.* 2018).

The south-eastern side (III) of the hexagon seems to have played a key role in the movement of cargoes through the port. The warehouses here ran parallel to the Canale Romano, enabling cargoes unloaded from sea-going ships in the hexagonal basin to be stored in them before being transhipped onto smaller river boats or barges bound for Rome. It is unclear whether all cargoes unloaded in the hexagonal basin would have passed through here, and if so, how they might have been easily moved to here from their original point of storage. Marble followed a different trajectory. It was deposited in the marble yards (*statio marmorum*) on the southern bank of the Fossa Traiana, prior to being moved upriver to the marble yards (*statio marmorum*) at Rome from the late first century CE onwards (Pensabene 2007: 389–430). Analysis of the surviving material found at the site in the late nineteenth century points to the presence of a wide variety of material from the east Mediterranean and to a lesser extent from North Africa.

Aside from the buildings related to commercial activities and storage, our knowledge of other kinds of building is limited. The western side (II) opposite the entrance to the hexagonal basin (V) was dominated by a temple within a monumental *temenos* that was fronted by a large statue of the emperor Trajan (Keay *et al.* 2005: Area 12, figure 5.34). This complex lay on axis to the entrance to the basin and was flanked on each side by double pairs of oblong warehouses. There may also have been a sanctuary to Serapis on or near the central isthmus (Keay 2020), and an *Isaeum* to the south of the Fossa Traiana.

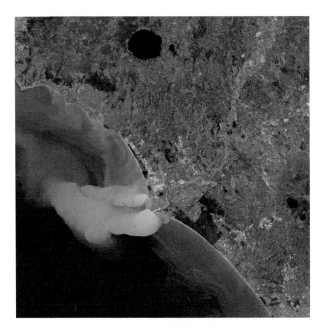

*Figure 16.6* Satellite image of sediment being discharged from the Tiber mouth and the Canale di Fiumicino (Fossa Traiana) (north) during a flood in 2019, illustrating the force of the currents (European Space Agency).

There is no evidence for the civic buildings that abound at Ostia, although the area lying between the Trajanic basin, the Fossa Traiana to the south, and the Canale Trasverso was occupied by some kind of administrative complex, a *statio* of the *vigiles* stationed at the port and perhaps some residential buildings. On the south side of the Fossa Traiana, however, there was a settlement comprising baths (Veloccia Rinaldi and Testini 1975) and a cemetery (Necropoli di Porto; Baldassare 1978) that was in use into the fourth century CE. A further cemetery lay in the flat land between the hexagonal basin and the Tiber to the east (Keay *et al.* 2005: 288–90; 295).

## Modelling the water spaces (Peter Campbell)[2]

### *Approaching the harbour*

Most research on ancient navigation focused on open waters, where mariners relied on winds, water colour or marine species to negotiate the seascape. Indeed, the seascape would have been important on the approach to Portus, as mariners would have noticed a change in colour and turbidity of the water as they approached the coast, due to Tiber sediments flowing into the sea. During normal conditions, the change might be relatively close to shore, while at times of flood and increased sediment transport, the change would be evident from miles away. This would indicate periods when the harbour might not be functioning properly, prior to the ship actually arriving in the port.

The *pharos* at Portus was the primary navigational feature on the coast. It would have increased visibility for those at sea and in the harbour and would have also guided movement across the open waters around the harbour. During the day, smoke from the lighthouse would be the first visual reference for sailors seeking the harbour's location. Significantly, the behaviour of the smoke would indicate wind dynamics at the entrance to the harbour, informing mariners both entering and exiting the Claudian basin as well as lightermen and stevedores as to what vessels would do when entering with the wind. Serving as a wind compass in this way, it would be possible for harbour workers to know whether ships could travel from the north or south on any given day. The lighthouse also indicated where vessels should anchor by night, usually offshore unless gale conditions forced them to seek shelter in the harbour. The offshore anchorage would have probably been off the bank near Ostia, as this would provide ships with a fast hold on the seafloor as well as sea room to drift if they lost this.

### Constraints upon movement within the harbour

Movement within a harbour's water spaces is contingent on environmental forces, making movement complex to model and different from that on land. While the water spaces may appear to be wide open, watercraft can only move at certain angles to marine and atmospheric forces. Sea transport, therefore, involves routes that are more complex than roads but nevertheless follow prescribed paths. A maritime perspective of Portus can, therefore, contribute to our understanding of flows and rhythms within the harbour.

The key parameters for understanding movement within the water spaces at Portus are the sea state and vessel propulsion. The sea state is a product of winds and currents, which are the natural factors for the movement of any watercraft. Previous research has modelled the currents at Portus by means of a two-dimensional (2D) wind-driven current model, with the aim of understanding sediment transport and deposition (Millet *et al.* 2014). However, movement within harbours would have been dictated by wind as well as currents operating within three-dimensional (3D) space. Since the built environment of any harbour is intended to mitigate natural forces, it is particularly important to factor 3D buildings into the consideration of winds within a port. While the natural environment of Portus has changed considerably since antiquity, wind patterns in the Mediterranean generally remain the same (Murray 1987; Morton 2001: 5–6), particularly in terms of direction and duration.

A proxy of the Portus environment was simulated by means of a general model of wind direction. This is illustrated in Figures 16.7 and 16.8, and drew upon data from the Italian *Aeronautica Militare Centro Operativo per*

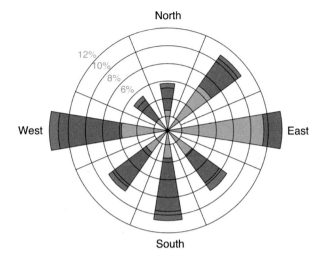

*Figure 16.7* Relative wind direction and frequency from the Fiumicino weather station 1958–1979 (Noli *et al.* 1996: 289, figure 1b).

*la Meteorologia* from 2008 to 2018, the Mediterranean Pilot wind rose and data from the 1940s to 1980s that were collated from ten weather stations along the Tyrrhenian coast (Noli *et al.* 1996). However, wind strength cannot be incorporated into the model in a straightforward way as it may have changed since the Roman period. Since the built environment at Portus was created to manipulate the sea state, modelling movement through Portus also incorporates 3D data relating to the harbour buildings and associated infrastructure.[3] Autodesk's wind modelling software Flow Design was used to understand the wind dynamics within Portus, with particular reference to the enclosed Trajanic basin (Figures 16.9 and 16.10). Volumetric models of the buildings belonging to each phase of the port were imported into the software, and changes to the localized wind patterns were documented. While the wind modelling does not directly provide information about the movements of ships and boats within the basins, the localized wind patterns would have had an effect upon how they used it. It is hoped that further 3D modelling of this kind will refine these results.

The other consideration in sea state is the current. There are longshore currents that run north along the coast (Heikell and Heikell 2015: 30), but the harbour moles would have deflected these away from the inner space of the harbour. Today, the most significant currents in the area are the Tiber outflow, through the Canale di Fiumicino, which continues the line of the Roman Fossa Traiana, and the section of the Tiber that flows into the sea just west of Ostia Antica, the Fiumara Grande (Figure 16.6). These currents measure 3–4 knots W or NWN depending on the orientation of the outlet (Heikell

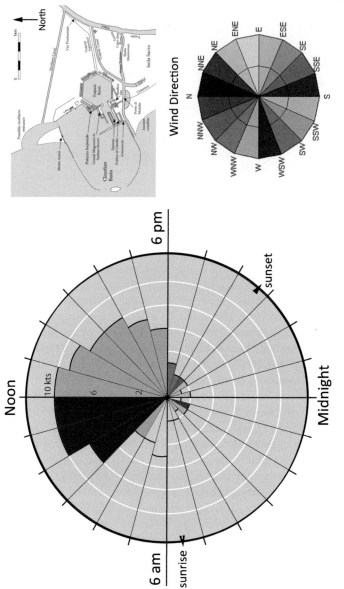

*Figure 16.8* Wind strength at Portus by hour over the course of 1 June 2017, with an inset map of Portus and its orientation (P. Campbell after *Aeronautica Militare Centro Operativo per la Meteorologia* and Keay 2016: figure 2).

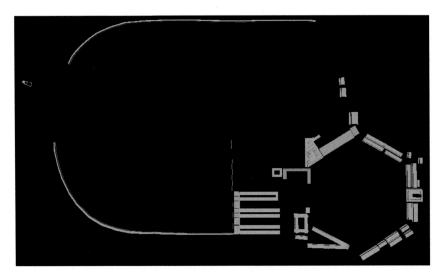

*Figure 16.9* Computer graphic model of the main volumetric elements of Portus during the later second century CE (Portus Project/Artas Media).

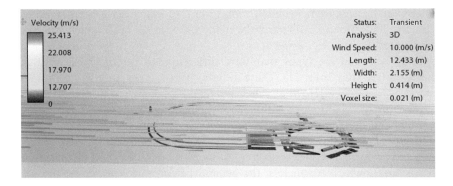

*Figure 16.10* Wind model of Portus showing an SW wind during the later second century CE (P. Campbell).

and Heikell 2015: 167), though sometimes reaching 6–7 knots during flood. They could prove problematic during an onshore wind, such as that coming from the W or WSW, in which contrary winds and currents cause the sea to build up and form a confused sea state in the area where they meet. This still occurs today at the mouths of the Canale di Fiumicino and the Tiber (Heikell and Heikell 2015: 167) and may well also have occurred at the entrance to the Claudian as in the manner represented by Danti in his 1582 reconstruction in the Gallerie delle Carte Geografiche in the Vatican. In such conditions, a ship would require good speed to enter the port through the breaking waves and make headway against the contrary current. By contrast, vessels exiting with the NE wind would have travelled with the current. Ongoing research into the prevailing winds operating off the Roman coastline suggests that this entrance was especially prone to wind and waves in the summer months, which might have affected the regularity of ships being able to enter the Claudian basin at the height of the main sailing season.[4] Noli and Franco modelled wave period and strength entering the Claudian basin from the open sea from the predominant direction, demonstrating that the sea state inside the basin would be affected by the exterior wave forces (2009: 198–199).

The second set of parameters to consider is the propulsion of the vessels. In the Roman Mediterranean, the sail and the oar were two means by which this was achieved. The merchant vessels serving Portus would have been fitted with square, sprit- or lateen sail (Whitewright 2018). Traditionally it has been argued that these sail types allowed for movement at different angles to the wind, but recent comparisons have shown that the square sail could point as close as 60–65° into the wind and the lateen as close as 56–67° (Whitewright 2011: 14). This performance was also limited by the sea state, with a rougher sea state resulting in decreased performance into the wind (Whitewright 2011: 7). The closeness of these angles indicates that performance of this rig was not significantly different, but there must be some underlying importance. The lighters (*naves caudicariae*), several of which have been excavated (Boetto 2008; Boetto 2011) and the many other small craft which will have frequented Portus (e.g. *lenunculus, linter, ratiaria, ratis, scapha, utricularius, stlatta*), featured rig types that were differentiated on the basis of their function (Arnaud 2011: 21). These different vessel types are not fully understood by researchers. However, mosaics and reliefs depicting Roman harbours show large merchant ships with square rigs, and occasionally *artemons*, and lighters and small craft with lateen or spritsail rigs (Figure 16.11). Hull form and sailing rig combined to suit a vessel's work environment and would have affected performance in certain conditions, although the extent of this is currently unknown. Nevertheless, the general performance of the square and lateen sails offers us an insight into movement within Portus.

Rowing provided a means of moving a craft much closer to the wind than sailing. Depending on the design of a vessel's bow, it could be rowed directly into the wind. Vessels could be rowed themselves, or they could be moved through towing by a tugboat and, more labour-intensively, through warping (Casson 1995: 336). Merchant ships, even the larger ones, were probably fitted with oars for moving around a harbour (Arnaud 2011: 159). Reliefs, such as one from the Isola Sacra (Casson 1995: figure 193), and textual sources show that tugboats operated with regularity at Portus. It should also be noted that not every merchant ship would traverse the basins to reach the quayside, but that much of their cargo could have been unloaded onto lighters while they were at anchor in the basins. It should be noted, however, that vessels at

*Figure 16.11* Mosaic from the Piazzale delle Corporazioni at Ostia depicting two types of vessels and rigs. A sea-going square rigged with an artemon is represented on the right, and a coastal or riverine vessel with what is likely a staysail is illustrated on the left (Source: Becatti 1961: pl. 181 no. 106).

anchor are also subject to the sea state (Greenhill and Morrison 1995: 32), meaning that the behaviour of ships moored in the Claudian basin would change based on the wind.

All of these factors would have influenced movement within and between the Claudian basin, Darsena, Trajanic basin and the internal canals, and along the other external canals to the Tiber and Ostia. The different options did not complicate movement but maximized them at different times and in different conditions. It needs to be remembered that a built harbour is an attempt to control the environment, and that Portus is perhaps the most ambitious example in the ancient world. Its various water spaces served different conditions and vessels. Juvenal (Satires XX.75–82) describes a ship entering Portus, which provides us with a concise image of different stages of its passage:

> At last the vessel enters the harbour of Ostia, passing/ The Tyrrhenian lighthouse, gliding between those massive/ Piers that reach out to embrace the deep, and leave/ Italy far behind – a man-made breakwater/ That no natural harbour could equal. The captain nursed his lame/ vessel through to the inner basin, its waters so still/ That a rowboat could safely ride there.
>
> (Green 1998: 243)

The movement of the watercraft described above corresponded to the sequence of open water, outer basin and inner basin. Furthermore, the flows of people across the port scape – lightermen, stevedores, measurers, administrators, shipwrights and so forth – would have been broadly conditioned by them. The built environment of the harbour mitigated the natural forces, even though it could not always prevent them. This is most evident in the raging tempest of 62 CE, in which some 200 ships were sunk *in portu* (Tacitus *Annals* XV.18.3), a term generally taken to refer to the Claudian basin. Similarly, certain vessels would have been able to operate in particular conditions, while others would not.

### Movement through the water spaces

Entering the Claudian basin, vessels would moor or make their way to the quay. The basin must have been filled with hundreds of moorings. The Claudian basin served as protection from waves and swell, which would have allowed the cargoes of merchant ships to be unloaded on to lighters as well as offering offshore anchorage for ships awaiting clearance or provisions. However, the vessels anchored or moored in the basin were still susceptible to the winds. Shifting winds would have pivoted the vessels around their moorings, while strong winds could drag the moorings. Either scenario had the potential to cause vessels to foul and become damaged.

Vessels making their way to quays would have made use of visual transects to navigate to their prescribed destination. Depictions of Roman harbours are filled with monuments such as arches, columns and statues as well as architecture such as lighthouses and temples. The Torlonia relief (Lugli and Filibeck 1935: Tav.1) is a case in point. While these features played a role in expressing political and religious statements, they are rarely discussed in terms of their likely role within the navigational landscape of harbours. Navigation with visual transects would have been critical at Portus and other harbours, requiring bearings into and out of the harbour as well as to reach specific areas and berths. Safe bearings composed of visual transects, such as lining up the lighthouse and temple, or a column and a rooftop, would be part of the shared navigational knowledge within the maritime community.

The Darsena was integral to the first phase of the harbour and the most sheltered area within the Claudian basin. The buildings around its waters protected vessels from the west winds, though northern or eastern winds would have confined vessels within their berths. While the basin provided shelter from one aspect of the sea state, the waves, the Darsena would have offered limited shelter from the other, the wind. However, it was the Trajanic basin that was more specifically designed to address the wind. Although Roman knowledge of wind dynamics is not well known, it is likely that the size of the hexagonal basin, as well as the size of the buildings bordering it, was designed to create a microclimate conducive to the safe anchorage of large, unwieldy ships. Today it is understood that wind passing over an object does not regain its strength until it has travelled a length 30 times the height of the object (Gooley 2016: 123). The diameter of the Trajanic basin is 715.5 m or radius of 357.8 m. At this scale, an obstacle standing at a height of 24 m would keep the entire basin from experiencing the full strength of the wind. The Palazzo Imperiale and the Imperial *navalia* had an estimated height of c. 18 m, which would have been effective in obstructing much of the wind entering the basin. Even though they may not have understood wind dynamics in the modern sense, the architects and engineers who designed and built the Trajanic port did a laudable job in creating a protected harbour.

The emerging picture, therefore, is that the Claudian basin was effective at breaking waves but left vessels susceptible to the winds. The Trajanic basin, by contrast, offered protection from both waves and wind. The larger sea-going ships that arrived entered it would have either anchored at the centre of the basin before moving to an assigned berth along the quay or remained at the centre, with their cargo being unloaded onto lighters for carrying to the quays.[5] Evidence for the latter can be seen on the bottom right hand corner of the Torlonia relief, where a *saccarius* is represented unloading from a small boat which is adjacent to a seagoing ship, and whose bow faces the quay and is fastened by a mooring ring.

From the Trajanic basin, movement in the harbour shifted from the marine spaces to roads, warehouses, canals and the Tiber. Cargoes would have been transferred to the Caudicarii who were in charge of towing vessels along the banks of the river. Propulsion within these spaces would have been more controlled and achieved by means of rowing, poling or towing by ox or humans or – in the case of cargoes coming downstream to Portus from Rome – the current.

### Harbour rhythms

While wind and sea state would have been the most significant features affecting the movement of ships and boats within the constricted spaces of the port, daylight, human behaviour and seasonal environmental changes would have also been contributory factors, with activity following certain rhythms over the course of a day, month or season.

On the daily scale, the key rhythms for the movement of ships in and out of a port are set by the winds (Figure 16.8). For example, at Fiumicino near Portus on the 1 June 2017, the sun rose at 5:37 A.M. It was followed by the diurnal wind, which was driven by temperature differences between the land and sea. This morning offshore wind came from ENE at 4–5 knots. After the ground temperature warmed, the diurnal wind stopped and was followed by a strong 6–10 knot WSW wind from 9 AM to 12 PM, which shifted to a W wind which gradually declined from 10 to 4 knots over the course of the afternoon until 6 PM. The wind then dropped to a 2- to 3-knot WNW and NW wind until sunset at 8:39 PM, which then shifted to a 2-knot NE wind until midnight.

At Portus, the WSW mid-morning wind is aligned with the orientation of the Claudian and Trajanic basins, which in antiquity would have maximized manoeuvrability for vessels that could operate from 0 to 67° to the wind. Changes in the morning offshore and evening onshore winds such as these would have clearly dictated the periods and types of activity for Roman mariners as they do today (Morton 2001: 51). Indeed, the discovery of a Roman wind rose (anemoscope) of second century CE date just outside the Porta Capena at Rome (Dilke 1987: 249), close to the Via Appia, is a clear evidence that Roman travellers would have factored wind patterns into their planning when setting out on maritime voyages from Portus, Ostia and other ports along the Tyrrhenian coast. The hours of daylight and darkness were also important to the rhythms of maritime activity at Portus, with certain activities, such as loading and unloading, shipbuilding or repair being based upon hours of daylight.

The movement of ancient ships and boats against river currents was another significant consideration, as has been demonstrated in reference to the Nile (Cooper 2011). Portus would have also been affected by the seasonal behaviour of the Tiber, as is evident from satellite imagery of the Tiber in flood (Figure 16.6). Whereas the Nile reaches its peak discharge during the summer, this happens in the Tiber between November and February (Aldrete 2007: 66). As discussed above, the average current of 3–4 knots would have been difficult enough for river boats with a contrary wind, but when the river was in flood with a current of 6–7 knots, movement upriver would have become significantly harder. Given that ancient vessels travelled at c. 4–6 knots with a favourable wind (Casson 1995: 282), a strong current would have stymied movement, and the only option would have been to row, tow or wait at anchor.

Much has been made of the timing of the ancient sailing season (Beresford 2012; Morton 2001; Casson 1995) in discussing ancient shipping patterns. Described as early as the seventh BCE by Hesiod in his *Works and Days* (II 618–694) and also discussed by Vegetius in the late fourth century CE (4.39), the so-called sailing season from May to September is often assumed to have been one of the primary rhythms for maritime trade. Sailing almost certainly occurred outside of this period, but it is often thought that it would have only been contemplated if there was a desperate need, it was undertaken for an important purpose or it was the choice of uncautious mariners (Tchernia 2016: 217). One has to assume, therefore, that at the very least there would have been a high and a low season for shipping to and from Portus.

## Movement around the harbour scape (Katherine Crawford)

Two related methods were used to assess accessibility to, and mobility through, built up space in the area lying to the east of the Claudian basin at Portus. Both were undertaken with reference to a palimpsest plan that was based upon the interpretation of the 1998–2004 magnetometry survey of the port (Keay *et al.* 2005: pull-out; Figure 16.3), with a few minor adjustments. When the results are interpreted in the light of our archaeological understanding of the site, they provide new insights into relationships between the distinctive hexagonal spatial configuration of the Trajanic basin and possible human interactions. The first method was based upon space syntax, which was developed to quantify the relationships that exist between the built environment and human phenomena (Hillier and Hanson 1984). The second method was urban network analysis (Sevtsuk and Mekonnen 2012), a form of network analysis that is used to question how the built environment of the port may have structured movement-based interactions.

### *Axial analysis*

Axial line analysis, a subset of space syntax, was used to identify potential movement pathways throughout the landscape immediately surrounding the Trajanic Basin. The analysis, undertaken within the software DepthMap, consisted of first generating an axial map by drawing the fewest and longest lines that pass between convex spaces of the built environment of the port. A convex space can be considered as any open space in which all points in space are visible from all other points within the space. At Portus, these spaces are identified as the fewest and largest areas in which a straight line can be drawn without encountering any obstacles, delineated by the Northern Canal, the Canale Romano and the Portus to Ostia Canal, lying to the south of the port. The axial graph is subsequently reduced to represent the fewest number of axial lines. Using this plan, two specific axial measurements were calculated, integration and choice, in order to understand how routes were connected and movement may have flowed through the port landscape.

Integration is generally used to measure the overall accessibility of a singular axial street segment when compared to an entire movement network (Hillier *et al.* 1993). It is calculated by determining how well connected each axial line is to every other line within the network, at both a global and a local scale. The results of applying this to Portus were interpreted in the light of how accessible different areas and buildings were within the port scape and suggest that the entire port was relatively well-integrated (Figure 16.12). The thickest and darkest lines show potential movement areas with the highest integration values, while the thinnest and lightest lines indicate the most segregated movement spaces. Taken together, they suggest that the most highly integrated areas were concentrated along the northern side of the Trajanic basin. While these results in part reflect the large amount of open space within this area, they also indicate a high degree of interaction along the line of northern warehouses and with the temple. The calculation of integration using a global radius (radius-n) illustrates highly integrated movement areas travelling past the warehouses located on the north and north-east sides of the Trajanic Basin (Figure 16.12 Left). Local integration, representing smaller scale movement, is calculated using radius-2. This measures how connected each axial line is to two other axial lines within the graph. It indicates that the

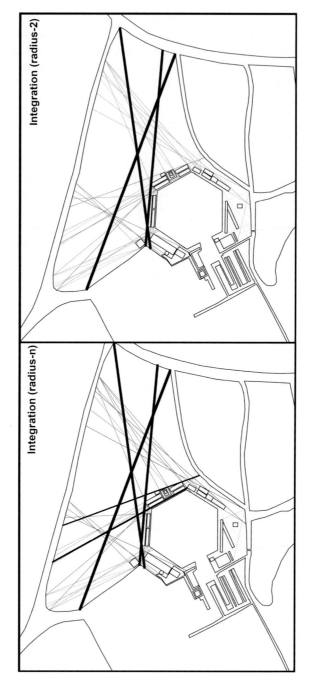

*Figure 16.12* Left – axial analysis graph showing global integration measurements (radius n). Right – axial analysis graph showing local integration measurements (radius 2). The areas with the highest integration are represented by the thickest and darkest lines.

most integrated movement routes were along the line of the warehouses lying alongside the northern side of the hexagonal basin (Figure 16.12 Right).

The calculation of choice, shown in Figure 16.13, illustrates the primary pedestrian movement routes that are shaped by movement through the port scape. Choice is estimated by measuring the shortest paths from all origins and destinations within the axial network. The calculation is undertaken at both a global and a local scale. The results provide an indication as to which movement pathways would have seen the greatest amount of use. The movement areas with the highest choice value are indicated by the thickest black lines and the lowest by the thinnest grey lines. The results of both global and local choice values indicate that the central isthmus would have seen the highest movement potential. A particularly marked pathway of movement ran eastwards past the northern end of the imperial *navalia*; another significant one extended north-wards along the isthmus from the Palazzo Imperiale (Figure 16.13, Left). The global choice visualization also indicates a high probability that movement occurred between the western side of the Canale Traverso, past the warehouses located at the southern end of the basin and ending at the southern mouth of the Canale Romano. At a more local scale, the results highlight the probability of movement travelling past the temple, which is consistent with the integra-tion calculations (Figure 16.13, Right). Both of the choice calculations suggest that there would have been less movement passage within the southern area of the Trajanic basin. Furthermore, when compared to the results of integra-tion, the choice calculations indicate that there was almost no potential for movement over the Ponte Matidia that would have crossed the Fossa Traiana and connects Portus to the Isola Sacra. This indicates that movement within the port was clearly structured around the Trajanic Basin.

The space syntax metrics of integration and choice both provide a gen-eral insight into the way in which the space surrounding the Trajanic basin would have structured movement patterns. Both sets of results indicate that the warehouses located at the northern area of Portus, as well as the Palazzo Imperiale and imperial Navalia, would have seen the highest degree of movement interactions.

### *Urban network analysis*

In order to understand how the various known buildings may have shaped movement patterns through the area around the Trajanic basin, urban net-work analysis (Sevtsuk and Mekonnen 2012) was applied to the plan of the port. This technique computed closeness and betweenness centrality measures, which are equivalent to the space syntax analyses discussed above. Most spa-tial networks are calculated using two network elements, which in the case of a street network includes street segments and intersections (Porta, Crucitti and Latora 2006). Urban network analysis, by contrast, is calculated using a tripartite network that factors buildings into the calculations and computes their positions along street networks.

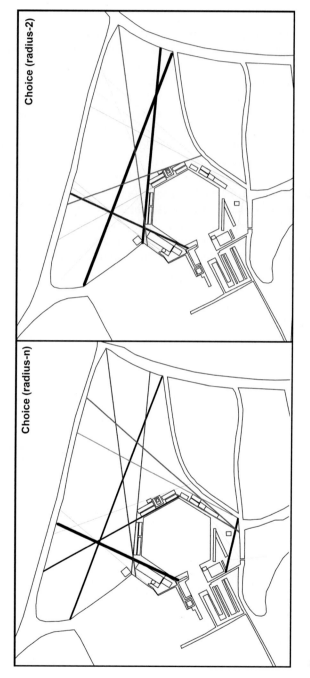

*Figure 16.13* Left – axial analysis graph showing global choice measurements (radius n). **Right** – axial analysis graph showing local choice measurements (radius 2). The areas with the highest choice value are represented by the thickest and darkest lines.

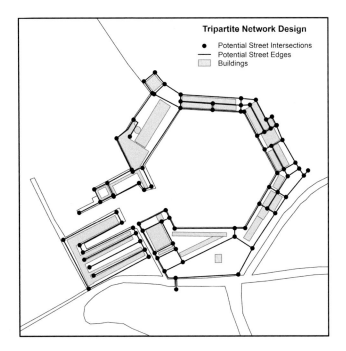

*Figure 16.14* Map showing the tripartite network design of urban network analysis.

In order to apply urban network analysis at Portus, a hypothetical street network had to be created (Figure 16.14). Consequently, all possible routes past the different buildings surrounding the Trajanic Basin were identified by following the axial graph generated during the space syntax analysis. The known existence of the Ponte Matidia over the Fossa Traiana was the justification for allowing for movement southwards out of the port into the Isola Sacra.

Two urban network analysis measures were calculated, closeness and betweenness centrality. The former measures how close a building lies to all other buildings within the surrounding built environment, following the shortest path along a network graph (Sabidussi 1966). Betweenness centrality, by contrast, allows one to visualize which buildings would have witnessed the greatest degree of passing movement. It is calculated by determining the probability of a certain building being bypassed when taking the shortest path between two nodes in a network graph (Freeman 1977).

Figure 16.15 represents those buildings with the highest closeness and betweenness centrality measures when all buildings within the network are unweighted. The calculations are shown on both a global scale using an infinite radius (n) and a smaller scale using a 1000-m radius to reflect local scale movement around the port. The calculation of closeness centrality indicates that the buildings aligned along the central isthmus have the highest

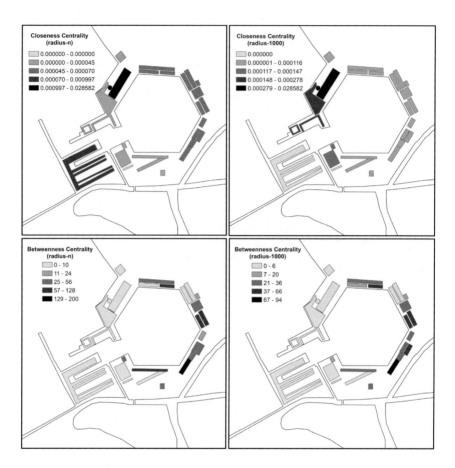

*Figure 16.15* Unweighted closeness and betweenness centrality graphs calculated using an infinite and a 1000-m radius.

value (Figure 16.15 upper left and right). This suggests that the central isthmus enjoyed one of the most desirable spatial positions within the port. Betweenness centrality results, by contrast, provide an indication as to where movement would have been channelled through the port (Figure 16.15 lower left and right). They suggest that most of it was structured to move along the eastern sides of the Trajanic basin. Both radii calculations show very similar results in terms of which buildings would have witnessed the highest degree of passing movement.

In the next set of calculations, the buildings on the central isthmus were weighted in order to gauge their role in structuring movement (Figure 16.16). When compared to the unweighted calculations, the results provide us with a more nuanced understanding. The weighted closeness centrality

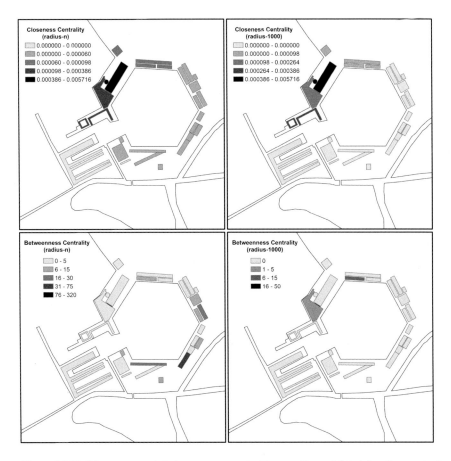

*Figure 16.16* Closeness and betweenness centrality results weighted by the central Isthmus using an infinite radius and a 1000-m radius.

measurements are almost identical to the unweighted calculations, with the main difference being that within the global weighted calculation, the Grandi Magazzini di Traiano does not have a high centrality measure. Instead, both the global and local weighted calculations emphasize the buildings located on the central isthmus. On a global scale, however, the betweenness centrality results indicate that the central isthmus, even when weighted, did not have a high degree of movement potential; the opposite, however, was true of the warehouses on either side of the temple. If the central isthmus was the principal administrative area of the port, as current research suggests, then the results may be indicative of the need to travel to and from the Palazzo Imperiale. The betweenness measures calculated using a smaller radius, however, indicate that the Palazzo Imperiale would have seen a high probability of passing movement. This suggests that the central isthmus would also have been a hub of port activity at a smaller scale, probably playing an important role in structuring movement around the Trajanic basin.

Both unweighted and weighted closeness and betweenness centrality calculations provide us with a slightly more nuanced understanding about how individual buildings may have structured interactions across the port scape. The former indicates that the buildings lying on the central isthmus were in a preferential area within the port, while the latter provides us with some indications as to how they may have structured different kinds of interactions related to port activity.

### *Interpreting movement patterns at Portus*

The axial and urban network analyses provide complementary information about how built space may have functioned within the port as well as giving us an indication as to how movement may have been structured. The analyses of the interconnection of space, detailed by both space syntax integration and closeness centrality within urban network analysis, produced similar results. Within space syntax, the northern area of Portus is shown to have had the greatest connection between different component spaces. The closeness centrality measures provide a more detailed picture, indicating that the central isthmus held an important spatial position within the overall port scape. The space syntax analyses and betweenness centrality calculations likewise present similar results, suggesting that movement was primarily structured to pass the warehouses on the eastern side of the port. This may be indicative of off loading of cargo from the Trajanic Basin and its subsequent transport through the built environment.

## Visibility and fluvial movement between Portus, Ostia and Rome (Maria del Carmen Moreno Escobar)

So far, this chapter has focused upon modelling movement through the water spaces of the harbours and the built space of the port scape. However, Portus was part of a bigger whole, which has been defined as the 'port-system of Imperial Rome' (Keay 2012a). This was geared towards supplying the City of Rome and developed in the course of the first and second centuries CE. It included Ostia and the Tiber river ports as well as *Centumcellae* (Civitavecchia) and the Tyrrhenian ports down to the Bay of Naples. Any meaningful analysis of movement at Portus, therefore, also needs to consider the lower Tiber from Ostia, past Portus northwards in the direction of Rome.

However, undertaking this is not without its challenges. The course of the River Tiber has experienced important modifications since antiquity caused by the natural dynamics of the river itself and also as a consequence of artificial canals excavated at, and in the vicinity of, Portus. Some of these changes may be observed through the analysis of historical maps (e.g. Meijer 1685; Amenduni 1884), but many others are invisible to the naked eye on account of having silted up since antiquity, such as in the case of the Canale Traverso (Salomon *et al.* 2012) within Portus, or the cutting of the Spinaceto meander in 1930s (Aguilera Martín 2012), which modified the course of the Tiber to the north-east of the site of the port. Transformations such as these are being identified along different stretches of the river by means of geoarchaeological studies (Figure 16.17). The evidence is still too scattered, however, to gain a full understanding of the historic course of the Tiber between Rome and the Tyrrhenian Sea, since long stretches of it remain to be investigated. Nonetheless, integration of the available cartographic, archaeological, environmental and geoarchaeological evidence for these changes within a GIS environment has provided interesting insights into their impact upon the route of the river that connected Rome with the Tiber ports and the sea. In this sense, the temporal analysis of these transformations allows for the

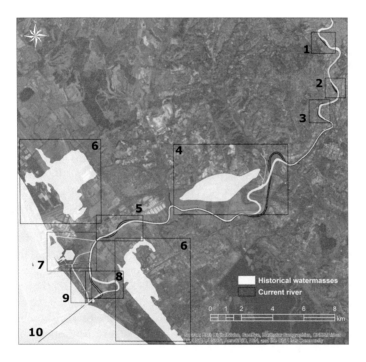

*Figure 16.17* Areas in the Lower Tiber Valley where previous research has identified transformations of the ancient river course. 1. Campo Marzio (Taylor 2018); 2. Ex-Mercati (Mellace *et al.* 2011); 3. Santa Passera (Mocchegiani Carpano, 1981); 4. Magliana and Campo Merlo (Catalli *et al.* 1995; Meijer 1685); 5. Fiera di Roma (Arnoldus-Huyzendveld, 2014); 6. Stagno di Ostia and Stagno Maccarese (Amenduni 1884); 7. Portus (*e.g.* Keay *et al.* 2005; Salomon *et al.* 2014); 8. Fiume Morto (Salomon *et al.* 2016); 9. Portus to Ostia canal on the Isola Sacra (Salomon *et al.* 2016); 10. Progradation of the coastline (Salomon *et al.* 2016; Arnoldus-Huyzendveld 2005) (Source: M.C. Moreno Escobar).

creation of models and simulations of the river at the different stages during the Imperial period (Figure 16.18). Most important of all, these models make it possible for us to move beyond a mere description of the changes along the course of the Tiber towards a better understanding of their impact upon the river as the fluvial axis of the port system of Imperial Rome. They also make it possible to explore general historical dynamics in the area and test earlier hypotheses about the role of the river in supplying Rome.

A first line of approach was to investigate how far an increase in the extent of waterways might have affected the capacity of the port system for moving cargoes along the Tiber between Rome and its maritime ports at different periods. In order to do this, the length of the course of the Tiber and the associated canals at different periods was calculated. This suggested that it increased from 35.5 km between the late first century BCE and early first century CE (period 1) to 39.9 km after the construction of Portus and the excavation of the Northern Canal (period 2), the Canale Traverso and the Fossa Traiana, and 43.9 km after the Trajanic expansion of Portus and the excavation of the Canale Romano and the Portus to Ostia canal on the Isola Sacra (period 3).[6] These figures roughly equate to increases of 12.39 % in period 2 and of 23.66 % in period 3, which may reflect a relationship between the growth of the port system and the increasing need for supplies to Rome (Figure 16.19).

These estimates become more meaningful when they are connected to the development of the port system's capacity to move goods and foodstuffs towards Rome, an issue which may also be explored by means of models and simulations of navigational possibilities between ports along the waterways of the port system. A hypothesis proposed by Malmberg (2015) postulated the existence of three lanes of river traffic on the Tiber between Rome and Ostia: two of these were lateral lanes used for towing boats upriver to Rome, while the central one was used to conduct them downriver back to Portus and Ostia (Figure 16.20.1). However, estimates based upon the historical models of the Tiber discussed earlier, together with a consideration of the space required for river boats to manoeuvre within the Tiber, suggest that such a system would not have worked. Even after one dismisses such factors as the shallow depth of the river bed close to the river banks, or the difficulty of navigating the concave or convex sides of river meanders, Malmberg's model would have required repeated changes between three- and two-lane stretches and vice versa (Figure 16.20.2), thereby multiplying potential areas of river traffic congestion along the whole course of the river. In view of this, the existence of only two lanes of circulation on the Tiber appears as the most plausible solution for organizing the river traffic within Rome's port system during the High Empire.

These conclusions may help us understand how the capacity of the river for carrying commercial traffic might have changed through time. This was achieved by using spatial simulations to calculate the maximum number of river boats that could have been towed upriver simultaneously in the different

*Figure 16.18* Topographical models of the River Tiber and the Lower Tiber Valley in the different periods under study: 1. Period 1: The late first century BCE and early first century CE; 2. Period 2: The middle-late first century CE; 3. Period 3: The end of the first century CE to the middle second century CE (Source: M.C. Moreno Escobar).

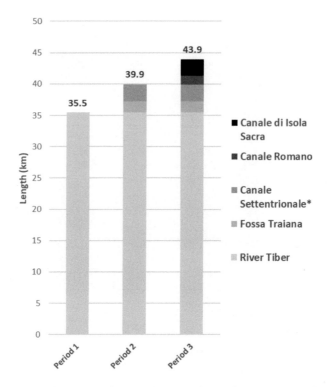

*Figure 16.19* Increase in the total length of the waterways in port system of Imperial
Rome between periods 1 to 3 (Source: M.C. Moreno Escobar).

periods of development of the waterways. The simulations took account of
the requirements for safe navigation along the river[7] and the capacity of a
*navis caudicaria*, as exemplified by the Fiumicino 2 shipwreck found at the
Claudian basin (Boetto 2010), whose deadweight was estimated in 70 tonnes.
By comparing the space needed for one such boat, its storage capacity, and
the total length of the waterways between Rome, Portus and Ostia at each
of the three different periods, it was possible to approximate the tonnage of
goods and foodstuffs that could have been moved simultaneously along the
river towards Rome (Table 16.1).

However, it is important to note that these estimates do not factor in other
modes of river transport, such as linking two or more *naves caudicariae*, so that
they could be towed simultaneously using larger or smaller river vessels; nor do
they take into account seasonal differences on the river flow which may have
affected the volume of river traffic. As a result, these estimates and calculations
must be considered only illustrative of possible ancient river capacity.

The discussion so far has focused upon the benefits of the role played by the
river and canals in supplying the City of Rome. Against this, however, must

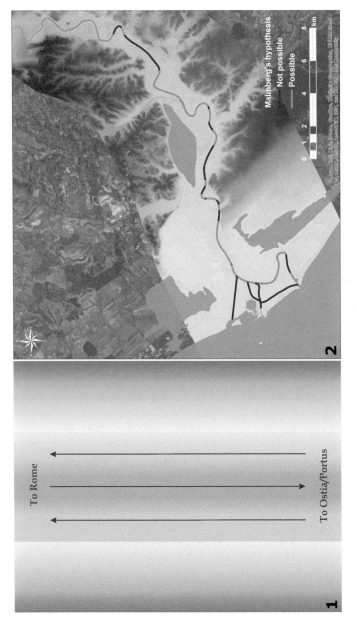

*Figure 16.20* 1. Malmberg's model of the organization of river traffic on the Tiber in the Imperial period (Source: M.C. Moreno Escobar, after Malmberg 2015). 2. Stretches of the Tiber where Malmberg's hypothesis would have been possible and not possible between the end of the first century CE and the middle second century CE (Source: M.C. Moreno Escobar).

*Table 16.1* Estimates of the maximum transport capacity of Rome's port system between the late first century BCE and the middle second century CE

|  | Waterway length | Number of naves caudicarii | Tonnage transported |
|---|---|---|---|
| Period 1 | 35.5 | 910 | 63,733 |
| Period 2 | 39.9 | 1023 | 71,615 |
| Period 3 | 43.9 | 1126 | 78,795 |

Source: M.C. Moreno Escobar.

be set the considerable costs that would have been incurred in the excavation of the canals and the construction of related infrastructure. There was also the major logistical of organizing the movement of *naves caudicariae* in order to avoid congestion at pinch points where canals flowed into the Tiber close to Portus and also along the many meanders closer to Rome (Figure 16.21). There is a strong argument that a signalling system would have been needed to ensure the smooth flow of goods and foodstuffs through the different nodes of the port system and their safe arrival at the landing stages and warehouses at Rome. However, the changes in the river course already described, as well as the major transformations that have taken place in the Lower Tiber Valley on account of successive floods, the development of infrastructure and other alterations to the landscape, have erased any traces of this system.

Computer modelling makes it possible to simulate this system by recreating the contemporary topographic and geographic conditions and analyse specific past dynamics. In this way, it was possible to explore locations for signalling posts along the lower Tiber. A computer-generated simulation of movement along the river made it possible to pick out those adjacent areas that would have been most visible to an observer on a *navis caudicaria* similar to the Fiumicino 2 that was travelling from Ostia to Rome. The computing technique employed combined movement and vision through spatial statistics and the modelling of fuzzy visibility in a GIS environment.[8] The maps generated in this way (Figure 16.22.1) were further processed by comparing them with cumulative viewsheds based on binary maps which defined the visible and non-visible areas of the Lower Tiber Valley (Figure 16.22.2) and resulted in the creation of a map of enhanced visibility (Figure 16.23). This made it possible to identify the most likely locations of possible signalling positions. Furthermore, these visible and non-visible areas were compared with the distribution of sites dated in each of the three periods under study, which suggests that certain sites may have played a role in the organization of the river traffic. This may have been the case, for example, with the early river port close to the junction between the Fossa Traiana and the Tiber in periods 2 and 3. It was also interesting to note the lack of correlation between the identified archaeological sites and the most probable locations of signalling positions in period 1, which may suggest a lack of concern about the organization of the

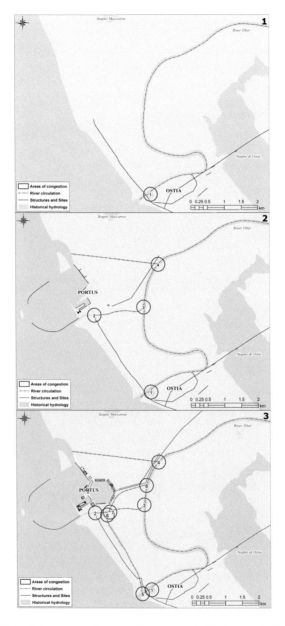

*Figure 16.21* Potential areas of congestion around Portus and Ostia in period 1 (1), period 2 (2) and period 3 (3). The circles define the congestion areas: 1. Harbour at Ostia; 2. junction between Canale Traverso and Fossa Traiana; 3. junction at Capo Due Rami; 4. junction between Canale Settentrionale and River Tiber; 5. junction between Portus to Ostia canal; 6. junction between the Portus to Ostia canal and the Fossa Traiana; 7. junction between Canale Romano and Fossa Traiana; 8. junction between Canale Romano and River Tiber (Source: M.C. Moreno Escobar after Keay 2012b).

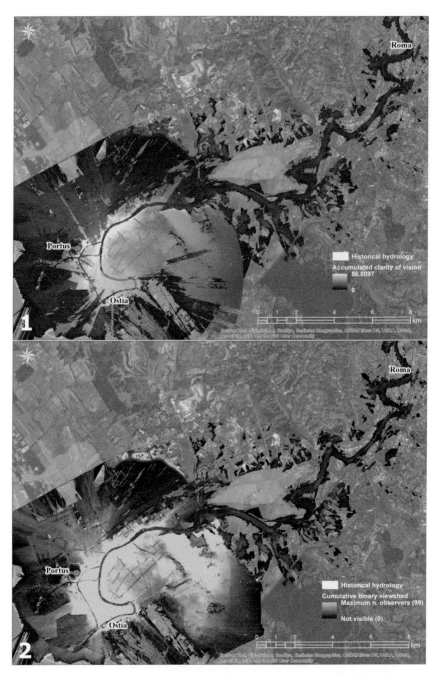

*Figure 16.22* 1. Map of accumulated clarity of vision in the lower Tiber Valley for period 3; 2. Map of cumulative binary visibility for period 3 (Source: M.C. Moreno Escobar).

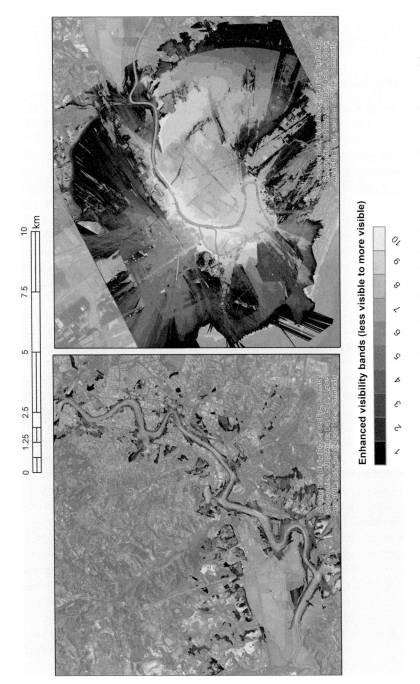

*Figure 16.23* Map of enhanced visibility bands for period 3, defining in lighter shades the areas where the signalling positions were most possibly located (Source: M.C. Moreno Escobar).

river traffic by the river authorities prior to the construction of Portus and its canals in the Claudian period. If so, there is an argument that if there was a signalling system, then its development was directly linked to the broader provision of port infrastructure at Portus under Claudius and Trajan.

## Discussion (Simon Keay)

What has the study of movement on water and land been able to tell us about the accessibility of Portus to commercial traffic? In the first instance, the movement of ships and boats through the water spaces of the port was clearly a complex process subject to winds, currents, the hours of daylight and the sailing seasons, and the effects of which were constrained by the technological abilities of the ships and boats, the skill of the mariners and the harbour infrastructure. The movement of ships and boats through the port, therefore, was not entirely predictable or necessarily unproblematic. Furthermore, the likely greater use of lighters implied a greater risk of the loss of cargoes during the process of transhipment. Consequently, a largely unquantifiable time element needs to be factored into any consideration of the 'efficiency' of the port in the processing of cargoes.

The access and network analyses of the land-based areas of the port suggest that the central isthmus was the main focus of activity for the port as a whole, something which helps to support the argument that the Palazzo Imperiale was its principal administrative complex. It is also clear that in spatial terms, access to and movement around the Grandi Magazzini di Traiano complex were more related to the south-eastern side of the Claudian basin, the Fossa Traiana and the Canale Traverso than it was to the rest of the port. Aside from this, it is clear that there were two dominant areas of terrestrial movement. One, north-westwards along the central isthmus past the Palazzo Imperiale and the Imperial navalia in the direction of the Tiber, and another along the line of the warehouses and temple along the north-eastern side of the Trajanic basin, in the direction of the Canale Romano. Furthermore, the eastern side of the Trajanic basin seems to be confirmed as a transitional area, underscored by its key transhipment position between the basin and the Canale Romano (Keay *et al.* 2005: Area 11, figure 5.32).

This evidence points to an organizational differentiation within the port scape comprising (1) an administrative area in the central isthmus with a primary land-based communication with the Tiber and Via Campana/Portuense; (2) a grain storage area around the Darsena only accessible by sea and canal; (3) a suite of warehouses and temple along the north-eastern side of the hexagon and (4) a suite of warehouses between the Trajanic basin and Canale Romano. Presumably, this topographic logic was dictated by the ways in which the port authorities organized the movement of different kinds of cargoes through and around the port. Further evidence for this attention to control is provided by the numbered columns that were placed on the quays of the Trajanic basin, presumably in order to guide ships to assigned berths

(Keay 2019: 150). Furthermore, at a later stage, presumably in the later second century CE, the port authorities built the internal wall circuit (Contramura Interna) to run around most, if not all, of the quayside of the Trajanic basin and was pierced by narrow doorways at regular intervals to control the flow of movement between quays and warehouses.

The spatial analyses of visibility along the river help us to better understand how the river authorities may have met the challenge of coordinating river traffic. It supplements earlier arguments (Keay 2012b) that the movement of cargoes to Rome and back to Portus was a complex process that would have required careful coordination. The identification of possible sites for signalling stations, and the pivotal role that may have been played by the river port, are an index as to how some of these challenges might have been met, although these need to be verified with careful ground survey. At the same time, analysis of river traffic suggests that its volume may have been less than has been argued previously. Furthermore, during the *pieni* of the Tiber in the winter months movement along the river will have become further compromised, particularly on those occasions when there were major floods, such as during the reign of Hadrian and in the years 147 and 162 CE (Aldrete 2007: 29–30).

Much still remains to be learned, however, particularly in relation to the volume of traffic and the size of ships and boats passing through the port. More information is needed about the maximum depth of the harbour basins and canals at different periods, since this is a significant index of the maximum draft of ships and boats that would have used them at different periods in the history of the port (Keay 2019: 159–60). It is also very difficult to estimate the number of ships and river craft that might have used the port at any one time, with the only evidence coming from the Trajanic basin, which could have accommodated up to c. 116 sea-going ships and an unquantifiable number of smaller ships and boats. These would have anchored at the centre of the basin until such time as mooring spaces along one of its six sides became free (Keay 2019: 158–9). We also need to better understand the width and accessibility of the quays between the water spaces, the warehouses and other buildings bordering the harbour basins and canals. This would complement our understanding of the centrality and accessibility of the spaces identified in the access and network analyses. In particular, it would help us better understand the degree to which it was possible to manoeuvre bulky cargoes between moored ships and adjacent buildings. Another major challenge is identifying places where the registration and control of cargoes might have taken place. It has been argued elsewhere that the Palazzo Imperiale and the Grandi Magazzini di Settimio Severo were the principal administrative focus of the port (Keay 2019: 151–2). However, the width of quays combined with the centrality and accessibility of certain spaces around the port might also be indicative of spaces where weighing, measuring and sampling might have taken place. A final, and particularly challenging, problem is that it is still challenging to calculate the warehouse capacity at the port. While global figures have been calculated for the first, early second and late second centuries CE (Keay *et al.* 2005: table 9.1), these are almost certainly a considerable underestimate, since they are calculated on the basis of the ground floor area, when recent work at the Grandi Magazzini di Traiano suggests that this particular complex at least would have stood to two stories (Bukowecki 2016).

There is little doubt that the Portus complex was one of the great engineering achievements of the ancient world. The artificial creation of the three basins, canals, roads and built infrastructure represented an attempt to control the unpredictable maritime and fluvial environments on an unprecedented scale. However, even though the port was planned in such a way as to ensure the smooth throughput of cargoes bound for Rome, the movement of ships, boats and their cargoes through it was still complex and unpredictable and could also be time-consuming.[9] Account also needs to be taken of the controls and checks that would have been imposed by imperial officials upon the goods being moved through the port by merchants, shippers and their representatives. These can be broadly broken down into broad categories related to tasting, weighing, measuring, registration and payment of taxes,[10] and there are grounds for suggesting that the architecture of individual buildings and topography of the port as a whole was planned in order to facilitate this. The implication must be that these activities that would have been more time-consuming than time that is generally assumed, and that they would have acted as a further brake on the smoothness and fluidity with which cargoes would have moved through the port. Indeed, it could be argued that they represent a significant 'transactional cost' which needs to be factored into our understanding of the scale of commercial activity that the port could support.

## Notes

1 The work for this was undertaken in the context of the ERC-Advanced Grant funded PortusLimen Project.
2 The research in this section was undertaken as part of a fellowship at the British School at Rome funded by Peter Smith, a long-standing friend of the institution, whose support is gratefully acknowledged here.
3 This was derived from the Portus model produced by Artas Media in conjunction with the Portus Project. This is discussed in Earl *et al.* 2020.
4 The research is being conducted by Nicolas Carayon as part of the PortusLimen Project. His work also suggests that in this regard access to Portus was much more problematic than, for example, neighbouring *Centumcellae*, which was exposed to summer offshore winds for much less time (Carayon, Forthcoming).
5 The celebrated commemorative Trajanic *sestertius* (Woytek 2010: plate 94: 470b1–3; 470c; 470f; 470v1–v4) shows a range of different kinds of ship in the basin, including what appear to be merchant ships and possibly a galley.
6 The measurements of these geographical features were taken on the coordinate system ETRS89 UTM32N.
7 Defined by the formula "Space for manoeuvre (per side) = boat's length * 1,5". I would like to thank Dr Cerezo Andreo for his help in defining this formula.

8  The parameters of these analyses were observer height = 2.6 m (1 m above water level + 1.6 m of person height); observed feature = a person or feature 2 m height; algorithm of analysis based in Ogburn (2006) and automatized by Rášová (2014); clarity zone defined at 1000 m radius; one fuzzy viewshed performed every 200 m on the way of Ostia/Portus to Rome.

9  The possible delays in the movement of cargoes through the port is discussed in Keay 2019: 168.

10  This is the subject of a doctoral thesis on the legal framework of commercial activity at Roman Mediterranean ports by Emilia Mataix at the University of Southampton. See also Keay 2019: 161–3.

# References

Aguilera Martín, Antonio. "La sirga en el Tíber en época romana." Pages 105–26 in *Rome, Portus and the Mediterranean.* Edited by Simon Keay. Archaeological Monographs of the British School at Rome 21. London: The British School at Rome, 2012.

Aldrete, Gregory S. *Floods of the Tiber in Ancient Rome.* Baltimore: Johns Hopkins University Press, 2007.

Amenduni, G. *Sulle opere di bonificazione della plaga litoranea dell' Agro Romano che comprende le paludi e gli stagni di Ostia, Porto, Maccarese e delle terre vallive di Stracciacappa, Baccano, Pantano e Lago dei Tartari.* Rome: Tipografia Eredi Botta, 1884.

Arnaud, Pascal. "Sailing 90 Degrees From the Wind: Norm or Exception?" Pages 147–60 in *Maritime Technology in the Ancient Economy: Ship-Design and Navigation.* Edited by William Harris and Kenneth Iara. *Journal of Roman Archaeology* Supplementary Series 84. Portsmouth RI: *Journal of Roman Archaeology*, 2011.

Baldassare, Ida. La necropolis dell'Isola Sacra. Un decennio ricerche archeologiche. *Quaderni della Ricerca Scientifica* 100 (1978): 487–504.

Becatti, Giovanni. *Scavi di Ostia IV: Mosaici e Pavimenti Marmorei.* Vol. 1. Rome: Libreria dello Stato, 1961.

Beresford, James. *The Ancient Sailing Season.* Leiden: Brill, 2012.

Boetto, Giulia. L'épave de l'Antiqué Tardive Fiumicino 1: Analyse de La Structure et Étude Fonctionnelle. *Archeonautica* 15 (2008): 29–62.

Boetto, Giulia. "Le port vu de la mer: l'apport de l'archéologie navale à l'étude des ports antiques." Pages 112–128 in *Ostia and the Ports of the Roman Mediterranean. Contributions from Archaeology and History.* Edited by Simon Keay and Giulia Boetto. *Meetings between Cultures in the Ancient Mediterranean. Proceedings of the17th AIAC International Conference of Classical Archaeology: Rome, 22–26 September 2008.* Edited by Helga Di Giuseppe and Martina Della Riva (Bollettino di archeologia on line, Vol Speciale; I) Rome: Ministero per i Beni Culturali e Turismo, 2010. http://bollettinodiarcheologiaonline.beniculturali.it/wp-content/uploads/2019/01/9_Boetto_paper.pdf (last accessed 15/2/2019)

Boetto, Giulia. Tra il fiume e il mare: Le Caudicariae di Fiumicino. Pages 110–2 in *Maritime Technology in the Ancient Economy: Ship-Design and Navigation.* Edited by William Harris and Kenneth Iara. *Journal of Roman Archaeology* Supplementary Series 84. Portsmouth RI: *Journal of Roman Archaeology*, 2011.

Bukowiecki, Évelyne I Grandi Magazzini c.d. di Traiano Portus. Archeologia alle porte di Roma. *Forma Urbis* Dicembre (2016): 38–41.

Bukowiecki, Évelyne and Panzieri, Camilla. Portus. Les entrepôts dits de Trajan. *Chroniques des activités archéologiques de l'École française de Rome: Italie centrale. Mélanges de l'Ecole française de Rome* 125–1 (2013). http://cefr.revues.org/935

Bukowiecki, Évelyne, Panzieri, Camilla and Zugmeyer, Stefanie. Portus. Les entrepôts de Trajan. *Chroniques des activités archéologiques de l'École française de Rome. Italie centrale, Mélanges de l'École française de Rome* 124–1 (2012): http://cefr. revues.org/286

Bukowiecki, Évelyne, Mimmo, Millena, Panzieri, Camilla and Sebastiani, Renato. "Le système des sols surélevés dans les entrepots d'Ostie, de Portus et de Rome: nouvelles découvertes en cours." Pages 231–67 in *Entrepots et circuits de distribution en Méditerrannée antique.* Edited by Véronique Chankowski, Xavier Lafón and Catherine Virlouvet. *Bulletin de Correspondance Héllenique Supplément* 58. Athens, École française d'Athènes, 2018.

Casson, Lionel. *Ships and Seamanship in the Ancient World* (2nd edition). Baltimore: The Johns Hopkins University Press, 1995.

Cooper, John P. "No Easy Option: The Nile versus the Red Sea in Ancient and Mediaeval North-South Navigation." Pages 189–210 in *Maritime Technology in the Ancient Economy: Ship-Design and Navigation.* Edited by William Harris and Kenneth Iara. Journal of Roman Archaeology Supplement 84. Portsmouth RI: Journal of Roman Archaeology, 2011.

Crawford, Katherine. "Rethinking Approaches for the Study of Urban Movement at Ostia." Pages 313–27 in *Finding the Limits of the Limes: Modelling Demography, Economy and Transport on the Edge of the Roman Empire.* Edited by P. Verhagen, J. Joyce and M. R. Groenhuijzen Springer, 2019. https://doi.org/10.1007/978-3-030-04576-0

Dilke, Oswald. "Itineraries and Geographical Maps in the Early and Late Roman Empires." Pages 234–57 in *Cartography in Prehistoric, Ancient, and Medieval Europe and the Mediterranean.* Edited by J. B. Harley and David Woodward. Chicago: University of Chicago Press, 1987.

Freeman, Linton. A Set of Measures of Centrality Based on Betweenness. *Sociometry,* *40*(1) (1977): 35–41. https://doi.org/10.2307/3033543

Germoni, Paola, Keay, Simon, Millett, Martin and Strutt, Kris. "The Isola Sacra: Reconstructing the Roman Landscape." Pages 231–60 in *Portus and Its Hinterland. Archaeological Monographs of the British School at Rome* 18. Edited by Simon Keay and Lidia Paroli. London: BSR, 2011.

Gooley, Tristan. *How to Read Water*. London: Sceptre, 2016.

Green, P. *Juvenal, The Sixteen Satires.* Harmondsworth: Penguin Books, 1998.

Greenhill, Basil, and Morrison, John. *The Archaeology of Boats and Ships: An Introduction.* London: Conway Maritime Press, 1995.

Heikell, Rod and Heikell, Linda. *Italian Waters Pilot.* St. Ives: Imray Laurie Norie and Wilson, 2015.

Hillier, Bill and Hanson, Julienne. *The Social Logic of Space.* Cambridge and New York: Cambridge University Press, 1984.

Hillier, Bill, Penn, A., Hanson, J., Grajewski, T. and Xu, J. Natural Movement: or, Configuration and Attraction in Urban Pedestrian Movement. *Environment and Planning B: Planning and Design* 20 (1993): 29–66. https://doi.org/10.1068/b200029

Keay, Simon. "Portus and the Alexandrian Grain Trade Revisited." Pages 11–22 in *Ostia and the Ports of the Roman Mediterranean. Contributions from Archaeology and History.* Edited by Simon Keay and Giulia Boetto. *Meetings between Cultures in the Ancient Mediterranean. Proceedings of the 17th AIAC International Conference of Classical Archaeology: Rome, 22–26 September 2008.* Edited by Helga Di Giuseppe and Martina Della Riva, Rome: Ministero per i Beni Culturali e Turismo, 2010. www.bollettinodiarcheologiaonline.beniculturali.it/bao_es_b_7.php

Keay, Simon. "Introduction." Pages 1–29 in *Rome, Portus and the Mediterranean. Archaeological Monographs of the British School at Rome* 21. Edited by Simon Keay. London: BSR, 2012a.

Keay, Simon. "The Port System of Imperial Rome." Pages 33–68 in *Rome, Portus and the Mediterranean.* Archaeological Monographs of the British School at Rome 21. Edited by Simon Keay. London: The British School at Rome, 2012b.

Keay, Simon. "The Role Played by the Portus Augusti in Flows of Commerce between Rome and Its Mediterranean Ports." Pages 147–92 in *Infrastructure and Distribution in Ancient Economies. The Flow of Money, Goods and Services. International Congress 28–31 October 2014.* Edited by Bernard Woytek. Austrian Academy of Sciences. Institute for the Study of Ancient Culture. Division Documenta Antiqua. Vienna: Austrian Academy of Sciences Press, 2019.

Keay, Simon. "The Buildings of the Central Isthmus and Their Broader Context." In *Uncovering the Harbour Buildings: Excavations at Portus 2007–2012 Volume I: The Surveys, Excavations and Architectural Reconstructions of the Palazzo Imperiale and Adjacent Buildings.* Edited by Simon Keay, Graeme Earl and Felici, Fabrizio. London: BSR Studies, CUP, 2021.

Keay, Simon, Millett, Martin, Paroli, Lidia and Strutt, Kris. *Portus, an Archaeological Survey of the Port of Imperial Rome.* Archaeological Monographs of the British School at Rome. London: British School at Rome, 2005.

Keay, Simon, Earl, Graeme and Felici, Fabrizio. "Excavations and survey at the Palazzo Imperiale 2007–2009." Pages 67–91 in *Portus and Its Hinterland. Archaeological Monographs of the British School at Rome* 18. Edited by S. Keay and L. Paroli. London: BSR, 2011.

Keay, Simon, Earl, Graeme, Felici, Fabrizio, Copeland, Penny, Cascino, Roberta, Kay, Stephen and Triantafillou, Christina. Interim Report on an Enigmatic New Trajanic Building at Portus. *Journal of Roman Archaeology* 25 (2012): 486–512.

Keay, Simon with Earl, Graeme and Felici, Fabrizio. *Uncovering the Harbour Buildings: Excavations at Portus 2007–2012 Volume I: The Surveys, Excavations and Architectural Reconstructions of the Palazzo Imperiale and Adjacent Buildings.* London: BSR Studies, CUP, 2021.

Lugli, Giuseppe and Filibeck, Goffredo. *Il Porto di Roma imperiale e l'Agro Portuense.* Bergamo: Officine dell'Istituto Italiano d' Arti Grafiche, 1935.

Malmberg, Simon. "'Ships Are Seen Gliding Swiftly along the Sacred Tiber': The river as an Artery of Urban Movement and Development." Pages 187–201 in *The Moving City: Processions, Passages and Promenades in Ancient Rome.* Edited by Ida Östenberg, Simon Malmberg and Jonas Bjørnebye. London, Bloomsbury, 2015.

Meijer, Cornelius. *L'arte di restituire a Roma la tralasciata navigatione del suo Tevere.* Rome, Stamperia del Lazzari Varese, 1685.

Millet, Bertrand, Tronchère, Hervé and Goiran, Jean-Philippe. Hydrodynamic Modeling of the Roman Harbour of Portus in the Tiber Delta: The Impact of the North-eastern Channel on Current and Sediment Dynamics. *Geoarchaeology* 29(5) (2014) https://onlinelibrary.wiley.com/doi/full/10.1002/gea.21485 (last accessed 2 April 2019).

Mocchegiani Carpano, Claudio. Indagine archaeologiche nel Tevere. *Archeologia Laziale* IV (1981): 142–59.

Morelli, Cinzia, Marinucci, Alfredo and Arnoldus-Huyzenveld, Antonia. "Il porto di Claudio: Nuove Scoperte." Pages 47–65 in *Portus and Its Hinterland. Archaeological Monographs of the British School at Rome* 18. Edited by Simon Keay and Lidia Paroli. London: BSR, 2011.

Morton, James. *The Role of the Physical Environment in Ancient Greek Seafaring.* Leiden: Brill, 2001.

Murray, William M. Do Modern Winds Equal Ancient Winds? *Mediterranean Historical Review* 2(2) (1987): 139–67.

Noli, Alberto, Girolamo, Piero Di and Sammarco, P. Parametri meteomarini e dinamica costiera. *Idrodinamica Costiera* (1996): 285–328.

Noli, Alberto and Franco, Leopoldo. The Ancient Ports of Rome: New Insights from Engineers. *Archaeologia Maritima Mediterranea* 6 (2009): 189–207.

Ogburn, Dennis. Assessing the Level of Visibility of Cultural Objects in Past Landscapes. *Journal of Archaeological Science* 33 (2006): 405–13.

Pensabene, Patrizio, *Ostiensium Marmorum Decus et Décor. Studi architettonici, decorative e archeometrici. Studi Miscellanei* 33. Rome: L'Erma di Bretschneider, 2007.

Porta, Sergio, Crucitti, Paolo and Latora, Vito. The Network Analysis of Urban Streets: A Primal Approach. *Environment and Planning B: Planning and Design, 33* (2006): 705–25. https://doi.org/10.1068/b32045

Rášová, Alexandra "Fuzzy Viewshed, Probable Viewshed, and Their Use in the Analysis of Prehistoric Monuments Placement in Western Slovakia." Pages 47–65 in *Connecting a Digital Europe through Location and Place. Proceedings of the AGILE 2014 International Conference on Geographic Information Science, Castellón, June, 3–6.* Edited by Joaquín Huerta, Guijarro, Sven Schade and Carlos Granell Canut. Castellón de la Pala: Springer, 2014.

Rickman, Geoffrey. *Roman Granaries and Store Buildings.* Cambridge: Cambridge University Press 1971.

Sabidussi, Gert. The Centrality Index of a Graph. *Psychmetrika,* 31 (1966): 581–603.

Salomon, Férreol, Delile, Hugo, Goiran, Jean-Philippe, Bravard, Jean-Paul and Keay, Simon. The Canale di Comunicazione Traverso in Portus: the Roman Sea Harbour Under River Influence (Tiber Delta, Italy). *Géomorphologie: Relief, Processus, Environnement* 18 (2012): 75–90.

Salomon, Férreol, Goiran, Jean-Philippe, Bravard, Jean-Paul, Arnaud, Pascal, Djerbi, Hatem, Kay, Stephen and Keay, Simon. A Harbour–Canal at Portus: A Geoarchaeological Approach to the Canale Romano: Tiber Delta, Italy. *Water History* 6 (2014): 31–49.

Salomon, Férreol, Keay, Simon, Strutt, Kris, Goiran, Jean-Philippe, Millett, Martin and Paola Germoni. ""Connecting Portus with Ostia: preliminary results of a geoarchaeological study of the navigable canal on the Isola Sacra." Pages 293–303 in *Les Ports dans l'Esapce Mediterranéen antique. Narbonne et les systèmes portuaries fluvio-lagunaires. Revue archéologique de Narbonnaise. Supplément 44.* Montpellier: Révue archéologique de Narbonnaise, 2016.

Sevtsuk, Andres and Mekonnen, Michael. Urban Network Analysis: A New Toolbox for ArcGIS. *International Journal of Geomatics and Spatial Analysis, 22*(2) (2012): 287–305. https://doi.org/10.3166/RIG.22.287–305

Taylor, Rabun. "The Soft-core City: Ancient Rome and the Wandering Tiber." Pages 49–75 in *River Cities: Historical and Contemporary.* Edited by Thaïsa Way and John Beardsley. Washington DC: Dumbarton Oaks, 2018.

Veloccia Rinaldi, Maria Luisa and Testini, Pasquale. *Ricerche archeologiche nell'Isola Sacra. Monografie III.* Rome: Istituto Nazionale d'Archeologia e Storia dell'Arte, 1975.

Whitewright, Julian. The Potential Performance of Ancient Mediterranean Sailing Rigs. *International Journal of Nautical Archaeology* 40(1) (2011): 2–17.

Whitewright, Julian. Sailing and Sailing Rigs in the Ancient Mediterranean: Implications of Continuity, Variation and Change in Propulsion Technology. *International Journal of Nautical Archaeology* 47(1) (2018): 28–44.

Woytek, Bernard. *Die Reichsprägung des Kaisers Traianus (98–117). Moneta Imperii Romani 14.* Vienna: Österreichische Akademie der Wissenschaften, 2010.

# PART IV
# Conclusion

# The economics of space and mobility in Roman urbanism

*Frank Vermeulen and Arjan Zuiderhoek*

The Roman world offers a great diversity of economic spaces due to its size, geographic contrasts and duration. Natural conditions such as the presence of mineral resources, soil fertility or climate influenced the economic development of its various regions, but the role of cities and their connecting communication routes, as commercial hubs and arteries, was certainly equal if not more important. In this volume, a group of researchers have explored how the spatial structures of Roman cities and the patterns of movement and mobility through and between urban spaces influenced Roman economic processes and developments, and, conversely, how urban spaces were themselves shaped and moulded by the rhythms and demands of the economy. As signalled in the introduction, with its resolute focus on the *local* urban and spatial context of economic activities rather than on empire-wide models, this volume offers a different perspective on many issues that currently characterize the debate on the nature of the Roman economy. Some chapters focus more specifically on the uses of space in and around cities, while others are more concerned with the flows of goods, people and technology that link towns together or strengthen the cohesion of town and countryside. But throughout the volume, the individual authors agree that it is essential for our understanding of Roman urban history to develop more and better tools to construct historical narratives on the basis of archaeological and textual evidence from multiple kinds of cities and in a wide range of regions.

Central Tyrrhenian Italy is the starting point of many investigations in this domain, as most models of the use of economic space and mechanisms of movement observed in the Roman world originated here. Nevertheless, the well-studied or better preserved contexts in *Latium* and *Campania*, such as *Ostia* or *Pompeii*, should best be seen as good models for comparative exercises that allow an appreciation of regional diversity and specific solutions elsewhere in the Roman world. This is particularly well demonstrated in Flohr's contribution (Chapter 3) on retail landscapes. The author attempts to confront the picture that can be reconstructed for the spatial distribution and organization of *tabernae* in *Pompeii* and *Ostia* with realities in many other medium-sized and small towns that made up the bulk of cities in Roman Italy. On the basis of his analysis, it becomes clear that even after the commercial boom of the late Hellenistic Period, the *taberna* had not become omnipresent in every city in Italy. This seems to show that, as globalization theory suggests, the broader political and economic developments that shaped and transformed the Italian peninsula in the late Republican and Early Imperial Period had very different local outcomes. Flohr's analysis also underscores how important it is to contextualize particular types of commercial buildings within their specific urban settings. Thus, his chapter suggests one fruitful strategy for moving away from what we in the introduction termed 'the Vesuvian model' of Roman urbanism that has dominated studies of Roman urban space for so long. As Leder-Slotman (Chapter 4) demonstrates for another type of (supposedly) economic architecture, the so-called market buildings found along the agoras of cities in *Asia Minor*, contextualization and a critical study of the varying possible functions of buildings can lead to more nuanced conclusions. She argues that it is necessary to break away from the methodologically haphazard ways in which functions of market buildings have been proposed in the past, among which is the habit of suggesting functions on the basis of individual details. These buildings were part of a versatile urban environment and the presence or absence of other commercial buildings or spaces in a specific town could have a serious impact on the variety of functions of a specific market building. That the diversity and the flexibility in the use of ancient buildings and spaces are all too easily obscured by the labels we attach to them is well illustrated again by Dickenson (Chapter 7) for a province, *Britannia*, located at the other end of the Empire. Certain identifications should cause us to question the appropriateness of ascribing single functions to buildings, as is evident from his analysis of the forum–basilica complexes of Roman Britain. Their commercial function has often been downplayed in the past by scholars keen to emphasize the civic and political nature of these buildings as settings for local administration, political meetings and legal hearings. Yet, not only were these provincial forum–basilicas crucial *loci* for trade, but it can also certainly be argued that their commercial aspect should be given primacy in our understanding of why they were built and how they were used and experienced by people in everyday life. As Zuiderhoek illustrates with a case study of local elite intervention in the urban landscapes of *Asia Minor* (Chapter 6), the 'economic space' produced by urban elites often remained largely implicit within the broader civic structures that constituted the primary focus of their munificence or their activities as civic magistrates. Beneath the veil of civic ideology and euergetic public mindedness, urban elites, in fact, created a great deal of economic space, and the forum–basilica complexes of Italy, Britain and many other provinces are perfect examples of this architectural embeddedness of economic space in Roman cities.

But the impact of the urban populations and elites on the organization of economic space does not remain confined to the grandeur or efficiency of architectural complexes centrally placed within the intramural cities. A series of contributions in our volume emphasize the strict nexus between town and territory to understand the economics of space in Roman antiquity.

Examples from Adriatic Italy presented by Vermeulen, Lepore/Silani and Basso (Chapters 2, 8 and 9) demonstrate a trend towards a more regional approach of analysing the urban and spatial economy often helped by recent results from large-scale non-invasive fieldwork operations on a series of towns and their countryside. Through their detailed case studies of Adriatic coastal cities like *Potentia*, *Aquileia* and *Sena Gallica*, the researchers stress the prime importance of road and river networks as the arteries of economic movement, in close interplay with maritime connections, and the fundamental impact that a dense network of towns, villages and other transport nodes had on economic space. Part of the commercial vocation of these maritime centres of trade in Italy can be traced back to their origins as discrete *emporia* or landing stages, which pre-Roman populations drew on for some of their wealth and which provided them with incentives for social stratification. As suggested in the introduction, such landscapes consisting of large numbers of densely interwoven small towns and settlements may well have constituted a typically Mediterranean Roman, and economically viable, alternative to the model of regional primate centres interconnected with small-town satellites that scholars usually associate with pre-modern economic development.

Another factor is, of course, the impact of Roman colonization and the resulting construction of new towns, arguably stimulated by economic motives as well as military and strategic ones. The coastal towns mentioned here, as well as many others spread over the wider Mediterranean, illustrate well that the foundation of these colonies was a complex operation, which soon involved a complete reorganization of space, including economic space, in and around the urban centre and in its wider territory. The arrival in these new towns of various categories of specialists with specific technological skills, alongside the creation of new production facilities, soon led to a different lifestyle in these conquered regions. Extensive land reclamation in depressed areas, central Tyrrhenian- and Roman-style living standards in town and countryside, specialized crops such as vines and olive trees, new roadside facilities: these are just a few of the introductions that transformed the economic landscape of these areas.

As the analysis of the economic relationship between city and countryside in *Asia Minor*, and especially at the upland city of *Sagalassos* shows (Chapter 5), this tight economic relationship between city and countryside was also characteristic for inland centres and in other areas of the Roman world. The findings presented by Poblome and Willet not only support the idea that settlements in the territories of autonomous cities constituted the socio-economic foundation from which Roman regional urbanism emerged but also illustrate that local and regional markets and fairs, both urban and rural, played a crucial role in the strong integration of a Roman city with its hinterland. The monumentalization of a town, partly expressed by architectural complexes with commercial and economic finalities, was in large part the result of the intensification of agriculture and/or the exploitation of larger areas, even if what was built did not necessarily act as a catalyst to further improve the return on investment in agriculture.

The town–countryside relationship and the exploitation of urban hinterlands, as well as the connection of Roman cities to wider networks of trade and communication, brings us to the other main topic of this volume: economic movement. On the one hand, an urban centre can fulfil the role of place of easy transit on longer routes towards other destinations, as the case of *Aquileia*, with its centuries-old function as transit node directly linked to transhumance routes, possibly shows (Chapter 9). This would partly explain the probable location of the local cattle market in an extra-urban position at some distance from the city centre. On the other hand, many cities were precisely the motor for the movement of goods in many directions: from town to countryside, from its territory to the urban centre and to and from wider destinations. The example of *Munigua* in *Baetica* (Chapter 14) demonstrates well this pluri-directional movement of goods. With Schattner's attempt to determine *Munigua*'s place in the production chain of the goods that the city itself produced or that came into and went out of the city, an interesting theoretic framework is developed comparable to the study of production chains in modern industrial and commercial enterprises. In terms of its intake of a whole range of goods, which include not only food such as fish sauces, wine and flour but also expensive construction materials (marble), sculptures and luxury goods, *Munigua* will not have differed significantly from other cities in the region. But compared to exports from other cities, the metal exploited and produced near the town gives *Munigua* a special status; it must have been the reason for the wealth of the city and its inhabitants, which is reflected in the buildings and the specific spatial organization of its very small urban centre. The monumentality of *Munigua*'s urban centre no doubt also impacted on the strength and attraction of the economic movements within the town, a phenomenon which is perceptible in many Roman cities. As Dickenson shows for Roman Britain (Chapter 7), the prime commercial spaces materialized in the monumental forum–basilica complexes and their often grand entrances would have been visible from far off, creating an imposing impression in contrast to the modest houses that made up most of the urban landscapes. Their looming bulk would have worked to draw in visitors from afar and to promote trade and economic activity of all sorts. As Hoffelinck shows with her spatial study of the *macella* (Chapter 10), other types of commercial buildings also fulfilled this role of attraction pole for movement. The *macellum*, as one of the main market buildings in the Roman city, must have provoked two important flows of movement throughout the town. A first flow was caused by the city's residents who did their daily shopping in this market, and a second flow, perhaps the most important one, was generated by the transportation of products to the market. How exactly goods circulated in the urban centres is carefully analysed for *Pompeii* and *Herculaneum* by Wallace-Hadrill (Chapter 11) who proposes a model whereby the elite maintained the 'dignity' of their city without discouraging the trade in which they were also implicated. On the one hand, the ancient city is supposedly characterized by an open street network: preferably a rationally organized grid pattern, but in any case a system of capillary connections whereby the main roads ran from the gates to the centre, opening up the city to communication locally and externally, with a place of exchange, agora or forum, at its heart. On the other hand, there seems to have been an urge in the Imperial period to 'pedestrianize' the city centre, or rather to restrict the circulation of wheeled traffic. As with modern pedestrianization, this was not a strategy designed to prevent commerce but instead to promote it by separating the wheeled traffic from the pedestrian shopper. The traffic that enables the movement of goods may impede retail by obstructing the movement of persons, and successful planning depends on the delicate management of conflicting needs. But even if wheeled traffic was relatively discouraged, alternatives for the ox- or mule-drawn waggon existed, and especially the role of mules and human porters (*saccarii*) needs to be emphasized. Alongside this, as Corsi stresses in Chapter 13, the spatial analysis of the location in town of the commercial operations related to the economy of transport and mobility provokes interesting observations about the economic strategies (e.g. the ratio between investments, property market and revenues) as well as about the social urban landscape (e.g. the relationship between areas where public activities are carried out versus alleys for secluded activities; residential districts versus more 'touristic' sectors). In general, investments not only in commercial operations related to the movement of people (such as inns and taverns) but also in simple infrastructure related to transport and logistics (such as ramps, loading bays and stables) prove how strong the impact of the commercial sector on the urban tissue was. After all, the economy of mobility stands as one of the driving forces in the development of cityscapes, from the spatial as well as the social point of view.

Finally, the movement of goods over longer distances, connecting cities with extra-regional sources of origin, triggers yet another set of studies and models. As Taelman demonstrates with his analysis of land transport of overseas marble to central Adriatic cities in inland locations (Chapter 12), the lack of direct archaeological data on the organization of transport can be overcome with focused modelling. He presents a formal model for predicting the energy costs of transporting heavy loads over land through the study of the provenance, spatial distribution and consumption of material culture, thus improving our understanding of the functioning of this area of Roman trade. Interestingly, the study shows no clear or direct connection between marble consumption and transport costs, suggesting that the distribution and consumption of marbles was not completely market driven, but that other factors such as state intervention, fashion or ideology played a role in the movement of these high-quality goods. The modelling of economic movement also lies at the base of the work presented by Keay's team on the *Portus Augusti*, the maritime port of Imperial Rome (Chapter 16), which has seen much intensive research in recent years, and which is an important proxy for the commercial connections between Rome and the Mediterranean at large for at least 400 years. Here the contributors use different spatial techniques to model the movement of ships and people through the port as an index of its permeability to commercial traffic, and thus its efficiency in mediating the import, export and re-distribution of cargoes. Their impressive study connects very well with the thorough analysis by Malmberg of the river ports of Rome (Chapter 15). Both studies of the respective maritime and river harbours show how the strain of supplying up to a million urban inhabitants in a pre-industrial society necessitated harbour facilities on an unprecedented scale, transforming the Tiber estuary and the banks of the Tiber near the *Urbs* into major commercial and industrial zones. Deep inland, away from the imposing maritime harbour infrastructure developed from the time of the emperor Claudius, there were essentially two types of river ports at Rome. One type was adapted to the river craft arriving from the inland regions to the city's northern harbours, while another type in the southern part of Rome catered to larger ships going upstream from *Portus* and *Ostia*, or arriving directly from the Mediterranean. Although all these systems were developed over a long stretch of time, from Republic to Empire, they exemplify brilliantly how the Rome superpower invested in a highly efficient infrastructure for the facilitation of economic movement, as is reflected in many instances, large and small, that can be found throughout the wide geographical expanse of the *imperium Romanum*.

After considering the various arguments developed by the contributors to this volume, we would like to end with some brief reflections on where the study of economic space in and around Roman cities in Italy and beyond, in the provinces East and West, might go next. Methodological and technical innovation in archaeological and historical analysis will without doubt continue to invigorate the field in the near future, as it has done in the recent past (for instance, with the development of non-invasive archaeological techniques, or with the application of space syntax analysis, to mention but two relatively recent novelties). Yet where might the focus of future work lie? In the introduction, we asked how and to what extent urban space and movement were shaped and determined by the needs and requirements of economic life, and what the close study of urban space and movement can teach us about the kind of economy that the Romans had. We also began our introduction with a sketch of the 'agglomeration economics'-approach developed by modern economists to explain urbanization and urban growth, which is based on the assumption of a fully integrated market economy. Yet it is clear from the contributions in this volume that economic spaces in Roman cities were shaped by a far more complex and varied set of influences. The requirements of production, distribution and consumption, often moulded by commercial incentives, certainly had a strong impact on the shape of urban space and the structure of urban networks in the Roman empire. As our contributors make clear, however, many other factors that were not specifically economic in nature also played an important part in the creation of urban economic space, such as civic social and political relations, colonization, local elite competition, euergetism, elite and popular tastes and fashions as reflected in preferences for certain types of leisure facilities, architectural styles or building materials, area-specific geographical and ecological factors and so on. Future analysis should in fact move away from the false and anachronistic dichotomy of 'economic' versus 'non-economic' factors and concentrate on the multiplicity of forces that shaped and influenced Roman economic spaces and their uses. Tied to this is the realization that we should not be too eager to ascribe function (economic or other) simply on the basis of the surface appearance of buildings, monuments or urban spaces only, but rather study their use through time, and their often intricate relationships and connectivity with the rest of the urban landscape, even their connections with spaces and settlements beyond the city gates, before we draw our conclusions. Moving beyond the city gates, various contributions to this volume also suggest that it might pay off to concentrate more on the specific character of *regional* settlement and transport networks in different parts of the empire to see what forces shaped their history and structure and on the local ecological conditions in which individual cities found themselves. Finally, in closing our introduction, we mentioned the desirability of historical-comparative studies of urban economic space. The contributions to this volume suggest, however, that when we employ the comparative method, we would do well to be as sensitive to differences as we are to similarities. Roman urban landscapes and economic spaces were often shaped differently from those in other societies, particularly from those in the cities of early modern western Europe which through the accident of history have become so strongly associated with the development of capitalism and modern economic growth. As the contributions to this volume make clear, Roman urban landscapes and spaces were very capable of generating their own forms of economic dynamism, sufficient to sustain a highly urbanized pre-modern empire for many centuries. How this happened precisely, in the different areas of the empire, during the various periods of Roman Imperial history, is an issue that should indeed remain at the forefront of research into Roman urban economic space.

# Index